The Great Introduction

to the Science of the Judgments of the Stars

by Abū Ma'shar

The Complete Edition from Arabic

TRANSLATED & EDITED BY
BENJAMIN N. DYKES, PHD

The Cazimi Press
Minneapolis, Minnesota
2020

Published and printed in the United States of America
by The Cazimi Press
Minneapolis, MN 55414

© 2020 by Benjamin N. Dykes, Ph.D.

All rights reserved. No part of this publication may be reproduced, stored in or introduced into a retrieval system, or transmitted, in any form or by any means (electronic, mechanical, photocopying, recording or otherwise), without the prior written permission of both the copyright owner and the above publisher of this book.

The scanning, uploading, and distribution of this book via the Internet or via any other means without the permission of the publisher is illegal and punishable by law. Please purchase only authorized editions and do not participate in or encourage electronic piracy of copyrighted materials. Your support of the author's rights is appreciated.

ISBN-13: 978-1-934586-52-5

Acknowledgements

I would like to thank the following friends and colleagues, in alphabetical order: Steven Birchfield, Chris Brennan, Margherita Fiorello, Philip Graves, and Sharon Knight.

Also available at www.bendykes.com:

Designed for curious modern astrology students, *Traditional Astrology for Today* explains basic ideas in history, philosophy and counseling, dignities, chart interpretation, and predictive techniques. Non-technical and friendly for modern beginners.

This new translation of six works by Sahl b. Bishr is a required text for Benjamin Dykes's traditional natal astrology course, and is the first translation of Sahl's huge *Book of Nativities* from Arabic.

Dorotheus's *Carmen Astrologicum* is a foundational text for traditional astrology. Originally written in a lost Greek version, this is a translation of the later Arabic edition. It contains nativities, predictive techniques, aspect and house combinations, and a complete approach to elections or inceptions.

This excellent and popular introduction to predictive techniques by contemporary Turkish astrologer Öner Döşer blends traditional and modern methods, with numerous chart examples.

The first two volumes of this medieval mundane series, *Astrology of the World*, describe numerous techniques in weather prediction, prices and commodities, eclipses and comets, chorography, ingresses, Saturn-Jupiter conjunctions, and more, translated from Arabic and Latin sources.

Two classic introductions to astrology, by Abū Ma'shar and al-Qabīsī, are translated with commentary in this volume. *Introductions to Traditional Astrology* is an essential reference work for traditional students.

The classic medieval text by Guido Bonatti, the *Book of Astronomy* is now available in paperback reprints. This famous work is a complete guide to basic principles, horary, elections, mundane, and natal astrology.

This first English translation of Hephaistion of Thebes's *Apotelesmatics* Book III contains much fascinating material from the original Dorotheus poem and numerous other electional texts, including rules on thought-interpretation.

The largest compilation of traditional electional material, *Choices & Inceptions: Traditional Electional Astrology* contains works by Sahl, al-Rijāl, al-'Imrānī, and others, beginning with an extensive discussion of elections and questions by Benjamin Dykes.

The famous medieval horary compilation *The Book of the Nine Judges* is now available in translation for the first time! It is the largest traditional horary work available, and the third in the horary series.

The Search of the Heart is the first in the horary series, and focuses on the use of victors (special significators or *almutens*) and the practice of thought-interpretation: divining thoughts and predicting outcomes before the client speaks.

The Forty Chapters is a famous and influential horary work by al-Kindī, and is the second volume of the horary series. Beginning with a general introduction to astrology, al-Kindī covers topics such as war, wealth, travel, pregnancy, marriage, and more.

The first volume of the *Persian Nativities* series on natal astrology contains *The Book of Aristotle*, an advanced work on nativities and prediction, and a beginner-level work by his student Abū 'Alī al-Khayyāt, *On the Judgments of Nativities*.

The second volume of *Persian Nativities* features a The second volume of *Persian Nativities* features a shorter, beginner-level work on nativities and prediction by 'Umar al-Tabarī, and a much longer book on nativities by his younger follower, Abū Bakr.

This compilation of sixteen works by Sahl b. Bishr and Māshā'allāh covers all areas of traditional astrology, from basic concepts to horary, elections, natal interpretation, and mundane astrology. It is also available in paperback.

Expand your knowledge of traditional astrology, philosophy, and esoteric thought with the *Logos & Light* audio series: downloadable, college-level lectures on MP3 at a fraction of the university cost!

Enjoy these additions in our magic/esoteric series:

Astrological Magic: Basic Rituals & Meditations is a basic introduction to ritual magic for astrologers. It introduces a magical cosmology and electional rules, and shows how to perform ritual correctly, integrating Tarot and visualizations with rituals for all Elements, Planets, and Signs.

Available as an MP3 download, *Music of the Elements* was composed especially for *Astrological Magic* by MjDawn, an experienced electronic artist and ritualists.

Nights is a special, 2-disc remastering by MjDawn of the album GAMMA, and is a deep and powerful set of 2 full-disc MP3 soundtracks suitable for meditation or ritual work, especially those in *Astrological Magic*.

Aeonian Glow is a new version of the original ambient work mixed by Steve Roach, redesigned by MjDawn and Vir Unis from the original, pre-mixed files. This MP3 album is entrancing and enchanting.

Table of Contents

Table of Abbreviations viii
Table of Figures ix
INTRODUCTION 1
   §1: Contents and sources of the *Great Introduction* 1
   §2: The dating of the *Great Introduction* 4
   §3: Abū Ma'shar's theory of astrology (Books I and IV) 6
   §4: Planetary qualities and mixtures 20
   §5: Hermes and Agathodaimōn 27
   §6: The faces and parans in VI.1 29
   §7: Classical aspects in VI.3 and Book VII 30
   §8: Lots in Book VIII 35
   §9: Manuscripts and sentence numbering 40
BOOK I: DEFINITION & DEFENSE OF ASTROLOGY 41
   Chapter I.1: On the beginning of the book, and the seven headings 42
   Chapter I.2: On the existence of the science of the judgments of the stars 46
   Chapter I.3: On the manner of the planets' activity in this world 62
   Chapter I.4: On the forms, natures, composition, and the "natured" 69
   Chapter I.5: On arguing for the confirmation of judgments, and responding to everyone claiming that the planets have no power in their motions, nor an indication for things which come to be in this world 78
   Chapter I.6: On the benefit of the science of judgments, and that foreknowledge of things which come to be in this world from the power of the planets' movements, is very beneficial 102
BOOK II: FIXED STARS, THE ORDER OF SIGNS, QUADRUPLICITIES, & SECT 117
   Chapter II.1: On the number of the stars of the sphere both fast and slow in motion, which the ancients measured, and the knowledge of their six magnitudes, and how many planets there are in each magnitude, and the number of images in the sphere, and the name of each image 118
   Chapter II.2: It is stated why twelve images were made more fundamental in indication, than the rest of the images of the sphere 127

Chapter II.3: On the reason for the number of signs, and that there are twelve, neither less nor more 129
Chapter II.4: On the sequence of the natures of the signs 134
Chapter II.5: It is stated why one begins with Aries rather than the rest of the signs 137
Chapter II.6: On the reason for the convertible, fixed, and double-bodied signs 140
Chapter II.7: On the knowledge of the quarters of the sphere, and the reason for the convertible, fixed, and double-bodied signs, and the reason for the number of the signs (and that they are twelve), and why one begins with Aries in the sequence of their natures, and the knowledge of their triplicities, according to what Hermes reported from Agathodaimōn 141
Chapter II.8: On the knowledge of the masculine and feminine signs . 146
Chapter II.9: On the diurnal and nocturnal signs 147

BOOK III: DEFINITION OF ASTROLOGY, WEATHER, TIDES, & GROWTH **149**
Chapter III.1: On the reason for the masters of the stars' using the seven planets in the general indication of things, rather than the rest of the planets of the sphere, and the special property of action of each one of them in the conditions of the four principles 150
Chapter III.2: On the definition of the "judgments of the stars," "astrologer," and into which matter he looks 153
Chapter III.3: On the special property of the Sun's indication for the moderation of atmospheric things, natures, compositions, and the planets' partnership with him 159
Chapter III.4: On the special property of the Moon for the flow and ebb [of the tide] 166
Chapter III.5: On the cause of the flow and ebb [of the tide] 171
Chapter III.6: On the strength of the flow and its weakness, and the abundance and scarcity of its water 177
Chapter III.7: That the Moon is the cause of the flow and ebb, and the response to those opposing that 191
Chapter III.8: On the different conditions of the seas, and the quality of the seas in which the flow and ebb is made obvious (and in which it is not obvious), and on the special property of the Sun's action in the seas 193

Chapter III.9: On the Moon's indication for animals, plants, and minerals, through the increase and decrease of her glow..................200

BOOK IV: THEORY OF ASTROLOGY & CLASSIFICATIONS OF THE PLANETS..................204

Chapter IV.1: On the natures of the seven planets quick in motion, according to what Ptolemy said..................205

Chapter IV.2: On the natures of the planets, and their fortunes and infortunes, and what is blended of them, according to what the generality of the masters of the stars claimed..................209

Chapter IV.3: On our response to one claiming that the natures of the planets, and their fortunes and infortunes, are known from their colors..................215

Chapter IV.4: On our establishing the existence of the fortunes and infortunes, according to the teachings of philosophy..................217

Chapter IV.5 On knowing which of the planets is a fortune, and which of them an infortune..................222

Chapter IV.6: On the different conditions of the fortunes and infortunes, and the shifting of one of them over to the nature of the other..................234

Chapter IV.7: On the natures of the planets, and their shifting from nature to nature, and the strength of their nature inherent in them (and its weakness)..................244

Chapter IV.8: On the masculinization of the planets, and their feminization..................249

Chapter IV.9: On the diurnal and nocturnal planets..................251

BOOK V: ON THE SHARES OF THE PLANETS IN THE SIGNS..................254

Chapter V.1: On the shares of the planets in the signs..................255

Chapter V.2: On the reason for the planets' houses, according to what some of the masters of the stars claimed..................256

Chapter V.3: On the reason for the planets' houses, according to what fits with the statement of Ptolemy..................258

Chapter V.4: On the reason for the planets' houses, according to what fits with the statement of Hermes, from Agathodaimōn..................261

Chapter V.5: On the reason for the planets' exaltations, according to what some of the astrologers claimed..................268

Chapter V.6: On the reason for the planets' exaltations, according to what Ptolemy claimed..................271

Chapter V.7: On the reason for the planets' exaltations, according to what fits with the statement of Hermes 273
Chapter V.8: On the different bounds of the planets, <and their conditions>.. 284
Chapter V.9: On the bounds of the people of Egypt............................... 287
Chapter V.10: On the bounds of Ptolemy.. 288
Chapter V.11: On the bounds of the Chaldeans.. 290
Chapter V.12: On the bounds of Astrātū... 292
Chapter V.13: On the bounds of the Indians... 293
Chapter V.14: On the lords of the triplicities.. 293
Chapter V.15: On the faces and their lords, according to what fits with the statement of the scholars of Persia, Babylon, and Egypt............ 295
Chapter V.16: On the faces and their lords according to what the Indians said: and they call them the *darījān*.. 297
Chapter V.17: On the *nawbahr* of the signs (and it is the ninth-part), according to what fits with the statement of the Indians 298
Chapter V.18: On the twelfth-parts of the signs, and the lords of each degree of every sign.. 301
Chapter V.19: On the male and female degrees.. 303
Chapter V.20: On the bright, dark, dusky, and empty degrees............... 305
Chapter V.21: On the wells of the planets in the signs 307
Chapter V.22: On the degrees increasing in good fortune 309

BOOK VI: ON THE CLASSIFICATIONS OF THE SIGNS 311
Chapter VI.1: On the natures of the signs, their conditions, and what images ascend in the faces.. 313
Chapter VI.2: On the ascensions of the signs on the equator and in the seven climes, according to what Theon claimed.................................... 342
Chapter VI.3: On the symmetry of the degrees of the circle 347
Chapter VI.4: On the signs loving one another, hating one another, and hostile to one another, and straight and crooked in ascensions, and obedient and disobedient to one another.. 355
Chapter VI.5: On the signs agreeing in the belt and ascensions, agreeing in power, and agreeing in manner... 357
Chapter VI.6: On the signs which harmonize with each other in a "natural" opposition and sextile, but do not look at each other 362
Chapter VI.7: On the signs which harmonize with each other from the square.. 364

Chapter VI.8: On the years of the signs, and their months, days, and hours 365
Chapter VI.9: On the indications of the signs for collections of countries and locales in lands 367
Chapter VI.10: On the signs indicating motion and rest 371
Chapter VI.11: On the rational signs which indicate a class of people and their conditions 371
Chapter VI.12: On the division of what belongs to each sign, in terms of the limbs of the human body 372
Chapter VI.13: On the signs indicative of grace and beauty, and the signs indicative of generosity and liberality, and the signs which accumulate and become full, and which grant ease, and which pour forth, and which seize and take 374
Chapter VI.14: On the signs indicative of lewdness and illnesses 376
Chapter VI.15: On the signs indicative of women's chastity and their modesty 377
Chapter VI.16: On the signs of many children, twins, and few children, as well as sterility 377
Chapter VI.17: On the signs of cut limbs, and the signs of much sharpness and anger 378
Chapter VI.18: On the signs indicative of the conditions of voices 378
Chapter VI.19: On the signs indicative of mange, leprosy, spots, itching, ringworm, deafness, muteness, baldness, thinness of the beard, stringy hair, and an armpit which does not have hair 379
Chapter VI.20: On the positions in the signs indicative of defects in the eye 380
Chapter VI.21: On the signs indicative of culture, beguiling speech, deception, cunning, the signs of anxiety, and the dark signs 382
Chapter VI.22: On the signs indicating types of birds, and everything having four feet, and predatory animals and venomous things, things scratching the earth, and animals of the water 382
Chapter VI.23: On the signs indicative of trees and vegetation 383
Chapter VI.24: On the signs indicative of types of waters, and the signs indicative of what is worked by fire 383
Chapter VI.25: On the directions of the signs 384

Chapter VI.26: On the stakes of the circle and their quadrants, and the the twelve houses, the sum of their indications, and the reason for that, and the houses of the planets' joys 385

Chapter VI.27: On the quadrants of the circle being attributed to what is bodily and spiritual, and other things 397

Chapter VI.28: On the blending of the natures of the stakes of the Ascendant 398

Chapter VI.29: On the colors of the quadrants of the circle, and the twelve houses 398

Chapter VI.30: On the rising quadrants of the circles, and those falling, and the tall and the short 399

Chapter VI.31: On the distribution of the four natures, to things 399

Chapter VI.32: On explaining the quarters of a single day and single night, and their twenty-four hours 400

Chapter VI.33: On the lords of the days and hours 402

BOOK VII: ON THE CONDITIONS OF THE PLANETS, & THEIR SPECIAL INDICATIONS FOR THINGS **406**

Chapter VII.1: On the conditions of the planets in themselves 407

Chapter VII.2: On the conditions of the planets relative to the Sun, in front of him and behind him 412

Chapter VII.3: On the conditions of the planets in the quadrants of the circle and their houses, and the range of the power of their bodies.. 424

Chapter VII.4: On the planets' assembling with each other, and the mixture of their qualities, and which of them is stronger, and which weaker 425

Chapter VII.5: On the planets' looking at each other, and their connection and separation, and the rest of their similar conditions which follow upon that 443

Chapter VII.6: On the planets' good fortune, strength, weakness, and misfortune, and the corruption of the Moon 478

Chapter VII.7: On the casting of the planets' rays, according to the work of Ptolemy 485

Chapter VII.8: On knowing the years of the planets' *fardārs*, and their mighty, greater, middle, and lesser years 487

Chapter VII.9: On the natures of the seven planets, and their special indications for existing things 488

Contents

BOOK VIII: ON LOTS **499**
   Chapter VIII.1: On the reason for deriving the Lots...................499
   Chapter VIII.2: On the classification of the Lots, and their names 502
   Chapter VIII.3: On the Lots of the seven planets.......................506
   Chapter VIII.4: On the Lots of the twelve houses......................517
   Chapter VIII.5: On stating the Lots which are not mentioned along with the seven planets nor with <the Lots of> the twelve houses......554
   (And they are used in nativities and on many occasions along with those Lots which we mentioned above)..554
   Chapter VIII.6: On stating all of the Lots in an abbreviated way...........560
   Chapter VIII.7: On the Lots' coinciding in a single position 570
   Chapter VIII.8: On knowing of the indicators of the Lots in their entirety 572
   Chapter VIII.9: On knowing the positions of <any of> the indicators relative to each other..575
APPENDIX A: ASCENSIONAL TIMES **579**
APPENDIX B: TABLE OF LOTS..**582**
BIBLIOGRAPHY **585**
GLOSSARY..**588**
INDEX..**615**

Table of Abbreviations

Anth.	Valens, *Anthology*
Aphorisms	Sahl, *The Fifty Aphorisms* (in *ASB1*)
ASB1	Sahl, *The Astrology of Sahl b. Bishr Volume I*
AW1	Dykes, *Astrology of the World, Volume I*
AW2	Dykes, *Astrology of the World, Volume II*
BA	The *Book of Aristotle* (in *PN1*)
Carmen	Dorotheus, *Carmen Astrologicum*
Gr. Intr.	Abū Ma'shar, *The Great Introduction to the Science of the Stars*
Heph.	Hephaistion of Thebes, *Apotelesmatika* I-III
Introduction	Sahl, *The Introduction*, (in *ASB1*)
ITA	Dykes, *Introductions to Traditional Astrology*
Mathesis	Firmicus Maternus, *Mathesis*
Nativities	Sahl b. Bishr, *On Nativities* (in *ASB1*)
PN1 – PN3	Dykes, *Persian Nativities* Vols. I - III
PN4	Abū Ma'shar, *On the Revolutions of the Years of Nativities* (= *Persian Nativities IV*)
Questions	Sahl b. Bishr, *On Questions* (in *ASB1*)
TBN	'Umar al-Tabarī, *Three Books on Nativities* (in *PN2*)
Tet.	Ptolemy, *Tetrabiblos*

CONTENTS

Table of Figures

Figure 1: Passages defining astrology 8
Figure 2: Some arguments about change and causation 12
Figure 3: Planetary elemental principles 20
Figure 4: Proposed planetary positions on cycle of principles 21
Figure 5: Hermes-Agathodaimōn passages in Gr. Intr. 28
Figure 6: Special Arabic terminology in Ch. VI.3 32
Figure 7: The quintile or fifth "harmonic" 33
Figure 8: No out-of-sign aspects by degree 35
Figure 9: Sources of two "Hermetic" Lots in Gr. Intr. VIII 39
Figure 10: Special properties of natures and forms (I.4, 38-45) 73
Figure 11: Special dim stars in Almagest VII.5-VIII.1 119
Figure 12: Constellations 1-9 121
Figure 13: Constellations 10-18 122
Figure 14: Constellations 19-27 123
Figure 15: Constellations 28-36 124
Figure 16: Constellations 37-45 125
Figure 17: Constellations 46-48 126
Figure 18: Cycles of the four principles 131
Figure 19: Order and characteristics of the natures and principles in the signs 135
Figure 20: Diurnal (white), nocturnal (black), and mixed signs (gray) according to others (II.9, 2) 147
Figure 21: Planetary qualities (III.1, 11-19) 151
Figure 22: Principles, humors, and tastes (IV.2, 8-11 and 27-30) .. 210
Figure 23: Reading guide to astrological theory in IV.4 217
Figure 24: Fortunes and infortunes (IV.5) 226
Figure 25: Theory of accidental fortunes and infortunes (IV.6, 1-11) 234
Figure 26: Infortunes as accidental fortunes (IV.6, 14-22) 237
Figure 27: 2020 apogees 244
Figure 28: Alteration of qualities in circle of apogee 245
Figure 29: Fixed and variable qualities of planets (IV.7) 246
Figure 30: Alteration of qualities in Lunar phases 248
Figure 31: Superiors' phases 249
Figure 32: Inferiors' phases 249
Figure 33: Masculine and feminine classification of planets 250

Figure 34: Masculine and feminine quadrants 251
Figure 35: Diurnal and nocturnal planets (IV.9) 252
Figure 36: A *Thema Mundi* with lunar and solar halves (V.3, 13-19) 260
Figure 37: Similarity of planets' houses with their figures and moderation (V.4, 35-43) 266
Figure 38: Standard exaltation degrees (V.5) 268
Figure 39: Hermes's exaltation degrees (V.7) 273
Figure 40: Exaltations of Jupiter and Sun (from Hermes, V.7, 27-30) 277
Figure 41: Exaltation of Mars (from Hermes, V.7, 35-37) 278
Figure 42: Exaltation of Venus (from Hermes, V.7, 38) 279
Figure 43: Mars and Venus adjusted (from Hermes, V.7, 39) 279
Figure 44: Exaltation of Mercury (from Hermes, V.7, 42) 280
Figure 45: Exaltation of Saturn (from Hermes, V.7, 46) 281
Figure 46: Exaltation of Moon (from Hermes, V.7, 51) 282
Figure 47: Table of Egyptian bounds 287
Figure 48: Table of Ptolemaic bounds according to Abū Ma'shar 288
Figure 49: Table of Ptolemaic bounds (Hübner critical edition of *Tetrabiblos*) 289
Figure 50: Table of Chaldean bounds (Tet. I.21) 291
Figure 51: Table of the bounds of Astrātū (V.12) 292
Figure 52: Table of Indian bounds (V.13) 293
Figure 53: Dorothean triplicity lords (V.14) 295
Figure 54: Table of Chaldean faces (V.15) 296
Figure 55: Table of Indian *darījān* (V.16) 297
Figure 56: Table of Indian ninth-parts (V.17, 1-13) 299
Figure 57: Table of twelfth-parts (V.18, 1-3) 301
Figure 58: A *monomoria* system from Hermes (V.18, 4-7) 302
Figure 59: Male and female degrees (V.19) 304
Figure 60: Four categories of brightness 305
Figure 61: Degrees of brightness (V.20) 306
Figure 62: The wells of the signs (V.21) 308
Figure 63: Degrees increasing in good fortune (V.22, 1-3) 309
Figure 64: Degrees of elevation and power (V.22, 4-5) 309
Figure 65: AT, Clime 1 343
Figure 66: AT, Clime 2 344
Figure 67: AT, Clime 3 344
Figure 68: AT, Clime 4 344

Figure 69: AT, Clime 5 345
Figure 70: AT, Clime 6 345
Figure 71: AT, Clime 7 346
Figure 72: Seven climes in the *Almagest*, with modern latitudes 346
Figure 73: Geometrical affinities (VI.3, 4-16) 350
Figure 74: Summary of harmonies (VI.3, 17-24) 351
Figure 75: Straight and crooked signs (VI.4, 7-8) 357
Figure 76: Abū Ma'shar's commanding and obeying signs (VI.4, 9-11) 357
Figure 77: Signs agreeing in the belt and ascensions (VI.5, 2-5) 358
Figure 78: Signs agreeing in power, Persian signs obeying each other, antiscial signs (VI.5, 6-9) 359
Figure 79: Detail of signs agreeing in power, Persian signs obeying each other, or antiscial signs (VI.5, 10-11) 360
Figure 80: Signs agreeing in manner (VI.5, 12-14) 361
Figure 81: Signs in aversion but with "natural" opposition (VI.6, 1-2, 4) ..362
Figure 82: Signs in aversion but with "natural" sextile (VI.6, 1-3, 5) 363
Figure 83: Signs harmonizing by square (VI.7) 364
Figure 84: Planetary years and months, from Valens (VI.8) 367
Figure 85: Rational signs (VI.11) 371
Figure 86: Signs of lewdness and illness (VI.14) 376
Figure 87: Signs of skin diseases and little hair (VI.19) 379
Figure 88: Stars harming eyes (VI.20), corrected by Dykes 381
Figure 89: Terrestrial directions by sign (VI.25) 384
Figure 90: Advancing and withdrawing quadrants (VI.26, 3) 386
Figure 91: Quadrant divisions by angularity (VI.26, 5) 387
Figure 92: Basic topical meanings of the twelve places or houses (VI.26).388
Figure 93: A planetary scheme to explain topical place meanings (VI.26) 391
Figure 94: Planetary joys in the places (VI.26) 396
Figure 95: Spirit and body in the quadrants (VI.27) 397
Figure 96: Rising-falling and tall-short hemispheres (VI.30) 399
Figure 97: Planetary hours and days 404
Figure 98: Speed relative to apogee (VII.1, 10-13) 408
Figure 99: Inferiors right and left of Sun (VII.2, 3) 413
Figure 100: Superiors right and left of Sun (VII.2, 2) 413
Figure 101: Moon right and left (VII.2, 4) 413
Figure 102: Synodic cycle of superiors (VII.2, 6-34) 415
Figure 103: Synodic cycle of inferiors (VII.2, 35-53) 420

xii   ABŪ MA'SHAR: THE GREAT INTRODUCTION

Figure 104: Synodic cycle of Moon (VII.2, 58-74) 421
Figure 105: Bodies or orbs of planets 424
Figure 106: Assembling with planets' bodies or orbs (VII.4, 5-8) 426
Figure 107: Planets visually united (VII.4, 17-20) 427
Figure 108: Cycle of simple principles 433
Figure 109: Mars-Saturn conjunctions (VII.4, 59-64) 434
Figure 110: Argument against planets mixing like material bodies (VII.4, 97-109) 440
Figure 111: Saturn looking at signs (VII.5, 2-7) 444
Figure 112: Assembling in same sign (VII.5, 10-13) 445
Figure 113: Mixing natures across signs (VII.5, 14, 23, 32) 446
Figure 114: Moon separating, still strongly in nature of Saturn (VII.5, 18) 446
Figure 115: Assembly at end of sign, bodies extend into next sign (VII.5, 23) 448
Figure 116: Moon leaving the nature of Saturn (VII.5, 23) 448
Figure 117: Square connection from signs which see each other (VII.5, 25-26) 449
Figure 118: The power of the square connection begins (VII.5, 27) 449
Figure 119: Moon connects with Saturn first (VII.5, 29) 450
Figure 120: Jupiter connects with Saturn first (VII.5, 30) 451
Figure 121: Moon and Saturn mixing natures until sign changes (VII.5, 32-33) 451
Figure 122: Connection in latitude by assembly (VII.5, 39) 452
Figure 123: Connection in latitude by opposition (VII.5, 40-41) 453
Figure 124: Emptiness of course (VII.5, 78) 458
Figure 125: Wild Mars (VII.5, 79) 459
Figure 126: Transfer (VII.5, 83-85) 460
Figure 127: Collection (VII.5, 86) 461
Figure 128: Reflection as collection from aversion (VII.5, 87-88) 462
Figure 129: Reflection as transfer from aversion (VII.5, 89) 463
Figure 130: Blocking #1 (VII.5, 91-92) 464
Figure 131: Blocking #2 (VII.5, 93-94) 465
Figure 132: Handing over nature (VII.5, 95) 466
Figure 133: Handing over power (VII.5, 96) 467
Figure 134: Handing over two natures (VII.5, 97-100) 468
Figure 135: Handing over management (VII.5, 101-02) 469
Figure 136: Returning with suitability and corruption (VII.5, 104-14) 470

Figure 137: Revoking (VII.5, 117) 471
Figure 138: Resistance (VII.5, 118) 472
Figure 139: Escape (VII.5, 119) 472
Figure 140: Cutting #1 (VII.5, 121-22) 473
Figure 141: Cutting #2 (VII.5, 123-24) 473
Figure 142: Cutting #3 (VII.5, 125) 474
Figure 143: Favor and recompense (VII.5, 126-28) 475
Figure 144: Reception (VII.5, 129-30) 476
Figure 145: Enclosure or besieging by degree (VII.6, 56-57) 483
Figure 146: Planetary years 487
Figure 147: Four classes of Lot calculation 507
Figure 148: Projecting from beginning of rising sign 508
Figure 149: Ptolemy's theory of the Lot of Fortune (Tet. III.10; Gr. Intr. VIII.3, 25) 510
Figure 150: Relations between four Lot positions (VIII.9, 10) 577

INTRODUCTION

I am pleased to present my translation of the complete Arabic edition of one of Abū Ma'shar's two most celebrated works, *The Great Introduction to the Science of the Judgments of the Stars*, or the *Great Introduction* (*Gr. Intr.*). The other is a work on political and historical astrology, *The Book of Religions and Dynasties*, also known from the Latin version as *On the Great Conjunctions*. (I plan to translate this in the near future.)

In the Middle Ages the *Gr. Intr.* was translated into two Latin versions, by Hermann of Carinthia and John of Spain, both in the 12th Century. It was published in manuscript and printed editions, before disappearing from the astrological scene along with most other traditional works. In 1995 an American scholar, Richard Lemay, published critical editions of both the Arabic and Latin versions but without translating them. In 2019 Charles Burnett and Keiji Yamamoto (here abbreviated as BY) published their critical edition of the Arabic, along with an English translation. Since they had access to more Arabic manuscripts than Lemay did, they could be more certain about correct readings; I generally follow them where they and Lemay disagree.

Many years ago I began to translate the Latin version of John, and later began my own translation of Lemay's Arabic, but decided to delay publication until I could check uncertain readings against BY. I think my edition has benefited from this comparison, and is also more helpful for the average reader who does not need access to the Arabic. Throughout I have added numerous footnotes, cross-references, tables, and diagrams, to explain what Abū Ma'shar wants to do in his *Great Introduction*. I hope that future generations of astrologers and scholars of cultural history will find it useful.

§1: Contents and sources of the *Great Introduction*

Abū Ma'shar Ja'far b. Muhammad b. 'Umar, known as Abū Ma'shar (and in Latin as Albumasar), was one of the most famous astrologers of the Middle Ages. He was active during most of the 9th Century, during the "golden age" of the 'Abbāsid Caliphate, and for a variety of reasons attracted both acclaim and criticism. In my translation of his *On the Revolutions of the Years of Nativities* (2019), I described something of his career and my doubts about some of the claims made about him, and I refer the reader to my introduction there. What I want to emphasize here is that the *Gr. Intr.* was probably his first major foray into astrological writing.

As the story goes, Abū Ma'shar had been a religious and philosophical scholar before being introduced to astrology by al-Kindī, a major philosophical figure in Baghdad in the 800s. The *Gr. Intr.* can be viewed as a synthesis of Abū Ma'shar's two primary interests, and can be divided into two parts. The first part (Books I-IV) contains his own definition, theory, and defense of astrology, especially as expressed in the language of Aristotelian physics and metaphysics. The second part (Books V-VIII) is more strictly astrological, describing categories of the signs, dignities, planetary conditions and significations, house meanings, and Lots. In other words, he needed his Aristotelian background to write the first part, but needed wide astrological reading and some practice to write the second part. Taken together, the eight books of *Gr. Intr.* are a major contribution to theoretical astrology.

In later sections I will discuss Abū Ma'shar's theory of astrology and other topics at length, but here I would like to mention some of the source material we can be sure that he used in *Gr. Intr.*:

- **Agathodaimōn** ("Good Spirit"), who according to some traditions is the father of **Hermes Trismegistus**; his views are put into the mouth of Hermes in many places in *Gr. Intr.* This term (as *Agathos Daimōn*) was also used for the 11th house or place, and in the form of a spiritual being was paired with *Agathē Tuchē* (Good Fortune), attributed to the 5th house or place.
- **Al-Andarzaghar** (active perhaps 650 AD?), a Persian astrologer whom I have argued wrote the Arabic original of the later *Book of Aristotle*, which Sahl quotes extensively in his *Nativities*. Abū Ma'shar quotes him in relation to Lot calculations, in Book VIII.
- **Antiochus** (perhaps 1st-2nd Centuries AD), an astrologer whose work on astrological principles is known today only in summary and by later quotation (see Schmidt 2009). Abū Ma'shar mentions him in VI.1, on the fixed stars.
- **Aratus** (3rd Century BC), a poet who wrote the *Phenomena*, describing the fixed stars based on a lost work of Eudoxus. Abū Ma'shar mentions him in VI.1, on the fixed stars.

- **Aristotle**, or more likely some summary or digest of Aristotelian natural philosophy based on *De Caelo, On Generation and Corruption*, the *Categories*, and other works. According to Gutas,[1] Arabic translations of most of these works were not available until the middle of the 9th Century. I suspect that the works of someone like Alexander of Aphrodisias, an Aristotelian commentator of the 2nd-3rd Centuries AD, might have been involved.
- **Astrātū or Istrātū** (اسطراطو), an unknown astrologer or astronomer who might be Erasistratos or Aristarchus.
- The *Bizidaj*, a 6th-Century Persian compilation and perhaps commentary on past astrologers, including **Dorotheus** and **Vettius Valens**. It has been attributed to a Persian vizier named Buzurjmihr (ca. 500 – 580 AD). According to al-Bīrūnī, the *Bizidaj* included categorizations of zodiacal signs which Abū Ma'shar partially represents in *Gr. Intr.*VI.5.[2]
- **Claudius Ptolemy** (2nd Century AD), both the *Tetrabiblos* and *Almagest*, and perhaps some version of Ptolemy's *Planetary Hypotheses*. Abū Ma'shar praises the *Almagest*, but is very critical of Ptolemy's theory of the planets' elemental qualities—so much so, that he doubts the two books are written by the same man (see below).
- **Dorotheus of Sidon**, the 1st-Century Hellenistic astrologer, via the Pahlavi translation of his *Carmen*, or more likely an Arabic translation of it other than the 'Umar al-Tabarī translation which I published in 2019.
- **Galen**, the ancient physician, in some translation or summary.
- **Hermes**, most likely supposed to be Hermes Trismegistus, probably from two books: a work on basic principles and one on Lots (see below). Hermes is sometimes depicted as reporting the view of **Agathodaimōn**, who in some traditions was his father.

---

[1] See Gutas 1998, pp. 182-83.
[2] See al-Bīrūnī 1959, pp. 4-7 and 124-25. Apparently there was some disagreement about the proper names of these categories, as al-Bīrūnī reports other versions as well.

- **Hippocrates**, the ancient physician, in some translation or summary.
- **Rhetorius of Egypt**, a late Hellenistic astrologer whom I have argued was most active in the late 5th or early 6th Centuries.[3] Abū Ma'shar probably did not have access to Rhetorius under that name, but in Arabic translation or excerpts in some other source (such as **Theophilus of Edessa**).
- **Teucer of Babylon** (perhaps 1st Century BC), a Hellenistic astrologer. Abū Ma'shar uses some version of his work on fixed stars and constellations in VI.1.
- **Theon of Alexandria** (4th Century AD), an Alexandrian mathematician known for his editions and commentaries on Euclid and Ptolemy. Abū Ma'shar claims to use his *Handy Tables*.
- **Theophilus of Edessa** (ca. 695-785 AD), one of the last truly Hellenistic astrologers working during the 'Umayyad and 'Abbāsid Caliphates. Abū Ma'shar refers to him in relation to Lot calculations (Book VIII), where he always disagrees with Theophilus.
- **Vettius Valens** (2nd Century AD), a Hellenistic astrologer known to Persian and Arab astrologers mainly through the *Bizidaj*.
- Certain astrologers who **"do not understand nature."** Abū Ma'shar refers critically to such unknown astrologers in several places, such as II.8 and II.9. A similar reference appears in V.2 and V.5, **15-27**. (In the latter case he states that they are not Persians, Indians, or Greeks, so perhaps some Egyptians or Babylonians?)
- Numerous unnamed astrologers and critics of astrologers, including unnamed **Babylonians**, **Egyptians**, **Indians**, and **Persians**.

§2: The dating of the *Great Introduction*

The precise dating of *Gr. Intr.* does not really affect its contents. On the one hand, the astrology and astronomy in it is wholly traditional (even when various authors disagree on certain points). For the Aristotelian philosophical portions, we only need to assume that some summaries of

---

[3] See my Introduction to Theophilus of Edessa (2017), p. 29.

Aristotelianism were available to Abū Ma'shar in Arabic—and these were indeed available by about the middle of the 9th Century. However, something unusual emerges about his relationship to history when Abū Ma'shar tells us what year his fixed star positions are calculated for, and in light of some comments he makes about Ptolemy.

First, in Ch. VI.1, **20**, Abū Ma'shar tells us that he has precessed the star positions of the *Almagest* for his own era, which he describes as year 1,160 of Alexander the Two-Horned, a calendar which began when Alexander the Great was 26 (namely in 330 BC).[4] If so, then adding 1,160 years to Alexander's epoch gives us about 830 AD (-330 + 1,160 = 830).[5] It may seem strange that he uses the Alexander calendar, but he must be doing it right because this is the correct era for Abū Ma'shar's life, and for the known Arabic translations of the *Almagest* which he would have worked from. So, the *Gr. Intr.* was written around 830 AD, or used star positions calculated for that year.

But when Abū Ma'shar actually provides some of the longitudes for his fixed stars in Ch. VI.20, the amount of precession he applies is surprising. If we allow for scribal errors, the positions are on average about 10° 30' greater than those in Ptolemy's *Almagest*. Since Abū Ma'shar uses Ptolemy's incorrect precession rate of 1°/100y, this amount equals 1,050 years (10.5° * 100 = 1,050). So based on these averaged values, Abū Ma'shar believes that he is living about 1,050 years after the *Almagest* was written: that would put the *Almagest* at about 220 BC, instead of the mid-100s AD (as we know it to be).

What accounts for this 370-year discrepancy between the real *Almagest* (mid-100s AD) and Abū Ma'shar's presumed date (220 BC), given that Abū Ma'shar does have his own era correct (820-830 AD)? The answer comes from Abū Ma'shar's own opinion of the *Tetrabiblos* and a quirk of regnal names in Hellenistic Egypt. While Abū Ma'shar had great respect for Ptolemy the author of the *Almagest*, in Ch. IV.1 he severely criticizes Ptolemy the

---

[4] See al-Bīrūnī's *Chronology of Ancient Nations* p. 26.
[5] In later years, in *PN4* Abū Ma'shar claimed that his values were calculated for year 1,150 of Alexander, which would give us 820 AD (see *PN4* IX.8, **51**). But it's unlikely that he recalculated everything for *PN4*, since he gives Praesepe exactly the same longitude and latitude in both (*Gr. Intr.* VI.20, **5** and *PN4* IX.8, **45**). Simple scribal errors can account for the difference in dates.

author of the *Tetrabiblos*—so much so, that he finds it hard to believe the same Ptolemy could have written both books. By coincidence, after Alexander the Great's death, Egypt was ruled by a dynasty of Greek kings (and one queen) who bore the name "Ptolemy": this happened to be in the 275 or 276 years following Alexander's death, from 323 BC until Julius Caesar conquered Egypt in 47 BC.[6] Abū Ma'shar must have thought it more fitting that a royal Ptolemy of this era had composed the *Almagest*, and so in IV.1, 3 he says "They were generally sages, and among them was Ptolemy the Sage, who wrote the book *Almagest*." And indeed, Abū Ma'shar's assumed date of 220 BC for the *Almagest* falls approximately in the reign of Ptolemy III, when Hellenistic Egypt was very powerful, and this respected king added to the library at Alexandria; the astronomer and geographer Eratosthenes was also active in Egypt at this time.

In this way, Abū Ma'shar's dissatisfaction with the *Tetrabiblos* led him to accept another, more suitable Ptolemy as the author of the *Almagest*, one living 370 years before the real one.[7] The consequences of this error are important: not only was Abū Ma'shar using the wrong rate of precession, but adding it four centuries too early. This means that we must reevaluate Abū Ma'shar's star positions in other books, such as his *Flowers* (also known as his *Report*), which I translated in my *AW2*. This error also affects the fixed star positions in *PN4*.

§3: Abū Ma'shar's theory of astrology (Books I and IV)

In this section I will describe the basics of Abū Ma'shar's theory of astrology, with some handy tables for further reading. Let's take this in three stages, from general considerations of what astrology is and does, to Abū Ma'shar's adaptation of Aristotelian physics and metaphysics, to his "complete" theory of planetary activity. I will omit his lengthy discussion of necessity, possibility, and impossibility in his defense of astrology in Ch. I.5.

---

[6] See the list in al-Bīrūnī's *Chronology* p. 103.
[7] (We should also consider that the inspiration for Abū Ma'shar's calculation was his own translation of the *Almagest*.)

Stage 1: What astrology is (I.2 and elsewhere)

Historically there have been two broad conceptions of what astrology is. The first is that astrology is akin to physics, because the planets more or less directly *cause* things to happen: thus astrologers directly observe causal activity produced by the natures of the planets. We can associate this view generally with Ptolemy. The second is that astrology is akin to medicine, because the planets primarily *signify* things: so the astrologer is like a doctor who diagnoses by observing symptoms rather than the underlying disease. We can associate this view broadly with the Stoics. Abū Ma'shar's view is a combination of the two. On the one hand, he believes that the planets' motions do cause change on earth, but the planets do not do so directly via heating, cooling, and so on. So unlike with Ptolemy, Saturn does not have a natural power of cooling and drying. Instead, we are limited to observing the planets' *effects* and making inferences about them: that is to say, correlating patterns of effects with patterns of motions. Abū Ma'shar summarizes this neatly in III.2, **4-14**, where he points out that celestial activities and patterns "indicate something even though they are not that thing." This shows a familiarity with ancient theories of knowledge by signs or signification, which was a part of medical debates (such as in symptomology). As an example, Venus causes changes in the world through her motions; these changes eventually produce romantic relationships. But for the astrologer, she can only *indicate* relationships and their qualities, since we do not actually observe how this causal power works. And Venus herself is not a relationship: she is a body, moving on an epicycle at a certain rate, and so on. From patterns of motions in the heavens we build up a set of mental concepts, which *describe* the earthly events actually *caused* by those motions. For Abū Ma'shar, that is what astrology fundamentally does.

So as a form of knowledge, astrology is knowledge about heavenly *signs*. But the signs are signs of what the planets *cause*, and that causal process is unobservable. Ultimately we want to know what this causal power is, and where the formative principles which structure matter actually come from. Abū Ma'shar does not fully answer the question, and perhaps he thinks it's a matter of for metaphysicians. Nevertheless he makes some suggestions we will return to below.

Passage	Topic
III.2, 4-14	Definition of astrology and the astrologer.
II.3, 8	Planets are causes of elemental change.
I.2, 95-96	Astrology describes earthly effects which are caused by planets' motions.
I.2, 11-13; 16-31	Astrology vs. astronomy (with a description of changes).
I.2, 80-81	Loftiness of astrology; comparison with medicine.
I.6, 99-114	Why astrological prediction is beneficial.
I.2, 100, 106-08, 119-22	Rules for being an honest and effective astrologer.

Figure 1: Passages defining astrology

It should come as no surprise that Abū Ma'shar rates astrology very highly, both because of its source (the planets) and what can be done with it. He explains this in numerous passages, which I will mention briefly. If we contrast it with astronomy, astrology depends on astronomy but takes astronomical measurements further and describes what they *mean*, in the form of astrological judgments about earthly events. So in this sense, astrology fulfils an important purpose of astronomy, which is to contribute to our understanding and ability to live happily. Astrology also compares favorably to medicine, for doctors monitor, predict, and manage health and disease through their knowledge of changes in "natures" (i.e., physical changes); but astrologers go a step further by studying the planets whose motions *cause* those natural changes. Moreover, astrologers can correlate those celestial changes with areas of life that go beyond medicine (like relationships, profession, and so on).

With this lofty purpose, we can understand that astrologers need to know a lot about life in order to counsel people. (For instance, mundane astrologers should know something about macroeconomics). But Abū Ma'shar points out that one shouldn't be discouraged by this requirement: don't give up astrology just because you're not perfect, and indeed you should still try to use what you *do* know. But of course you should not advertise yourself as being good at things you aren't, and the worst thing would be to be a charlatan for the sake of raw profit or fame.

Stage 2: Adapting Aristotelian physics and metaphysics (I.3 and I.4)

At this point we must turn to Abū Ma'shar's physical theories, and the traditional vocabulary he uses. First, a background note.

In 1962, Richard Lemay (the first publisher of a critical edition of the *Gr. Intr.*) argued that Abū Ma'shar's work was one of the earliest avenues for introducing Aristotelian natural philosophy into the Latin West. Lemay spent a lot of time correlating the two Latin editions of *Gr. Intr.*, trying to show how it influenced later original works of the translators, and tracing Abū Ma'shar's theory of astrology to Aristotle's authentic works. He remarked that most scholars have dismissed this notion of transmission via Abū Ma'shar, and so it is today with scholars like David Pingree and Charles Burnett. But their interest, like Lemay's, had to do with what was new to the *Latins*; I am more interested in the appearance of Aristotle himself in the *Gr. Intr.*, and we can't deny that technical Aristotelian terms like "form" and "special property," and teachings about circular motion, do appear in the *Gr. Intr.* What can we say about them?

As I translated, I found it difficult to identify clear, specific source texts in the works of Aristotle, even when I used BY's occasional footnotes which pointed to them. An indirect way to look at the matter, is to identify if and when the works of Aristotle were actually available to Abū Ma'shar in Arabic. According to Gutas,[8] many of them may have been available in some form before 850 AD, but to me it seems unlikely that by 830 AD Abū Ma'shar would have had, and mastered, the wide variety of texts needed here—from *On the Heavens*, to the *Metaphysics*, *Topics*, and others. To me it makes more sense that Abū Ma'shar relied on some intermediary text, such as a Neoplatonic summary or commentary on Aristotle. (The passage in Ch. VII.4, **97-98** suggests that he had some version of the Stoic theory of mixtures from Alexander of Aphrodisias, an Aristotelian of the 2nd-3rd Centuries AD.) But that is all right, because his theory is already a blend of generic Aristotelianism, astrology, and perhaps some Neoplatonism. So we don't need to insist on pointing to the "real" Aristotle at every turn.

Now let's turn to the physical theories. Our primary chapters here are I.3 and I.4, which outline basic concepts in causation and natural change.

---

[8] See the table in Gutas 1998, pp. 182-83.

Change and causation (I.3). Here Abū Ma'shar's goal is to explain several things: the regions of the universe in which change occurs, the types of change stimulated by the planets, and something about how this change is caused.

In the traditional worldview described here, there are two distinct physical realms: a higher planetary and starry realm in which change does not occur, and a lower natural world in which it does. The kind of change I mean here is of a special sort. In classical philosophy (especially in Aristotle), change is of many types: for example, spatial motion is a form of change, and so are many other types of "alterations" which beings undergo. We can think of this first kind of change as "feature change," because it is only the incidental changing of something's features, not its very essence. This is *not* the kind of change which divides the universe into two regions, because both planets and terrestrial objects do exhibit feature changes: planets change their spatial positions, as do humans, without changing their essences as planets or humans.

The second kind of change is the most important, and divides the world into two spheres. It is often called "substantial change," and this occurs when something changes by transformation into something essentially different; a related phrase is "generation and corruption," or "coming to be and passing away." Classic examples of this would be the natural generation of a human being through reproduction, and the human's change into a corpse after death (and its eventual disintegration). But in Abū Ma'shar we can also consider elemental change as substantial change, because the principles of hot, cold, wet, and dry, are part of a process in which the elements transform into each other (which ultimately produces substantial change in complex beings). So, when Abū Ma'shar begins his discussion of change, he reminds us that the planets occupy a higher realm in which their incidental features alter, but substantial change only occurs in the realm of the four elements where we live (**13-14**).[9]

---

[9] For this reason Abū Ma'shar rejects the view of Ptolemy in the *Tetrabiblos*, that the planets are actually heating, cooling, etc.: see especially *Gr. Intr.* IV.1, **25-27** and **37-39**. And in IV.2-IV.3 he rejects the views of others on deriving planetary natures by analogy with terrestrial colors, humors, and principles.

In general, things were not thought to cause change in *themselves*, at least not in their own right. That is, a stone does not drive its own change, but it is susceptible to external pressures and stimuli which make it change position or in other ways. According to much ancient thought, this is also generally true of living beings, both animal and human. On the one hand, it's easy to see that we change mechanically because of physical pressures outside us and inside us. But even with psychic functions which we normally consider spontaneous, like desire and choice, we are partly driven by external causes. And Abū Ma'shar affirms that we have both animal and rational souls[10] (which are responsible for desires and choices). But desires are stimulated by, and respond to, external objects and change;[11] and choices are framed in terms of present stimuli and possible changes we can make via action. Even if desires and choices are not direct responses to external stimuli, we can generally trace them back to a concern with externals. So most (or maybe all) of the changes in the world occur in relation to external changes, and these are precisely what the planets cause. The planets' cosmic role within their own unchanging realm, is precisely to *externally produce and stimulate* certain feature changes as well as substantial change in the lower realm (**22-26**): this is how things which are only potential, become actual, and how things are generated and then corrupted over time. Sometimes planets produce things for the first time, such as when humans are generated; at other times they stimulate feature changes to existing things, like in illness or physical development.

How exactly the planets do this is a mystery. For since they are above the world of natural principles and change, they do not actually emanate the cold, dry, and so on: those pertain to terrestrial changes which we can only say are *caused by* the planets. But Abū Ma'shar gestures at familiar ways of causing change, in search of the right model for the planets (**27-47**). He begins with common ones, like fire directly burning wood by touching it (**28**), or indirect ways like heating water by applying fire to the container which holds it (**34**). He concludes by saying that planetary causality works in a way

---

[10] I.4, **59** and **61**; I.5, **87**.

[11] Even hunger is "external" in the sense that it is something which affects the mind due to changes in the stomach. The mind does not produce hunger in an absolutely spontaneous way.

similar to the magnet's effect on iron at a distance (**35-41**). For the magnet has a power of drawing certain things to it, the iron has a specific receptivity to magnetism, and this cause-and-receptivity relationship occurs in the medium of air. If the magnet's power were not attuned to iron it would not attract it, and if the iron were wood it would not be receptive to the magnet's power. In a similar way, the planets have specific causal powers to produce certain planetary changes (such as Saturn producing Saturnian changes), and terrestrial beings are susceptible to taking on these changes (such as the sea being susceptible to tidal changes due to the Moon's power).

Passage	Topic
I.3, **13-14, 22-26**	Two realms of change; direction of causation.
I.3, **35-41**	Model of planetary causation: at a distance, in susceptible beings.
I.3, **43, 46-54**	Much individual behavior and differences not directly caused by planets.

Figure 2: Some arguments about change and causation

This does not mean that everything we do occurs because of direct planetary causation. Most of the planet-induced effects happen at the elemental level, such as Saturn producing cold and dry effects in receptive beings. Many fundamental effects take place by the time the native is born. But once the causal agent (the planet) affects things at the elemental level, these beings then go on to behave independently in other ways (**46-54**): Abū Ma'shar says these behaviors are "stimulated" by the elemental effects (**46**). This is just like saying that someone with a weak body will later go on to be sick, or even take precautions against sickness, because of that original weakness. Thus if Saturn's effect on the native is to produce a Saturnian body and temperament through cold and dryness, such a native will go on to exhibit other typical Saturnian behaviors and responses because of it, even though Saturn is not directly causing them.[12] Now suppose that Mars has

---

[12] One of Abū Ma'shar's examples has to do with blushing (I.3, **47**). He means that shame is caused by something else (the mind, some experience), but that shame *in turn* causes the blushing. The original experience does not cause the blushing, but rather the shame does.

some effect on this Saturnian native (let's say, by a later transit or solar revolution). Such a native will be receptive to those hot and dry effects of Mars, in both his body and behavior, but only in certain ways and to a certain extent, because the original Saturnian makeup of his body places limits on how fundamentally he can be changed by Mars. So not every change we undergo, choice we make, or desire we have, is directly caused by planets; but our experiences are conditioned by the natural processes which they influence, and by how susceptible each of us is to this or that effect (**49-51**). An unresolved question is whether or not the influence occurs through a certain medium, or in some other metaphysical way.

Metaphysical principles (I.4). In Chapter I.4, Abū Ma'shar introduces some generic Aristotelian vocabulary, and is more specific as to how the planets contribute to earthly beings. Let's look at this metaphysical picture and try to build up a creature such as a human being.

The four principles and natures. We begin at the lowest physical level with the four simple "principles" (sing. رکن) which today are often called the four elemental "qualities": the hot, cold, wet, and dry. These are simple states of matter. When one of the active principles (hot, cold) is paired with a passive one (wet, dry), they produce "composite principles,"[13] which we usually call an "element." Thus fire is said to "be" hot and dry, earth cold and dry, water cold and wet, and air hot and wet. This is the Aristotelian physical theory, which dominated astrology and traditional medicine for many centuries. (The Stoic version only used one quality for each element: fire is hot, water wet, earth dry, air cold.) In Abū Ma'shar, each composite principle or element is also called a "nature" (طبیعة). The reason is probably this: in Aristotelianism, a "nature" is an inner cause of change and stability.[14] Since the processes of heating, cooling, moistening, and drying produce material change at the most basic level, and the four principles also directly constitute changeable material things, the elements must themselves be natures (**4**).

---

[13] See II.3, **4**. The Arabic word can also be translated as "element," but since we are not normally used to speaking of "composite" elements, I have decided to stick with "principle."

[14] See Aristotle, *Physics* II.1, 192b20.

So at the lowest physical level of the material world exists an unstructured, swirling process of elemental transformation—or at least, it *would* be that if there were no principle which organized this mess into determinate beings and structures, from the primitive to the complex, such as metals, animals, or humans. Without an organizing principle which states *what* things are, with some stability, we would not have proper beings **(15)** and could not even speak intelligibly about change from one thing to another. This principle is "form."

Form. In classical philosophy, form is a special term used in many ways. But it was generally agreed that form denotes "what" something is, its "essence," or its actual being: it's what makes something determinate rather than indeterminate. It is usually the correlate of "matter," and can be extended up and down the hierarchy of any kind of being: I am a human (my form) composed of certain matter (organs), but each organ is determined by its form and is composed of matter. We could speak in similar ways about musical notes, words (of a certain form, composed of letters), and so on. Let's look at two broad traditions in Western metaphysics which deal with form.

In the Platonic and Neoplatonic tradition, Forms (usually capitalized, and sometimes called Ideas) are practically the only things which have genuine being: they are immaterial, exist on a higher level of reality, and are so to speak projected into matter, structuring nature into determinate things. Platonists usually claimed that numbers, geometrical relations, certain values like Beauty, and conceptual structures like the Different, are all Forms. The Sephiroth of Qabalism are part of this tradition.

In the final version of Aristotle's metaphysics, the forms of changeable material things are more down-to-earth. They have an active role in subsuming matter into themselves, so that matter no longer exists separately. As a human, "what" I am is human, and my material nature is subsumed into that: my material aspects aren't just a bunch of indeterminate stuff, but actively crafted by form to help constitute my humanity. Perhaps a biologist would say that my DNA—or its information—is my form, and the final result of its crafting is the physical, independent me.

Abū Ma'shar draws on Aristotelianism, but it is sometimes hard to tell whether he is relying on the *Categories* or the *Metaphysics*.[15] (This is probably because, as I've suggested, he has an Aristotle partly filtered through Neoplatonic commentators—who paid special attention to the *Categories*.) The word he uses for "form" (صورة) is the same word which means "image," when speaking of chart diagrams. It comes from a root verb which means to shape or mold something so as to *incline* a certain way, to give it a certain direction; hence he says in Ch. IV.4, **17** that humanity and bestiality "incline" (صارت) towards certain things. The word was then taken to refer to the abstract quality, essence, or description of something. So when speaking of forms, particularly human forms, Abū Ma'shar is capturing the notion of activity, crafting, essentiality, and also that living beings are inclined in certain ways because of what they are. (And the less we follow this inclination, the more we stray from our humanity: see IV.4, **17**.) He then explicitly endorses the notion that forms actively craft matter, in speaking of how various animal forms adopt, subsume, and craft elemental natures into structures suitable for those animals (I.4, **21-34**). We can undergo feature-changes or "incidental" changes like increasing and decreasing in size, and becoming sick or healthy, due to the material changes in us: but we still remain what we are, due to our form (**48-51**). What we don't know yet is how astrology plays a role: see below.

Natured individuals. The combination of forms acting upon the four natures, produces the natur*ed* individual, which for purposes of analysis is a "composite" (**6, 21**), even though it is designated simply by the name of its form (**2**). So a single horse "is" its form, "horse"; but considered as a natured individual it is a composite of the form of horse and all of the material structures actively subsumed by the form and converted into *this* material horse. Interestingly, the original Arabic verb root for "individual" (شخص) meant to rise up out of indistinctness into distinctness, like a star rising up from the horizon and standing out; or a man raising his eyes and looking fixedly at something. So the natured individual "rises up," so to speak, from the mate-

---

[15] Aristotle's metaphysics went through two stages: the earlier version in the *Categories*, which was meant to be the polar opposite of Plato; and the final version in the *Metaphysics*.

rial mass of potentials and becomes an actual individual through its form. (We might also point out that crafting one's own individual *life* beyond what is simply standard and mass behavior, is an activity that takes effort.)

Special properties. One final bit of terminology is a "special property" (خاصّيّة), which is defined briefly by Aristotle in *Topics* I.5, but elaborated upon by the later Neoplatonist Porphyry in his *Isagoge* §4 and elsewhere. A special property is a feature or function of a being, which is not directly part of its essence, and may belong to one species uniquely or to many species. Thus it is a special property of horses uniquely to neigh, and of many animal species to sleep,[16] even though neighing and sleeping does not define their essences and they don't have to do those things all of the time. A horse remains a horse even when not neighing or sleeping, which shows that it's not essential to being a horse—but it is a special property. "Doing astrology" could be considered a special property of humans.

Special properties have a huge role to play in Abū Ma'shar's theory of astrology, because they pretty much describe all of the interesting things about our lives and how they change. The four natures have special properties, such as increasing and decreasing in intensity (**37-41**); forms generally have special properties, which are contrary to the natures (**42-45**); and these features are present in natured individuals (**46-53**). But Abū Ma'shar says that the planets account for the other features of individuals, including human special properties (**36, 55**), such as *how* each natured individual is composed by organs and the harmonization of soul with body (**54-74**). Once the individual is created, ongoing planetary motions will alter the activity of natural characteristics within them, such as producing imbalances that lead to illness.

But it is precisely where astrology overlaps with physics and metaphysics, that things become a bit puzzling. Among the things contributed by the planets are an individual's species, how one individual differs from another, each person's internal composition, the harmony of soul and body, and various moral qualities (**54-57**). Some of these are understandable, such as how certain organs and tissues are attributed to certain planets or their combinations, like Mercury and the tongue (**63-64**). We can understand that a

---

[16] Do amoebas sleep?

Saturnian person would have Saturnian personality traits, and that Solar and Saturnian people differ from each other in various ways. But the issue of determining the species and the harmony of soul and body needs to be explained.

In **59** and **61**, Abū Ma'shar says that Mercury contributes the species-indication of the individual human. And human is "what" a person is. But we would expect that to be his form, and this form was *not* contributed by the planets, just as was stated in **2**; indeed in **76** he affirms that the human is produced by the sperm (the parental contribution). Even if we say the form is only supposed to designate an *individual* human (**2**), he is a human nonetheless. So what does Mercury contribute here, that the form does not?

One possibility is that Mercury contributes the form and species by affecting only a suitable fetus: that is, the potentially human fetus only contains the *material substrate* to become human, and Mercury's causal activity converts its natures into an *actual* human. This is made more likely because the Sun "fulfils the animal indication" in living things by granting generic life (**59, 61**): if so, then perhaps the fetus is made living by the Sun, but a human by Mercury. And that is due to the susceptibility of the human fetus's matter to take on such a formal structure from the planets. (For the planets are always active, but do not produce humans or metals or plants everywhere.) Some other being might be alive due to the Sun, but become a different animal due to another planet. But this means that the astrology is present all the way down to the presence of life itself, and this changes the question: what do the parents contribute, that the planets do not? In order for a fetus to be susceptible to life, surely it must have a form in it already, to make it susceptible to the planets in the first place, and making it different from a stone or sprout. (I ignore here Abū Ma'shar's apparent acceptance in **77-79** that some beings are generated from other species.) So perhaps there is some kind of embedded *material form* in all potentially living things, which is contributed by the parents, but it somehow needs "finishing" by the planets. Some Neoplatonic philosophers suggested that there were material forms somewhat like this, but they were introduced as a concession because they believed that the *real* work was being done by immaterial Forms. For example, in Platonism there is a Form of Animal or Living Thing, which all living things partake in if they are suitably composed. Abū Ma'shar may have had this in mind: if so, then the Sun transmits an immaterial Form of Animal, and Mercury an immaterial Form of Human, in addition their mechanical influence on the four elements. That would be a type of Platonism.

A similar question could be raised about the harmony of body and soul. In Aristotelianism there was some debate over whether Aristotle's types of soul (or levels of soul), which were responsible for being alive, moving and perception, and rational thought, were only functions of the body or were partly immortal by being immaterial. Certainly in Platonism, some aspect of the soul is immaterial and immortal. Abū Ma'shar claims that the human body is harmonized with both animal and rational soul (**29**), but it's unclear where the rational soul comes from—it does not seem to be a function of the body, however we describe the natured, living body. So it could be that Abū Ma'shar has some other kind of soul in mind, which is granted by God: perhaps it is transmitted independently of the planets but they must harmonize it with the body.

At this point let us turn to Abū Ma'shar's model of astrology, and how the key categories of benefic-malefic or fortune-infortune, appear in it.

Stage 3: Abū Ma'shar's model of astrology (IV.4-IV.5, and IV.6-IV.9)

In Book IV Abū Ma'shar resumes his theory of astrology. After reviewing and rejecting the views of others (IV.1-IV.3), he outlines his theory in IV.4-IV.5. Following that, he ends by deducing certain astrological categories in IV.6-IV.9, such as accidental fortunes and infortunes,[17] elemental variations among the planets,[18] gender,[19] and sect.[20]

Chapter IV.4 again talks about the effect of the planets on terrestrial beings, but the concern is more strictly astrological: right away in **1-3**, Abū Ma'shar lays the groundwork for the all-important categories of fortunes and infortunes (or benefics and malefics). When planetary activity upon earthly things produces harmony and moderation in the things typically needed for a happy life, those effects are "good fortune"; when they produce disharmony and excess, the effects are "bad fortune."

---

[17] IV.5, **49-65**; IV.6, **1-11** and **64-69**; IV.7.
[18] IV.6, **12-63**.
[19] IV.8.
[20] IV.9.

I have provided a detailed reading table in Ch. IV.4 for the student to follow, and we can think of this cosmic picture in four levels. At the highest, first level, each planet exists in its own unique planetary system (such as its deferent circle and epicycle); at the second, each planet is distinguished from the others by having its own properties. This is what makes Mercury Mercury, and Saturn Saturn. It is also the source of why Mercury produces certain Mercurial effects on earth, and Saturn Saturnian ones. But the categories of fortunes and infortunes do not exist at these levels: Saturn is not an infortune in himself, but only *in relation to* things on earth.

The third level is where astrology properly enters the picture. Here, at the terrestrial level the planets produce their initial effects of drawing forth individuals from the mass of natural change, manifesting their excess and moderation in the four natures, and dividing beings into different species. But this really only sets the stage for the fourth level.

At the fourth level, planetary activity is paired with astrological judgment. Each planet's own motions, its relationships to other planets, and the quality of elemental natures, are described astrologically. That is, a planet may be slow, or going under the rays, or trining another planet—and this distinguishes each individual's qualities and destiny. Here we can properly say that planets are fortunes or infortunes, based on their own conditions and what kinds of earthly activities they act upon (**22**). So for example, Saturn is slow: at a basic level this could indicate slowly-moving events in human life. Such events are not necessarily bad in themselves, although they can be in relation to someone's life if they retard growth or hinder projects. But if Saturn is moderated by various planetary conditions, he can become an accidental fortune by indicating more moderate Saturnian effects like determination and hard work—subject to the receptivity of the person involved (**18, 22-26**). Thus, astrological judgments are made for events *at* the fourth level, but they are fundamentally *about* the individuals produced at the third level.

In the rest of Book IV Abū Ma'shar uses these ideas to develop interpretations of planets in different conditions, as well as deducing the kinds of categories I mentioned above. A fine passage which matches interpretive theory to chart conditions can be found at IV.6, **4-11**, wherein first Saturn and then Jupiter are considered as the triplicity lords of the Ascendant, and in terms of the second and fourth houses.

§4: Planetary qualities and mixtures

In the previous section I described the four simple natural principles (hot, cold, wet, dry), and their combinations as the four "natures" or elements. In this section I will describe Abū Ma'shar's version of how the principles are attributed to the planets, and his theory of planetary mixtures. This is necessary for the following reasons. First, if the planets produce natural change, then since each planet produces its own particular kinds of change, we need to attribute elemental principles to them which describe that change. So, Saturn "is" or causes the cold and the dry, because some of his significations are relatable to, and explained by, coldness and dryness. Jupiter "is" or causes the hot and the wet. But secondly, when planets combine by conjunction or aspect, these causal powers have to be taken into account. For if cold and dry Saturn combines with a wet planet like Venus, their combination must mean something different than when Saturn combines with Jupiter. If so, then we need a theory of mixtures in order to explain why planetary combinations mean what they do. In short, it doesn't matter whether you believe that the planets cause things, or only signify them: if change can be described by elemental natures, we need to know which natures go with which planets, and how they combine.

	Ptolemy	Gr. Intr.
♄	C D	
♃	H W	
♂	H D	
☉	H D	
♀	H W	C? W
☿	Varies: D-W	(C) D
☽	H W	C/H W

Figure 3: Planetary elemental principles

The standard view of the planets' principles in antiquity was Ptolemy's, in *Tet.* I.4-I.5. Figure 3 reflects his and Abū Ma'shar's views, apart from certain refinements such as whether certain principles were excessive or moderate. Thus for example, both agree that Saturn is cooling and drying (C, D)—Ptolemy being explicit that these are causal powers rather than mere properties of "being" cold and dry. In the *Gr. Intr.*, I have tried to be clear when Abū Ma'shar speaks in this causal way, although he does not do so consistently. Note that for Ptolemy, the three planets used most for the prediction of children and fertility (Jupiter, Venus, Moon) are all hot and wet (H, W). This reflects his view (which Abū Ma'shar shares) that heat and wetness are productive of generation and life.²¹ The infortunes (Saturn, Mars) predominate in the cold and dry, which inhibit and destroy life. Again following Ptolemy, Abū Ma'shar uses these ideas to justify and explain what it means to be a fortune and infortune: fortunes and moderation produce generic goods, and infortunes and excess produce generic evils.²²

Abū Ma'shar himself rejects Ptolemy's explanations for why the planets had these qualities (see IV.1), although his attributions remain similar. This Figure also shows some ambiguities and differences in Abū Ma'shar's approach. For Mercury, Abū Ma'shar agrees that he is primarily dry, but instead of letting him alternate with wetness as Ptolemy does, he associates him with the cold by nature,²³ and with the hot because dryness is akin to the hot.²⁴ Abū Ma'shar also prefers to makes the Moon phlegmatic (or cold and wet) instead of hot and wet, but he does say that she is primarily wet and has some incidental heat in her.²⁵

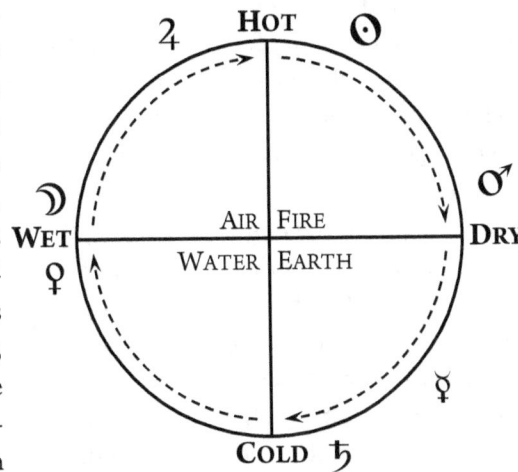

Figure 4: Proposed planetary positions on cycle of principles

The most important difference involves Venus. According to Ptolemy she is hot and wet, and this makes sense in terms of her status as a fertile planet. But Abū Ma'shar makes eleven statements about her, which we can divide

---

[21] *Tet.* I.5.
[22] See for example IV.4, **1-3**.
[23] IV.7, **32**.
[24] IV.8, **8-9**.
[25] VII.9, **33**.

into three classes. (1) In one statement,[26] Venus is made to be moderately hot and wet in a way similar to Jupiter; this is virtually identical to a couple of sentences in *Tet.* I.4 and I.5. (2) In five statements, she is said to be moderately wet, or moderate and wet.[27] These statements emphasize wetness. (3) In five other statements she is said to be cold and wet,[28] but especially in a way that is conducive to generation. So is Venus hot or cold?

I propose that we think of Abū Ma'shar's planets in the following way. Figure 4 shows where I believe Abū Ma'shar would place the planets in the cycle of elemental principles.[29] We can see that the planets least generative of children are on the dry side, and the most generative on the wet; the most benefic planets cluster around the hot and wet, and the most malefic around the cold and dry. Also, note that the nocturnal planets fall on the passive, wet-dry axis, and the diurnal ones along the active, hot-cold axis. Now, by putting Venus just on the cooler side of wetness, we can see another pattern.[30] In many traditional texts, it is said that certain fortunes can "break" the evil of the infortunes: specifically, that Jupiter breaks the evil of Saturn, and Venus breaks the evil of Mars.[31] In this Figure, Jupiter and Saturn are roughly opposite each other, while Venus and Mars are roughly opposite each other. Each infortune is opposite the fortune and luminary of its own sect, in such a way that their contrariety produces some balance and moderation.

At this point we can move to the topic of planetary mixtures: this pertains to planetary conjunctions, where the qualities of the planets, or their effects, are directly mixed. We will examine this in a couple of stages.

Fixed and variable principles. Although each planet "has" (or rather, causally produces) two principles, Abū Ma'shar is careful to point out that one of

---

[26] IV.7, **31**.
[27] IV.5, **18** and **35**; IV.6, **36** and **58**; IV.8, **11**.
[28] III.1, **14** and **18**; VII.4, **67**; VII.9, **19**; VIII.4, **132**.
[29] This is almost the same as his scheme in III.1, **11-19**. I have omitted the Head and Tail, and made the Moon a bit warmer. But the Moon and Venus could possibly switch places here.
[30] Remember that fertility and generation are functions of heat and wetness, so if Venus is cold, she cannot be very cold: perhaps cool, verging on lukewarm.
[31] See Sahl, *Aphorisms* #34.

them is fixed, while the other one varies and alters.³² The fixed principle may intensify and become excessive, become moderate, or may weaken, but it still remains the same quality; the variable principle may change into its contrary. Thus Saturn is cold and dry, but since cold is his fixed quality, he will always be cold to some degree; but the dry, being his variable quality, can sometimes alter into the wet. This, I suppose, could be one reason why Saturnian significations sometimes include stinking and water-related professions and activities: these are his cold and *wet* significations. Now for most of the planets, the fixed principle is explicitly or implicitly the active one (hot, cold), while the variable principle is the passive one (wet, dry). However, I want to suggest that this may not be correct, even on Abū Ma'shar's own terms. He says that Mars is hot and dry, and dry is the variable quality; but we have seen above that the nocturnal planets cluster around the passive qualities, and in the case of the Moon and Venus he always emphasizes their moisture. Indeed, their moisture is one reason why they are so easily affected by other planets. Likewise, Ptolemy says that Mars is hot but *excessively* dry. To me this suggests that perhaps the wet and the dry are the fixed qualities for the nocturnal planets, not the hot and cold. But this requires more research and thought.

There are many ways in which a planet's principles may change, either in intensity (for the fixed principle) or in intensity and by altering (for the variable one). This seems to be controlled in part by the planet's natural ability to be affected: thus Saturn, who is not easily affected, is less susceptible to becoming wet; but a planet like the Moon may easily change. Abū Ma'shar gives lists of such conditions in a couple of places, with examples,³³ and the four most common ones are these: (1) a planet's position relative to its apogee, (2) the elemental principles of the sign it occupies, (3) its quadrant, and (4) its solar phase. So for example, Saturn is cold and dry. As he moves down from his apogee towards his perigee, the fixed quality of cold will be weakened, and he becomes more wet; in a watery sign his cold is reinforced but he becomes more moist; and so on. But it is not just a matter of adding or subtracting individual qualities. Remember that the cycle of elemental principles is a *process*, so that when one principle is affected by its contrary, it

---

³² See IV.7.
³³ See IV.7, **2-16**; and VII.4, **34-40** and **46-57**.

affects the second principle as well. For instance, when Saturn is in a watery sign, I said it "reinforces" his cold because both he and water are cold. But in the elemental process, wetness veers towards the hot: so the way in which the cold of *water* affects his cold, is different from the way that the cold of *earth* does. The position of water's moisture in the process has a weakening effect on his cold. Likewise we may speak of the dry—but the dry itself is a result of heating, and will still bear similarity to the hot until it becomes much more cold. This is one reason why a theory of planetary mixtures is complicated, apart from the fact that many factors may affect a planet's principles.

Planetary mixtures: assessing the qualities. In Ch. VII.4, **58-64**, Abū Ma'shar proposes a method for assessing how two planets will mix their qualities in a conjunction: in one quality, or two. The terminology is a little odd, so one way to look at it is this: a "mixture" happens when the planets' qualities are different, or have undergone change. Suppose that we have a Mars-Saturn conjunction, and ignore the question of sign, quadrant, and so on. Mars is HD, Saturn is CD. Their variable quality of dryness (D) is the same, so they do not "mix" in that quality but just reinforce it. Instead, only their fixed qualities (H, C) differ: thus, they mix in "one quality." On the other hand, suppose that they conjoin in some sign or situation in which one or both of them has become more wet (W): in that case, they will mix in "two qualities": the fixed quality which is always different, and also the variable one which has been altered for at least one of them.

The meaning of this mixture has to do with their fortunate and unfortunate significations. Mars and Saturn are infortunes due to their excessiveness in two principles which are hostile to life: cold and dry. If they only mix in their fixed quality and both remain dry, not only will Saturn's dryness draw Mars's heat closer to dryness, but it will reinforce Saturn's coldness (which is further along in the process of dryness). If so, then their indications will be more malefic and troublesome in nativities, elections, revolutions, and so on. But if they were in a wet sign which added some moisture, then the wetness would draw away some of Mars's heat, and warm up some of Saturn's cold, and their indications would be more moderate and fortunate.[34]

Planetary mixtures: burning by the Sun. Being burned by the Sun is always an important consideration for a planet, and in VII.4, **65-85** he applies his rules of mixture to assess the damage. In general, the stronger a planet is by dignity, or by latitude and in its apogee, the less it is harmed by the Sun. But as for the individual planets, the worse damage is to Venus and the Moon because of their moisture. Jupiter's harm is middling because he at least shares the quality of heat with the Sun. Mercury is worse retrograde than direct, but is not terrible overall because he shares in the dry and is always close to the Sun anyway. Saturn's harm is middling, and he will also harm the Sun to a lesser extent. Mars is better direct than retrograde, and he will also harm the Sun somewhat, more so than Saturn will. And in all cases, the exact mixtures will matter: if the Sun and Saturn are made wetter by sign or some other condition, their mixture will be moderated and improved.

Planetary mixtures: theory. In the midst of these discussions in VII.4, Abū Ma'shar entertains a number of questions about mixtures, and introduces some technical vocabulary regarding mixtures—such as "aggregates," "blending," and so on (**21-29** and **93-109**). Why?

The immediate reason is that, in **17-20**, Abū Ma'shar has just pointed out that planets which *appear* to be exactly conjoined, are not, exactly. If we observe a conjunction of Saturn and Venus, that conjunction only exists relative to our vantage point. The bodies of Venus and Saturn are not actually conjoining, but are millions of miles apart. So what is the astrologer—especially a naturalistic astrologer—actually referring to when he or she

---

[34] VII.4, **60-64**. However, this does not explain why the Saturn-Mars conjunction in Cancer was taken to be so bad in mundane charts by al-Kindī and some others who followed him (like Abū Ma'shar). For it is true that Cancer is the detriment of Saturn and the fall of Mars (which is bad), but according to this elemental theory a conjunction in Cancer would moderate them, not make them worse. But as I suggest in my footnote to **77**, it could mean that the government and army (Saturn, Mars) are both *weakened* by such a conjunction, and in mundane events weakness can kill just as much as violent aggression.

speaks of such a conjunction indicating this or that event? The second reason is that when we do speak of planetary mixtures, we naturally start by making analogies with familiar material things, and this might not be appropriate because the planets exist above the realm of material change. For example, an acid and a base change each other to produce water and salt, and adding water to water makes more water; but what is the right way to think about the planets? Do a fortune and infortune cancel each other out? Or do they still do separate things? Do they produce a third thing, and if so, what? This is not just an idle question, because certain ancient texts contain puzzling interpretations. For example, we might expect that a Mars-Saturn conjunction is "very bad," on the theory that bad + bad = worse. But part of the interpretation of this conjunction in *Carmen* II.18, **2** is favorable. Likewise in transits: the transit of Mars to natal Saturn is favorable, but Saturn to natal Mars is not; the transit of Jupiter to natal Venus is favorable, but Venus to natal Jupiter is not.[35]

Thus Abū Ma'shar needs to review several types of mixture and blending, from the most crude (fastening or juxtaposition) to true chemical change (true blending), in order to come up with the right model.[36] I direct the reader to the passages there and my table summarizing them, but the bottom line is that two planets will blend in their *effect* and in some elemental *quality*, but not in a true chemical sense or in their own essence (ذات): they will not produce a third thing different from them both. In a Mars-Saturn conjunction, each planet will still produce its own Martial and Saturnian essence, but these effects will be modified according to the sign, quadrant, and so on: if they are moderated properly, the combined Martial and Saturnian essences may come to have the character or stamp of fortunes (such as we see with discipline, strong leadership, or energetic striving).

Abū Ma'shar's solution via mixtures is designed to explain conjunctions in a single chart, such as a nativity. However, the question of transits requires something extra. Suppose we have Mars transiting natal Saturn. Abū Ma'shar's mixtures could help explain why two natives will experience this

---

[35] *Carmen* IV.4, **38**. See also Schmidt 1995, pp. 31 and 42.
[36] The passage in which Abū Ma'shar introduces these terms is based on Stoic theories of mixtures, probably filtered through Alexander of Aphrodisias, an Aristotelian commentator from the 2nd-3rd Centuries AD.

differently: perhaps one native's Saturn is in Pisces, and another's in Aries: Mars and Saturn would be mixing differently due to the difference of signs. But it does not explain why there are fundamentally different interpretations for Saturn transiting natal Mars, and Mars transiting natal Saturn, since the same two planets are involved in each transit. In the case of transits, the natal planet has established a baseline natal quality, and the transiting planet has come along later to change it. Thus if Mars transits natal Saturn, Mars's heat and energy will stir up natal Saturn and allow him to perform with effort and determination; but if Saturn transits natal Mars, Saturn's coldness will make Mars's original significations sluggish. So it does matter who is doing what to whom, in explaining these transit significations. Still, Abū Ma'shar's theory of mixtures could make an important contribution to this whole topic.

§5: Hermes and Agathodaimōn

One of the valuable features of the *Gr. Intr.* is its presentation of divergent explanations for astrological categories. In Book V especially, Abū Ma'shar gives us the opinions of three groups or personages. The first is a rejected group whom he says do not understand natural things.[37] It is hard to say exactly who they are, but they seem to be a combination of unnamed Indians and earlier Persians. The second is Ptolemy of the *Tetrabiblos*, whom he also rejects: recall that Abū Ma'shar thinks it unlikely that the same man wrote the *Almagest* and the *Tetrabiblos*. The third is Hermes, who is also portrayed as reporting the view of Agathodaimōn: in some versions of Hermes Trismegistus, Hermes is the son of Agathodaimōn. Abū Ma'shar accepts the views of Hermes, both here and in Book VIII, where he prefers Hermes's view of Lot calculations when they differ from others'.

In Ch. V.18, **7**, Abū Ma'shar recognizes many books written by Hermes, so I don't think we can assume that Abū Ma'shar was working from a single source. More likely, he had one Hermes-Agathodaimōn book which dealt with signs and principles (used in Books II and V), and a separate one attributed to Hermes on Lots (used in Book VIII). This book on principles

---

[37] See V.2 and V.5, **15ff**. These may be some of the same people mentioned in IV.2. See also II.9, **2-5**.

might have been much more extensive than we think, as Abū Ma'shar notes here that Hermes "stated many judgments in his books, degree-by-degree for every sign, in different categories, in the topics of nativities and questions." Perhaps many different Hermetic books were bound together in a single volume.

In this section I simply want to provide a table of the certain and likely Hermetic passages in the *Gr. Intr.* which Abū Ma'shar uses. If read together, they show several thematic overlaps which involve the principles of light versus darkness, generation and corruption, seasonal changes, and intermediates or middles between two extremes. To me, the big payoff occurs in V.7, where Hermes explains in detail how *exactly* the planets' exaltations may be derived—not just the signs, which the other groups also attempt to explain, but the degrees themselves. It is a fascinating account which I have worked out mathematically and illustrate with many diagrams. When deriving the exaltation of the Moon, there are certain details which might reveal when this Hermes lived, or in what cultural milieu. I have not seen this kind of Hermetic astrological treatment presented anywhere else.

Hermes passages	Description
II.2	(Probably) Justifying certain fixed stars; dividing the sphere into three parts.
II.3, **4-34**	(Probably) Contains the use of beginnings, middles, and endings.
II.7, **1-31**	Quadruplicities, seasons, elemental processes.
II.9	Possibly **2-5**, due to making Aries and Cancer diurnal.
V.4, **1-20, 35-43**	Explaining the planets' domiciles; relating planetary phases to domicile rulership.
V.7	Explaining the planets' exaltations.
V.8, **12**	Possibly a reference to Hermes on the bounds.
V.14, **1-3**	References to middles and earlier Hermes statements
V.18	Twelfth-parts and *monomoria*.
VI.1	The stars and constellations which co-rise with the faces or decans.

Figure 5: Hermes-Agathodaimōn passages in *Gr. Intr.*

§6: The faces and parans in VI.1

Chapter VI.1 presents three descriptions of the "parans," or which fixed stars rise together with different parts of the zodiac. Abū Ma'shar follows his earlier sources by dividing each sign into its three faces or decans (of 10° apiece), and slowly works his way around the zodiac in each description. His three bodies of source material are (1) the Persians, Babylonians, and Egyptians, (2) Indian astronomers or astrologers, and (3) a classical Greek zodiac attributed to Ptolemy (or more likely, a pseudo-Ptolemy) and Aratus. He specifically includes the names Hermes, Dorotheus, Teucer, and Antiochus, but without stating which group they belong to. Teucer definitely belongs in (1), and probably Hermes as well; my guess is that Dorotheus and Antiochus belong in (3), but it is hard to say since several constellations in (1) and (3) are given the same names.

Group (1) seems to be a hybrid zodiac from several traditions, often called the "barbarous" sphere because it mixes several non-Greco-Roman nations' constellations. We know for example that Teucer of Babylon's Egyptian constellations are used here, as confirmed by comparing Abū Ma'shar with Appendix I of Holden's translation of Rhetorius. Abū Ma'shar also uses some Persian terminology (and not always consistently, it seems). Plenty of Greek names of heroes and divinities also appear here. However, many of the constellations here also appear in group (3), with slightly different descriptions.

Group (2) relies on Indian traditions, and at first many of the images are quite fanciful, such as the one-legged woman in a red garment with the face of a horse (Aries #2). We might chalk some of this up to the exotic Indian deities which combine human and animal features. But some are obvious adaptations from the Greek zodiac, such as the man with the face of a lamb and cloven hooves (Taurus #2), while others are thinly-disguised animals from other sources, like the young man with crooked fingers and white legs, which in context are evidently versions of elephant tusks (Cancer #1). In other cases, the images seem closely aligned with professions and activities, such as the accountant in Virgo #2 or the hunter in Libra #3, and resemble the kinds of things we might find in Tarot cards. There is also a hint that some images are connected with the Indian theory of decan rulership: in Aries #3, the male figures wants to do good because that decan is ruled by Jupiter in the Indian theory; but because the sign is ruled by Mars, he cannot help doing evil. A surprising image is Gemini #2, which is described as a *zanj* but with the color of a white animal. In medieval Arabic, *zanj* was the name for black Africans on the eastern coast of Africa around Somalia and Kenya (hence the name *Zanzibar*), so this sounds like an African albino. How did this image make its way into an Indian catalogue of faces? It probably reflects a migration of the tradition westward, picking up and amalgamating different images along the way.

Since there is much overlap between the three groups, at some point it would be nice to recreate each zodiac, and especially to see how the Indian faces do and don't match the others. For more on this topic, see Boll 1903, Gundel 1935, and Piperakis 2017.

§7: Classical aspects in VI.3 and Book VII

In Ch. VI.3 and in several places in Book VII, Abū Ma'shar makes some important statements about aspects, and especially aspects by exact degree. In this section I want to explain the two central claims: that (1) only the classical or "Ptolemaic" aspects are proper aspects, and that (2) there are no proper "out-of-sign" conjunctions or aspects. Both of these claims are denied in modern astrology.

(1) Classical aspects. Before introducing Abū Ma'shar, let's review some traditional aspect theory. Most readers should know that the "classical" or "Ptolemaic" aspects are the sextile, square, trine, and opposition; the conjunction is not exactly an aspect, because "aspect" means "to look at," and planets whose bodies are joined are not looking at each other. The other important point to make is that the signs themselves are the basis of aspects: aspects are fundamentally between *signs*, so that Aries bears a sextile relationship to Gemini, a square to Cancer, and so on. When planets dynamically approach each other from specific degrees, this is usually called a "connection" (اتّصال); when they separate from each other this called "separation" (انصراف), or more rarely "flowing away" (انصباب). So, a planet anywhere in Aries sees another planet anywhere in Gemini from a sextile *aspect*, but a planet in 15° Aries connects with or applies to a planet in 18° Gemini by a sextile *connection*. This distinction between looking by sign and connecting by degree is well established in Greek, Latin, and Arabic, and in the decades before Abū Ma'shar wrote, Māshā'allāh had put it plainly (as

quoted by Sahl): "Looking is from sign to sign, and connecting is from degree to degree."[38]

Both aspects by sign and exact connections by degree are defined as intervals of precise numbers of degrees: the sextile is 60°, the square is 90°, and so on. To put it more specifically, any particular degree in Aries bears an exact sextile relationship to its corresponding degree in Gemini: 0° Aries to 0° Gemini, 12° Aries to 12° Gemini, *et cetera*. If we map out these intervals of degrees from one sign to the next, they mostly form shapes: the sextiles form a large hexagon, the squares a large square, the trines a large triangle, and the opposition a single line dividing the circle into two halves. The point here is that the classical aspects divide the ecliptic into symmetrical polygons or regions, which fall into separate signs which see each other. This means that some signs do not see each other at all because the exact aspects by degree or corners of the polygons do not fall in them: these are said to be in "aversion" to each other, and although they are not configured by aspect they still mean something. (The material on aversion is vast and sprinkled throughout all texts, so it is not a boutique notion but a direct function of aspect theory.)

Since the early modern period, astrologers have been used to hearing about "minor" aspects and so-called "harmonics," which are supposed to allow a greater variety of aspectual relationships. An example of a minor aspect is the "inconjunct," a so-called aspect of 150°: this would allow planets in Aries to see planets in Virgo, which is not possible in classical aspects. "Harmonics" are taken to be any division of the circle without remainder: so since we can divide 360° / 5 to yield 72°, there must be a special "quintile" aspect or relationship between any planets which are 72° apart. Note that in the case of the inconjunct, multiples of 150° do not form a polygon. In the case of the quintile, there is a doubling-up of aspects between signs: both the sextile (60°) and quintile (72°) fall within the same signs. So the modern use of minor aspects and harmonics removes the concept of symmetrical polygons or shapes, and detaches connections by degree from the relationships by sign. It also subverts the key interpretive tool of aversion, which means that many traditional texts cannot be properly understood as a result.

---

[38] Sahl, *Introduction* Ch. 3, **23**.

Special terms	Verb form	Translation, meaning
نسب : "to relate"		
نسب \ نسبة	1	Relationship. A one-way correspondence or attribution.
ناسب \ مناسبة	3	Affinity. Translates Ptolemy's "familiarity" (*oikeioutai*).
تناسب \ متناسب	6	Proportion.
نظر : "to look at"		
ناظر \ مناظرة	3	Exact aspect. (Lit., to closely compare.)
تناظر \ متناظر	6	Symmetry. (Lit., to face each other.)

Figure 6: Special Arabic terminology in Ch. VI.3

But it turns out that the use of these lesser harmonics was not only proposed in the modern period. It was also proposed among the Arabic-speaking astrologers, which brings us to Abū Ma'shar. In Ch. VI.3, Abū Ma'shar partly adapts a chapter from the *Tetrabiblos* (I.13), to explain in his own way why only the classical aspects are valid. Key to this discussion are two sets of related words which must have played an important role in mathematics at the time but which are difficult to distinguish exactly (see Figure 6). The most important word is *munāzarah* (مناظرة), which here means an "exact aspect"; in other contexts I have translated this as "inspection," because it means to closely examine two things. It seems to be the intentional Arabic equivalent of the Greek word to "scrutinize" (*katopteuō*), which sometimes appears in Greek texts and which Robert Schmidt argued meant a very close connection by degree. In light of Abū Ma'shar's discussion, I think Schmidt was right. So, Abū Ma'shar is interested in the geometrical relationship between two degrees in an exact aspect, such as the 60° between a degree in Aries and its corresponding degree in Gemini.

We might ask, "why *should* some degree in Aries have any special relationship to some degree in Gemini in the first place?" I think there are two principles at work here. First is the fact that the basis of all relationships is a circle with twelve units: the signs. The signs are a balanced set of interrelated qualities or natures: quadruplicities, triplicities, and gender. So, any relationships between signs, or degrees in those signs, must reduce to and thereby harmonize with these twelve units *as* integer numbers of whole signs. Second, we have the traditional Pythagorean set of relationships in music, which mesh well with these units. The numbers 2, 3, and their inverses (1/2 and 1/3) produce these aspects, so that 1/2 of the circle is 180° or the opposition; 1/3 is 120° or the trine.

Abū Ma'shar emphasizes that true aspects must harmonize both with *each other*, and with the *whole circle* (considered as twelve units), through these simple relationships. He proposes two ways, which he treats as producing equivalent results: a shape-based, geometrical approach (**2**, **4-16**), and a numerical, ratio-based approach as in the Pythagorean system (**3**, **17-25**). That is, it's not enough for some number to be divisible into 360° without remainder: the result has to be convertible into the other aspects, and also reducible to integer numbers of whole signs. Thus the square (90°) is equivalent to a sextile (60°) plus 1/2 of a sextile (30°), and both the square and sextile equate to integer numbers of signs. It also implies that each sign has one, and only one, relationship with any other sign: for example, Aries has only one aspect with Cancer.

These requirements mean that any exact aspect between individual degrees will also have the same properties as their signs: the exact square between the corresponding degrees of 5° Aries and 5° Cancer preserves the same relationships as exist between the signs themselves. But it rules out other so-called aspects: the quintile (72°) is not reducible to an integer number of signs, because it is equivalent to 2

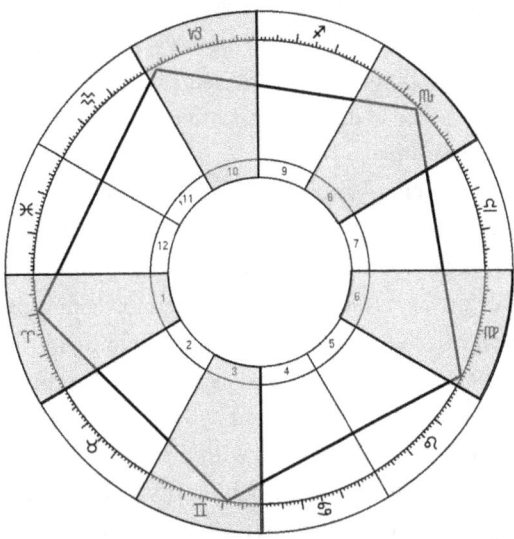

Figure 7: The quintile or fifth "harmonic"

signs (60°), with a remainder of 12°. Nor can it be converted into other aspects by simple proportion, nor does it preserve symmetry between the signs, halves of the zodiac, or even corresponding degrees. It also implies that multiple aspects can fall on the same sign, so that each sign has multiple relations to others—which is also changeable. Figure 7 shows what I mean. If we begin our quintiles with 9° Aries, the relationships between the signs are uneven, the degrees within each sign do not correspond, and the signs in which the angles of the pentagon occur do not all look at each other, either: Gemini has no aspect to Scorpio or Capricorn. If the pentagon were rotated only a few degrees clockwise, the angle which now rests in Virgo would switch to Leo, further changing the relationships between the signs and their qualities, such as quadruplicity, triplicity, and gender.

Abū Ma'shar discusses precisely just this division by quintile in VI.3, **40-46**, where he adds that some people have also proposed divisions by 8, 9, and 10. But as I noted, it is not enough to divide 360° by some number without remainder: aspects must be interdefinable through simple proportions, and their degrees preserve integer numbers of signs. For these reasons, he argues, only the classical aspects are valid.

(2) No out-of-sign conjunctions or aspects.[39] Another claim that might be a surprise, is that there are no "out-of-sign" conjunctions or aspects. This is closely related to the concept of an "orb." The Arabic word which we commonly translate as "orb" is *jirm* (جرم), which means a "body" or something's mass, bulk, or volume. When astrologers assigned each planet an orb of a certain size in degrees, this orb only pertained to the planet's body: *aspects do not have orbs*.

Let's take Venus as an example. In VII.3, Abū Ma'shar lists the standard size of each planet's orb or body, and we can see that Venus has an orb of 7° on each side of her exact degree. If she were in 25° Gemini, then the power of her orb would extend to 18° Gemini behind her, and 2° Cancer in front of her. Anything within this range would be in the power of her orb. However, because conjunctions and aspects are determined by sign relationships, only planets actually in Gemini can be conjoined with her. If some other planet were in early Cancer and within range of her orb, it could be weakly affected; but being in a different sign means being in a different state, a different situation, a different house. It is not a proper conjunction.

---

[39] For the key texts here, see VII.4, **3**, **13-14**; and VII.5, **10-14**, **22-24**, **32-33**.

As for aspects, because she is in Gemini she is configured to Leo by a sextile. She can also send an exact aspect by degree from 25° Gemini to 25° Leo. Now suppose there were some planet in early Virgo, such as Mars at 1°. In modern thought, it's as though the aspect itself has an orb of some size around it, and

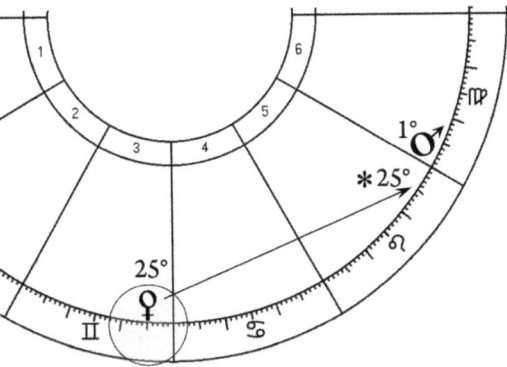

Figure 8: No out-of-sign aspects by degree

because her sextile ray is so close to Mars, she can make an "out-of-sign" sextile to him—out of sign, because he is not in the correct sign to be in her sextile. But Abū Ma'shar says this is not so. This ray may be touching *Mars's* orb, so that there is some weak relationship there, but she cannot really sextile him. She is in Gemini, he in Virgo: that is a square relationship. So she *aspects* or sees him by *square*, even though her sextile ray is somewhat within the power of his body and is getting closer to him. But the sign boundary is the real problem. If this were a horary chart and we wanted Venus and Mars to connect so as to show some event occurring, this would not be enough. We would need her to cross over into Cancer and actually connect with him by a sextile ray; if she suddenly went retrograde and never completed the connection across the sign boundary, the matter would not perfect. In a natal chart, this relationship would be even more tenuous because she is permanently in this natal state. Fundamentally, her relationship to Mars is by a whole-sign square.

§8: Lots in Book VIII

Book VIII became an important source for later work on Lots (falsely called "Arabic Parts"). A large portion of Tr. 8 of Bonatti's *Book of Astronomy* is nothing but a Latin translation of it. Abū Ma'shar discusses 97 Lots (including variations), many of which are familiar from Hellenistic and Arabic natal sources, but others were evidently invented or adapted for horary purposes, such as [61] the Lot of whether a report is true or false.[40] Known sources for his Lots include Ptolemy, al-Andarzaghar, Theophilus of Edessa, and Hermes. He also includes unnamed groups of people such as "the Egyptians" and "the Persians," but I suspect he also uses the *Bizidaj* (a Persian compilation) and either a separate translation of Dorotheus or a version of Dorotheus from the *Bizidaj*.

Abū Ma'shar's treatise is a good place for moderns to begin learning about Lots. Two passages present general and interesting methods of interpretation: VIII.1, **3-4** and VIII.8. In VIII.1 he also introduces a reason for using Lots, and makes an interesting claim about their calculation: the reason we must project the distance between two points from a third one (normally, the Ascendant), is because we want to put the topics of the Lots in the context of the good and the bad. Since the good and bad places of the chart are determined relative to the Ascendant, projecting from it illustrates how the celestial distance between two general significators, is personalized into good and bad for *this* native.

There are two more observations to make about calculations. First, most moderns have learned the algebraic formula for Lots, such as "ASC + Moon − Sun." This was not the traditional way: instead, one began from one point or planet, counted forward to the second one, and projected that distance from a third point. This makes the counting easier, but also allows us to understand *why* the calculations are as they are. For instance, in diurnal charts one usually begins with the diurnal planet (or the more diurnal of the two): thus, although two diurnal planets (the Sun and Saturn) are used to calculate the Lot of the father, by day one begins from the *more* essentially diurnal one (the Sun) and counts forward to the other (Saturn). In this vein, Abū Ma'shar presents several classifications of Lots in order to help the reader understand and remember the calculations (VIII.3, **1-8**). We cannot say that his classification always works, but it is a good way to become familiar with the thinking around Lots.

The second point about calculations concerns reversals. Most Lots—except for those which measure from the lord of a house or place to that

---

[40] Because Abū Ma'shar's names for the Lots vary slightly, and he mentions them several times, I have numbered each one with brackets for the reader's convenience.

place—are reversed by night. Thus for the Lot of the father, we measure from the Sun to Saturn by day, and from Saturn to the Sun by night. Now, the oldest sources tend to be consistent in reminding us to reverse the calculation by night, although sometimes they seem to give us the diurnal formula and assume we know the rest. But by the time of Olympiodorus (6th Century AD), the philosopher and commentator on Paul of Alexandria, we sometimes find lists of Lots organized only by their diurnal formula; on rare occasions a Lot is explicitly said *not* to be reversed by night. When we reach Abū Ma'shar in the 9th Century, it is not always clear what his sources actually report. There are numerous Lots which Abū Ma'shar reports as being the same by day and night, and to my mind this is most likely because the ancient source was simply being economical: it is tedious to explain the nocturnal reversal every time. For example, in VIII.4, **108-11** Abū Ma'shar notes that while the Lot of children ought to be reversed by night, Theophilus does not reverse it. But if we look at the known passage of Theophilus which gives the formula,[41] he simply omits to mention nocturnal charts at all. Thus, Abū Ma'shar may sometimes take a source's silence about reversals, as an instruction *not* to reverse. For these reasons we ought to be careful about accepting Abū Ma'shar's reversals and non-reversals. To my mind probably every Lot needs to be reversed, except for the house-based Lots (such as [55] the Lot of travel, taken from the lord of the ninth to the ninth).

A final topic on the subject of Lots, is Abū Ma'shar's use of Hermes. Above I stated that Abū Ma'shar probably had at least two Hermes texts: one on principles, and one on Lots. We will now turn to the latter. As in other parts of the *Gr. Intr.*, Abū Ma'shar favors Hermes when there is disagreement on astrological matters, and in this case he always favors Hermes on Lot calculations. He mentions other famous astrologers like al-Andarzaghar and Theophilus several times, only to reject them. (But he does approve of Valens.) We could understand that the authority of someone like Hermes is hard to resist, but does the text give any clues as to who this Hermes might have been?

Abū Ma'shar attaches the name of Hermes to 14 of his Lots (see below). Most of them are common natal Lots reported in just the kinds of sources we would expect, such as Dorotheus, al-Andarzaghar (who also had a ver-

---

[41] In *On Various Inceptions* Ch. 5.4, **15**.

sion of Dorotheus and Rhetorius), and Māshā'allāh. But two of them stand out as unusual: [17] the Lot of the father variation, and [21] the Lot of immovable property. If we ignore the question of reversal by night, two other traditional authors have these or almost exactly these Lots.

As for [17] the Lot of the father, this is usually calculated by day from the Sun to Saturn. But if Saturn is under the rays of the Sun, we are told by some authors (notably Dorotheus) that we must use a different formula instead: Mars-Jupiter.[42] Now, Abū Ma'shar does mention this Mars-Jupiter variation,[43] but only says that "some of the people" use it; instead, he recommends the Hermes variation, which is Sun-Jupiter—that is, if Saturn is under the rays, substitute Jupiter for Saturn and recalculate. Now, the obvious flaw in this logic is that Jupiter could equally be under the rays: what then? But never mind, that is what he reports about Hermes's variation. I have only been able to find one source for the Sun-Jupiter variation, and it is Valens *Anth.* II.32, where Valens does not give it as a variation when Saturn is under the rays, but simply as an alternative which, again, "some" people use. If Valens is a source of the Sun-Jupiter calculation, it could be that some compiler reported the Dorothean Sun-Saturn Lot, with a Mars-Jupiter variation, but somehow Valens's totally separate Sun-Jupiter Lot was taken to be another variation when Saturn is under the rays. (Remember that Valens was excerpted in the Persian *Bizidaj*, so this could be the reason Abū Ma'shar thinks it is a Persian variation.) It is also possible that the "some people" who use Sun-Jupiter are indeed followers of a Hermetic book of Lots.

As for [21] the Lot of immovable property, its calculation is the same as a Lot of "dwelling" or "inhabiting" (*oikēsis*) in Ch. 22 of Olympiodorus,[44] part of a long list of alternative Lot calculations. The name is not identical to Abū Ma'shar's, but the idea of occupying and owning land is the same.

---

[42] *Carmen* I.14, **5**. This is confirmed by Paul Ch. 23.
[43] Ch. VIII.4, **74**.
[44] Greenbaum translates this as the Lot of "family/household."

Hermes Lots in *Gr. Intr.*	Olymp.	Valens
[14] Siblings: ♄→♃		
[17] Father: ☉→♄, ☉→♃		✓[45]
[21] Immovable property: ♄→☽	✓[46]	
[25] Children: ♃→♄		
[27] Male children: ☽→♃		
[28] Female children: ☽→♀		
[30] Illness: ♄→♂		
[32] Slaves: ☿→☽		
[34] Men's marriage: ♄→♀		
[39] Women's marriage: ♀→♄		
[45] Men's and women's marriage: ♀→DSC		
[46] Time of marriage: ☉→☽, ASC[47]		
[50] Death: ☽→8th, ♄		
[86] Enemies: Lord 12th→12th		

Figure 9: Sources of two "Hermetic" Lots in *Gr. Intr.* VIII

We know from the work of Paul that Hermes wrote a book on seven planetary Lots (the *Panaretus*), and Abū Ma'shar includes a version of these, also attributing them to Hermes.[48] We have also seen that Olympiodorus, a commentator on Paul, contains the land-related Lot in a separate listing. In addition, many of the other Lots which *Gr. Intr.* attributes to Hermes would be commonly found in any single author or compiler. Finally, the Sun-Jupiter calculation for the Lot of the father comes from Valens, who was

---

[45] In *Anth.* II.32, the Sun-Jupiter calculation is simply given as an alternative that "some" people use—not specifically in cases where Saturn is under the rays.
[46] In Paul, this is a Lot of "dwelling" or "inhabiting" (*oikēsis*).
[47] This Lot should be projected from Venus, as other sources have it; but Abū Ma'shar projects it from the Ascendant.
[48] Ch. VIII.3, **52**. But as so often happens, there is confusion about the calculation of the Venus and Mercury Lots.

partly available through the *Bizidaj*. I want to suggest that (1) Abū Ma'shar's Lot material came from a late compiler either passing himself off as Hermes, or as handing down Hermetic wisdom, or perhaps simply using the name Hermes at the head of his list of planetary Lots, and (2) this compiler was relying on at least three Greek sources: some version of the *Panaretus*, Valens (with his alternative version of the Venus and Mercury Lots), and a third set of lesser-known Lots such as this Lot of immovable property. (Since so many of the other Lots are readily available, we don't need to establish whether he had included those as well.) I suspect that this was the compiler of the *Bizidaj*.

§9: Manuscripts and sentence numbering

Following are the manuscripts which BY used for their edition; I occasionally reference these in my footnotes:

B Oxford, Bodleian Library, Or. 565
C Istanbul, Carulla 1508
D New Delhi, Hamdard University Library 1325
E Eton, Eton College 65
H Istanbul, Halet Efendi 541
L Leiden, University Library, Or. 47
N Istanbul, Nuruosmaniye 2806
O Oxford, Bodleian Library, Hyde 3
P Paris, BNF, Ar. 5902
R Rampur, Raza Library 4193
S Tehran, Danishgah 470
T Tehran, Majlis 6514

As I have been doing for a few years, I have added sentence numbers to the text in bold. My standard citations for any sentence have the following form: IV.4, **5** (Book IV, Chapter 4, sentence **5**).

In addition, in a few places Abū Ma'shar presents material which is or should be in tabular form: I usually treat this as a single sentence and insert the number in the upper corner. An example may be found in V.22, where sentence **3** is a list of signs and degrees but framed as a table.

THE BOOK OF THE INTRODUCTION TO THE SCIENCE OF THE JUDGMENTS OF THE STARS

In the name of God the Merciful, the Compassionate:

Praise be to God Who created the heavens and the earth, and the wonders which are in them, and Who made the planets as embellishments and lamps, and appointed them as indicators and guidance to follow, and made the earth a resting place, and decreed its nourishment in it; and there is no God but God alone, He has no partner; and the praise of God be upon Muhammad the prophet, his slave and messenger, and upon his family[1] much peace.

BOOK I: [DEFINITION & DEFENSE OF ASTROLOGY][2]

1 This is the book which the famous astrologer Ja'far b. Muhammad b. Abī Ma'shar,[3] of Balkh in Khurāsān, wrote on the art of the introduction to the science of the judgments of the stars; and it is in eight Books, and in each Book we will state the number of its chapters. **2** As for now, we will state the chapters of Book I, and there are six:

3 Chapter I.1: On the beginning of the book, and the seven headings.
4 Chapter I.2: On the existence of the science of the judgments of the stars.
5 Chapter I.3: On the manner of the planets' activity in this world.
6 Chapter I.4: On the forms, natures, composition, and the "natured."
7 Chapter I.5: On arguing for the confirmation of judgments, and responding to everyone claiming that the planets have no power in

---

[1] Although these blessings have become totally formulaic, it's worth remembering that Abū Ma'shar himself was closely associated with 'Abbāsid Caliphs, who justified their right to rule in part because of a claimed family relationship to Muhammad.
[2] Originally, the whole title read "The first treatise [*qawl*] of *The Book of the Introduction to the Science of the Judgments of the Stars*," but I have put the title above, and added my own description of Book I's contents in brackets.
[3] Sezgin reports the name as Abū Ma'shar Ja'far b. Muhammad b. 'Umar.

their motions, nor an indication for things which come to be in this world.

8 Chapter I.6: On the benefit of the science of judgments, and that foreknowledge of things which come to be in this world from the power of the planets' movements, is very beneficial.

Chapter I.1: On the beginning of the book, and the seven headings

1 Ja'far b. Muhammad, known as Abū Ma'shar the astrologer, said: The reason that called us to write *The Book of the Introduction to the Science of the Judgments of the Stars*, is that I saw that the lovers of science aspire to the knowledge of things and the discovery of the sciences, and compiling them, so when that is prepared for them their desire is fulfilled: because the fulfillment of scholars' goals happens through the fulfillment of the knowledge they aspire to.

2 And we have found many books which [our] predecessors among the people of the profession of the stars wrote, but have not seen a book among them in which this profession is established by means of sufficient arguments, nor a [sufficient] beginning in what someone looking into this science needs. **3** And we have found that people have disagreed about the essence of judgments: for [some] people said that the power of the planets' motions have no effect in this world at all,[4] while other people said that they have an effect in genera, species, and the four principles, but in no other thing.[5] **4** And [some] people said that they have an effect in just the shifting of the season and its alteration,[6] while other people said (within the torrent of differing statements) that they have an effect in *everything* in this world: and this is the teaching of the masters of the profession of the stars.

5 But I did not see one of them offer an argument for his statement in a clear way which wise people would accept: so I thought that I would write this book concerning an introduction to the science of judgments in the way that scholars write *their* books (when explaining what they need knowledge

---

[4] See Ch. I.5, **2ff**.
[5] See Ch. I.5, **12ff**.
[6] See Ch. I.5, **111ff**.

of in their books), and first putting forth what ought to go first, and putting last what ought to be put last. **6** And in it I begin with a statement of the seven headings which wise people begin with in their books, in imitation of them and the style of their procedure, and the aspiration of their path.

7 As for the first of the seven headings, it is the goal of the book; the second, its benefit; the third, the name of the book's author; the fourth, the name of the book; the fifth, at what time one should read [it] (prior to which book or after which book); the sixth, which of the parts [of this profession] it belongs to (the part of theory, or the part of practice); and the seventh, on the division of the parts of the book into Books and Chapters.

8 As for [1] our goal in this book of ours, we make clear in it the reason for everything which the beginner needs, for instruction in the judgments of the stars. **9** And indeed we have done that because we have found many books which people among those of this profession have written on this topic, but we have not seen a single book by any of them on all of what is needed in this profession.

10 Many people have thought that the judgments of the stars are something which people found by guesswork and estimation, without their having a sound basis to work on or measure against, and indeed that they have no explanation nor proof, nor defense against objections,[7] and that all people among those of this profession follow the ancients of the old eras in all things of this science, and if one of the ancients had not set forth a prior statement on one of the topics, the scholars of this profession were unable to generate knowledge about that matter. **11** So we have written this book of ours on the establishing of judgments by sufficient arguments and proofs, and in it we have made clear the explanation of the conditions of the planets and signs, and their natures and conditions (both separately and in composite), according to the detailed examination which is needed in this book. **12** And

---

[7] تثبيت على الاحتجاج. This reads literally as "confirmation by argumentation," but that would be redundant given the previous phrases.

indeed, the knowledge there is of it, is not "found,"[8] but its derivation is possible for scholars by means of the foundations of this profession.

13 As for [2] the benefit of this book, it is manifest and clear: because for everyone wanting to begin in the instruction of judgments, he will be satisfied in reading and understanding it with this book, without needing to read every book on the introduction to the knowledge of judgments. **14** And by his reading this book alone he will gain information about things which he would not be informed about by reading the book of any other predecessor: because I have already gathered together in it the foundations of this profession, and among the secrets of its knowledge I have revealed what was unknown to many predecessors of the scholars of this profession, and among those things which are needed (of the foundations of the science of judgments) I have exposed the inner [workings] of what was unknown to those who read something of it.

15 Now as for [3] whose book it is, we have already stated at the beginning of this book of ours that it is by Ja'far b. Muhammad, known as Abū Ma'shar the astrologer. **16** And the wise needed to know the name of the author of the book, because when the reader is aware that the author of a book is knowledgeable in the doctrine of the book [and] sincere in talking about it, he will accept its teaching and be confident in the truth of what he reads. **17** (And also, it is so that the ignorant do not discover a book whose author they do not know, and attribute it to themselves so as to gain fame and profit by it.)[9]

18 And one needs [4] the name of the book, because sometimes the name of the book indicates its goal.

19 As for [5] at which time one should read [it] (prior to which book or after which book), one should read it prior to every book among the books of judgments, because it is an *introduction* to the knowledge of the science of judgments. **20** And indeed, one needs knowledge of this because sometimes a man will read one of the books but not understand it unless he has read another book prior to it.

---

[8] **BY** read this as "If any part of this science is omitted," (or rather, "the knowledge of it that is not found..."). But I believe Abū Ma'shar is referring back to **10**, where knowledge was claimed to be found by mere guesswork and estimation.

[9] Compare this with the approach of Ptolemy as described in V.8, **13-14** below.

21 As for [6] which of the parts of this profession it belongs to, it is of the part of theory: and indeed in it there is something of the theoretical part which the follower of an introduction needs for the knowledge of judgments.

22 As for how [7] many Books it is divided into, it is divided into eight Books:

23 In Book I there are six chapters: [I.2] on the existence of judgments, [I.3] confirming them by the power of the planets' motions, [I.4] the quality of their action in this world, [I.5] responding to one asserting their emptiness by means of sufficient arguments and proofs, and [I.6] benefiting by foreknowledge of things, due to the science of the stars.

24 In Book II there are nine chapters: [II.1] on the number of the images of the circle and their names, and [II.2-II.9] the conditions of the signs and their individual natures.

25 In Book III there are nine chapters: [III.1] on the reason for the astrologers' using the seven planets rather than others, in matters quick to alter, and their indications for the conditions of the four principles, and [III.2] the [proper] definition of "the judgments of the stars" and "astrologer," [and] what matter one following the science of judgments should look into, and [III.3-III.9] the special property of the indications of the Sun and Moon, and the collaboration of the planets with them both, according to what takes place in this world.

26 In Book IV there are nine chapters: [IV.1] on stating the natures of the planets [according to Ptolemy], [IV.2] their fortunes and infortunes according to what the generality of the ancients stated, [IV.3] our response to their statements, [IV.4-IV.6] what we have stated about the fortunes and infortunes among the planets, and [IV.7-IV.9] the difference of their conditions and natures.

27 In Book V there are twenty-two chapters on [V.1] the shares of the planets in the signs: such as [V.2-V.4] the houses, [V.5-V.7] exaltations, [V.8-V.13] bounds, and [V.14-V.22] the rest of their shares.

28 In Book VI there are thirty-three chapters: [VI.1-VI.7] on the conditions of the signs, and [VI.8-VI.33] the special property of their indications for things.

29 In Book VII there are nine chapters: [VII.1-VII.8] on the conditions of the planets, and [VII.9] the special property of their indications for things which come to be.

30 In Book VIII there are nine chapters on the derivation of the Lots and their explanations.

31 And indeed the book is divided into Books and Chapters, because when a book is understood [only] with difficulty but is then divided and rendered into parts, it is easier for the reader's comprehension, and more convenient for him.

Chapter I.2: On the existence of the science of the judgments of the stars

1 Regarding the stars and their motion, there are two species of the science, wonderful to consider and great in value:

[The science of "the whole"]

2 The first species is called [1] "the science of the whole,"[10] and it is the knowledge of the quality and size of the higher spheres and the spheres of the planets, each sphere by itself as well as the distance of each sphere from its neighbor, and the inclination of one relative to the other, and their size, and the scope of each sphere in itself as well as its distance from the earth. **3** Now the earth is round, and the spheres are round [and] encompass it; the highest sphere rotates in its own right, and these [other] spheres and what is in them in terms of the planets [all] rotate about the earth by one rotation in a [single] day and night, from the east to the west. **4** And the Sun arises over nation after nation, so that at one time it will be day for one nation, and night for other nations. **5** And all of the higher bodies move in two motions: many of the spheres travel in a way that is in agreement with the course of the highest sphere, from east to west,[11] while as for the planets, they travel from west to east,[12] contrary to the course of the highest sphere. **6**

---

[10] Aristotle uses this language in *De Caelo* Ch. 2, 268b11, but the description which follows is more likely based on Ptolemy's *Almagest* Ch. 1.2.
[11] This is "primary" or diurnal motion.
[12] This is "secondary" or zodiacal motion.

And many of the spheres' motion is in agreement with the motion of the planets.

7 And we have already discussed all of that in our own *zīj*,[13] and in it are stated the types of motions of the spheres and planets, each sphere and each planet on its own, and what the special property of each one of them is, and which of them is faster in motion, and which of them slower, and which of them higher than its neighbor, and that the size of the earth as compared with the highest sphere is like the point in a circle in smallness, and the knowledge of the planets' eclipsing of each other, and the eclipse of the luminaries. **8** The knowledge of this and everything one needs of this genus, in terms of the quality of the spheres and their sizes, and the amount of the planets' motions and their conditions—this is called "the science of the whole."

9 Now as for much of the quality [which is] evident [in] the science of the whole, it is discovered by direct observation; and what is not discovered by that observation is by inference from it, compelling [us] to accept it: because the indications and proofs of it are due to plain and clear reasons agreed upon in the science of calculation, geometry, and land-measurement which doubt does not enter into, and rational minds will not refrain from accepting, nor would one push away this science unless he stubbornly resists the truth.

10 And Ptolemy the Sage wrote a book called *The Book of the Almagest*, in which is everything one needs for the science of the conditions of the spheres and planets, in a detailed examination.

[The science of judgments]

11 The second species is [2] the science of judgments, and it is the knowledge of the nature of each planet, and each sphere, and the special property of their indications, and what is produced and occurs from the powers of their various movements, and their impression upon this world which is below the sphere of the Moon—among the different seasons, the alteration of the natures (which are fire, air, water, and earth), and in the

---

[13] According to King and Samsó (p. 31, n. 53), this is the *Zīj al-Hazārāt* (date uncertain).

things which take place from these natures in terms of individual animals, planets, and minerals. **12** The first species, on the science of the stars (which is the science of the whole), is relied upon for information about the second species (which is the science of the judgments of the stars).

13 As for most of the science of judgments, it is apparent, clear, and ready-to-hand; but what is *not* apparent in it is inferred by clear analogies from the science of the natures of things,[14] and what is apparent from the powers of the planets' motions over this world at the time of their culmination[15] over some places, and their distance from the earth (and their nearness to it).

14 And no one would push away this second species of the sciences of the stars unless they were people who are far from knowledge, discrimination, and thought about the conditions of the higher bodies.

[The use of judgments in other areas of life]

15 Now, there are many analogies found which we have mentioned concerning the correct definition of judgments about the stars, some of them apparent among the general public, and some of them not apparent among them.

16 Of the apparent ones which the general public understands by their clear experience, is that they find the seasons (spring, summer, autumn, and winter) existing by means of the Sun's shifting in the quarters of the [zodiacal] sphere; and they find that the natures alter and shift from one to another, and some of them are strong and some weak in the seasons, and in their agreement with [the seasons] and their being contrary to them. **17** For if the natures alter with the seasons, and the seasons alter by the Sun's shifting in the quarters of the sphere, then the shifting of the natures from one to another will therefore be by means of the Sun's shifting in the quarters of the sphere.

18 And we also find that on every day and at every time the Sun has a function in the altering of natures which is contrary to his function at another time: and that is because the more that he passes to the east of one of the

---

[14] That is, physics ("physics" comes from the Greek *phusika*, meaning "natures").
[15] مُسامتتها.

places [on earth], or is raised up over them, or is lowered below them, he alters their natures and constitutions, and from the heating, cooling, moistening, or drying, there will occur in that place, among its animals, plants, and minerals, at every time of the day and night, some alteration, generation, and corruption, that is contrary to what it had been at another time.

19 And that is like what we see at the beginning of the stirring of a man and the rest of the animals upon the Sun's reaching their east: for so long as the Sun is rising up to their Midheaven, their movement is in [a state of] increase and power; but when the Sun inclines away from the Midheaven, their motion weakens and decreases up to the setting of the Sun. **20** Now when the Sun sets from them, it is night and bodies become still in it, and become tranquil and weaken, and they become relaxed for sleeping and quiet, and generally animals go to their homes and lairs. **21** And when the Sun ascends over them a second time on the next day, they return to the first condition of stirring. **22** As for plants, the effect of the Sun is apparent in them, because many of them appear, become strong, flourish, and increase upon the rising of the Sun: such as the fragrant herb which is called the *nīlūfar*,[16] the marigold, the mallow, and the leaves of the castor-oil plant, and many other things among vegetation which stir and flourish along with his motion. **23** But when the Sun sets, they decline, weaken, and droop: and what is most apparent of this from the Sun's activity is that seeds and plants do not flourish and grow, except in places over which the Sun rises or the power of his heat affects them. **24** As for minerals, precious stones are born in them in accordance with their nearness to the orbit of the Sun (or their distance from it), because when the Sun culminates over some place, there is heat; while when he moves away, there is cold. **25** The general public understand this and much of this genus as being an evident effect of the Sun.

26 And an evident effect is also found for the Moon in many things, because the more that the Moon changes from condition to condition, many alterations take place in animals, plants, and minerals, and in the water of the sea, and in the falling of the sperm, the birthing of animals, and the inception of offspring and pollination: and that is in accordance with her increase in glow and her decrease in it, and the rest of the variation of her conditions. **27** And many different nations understand what occurs in the days of the year

---

[16] The European white water lily.

with respect to heat, cold, winds, and rains, and the types of changes in the air due to the Moon's alighting in each of the 28 mansions. **28** And for many of them, when they see each of these mansions in the west in the morning, they say that the air will be changed on that day by wind, clouds, heat, or cold, in accordance with what their experience has shown before.

29 And all of the planets are found to have various effects in this world, except that their effects among the general public are more hidden than the effects of the Sun and Moon. **30** But what the general public is guided by concerning the activity of the planets in this world, is what they find concerning the different conditions of the seasons in the quality of increase or decrease: because their variation in increase and decrease is by means of the planets' partnering with the Sun and Moon, upon [the luminaries'] alighting in any of the places of the circle. **31** For if there were no partnership of the planets with them, no summer would be hotter than another, nor one winter colder than another.

32 And of course the people of all nations and climes find and know what we stated about the alteration of natures and their shifting from condition to condition (from what little experience they have), and from this obvious situation they are certain that growth and corruption both come to be in accordance with the changing of the seasons and natures, and indeed the alteration of these things comes to be by means of the Sun and the rest of the planets. **33** But as for people with prior experience and whose days and years are long in it, they have learned some of that from their predecessors; but when they drew analogies from these evident matters which they found of the activity of the planets in the seasons and these natures in terms of alteration, they knew recondite and subtle things from them.

34 And each one of the professionals of different crafts (I mean, those who apply the craft of management and the sciences of all peoples, such as the masters of sowing, planting, the herdsmen of riding animals, sheep, and the rest of animals, and the managers of ships, and the rest of the managing professions) understands from subtle experience in the courses of the planets which of the times and periods is preferable, and which of them bad, for everything they want to do in terms of the inception of sowing, planting, sending male stallions to breed, and the reproduction of the rest of the animals. **35** As for sowers, they know the time in which sowing is better for plants greater for profit and growth, so they sow in that time. **36** And the masters of planting know the time in which it is suitable to plant types of plantings, and the time when that is not suitable; and for every species of planting, in which season it takes root better, and is more excellent and better for sprouting, and stronger: so they plant every species in the season which is suitable for it. **37** As for the masters of breeding, they understand the season in which it is suitable to send male stallions to females in order to reproduce, so they aim to send them at the right time so as to complete their pregnancy, and their birthing is at a time for their growth and upbringing to be good. **38** And sailors and the managers of ships understand the time in which the sea is stirred up due to the blowing of winds, and waves, and the time in which it is calm, and at which time of the year every wind blows: so they refrain from sailing the sea during a time when they know that the sea is disturbed by bad winds and waves, and sail it during times of the year when they know that the wind will be with them and not harming them.

39 And all of these will say beforehand what will be, in terms of the excellent and the bad, and they teach that to one who is not good at it, and has not examined it, and has not been concerned with it in the same way as their own concern. **40** They report that they know it by long examination and their experience in the divisions of the year and its conditions, and the course of the Sun and Moon, and the Moon's being in any of the 28 mansions, and from the Moon's increase and decrease in glow, and from the planets' easternization and westernization in that time.

41 And many of them also gain information about recondite things from what they discover at that time, from the blowing of some of the winds, and the alteration of the air by an increase of heat or cold, or temperateness: so that sometimes on the day of letting out a male animal to the females, a breeder will say that the clarity of the atmosphere, and the strength of the blowing of the north wind, or the blowing of another wind, indicates that more of the sheep which become pregnant on that day will give birth to males or females, and that more of their colors will be such-and-such, in accordance with what their knowledge by experience predicts. **42** And also, upon their birth they report that they will be healthy or not, and that their growth will be quick or they will die. **43** And sometimes they say that in this year death will occur in the species of such-and-such a riding animal, sheep, cow, or the rest of the animals, in accordance with what they find in their experience of the course of the Moon and the alteration of the air. **44** Likewise, those among the managers of ships having experience say that the wind which blows before the disappearance of the Sun will be altered upon the

Sun's disappearance, or will come to rest. **45** Likewise, the masters of planting say that for one species of planting which they have planted in one season, this tree will bear [fruit] more quickly than this one, or more slowly than that, in accordance with what they see of the special property in each one of [the seasons], by long experience. **46** Likewise, the people of all crafts: for in their crafts they have subtle things they know by long experience and do not make mistakes in it, and they say that the reasons by which they know these things, is by their long experience in the alterations of the air, its variation, and the mansions[17] of the Sun and Moon.

47 And people do also perceive many things by experience, apart from the indications of the stars. **48** And that is like midwives, for they understand by experience whether a woman is pregnant or not, and [whether] the fetus is male or female; and they also understand from a first-born child whether the woman will give birth after that or not, and the number she will give birth to: and their errors are few in what they report about these things due to the length of their experience and the abundance of what they have heard from the ancestors who had experienced these things from ancient times. **49** So as for their knowledge of whether a woman is pregnant or not, they looked at the woman whom they suspect to be pregnant, and if they saw the tips of her breasts to have expanded and changed from the color which they had, she was pregnant. **50** And what they also drew inferences from about a pregnant woman, was looking at the eyes of that woman: for if they saw they were sunken, and droopiness in her eyelids, and they saw she was sharp of gaze, with clear, full pupils, the white of the eye thick, they knew that she was pregnant.

51 As for their knowledge of masculinity and femininity, they looked at the woman's belly: if they saw it full, round, and coarse, with firmness in it,[18] and they saw her having a clear color,[19] they knew that the fetus was male. **52** And if in the woman's belly there was distension, droopiness, and ugliness,[20]

---

[17] Or more simply, "stopping-points" (المنازل). But since the mansions of the Moon are known, I have retained it. There are no mansions of the Sun, only special positions, which is what Abū Ma'shar means.
[18] These suggest the qualities of heat and dryness.
[19] Or, "complexion," as **BY** translate it.
[20] These suggest the qualities of wetness.

and in her color there appeared discoloration and freckles,[21] they knew that the fetus was female. **53** Then after that they looked at the tips of her breasts: for if they had changed to black, they knew that the fetus was female; while if they had changed to red, they knew that the fetus was male[22]—except that this indication by itself is sometimes misleading from woman to woman. **54** And also, the milk of the pregnant woman is taken between two fingers, and one looks: for if there was thickness in the milk and strong stickiness, they knew that the fetus was male; but if that milk was fluid, inclining to thinness, and there is no stickiness in it, they knew that the fetus was female. **55** And also, the milk of the pregnant woman is dripped onto an iron mirror and placed gently in the Sun so that it is not disturbed, then left for an hour: if it comes together so as to resemble a pearl-bead, they knew that the fetus was male; while if it spreads out, they knew that it was female.

56 Now as for their knowing what will come to be after the birth, when she gives birth and it falls to the ground they looked at its head (whether the one born was male or female): for if it resembled a crown of thin hair on its head, they knew that a native whom the woman would give birth to after that would be male, at whatever time she gave birth, after a year or more. **57** And if they saw two crowns on its head, they knew that she would give to two boys in a single belly after that. **58** And she would be blessed by every male or female born,[23] who had a crown upon its head at the time of her childbirth. **59** And what is a blessing for the one born is that its sac is whole when its mother gives birth, because the native's sac is sometimes ripped before it comes out from the belly of its mother.

60 As for knowing the number of children which the woman will give birth to, they look at the first-time mother when she first gives birth to her child. **61** For when the one born falls upon the earth, in the length of its umbilical cord are lumps and knots: so they saw how many lumps and knots there were, and said that that woman would give birth to as many individual children as there were lumps and knots in the length of that cord. **62** And if

---

[21] This sounds like the quality of coldness: the condensation or retraction of color into spots. This seems to be confirmed in III.3, **34**.

[22] Again, the blackness or darkness suggests cold and wetness, while the redness suggests heat and dryness.

[23] Something is wrong here, because a crown of hair was supposed to indicate males.

they do not see lumps, they say that she will not give birth to any after that. **63** But if the woman miscarries her first-born and then gives birth after that, this indication is sometimes invalid.

64 And also, those herdsmen of sheep and types of riding animals who have experience, have signs for every species by which they know that that type is pregnant, and its masculinity, femininity, and color; and their errors in it are few. **65** And indeed, these people understand these things due to the length of their experience in what they are in.

66 As for doctors, they know what occurs in the seasons of the year in people's bodies, with respect to the dominance of the heating, cooling, moistening, or drying. **67** And the skilled experts among doctors predict what will be in each season in the bodies of living things: of the types of illnesses, fevers, swellings, and the variation of condition in every ailment and illness, in terms of its strength or weakness, increase or decrease, and the length of its stay or speed in disappearing, and whether it will be benign or not benign, in accordance with what they see of the variation in the air of countries, and the ages of living things, and the dominance of some natures over the bodies. **68** And they say that one may gain information about these things from the mixture of the year, and the variation of the air (in its suitability and corruption) upon the shifting of the season and the alteration of natures. **69** And these things by which the doctors gain information (among the difference of the seasons of the year, and the air of countries, and the alteration of natures), comes to be through the power of the planets' motion: like the warming power of the Sun, and the moistening power of the Moon, and what appears from the action of the planets upon their blending with the Sun and Moon in every season.

[Medicine and astrology]

70 Now doctors are more knowledgeable about the reasons and causes, and the knowledge of the natures [themselves], than the masters of breeding, herdsmen, and others, for [the doctors'] profession is closer to the profession of the stars than the professions which we stated above: because the profession of medicine is the knowledge of the natures of the four principles, and the bodies of animals, plants, stones, waters, and their blending, as well as the knowledge of their special properties and what harmonizes with that and differs [from that] in countries.

71 And as for the profession of the stars, it is the knowledge of what is stimulated by the motions of the planets, in the different air of the countries, and the conditions of their people, and the alteration of natures, and their shifting from thing to thing, and their composition in individual animals, plants, and precious stones, and the knowledge of their powers in increase and decrease. **72** So, for the reasons we have stated, the profession of medicine is closer to the profession of the stars, and more noble than the professions which we stated before.

73 And indeed, doctors understand the natures of things and what is in them, in terms of general and particular powers, by means of what is evident from their actions and their alterations which belong to bodies; then, they relate everything to the nature which they find it to have by analogy with what is apparent from their powers and activity in bodies. **74** Thus they say: "This is heating, this is cooling, this moistening, and this drying, and the special property of each one is that it does such-and-such." **75** In this way then, doctors understand the natures of drugs and treatments, their special properties, and the natures of ailments and illnesses. **76** Then, they tell what will be and occur in every single [case] of that, prior to its being at [some] time.

77 As for the astrologers, they understand the powers of the planets by means of what appears from their activity in this world. **78** So, they say the Sun is heating due to what they see of his heating power, and the Moon is moistening due to what they see of the power of her activity in the water of the sea and the rest of waters, and likewise they understand the powers of the rest of the wandering and fixed stars by analogy with what appears from the powers of their movements upon this earth. **79** And in this way they tell what will be and occur in this world in general and in particular, and they seek information about that from the powers of the planets' movements acting upon the natures and altering them.

80 And for all of those whom we have stated, among all of the masters of these professions, such as farmers and the masters of ships, and the rest of the various professions, their profession is "partial" because in their profession they make use of a single type [of knowledge], even though they do understand much of the sciences of their profession and its management by experience in the courses of one of the planets. **81** But as for doctors and astrologers, their profession is "universal," because it makes use of all types of existents, and indeed they understand the science of their profession in its essence by means of what appears to them of the activity of the planets in the natures, and the activity of the natures in individuals, and by analogy with what they discover from things whose causes are hidden from them—except that the science of the stars is more noble, elevated, and lofty than the science of medicine, because doctors seek information about health, ailments, illnesses, and their conditions from the *natures*, their composition and blending, and the combination of powers which are in animals, trees, and minerals. **82** As for astrologers, they seek information about what will be and occurs in this world by means of the motions of the *planets*, their activity *in* these natures, and their alteration *of* them or shifting them from condition to condition. **83** For the planets are a cause for the alteration of natures by means of their motions, and the natures are altered by the motions of the planets: and the astrologer seeks information from the planets and the powers of their actions in the natures. **84** But the doctor seeks information by means of the *powers* of the *natures* and their alteration and shifting from condition to condition—and indeed the alteration of the natures and their shifting comes to be through the activity of the planets in them.[24] **85** So therefore, the profession of the stars is more elevated than the profession of medicine, as well as all of the [other] professions. **86** And what may also be inferred by that about the nobility of the profession of the stars, is that the profession of the stars is a heavenly profession, and its object is the stars—which do not change, nor are they susceptible to generation and corruption, until the time when God wills it. **87** But the profession of medicine and the rest of the professions are earthly, and their object is bodies and vanishing, changing individuals susceptible to increase and decrease, and generation and corruption. **88** So therefore, the profession of the stars is more noble than all [other] professions, and more lofty in rank.[25]

89 Now since the science of the stars is as we have stated, and it is obviously the science of the motions of the stars and the knowledge of their powers which appear in this world (which we have explained in relation to many of the common people and professionals making inferences about

---

[24] Abū Ma'shar's sentences are sometimes hard to follow, but his point is that astrologers focus more on the planets, while doctors focus more on the elemental natures which are *changed* by the planets.

[25] Astrology describes a wider class of events (see **95-96**), but makes more thorough use of the ultimate, celestial causes. See also Ch. I.6, **108-12**.

much of what comes to be in all of these professions, from their narrow experience and knowledge, [and] what occurs at any time and season of the year by means of the harshness of heat, cold, wetness, or dryness, in relation to the varied motions of the planets in their transit, course, and shifting in the quarters of the sphere), then why should it be denied to one knowledgeable in the movements of the planets and their natures (and the natures of the season, with the most experience, and who has attained what the scholars of old antiquity have tested out by means of the science of the stars, and what the scholars and philosophers have extracted by its wisdom and science, and its subtle reflections), that he should say, if he saw the *time* to be moderate [and] with a good mixture, "this time is healthy for bodies, their survival, and the moderation of their natures, and what is indicative of it is such-and-such a planet"? **90** And if the time was not moderate, with a predominance of one of the natures over it, [why shouldn't] he say, "this is a time for the illness of bodies, their shifting, corruption, and the weakness of their natures, and what is indicative of it is such-and-such a planet," and that planet be attributed that thing of excellence or badness?

91 And this was understood among all of the predecessors among the people of the profession of the stars, and was agreed upon by them through prior knowledge and length of experience; and what was apparent as well as hidden in the indication, was that what was indicative of that thing, was what they *attributed to* that planet (of health and illness, or good or evil).[26] **92** Then he looks at that planet indicative of the corruption of the time (or its fitness): for if it stood alone in indicating some individual animals, and its condition was like the condition which indicates the fitness of the time (or its corruption), he would say that that individual's condition would be such-and-such, in terms of survival or destruction, or fitness or corruption. **93**

---

[26] This is a confusing sentence, but Abū Ma'shar is saying that ancient astrologers attributed certain things to the planets, even though they knew that the planet itself was not overtly causing these things. Rather, they attributed the elemental qualities of (say) an illness to the planet whose motions indicated it—when an illness is really caused directly by various changes in the temperament and qualities of the body, the person's diet, the season, and so on. These things are influenced by the planets in a regular way, but not directly caused. Thus by convention Saturn "is" an infortune and "is" cold and dry, because his motions and conditions ultimately lead to those kinds of natural effects. But this attribution is not exactly scientific.

And he would gain information about all conditions of that individual (in terms of good or evil) in accordance with what he would infer from about the condition of the time (in terms of moderation or something else), because the planets are what indicate the whole, and their conditions indicate a portion of that whole. **94** For if a planet was indicating a time period and its conditions, as well as what was in it in terms of individual [things] and their conditions, of course it will indicate the single individual and its conditions, too.

95 And because bodies and souls, [one's] disposition and morals, and the rest of things differ in accordance with the different powers of the planets' motions in the situations of the year, and in the conditions of the time, and in the place, [the astrologer] will ascend from this world as though up these steps, until he can describe—from the different powers of the planets' motions in the time and place, and in the conditions of the year, and of the falling of the seed, and the inception of a man's birth—his character, generation[27] and standing, nourishment, growth, and movement, strength and weakness, courage and cowardice, generosity and stinginess, and other things of his conditions; and a way like this one may know the conditions of the rest of the animals, plants, and minerals. **96** Then, from all of the planets' motions he would gain information about all of the conditions of individuals, in terms of survival or destruction, fitness or corruption, excellence or badness, and the rest of things. **97** Thus if he had foreknowledge of the planets' motions and their conditions, he would also have prior information about the conditions of individuals, and [his] statement concerning them about what will come to be from all of their conditions, will be prior to their existing at a [particular] time. **98** So, the ancients mastered the science of the judgments of the stars in a way like this one we have stated.

[Errors in the sciences]

99 Now if error happens to occur in it, that is not due to this profession [itself], but rather that is from a failure of many people looking into this profession to comprehend its knowledge, and their weakness in understanding

---

[27] خلفة. According to Lane, this especially refers to how someone takes after his own parents, or how the current generation compares to the last one.

the subtleties of causes and reasons by which one may make inferences about its essence, and their scanty cleverness in making the connection between the powers of the planets' motions, and their natures in harmony and difference, in this world. **100** And that is because the master of this profession needs to be knowledgeable in the paths of the planets and their courses, conditions, their exact degrees and minutes in the signs at any time he needs them, and knowledge of the planets' natures and active powers in this world, in the conditions of the year, and the composition of natures, and their harmony and difference, and the natures of things and their composition and blending, and the manner of growth and birth, and the different conditions of animals, plants, and minerals, and what occurs in every one of them upon the changing of the seasons in all of the climes, and things which we will state in what follows. **101** So, if one of the masters of this profession lacked knowledge of something which we stated, he would not be complete in what he needs for the profession of the judgments of the stars.

102 And because many of those using this profession are unable to have comprehensive knowledge of all of these things, due to [these things'] subtlety and reconditeness, and the variety of their causes and powers, they are not safe from errors at certain times, and from oversights in what they need when looking into it. **103** And sometimes, some of the scholars of this profession were unable, at the time of their looking into some of the matters, to reach [a level of] truth and comprehension in it so as not to err in it, due to their inability at that time to make use of thought in every matter they needed to know in that very topic. **104** Sometimes that error was due to the doubtfulness of its indications, and the difficulty of distinguishing one of them from another. **105** And likewise for all of the subtle and recondite sciences: sometimes many of the people are unable to have comprehensive knowledge of it, and sometimes its scholars are not safe from error and oversight at certain times (and especially if it was like what we stated about the knowledge of this profession).

106 Now since the knowledge of this and the rest of the professions which are in need of foreknowledge, is in accordance with what we stated about reconditeness and its distance from the senses, one should not nullify what the person knowing it *does* attain, based on what he has *not* attained in it; nor should the ignorance of one who is ignorant of it, or who distorts it from [its true] position, be imputed to one knowing it [who] speaks truth about it. **107** Nor should he abandon what he is able to do in that, having indifference to it because he is not able to do more with it; nor should his being weak in what he does not know, prevent him from using what he *does* know of it; nor should fear of what error might occur in it (in his weakness) deter him from enjoying what he *is* able to do in it. **108** So, one should carry out what one needs to, because a little knowledge has great benefit, and especially foreknowledge of what is coming to be, and what will be coming.

109 And we already see doctors and other masters of the professions make errors in the foreknowledge of illnesses and ailments, when they report what the illness comes from and [what will] occur with the sick person, in terms of the harshness of his ailment or its ease, and the quickness of his recovery or the length of his illness, and his safety or death, and the rest of the conditions of illnesses, of what occurs in them and [what] his condition will revert to due to them. **110** But, their few errors do not prevent doctors from having a desire for their own profession, looking good in it and using it. **111** And the rejection of the people does not make that unbearable for them, nor does the small error these people see in their profession prevent them from seeking benefit from their treatments and relying on their therapies, and hastening to get confirmation in their reports of what is coming to be in the fitness and corruption of their bodies,[28] since they had already gotten benefit and proper [treatment] from them (which [the doctors] had understood about [those patients] in prior days by long examination and experience). **112** And likewise the managers of ships: the sailor does not give up navigation, nor do the people give up traveling by water due to the small error of the sailor. **113** And likewise the rest of the sciences and professions: their people are hardly safe from the accidental occurrence of error or the incidence of harm made possible by them,[29] nor does it nullify their professions because of that.

---

[28] Reading the rest of the sentence in a somewhat streamlined way. Abū Ma'shar sometimes gets carried away with his long sentences, and the rest of this one is an unpleasant mess of clauses.

[29] يتهيأ لهم. Normally this would be "being *prepared for* them," which could be Abū Ma'shar's intent: that the complexity of the professions and the world means that some error is always being "prepared," as it were. But this verb with this preposition also means "to be possible" for someone. If it is made possible *for* them, it again attributes independence to the world, as though it's working against the professional. Instead, I have translated لهم in parallel with لذلك ("because of that") and treated the

BOOK I: DEFINITION & DEFENSE OF ASTROLOGY

114 But the error of all whom we have stated, is greater in harm than the error of a master of the profession of the stars: because when the doctor errs in the foreknowledge of illnesses, treatment, and remedies, sometimes his error is a cause of killing people, and their death. **115** And if the sailor errs, sometimes that is the cause of people drowning and their destruction; and if herdsmen and the masters of breeding err, sometimes that invites the corruption and destruction of that kind of animal; and if the master of planting and sowing errs, sometimes that is a cause of the corruption of the crop and planting. **116** But if the master of the profession of the stars errs, for the most part it will be that its master is ignorant of the foreknowledge of the thing which happens and comes to be, so he will omit making advance warning of harm and detestable things prior to their arrival; and sometimes his neglect of advance warning will invite something detestable (though transitory), and sometimes there will be destruction in it; but sometimes there will not be a single thing of what we have stated, and that error will not harm its master.[30] **117** As for the rest of the other professions, for the most part there is definitely destruction, corruption, and ruin in the error of its people.

118 And this is also what we have said about the merit of the profession of the stars: since the science of the profession of the stars is the most noble of these professions, and the path of error for its people at certain times is less than the path of others (among the masters of the rest of the professions), and their error is safer and has less harm, and their correct [statements] have mighty benefits, what is more right for people who have

---

preposition as causative or explanatory: error is made possible by them because of their own ignorance, lack of experience, and general human fallibility (which has been Abū Ma'shar's point for many sentences).

[30] This is a pretty weak defense of astrology: it means that if the astrologer is helping powerful people make big decisions, his errors will either be unimportant (in which case, he is less useful) or disastrous. Imagine the astrologer advising the 'Abbāsid Caliph al-Amin after the complete sack of Baghdad saying, "Well, the city was sacked, and I sure didn't see that coming, but it's only transitory, and look at how many other errors I made which had no effect on the outcome at all!" The same would also be true for the ordinary client who is relying on his local astrologer for advice on important life decisions. But Abū Ma'shar assumes that a mundane astrologer would also have comprehensive astrological *and* normal knowledge of war and many other mundane matters (**99-104**).

discernment and knowledge than receiving and listening to them, and trusting in what they say, and making use of this profession in everything they want to do, and giving it precedence over other sciences and secular management? **119** And what is more right for the masters of this stellar science than to use what they have attained in it, and abstain from what is hidden from them, and to leave off from undertaking what their understanding has not attained? **120** For, most of the blame which clings to the scholars of this profession is because ignorant people intend to look into it seeking profit, acquisition, and an increase in rank and power: so, they will claim knowledge in this profession which they have not achieved and are unable to comprehend, and they have no aptitude in its knowledge. **121** So for this reason many of the common people find a way to reject this science and accuse it of lies and the inadequacy of its scholars and people. **122** And just this kind of bad impediment occurs in all professions.

Chapter I.3: On the manner of[31] the planets' activity in this world

1 Anyone who composes a book must make clear the concept of the book at the beginning of what he is undertaking. **2** As for us, in this book we have sought to communicate the indications of the planets over the things which come to be and pass away[32] in this world, then after that to report their natures and the rest of their conditions. **3** And in the knowledge of things, the Sage[33] has determined for us four definitional points which anyone wanting knowledge of things must adhere to:

---

[31] Reading with the title in the table of contents, for "On the *explanation of* the planets' activity...".

[32] Or, "are corrupted" (تفسد), as in "generation and corruption."

[33] **BY** point to Aristotle, *Cat.* Ch. 4, 1b25, but this reference is incorrect. It may come from a later summary of Aristotle.

Book I: Definition & Defense of Astrology

4 The first is that one must understand [1] "whether" or not the thing asked about or sought, exists.
5 The second is [2] "what" it is.
6 The third is [3] "how" it is.
7 The fourth is [4] "why" it is.

8 Now, natural things are perceived by one of the five senses, which are: sight, smell, hearing, taste, and touch. **9** As for the planets, [1] they are discovered by the sense of sight, and those who possess discernment are not able to deny their existence.

10 But as for [2] the "what-it-is" of the planets, all of the ancient philosophers (among those who discussed higher things), were agreed that their essence is of a nature contrary to these four natures which are below the sphere of the Moon (I mean, fire, air, water, and earth). **11** Because if they were of these four natures, there would inhere in them what inheres in these natures, with respect to the transformation of one into the other, and generation and passing away, and increase and decrease: and because of that the sages said that the essence of the sphere and what is in it (of the planets) is of a fifth nature.

12 As for [3] the "howness"[34] of the planets, the philosophers stated that they are spherical bodies, luminous, moving with a natural motion.

13 And as for [4] "why" they are, it is so that by their natural motion about this world, natural transformations may be stimulated in these four principles, from one to the other, due to the connection of these principles with [the planets] by nature. **14** Due to that, the philosophers said that the terrestrial world is connected to the celestial world and its motions by necessity; and because of that, from the power of the celestial world and celestial motions it happens that in this terrestrial world things are stimulated to come to be and pass away, by the permission of God.[35] **15** And that is because the higher sphere surrounds this world and is in motion about this world (along with the stars which are in it) in an eternal circular motion: so by its eternally moving the stars, and by the motion of the stars about this world, hotness is stimulated in this terrestrial world which is connected with

---

[34] That is, in what state or manner they exist (كيفيّة).
[35] This is similar to Aristotle, *De Gen. et Corr.* II.11, around 338b1.

them, and it heats up. **16** But when this world becomes hot, it softens and moves, and by its motion there occurs in these bodies a transformation of one into another, and in them there comes to be generation and corruption, by the permission of God (be He exalted!). **17** So in this way the higher bodies have an effect and management in this terrestrial world.

18 And also, it is because none of the motions are complete except for circular motion, since what moves in circular motion is not able to come to a rest (because its motion has no beginning nor end). **19** But things which move in varied ways are not complete, [and] have a limit: so when they reach the limit of the place in which they move, they come to a rest, and they are isolated from each other due to the situation of their limit. **20** And because their motion has an end, by necessity it has a beginning.

21 So whereas [a] the higher bodies (I mean, the sphere and the planets) surround this world and move about this world with a regular, circular, complete motion, in a certain understood rank and order, and [b] these bodies which are below the sphere of the Moon have two motions—one of them being [b1] direct and incomplete (by which they seek [their] limits and [their natural] place, so when they reach their limits they would come to rest—and that is like the motion of fire and air up above, and the motion of earth and water down below), and the other motion is [b2] cyclical, by which they are converted and shift into each other—due to that, those higher bodies surrounding this world (which move with a complete motion) move[36] these terrestrial bodies (which move with a varied motion). **22** So the cause of the motion of these terrestrial bodies comes to be from the motion of the celestial bodies, and the power which comes to these terrestrial bodies is from those celestial bodies. **23** And from the higher bodies' setting the terrestrial bodies into motion, the terrestrial bodies come to be shifted and transform into each other, because some of them are in each other potentially: and by their transformation into each other, there occurs generation and corruption in this world, by the permission of God.

---

[36] كانت...بتحرّك. This does not literally mean "move" (which Abū Ma'shar could have said), but rather they "have the motion" or are "with the motion." I think Abū Ma'shar is speaking instrumentally and indirectly here: the higher bodies do not directly push and pull elemental things below the sphere of the Moon, but they are indirectly responsible for their motions.

24 And an analogy for that is what we see of the effect of fire. **25** For when fire produces burning in wood, and a change from something to something through its motion and special property, smoke is stimulated from the wetness which is in the wood: because the smoke is in the wood potentially, so through the motion it emerges into actuality. **26** Likewise, change and a shifting over from one thing to another is stimulated by the motions of the planets in the four principles, so that generation and corruption occurs from [the change and shift]: because generation and corruption are in the four principles potentially, so that by the planets' setting them into motion, they emerge into actuality.

[Change in the terrestrial world]

27 Now for any of the terrestrial bodies, its action in other things comes to be in one of two ways: [1] by [direct] contact, and [2] through an intermediary.[37]

28 Something whose action is in other things by [1] contact, is like fire's activity of burning in wood by coming into contact with it, and like ice's activity of cooling by coming into contact with any body receptive of cooling.

29 But something whose action is in other things through [2] an intermediary, is in three ways. **30** One of them is [2a] what occurs from the voluntary action of a man upon another body by means of a medium which is between them both. **31** And that is like his setting some body into motion, so that from the man's setting that [mediating] body into motion, some other body (or many bodies) moves. **32** Or, it is like the man's throwing some body a certain distance away from himself, so that from his setting the thrown body into motion there will occur some effect in the thrown thing: thus from the man's setting into motion the intermediate thing which is between him and the other body, there occurs an effect in that other thing far away from him.[38]

---

[37] Or, a "medium" (بمتوسّط).

[38] For example, let the man throw a spear (the intermediate thing) at an astrologer's face (the other body): he produces a motion in the spear, which produces an effect in the face of the astrologer.

33 And the second is [2b] what any body effects by its impressing[39] on another one through a proximate intermediary. **34** That is like the heating activity of fire on water through the medium of the vessels which the water is in; or, like the chilling activity of ice on water through the intermediary of the vessels which the water is in.

35 And the third is [2c] what any body effects by its impressing on another one through a distant medium. **36** And that is like a magnetic stone which, by its character, moves iron and attracts it to itself from a certain distance through the medium of air, due to what is in that stone (of the character of setting iron into motion and attracting it), and due to what is in the character of the iron (in terms of a receptivity to being moved by the stone, and the attraction to it because of its connecting with it by nature). **37** And of course this stone would also set the iron into motion in the rest of the ways which we stated: because if there was a proximate intermediary between them (like copper or brass), it would move it and attract it; and if it touched it as well, it would move it and cleave to it; and sometimes iron which borders on the stone is moved so as to go towards it, and it is moved and attracts along with it something of its own kind which happens to be connected with it or is close to it at that time, due to the strength of the impression of that stone. **38** And many things are found among precious stones and drugs which effect motion and attraction in other bodies through their character, both from nearby and a distance.

39 Now, the celestial bodies' setting the terrestrial bodies into motion, and their alteration of them, and their changing of one of them into another, is in accordance with [2c] this third way: and that is due to what is in the celestial bodies (in terms of the motion producing alteration and change in terrestrial bodies), and due to what is in the terrestrial bodies (of a receptivity to motion, alteration, and transformation from the motion of the higher bodies), from their connection to them by nature. **40** And since these terrestrial bodies shift over into each other through the power of the motions of the celestial bodies, and generation and corruption occurs in them, natural transformations as well as generation and corruption are stimulated by their

---

[39] طبع. This is the same word sometimes translated as "character" below. It comes from the same root as the Arabic word for "nature," but specifically refers to a more superficial pressure, stamp, or influence on something.

natural motions about this world within these four principles. **41** And since generation and corruption in this world are stimulated by their motions, [the planets] come to have an indication over what is generated and corrupted.

[Direct action vs. stimulation at a distance]

42 Now [some] people have thought that what is acted upon by another, and what is stimulated by another, are one [and the same] thing, and [also] that motion and alteration are not stimulated in something by another when it is at a certain distance from it. **43** But these people have made a mistake, because the "things" in this topic are of three types: one of them is [1] the activity of a thing, the second is [2] what is acted upon by the thing, and the third is [3] what is stimulated by the thing.

44 As for [1] the activity of the thing, it is of two types: one of them is [1a] voluntary (and it is what a man does voluntarily, in terms of moving, standing, and sitting), and the other is [1b] through its nature (and it is like the burning activity of fire through its own nature, upon some body receptive of burning).

45 And as for [2] what is acted upon by another, it is also of two types: one of them is [2a] by volition (and it is like a built wall, and a carved door, and a written line, for these things are acted upon by the motion of a man from his volition),[40] and the second is [2b] through its nature (and that is like what is burned by fire, for what is burned by it is acted upon by its activity in it through [the fire's] nature).

46 But as for [3] what is stimulated by another, it is different from these two types: for it is what occurs in the thing from the other, in terms of motion and change—even if it is at a certain distance from it. **47** And that is like the blushing of shame due to shame, and the pallor of terror due to terror; and like the movement of the soul and limbs which is stimulated in a man by the song of a singer skilled in melody; and the motion, shivering, wonder, and confusion in the lover upon his seeing the beloved (and the bashfulness

---

[40] To my mind this is imprecise. I think Abū Ma'shar should have said the following, using the door as the example: what is acted upon is the *door, insofar as* it is carved. For it is not the "carved door" that is acted upon, but the *uncarved* door which is acted upon *by the carving*.

in the beloved when he sees his lover); and like the effect of the motion and attraction in iron from a magnetic stone.

48 So in this, and much of this category, various movements are stimulated by another,[41] due to the variety of their causes, even though it is at a certain distance from it. **49** Then, in individual people different qualities are stimulated by those various movements in accordance with the variety of those movements and the variety of the condition of the individuals receptive to them. **50** So likewise, since every planet moves about this world with a natural motion, motions and natural change are stimulated in these four principles by means of its natural motion, by which they take shape and combine with each other in a condition generated by that shaping and mixing, in the individuals of different species, by means of what is in each individual (of the different qualities which are not in other individuals of that species). **51** And indeed, the variation of individuals and their qualities is in accordance with the motion of the planets, in proportion to the reception of these influences from them.

52 And we will posit an example of this from the Sun: because when he passes into the first quarter of the [zodiacal] sphere and travels in it so as to mark off a section of it, an effect is produced from his alighting in it, and his natural motion about us, and what is found in his varied course among us, such that the nature of that season and the four principles takes shape, in a condition in which there are natural things of varied species: of the emergence of trees' leaves and their growth, and the sprouting of grasses and crops, and many species of fragrant herbs, fruits, trees, precious stones, animals, and the generation of one thing and the corruption of another. **53** And it is not from the Sun's "choice" that he alights in this quarter, or that those things are generated or corrupted, but it is due to his reaching this quarter by natural motion, and from his motion about us, that there is a stimulation of these natural things of different species. **54** And in this way there [also] comes to be a stimulation of things coming to be and passing away in this world, from the motions of the planets and from their reaching all of the positions of the circle, by the permission of God.

---

[41] Omitting "in every one." Abū Ma'shar is trying to be universal while at the same time only saying that it is in "much" of this category. But we get the point.

55 And in order to point out that the motion of the sphere is due to the power of the First Cause, I will state the view of the Philosopher when he said: Since the sphere is in motion, it is necessary that its motion comes to be from something other than what is moving, because if the mover was moving, that would inherently go on endlessly.[42] **56** But the sphere has eternal motion, so the power which the mover has, is endless. **57** And if its power is endless, it cannot be a body, but rather it is required to be a mover of bodies; and because its power *is* endless, it does not fade away nor pass away.

58 So, observe how we have comprehended the Maker as a mover of things, *from* apparent, known things perceived by the senses: and that He is eternal, possessing endless power, and that He is neither moving, nor coming to be, nor passing away, be He blessed and exalted, highly and greatly!

Chapter I.4: On the forms, natures, composition, and the "natured"

1 In what preceded we spoke of the "howness" of the planets' activity in things which come to be and pass away in this world, among these four principles;[43] now we will mention [1] the forms, [2] the four natures, [3] natural composition, and [4] the "natured."[44]

2 As with the current practice among philosophers, I say that we call [1] "human" forms those things which designate[45] individual people, and the "equine" those which designate every horse, and the "asinine" what designates every ass. **3** And of the things which exist in this way, we call them "forms." **4** And we designate as [2] the four "natures," fire, air, water, and earth. **5** We call [3] natural "composition" the combination of the parts of natural individuals, and the composition of every individual [considered] by

---

[42] Here and below, for "endless" one can also read "infinite." Abū Ma'shar may be referring to Aristotle, *Physics* VIII.5, especially 256a15-20.

[43] See Chs. I.3, **12** and the general theory of astrology in the rest of that chapter, especially **22-23, 35-41, 43,** and **46-51**.

[44] These are in "descending" order of reality, in which the immaterial form is [1], and the complete material being is [4].

[45] Or, "which are said about" (التي يقال على).

itself. **6** And we call [4] the "natured" what has been characterized by[46] the four natures (among all individual animals, planets, and minerals). **7** And so, four things are found in what is "natured" (I mean, natural, visible, sensed individuals):

8 The first of them is [4] the existence of the essence[47] of the natured.
9 The second, is [3] composition.
10 The third, is [2] the four natures.
11 The fourth is [1] the species which it belongs to.

12 Since we have set forth these things which we need to state for what follows, let us state the view of the Philosopher when he said: For everything caused, its cause is prior to it in rank; and the caused leads us to the cause, and we understand the cause by means of the caused.[48] **13** And[49] the natured leads us to the natures, and we understand the natures by means of the natured. **14** And for everything which occurs due to something, the thing due to which it occurs, is prior to the [caused] occurrence: and that is like "what bears" and "what is borne": for what bears is land, and what is borne is the animal, since the land is prior to the animal due to the animal being borne [upon it], and the land had already existed when there was no animal on it. **15** And it is likewise said that the natures are prior to the natured in rank, since the natures existed when there was nothing natured, and the species of animals, planets, and gems exist in the natures *potentially* when not natured. **16** And there is no subsistence[50] for the natured except through a balance of the natures, nor a subsistence for the natures within the natured except through a balanced composition, and there is no composition except by what composes, and nothing natured except by a cause. **17** And indeed, the composer is prevented from composing its own essence, and the natured

---

[46] Lit., "stamped" by (ينبطع). In the most literal sense, this phrase reads as follows: "we call 'the stamped' what has been stamped by the four stamps"; or, "we call 'the characterized' what has been characterized by the four characterizations."
[47] وجود ذات.
[48] **BY** refer to Aristotle, *Met.* V.11, 1018b8ff, but this is not quite right. There may be a Neoplatonic intermediary involved here.
[49] I believe what follows is now from Abū Ma'shar.
[50] قوام, here and later in the sentence.

from being the cause of characterizing its own essence. **18** And if it is like that, there is no escaping the fact that the cause characterizes the natured from the natures, and they compose[51] what is composed, and generate divisions among the species of animals, planets, and gems, due to the natures and forms.

19 So it is now clear that God, the Maker, the Creator, the Blessed and Exalted, assigned natural indications and movements to the planets, and that by means of what is stimulated by the powers of their natural motions in the four principles, there comes to be a composition of things which are natured, and a division of all species (due to the natures and forms) into the divisions which are in the species. **20** Then it will be clear in the future, that what is stimulated in them by the power of the Sun is more powerful for the composition of natural individuals and the division of all species from each other, and the harmony of the animal soul and the body, by the permission of God.

21 As for things which are natured, they are all of the individuals which are characterized by these four natures. **22** And the forms are what have been appointed as rulers over the natures, and they fashion [the natures] into their substantiality, and they draw forth and adopt, from the natures, tools adequate for them, so that what is in the natures potentially, is manifested into actuality. **23** This is the activity of the forms in all animals, plants, and minerals.

24 And the philosophers made an analogy like that, because they likened the forms to craftsmen, and the natures to tools, and said the forms were skillful craftsmen while the natures are various tools. **25** And craftsmen are varied, like a plowman, ironsmith, goldsmith, and carpenter. **26** But there is no craftsman among them unless it is with a tool which differs from the tool of another, and his knowledge is not practicable unless it is with a tool adequate to his craft: because the tool which is practicable for a goldsmith is different from the tool which is practicable for a carpenter. **27** And crafts are not attributed to the tools, but rather they are attributed to the craftsmen: because it is not that since the carpenter needs to saw with a saw in his profession, and to hew with an adze, that the profession is attributed to the saw and the adze, but rather that the profession is attributed to the carpenter. **28**

---

[51] Reading as though the natures do the composition. But **BY** read this as though the *cause* is doing the composing as well as generating the divisions.

And the various forms of a man, beast, predatory animal, and bird, are likewise: for what is suitable (among the natures) for the man is not suitable for the beast, and what is fit for the predatory animal is not suitable for the bird.

29 Now, the forms adopt from [their] "tools" what is adequate to them, because they adopt the human (I mean, the species) from the hot and wet natures (and the rest of them) as agreeable tools suitable for receiving the animal and rational soul, and adequate for laying down, standing up, resting, and the rest of the motions. **30** And the predatory animal species adopts from the hot, drying natures (and from the rest of them) tools suitable for claws, fangs, roughness, force, and strength. **31** And the bestial species adopts from viscous, drying natures what is suitable for hooves, cloven hooves, and the hock. **32** And the bird species adopts from light and subtle natures what is suitable for feathers, wings, and flying. **33** And likewise every species of them employs from among the natures what is suitable for, but that activity is not attributed to the natures, but rather it is attributed to the *forms*: because they are what are appointed as rulers over the natures, and they act in them; and they adopt from them what is adequate to them. **34** Because of that, the activity is attributed to the forms, and [the philosophers] liken them to craftsmen, and they make the natures be like tools.

[Special properties of the four natures and the forms]

35 Now we will state the special property of the natures and forms, so that it may be made clear to us what occurs[52] in what is natured by them. **36** And we know that everything in them which is not from their special property, is what is stimulated in natured things due to the power of the planets' motions,[53] by the permission of God. **37** As for the special properties of the four known natures, there are three:

38 The first special property is that they are antithetical to each other: because the hotness and the dry which are in fire, are antithetical to the coldness and wetness which are in water.

39 The second special property is that they transform into one another: because when earth becomes fine it transforms to become water; and when

---

[52] يعرض. Or perhaps, "occurs *incidentally*."
[53] See **54ff** below.

water becomes fine it transforms to become air, and when air becomes fine it transforms to become fire. 40 And when fire thickens it transforms to become air, and when air thickens it transforms to become water, and when water thickens it transforms to become earth.

41 The third special property is that they are susceptible to increase and decrease: because one air is wetter than [another] air, and one earth is drier than [another] earth, and one water colder than [another] water, and one hotness is less than [another] hotness—all of the four natures taking on increase and increase.

Special properties	
Of the 4 natures	Of forms
Antitheses	Not antitheses
Transform into each other	Do not transform into each other
Increase, decrease	No increase, decrease

Figure 10: Special properties of natures and forms (I.4, 38-45)

42 As for the forms, they have three special properties different from the special properties of the natures:

43 The first special property is that they are *not* antithetical to each other: because in his essentiality[54] and rationality the man is not the antithesis of anything.

44 The second special property is that they do *not* transform into each other: because the man does not transform from his humanness into something else.

45 And the third is that they are not susceptible to increase and decrease: because a man does not have more or less in his [essential] life and rationality than another man.

46 So these are the special properties of the natures and forms, and all of them meet together in everything which is natured, along with the other things: so that everything in natured individuals which is due to the natures, is susceptible to increase and decrease, and transforms from thing to thing, and is the antithesis of another; but what is due to the form in them, is not less in one individual than in another of its species, nor is one the antithesis of another, nor does it transform from thing to thing, nor does it take on in-

---

[54] جوهریته.

crease and decrease. **47** And what does not belong to the form nor to the nature inevitably has a cause, and its cause is the celestial power.

48 And that is like the man: for due to what is in him of the special properties of the natures, he will be at one time hot, at [another] time cold, and at one time healthy, and at [another] time sickly; and each one of these is the antithesis of the other. **49** And the second [cause] is what transforms one of them into another, so that he will be changed from health to sickliness, and from sickliness to health. **50** And the third [cause] is what takes on increase and decrease, so that at some times the man has greater or lesser hotness than he is at other times. **51** But these are the accidents which appear in the natured man, due to the natures.

52 As for what is in the man of the special property due to the form, he does not take on increase and decrease, because a man is not greater or lesser than another man in life, rationality, and death, nor does he transform from humanness into something else; nor is he the antithesis of anything in his essentiality and rationality. **53** And this is what is in the natured man due to the special properties of the form, and the special properties of the natures.

[What is stimulated by the planets apart from the natures and forms]

54 But as for what is stimulated in him from the powers of the planets' motions (by the permission of God), of what does *not* belong to the natures nor the form, that is made clear: and it is their indication over the distinguishing of [1] his species and [2] its individuals from the rest of the species and individuals, and their indications over [3] the composition of every natural individual, and [4] the blending of the form and the natures in natured things, and [5] the harmony of the animal and rational soul with the body, as well as [6] other things like the handsomeness of his shape (and its ugliness), tallness and shortness, masculinization and feminization, colors, movement, courage and cowardice, a good character, fatness and skinniness, coarseness and refinement, and the rest of what resembles this.[55]

55 So it is apparent to us that in a single individual the four things[56] come together, because he is an individual of the species which he belongs to, and

---

[55] Abū Ma'shar will explain this further in I.5, **12-24**.
[56] See **8-11**, and **21-22**.

BOOK I: DEFINITION & DEFENSE OF ASTROLOGY   75

is composed of the four natures. **56** And it is clear to us what is in every individual, in terms of the special property of the natures and the special property of the forms,[57] and what is in it in terms of what is stimulated by the powers of the planets,[58] by the permission of God.

57 And indeed, everything is characterized by these four natures, and [1-2] the distinguishing of all of the species and individuals from the natures and forms, and [3] the composition of natural individuals is by means of their [4?] different qualities, and [5] the harmony of the animal and rational soul in the body, and [6] the rest of their conditions are from what the power of the motions of the planets indicate, by means of the movements which the Maker, the Creator, assigned to them, from whose powers these things are stimulated.

[How individual planets indicate individuals, their, parts, and qualities]

58 And all of the seven planets, in the harmony and difference of their conditions, collaborate in indicating the conditions of every individual in this world, be that individual small or large, except that one of them will have a greater indication in some kinds or species or individuals, than what another planet has. **59** And that is like the indication of the Sun for generic life which belongs to every breathing, developing, moving animal, while the indication of Mercury is over the species of man.

60 Now when one of the planets has an indication over something, and then fulfills its indication over that thing in some individual, it will collaborate afterwards with the rest of the planets in the indication of fulfilling the parts of that individual. **61** And that is like a single individual among people: the Sun fulfills his animal indication in [the man] through the generic life which he has, and then Mercury fulfills his species-indication in him by means of the humanity and rationality he has: then they and the planets will collaborate in the indication of the completion of his limbs and qualities.[59] **62** For in an individual man, the Sun has the sole indication over the general life which is the genus, and the indication over the brain and heart through

---

[57] See **37-51**.
[58] See **54**, but also the following discussion in **58-75**.
[59] That is, in the womb.

his partnership with the [other] planets. **63** Mercury has the sole indication of humanity which is the species, and the indication over the tongue and mouth through his partnership with the [other] planets. **64** Saturn has the indication over the spleen, Jupiter the indication over the liver, Mars the indication over the blood, Venus the indication over the kidneys and the spermatic duct, and the Moon the indication over the stomach.

65 And likewise the indication of each one of them is over one part of the body so that all of its parts may be completed; but sometimes a single planet will come to have the indication over several parts of an individual man through [those parts'] qualities, due to [the planets'] collaborating in him in the way we stated. **66** And each limb comes to have a place in the body, a nature, a function, and a condition which does not belong to the other limbs. **67** A single citron is like that: it has a shape, a rind, flesh, acidic pulp, and seeds, and its seeds have two skins, and in the cavity of that seed is another seed; and each one of them has a nature and special function. **68** So one of the planets has the indication of the "fragrant plant" which is its genus, and another the indication of its "citronicity" which is its species; then after that all of them collaborate in the indication of its parts, so that one of them has the indication over the rind, and another the indication of the flesh, until the indication of all of them is fulfilled in the completion of its parts in their qualities, through the collaboration of all of them in them. **69** And likewise a single sapphire: it has a nature, size, shape, color, clarity, and indeed its hardness and opulence is more intense than other gems of its genus, and it has a special function.[60] **70** So, one of the planets has the indication of the stone which is its genus, and another the indication of the species of sapphire, and another planet has the indication of something else so that its parts are made complete through the collaboration of the planets in it.

71 And if there were no collaboration of all of the planets' indications in a single individual, it would not have different parts, qualities, and conditions, nor these portions with their qualities: it would come to be part-by-part, and their collaboration would be sporadic:[61] but all of them do collaborate in the indication over the parts of a single individual, and its qualities and conditions, in one fell swoop. **72** And likewise for every individual among animals,

---

[60] حاصّية فعل.

[61] Lit., "time after time" (مرّةً بعد مرّةٍ).

plants, and minerals: one of the planets has an indication of the genus in it, and another the indication of the species, and then they both collaborate with all of the planets after that in the indication of the completion of its parts and qualities.

73 But even though all of them collaborate in the indication over a single individual, each one of them has, in terms of a special indication for any single individual of a single species, an indication different from what it has for another individual: and that is due to the difference of their conditions, and their strength and weakness, at any time, as well as the difference in the condition of these principles which are susceptible to its powers. **74** So this is the reason we see one mixture predominate in one individual, and we see another individual having qualities and special properties which do not belong to other individuals which are of its species.

75 And all natural individuals are composed of the four principles in one of two ways.

76 One of them is [1] from the transformation of the materials which are of its genus, so that upon its transformation something else is stimulated from it: and that is like the stimulation of the human from the sperm, and the ear of grain from a seed of wheat, and a tree from a twig of a tree which is of its own genus.

77 And the other is [2] like the stimulation of any of the animals, plants, and gems from the four principles, not from some other thing just like it: and that is like vegetation and many plants and trees, for they come to be from something other than their own genus. **78** And mineral essences come to be from different vapors, not from something like them. **79** And many animals and land and sea, like flies, bedbugs, frogs, mosquitoes, worms, and many species of fish and aquatic animals, and snakes which are found in the Egyptian willow tree between the inner bark and the pulp, and some scorpions and things that scratch upon the earth, and flying animals, come to be at certain times of the year from out of the four principles without being birthed. **80** And in this second way is a refutation of those saying that nothing comes to be except from something of its own genus, and an indication that it comes to be through the decree of the Almighty, the Knowing, and His arranging it.

Chapter I.5: On arguing for the confirmation of judgments, and responding to everyone claiming that the planets have no power in their motions, nor an indication for things which come to be in this world

1 Some people reject the science of the judgments of the stars, and they are in ten categories:

<The first category:> [The planets have no indication for sublunary things]

2 As for the first category, they say that the planets do not have an indication over anything which is generated and corrupted in this world which is below the sphere of the Moon. **3** But we say that all sages agree that every essence[62] moves by a natural motion, and natural transformations are stimulated (by its natural motion) in other things connected to it by nature. **4** And if natural transformations are stimulated by its natural motion in other things connected to it by nature, then the moving is a cause of those transformations, and they are effects of it. **5** And an example of that is what is found of the movement of fire: for natural transformations are stimulated by its own special property and natural motion in things connected to it by nature, that is, burning: for fire is a cause of burning things which [can] be burned by it. **6** So, burned things are the effects of it. **7** And many things are found of this kind.

8 And likewise these heavenly bodies: since they are in natural motion about this world, a transformation is stimulated by their natural motion in these four principles connected with them by nature, from one [principle] to another: and upon the transformation of one of them to another there is generation and corruption, by the permission of God. **9** Therefore, the transformation of one to another, and the generation and corruption which exists from them, is an effect of the higher, moving bodies, and they are a cause of them; and their motions which belong to generation, are [also] what belong to corruption, except that the direction of generation is praiseworthy, and

---

[62] جوهر.

BOOK I: DEFINITION & DEFENSE OF ASTROLOGY

the direction of corruption is blameworthy.[63] **10** And that is like wood which is burned so that it becomes charcoal: for even though it is corrupted from the woody nature by the motion of the fire in it, from that motion comes the generation of charcoal, because the corruption of one thing is the generation of another things. **11** So due to that, the generality of preceding philosophers said that eternal, natural generation is stimulated by the eternal, natural motions of the planets, until the time when God wills that [to cease].

The second category: [Planets do not indicate individuals, their parts, nor their conditions]

12 As for the second category, they state that the planets do have indications over general things like the four principles (which are fire, air, water, and earth), and over the transformation of one into the other, and over genera and species in a general way—like their indications in the sense of a genus, over "the living" in general (which is stated about each body which has life), and indicating in the sense of a species, over man, horse, donkey, and the rest of species in a general way.[64]

13 So, they claim that [the planets] do indicate the four principles, and the transformation of one into the other, and their shifting from condition to condition, and genera and species in general—but they do *not* indicate [1] the single individuals which [derive] from these four principles: like Sa'īd, Khālid,[65] a single horse, and a single donkey. **14** Nor do they indicate [2] the parts of individuals either, like the head, hand, leg, and the rest of limbs; nor [3] their conditions, like standing, sitting, illness and health, and the rest of the various general and partial conditions which belong to each individual in the world.[66]

15 We will respond to their statement with two arguments. **16** One of them is that a foundation agreed upon by the philosophers is that every indi-

---

[63] This will later be a basis for classifying planets into fortunes (or benefics) and infortunes (or malefics): see IV.4, **2-3** and IV.5, **3**.
[64] Examples of this would be the Sun for living things, and Mercury for humans: see Ch. I.4, **59**.
[65] In Greek texts the typical names would be Socrates and Callias.
[66] So, they deny Abū Ma'shar's statements in I.4, **54-74**.

vidual in this world (of natural individuals), is composed of the four principles (which are fire, air, water, and earth), because these principles exist in every individual in this world. **17** Now the Creator made the genera and species be active in these principles by reason of the motions of the planets around them, because each individual which is generated or corrupted in this world comes to be by means of the motion of the principles, and the shifting of one to the other, and by the motion of the Sun and planets about them, stimulating in them that motion which is the shift and transformation [into that thing]. **18** So since the planets are the cause of the motions of these principles, and the transformation of one of them into the other, and they have an indication over genera and species (as they claim), therefore they are the cause of generation and corruption which exist in these principles, by the permission of God. **19** And because the genus, species, the four principles, and generation and corruption exist in every individual, and the planets are indicative of genera, species, the four principles and the transformation of one of them into the other, and the motions which are the inception of generation and corruption, the planets are therefore indicative of single individuals. **20** And since they indicate single individuals, they are indicative of the parts of individuals as well as their conditions.

21 The second argument is that wholes are said to be wholes in virtue of their parts, and parts are parts of a whole: and [therefore] a single individual is one of the parts of a whole species, and a species is a whole in virtue of the single individuals which fall under it. **22** So if the planets indicate a species, then they also indicate the single individual which belongs to that species, because when they indicate the general species of human (which is predicable of each individual human), and the species of horse (which is predicable of each individual horse), then they also indicate [1] the single individuals: which are the individual human (such as Sa'īd and Khālid) and the individual horse. **23** And if they indicate single individuals, they therefore indicate [2] the parts of those individuals, which are the head, hand, and leg, as well as [3] the qualities, which are whiteness, blackness, and other qualities, and [the individuals'] conditions, which are illness and health, standing and sitting, and the rest of the conditions.

24 So, the planets do therefore have an indication for [1] single individuals, the [2] parts of individuals, and [3] their general and special properties and conditions.

BOOK I: DEFINITION & DEFENSE OF ASTROLOGY

The third category: [The stars do not indicate the possible]

25 As for the third category, they are those among the people of examination and debate [who] reject the science of the judgments of the stars, and say that the planets do not have an indication over anything which comes to be in this world, and they argue for that by saying that the stars do not indicate the possible. **26** We will now [1] state the argument of some of the ancients who rejected the possible,[67] then we will [2] establish the possible,[68] then we will make clear that [3] the planets do indicate the possible.[69]

27 The people who [1] rejected the judgments of the stars by reason of the possible, argued by saying that the Philosopher stated that the conditions of things in the world are three: the necessary (like that fire is heating), the impossible (like that a man flies), and the possible (like that a man writes).[70] **28** But, [they say], the stars indicate [only] two of the factors, the necessary and the impossible; but as for the possible, they do not indicate it: so the profession of the stars is invalid.

29 Now as for the people among the masters of the stars and many of the ancient philosophers, who used to confirm the indications of the stars over things coming to be in this world in a compelling way, when this difficult question came to them and they were unable to answer it, they rejected the possible. **30** They said that there are [only] two factors: the necessary and the impossible, for we understand two things: "yes" or "no," and the meaning of them is "the existent" and "the nonexistent." **31** As for "yes," it indicates the existent, while as for "no," it indicates the nonexistent; and the existent is the necessary factor, while the nonexistent is the impossible factor. **32** And these are called "mutually exclusive" propositions, because when one side is true, the other side is false, and they cannot both be true together in a single matter at a single time.[71]

---

[67] See **27-39**.
[68] See **40-81**.
[69] See **82-110**.
[70] The ideas of Aristotle's *De Interp.* Ch. 9 may be the basis of this discussion, but there might still be Neoplatonic intermediaries involved.
[71] Thus there were even astrologers who denied that astrology was about possibilities (rather than necessities).

33 And that is like two men, one of whom says, "tomorrow there will be rain," while the other says "tomorrow there will not be rain": for there is no escaping it but that one of them is true (and it is the necessary), and the other false (and it is the impossible). **34** And likewise, if a speaker today says that tomorrow something will occur, and then that thing does occur tomorrow, it occurs because its occurrence was necessary. **35** But if he says it will not occur, and it doesn't occur, then it doesn't occur because its occurrence was impossible. **36** So, if one of them is true, the other is false. **37** And likewise, if so-and-so says, "he will walk," and he walks, then he walks because it was necessary that he should walk; and if he said "he will not walk" and he does not walk, he does not walk because it was impossible that he should walk.

38 And they said that people are compelled to do things, for when they do something they do it because they are compelled to do that (and it is the necessary); while if they do not do it, they are prohibited from doing it, because it is impossible that they should do it. **39** So for everything that is, its being is necessary;[72] and for what is not, it is prohibited from being—and the stars only indicate these two things, while the possible does not exist at all.

40 But [2] the Philosopher refuted their statement and confirmed the possible by many arguments; then after that[73] he stated that the possible leads to either the necessary or the impossible:

41 The first argument in his confirmation of the possible, was that he said necessary and impossible things[74] are known at the three times[75] by what is necessitated or made impossible through their *natures*. **42** But as for our *actions*, they are different from that because they are possible. **43** And that is like our knowledge of the Sun, namely that he was glowing in past time, and he is glowing now, and he will be glowing in the future; or like our knowledge of fire, namely that it was heating, it is heating now, and it will be

---

[72] "Is" and "being" in this sentence could also be understood as "coming to be" or "generation," but Abū Ma'shar means this is a much broader sense about existents themselves.

[73] See **79** below.

[74] Abū Ma'shar does not say "things," but is the general term implied by the word endings.

[75] That is, past, present, and future.

heating. **44** Likewise if we say that fire, air, water, and earth, just as they are now, they were like that, and will be like that, so one knows that in the three times it is true. **45** And this is the necessary factor. **46** As for the impossible factor, it is like our saying that a man was flying, and the man flies now, and it is possible that he will fly in the future; and likewise if we say that fire was cold, and it is cold, and it will be cold. **47** For that is known to be impossible in the three times, and is false. **48** Thus the necessary and the impossible come to be known in the three times by what is necessitated and what is made impossible by their natures. **49** But as for our actions, they are not like that because when a man says "I was doing good in what is past, and am doing good now," then he cannot say "I will definitely do the good in the future," because he does not know whether or not he will be able to do that. **50** But if a man does not know what he will want to do without question, this is not compelled but rather it is possible: so the possible exists.

51 The second argument is that he says the necessary and the impossible are each in the whole species equally, while the possible is not in it equally. **52** And that is [like how] life exists in all people equally, and hotness is equally in all fire, with nothing of it being susceptible to increase and decrease;[76] and likewise all impossible things are equally distant from all people of the species, because it is equally predicated of all people that they do not fly, and that fire is not cooling. **53** But as for actions, they are not like that because in the species of humans one may do the good, and another may do evil, and the action of one might be greater for the good or for the evil than the action of another. **54** And [even] if all necessary things were not true of all people of the species equally, nor the impossible equally distant from all people of the species equally (and they do not change), our actions would [still] not be equally in the species, but rather they would [still] change from good to bad, and from bad to good, at various times, and from little to much, and from much to little, and they are susceptible to increase and decrease—so they are the possible, and so the possible exists.

---

[76] These are examples of the necessary, or what is necessary "by nature." But Abū Ma'shar did say that hotness is capable of increase and decrease, in I.4, **41**, and in **84** below. On the other hand, at the end of this sentence he may just mean that fire is "not cooling." Nevertheless he is saying it awkwardly because he wants to say that (for instance) all living people are equally alive.

55 The third argument about the existence of the possible is that a man does deliberate and take counsel in what is possible: like if a man wanted to build a building, he would deliberate about the quality of what he wanted to build, and would take counsel in it. **56** And if his resolve to build was firm, he would deliberate and choose on which day he would begin it. **57** And if he wanted to travel, he would take counsel on whether or not he should travel, and whether travel by land would be good for him, or by sea: and if his resolve to travel was firm, he would deliberate and take counsel on which day he should travel—then he would travel on the day he wanted. **58** And if he wanted to sow, he would deliberate and take counsel in what he wanted in relation to the sowing, and in the place he wanted to sow: then he would choose what he wanted based on his deliberation and what he was advised to do. **59** And if he wanted the companionship of a man, he would deliberate and take counsel on which of the people is good for him: then he would choose the one he wanted.

60 And it is done like that in particular things, such as a man who deliberates and says, "which thing will I eat today," or "which thing will I drink," or "which garment will I wear," or "in which chair will I sit?" **61** And if he had healthy limbs and senses, he would say, "I will pay attention to such-and-such" (or not), or "I will speak with so-and-so" (or not). **62** For this and things of this type are able to be chosen, and for all of these possible things, they first arise in thought, and next they come to doing it or leaving it aside.

63 Now as for the necessary and the impossible, they are both discovered in things having natural existence by means of thought alone:[77] because a man knows by thought that life is necessary for a living man, and that it is impossible that he should fly. **64** And if things had only been necessary or impossible—and the necessary and impossible derive from compulsion—people would not need thought nor advice. **65** And deliberation and advice would be futile when choosing one thing over another: because a man is not able to deliberate with true thought or take advice from another, on whether fire burns or doesn't burn (since burning is by compulsion). **66** And he does not deliberate with true thought and say "will a man fly, or not," because it is impossible that he should fly.

---

[77] That is, choices and deliberation are irrelevant when it comes to identifying necessary and impossible things.

67 And the fourth argument is that there is a single potential in necessary things: that is, they come to be by compulsion. **68** Or, impossible things also have a single potential: namely, they do not come to be at all. **69** But we do see many things in which there are two potentials, that something should come to be just as it is, and that it will not come to be: such as a whole cloth which, if it is left in its state it will remain (until the day it wears out); while if it is cut, it will take on cutting. **70** And like iron, lead, and the rest of what is like them: if they are left alone they will remain solid; but if they are melted they take on melting—and they will be susceptible to melting less or more so than others. **71** And likewise air already takes on the hot or cold, [whether] little or a lot.

72 Thus it is made clear that the possible exists and it is of three types. **73** The first of them is "natural," and it is easy: that is like hoping for rain with a uniform [covering] of stormy clouds in winter, for the possibility that there will be rain is greater than that there will not be. **74** Another is "by desire," and it is difficult: that is like the ambition of some of the underclass and miserable people to attain rulership and nobility. **75** An example of this possibility is that he will *not* become a ruler, more so than that he will; but if he was a ruler, it would be due to a powerful contingency. **76** The third [type] of the possible is the "equal," and it is what comes to be by thought: and that is like the hope of a pregnant woman that she would give birth to a male, for her hope of that has no more power than her fear that she should give birth to a female.

77 And among the possibilities is what appears in bodies due to their susceptibility to the thing and its contrary: and that is like water, which is able to become cold, then heats up: it takes on cold less or more so, and heating less or more so.[78] **78** And among them is what comes to be through deliberation, and choosing one thing rather than another: and that is like how a man with healthy limbs is able to deliberate on whether to stand or not stand, to speak or not speak, and to turn around or not turn around—then he chooses one of the two and does it due to soul's power of deliberating on it and choosing one of them, and due to the ability of his body to be susceptible of action.

---

[78] Lit., "it takes on cold less or more so than cold, and heating less or more so than heating."

79 Once the Philosopher finished confirming the possible, he reported that the possible reverts to the necessary or impossible: and that is like the speaker who says "I will walk tomorrow" or "I will not walk," because both walking and its contrary are possible for him. **80** But when he does walk, then his walking has become necessary: because before he walks, the walking is possible for him; but once he walks the possibility is eliminated from him and he comes to be in the realm of necessity. **81** But if he does not walk tomorrow, he will come to be in the realm of the impossible, because the walking will not be readied for him.

82 Since [3] we have made the conditions of possibility clear, it should be clear that the planets are indicative of the three factors [mentioned before], which are the necessary, the possible, and the impossible.

83 And[79] we say that every individual in this world (of the individual animals, plants, and minerals) is composed of the four principles (which are fire, air, water, and earth), because they exist in every individual. **84** And every principle among them is susceptible to increase, decrease, and transformation from one of them to the other, because one hotness is less than another hotness, and one air wetter than another, and one water colder than another, and one earth dryer than another, and some of them transform into others.[80] **85** So, if each principle by itself has the potential to take on change, and individuals are composed of these four principles, then individuals [so] composed therefore have the power to take on increase and decrease, and transformation from one of them to another, and their motions and susceptibility to alterations and compositions are by means of the motion of the signs and planets about them. **86** And the signs and planets are therefore indicative of the conditions of the four principles and their alterations, and compositions in individuals, by the permission of God.[81]

87 As[82] for a living man, he is composed of an animal and rational soul, and the four natures; and the Philosopher has stated that the planets are liv-

---

[79] The argument of this paragraph is that natural things have the potential to undergo contingent changes.
[80] See I.4, **37-41**.
[81] See **17-19** above.
[82] The argument of this paragraph is that our rational souls deliberate about possible things.

ing, and they have rational souls:[83] so, by the permission of God they indicate the harmony of the rational and living soul in the body, by the rational soul they have, and by their being alive, and by their natural motions—just as we stated in what preceded. **88** And the rational soul has the potential for thought and choice, and the body the potential to take on what possible. **89** So, if the planets indicate the harmony of the animal and rational soul as well as the body, then they indicate necessary, impossible, and possible things, because a living man has the life which is necessary for him, and the impossibility of flying, and possibility because he is susceptible to illness and health, hotness and coldness, wetness and dryness, and it is in him to deliberate on many things and choose one of them. **90** The power by which he chooses one thing over another is the thought within him, for it belongs to a man apart from all [other] animals; the potential for taking on the thing and its contrary belongs to bodies; and our actions come to be by our prior thought about the thing which we want to do. **91** So if a possibility exists first in the soul (to do one thing and its contrary), we do one of them or seek counsel about it.

92 The astrologer looks at things which have the ability to be potentials for taking on a thing and its contrary, up to whatever the matter will end up as, and he does not look at its special property: for within the profession of the stars the astrologer does not see whether fire burns or not (since he knows that it burns); and within the indications of the planets he does not see whether ice is cooling or not (because he knows that it cools). **93** But he does see whether or not fire will burn some [particular] body which is susceptible to burning, tomorrow; and whether or not ice will chill something susceptible to being chilled, tomorrow; and whether or not there will be rain tomorrow, and whether or not a man will choose to say such-and-such tomorrow, or whether or not to walk tomorrow. **94** And indeed, he looks into these things because it is possible for these things to be as well as not to be.

---

[83] Aristotle does say that the heavens are alive (*De Caelo* II.12, 292a19-22), but he does not attribute rational souls to them in that place. On the other hand, they do not need nutrition or have animal desires, so perhaps rational soul is appropriate to them.

95 So if by their natural movements the planets indicate that something will not come to be, then it is prohibited from being.[84] **96** And if they indicate the being of something together with the time of the indication,[85] its being comes from what is necessary. **97** But if they indicated that it would come to be at a future time, their indication for the being of that thing would be in potential *until* the time in which it exists—and when the thing does exist, its being would come to be from the necessary. **98** And likewise a man who is not prevented from speaking by some problem: for the speaking in him will be in potential until the time in which he speaks, and when he does speak, that speaking in that time will come to be from the necessary. **99** And indeed fire too, even though it is burning, the burning in it is in potential prior to its activity: so when it does burn, the burning comes to be from necessity.

100 So it is now clear to us that the planets do indicate the possible as well as choice, and that is in two things. **101** One of them is in composition, such as the possible which is in an individual man due to being susceptible to the thing and its contrary,[86] and the choice which is due to his soul. **102** The second is in the things whose generation is in a future time, just as we stated.

103 And just as the planets indicate the possible and the choice which belong to a man, so likewise do they indicate that the man will *not* choose apart from what the planets indicate: because his choosing the thing or its contrary is by means of the rational soul which mixes with the animal soul in individuals, through the indications of the planets. **104** And that is like the man who, in his body, is receptive of the possibility of moving as well as desisting from it, and of standing or not standing, and in him is the soul's power of choosing one of them. **105** So when he chooses, he does one of them or desists from it, and will pass into the realm of the necessary or impossible, since possible things and choosing definitely pass into one of the two: except that the man does not choose except for what the planets indicate about him, in terms of the necessary or the possible. **106** As for being susceptible to possi-

---

[84] I.e., it is impossible.

[85] This means that the event and the planetary indications exist at the same time, such as if something of the nature Mars-Mercury occurs in real time during a Mars-Mercury transit: for then it is necessarily happening at that moment.

[86] That is, because of his body, as mentioned in **88**.

ble things, it is found in these four principles which are below the sphere of the Moon, and in the bodies composed of them. **107** But as for the planets, they do not have that because they are simple bodies.[87]

108 And as for the choice which comes to be by thinking about things, it belongs to the human apart from all [other] animals because he has the rational soul by which he meditates on something or its contrary, then chooses one of them so as to repel detestable things and troubles from himself through that choice, by the power of his knowledge. **109** But as for the rest of the animals, their actions are by nature because they do not have a rational soul by which thinking comes to be. **110** And as for the planets, even though they have rational souls, they do not need it due to their distance from troubles.

The fourth category: [The planets only indicate seasonal changes]

111 As for the fourth category of those who reject the indications of the planets, they are people who have looked into the science of the whole (I mean, the science of the spheres and their conditions),[88] and said that the planets have no indication over things which come to be and occur in this world, in terms of individual animals, plants, and minerals, but their indication is only over the changing of the seasons.

112 Now, these people who have looked into the science of the whole are not able to deny this range of power belonging to the planets' activity, be-

---

[87] In this discussion Abū Ma'shar comes close to saying that although the planets indicate things which fall into the *category* of the possible (such as marrying or not marrying), as a matter of *fact* someone *will* choose what they happen to indicate about his character. This sort of abrogates the whole point of the discussion, which was to say that people have the power of choosing one thing over another. Luckily, he later talks about the importance of using choices to enhance or inhibit other types of events which are indicated. The greater problem for the concept of choice is that since the chart also predicts things about other people in the native's life (such as the spouse), it implicitly includes *other* people's choices in the indication: and it is hard to see how the power of choice works for someone if their choices are also described in the nativities of other people. So we still have to ask how likely it is that someone might *actually* choose something *contrary* to what the chart indicates.
[88] See I.2, **2-10**.

cause this is of their felt, manifest activity, and rejecting it is a bare-faced lie: because one does not reject the science of judgments and [also] confirm the indication of the planets over the changing of the seasons unless one has little knowledge of the natures of things, and what is born of the shifting of one of them to another. **113** Because one knowledgeable in what we have stated knows that the alteration of natures and the variation of their conditions comes to be *by means of* the changing of the seasons; and the changing of the seasons comes to be by means of the power of the planets' motion; and the things which occur in this world are by means of the changing of natures and the shifting of seasons from one condition to another. **114** So therefore the planets, by the power of their motions and their changing the seasons, and the shift from one of them to another, do indicate what occurs in this world.

115 And all of the philosophers claim that the planets have indications over things which come to be in this world, and all of them employ this second species of knowledge of the stars (in every one of their situations and motions), in religious and earthly affairs. **116** And that is evident from their actions, for one who understands their teaching; and indeed they do that because [the planets] are the highest bodies, and the most noble of them. **117** And among the philosophers it is not doubted that generation and corruption exist in this world through the power of their movements, by the permission of God.

118 And [the philosophers] say that what is necessary for one looking into the first species of knowledge of the stars,[89] is to look into the second species of it afterwards,[90] because they are two sciences connected to each other. **119** For the second science is the fruit of the first science, because when the knowledgeable person understands the quality of the movements of the spheres and planets, and their quantity, then the fruit of that is to understand what the powers of those movements and conditions indicate for things which come to be in this world. **120** And if he does not know what the planets indicate through their movements, then there is no fruit for the first species of the science of the stars.

---

[89] That is, astronomy or the science of the whole.
[90] That is, astrological judgments.

121 And the situation of these people who look into the first science but do not understand this science connected with it, is like the situation of people who have drugs and medical creams but do not understand how to use them, nor for which thing the drugs and remedies are appropriate, in treatments and the repelling of illnesses.

122 And likewise, these people also understand the conditions of the planets and their positions in the signs, but they do not know what thing the planet has an indication for in its sign and condition. **123** And what these people's rejection of the second species of the science of the stars comes to, is that they are people not [actually] applying themselves to it. **124** So they reject it, because if they acknowledged it, the people would blame them for neglecting its knowledge; and it would be said about them that of the two species of knowledge (one of them being connected to the other), they were good at one of them but not the other.

The fifth category: [Planetary indications cannot be replicated in experience]

125 As for the fifth category, they are also people who have looked into the science of the whole, and consider the science of the judgments of the stars from the perspective of experience. **126** And they say that judgments concerning the planets are not sound because things are known by experience, and the minimum [needed] for knowing the truth of a thing by experience, is if it is found to be in a single condition twice. **127** But the planets are not able to be in that [situation], because if a planet was in some position in the signs and the other planets were looking at it or assembling with it, it will not return to that condition in that sign in which it was, except after thousands of years. **128** And the lifespan of a single man doesn't reach this amount of years, so how is a man able to find the planets twice in a single condition, so that he may experience what they indicate from their returning to their place?

129 We say[91] that the ancients understood the natures of the planets and their indications from many things, some of them particular [and] manifest, some of them general. **130** As for the particular [and] manifest ones, it is like

---

[91] Abū Ma'shar's basic point in his response is that we can replicate many smaller and short-term things: we are not limited to replicated everything at the same time.

what is found from the influences of the Sun for warming, and the Moon for moistening and putrefying, and from the influences of the planets on the alteration of the air every day and night. **131** As for the general ones, it is like what is found from their indications in the revolutions of the years of the world[92] and nativities, from the variation of condition in the hot, cold, and the moderate, and health and illness, and death, travel, and the rest of the general and particular conditions.

    132 And these are manifest things which the philosopher will discern from the people[93] in a short time if he compares planets and their conditions for several years to the planets of other years, from their alighting in the fiery, earthy, airy, or watery signs, in whichever position of the sign they are, after the nature of the sign and its indications are [already] known. **133** And the ancients who observed the stars did likewise, for no man among them observed the stars for 1,000 years, or 500, nor did the lifespan of [any] knowledgeable man among them reach these years.

    134 But the knowledgeable man did determine by measurement the planets at one time of his lifespan, so that he understood the positions which he found them in during those times of his, and he wrote down their positions in the signs and the dating of his measurements. **135** So when many years had passed by that measurement, one of the scholars of the people of that period would be charged with measuring the planets [again] and consider [the difference] between their places at his measurement of them, and their places at the time of the measurement of the one who had been before him (whose measurement he relied on), so as to know the correct [value] of that. **136** And as a model of this work, Ptolemy the Sage perceived the true positions of the planets, because he looked at the measurements of the planets which had been measured by one a long time before him, such as Hipparchus and others among the sages relied on for their measurements, and he understood them. **137** Then in his own time he measured the positions of the planets for many years, and saw what the difference was between his own measurement and that of those ancients: he understood it and ex-

---

[92] That is, mundane ingresses (but probably also Full and New Moon charts).
[93] **BY** read this as though the philosopher is one of the people, but this seems wrong. Yet it does not seem right that he would simply learn it from just any casual person.

amined it in a clear way until he understood their explanations and proved their positions for himself through the prior measurement of the ancients.

138 And if Ptolemy and all of the predecessors who took an interest in the true positions of the planets had observed them when they were at the apex of their epicycles or in some [other] known position in them, [and] then the position of the planet in its epicycle exactly matched its position relative its eccentric center, [and] then they did nothing until the planet returned to that position relative to its epicycle and eccentric center, [and] then they measured it another time, the true position of the planet would not be found at all, and the number of planetary spheres would not be understood, nor the apex of each sphere, nor its perigee, nor the rest of its positions. **139** For it is [only] by much observation, many times, in different years, in season after season, that they understood the positions of the planets and their course in year after year, and their cycles, and the number of their spheres, and the utmost elevation of every sphere as well as its lowest point,[94] and the rest of its positions and situations.

140 And likewise the sages understood what had been doubtful to them concerning the natures of the planets and their indications: for they looked at their positions or conditions in one of the signs at one of the periods, and found that [the planets] had indications for determinate things. **141** So they understood those indications and wrote them down, and made their positions and conditions be models for making comparisons. **142** Then after many years some of the sages searched for those indications, taking into account the positions of the planets in their own time [as compared] with what the predecessors found, and they discovered they had indications over things resembling the original indication, so they made those indications be models and considerations [to follow]. **143** Then the philosophers looked at those things which the planets had indicated, time after time, and they drew conclusions from them about their indications which had been hidden from them, and what they wanted from the indications of the planets turned out to be correct for them.

144 And if they had searched for their indications upon [the planets] returning to their positions after 1,000 years, nothing at all would have been clarified for them; but what they wanted of the indications was made clear to

---

[94] Lit., "its fall" (هبوطه): that is, the perigee.

them when they understood the different positions of the planets and their indications in time after time, over many years. **145** So, they drew conclusions about what had been hidden from them based on what they did find, until they knew their indications over things.

146 And likewise the scholars found hidden things because they drew inferences about them by what was manifest to them in that category: because truthful reports about something, in case after case, at different times, and clear indications about it, can stand for observation and a [directly] present existing thing.

The sixth category: [That the zījes differ and have errors]

147 As for the sixth category, they are people among the masters of calculation who are unable to look into the calculation of the stars and find the true position of the planets from the book in which the knowledge of the whole is (I mean, the *Almagest*): so they calculate the positions of the planets by partial, conflicting *zījes*, and when they calculate each planet by one of the *zījes* they find it in certain degrees of one of the signs—but if they calculated that planet by another *zīj*, they would find it in another degree in the signs. **148** So these people state that judgments are not valid, and they present two arguments for their claim:[95]

149 One of them is that they say if a man wanted to erect the planets by one of the *zījes*, there would be a compensatory addition or subtraction in the calculation of the [*zīj*] by which he erected the planets from their mean [positions] and equations, such as seconds and thirds, so that error would affect the length of the days in the position of the degree of the planet.

150 The second argument is that they say judgments are based on the true degree of a planet, but none of the planets is accurately determined in

---

[95] In these descriptions Abū Ma'shar is referring to the use of tables in the *zījes*. The tables showed how far each planet moves in certain units of time, such as in 100 years, 1 year, 30 days, and so on. That way, one could quickly count how much time had passed since the day which the tables were calculated for, and determine the planet's position. But because different *zījes* used years of different lengths (such as Ptolemy's tropical year, or the *Sindhind*'s sidereal year), the calculations of different *zījes* would yield different results. Some *zījes* were also combinations of previous ones with differing values.

the true degree of its sign: because when one of the planets is found by one of the *zījes* to be in one of the signs, in a certain degree, its position by another *zīj* will be different than that degree, and one will not know which of them is more correct. **151** And if he does not rely on the true degree of the planet in its sign, then the judgment about it is not valid.

152 But these people are wrong and have not come across any correct *zījes*, so they turn to imagining that their *own* error is what enters upon the master of the profession of the stars. **153** We respond to their statement with two arguments. **154** One of them is that we say if the astrologer wanted to make a judgment about something, he would rely on looking at the nature of the planets, and their special properties, and the lord of the sign of each one of them, and its exaltation, and the lords of its triplicities, and its position relative to the stake and what follows it, and the falling [planet], and its alighting in the house of assets, siblings, and the rest of the houses of the circle, and their indications for the climes and the rest of the general indications they have—then he would judge in accordance with what it indicates. **155** But as for the degree of the planet, it has a partial indication, for the masters of the stars use it in special things; but if there was an error of [some] minutes or a degree, that would not harm the owner of the judgment.[96]

156 The second argument is about the one making use of the profession of judgments, when the mathematician gives him the places of the planets in the signs for certain times, [namely] that he will report that those positions which the planets are in, indicate such-and-such. **157** But as for the correct determination of the degrees of the planets, and in which position of the signs they are in truth, that is up to the masters of calculation [alone].

158 And an analogy to that is the one practicing medicine, for it is up to him to report the nature of each treatment for each thing it is good for, and for each of the illnesses it will benefit. **159** But as for seeking out the remedies in [various] countries, grinding them, and sifting them, that does not fall to the doctor but to the masters of remedies.

160 And likewise it is for the one justifying the professions of judgments, establishing them, [and] judging what the planets indicate, to make clear that the planets have an effect in this world by means of argument, to be ac-

---

[96] That is, the client. In Arabic the client or native is often called the "owner" of the chart.

quainted with their causes, and with what they indicate in terms of their natures, special properties, and culminating in places, and their positions in every sign—but [it is] for the mathematicians to correctly determine their degrees. **161** For if one of one of them is ignorant of the truth of [the positions], the fault for that ignorance refers back to the mathematician, because he is ignorant of what he ought to know about his profession—although people who are limited in the knowledge of the whole to adjusting positions by particular *zījes*, are limited in it to something with a weak foundation, because when they search for their foundations they discover corruption and discrepancy, which does not support them in [finding] the truth about them. **162** And if they did erect the planets by each one of [the *zījes*], then examined their positions in the signs and their assembling with each other, they would find—between the calculation which resulted for them and what they see by sight (or their results by measurement with sound instruments)—something far from being contrary, even though in their perplexity and confusion about the difference there is, they are preoccupied by a defect in the science of the judgments of the stars. **163** (And what prevents us from stating the corruption which is in each of the *zījes*, is preserving the affection of many of our brethren who use them and profit from them).

164 What the masters of judgments, and all of those working with the calculation of the planets both fast and slow in course, ought to rely on, are the positions which are found by valid measurements in every period by the rings and instruments explained in the *Almagest*: because by those instruments are discovered their positions as found by the naked eye, with no doubt about their correctness. **165** And from that book, one who is looking into the science of the judgments of the stars ought to have foreknowledge of everything he needs for the quality of the science of the spheres and planets, and the quantity of their motions, and the rest of the conditions.[97]

The seventh category: [The jealousy of those who are not good at astrology]

166 As for the seventh category, it is those who reject this science because they study it but are not able to attain what they want. **167** So, they envy the masters of this profession for their knowledge of it and reject the

---

[97] See I.2, **2** and **8**.

science of the profession of judgments due to their envying its people and their incapacity for knowledge of it. **168** And these people are not overcome by force of argument, since their repudiation of this profession is not based on knowledge—and a denier cannot be spoken to except by what will curb him and return him to necessary truth.

The eighth category: [Profit-seekers with superficial knowledge]

169 As for the eighth category, it is those who appeal to medicine for the sake of profiting by it, not the skilled doctors knowledgeable in the profession of medicine who have read the books of the ancients on the science of medicine and understand the foundations of their professions, the different natures and seasons, and their change, and the rest of the simple and compound things they need in their profession. **170** For *they* understand the merit of the science of the judgments of the stars, and they know that the science of the stars is fundamental to the science of medicine, and they use the profession of the judgments of the stars along with the profession of medicine on a continuous basis, in knowing pains as well as their increase and decrease, and the times of treatment. **171** So, their accuracy increases in their profession, and sick people are protected by them and recover at their hands, and the benefit of the people multiplies by means of them.

172 But as for that number of doctors whose ignorance is great and whose minds are incapable of knowing what they need to do, in their profession they aim first at profit, and lastly at knowledge. **173** So they reject the profession of the judgments of the stars, and say that the planets' movements have no power in this world, while the profession of medicine exists and is firm: so they consider the profession of judgments is worthless by [this] claim and affirm the profession of medicine. **174** And of these doctors, one will look in medicine at a particular science, like [applying] kohl [to the eyelids], setting broken bones, and external treatments for the sick: and indeed this easy ability brings benefit from having [only] superficial knowledge and little time. **175** But he is also not knowledgeable in what is practiced in that, because he has not read deeply the books of the ancients in the profession of medicine and its structure, nor does he understand the natures of things, nor the natures of time periods, and their harmony and difference, nor does he understand different treatments, even if perhaps he has read a small part of some of the books. **176** Those who are like these doctors affirm the profession of medicine because they profit due to it, and they reject the science of the judgments of the stars due to their scanty knowledge of it; but they do not reject this science alone, but every science which is needed for thinking. **177** And if these people had read the books of medicine, they would have understood that knowledge of the judgments of the stars is beneficial for them in their own profession, and they do need it.

178 And the Sage Hippocrates said in the *Book of Airs* (when he mentioned the different airs and natures),[98] that what we have stated about the changing of the airs does belong to the science of the stars: for the science of the stars is no small part of the science of medicine. **179** And indeed this wise man stated this view because doctors seek information about things by means of the difference of the seasons and the alteration of natures: and indeed this difference and change comes to be through the power of the motion of the Sun and planets (and this belongs to the science of the stars). **180** Doctors, therefore, are compelled to know the science of the stars so that they may truly understand the foundations of their own profession. **181** And also, one practicing medicine ought to treat the sick person once the astrologer has seen from the indications of the stars that his lifespan has not run out, and that he will benefit from the treatment and will recover from his ailment. **182** And if the astrologer does not see a lifespan for him nor recovery from his ailment, then there is no point to the medical practitioner's treatment of that sick person.

183 Now as for the known days (that is, the critical days) which the doctors need for knowing the condition of the sick person's strength and weakness, and his increase and decrease, they understand those from the course of the Moon and the mixing of the planets with her. **184** Hippocrates and Galen mentioned those in their books, and all of the scholars of medicine stated that the science of the stars is the reason for the science of medicine.

185 But this [other] category of doctors who do not understand that the foundation of their profession is from the science of the profession of the stars, find fault in the profession of judgments. **186** And since they find fault in the profession of judgments, they must find fault in their own profession: because the profession of judgments is the cause of the profession of medi-

---

[98] See Hippocrates, Section 2.

cine, except that this category of doctors is ignorant of this relationship and their understanding is deceived about this knowledge.

The ninth category: [Those who do not value science]

187 As for the ninth category, they are the common people, and in the rejection of the science of judgments they are of two types.

188 As for one of the two types,[99] they do not understand the merit of the science of judgments, nor the merit of the rest of the sciences, nor the merit of foreknowledge in things. **189** The most superior person among them is the one with the most assets, and the allotment of assets is more than the allotment of knowledge: so, they say that if a man was rich, having assets, it would not harm him to be ignorant of the science of the stars, medicine, and the rest of the sciences. **190** But they make a false analogy, because they compare knowledge with assets and this analogy is an error: because a thing ought to be compared to [another] thing of its own kind, such as knowledge with knowledge, and assets with assets, not comparing a thing with something not of its own kind. **191** Therefore, one should not compare assets with knowledge. **192** And if one did not often hear this thing from the common crowd (who affect [even] the masters of the sciences by it), we would not have to bother ourselves with thinking about their view; but we will respond to their statement in a courteous way. **193** So we say that assets and good fortune are prepared for both the ignorant and the intelligent, and the strong and the weak: but a man is not praised for what is prepared from him from that, because this is not available to him through his knowledge nor ignorance, nor strength or weakness. **194** A man is praised for discernment and knowledge, because the human's superiority to the rest of the animals is due to the discernment which is in him through the instrument of reason, and his knowledge of things which are and will be.

195 So the more that a man increases his knowledge in what we have stated, he will increase his distance from the beasts due to what is in him in terms of knowledge and the foreknowledge of things coming to be; and the more that his knowledge is scanty, he will increase his closeness to the beasts by the scanty discernment which is in him. **196** And if there was no merit to

---

[99] The second type is the tenth category below (**200ff**).

knowledge and discernment, the human would have no superiority to the beasts, because all of them collaborate in eating, drinking, and procreating, but the superiority of the human over the rest of the animals is due to reason and discernment. **197** So those people who are more abounding in intellect and have more knowledge, are superior in humanity than others. **198** For the allotment of knowledge and discernment (in the sense of being human) is superior to the allotment of assets, and the most superior thing for a human is his knowledge of things coming to be; and the most that this can be is in the knowledge of the profession of the judgments of the stars. **199** So, the allotment of the knowledge of the stars and the rest of the sciences (in the sense of being human), is superior to the allotment of assets.

The tenth category: [The prevalence of ignorant astrologers]

200 As for the tenth category, they are also the common people, but they reject the knowledge of this profession because they have seen an abundance of error from those making claims for it. **201** And that is because the common people accept things based on manifest discernment, but when they see an abundance of error by those making a claim for this profession in the judgments of the stars they are asked about, they accuse it of deception and reject it, and ascribe ignorance to its people. **202** And they say: "This profession is worthless; for if it told the truth, why do those making claims for it have so much error in what they are asked about?"

203 And these people are not to be blamed in their rejection of the science of this profession, because the majority of those [astrologers] making claims for it are ignorant people and the disreputable people of nations who ascribe knowledge of the science to themselves, even though they are ignorant, and they portray themselves (in terms of their knowledge) as though they are unable to err in understanding and discernment, while they put themselves beyond associating with scholars and learning from them. **204** But they do read some books with obscure meaning which they do not understand, or books which one cannot rely on knowing who wrote them. **205** So, in a single concept they will find two different things, not grasping which of them is more true; and if they were asked about the category of that concept several times, when looking into it each time they would employ a principle contrary to the first principle, due to the scarcity of their knowledge of the natures of the planets, their conditions, and indications, and in the name of this profession they practice kinds of pretense and deception, and they deceive weak minds among women and afflicted people, and those distressed by those having power, and groaning, hoping, or expecting types of good fortune from assets, power, and an increase in them.

206 And sometimes something right is made possible for them among some of these [gullible people] due to the correspondence of the statement [with reality], without their being aware of the meaning of that statement, so that they mention it and boast about it, and seek to take advantage of others while ignoring their many errors which have occurred, and their lies in previous times.

207 And these people aim at profit and gain, not knowledge, wisdom, and delving deeply into this profession, because one wanting to delve deeply into the science of the judgments of the stars needs the knowledge of the things which we have stated before, so that these things come to be a cause for the knowledge of this profession. **208** And they are: the different conditions of the planets, the knowledge of the natures (and their harmony and difference), the difference of the climes and their conditions, the different conditions of animals, plants, and minerals, and what occurs in each one of them upon the shifting of seasons in the climes, and the rest of what we stated in what preceded, and what we will state in what follows. **209** And the knowledge of these sciences is possible [only] over much time, and hard labor, but these people are incapable of knowing any of it.

210 But they are led into their errors from two directions: as for one of them, it is their scanty knowledge of this profession; as for the second, their purpose is [personal] benefit. **211** So if a querent with power asked them about something, in responding to him they would focus on whatever harmonious thing he rejoices in: so they would report to him that the stars indicate that thing, having their sights set on his pleasure and hoping for his wealth, and laying out false time periods for him, so that the heart of the querent depends on them. **212** They hasten away from him with those benefits and good opinion, and an increase in rank and power: and their manner of treating all kinds of people is in just this way we described.

213 So the common crowd blames all of the people of this profession, and says detestable things about them, lying about them, so that scholars suffer from the common crowd saying detestable things about them, because of the ignorant people we described before, who claim knowledge of it. **214** And the common crowd is not acting badly in their blaming the people of this profession, because there are those among them who are aware of just these things. **215** And indeed one who does have discernment and knowledge is astonished, for these situations of lying and pretense by some of them have been made clear to him: for he has heard of [such people], and received their words, and trusted in what was reported to him (or supposed that their words had truth).

216 So it is incumbent upon those laying claim to this profession that they apply themselves to what is necessary for training in it *before* they study it, and then with their knowledge in those things they may progress to this noble, lofty profession which is delightful to the soul.

Chapter I.6: On the benefit of the science of judgments, and that foreknowledge of things which come to be in this world from the power of the planets' movements, is very beneficial

1 Some people have said, "Even if the science of the stars is true (as you claim), it is a science without benefit in it, because what the stars indicate are things which will be. **2** And this is something a man does not need, because if that thing is a good or delight, he will get it at its own [appropriate] time, and foreknowledge of it is no benefit for him. **3** And if it was something detestable, he will anticipate distress through his foreknowledge of it, and then distress will [actually] follow upon that knowledge, and meditating on the fear of it until the time of its arrival—and the person knowledgeable in the profession of the science of the stars is not able to repel the detestable things which are coming to be!"

4 But these people are wrong and have left the path of discernment and knowledge, and do not understand the merit of this science, nor its benefit. **5** He who knows the benefit of foreknowledge in things, knows the benefit of this science: but these people who reject benefiting from this science reject only the *name* of the thing, because they do not understand it. **6** As for the *concept* of the thing, they do employ it: because all people who have discernment employ foreknowledge in things which they are able to have knowledge of, and wariness of a detestable thing which they fear. **7** And if they are unable to repel that thing itself, they repel from themselves much of the harm and unpleasantness which affects them from that thing, according to their ability.[100]

[That people do use foreknowledge in daily life and medicine]

8 As for some of the people, their foreknowledge of things is by experience: for they repel from themselves the unpleasantness which their knowledge predicts: and they are the common people. **9** For others, their foreknowledge of things is due to the shifting of the seasons and the conditions of the natures, so that in the repelling of the unpleasantness they prepare in advance by means of what their knowledge foretells: and they are the doctors. **10** And as for others, their foreknowledge is by means of the power of the planets' actions in this world, so that in the repelling of unpleasantness they act in advance based on what their knowledge foretells: and they are the astrologers.

11 Now as for those whose foreknowledge exists by experience (such as the common people), when they have foreknowledge by experience of a time of hot or cold, they also act in advance for self-preservation and protection against them before being surprised by it: thus they prepare cooling and cold places for the heat, and heating, concealed places, and heating things for the cold, in order to ward off harm from them by what they prepare for them both. **12** And sometimes in the sky they will see clouds suggesting rain in accordance with what they have experienced when they are on a journey or in town, so before the rain falls they go in advance to places which will hide them from the rain when it does fall, or they will already be carrying clothing to keep them from the rain when it occurs. **13** And if a man knows beforehand that his enemy wants to take him by surprise, he will set a time before that in order to prepare himself to repel that enemy's evil when he does strike.

14 So none of the common people wards off the *essence*[101] of the thing [itself] from occurring. **15** But when they know from experience over a long time, or for some reason they know the times of things which will harm

---

[100] With this paragraph, the substance of Abū Ma'shar's response is concluded. But he will beat this dead horse for a lot longer, often repeating phrases unnecessarily.
[101] ذات

them, they are on guard against them with what they have for repelling the harm from themselves, so that their unpleasantness does not reach them: because one who knows that there will be hot or cold, or rain, at such-and-such a time, will be on guard by acting in advance in what will repel its unpleasantness from himself before it strikes him. **16** So he does not repel the generation of the heat or cold, nor the falling of the rain, but when he has advance knowledge of its times by experience, he will use clever means for repelling the unpleasantness of that thing from himself. **17** And this, and much like it of this kind, is what the foreknowledge of the common people is by experience, and they get ready for it before its occurrence and onset.

18 And of course all professionals employ foreknowledge by experience in their crafts: like the masters of sowing and planting, herdsmen, and midwives, and in their wariness of the detestable thing which they fear, they act ahead of time before its onset. **19** As for doctors, they make use of foreknowledge in things from the perspective of different conditions in the season, and the changing of natures and humors, and they understand from this what others among all of the professionals we mentioned before, do not: because doctors have foreknowledge of the benefit of a treatment during the time of the seasons' shift from one condition to another.

20 And the common people also act beforehand at that time by protecting their bodies from ailments and illnesses, because if it was in the time of spring, the common people act in advance based on what has happened with long experience in the alteration of the mixture of their bodies at the shifting of the seasons, in the preservation of bodies from illnesses and ailments by medical treatments. **21** And doctors act in advance through their foreknowledge of what they will face with the changing of those bodies when the season comes upon them, by taking medicine, bloodletting, and the rest of the treatments, for fear that the summer season will set upon them, with its hotness. **22** For [in the summer] one finds bad, rotten, [and] sharp humors in their bodies, so the sharpness of those humors comes together with the hotness of the air, and the hotnesses which are corrupting to bodies gain dominance over their mixtures, and they become sick. **23** And likewise they act in advance in applying medical treatments and in guarding against illnesses at all times of the year and its days, so that in that time they are in [now], they guard against what they fear in future times, when it will befall them.

24 Of course the common people already seek protection from illnesses for their bodies by means of doctors' treatment of them: and that is why there is advance knowledge among them by experience, that many bodies become ill and sick when the variation of the season and natures befall them. **25** Also, there might be an ailment in a man due to the corruption of some of the humors, so that it is agitated at a certain time of the year or day: thus he will act before its agitation so as to guard against that illness by employing a remedy which draws it out, reduces it, or soothes it, and repels all or some of the harm of that bad humor from himself, in accordance with his ability in it.

26 And the doctor also draws conclusions from some of its causes due to his foreknowledge, when he sees that some of the bad humors have already begun to predominate in the body of the man, based on knowing that the treatment will repel the likes of it, or soothe it. **27** Thus he acts in advance to be on guard against the power of that bad humor (or an increase in it) by treatments which soothe or weaken its power, so that it is not stirred up in him (and with it some [other] bad humors are stirred up)—for a strategy to draw it out or soothe it, is difficult.[102] **28** And if the doctor did not have advance knowledge that that bad humor would be stirred up and aroused in the man if he left it alone in its [current] condition, it would cause [the patient] pain, and he [could] not act to draw it out or soothe it with an advance treatment for him. **29** But the skillful doctor will soothe the power of the bad humors through his foreknowledge, and will repel illnesses, pain, and insomnia through his prior knowledge of treating him,[103] and reduces or draws out the bad surpluses from the body, so that the man will not be harmed by them. **30** So if the doctor knew some of what he sought information about, [namely] concerning truthful indications that that illness would not disappear, and that its sufferer would not recover, and that he would die in that illness, he could inform the sick person that he would perish, and the sick

---

[102] I take this to mean that it is more difficult to draw it out once it has already flared up—hence the importance of foreknowledge.

[103] بما يتقدّم فيه من العلم بعلاجه إيّاه. I take the key word here to be إيّاه, which means there is prior treatment of *this* patient. In traditional medicine (but even in modern medicine), while one can work with general categories of disease and healthy mixtures in the body, everyone is a little different: therefore the doctor needs to know what really works for a particular patient.

person would act in advance in what he needed to, in the settling of his affairs. 31 So, foreknowledge of illnesses and treatments by those practicing medicine, is very beneficial.

[Why foreknowledge is good in astrology]

32 And in what we have stated about the foreknowledge of the common people and doctors about things, we wanted to draw an analogy with the profession of the stars. 33 Because when the knowledgeable astrologer sees (from foreknowledge of the power of the planets' movements) that something detestable will afflict some of the people, he will approach them by speaking about that because foreknowledge in the profession of the stars concerning the unpleasantness which will afflict a man at a future time is very beneficial. 34 And that is in five ways, one of them general and four particular:

35 As for the first, it is [1] the detestable thing which, when a man understands it, he is sometimes able to repel it, and sometimes not able to—and this is general.
36 The second is [2] the detestable thing which, if a man has foreknowledge of it, he has the power to repel it from himself in its entire substance.
37 The third is [3] the detestable thing which, when he has foreknowledge of it, he is able to repel some of it from himself through his foreknowledge.
38 The fourth is [4] the detestable thing which he knows, through his foreknowledge, that it will afflict him, [but] then it will withdraw from him after a certain time.
39 As for the fifth, it is [5] the detestable thing which, when he has foreknowledge of it, he is totally unable to repel it from himself.

40 Now as for [1] the first, general one, which is when he has foreknowledge of it due to the science of the stars, sometimes he is able to repel it, and sometimes not. 41 And that is understood from the revolutions of the years of the world: such as a general epidemic, plague, earthquakes, wars, killing and fighting, drought, and the destruction of beasts and fruits which are common to the people of a clime or city. 42 Foreknowledge of this and what is like it is beneficial, because when a man has advance knowledge of

that, he will be on advance guard against it for himself and others, insofar as he is able to guard against this and the like before its occurrence, by changing and transferring from that place, and what is like that. **43** And sometimes he will be able to repel a detestable thing like this from himself with a similar strategy. **44** But if he did not have advance knowledge of the occurrence of that thing, and then it happened, his anxiety would intensify upon the arrival of that unpleasantness, and the strategy of repelling it from himself would not be possible, so he might be crushed in it. **45** Or, it is like people who understand by advance knowledge of the stars that they have an enemy who will strike at them, so sometimes they are able to repel him from themselves by means of a stratagem, but sometimes they are not able to—and other things are of this sort.

46 As for the second [way], it is [2] the detestable thing which, if a man has foreknowledge of it, he has the power to repel it from himself in its entire substance: and indeed, that is known from the nativity of the man, or from the revolution of his year, or from a question about his situation. **47** And it is like an illness or the victory of one of his enemies over him, or unpleasant reports, or the rest of the categories of evil and detestable things: for foreknowledge of it is very beneficial, just like our previous statement about it. **48** Because when the astrologer sees through his foreknowledge that some ailment will be stirred up in one of the people at a certain time of the year or day, the like of which can be repelled by a treatment, the astrologer will notify him of that, and that man will take advance action in treatment and medicine to remove that ailment from his body (or soothe it), so that the ailment will not be agitated at that time. **49** Thus the astrologer has repelled the unpleasantness of that ailment in its entire substance from that man by informing him about it. **50** Or, [it is] like an enemy whom a man fears, so he sees by advance knowledge through the starry profession that [the enemy] wants to attack him, and acts in advance to be on guard before his attack; and if he does attack him he will not suffer harm from him and repels the unpleasantness from himself in its entire substance.

51 As for the third, from [3] the detestable thing which, when he has foreknowledge of it, he is able to repel some of it from himself through his foreknowledge, it is like the man who fears (by means of starry foreknowledge) that some ailment will be stirred up at some time, so he has advance treatment before that time, and repels most of that ailment from himself upon its being stirred up, through the advance treatment. **52** And it is like the man who already knows through his foreknowledge in the stars, that [some] man has open hostility towards him: so he is on guard against him with some wariness, and through that little bit of guarding he repels from himself some of the enemy's harm.

53 As for the fourth, from [4] the detestable thing which he knows, through his foreknowledge, that it will be, [but] then it will withdraw from him after a certain time, it is like the man whom he knows through his starry foreknowledge that he will be sick for certain days but then recover; or like the enemy whom he knows will conquer him for some days but then he will be safe from him; or like the confinement which will afflict him for some days, but then he will be freed from it.

54 And as for the fifth, from [5] the detestable thing which, when he has foreknowledge of it, he is totally unable to repel it from himself, it is like the man who knows through his starry foreknowledge that he will die at such-and-such a time, so the foreknowledge in it is beneficial for him because when he knows it in advance, he will act beforehand in the preparation of his affairs which he wants, and putting things in order, or settling affairs between himself and [other] people, in the manner which one needs to in this subject. **55** For death *is* coming to him, and he is aware of it, and [should] take advance action in settling the affairs he wants to. **56** But if he did not have advance knowledge in that, death would visit him even if his situation is one of conflict, being scattered in his affairs, so that the harm of that would redound upon those succeding him among his heirs and family, and they and his offspring would remember the unpleasantness in the days to come.

57 These examples which we have stated, indicate that advance knowledge in things from the profession of the judgments of the stars is beneficial in all things.

58 And I also say that foreknowledge of unpleasant things is very beneficial, because if evil came to a man by surprise, it would intensify his anxiety and perplex him, and snatch away his intellect, and he would not be capable of stratagems in it. **59** And sometimes, due to the harshness of the anxiety which [which occurs] with the arrival of that unpleasantness, another detestable thing is stirred up; and sometimes [when] being on guard against that unpleasantness has been neglected, an increase in the unpleasantness will get a hold of him; and sometimes he will die suddenly from the harshness of the worry. **60** But if he had foreknowledge of that unpleasantness before its arrival, it would come upon him and his firmness would repel it, and he would have informed himself about it and understood its cause, and would have done what was needed in advance in terms of managing its cause, working to repel from himself what he could in that, so that the evil would be more fragmented and smaller.

61 So even if the skilled astrologer is not able (through his foreknowledge) to repel all of that unpleasantness, he would use clever means in his foreknowledge to repel what he was able to of that unpleasantness. **62** And just as the planets indicate the detestable things which we stated, so they indicate being on guard as well as benefit from it; and indeed the astrologer [himself] is a cause of being on guard, through his foreknowledge and his informing the man about the occurrence of the detestable thing.

[Use foreknowledge for risk management]

63 Now[104] as for the argument which is closer to the understanding of the common people, [namely] in responding to those saying that a man ought not to look into the science of the stars because sometimes he will see in the indications of the stars that a detestable thing will find him at some time),[105] and anticipate the distress by his knowledge of that, [and] then distress will follow upon that, and thinking about it until the time of its arrival—I say [the following].

64 If a man had avoided doing everything he anticipated distress from, it would be necessary for him not to travel in search of gains, power, and authority: because before he traveled he would anticipate distress in the outlay of assets and expenses because of that travel—then on his journey he would anticipate being away from his own home, toil, harm, detestable things, and fear of his body, assets, and servants. **65** And perhaps something of what we stated about the unpleasantness will find him soon on his journey before accomplishing any of the things for which he traveled. **66** And he ought not to become the companion of a man in order to seek the good, advantages, and an increase in rank and power, because in that way he might be hasty in

---

[104] Sentences **63-74** are about avoiding making plans in areas you *expect* distress in, or worrying about what might happen until success actually comes.

[105] This is a direct rebuttal to the modern claim that astrology clients should never be told something "bad."

seeking the means for becoming the companion of that man, and then anticipate disgrace and degradation because of his service to him before [trying to] use him for benefit. **67** And he ought not to hope for anything, nor wish for it, because if he hopes for something and wishes for it, he will anticipate distress by thinking about and pursuing it until the time he is successful in it. **68** And all of these things we have mentioned, and others besides them which are of this type, people may anticipate unpleasantness and distress because of seeking them; and sometimes one of them will perish before succeeding in the thing he seeks.

69 Now if one of them was sound in his body and successful in what he sought, he would still anticipate the grief, hard toil, expense, and fear about [his] assets and body, loss of face, disgrace, and many of the unpleasant things and harm. **70** But if that [success] eluded him, [then] along with what he had already anticipated of these detestable things which we explained, regret, pain, and remorse would follow him in proportion to the assets he has squandered, and fatigue to his body, and sacrificing his rank, and having the types of unpleasantness; then he would have no strategy for restoring the assets he has squandered, nor for repelling the griefs and detestable things he anticipated, nor would the regret and remorse benefit him in proportion to what has eluded [him].

71 And as for the distress which follows a man with foreknowledge of the stars' indications for the detestable things which he sees will afflict him at another time, and the distress which follows him because of his thinking about it up until the time when they arrive, he benefits from them both: because when he has foreknowledge of the stars' indications for the unpleasantness which will find him, he will deliberate on a stratagem for repelling it, and in improving his affairs in orders just as we said. **72** So, the repelling of what unpleasantness he is able to, will follow upon his foreknowledge of it and his deliberation about it.

73 And also, if these people had had advance knowledge (from the indications of the planets) that the things which they sought would not be completed for them, nor would they be successful in them, they would cease their search and impulse for them, and their pursuing of them; then they would not anticipate the unpleasantness and distress, nor would the impulse for them ensue, nor brooding, regret, and remorse. **74** So, a man's knowledge of detestable things which will afflict him (from what the stars would indicate about that), is very beneficial.

Book I: Definition & Defense of Astrology

[Do not put off good things just because they are transitory]

75 And[106] I will also make a statement near to the understanding of the common people, in responding to people who claim that a man ought not to look into the science of the stars, because due to the knowledge of the detestable things he sees in it which will afflict him, distress will follow him until the time of their arrival [in his life].[107] **76** For if the man would avoid practicing everything which would make distress follow him because of it, then he ought not to listen to singing: because when the skilled singer pauses, grief would follow it due to the interruption of the delight which had been in him at the time of his hearing the song. **77** And he ought not to have sexual intercourse with women having grace and beauty, nor eat the best foods, nor drink the most pure and excellent drinks, because at the time he is finished with having sex, or interrupting the eating or drinking, distress will follow it due to his inability to make the pleasure of sex, eating, and drinking last. **78** And in accordance with his satisfaction with the girl's grace and beauty, and the exceedingly good food and drink, so likewise will be his distress when interrupting that, and his inability to do it [more]. **79** And he ought not to acquire many assets, because distress follows an abundance of assets (from [having to] protect them), and it procures him enemies, and envious people, and fear of them. **80** And he ought not to rejoice in an abundance of assets and slave girls in old age, because at that time he will not be able to enjoy the slave girls, nor rejoice in the assets, so distress will follow him because of his inability to feel pleasure and rejoice in that.

81 So if he stops using the science of the stars because he does not feel safe about seeing something unpleasant in it, so that distress follows upon his study of it and his knowledge of it, then he ought not to practice any [types of] good fortune, because grief, regret, sorrow, and remorse would follow them due to their being interrupted and his inability to [accomplish] them. **82** And he would have to devote himself to eating the worst of foods,

---

[106] Sentences **75-82** are about the absurdity of falling into despair and avoiding objectively good and pleasurable things because you anticipate they will *end*. This is different from **63-74**, which was about the fear of something actually bad that will happen.

[107] See **3** above.

and drinking the worst of drinks, and desist from sexual intercourse (and if he did have sex, it should be with the ugliest and most disgusting women), and in old age he should devote himself to poverty and deprivation in everything of the [types of] good fortune (just as we said before), until distress does not follow him due to his inability to take pleasure and delight in them.

[The danger in sudden delights]

83 For advance knowledge in both the good and the delightful is very beneficial, because sometimes something pleasing will reach a man by surprise, and he will be confused and startled, and sometimes he will die at that hour from the intensity of the joy, since from the excess of delight or distress a man will sometimes die suddenly. **84** But if something delightful happened to a man and he already had advance knowledge of it, he would not be confused nor startled due to it, and perishing would not be feared for him from the intensity of the joy; and he will think in advance about how he wants to manage it.

[Foreknowledge is particularly human]

85 And let us make clear what we have stated about grief and delight, using an understandable, natural analogy with all animals: we say that all animals, within their own character,[108] rejoice and are distressed. **86** So if an animal does not rejoice in what its own kind rejoices in, nor is distressed by what its own kind is distressed by, it is far from animality and is of the character of inanimate things, like stones, wood, and what is like those. **87** Now as for all animals apart from humans, they rejoice and are distressed when they come into *direct contact* with pleasing and distressing things; but *foreknowledge* of delight and grief belong to the human alone among the animals. **88** For the human being needs foreknowledge of beneficial and harmful things in all situations: because if that thing were detestable, advance knowledge of it would be better for him than delaying it,[109] for the reasons

---

[108] طبع. That is, of their own type, stamp, or nature.
[109] That is, better than delaying knowledge about it.

we stated before; and if it was good or a delight, the man will not be ignorant of its merit.

[Foreknowledge is important for happiness]

89 And indeed, his foreknowledge and the hastening of the delight by being informed of it before its existence, is more preferable than delaying it, because all people aspire to be happy[110] in this world, and their object in being happy is one of three states:[111] either [1] a distressed man who aims to repel that grief from himself and procure happiness; or [2] a man with diminished happiness who aims to complete that delight; or [3] a happy man who aims at enduring happiness.

90 And with respect to happiness, let us advance an analogy from the category of the musician (that is, singing). **91** I say that advance knowledge of pleasing reports (which are indicated by the profession of the judgments of the stars) have an amazing effect in the soul, because their praised actions manifest just as hearing the songs and the plucking of strings by a singer skilled in melody and knowledgeable in harmonizing the strings and playing them.

92 For just as the soul delights and is relaxed and rejoices in the balanced sounds of the combined strings when it hears them, and changes its character so that it increases in courage, generosity, and a good character, so likewise advance knowledge (from the profession of the stars) of pleasing reports which a man anticipates (such as rulership, victory over enemies, acquiring assets, and the generation of children) will produce more delight in him than what occurs in him from listening to singing and the plucking of strings.

93 And just as the repeated sound of the strings increases the man's delight, so likewise does his repeated hearing of pleasing reports which he anticipates, and his thinking about them increase his delight. **94** And just as when the man delights in some of the sounds he craves to hear many times over, so likewise does he crave to hear pleasing reports all of the time.

---

[110] This verb, here and below, technically means "delight," so one should not try to interpret this in the strong philosophical sense of "happiness."

[111] خصال.

95 And just as he craves to listen all the time to different songs (some of them being better than others), so likewise does he crave to listen all the time to different, pleasing reports about what he will face [in the future]; <and> his delight in them will be greater than his delight in what he has heard before that, except that his advance knowledge of pleasing reports which are in the future time (due to the indication of the stars) has a worthiness not in the musician (that is, in the singing). **96** And that is because the listener delights in the voices of the balanced [and] combined strings only so long as he hears them.[112] **97** Now if the musician (I mean, singing) pauses, he will interrupt that delight with his pausing and his ceasing to pluck the strings; but with a pleasing report which the astrologer informs him of (due to the advance knowledge of the profession of the stars), its recipient will delight in it from when he hears of it until that delightful thing reaches him.

98 So because of that, all of the people desire advance knowledge of pleasing reports from the profession of the stars.

[Foreknowledge also pertains to current situations]

99 Also pertaining to people's benefiting from the science of the stars' foreknowledge of things, is that the querent will ask an astrologer who is skilled in the profession, to inform him about the condition of an absent or fleeing man, so that he will be calmed by that. **100** Or, he will ask him about someone lost (who has already been lost for some time), and his family informs [him] of that, but they do not know whether he is living or dead: so he will inform them of what he sees about his condition, and they will act in accordance with that. **101** Or, he will ask about a traveler or runaway, not knowing in which direction he is headed, and he will report his direction to him so they may seek him there. **102** Or, he will ask about a man as to whether he has affection for him, or hostility: and he will report to him what he sees, so he may proceed in accordance with that.

103 And among those things which he may benefit from due to foreknowledge in the science of the stars, is that if a child is born to a man, and he knows that it will not be brought up, he will not marry [the child] off in its

---

[112] The listener can also *remember* the music, but it will be of something past and complete, not something anticipatory (which foreknowledge is).

childhood; but if he did not have advance knowledge about that, perhaps he would marry it off but the child will die before the end of [his] upbringing, and they will fall into confusion.[113]

104 So in this, and what is like it in this category, all people benefit very much by advance knowledge of the indications of the stars.

[Conclusion]

105 And we have already stated in what preceded, the benefit of the common people in their foreknowledge of things by experience, and their benefit by the foreknowledge of scholarly doctors in the variation of the season and alteration of the natures, and medical treatments. **106** And likewise, we have stated their benefit as being from the foreknowledge of the scholars of the masters of the stars, in what is evident to them from the power of the conditions of the planets in this world.

107 So it is made clear and apparent that knowledge of things is very beneficial for all people, except that in the knowledge of the stars it is more beneficial, superior, and noble than it is in the profession of medicine and in all of the [other] professions.[114] **108** As for its superiority over *all* of the professions, we have already stated that before. **109** But as for its superiority over the profession of *medicine*, the reason for that is that doctors seek information about things through the nature of the season and its changing from condition to conditions, and by fleeting, changing, and tangible things. **110** As for the astrologers, they derive information about things coming to be[115] from the higher bodies, and by what occurs from the power of their movements in the season and the natures. **111** And also, the astrologer gains information from what will be for a long time, and what did exist in an older time. **112** But the doctor gains information about what exists in a single season (among the seasons of the year), or in a single hour of the day; but as for what is past, what his knowledge is able to do is scanty.

---

[113] تخليط. This also connotes more serious emotional disturbance, but I am not sure that Abū Ma'shar means it that way.
[114] See I.2, **34-88**, but especially **80-88**.
[115] كائنات.

113 And I also say that the soul is the most excellent thing in a man, and it rejoices in the knowledge of things which will be[116] and are.[117] **114** And in all of the professions, with respect to the knowledge and science of past things and things coming to be,[118] there is nothing like what is in the profession of the stars: therefore the profession of the stars is the most excellent, and the foreknowledge of things coming to be[119] from them is the most beneficial of all the professions.

115 The First Book is completed, with praise to God and His blessing.

---

116 تكون.
117 كانت.
118 كائنة
119 كائنة

Book II: [Fixed Stars, the Order of Signs, Quadruplicities, & Sect]
And in it are nine chapters

1 Chapter II.1: On the number of the stars of the sphere both fast and slow in motion, which the ancients measured, and the knowledge of their six magnitudes, and how many planets there are in each magnitude, and the number of images in the sphere, and the name of each image.
2 Chapter II.2: It is stated why twelve images were made more fundamental in indication, than the rest of the images of the sphere.
3 Chapter II.3: On the reason for the number of signs, and that there are twelve, neither less nor more.
4 Chapter II.4: On the sequence of the natures of the signs.
5 Chapter II.5: It is stated why one begins with Aries rather than the rest of the signs.
6 Chapter II.6: On the reason for the convertible, fixed, and double-bodied signs.
7 Chapter II.7: On the knowledge of the quarters of the sphere, and the reason for the convertible, fixed, and double-bodied signs, and the reason for the number of the signs (and that they are twelve), and why one begins with Aries in the sequence of their natures, and the knowledge of their triplicities, according to what Hermes reported from Agathodaimōn.
8 Chapter II.8: On the knowledge of the masculine and feminine signs.
9 Chapter II.9: On the diurnal and nocturnal signs.

Chapter II.1: On the number of the stars of the sphere both fast and slow in motion, which the ancients measured, and the knowledge of their six magnitudes, and how many planets there are in each magnitude, and the number of images in the sphere, and the name of each image

1 The previous sages, both Ptolemy and those which were after him (of those concerned with the quality of the highest sphere), studied it in a satisfactory way so that they understood its circumference and size, and found it to encompass the earth on all sides, and found the size of the earth in it to be like a point of a circle. **2** But one wanting knowledge of that should look in the *Almagest*, for that is made clear in it.

3 And this sphere surrounds several [other] spheres in which there are many stars, and those of them which the sages measured were 1,029:

4 Seven of them are the quickest in motion (and they are Saturn, Jupiter, Mars, the Sun, Venus, Mercury, and the Moon). **5** These seven have different courses, each one of them having a sphere different from that of its associates.

6 And 1,022 stars are slow in motion, and they are called "fixed stars." **7** These 1,022 stars were reckoned by the sages as being in a single sphere, and the motion of each star is the same as the motion of its associates: and it is a change of approximately 1° every 100 years.[1] **8** And they made these stars be of six magnitudes.[2] **9** They assigned the greatest of them in glow to the first magnitude (and it is 15 stars). **10** The ones below these in glow are in the second magnitude (and it is 45 stars). **11** The ones below these in glow are in the third magnitude (and it is 208 stars). **12** The ones below these in glow are in the fourth magnitude (and it is 474 stars). **13** The ones below these in glow are in the fifth magnitude (and it is 217 stars). **14** And the ones below these in glow are in the sixth magnitude (and it is 49 stars). **15** Five of them resemble clouds and are said to be "nebulous," and nine are said to be "dark." **16** (And a single star is said to be a "tuft.")[3] **17** That makes 1,022 stars.

---

[1] This was Ptolemy's rate of precession.
[2] Lit., "grades" (مراتب).
[3] Or a "lock" of hair (الذؤابة). This is Coma Berenices, which is not a single star so does not count towards the 1,022.

Nebulous (5)		
Perseus #1	CGal. 884 and 869	On right hand
Cancer #1 (Praesepe)	CGal. 2632 / Messier 44	Chest
Scorpio #22	G Sco. and CGlo 6441	To rear of sting
Sagittarius #8	v^1 and v^2	Eye
Orion #1	λ Orion	Head
Faint/Dark (9)		
Ursa Major #32-#35	10 LMi, BSC 3809, BSC 3612, 31 Lyn	Near legs
Perseus #29	16 Per	Next to Gorgon
Equuleus #1-#4	α, β, γ, δ Equ	All
"Tuft" (1)		
Coma Berenices	15(c) Com	North part of nebulous mass

Figure 11: Special dim stars in *Almagest* VII.5-VIII.1

18 Then they assigned these 1,022 stars to 48 images, and called each one of these images by a name which was agreed upon among the ancients.

19 Of these stars, 360 stars are in 21 images inclining away from the path of the Sun in the direction of the north:[4]

20 The first of these images is [#1] the Lesser Bear.

21 The second is [#2] the Greater Bear.

22 The third is [#3] the Sea Dragon.

23 The fourth is [#4] the Inflamed One.

24 The fifth is [#5] the Howling Dog.

25 The sixth is [#6] the Northern Crown.

26 The seventh is [#7] the Kneeler upon his knee.

27 The eighth is [#8] Lyra[5] (and it is the Falling Vulture).

28 The ninth is [#9] the Hen.

---

[4] For all of the following, see *Almagest* VII.5 and the images in this chapter.
[5] The misspelled transliteration here is *Lūzā* (اللوزا).

29 The tenth is [#10] the Woman on the throne.
30 The eleventh is [#11] the Bearer of the ghoul-head.
31 The twelfth is [#12] the One clutching the reins.
32 The thirteenth is [#13] the Snake-charmer who clutches the Snake.
33 The fourteenth is [#14] the Snake of the Snake-charmer.
34 The fifteenth is [#15] the Arrow.
35 The sixteenth is [#16] the Eagle (and it is the Flying Vulture).
36 The seventeenth is [#17] the Dolphin.
37 The eighteenth is [#18] the First Horse.
38 The nineteenth is [#19] the Second Horse.
39 The twentieth is [#20] the Woman who does not see a husband.
40 The twenty-first is [#21] the Triangle.
41 And these are called the northern images.

42 And 346 stars are in the twelve images in the path of the Sun:
43 The first of these is [#22] the image of the Lamb.
44 The second is [#23] the Bull.
45 The third is [#24] the Twins.
46 The fourth is [#25] the Crab.
47 The fifth is [#26] the Lion.
48 The sixth is [#27] the Virgin.
49 The seventh is [#28] the Scales.
50 The eighth is [#29] the Scorpion.
51 The ninth is [#30] the Archer.
52 The tenth is [#31] the Goat.
53 The eleventh is [#32] the Bucket.
54 The twelfth is [#33] the Fish.
55 And these are called the images of the signs.

Book II: Fixed Stars, Signs, Quadruplicity, Sect

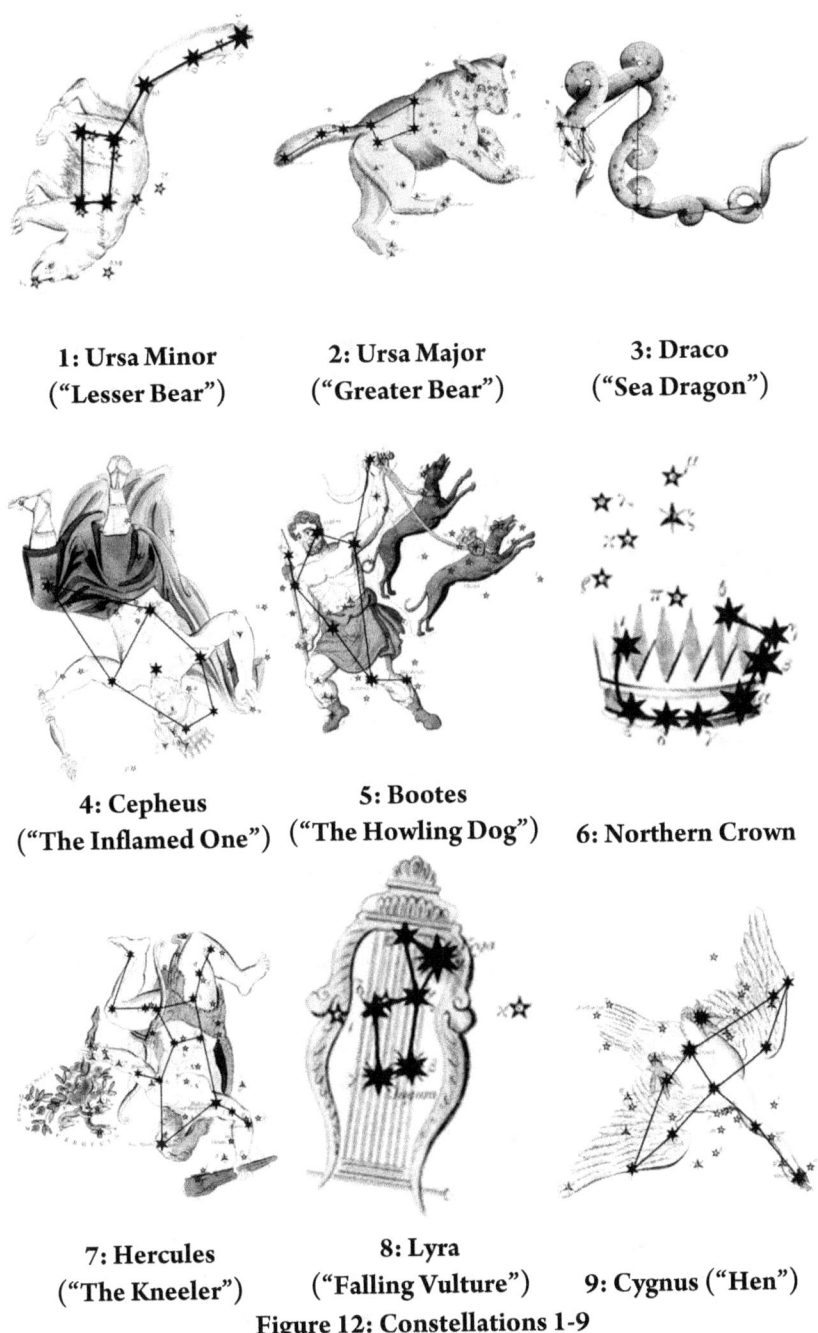

Figure 12: Constellations 1-9

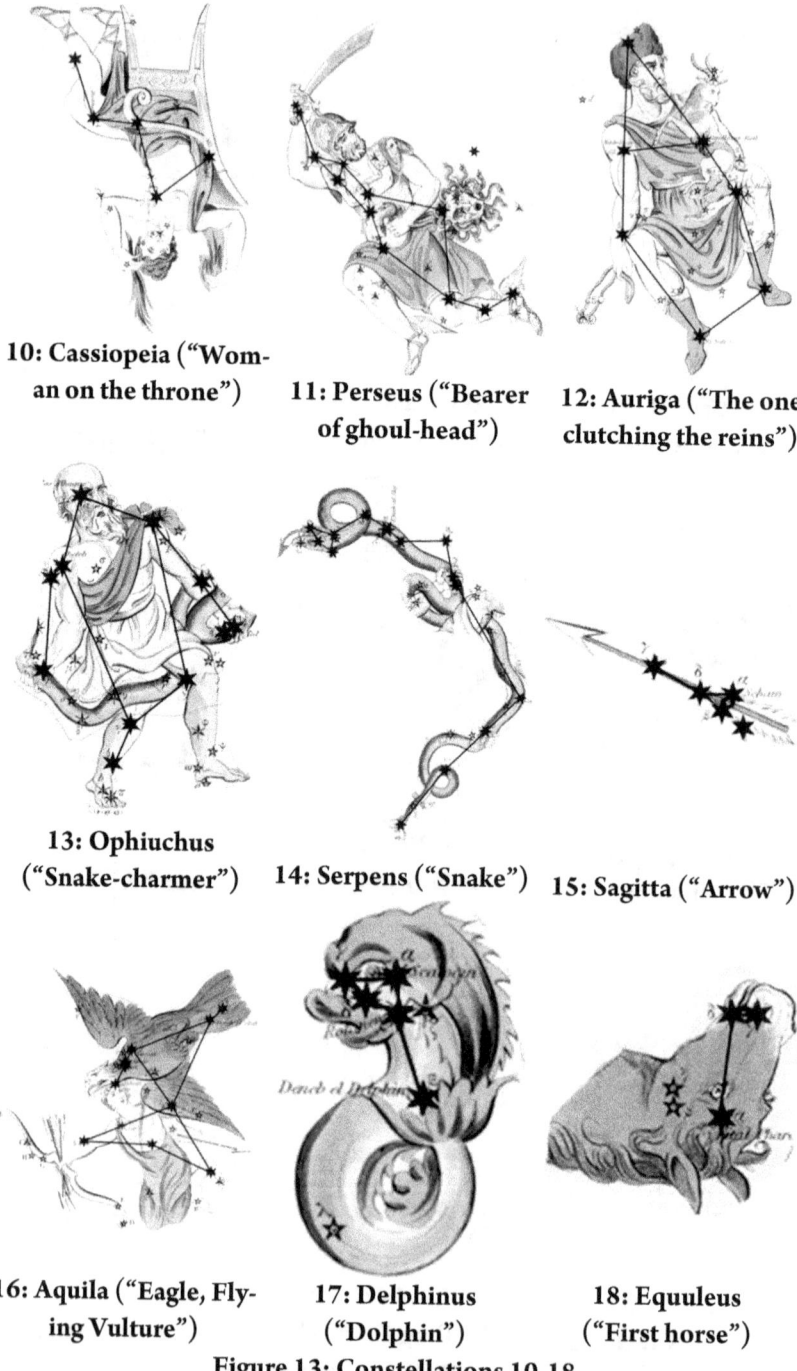

Figure 13: Constellations 10-18

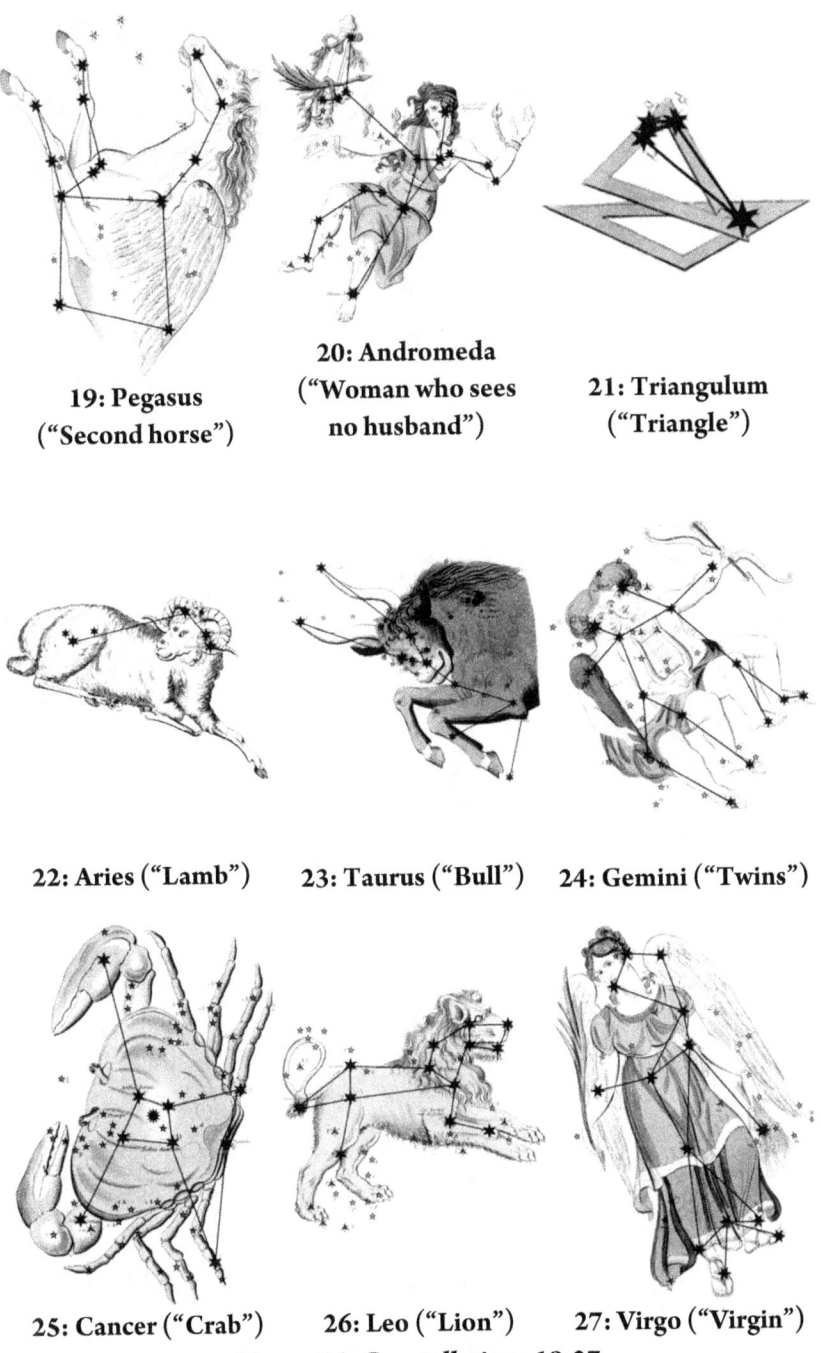

Figure 14: Constellations 19-27

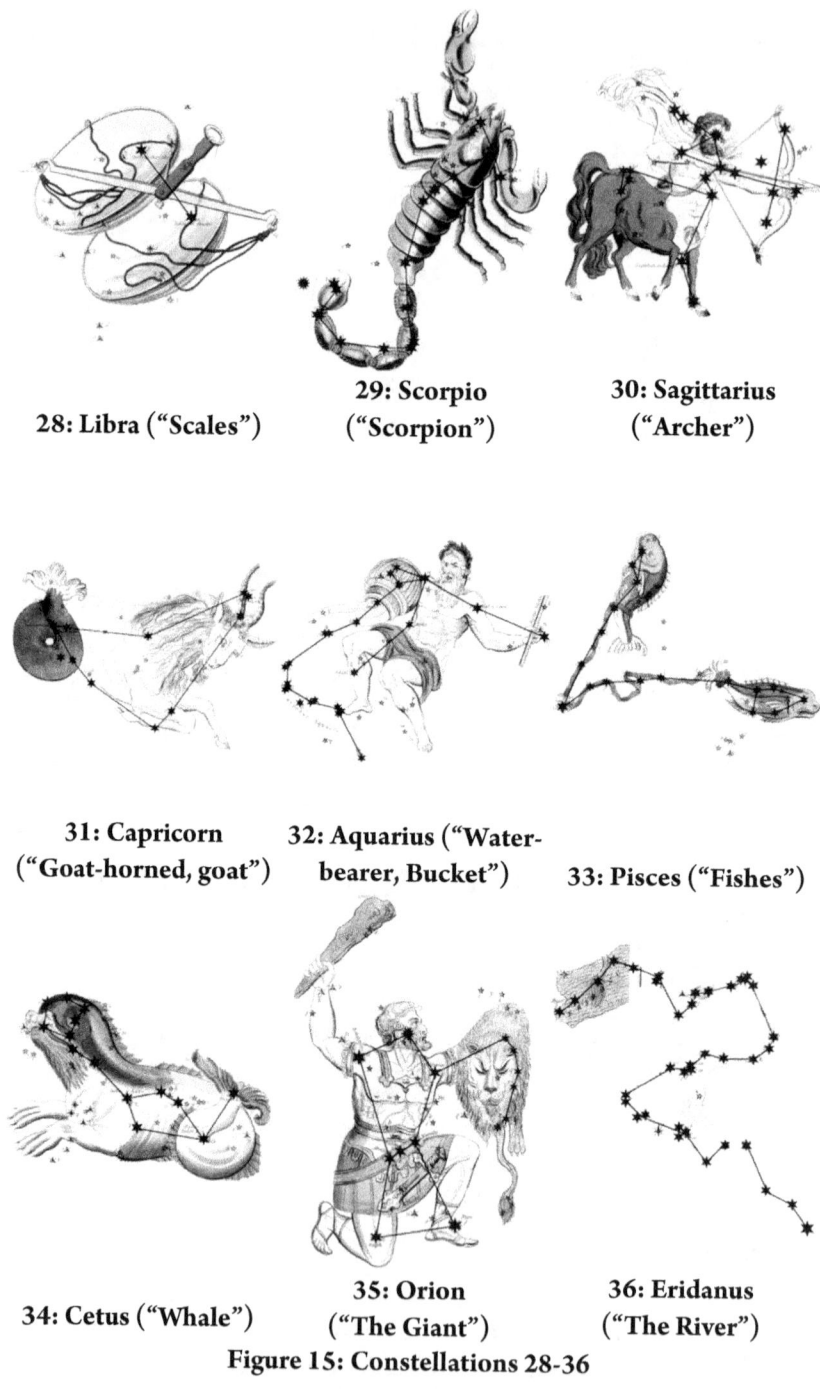

Figure 15: Constellations 28-36

BOOK II: FIXED STARS, SIGNS, QUADRUPLICITY, SECT 125

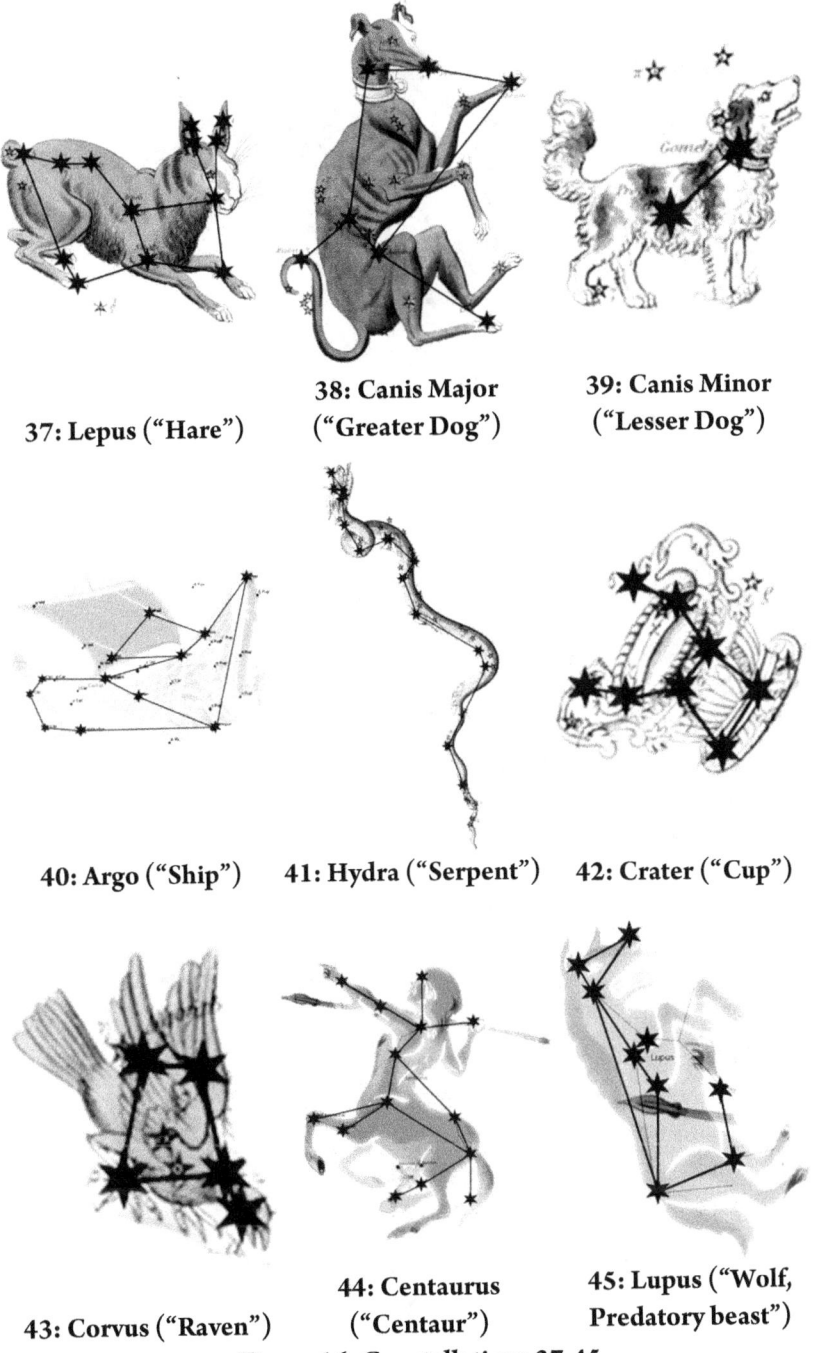

Figure 16: Constellations 37-45

46: Ara ("Altar, Brazier") 47: Corona Australis ("Southern Crown") 48: Piscis Austrinus ("Southern Fish")

Figure 17: Constellations 46-48

56 And 316 stars are in the fifteen images inclining away from the path of the Sun towards the direction of the south:[6]

57 The first of these is [#34] Cetus.
58 The second is [#35] the Giant.
59 The third is [#36] the River.
60 The fourth is [#37] the Hare.
61 The fifth is [#38] the Greater Dog.
62 The sixth is [#39] the Lesser Dog.
63 The seventh is [#40] the Ship.
64 The eighth is [#41] the Serpent.
65 The ninth is [#42] the Cup.
66 The tenth is [#43] the Raven.[7]
67 The eleventh is [#44] Centaurus.
68 The twelfth is [#45] the Predatory Beast.
69 The thirteenth is [#46] the Brazier.
70 The fourteenth is [#47] the Southern Crown.
71 And the fifteenth is [#48] the Southern Fish.
72 And these are called the southern images.

---

[6] For these, see *Almagest* VIII.1.
[7] Or, "crow."

BOOK II: FIXED STARS, SIGNS, QUADRUPLICITY, SECT

73 So that is 48 images, and all of these images are established in the imagination and thought alone. **74** We will get to know [them] thoroughly when we describe the special property of the classes of the signs and their conditions, and what portions of these images arise in each one of their faces. **75** But as for their indications for things, those are found in a different book.

Chapter II.2: It is stated why twelve images were made more fundamental in indication, than the rest of the images of the sphere

1 Since there are 48 images which are in the sphere, and 12 of them are in the belt of the circle of signs, they made these 12 become the ones to use, and they made them be a place for everything in the sphere, and they associated the rest of the 36 images with them, and the rest of the stars which are in the sphere (of those fast and slow in motion), and they made them be more fundamental in indication than other things.

2 And [some] people have rejected that, saying: If there are 48 images in the sphere, why did they refer the rest of the 36 images (as well as the rest of the stars which are in the sphere) to these 12, and make these 12 a place for other things, and make them be more fundamental in indication than other things?

3 But we say to them that they *did* indeed grant an indication over the conditions of the world to each image from among these 48: except that they assigned a universal indication to these 12, and assigned a special indication to these 36. **4** And indeed, they did that for many reasons.

5 As for the first [reason], since [1] the sphere of signs surrounds this world, rotating about it once in a single day, and [2] the rotation of this sphere is about its middle,[8] and [3] this middle rotates about the pole of the world which is the earth, and [4] generation and corruption are both found in this world due to the rotation of this sphere about it, and [5] these 12 images are in the middle of this sphere (while the rest of the images are set back from its middle in the north and south), they made these 12 images more fundamental in the universal indication over the generation and corruption

---

[8] The emphasis on middles in this section makes me think it derives from Hermes: see my Introduction.

which is in this world, rather than the remaining 36 images. **6** But they assigned a particular indication to the rest of the images. **7** Now as for the universal indication, it is the indication of a single sign over many things of varied kinds—like a man, horse, donkey, and other things. **8** And as for the particular indication, it is like what a single image indicates for man alone, or the donkey alone, or the characteristic⁹ of a thing alone.

9 And the second reason is that since [1] it is by means of the motion of the Sun (and his rising and setting) that there occurs among us things which the scholars are not ignorant of, such as actions, generation, and corruption (according to what has preceded in our account), and [2] he is the most evident of the planets in activity within this world, and [3] he turns around in these twelve images, and [4] these twelve are a place for him, they made these images (which are a place for the Sun) more fundamental for the universal indication than the rest of the images which are in the circle. **10** And they made them be a place for others, and referred the rest of the images and stars to them.

11 And the third reason is that [1] since they found the Sun going along in these twelve images, and [2] by his traversing these twelve images the completion of the year comes to be, with its seasons (which are spring, summer, autumn, and winter), and [3] by his being in each one of these twelve images the beginning of every one of these four seasons is known (as well as its middle and end), and [4] by his shifting into every one of them it indicates the generation of [some] things, and the corruption of other things, they assigned to these twelve images a general indication over generation and corruption in this world. **12** And they assigned a particular indication to the rest of the images.

13 And the fourth reason is that [1] since they found each one of the six planets which are quick in course transiting in the Sun's orbit and his path (except that they have latitude, and when they have latitude they incline away from the path of the Sun by the amount of their latitude), and [2] when each of these six planets which are quick in course alights in one of these twelve images, changes take place in this world, and generation and corruption (in accordance with what the nature of those images and that

---

⁹ صفة.

planet indicate), they assigned to these twelve a universal indication, and to the rest of the images a particular indication.

14 And the fifth reason is that since they found each one of these [fixed] stars which are slow in course (which are in any of the 36 images) manifesting more from the indication of the nature of that image which is of the 12 than what it manifests from the indication of the nature of that image which is of the 36, they made these 12 images be indicative of the universal conditions of the world, and assigned a particular indication to the rest of the 36 images, and they made [the 36] subordinate to the 12 in the indication.[10] **15** And [so], they associated these 36 images (and the rest of the stars of the circle which are quick in course, and the slow ones) to these 12, and made these 12 be a place for the images and stars which are in the circle.

16 They called these twelve images "signs,"[11] and called the middle of this circle the "belt of the circle of signs." **17** And they divided this belt into 360°, and every sign got 30°, and they made each degree have 60', and every minute 60", and every second 60'''; and likewise they divided down to fourths, fifths, sixths, sevenths, eighths, ninths, tenths, elevenths, and twelfths, up to what follows after that. **18** And indeed, they divided this belt into 360° because in this number are most of the portions (like the half, third, quarter, fifth, sixth, seventh, eighth, ninth, and tenth). **19** And, it is close to the days of the year of the Sun!

Chapter II.3: On the reason for the number of signs, and that there are twelve, neither less nor more

1 Some people among those who disagree with us have responded to what the ancients said about the number of signs, and said: Why did they claim that the signs are twelve, neither less nor more?

---

[10] What Abū Ma'shar means, is that a fixed star in a constellation like Pegasus, has indications which fit better with the indications of the zodiacal signs, than for things like flying horses. So even if that fixed star might have something to do with horses (or whatever), its significations still point to the zodiacal signs as the universal repository of indications.

[11] The word used for "sign" in Arabic (برج) actually means a "tower."

2 So we say that Aratus the Sage was the one who distinguished among these 48 images which are in the circles, and their names, and all of the wise predecessors confirmed his opinion and agreed about that, for the reasons which he stated in one of his books (which would be [too] long to relate here).[12] **3** But there came to be 12 of them in the belt of the circle of signs, so for this reason they said that the signs were twelve.

4 Now as for the philosophical reason due to which the ancients said the signs were 12 (neither less nor more), they found that things which come to be and corrupt in this world, are from the four composite principles (and they are fire, earth, air, and water). **5** And every individual is generated and corrupted due to these four principles, and has three conditions (a beginning, middle, and end). **6** These four principles, [multiplied] by the amount of their three conditions, make twelve, and these twelve conditions come to be by means of the indication of the signs and their number. **7** So, since the signs (through their number) are indicative over the four principles and the number of their three conditions, and the number of these four principles, [multiplied] by the number of their three conditions, is 12, we know that the signs are 12.

8 And indeed, the signs come to be indicative over the four principles and their three conditions because the signs are the place belonging to the planets: they do not indicate alteration in their own right, but indicate alteration, generation, and corruption due to the difference of their conditions (like rising, setting, and the alighting of the planets in them), and its[13] dominance over them. **9** And likewise, these principles are principles for generation and corruption, but do not take on change in themselves: they are receptive to alteration by means of the variation of the season[14] which befalls them, and due to the blending of one of them with the other, and the dominance of one over the other. **10** So for this reason they knew that the signs are indicative for the four principles, and that their number follows the number of the principles' conditions in the beginning of individuals' coming to be, their middle, and their end.

---

[12] This must be from his *Phenomena*, a didactic poem about the constellations.
[13] That is, the feature of difference and variation.
[14] الزمان. Or perhaps, "time period."

11 And that is in accordance with what I will make clear. **12** Since [1] the four composite principles (and they are fire, earth, air, and water), and what is produced from their three conditions (which are the beginning, middle, and end) are 12, and [2] what is indicative of the four principles and what is produced from their three conditions are the twelve signs (and they are Aries, Taurus, Gemini, Cancer, Leo, Virgo, Libra, Scorpio, Sagittarius, Capricorn, Aquarius, and Pisces), the indication over fire comes to belong to Aries, and to Taurus comes the indication over earth, and to Gemini comes the indication over air, and to Cancer comes the indication over water, so that the indication of the four signs for the four principles is complete. **13** Then, they began in the indication for a second time, and made it be like the first: so to Leo came the indication over fire, to Virgo the indication over earth, to Libra the indication over air, and to Scorpio the indication over water, so that the indication of the four signs for the four principles was completed for the second time. **14** Then, they begin a third time and made it be like the first: so to Sagittarius came the indication over fire, to Capricorn the indication over earth, to Aquarius the indication over air, and to Pisces the indication over water.

15 Thus, the four signs which are Aries, Taurus, Gemini, and Cancer, came to be those indicative over the conditions of the four principles which are the beginning. **16** The four signs which are Leo, Virgo, Libra, and Scorpio came to be those indicative over the conditions of the four principles which are in the middle. **17** And the four signs which are Sagittarius, Capricorn, Aquarius, and Pisces, came to be those indicative over the conditions of the four principles which are at the end.

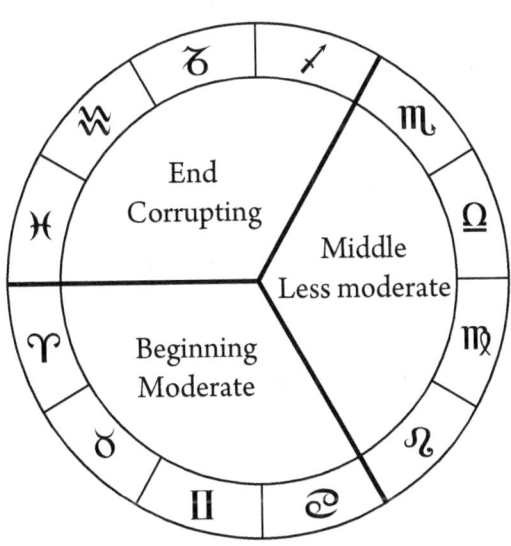

Figure 18: Cycles of the four principles

18 So three of them came to be fiery (and they are Aries, Leo, and Sagittarius), three earthy (and they are Taurus, Virgo, and Capricorn), three airy (and they are Gemini, Libra, and Aquarius), and three watery (and they are Cancer, Scorpio, and Pisces).

19 Now the indication of each one of the signs over existing things in this world, comes to be according to what I will make clear:

20 For to Aries (which is the first of the signs) came the indication over the condition of fiery, natural, moderate hotness and dryness by which the beginning of motion comes to be, and the generation of life and development. **21** To Leo came the indication over the condition of fiery, harmful hotness and dryness which subtracts the strength from moderation. **22** And to Sagittarius came the indication over the condition of fiery, corrupting hotness and dryness which is destructive to animals and vegetation.[15]

23 And the indication of Taurus came to be over the condition of earthy, moderate coldness and dryness which is indicative over generation and over pure soil in which there is vegetation. **24** To Virgo came the indication over the condition of earthy coldness and dryness which subtracts from moderation, and over all fertile[16] soil sprouting some types but not sprouting others. **25** To Capricorn came the indication over the condition of earthy, corrupting coldness and dryness, and over mud and all soil which does not sprout [plants].

26 And to Gemini came the indication over the condition of moderate hotness and wetness, indicative over generation and every breeze and good, moderate air strengthening individual animals and plants. **27** To Libra came the indication over the condition of hotness and wetness which subtracts from moderation, and over all thick, harmful, motley mixing[17] of air, and over thick, harmful winds and vapors harmful to animals. **28** To Aquarius came the indication over the condition of corrupting hotness and wetness, and over all corrupting air destructive to animals, and over all vapor and winds from which there is corruption, tremors, demolition, and what resembles that.

---

[15] But remember that the weather when the Sun is in Sagittarius (in the northern hemisphere) is *not* hot, so the scheme of interlaced beginnings, middles, and ends for the elements themselves, does not match the Sun's actual effect on weather.

[16] Or perhaps, "fertilized" (سبخ), as this word specifically designates manure.

[17] مختلط.

29 And to Cancer came the indication over the condition of moderate coldness and wetness, indicative over generation, and over all fresh water from which there is nourishment, and the life of animals and plants. **30** To Scorpio came the indication over the condition of coldness and wetness which subtracts from moderation, and over all changing water in which there is saltiness, and a small alteration in taste [away] from what nourishes, and which some animals benefit from but others are not nourished by nor do they benefit from it. **31** To Pisces came the indication over corrupting coldness and wetness which is destructive to animals and plants, and over all bitter, stinking water, of what does not nourish nor does one benefit from.

32 Thus, to the first four signs comes the indication over the condition of every moderate thing in which the beginning of generation is; and to the second four signs comes the indication over the condition of everything in the middle [which is] less than moderate, receptive to some [kinds of] generation but not receptive to others; and to the last four signs comes the indication over everything corrupting and destructive. **33** And to every one of these twelve comes the indication over the nature and special property of some thing different from that of the others. **34** For this reason, all three of them come to be a fitting, harmonious triplicity.

35 So look at these natures, how much more astonishing is their harmony: that of them two are light and high up (and they are air and fire), and they are in two grades, light and lighter than light (for what is airy is light, and the fiery is lighter than light), and that two natures are heavy, thick, and low (and they are water and earth), and they are in two grades, thick and thicker than thick (for the thick is water, and the thicker than thick is earth). **36** Thus all of the watery, thick, low things are opposed to the earthy things which are thicker than the thick; and all of the airy, light, high things are opposed to the fiery things which are lighter than light.[18]

---

[18] This kind of opposition is not very persuasive, because the "light" is not really opposed to the "lighter." But in this Aristotelian system at least some qualities of the dry and the wet are opposed: the fiery signs (hot and dry) are opposed to the airy ones (hot and wet); and the earthy signs (cold and dry) are opposed to the watery ones (cold and wet).

Chapter II.4: On the sequence of the natures of the signs

1 Some people among those who look into the natural sciences have rejected this sequence, and say: Why did they begin with fire, earth, air, and then water in the sequence of the indication of the *signs*, and why did they not make it be fire, then air, water, and earth, in accordance with how one ought to do it in the natural sequence?[19]

2 We say that among the principles is what is single (and that is hotness, coldness, dryness, and wetness), and among them is what is composite (and it is fire, earth, air, and water): and even though these four principles are composite, each one of them is associated with a simple principle which is more dominant in it. **3** That is, hotness is more dominant in fire, dryness more dominant in earth, wetness more dominant in air, and coldness more dominant in water: thus each one of these composite principles is associated with a simple principle which is more dominant in it.

4 And of these four single principles, two of them are active and antithetical to each other (and they are hotness and coldness), while two are passive and antithetical to each other (and they are dryness and wetness). **5** As for the two active ones, the motion of animals comes to be through one (and it is hotness), while the corruption of it comes to be through one (and it is coldness). **6** And the two passive ones are dryness and wetness: one of the passive ones is receptive to being acted upon (and it is dryness), more so than the other is receptive to it. **7** (So as for wetness, it is below dryness in receptivity to being acted upon.)

---

[19] See II.3, **35-36**. The natural sequence would be fire (which rises highest), air (next highest), water (sinks lower), earth (sinks lowest).

BOOK II: FIXED STARS, SIGNS, QUADRUPLICITY, SECT

Nature	Dominant principle	Activity / passivity	Role in generation and corruption
Fire	Hot	Active	Generation, motion
Earth	Dry	Passive (more)	Stronger, more receptive to activity
Air	Wet	Passive (less)	Less strong or receptive to activity
Water	Cold	Active	Corruption

Figure 19: Order and characteristics of the natures and principles in the signs

[Why fire and water form the extremes]

8 And since the four single principles are in this situation, they began with fire for [several] reasons:

9 One of them is that because hotness is dominant over fire, and neither motion nor the generation of animals[20] take place except through the innate hotness which occurs in that thing, they made it be at one extreme. **10** And they made water (in which the power of coldness is more dominant) be at the other extreme because, if hotness effects generation through the innate hotness which occurs in an animal, then since coldness is the antithesis of hotness, it effects the corruption of that generation.

11 And the second reason due to which they began with hotness, is that hotness is a component of generation, and coldness a component of corruption; and indeed a thing is first generated, then after that it is corrupted. **12** So, because of that they began with hotness as a component of generation, and they made it be at one extreme, and made the cold (as a component of corruption) be at the other extreme.

13 And the third reason is that the conditions which are added to an animal are those which come in between its generation and its corruption: so they made the two active principles (belonging to generation and corruption) be at the two extremes—and they are hotness and coldness. **14** And they made the two principles receptive to being acted upon, be in the middle: and they are dryness and wetness.

---

[20] حيوان. Really this should be "living things," but since Abū Ma'shar sometimes mentions plants separately I will restrict it to animals here.

15 And the fourth reason is that all generation and corruption occurs in this world which is below the sphere of the Moon, so its occurrence is by means of the indications of the upper bodies: and fire is the uppermost and most rarefied of these four principles, and the closest to the upper bodies and to the circle of the Moon (she being indicative of our general conditions).

16 So, for these reasons they made fire (in which the power of hotness is more dominant) be at one extreme when they arranged the natures of the signs, and they made water (in which the power of coldness is more dominant) be at the other extreme.

[The elements in the middle]

17 Thus when they put the two active ones at the two extremes (and they are hotness and coldness), in the middle there remained the two acted upon by them (and they are dryness and wetness). **18** And since the dry is dominant in earth, and wetness in air, earth was put below fire in the sequence, and air put under earth. **19** And indeed they did that for two reasons. **20** As for one of them, it is due to the kinship of the elements with each other, because the dry of the earth is akin to the hotness of fire, and the wetness of air is akin to the coldness of water.

21 The second reason is that since hotness is the strongest of the two active ones, and the dry the strongest of the two passive ones, and hotness is dominant in fire and dryness in earth, they began with the strongest of the two active ones (and it is fire), and made it be the first extreme; then they put the strongest of those acted upon (and it is earth) under it, because the dry is below hotness in strength. **22** But as for air, they made it be under earth because the dry is more dominant in earth, and wetness more dominant in air, and wetness is below the dry in strength. **23** So, air came to be below earth and above water in the sequence. **24** And indeed air came to be above water so that the two active ones (which are hotness and coldness) came to be at the two extremes, and the passive ones (which are dryness and wetness) in the middle.

25 So for these reasons, in the sequence of the natures of the signs they began with fire, then earth, air, then water, and they said: Aries indicates fire, Taurus indicates earth, Gemini indicates air, and Cancer indicates water. **26** And likewise the rest of the signs are in this sequence in indication.

Chapter II.5: It is stated why one begins[21] with Aries rather than the rest of the signs

1 Some people said: since the rotation has no beginning, why did they begin with Aries and make it the beginning of the signs?

2 We say: since [1] the single principles are four (and they are hotness, coldness, wetness, and dryness), and [2] when these four single ones are made composite some of them indicate generation, and some of them corruption, and [3] at one time of the year things will be generated and occur, while in another they will be corrupted, they made the beginning from the sign which, when the Sun alights in it, the nature of that season will be harmonious with the nature of the composite principle indicative of the beginning of generation, emergence, youthfulness, and desire.[22]

3 Now as for these four single principles, two of them are active (and they are hotness and coldness), and two of them passive (and they are dryness and wetness); and the activity of each of the active ones is apparent in generation and corruption, in one of the passive ones. **4** For when hotness acts in wetness, from them both there is motion, generation, growth, and life: and this harmonizes with the nature of air. **5** Also, when hotness acts in dryness, from them both there is hardening, rest, and death: and this harmonizes with the nature of fire.[23] **6** Also, when coldness acts in wetness, from them both there is survival and moderation: and this harmonizes with the nature of water. **7** And also, when coldness acts in dryness, from them both there is perishing and excess in badness: and this harmonizes with the nature of

---

[21] Reading بدئ with the table of contents, for "they began" (بدؤوا).

[22] الصبّا. This can also mean "childhood," but that would be redundant given the "youthfulness" just mentioned. This word can also mean "the east wind," which is associated with spring and the element of air, so there are layers of symbolic thinking here that make exact translation difficult.

[23] But remember that in II.4, **9-10**, the hot was associated with generation and motion (not death), and the cold was associated with corruption and death (not life). Perhaps Abū Ma'shar means that the simple principles form a natural sequence when considered by themselves (as in II.4), but when considered as pairs they make different patterns (as in II.5 here). But do also note that the two infortunes are excessive in the dry (Mars) and the cold (Saturn), and they are hostile to life. So this passage may also be preparing us for the classification of fortunes and infortunes.

earth. **8** So, that one of these composite principles which indicates motion, generation, growth, and life, is in the class of hotness and wetness.[24]

9 Then they looked at the conditions of the season and found that when the Sun alights in the first point of Aries, the season is altered by moderate hotness and wetness [as] he is elevated above them; and the day begins to increase until the Sun has traversed three signs (and they are Aries, Taurus, and Gemini). **10** And when the Sun passes to the end of Gemini, the day reaches the endpoint of its increase, and the night reaches the endpoint of its decrease.

11 Now when the Sun alights in the first point of Cancer, the season is altered by the hot and the dry, and the day begins to decrease and the night to increase, until the Sun has traversed three signs (and they are Cancer, Leo, and Virgo). **12** And the day decreases upon the Sun's being in Cancer just like it had increased when the Sun was in Gemini, and the day decreases when the Sun is in Leo just like it had increased when the Sun was in Taurus, and the day decreases when the Sun is in Virgo just like it had increased when the Sun was in Aries. **13** And when the Sun passes to the end of Virgo, the hot reaches its endpoint, and the night and day are equal.

14 Now when the Sun passes into the first point of Libra, the air is altered by the cold and the dry, and the day begins to decrease and the night to increase, until the Sun has traversed three signs (and they are Libra, Scorpio, and Sagittarius). **15** And the day decreases when the Sun is in Libra just like it had increased when the Sun was in Aries, and the day decreases when the Sun is in Scorpio just like it had increased when the Sun was in Taurus, and the day decreases when the Sun is in Sagittarius just like it had increased when the Sun was in Gemini. **16** And when the Sun passes to the end of Sagittarius, the night reaches the endpoint of its length, and the day reaches its endpoint in shortness. **17** And the length of the night when the Sun is at the end of Sagittarius is just like what the length of the day had been when the Sun was at the end of Gemini, and the shortness of the day when the Sun is

---

[24] For this paragraph, sentence **4** anticipates **22**; **5** anticipates **23**; **6** anticipates **24**; and **7** anticipates **25**. The dry is akin to death, the wet akin to life, the hot stimulates life, and the cold only preserves it. So, the hot and the wet are most indicative of life. Therefore, since Aries is the point where the hot is added to the wetness of winter, we begin the cycle of life in the airy quarter of Aries-Taurus-Gemini: see **22** and **28**.

at the end of Sagittarius is just like what the shortness of the night had been when the Sun was at the end of Gemini.

18 And when the Sun alights in the first point of Capricorn, the air is altered by the cold and wetness, and the day begins to increase and the night to decrease, until the Sun has traversed three signs (and they are Capricorn, Aquarius, and Pisces). **19** And the day increases when the Sun is in Capricorn just like it had increased when the Sun was in Gemini, and the day increases when the Sun is in Aquarius just like it had increased when the Sun was in Taurus, and the day increases when the Sun is in Pisces just like it had increased when the Sun was in Aries. **20** And when the Sun passes to the end of Pisces, the night and day are equal, and the Sun reaches the position which he had started from: and he will have traversed the belt of the circle of signs (and they are 360°, which is 12 signs), in 365 days plus 1/4 of a day, minus 1/300 of a day, according to what Ptolemy claimed.[25] **21** And this is the amount of a year of the Sun, and the year comes to be 12 months (following the number of signs), and the days of every month come to be like the number of days in which the Sun traverses one of the signs.[26]

22 And they found the conditions of the year to be four: the first of them heating and moistening according to the nature of air, and in it the generation of things and the emerging of plants begins, and the flowers of the earth come out, and the trees sprout leaves, and it is similar to the nature of desire,[27] and the beginning of generation, and it is what is called "spring." **23** And the second is heating and drying, burning and corrupting like the nature of fire, and it is what is called "summer." **24** The third is cooling and drying like the nature of earth, and in it is a general corrupting of what bears leaves and fruit, and vegetation, and it is what is called "autumn." **25** And the fourth

---

[25] That makes 365.24667 days (or 365d 5h 55m 12s), the tropical year as measured by Hipparchus and continued by Ptolemy in the *Almagest* III.1, p. 139. The tropical year is currently measured at 365.24219 (365d 5h 48m 45s).

[26] This is what Abū Ma'shar calls a "solar month" in *PN4* Ch. I.3, 12: namely, the length of time between Solar ingresses into each sign. Since the Sun moves at different speeds in different parts of the zodiac, his ingress period spent in each sign will differ slightly.

[27] الصبى, this time with a different spelling but the same meaning as in the end of **2**.

is cooling and moistening, clinging like the nature of water, and it is what is called "winter."

26 And each one of these four seasons has a beginning, middle, and end. **27** The beginning of each period is the sign in which the season shifts from nature to nature when the Sun passes into it; its middle is the second sign which follows that sign; and its end is the third sign from it.

28 So they made the beginning of the number of signs be from the beginning of the sign which, when the Sun alights in it, [1] there is a beginning of the season which is heating and moistening by its nature,[28] and [2] its [position in the] sequence is indicative of generation,[29] and [3] the nature of the sign in itself is indicative of the innate hotness by which the growth and movement of animals begins (based on what we have reported about the mixtures of the principles),[30] and [4] and in the corresponding nature of that time of the season it [really does] begin to generate things, and growth, and planets, and the fruit of trees [really] emerges,[31] and [5] upon the Sun's alighting in the beginning of this sign the day begins to increase over the night:[32] and this is the sign called Aries.

Chapter II.6: On the reason for the convertible, fixed, and double-bodied signs

1 Since [1] the conditions of the year are four (and they are the spring, summer, autumn, and winter), and [2] in every one of these four seasons the Sun traverses three signs, and [3] every season has a beginning, middle, and end, and [4] the beginning of [a season] is with the Sun's alighting at the beginning of any one of the four quarters of the circle, a sign is called "convertible" when it is at the beginning of one of the quarters, and when the Sun alights in it the season shifts over to another one. **2** And the sign which follows it is the "fixed" one, because when the Sun passes into it the nature of

---

[28] See II.5, **8**.
[29] See II.4, **5**.
[30] See II.4, **9**.
[31] See II.5, **22**.
[32] See II.5, **9**.

that season becomes fixed. **3** And a sign having "two bodies" is the one which blends the nature of that season which it is in, with the nature of the season it shifts over to, when the Sun passes into it.

4 So for this reason Aries is called convertible: because when the Sun passes into it, the season shifts from winter to the nature of spring. **5** And Taurus is called fixed, because when the Sun passes into it the nature of the season of spring becomes fixed. **6** And Gemini is called double-bodied, because when the Sun passes into it, the nature of the end of the season of spring is blended with the nature of the beginning of the season of summer. **7** And Cancer is called convertible, because when the Sun passes into it, the season shifts over from the nature of spring to the nature of summer. **8** And Leo is called fixed, Virgo having two bodies, Libra convertible, Scorpio fixed, Sagittarius having two bodies, Capricorn convertible, Aquarius fixed, Pisces having two bodies, for the reasons which we stated.

Chapter II.7: On the knowledge of the quarters of the sphere, and the reason for the convertible, fixed, and double-bodied signs, and the reason for the number of the signs (and that they are twelve), and why one begins with Aries in the sequence of their natures, and the knowledge of their triplicities, according to what Hermes reported from Agathodaimōn

1 Hermes said (from Agathodaimōn): Since we know that [1] a universal division is prior in rank to one based on parts, and that [2] every beginning is advancing and increasing, while every termination is retreating and decreasing, and [3] we want to know the number of signs, their conditions, and their natures, and where they begin from, it is necessary for us to know the quarters and their conditions before anything [else], so that from it we might know the rest of what is needed.

2 And indeed when we looked into the conditions of the quarters of the sphere, we found the two equalities which are when the Sun is at the end of Virgo and the end of Pisces. **3** And upon his alighting at the beginning of Aries, the day increases over the night and the Sun is lifted up, while upon his alighting at the beginning of Libra the day decreases as compared with the night, and the Sun is lowered. **4** And we have found all things among animals, plants, and metals to advance and increase along with the increase of the day and the Sun's being lifted up, while they decrease and retreat with the decrease of the day and the Sun's being lowered down.

5 So we know that the beginning in the number of the signs is from Aries, because the increase of the day is what begins at the Sun's alighting in the beginning of Aries, and its endpoint is when the Sun passes into the beginning of Cancer (and this is the end of the season of spring, and the beginning of summer). **6** And the decrease of the day [as compared to night] is what begins when the Sun is at the beginning of Libra, and its endpoint is when the Sun is at the beginning of Capricorn (and this is the end of the season of autumn, and the beginning of winter). **7** So, Aries and Cancer are called "having increase and power," while Libra and Capricorn "have decrease and weakness."[33]

8 So it has now become clear to us that the sphere has four turning-points: spring, summer, autumn, and winter. **9** As for the season of spring, it is heating and moistening; the season of summer is heating and drying; the season of autumn is cooling and drying; and the season of winter is cooling and moistening.

10 And we have found that for every one of these quarters there are three meetings,[34] and three images (each of the images being different from the others), and three conditions differing greatly (and they are the alteration of the day, the alteration of the inclination,[35] and the alteration of the season). **11** As for the alteration of the day, it is from increase to decrease, or from decrease to increase. **12** The alteration of the inclination is from being lifted up to being brought down, or from being brought down to being lifted up. **13** And the alteration of the season is from the beginning to the middle, or from the middle to the end.

14 Now the images in which there is a shifting of the season and day from one nature to another when the Sun passes into them, are called "convertible." **15** And the images in which the strength of the season is made clear, as well as its fixity (when the Sun passes into them), are called "fixed." **16** And

---

[33] See Ch. V.7, **6-7** for the use of this material in exaltations.

[34] اجتماعات. This is the usual word for the New Moon or "meeting," so Hermes must be talking about the lunar month.

[35] Normally this indicates latitude in the ecliptic, but in this Hermes-Agathodaimōn material it seems to mean declination.

the three images said to be "having two bodies" are because when the Sun is in the first half of them, the season resembles the past quarter, while when he is in the last half the season resembles the future quarter: and there the strength of the season is altered to an increase or decrease. **17** The increase is in Pisces and Gemini, and the decrease is in Virgo and Sagittarius.

18 And when we found, in every one of the quarters of the sphere, three meetings, three images, and three conditions differing greatly, we made each one of the quarters into three modes, then we multiplied the three modes by the four quarters, and they came to twelve: each one of them being one of the signs. **19** So the number of signs came to be twelve: four of them convertible, four fixed, and four having two bodies.

20 Since the number of signs has been sorted for us, we wanted to know their natures. **21** So we returned to the nature of the quarters of the circle, and we found the season when the Sun is in the first quarter to be heating and moistening, in the second quarter heating and drying, in the third quarter cooling and drying, and in the fourth quarter cooling and moistening.

22 Thus it has become clear to us that the second quarter (and it is Cancer, Leo, and Virgo) is the hottest of these quarters, and the driest: and half[36] of this quarter (and it is from the Sun's being in 15° of Leo) is the strongest that the hotness and the dry can be. **23** So since we know that Leo is the hottest of the signs, and the driest, and Sagittarius and Aries are in one triplicity with it, they are made to be harmonious with it in hotness and the dry. **24** And because there is nothing hotter nor drier than fire, Aries, Leo, and Sagittarius were made fiery.

25 We found in what preceded, that the first of the quarters is the heating and moistening season, and the last one is cooling and moistening: so since Aries and its triplicity are heating and drying, and it is the first of the triplicities, we knew that the last of the triplicities is cooling and moistening (and it is Cancer, Scorpio, and Pisces). **26** Thus we now knew the nature of Aries, Cancer, and their triplicities.

27 There remain the triplicity of Taurus and Gemini. **28** We knew that they are not cooling and heating, nor heating and cooling, nor are two consecutive signs of a single nature: so it is not that the one following Aries (which is heating and drying) is of a heating nature, but a cooling and drying

---

[36] نصف. I should have expected "the middle" (وسط).

nature follows it due to the resemblance of the season of one of them to the other—because the cooling and drying season is after the heating and drying season, due to the kinship of what is drying, to hotness. **29** So, Taurus and its triplicity came to be cooling and drying. **30** To complete the distribution of the four natures, there remains the heating and moistening nature, so the nature of Gemini and its triplicity came to be heating and moistening.

31 So it has now become clear to us that Aries and its triplicity are heating, drying, fiery; Taurus and its triplicity are cooling, drying, earthy; Gemini and its triplicity are heating, moistening, airy; and Cancer and its triplicity are cooling, moistening, watery.

[Abū Ma'shar's comments and argument?][37]

32 But [some] people among the masters of the stars have alleged that Aries is heating and moistening, and they argue for that by saying that the last of the triplicities is cooling and moistening, following the nature of the last division of the year, and following the nature of the last quarter of the day; but likewise, Aries is the first of the signs, so its nature should be heating and moistening (in accordance with the nature of the first division of the year, and the nature of the first quarter of the day).

33 We will respond to their statement with two arguments. **34** One of them is: we say that if the distribution of the natures of the signs had begun from the nature of the first division of the year, and from the first nature of the quarters of the day, what you said would have been necessary. **35** But[38] the natures of the beginning of the signs and their triplicities[39] are begun

---

[37] What follows is typical of Abū Ma'shar's style of debate, so I believe we have now left Hermes and Agathodaimōn behind. However, **35-36** repeat *Hermes's* argument: so this section could be Abū Ma'shar's reformulation of responses by Hermes to other people.

[38] These concepts are referred to in Hermes-Agathodaimōn's discussion of the exaltations in V.7, **1-5** and **22-24**. It's possible that Abū Ma'shar has adopted this Hermes-Agathodaimōn idea as his own for the purpose of organizing his arguments here.

[39] I believe this should probably read, "the natures of the beginning of the signs and *its triplicity.*" The argument here has little foundation, but what Abū Ma'shar seems to mean is the following. Since each triplicity has its own nature, but the three signs

from the nature of the *middle* of the summer season, and from the nature of the middle of the day corresponding to the nature of summer, and from the nature of the transiting of the signs in the *Midheaven*, because their transit in that position is equal over [all of] the climes. **36** And indeed the beginning was made from the day rather than the night, because the day is indicative of generation and motion.

37 The second argument is that we say wetness is more dominant than hotness in the period of the first division of the year, and things are indeed associated with the nature which is more dominant in them. **38** But if the nature of Aries had been associated with the nature of that period, one ought to have associated its nature to *wetness*, and not to hotness.[40]

---

form a developmental sequence, the middle sign (i.e., the fixed one) in each triplicity establishes the real nature of it. So it is true that the weather itself is warming and *moistening* in the spring, because we are just coming out of winter (which is moistening). But that does not mean that Aries itself as a member of the fiery *triplicity* is warming and moistening, because it is only the first in the sequence of Aries-Leo-Sagittarius. Therefore, we need to look at the corresponding natures of the middle of summer (the fixed sign Leo) and the middle of the day, to establish that this triplicity is really heating and *drying* (see **22-24** above). That is, since the middle of the season corresponds to the middle of the day, we need to look at the middle of the day to understand its qualities. (Still, something does not quite make sense here.)

[40] This argument could be taken in several ways: part of the problem is that we do not know enough about the physical theory of the objector, and Abū Ma'shar's response is somewhat incomplete. The objector has implied that in early spring, there is still plenty of moisture but a transition between coldness and hotness: therefore Aries should be considered heating and moistening, not heating and drying. Abū Ma'shar's response is that in early spring, the wetness is dominant, because there is still a transition between coldness and hotness. Therefore (he argues), if we really wanted the weather to guide our thinking, we would say that Aries is *primarily wet*, not heating. (And in Aristotelian physics, air is the wet element.) But Abū Ma'shar has gone too far: the opponent was objecting to Aries being *drying*, and did not make any claims about whether hotness or wetness was dominant. I think this dispute is difficult because the triplicities have their own distinct natures, and form a developmental series of three signs, but they are integrated throughout the zodiac instead of coming in discrete chunks. This means there is some artificiality in this way of combining weather, physics, and symbolic schematizing.

39 Thus the quarters of the circle have now become clear to us, and the convertible, fixed, and double-bodied signs, and their number, and their beginning, and the sequence of their natures and triplicities.

Chapter II.8: On the knowledge of the masculine and feminine signs

1 By the congruence[41] of the male and female, is produced generation: and what is active is hot [and] male, while the female is cold [and] passive,[42] and everything male precedes in rank and what is established, then the female follows it. **2** So, to Aries (which has an indication for hotness and activity) belongs the nature of masculinization, and to Taurus (which has an indication for cold and receptivity) belongs being acted upon [and] feminization; then to Gemini belongs masculinization, and to Cancer feminization—and likewise the rest of the twelve signs, according to this model: male, then female.

3 And [some] people have made a division of the male and female [signs] differently from this, and it is that they said: The east is hot, and hotness is indicative of masculinization, and [so] the sign which ascends from the east is hot [and] male; and since the female follows the male in rank, the second sign from the Ascendant is female; and the third sign from it male, and likewise the rest of the signs. **4** But we say that the first sequence is natural [and] has a fixed indication in masculinization and feminization; as for this second one, its arrangement is casual[43] because it is quick to change and shift from situation to situation—and a natural sequence is more sound in indication than a casual sequence.

5 Now if the two agreed in the indication of masculinization or feminization, that would be more sound; but if they differed, the sign indicative of masculinization and feminization in natural way is more fundamental in indication than a casual one; even though the ancients had sometimes used a casual sequence in the indication of masculinization and feminization in the characteristics of things.

---

[41] اتّفاق.

[42] Lit., "acted upon" (مفعول بها).

[43] Or, "contingent" (عرضيّ).

Chapter II.9: On the diurnal and nocturnal signs

1 Since these twelve signs rotate around us by one rotation every day and night, and a day is due to the Sun's arising from the horizon [in the east] up to his disappearance from the [western] horizon, and a night is from his disappearance from the horizon up to his arising from the horizon, and the nature of the day is heating while the nature of the night is cooling, and night follows day, they made the first of the signs (which is Aries) a heating one [and] diurnal, and Taurus (which follows it) cooling [and] nocturnal—then Gemini is diurnal, Cancer is nocturnal, and likewise the rest of the signs are diurnal, then nocturnal.

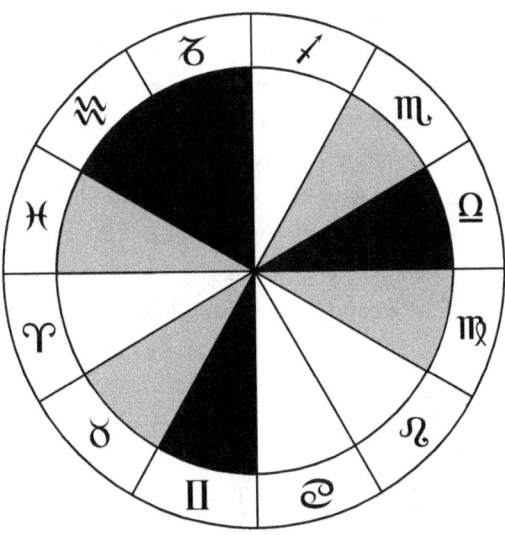

Figure 20: Diurnal (white), nocturnal (black), and mixed signs (gray) according to others (II.9, 2)

2 But as for those people who did not understand natural things and their sequence, they made four of them be diurnal (and they are Aries, Cancer, Leo, and Sagittarius), and four nocturnal (and they are Gemini, Libra, Capricorn, and Aquarius), and four blended with the diurnal and nocturnal (and they are Taurus, Virgo, Scorpio, and Pisces).[44] **3** Thus they made Cancer

---

[44] I am not sure what the overall rationale or pattern is here, but there are hints of Hermes and the Stoics. As for Hermes, note that Aries and Cancer (which he designates as increasing in light in II.7, **5-7**) are diurnal, while Libra and Capricorn (designated as decreasing) are nocturnal (II.7, **5-7**). Or, the signs of the luminaries (Cancer, Leo) are diurnal, while the signs of Saturn (Capricorn, Aquarius) are nocturnal. As for the Stoic theory of elements, the fiery signs (hot) are diurnal, while the airy signs (cold) are nocturnal—but the rest do not fully make sense. As for taking

(which is a female sign, according to what we have stated) be in the natural sequence belonging to fire, and they made Gemini, Libra, and Aquarius (which are male signs, in a natural order) be nocturnal. **4** And they made Taurus, Virgo, Scorpio, and Pisces (which are female signs in natural sequence) be blended with the day and night, and they said by day they are diurnal and by night nocturnal. **5** But they did not prove that with anything except to state it by way of a report in their books—and this is does not harmonize with what the ancients stated about the natural sequence belonging to the diurnal and nocturnal signs.

6 The Second Book is completed.

---

the diagram on its own terms, all four diurnal signs are opposed by the four nocturnal (black) signs, and all mixed signs (gray) are opposed to each other. All mixed signs are also in aversion to Aries and Libra.

Book III: [Definition of Astrology, Weather, Tides, & Growth]

And in it are nine chapters

1 Chapter III.1: On the reason for the masters of the stars' using the seven planets in the general indication of things, rather than the rest of the planets of the sphere, and the special property of action of each one of them in the conditions of the four principles.
2 Chapter III.2: On the definition of the "judgments of the stars," "astrologer," and into which matter he looks.
3 Chapter III.3: On the special property of the Sun's indication for the moderation of atmospheric things, natures, compositions, and the planets' partnership with him.
4 Chapter III.4: On the special property of the Moon for the flow and ebb [of the tide].
5 Chapter III.5: On the cause of the flow and ebb [of the tide].
6 Chapter III.6: On the strength of the flow and its weakness, and the abundance and scarcity of its water.
7 Chapter III.7: That the Moon is the cause of the flow and ebb, and the response to those opposing that.
8 Chapter III.8: On the different conditions of the seas, and the quality of the seas in which the flow and ebb is made obvious (and in which it is not obvious), and on the special property of the Sun's action in the seas.
9 Chapter III.9: On the Moon's indication for animals, plants, and minerals, through the increase and decrease of her glow.

Chapter III.1: On the reason for the masters of the stars' using the seven planets in the general indication of things, rather than the rest of the planets of the sphere, and the special property of action of each one of them in the conditions of the four principles

1 People have said: "Why have the seven stars [which are] quick in motion come to be more primary in the general indication [of things] than the rest of the stars [which are] slow in motion, when these ones slow in motion cooperate with those quick in motion, in their shifting within the signs, rising over us and setting from us, easternization and westernization, and in many things of their conditions and natures, and in the indication over generation and corruption?"

2 We say that all of the ancients did state that everything occurring in this world is by means of the power of the motions of the signs and stars about us. **3** And the signs are indicative of the four principles, in accordance with our previous statement in Book I.[1] **4** All of the stars therefore, [both] quick in motion and slow in motion, are indicative of what is produced and occurs from these four principles through their circular motions about us, except that [the ancients] discovered from these seven planets that they are the quickest of them in motion, and have the most variations in [their] conditions about us. **5** So due to the abundance of their varied conditions, and the quickness of their motions, the changes which are stimulated by them in this world came to be greater than those which are stimulated by the rest of the stars [which are] slow in motion.

6 In this way then, these seven planets came to have a general indication over the variation in conditions, and over the causes of change, and over the change which occurs in this world; and everything of them that is quicker in motion and in shifting in the signs, and with the most variation (in their conditions and alteration in themselves), has the most indication for things quick to change, and generation and corruption. **7** And because the Moon has the most alteration and variation in her conditions among the planets, she has come to be more indicative over general things [which are] quick in motion and shifting, and over the inception of works, than the other seven

---

[1] Abū Ma'shar may be thinking of Ch. I.3, but surely a better reference would be II.6—II.7.

planets are. **8** But as for the fixed stars, they have an indication over every particular thing [which is] slow in generation and corruption.

9 And the second reason is that whereas [1] the sphere and the [fixed] stars in it have eternal motion about this world, and these fixed stars are in a single sphere, and [2] the motion of each one of them is the same as the motion of another, and the distance of every star from one another is in the same state, not increasing in nearness nor distance beyond what it was and still is, and [3] they are slow in motion, with little variation in condition, while these seven stars have much variation in condition and are the quickest of the stars of the sphere in motion, and [4] each of [the seven] stars has a different sphere from its neighbor's sphere, and a motion in a path other than its neighbor's, and in a different motion, [5] and the conditions of each [of the quick] stars is different from the conditions of its neighbor, in [terms of] its body and motion, and [6] they have quick alterations and shifts from position to position, and from condition to condition (such as direct motion, stationing, and retrogradation, and rising and falling [in the apogee], and easternization and westernization), and [7] these seven stars do not cease in [their] motion and shifting of condition about this world, and this world does not cease [to have] generation, corruption, and alterations due to the motions of the sphere and the planets in it, they knew—by the abundance of motions of these seven planets quick in motion, and the variation of their conditions—that they have a general indication over everything in this world, among the things which have quick changes, and generation and corruption, and that the fixed stars which are slow in motion [and] have few changes have an indication over particular things which are slow in generation and corruption.

10 And because the signs are indicative over the four principles, while the planets are the cause of their alteration and conversion from thing to thing (in the manner we stated in Books I and II of this book of ours), and these seven have more action in them, and more alteration and conversion, than the others do, and they are varied in essence, nature, and condition, each one of

☉ ♂	Hot and dry	Generative Corrupting
☿ ♄	Cold and dry	Generative Corrupting
♀ ☽ ☋	Cold and wet	Generative Generative Corrupting
♃ ☊	Hot and wet	Generative Corrupting

Figure 21: Planetary qualities (III.1, 11-19)

them has a particular action of alteration and conversion in one of the principles, as well as generation and corruption, [which is] different from the others.

11 And indeed, the action of each one of them is more abundant in the principle which the nature attributed to it, resembles. **12** So, for the Sun and Mars the majority of their alteration, conversion, and action is in the principle of fiery hotness and dryness which their natures resemble. **13** For Mercury and Saturn, the majority of their alteration, conversion, and action is in the principle of earthy coldness and dryness which their natures resemble. **14** For Venus, the Moon, and the Tail, the majority of their alteration, conversion, and action is in the watery coldness and wetness which their natures resemble. **15** And for Jupiter and the Head, the majority of their alteration, conversion, and action is in the nature of airy hotness and wetness which their natures resemble.

16 But as for the Sun, the majority of his action in the principle of fiery hotness is indicative of generation, while for Mars the majority of his action is in the principle of corrupting, fiery hotness. **17** As for Mercury, the majority of his action in the principle of earthy coldness and dryness is indicative of generation, while the majority of Saturn's action is in the principle of corrupting, earthy coldness and dryness from which nothing sprouts or is brought into being. **18** The majority of the action of Venus and the Moon is in the growth-inducing, watery coldness and wetness belonging to animals and plants, while the majority of the Tail's action is in corrupting coldnesses. **19** And the majority of Jupiter's action is in the creative, airy hotness and wetness which is strengthening to animals and plants, while the majority of the Head's action is in the airy hotness and wetness in which there is some corruption.

Chapter III.2: On the definition of the "judgments of the stars," "astrologer," and into which matter he looks

1 In what has preceded we have already stated that the power of the stars' motions have an action in this world, and we stated the manner of finding those actions which come to be from the powers of their motions.[2] **2** Now as for the knowledge of those powers, that is called "the science of the judgments of the stars"; and as for the name of the man who is knowledgeable in their powers, he is called "the astrologer." **3** So let us define each one of these things which we have stated, in a true way, so that its meaning may be evident to us.

[Definition of astrology and the astrologer]

4 I say that the definition of the science of the judgments of the stars, is the knowledge of what the power of the stars' motions at a certain time indicates for *that* time, as well as for a defined, *future* time. **5** Now as for the knowledge which we stated in the definition, it is like the genus; and as for the rest of what follows from it, it is like [its] divisions.[3] **6** As for our saying in the definition "what the power of the stars' motions" indicates, we said that because the power of their motions has an action in this world—but many people have denied that something may indicate something [else] which is not that [very] thing.[4] **7** But we say that among the ancients it was agreed that what is indicative of a thing is not that

---

[2] Abū Ma'shar has done this in many ways, but may be referring to I.4, **54-74**.
[3] See **14-15** below.
[4] This is actually an important logical and metaphysical debate, as to how some things can be "signs" of, or indicate, other things. One of the most famous historical examples of this debate is in medicine, wherein we use relationships between symptoms to make inferences about underlying relationships between physical causes: the symptom indicates the disease, but is not the disease itself. Here, Abū Ma'shar is pointing out that astrology concerns visible signs within the heavens, which indicate other relationships like marriage, career, and so on, even though they are not relationships in the heavens, but processes and events on earth. Thus (say) Venus is a body and is not marriage itself, but we make inferences from the body of Venus about the physical and social facts of marriage.

[same] thing: and that is like how we see [it] in existing things like thunder and lightning, which indicate rain, even though they are not [themselves] rain. **8** And of course smoke indicates fire, though smoke is not fire; and a built wall indicates a builder who built it, though the wall is not the builder—many things indicate something even though they are not that thing. **9** And this is evident among scholars. **10** Likewise, through the power of their motions the stars indicate what occurs in this world, though they are not that occurrence which they indicate.

11 And as for our saying in the definition a "certain time" and the rest of what follows that, we mean by it the time at which one infers from the power of the stars motions what they indicate at *that* time (in terms of the conditions of things), as well as what they indicate about what will be after that time, in *future* times. **12** And that is because the astrologer who is knowledgeable in the judgments of the stars looks at some certain times into some thing, and says that the motion of the stars at this time indicates that the condition of this thing[5] at the very time of the indication *is* such-and-such, and after this (in a year or another definite time) its condition *will be* such-and-such. **13** Thus he has made an inference from a certain time about a thing at that time, as well as at a future time.

14 Now as for the astrologer, he is knowledgeable in the conditions of the planets and their indications, and he advises about what will come to be from them (based on a certain time), at *that* time, as well as at a defined *future* time. **15** As one who is knowledgeable, he is like a genus; but as for the rest of what follows upon that, he is like [its] divisions.

[Limitations in the astrologer's knowledge]

16 And although the stars indicate everything in this world, we are not able to know it in its totality due to our inability—because the stars' indications over things which are in this world [appear] in three ways. **17** The first of them is [1] the condition of subtlety and obscurity which the stars' indications are in, so that we cannot comprehend them nor the things which they indicate by means of their conditions, in terms of knowing species and indi-

---

[5] By "thing," Abū Ma'shar seems to mean some *earthly* state of affairs or concrete thing, which is indicated by the stars.

viduals. **18** The second is [2] that we do know *what* the conditions of the stars indicate, though we are unable to understand the *quantity* and *quality* of the indicated things, due to our weakness and the difficulty in it. **19** The third is [3] what we know their indications are about, and we know the quality and quantity of the indicated things.

20 Now as for [1] the first one, in which we are unable to comprehend the knowledge of it from the indications of the stars, nor also to understand the things which they indicate by those conditions, they are the stars' indications for the particularizing of species from the genera, and the particularizing of individuals from the species, and the knowledge of every species of animal which is on land and sea, and every species of plant and mineral which is in this world, and every individual of these species, and every grain of sand and pebble in the desert, or the amount [by which] every individual grows, on every day. **21** For indeed, all of these have quantities and qualities, and the stars are indicative of their quantities and qualities—except that we do not comprehend the knowledge of them, nor those indications which the stars have over these things.

22 And we are not able to have knowledge of the stellar indicators for single existing individuals which manifest from [those] actions and qualities, nor also the particularization of a quality among them: and that is like gestures, standing upright or bent, leaning or lying down, standing or sitting, and what is like these particular, subtle actions. **23** Or, the particularization of what is among two qualities when they are of a single genus and in two different individuals, and the particularization which is between them both is of that hidden quality: and that is like two individuals which partake in whiteness, blackness, redness, or fairness; or in the bigness or smallness of the eyes; or in the wideness of the mouth; tallness or shortness; smoothness or roughness; sweetness or bitterness; in a good odor or stench, or in any of the qualities which are of a single genus but in two different individuals, and each one of those qualities is defined in the same manner as the other, and the particularization which is between them both is found to be perceived [only] subtlely.

24 So even though the stars are indicative of this and what is like it, and over the particularization of what is between them, it belongs to the subtle and obscure indications which we do not understand in their totality—nor do we need to in the profession of judgments, because the goal of the master of this profession in the knowledge of this, is different.

25 And as for [2] the second, [it is] the stars' indications over a single species, or over the number of people in some city, the number of grains of sand in some specific place, the measures of water in a single river, the grains of wheat or barley in a plain,[6] or the area of one of the deserts in length and width, or any qualities which they have. **26** For, even if we had known the way in which the stars indicate the quantities and qualities of this and things like it which are defined by attribute and place, and known their number, measures, or areas from their indications, still we would not be able to count nor measure them, nor survey them, due the difficulty in it. **27** But the master of the profession of the science of the stars does not need knowledge of this and what is like it.

28 As for [3] the third, which comprehends with knowledge the indications of the stars, and knows the quantity and quality of the indicated thing, it is their indications for the knowledge of existing genera and species, the conditions of the four principles (which are fire, air, water, and earth) and their alteration, and the inception of the generation and corruption of every thing, and its conditions and qualities, whose like is able to be known from the evident powers of the stars' motions—*this* is the goal of the master of this profession.[7]

29 And so that I might summarize my view, I say that the planets have different conditions, movements, and powers; and every condition of theirs has an indication for something, except that some of their indications are evident, for [those] things whose existence and comprehension is possible, while some of them are subtle [and] distant, for [those] obscure things we are not able to understand. **30** (But due to their subtlety and obscurity, we have no need to know them in this profession.)[8] **31** But in this profession we do employ the indications of the stars which we are able to know and discover, and report about them and about the things indicated by them.

32 An analogy to that is that we know that the shifting of the season from one nature to another comes to be through the motion of the Sun in the

---

[6] Lit., "desert" (الصّحارى).

[7] See also **35-36**.

[8] I have abbreviated most of this sentence as it appears in Lemay, who repeats much of the last part of the previous sentence. (**BY** omits Lemay's repetition without comment.)

BOOK III: DEFINING ASTROLOGY, WEATHER, TIDES   157

quarters of the sphere, and that by this motion in every sign and degree, the season is changed from condition to condition, and the quality of that change in the season is evident—and the knowledge of his indications for what we have stated about the change of the season, is known and found. **33** But as for that whose indication we know and yet it is difficult to know *what* it indicates, we know that when the Sun travels in his sign by one second, third, tenth, or less than that,⁹ the air is altered somewhat; and we also know that when the highest sphere moves the Sun by a fourth, fifth, or rising or falling [in the apogee] by whatever motion, that it does produce an alteration of the air in the hot or cold, or due to the variation of its conditions some condition is altered which is contrary to the condition it had been in at another time,¹⁰ and it will produce the changes of generation and corruption in animals, plants, and minerals. **34** And it all of these changes will be produced in them due to the powers of the motions of the rest of the stars—except that we are not able to know the quantity nor quality of that change and variation.¹¹

35 Regarding these things and the indications of the stars which are like them, and the things indicated by them, even if the master of the profession of judgments is ignorant of their true quantity and quality, that does not harm him in his profession: because the goal of the master of the profession of judgments in his science, is to make inferences from the powers of the motions of the stars, about things coming to be in this world, in terms of existing genera and species, and the conditions of the four principles, and the shifting of one of them into another, and the inception of individuals' generation and their corruption, and their conditions whose like he is able to know, from the manifest indications of the planets and their existence. **36** *This* is the goal of the master of this profession.

---

⁹ That is, by fractions of a second in longitude.
¹⁰ Abū Ma'shar has let his tendency to create lists, and his promiscuous use of the word "condition," get away from him here. This sentence contains a "that" (ذلك) which lacks a referent, so I have smoothed out this last clause a bit.
¹¹ That is, we know that the Sun changes the atmosphere and can describe it up to a point; but we cannot say exactly how it will be changed as he moves in small amounts like 1/1000 of a degree.

[Six stages in the motivation and process of astrology]

37 We have therefore stated the definition of the judgments of the stars, and the astrologer, and into which matter the master of the profession of judgments ought to look, so we will [now] state the six things which follow upon that. **38** I say that the judgments of the stars have a [1] beginning, a [2] root, [3] branch, [4] proof, [5] fruit, and [6] completion:

39 The [1] beginning of judgments which are strongly desired, is understanding the merit of the knowledge of things coming to be, and caring about them.

40 Their [2] root is understanding the quality and quantity of the motions of the higher bodies.

41 The [3] branch of this understanding is that one judge by them about matters which are coming to be in this changing world.[12]

42 The [4] proof of judgments is the correctness which exists through foreknowledge in the conditions of the planets, and applying them in the matter in which one wants knowledge about the things which come to be. **43** And making good use of this science occurs through care and labor, for being correct about things which come to be by [mere] opinion and estimation may [only] be available for special people at any time. **44** So, from here our view is that we should begin with knowledge of the conditions of the stars, and then add judgments to it following [that], lest one suppose that judgment concerning the stars is done at random, by guesswork and opinion, without knowledge of the stars' positions, conditions, and indications.

45 The [5] fruit is the correctness, benefit, and advantages because of it, for those having understanding of the merit of correctness.[13]

46 And the [6] benefit of correctness is the completion: and whatever has no completion is deficient, and things are not established except by completion.

---

[12] This suggests that, like a tree, there are different branches of astrology based on the kinds of "matters" or "things" there are. And we know the four basic branches: nativities, choices or inceptions, questions, and mundane.

[13] See Ch. I.6, on the benefit of foreknowledge.

Chapter III.3: On the special property of the Sun's indication for the moderation of atmospheric things, natures, compositions, and the planets' partnership with him

1 People among those who disagree with us, claim that the moderation of natures, and their stability and foundation, and the composition of animals, plants, and gems, are not due to the Sun and planets,[14] but they are characterized by themselves without an [external] cause. **2** Others say that compositions have a cause apart from the planets.

3 Of our response to those claiming that the moderation of natures (and their stability) is not due to the Sun and planets but that they have a power in them of being characterized by themselves without an [external] cause, there is [the fact] that a composition does not come to be except as a compound, and that it is impossible that a compound should compound itself, or [that] what is natured be the cause of its own naturing: because if it was like that, the compound would make a composition like itself, and what is natured would nature what is like itself, and these principles would not have a transformation from one to the other, but rather they would be [only] in the [same] condition. **4** But we do see them transform and change, and we find them in natural things which come to be and corrupt: so from this we know that they do not change nor are they transformed from[15] themselves, but that that is from the action of something else in them. **5** So because of that, they do change and transform.

6 And also, if things were produced from themselves without an [external] cause, if a thing was existing at some time it would not change nor corrupt, but rather it would remain in its condition because the thing would not corrupt itself nor change itself. **7** So if we find it being produced after it did not exist, and we find it being corrupted after being generated, we know that the cause of the generation and corruption is something other than it. **8** So it has now become clear that the cause of the generation of a thing is not the thing, and that the thing is not produced from itself but rather from the character within it which is susceptible to being produced by another.

---

[14] At this point I transition from translating کواکب as the general term "stars," to the more narrow term "planets."
[15] That is, "due to." This could perhaps be read as "in virtue of."

9 Now we say that the Sun (with the partnership of the planets with him) is the cause of the moderation of natures and the composition of natural individuals, through what the Maker [and] Creator assigned to him in terms of natural powers, in accordance with what we stated. **10** And that is like how He assigned burning to fire by its nature, so that [fire] is the cause of everything burned by it; and the cold of water is the cause of everything chilled by it; and many natural things act in this way. **11** So likewise He made the diurnal luminary (that is, the Sun) be the cause of glowing, the day, and the total hotness which is in this world, and the cause of natural compositions: because for the places which are excessive in the cold (due to the distance of the Sun from them), or what is excessive in the hot (due to his nearness to them) animals are not formed in them. **12** Indeed, animals are formed in the places which are not very distant from his orbit nor close to it, and that is the place whose distance from the summer orbit of the Sun (which is the beginning of Cancer in the north) is 66°; and if you add the whole declination to it (and it is approximately 24°), that is 90°. **13** So animals are not composed in this place, nor do plants sprout in it, due to its distance from the orbit of the Sun and the harshness of its cold: because when [the Sun] passes to the southern signs, he does not ascend over them for six months. **14** Thus the vapors there congeal and do not rise, and violent winds blow in that place in the winter and summer, so that no animals or planets are composed there.

15 And one may gain information about that from the Armenian Sea:[16] for its distance in the north from the circle of the beginning of Cancer is 21°, and the violent winds grow harsh, and its gloominess is severe, so that people do not travel it. **16** And if this place was closer to the circle of the summer Sun than the position which we stated before, one would not be able to travel or be on it, due to the harshness of the cold and gloominess: for how could animals or plants be composed in a place which is at the extreme distance from the Sun, along with the cold and gloominess which is in it, and the violent winds? **17** And one may also gain information about what we stated

---

[16] That is, the Black Sea. In this paragraph Abū Ma'shar locates it at 21° north of the Tropic of Cancer, which he has already put at about 24° (in **12**): therefore, the Black Sea (or more specifically, the part around the Crimean peninsula) has a latitude of about 45° (see **19**), since 21° + 24° = 45°.

from those in the north, in the most extreme [parts of] Armenia, for they cannot appear from out of the snow for six months; and that is when the Sun passes into the southern signs. **18** And indeed, many of the animals which are among them die in those six months, while many of their birds remain in their nests for four months, neither spreading out nor feeding. **19** And the distance of that place in the north from the equator is 45°.

20 One may also gain information from the Syrian Sea, for when the Sun passes into the beginning of Scorpio until he comes to the beginning of Pisces, in these four months people are not able to sail it: and that is because the Sun is distant from it, and violent winds occur on it.

21 And these places which we have stated are in the direction of the north. **22** But as for the southern places, burned by the severity of the heat, neither animals nor plants are composed at the place whose latitude from the equator is 19°, and that is due to the harshness of the Sun's hotness in it: because when the Sun passes into Virgo at 5° [of it] until he reaches Pisces, he comes near to them and burns everything there.

23 And the two lakes which are tributaries of the Nile are in these burned countries, and in this burned place which we stated is the Sea of the Zanj:[17] and it is a sea in which there are no animals due to the intensity of its water's heat and density. **24** And that is because when the Sun rises over this sea, the subtle water which is in it is attracted to him by his hotness, so that the water of that sea becomes dense, becomes salty, and warms up intensely. **25** So due to the density of the water, and its saltiness, that heating remains within it for the whole night: and for this reason the water of this sea is dense, salty, with no people sailing it, nor on the whole are there animals on it. **26** And in that direction are many places which are not traveled by animals due to the intensity of the heat in them.

27 So from what we have explained, we have inferred that for the places from which the Sun is distant their cold is intensified, or for those which he is near to their heat is intensified, so that they are excessive in the hot and the cold and neither animals nor plants are composed in them; and indeed by their [mutual] moderation comes to be the establishing of natures and the natured. **28** And if the Sun had passed to the sphere of the fixed stars, na-

---

[17] If this is really a sea, it might be the portion of the ocean near the Zanzibar islands; if it is a lake, it is possibly Lake Victoria.

tures and the natured would be corrupted, while if he came down to the sphere of the Moon, they would [also] corrupt: and that is because corruption comes to natures and the natured in his distance and nearness. **29** So for this reason the Creator assigned to the Sun the middle of the seven planets, so that through his natural motion the moderation of natures and the natured would come to be upon this earthly world.

30 And of course we also find all places and countries differing in their conditions, and the conditions of their people, and what occurs in them, and indeed that is in proportion to the Sun's nearness to them or distance from them. **31** And a manifestation of that is the Turks, for due to their distance from the circle of the Sun at his rising and falling [in the apogee], snows are abundant among them, and the coldness and wetness predominates over their land, so due to that the bodies of their people are flabby and thick, and their joints become sunken [in the fat], not seen due to the abundance of their flesh, and their faces are round, their eyes small and elongated, their hair lanky, and their color whitish-red.[18] **32** And the cold predominates over their natures, and that is due to the cold of their atmosphere, and because the cooling mixture[19] gives birth to much flesh. **33** But as for the redness of their color, the coldness collects the hotness together and manifests it until it is seen. **34** And one may get an indication about that from what one sees in people whose bodies have much flesh and their color is white: when the cold affects them, their faces and lips redden, as well as their fingers and legs, because the cold gathers together the hotness and blood which is diffused in them. **35** And concerning the morals of the people of this direction, there is roughness, the rupturing of family relations, little certainty, little science, and an abundance of forgetfulness.

36 As for the Sudan and Ethiopia, they reside in countries which face[20] the signs between the circle of Aries up to Cancer: so due to the fact that when the Sun (in his rising and falling) is in those signs and occupies the Midheaven, he is at their zenith, he warms their atmosphere and burns them,

---

[18] Or more literally, "white, red" (بيضًا حمرًا).

[19] This can also be seen as "temperament" (مزاج). Water is primarily cold, and so the cooling temperament is the watery or phlegmatic temperament.

[20] That is, they are directly below them; another way to put it is that their terrestrial latitude is "parallel" to those celestial circles (تحاذيها).

and hotness and the dry are abundant in them. **37** So for this reason their color becomes black, their hair short and curly, their bodies dry and thin, and their natures hot; and their riding animals and trees are likewise. **38** And concerning the morals of the people of this region, there is levity,[21] and little cleverness.[22]

39 And as for the people who are distant from the circle of the beginning of Cancer towards the north (and that is like Babylon and its direction among the countries), due to the fact that the Sun is not distant from their zenith nor close to them, and yet his transit over them is moderate, their air has a fine mixture, and their location moderate, not having harsh heat nor harsh cold in it, and their colors, bodies, and natures are balanced, their minds and moral qualities fine, and science is abundant among them, as well as cleverness and foreknowledge of things, and good qualities in their morals—and this is the land of scholars and prophets.

40 And the difference between all of these places (which we stated as being in [their] bodies, forms, colors, sciences, minds, and morals), varies greatly, making [any] resemblance distant due to the variation of their locations relative to the sphere of the Sun, the variation in seasons of the year, and their alteration in them. **41** And just as these locations which we stated differ, and a special property comes to belong to each place which does not belong to another, so likewise does each city and every location which we have not stated, and their people, have a special property and nature in the difference of the people's form, the animals, plants, and minerals among them, and the heat and cold of the waters and springs, religions and ways of life, dress, moral qualities, and the rest of the things which do not belong to other cities. **42** And that exists [and] is evident in the places and major cities, such that a difference may [even] be found in one place that is near to another. **43** And indeed, that is in proportion to the Sun's nearness or farness from them in his sphere, and from the circling of the fixed stars around their zenith—except that these special, discovered properties which we stated belong to every city and place, in some [specific] matter: for even if they had lasting existence in their essences, we would still find them altering every

---

[21] الخِفّة. This can also connote fickleness and other types of instability.
[22] Lemay adds القطنة, which could be translated as something like "staying in one place." This would make sense for Sudanese herders and nomads.

year, towards increase and decrease. **44** For we know that that alteration is not from the special property of the Sun's circle, nor from the fixed stars' culmination for those places, but [it is] from the Sun's assembling with the fixed and wandering stars in his course, and from the mixing of the powers of the wandering stars in their shifting within the signs, with the fixed stars culminating in those places.

45 So in this respect we know that the rest of the planets have a partnership with the Sun in the indications over the atmosphere and the particularization of individuals of species, and the composition of every individual (and its generation), and the natures of cities and the conditions of their people, and the things in them—except that the Sun is more universal in his indication for the atmosphere and the composition of individuals, as well as animal souls and their blending with the body, character and morals, religions and religious allegiances, and minerals, planets, and growth (by the permission of God). **46** But as for the planets, their most universal indications are for the manner of their people's dress and the rest of their conditions.

47 And concerning their actions in the atmosphere too, the air is illuminated by the Sun and Moon, and darkened by their withdrawing away from it. **48** And when the Sun is distant from it, it becomes cold, while when he draws near it warms up; and we find the action of the Moon and planets to be like that in the warming of the air and thinning it out. **49** Due to that, Hippocrates the Sage said in the *Book of Sevens*[23] that the light of the planets breaks through the density[24] of the night, for the night is very dense and perception does not penetrate it—but the glow of the planets breaks through that density so perception does penetrate "into" it. **50** And if it were not like that, every living body would be corrupted by the harshness of the night's thickness. **51** But as for the day, the Sun warms the air by his hotness and breaks through it: so due to that the Maker [and] Creator, the Strong and Great, created the moving, luminous stars, that they would break through

---

[23] According to **BY**, this is actually from a pseudo-Galenic commentary on Hippocrates, which must have been available in Arabic.

[24] يسخّن صفاقة, which does not exactly mean "break through" or "density," but I follow **BY** in this more metaphorical translation.

the air with their light, protecting it and thinning it out with their movement, so that it is susceptible to the nature of generation and corruption.

52 And we do find things being generated and corrupted in a place, and the place is susceptible to change from the four principles by means of the alteration of the season and its shifting about it, and the seasons' alteration and their shifting from condition to condition is by means of the Sun's movement in the twelve signs: so it is therefore necessary that things be generated and corrupted by reason of the Sun's motion in the twelve signs, since the variation of the seasons comes to be through his motion in the signs, and the variation in natures comes to be through the variation of the seasons, and generation and corruption comes to be through the variation of natures (by the permission of God).

53 And among the things which come to be and occur in this world are things coming to be at a certain time of the year, and what comes to be at all times of the year (and their days). **54** The things which come to be and occur at a certain time of the year are like what we find occurring in the season of spring (such as the condition of the air, and the generation of many animals, trees, vegetation, and the birth of many beasts which does not occur in other quarters of the year. **55** And likewise the summer: in it we find, of the heat, the alteration of the air and bodies, the ripening of fruit, and the generation of things (and corruption of things) which we do not find in other quarters of the year. **56** And likewise autumn and winter, for we find for each quarter the generation and corruption of something which does not exist in other quarters of the year: and that is like how we see fruit, produce and vegetation, and many plants which come to be in the spring, corrupting in the autumn, and what comes to be in the summer corrupts in the winter. **57** And we find that each of the four divisions of the year comes to be when the Sun is in one of the quarters of the sphere. **58** So, it is clearly evident that those things which are generated and corrupted in the quarters of the year are by reason of the Sun being in those quarters.

59 And because we find that, in every year when the Sun is in that quarter, the condition of the air, heat, cold, the plants, and the rest of the things are not in the same condition as they were in the years before that, nor will they be after that in future years, but rather they will vary in increase and decrease, we know that that variation is due to the Sun's assembling with the planets. **60** For if the Sun alone had been the cause of the air and seasons, every spring would be the same as the other springs, and every thing the same as the others, and the division of each year would be the same as the divisions of other years. **61** The planets, therefore, have a partnership with the Sun in the indication of generation and corruption.

62 Now as for the things which come to be in all of the times of the year (and its days), they are like the procreation of people and their destruction, and the independent action of their conditions which is not absent from them for a single day in the whole year.[25] **63** And this generation and corruption comes to be through the motion of the whole (that is, the motion of the spheres and planets). **64** And just as the spheres and the planets in them give motion eternally to these earthly bodies, so likewise is there eternal generation and corruption in this world until the time when God wills its destruction—for He destroys as He wishes.

Chapter III.4: On the special property of the Moon for the flow and ebb [of the tide]

1 In what has preceded we made mention of the indication of the Sun and planets for things which occur in this world, for no composition of some nature comes to be in this world except by reason of the Sun and the partnership of the planets with him, by the command of God.[26] **2** Now we want to state the special property of the Moon for the flow and ebb [of the tide], and other things. **3** And it is that the Philosopher said the most universal indication of the Sun is for fire and air, and the most universal indication of the Moon is for water and earth;[27] and indeed, the indication of the Sun and Moon in this world becomes stronger and more evident than the indication of the rest of the planets, for two reasons:

4 One of them is that the Sun is the largest of the planets in size, and he occupies the middle distance from us, while the Moon is the closest of the planets to us. **5** But as for the rest of the planets, even though some of them

---

[25] That is, people's actions and qualities which are not dependent on seasonal changes.
[26] See III.3, **9** and **59-61**.
[27] Like many references to Aristotelian philosophy in the *Great Introduction*, this may be from a later summarizer or commentator.

are large, they are far from us, while others, even if near to us, are small in size (and the Moon is the closest of them to us).

6 And the second reason is that the luminous, glowing planets have no rays, so what appears from their action in this world is through the power of their motions and glow. **7** But as for the two luminaries, they do have rays with powerful action in this world, so they both act in us through their movements and rays; and they both convey the natures of the planets to this world, in the four principles. **8** And Hippocrates claimed in the *Book of Sevens* that the Moon is in the middle between the heavenly bodies and the earthly ones, she transmits from the superior bodies to the earthly bodies, and she alters the air.

9 So for these two reasons, the power of the luminaries' motion becomes more evident in this world than the power of the other planets does. **10** Now as for the Sun, we have stated that his power is in the moderation of the air, and compositions, and the rest of things. **11** But as for the Moon, her indication is stronger for waters, seas, and lands, and the condition of their animals, the alteration of bodies, health and illnesses, the days of the sick (which are the "crises"), different conditions, reproduction, trees, plants, and fruits, aromatic plants, and [other] things we will state.

[The Moon and the tides]

12 So as for her indication for seas, it is how we see the flow and ebb being connected with the Moon, because the Moon is the cause of the flow and ebb which is in the seas. **13** And of course people who look into natural matters have stated that with respect to the seas, something increases from when the Moon departs from the Sun up to half of the month (which is the fullness), [and] then it decreases after the fullness at the decrease of the Moon, until the end of the month (which is the waning).[28]

14 And pertaining to that is what flows and ebbs on every day and night along with the Moon's ascending, reaching the Midheaven, and setting: and that is found in the Persian Sea, the Indian Sea as it goes towards China, and

---

[28] المحاق. But this should rather be المحق, "the blotting out" of the Moon when she goes under the rays.

in the Sea of China, at every island[29] in them between these places, and in the sea which is between Constantinople and '*Ifranjah*,[30] and in its islands.

15 Now as for the times of the flow and ebb on every day and night, when the Moon [1] reaches one of the horizons of the sea (that is, one of the eastern rising-places of the sea) and rises above it, through her character and because of her closeness to us she moves the water of the sea and the water begins to advance with the Moon, increasing; and it does not cease to be like that until the Moon passes to the Midheaven of that place; and at that [time], the flow reaches its endpoint. **16** When the Moon [2] sinks down from its Midheaven, the water ebbs and returns to the sea, and does not cease to be like that, returning until she reaches its setting point, and at that [time] the ebbing reaches its endpoint. **17** Now when the Moon [3] withdraws from the setting of that place, the flow begins there for a second time, and does not cease to be advancing [and] increasing until the Moon passes to the stake of the earth: and at that time the flow reaches its endpoint for the second time in that place. **18** Then [4] the ebbing begins, and a returning [to the sea] for a second time, and the water does not cease to ebb and return to the sea until the Moon reaches the horizon of the east of that position, and the flow returns to what it was like the first time.

19 So on every day and night (and for the amount of the Moon's travel), and every position on the sea, there are two flows and two ebbs: because if the Moon on some day was in some degree of the sphere [and] then ascended over a place on the sea, the flow would begin in that place on the sea. **20** But when that degree on the horizon of that place on the sea ascends after that by a day, the Moon will already have withdrawn from that degree by the amount of her average travel for one day and night: so she will ascend over them *after* the ascending of that degree, by the amount of her travel on that day and night.[31]

---

[29] The word for "island" in Arabic can also refer to peninsulas, which may be intended here.

[30] This is the word for "France" or the "land of the Franks." Muslim geography was vague about everything European and west of the Islamic empires.

[31] I think Abū Ma'shar's point is that it is her *body* which matters: so since she travels about 6° over the course of a night, it is not the original degree which should be tracked. See also III.5, **49**.

21 And because the world is round and the sea encompasses its roundness, and the Moon ascends over all of it in the amount of a day and night, and in the amount of her travel in them,[32] therefore to the extent that a degree of the sphere is moved, the position of the Moon will become horizonal for one of the places on the sea, and that position will also become the Midheaven for another position, the setting for another position, and the stake of the earth for another position, and whatever is between each one of these stakes in some other situation for other places. **22** Thus at a single time on the sea in some of the positions, there will be the inception of a flow, and in another position the inception of an ebb, and in other positions other conditions belonging to flowing and ebbing.

23 Now as for the inception of the flow, its condition is not one [and the same] for all of the inhabitants[33] of the sea, the shores, islands, and estuaries, because people who are on the abyss of the sea find, at the time of the inception of the water's flow, a motion from the depths of the sea to its upper parts, and they see that it has a swell, and violent winds and waves are stirred up upon it, and so they know by that that it's the beginning of the flow. **24** But if it was the time of the ebb, those winds and waves would be reduced, and the swell would disappear from the water, and they would know that the water was already ebbing.

25 As for the inhabitants of the shores, coasts, islands, and estuaries, or those close to them, they find among them at the time of the water's flow, a motion and flowing from its lowest point up to its highest; then the water which is on the surfaces of these places and their highest points, flows, and the running of the water of the sea towards them intensifies, swells, and rises up, and goes over their land. **26** And it remains like that until it ebbs, and the water at that [time] returns to the sea and leaves the estuaries and islands, and decreases.

27 And indeed the water's coming and going, its flowing along, and its arrival and disappearance, is evident on the shores and estuaries of the sea. **28** But as for on the depths of the sea, that is not found [to be so].

---

[32] That is, in a day and night.
[33] أصحاب, which really means "associates," but I follow **BY** in this more straightforward translation.

29 But as for the winds which are on the water and leave it at the inception of the flow, that comes to be in places in which the inception of the flow is, and the places close to it. **30** But on the shores and estuaries of the sea, and places remote from the depths of the sea, whatever is in it [of] the blowing of winds, is reduced.

31 And the time of the inception of the flow and ebb which is on the sea is not the time when the inception of the flow and ebb is made evident to the people of the shores, coasts, and estuaries of the sea, but rather it is very different: so that many of the people suppose—based on what they see of the great difference in the inception in various places—that the Moon is not the cause of the flow and ebb. **32** Because the inception of the flow's strength on the seas occurs in every deep, expansive place with much, dense water, and hardness or an abundance of mountains predominates over its floor: and the position of the Moon is their horizon, and those places are close to the culmination of the Moon and her path. **33** So when the flow begins in these places at some time, she connects [immediately] with the rest of the waters of the sea, except that the flow does not pass to the shores and estuaries of the seas without a period of time having passed from the inception of the flow on the sea in the places we stated, in proportion to the closeness or farness of the shores and estuaries of the seas, from those places. **34** Because on the shores, islands, and estuaries of the sea which are close to the places in which the inception of the flow's power is made clear, the flow is made evident before it is made evident in the places which are distant from it.

35 And if the shores of the sea, its estuaries, and drainage places[34] were far from the places in which the inception of the flow is, the flow will reach them when it gets near to its endpoint on the sea; and likewise the ebb. **36** So, it is assured that the flow will be in some islands and shores distant from the places in which the flow begins, at the time of the ebb—and the time of their ebb will be ready at the time of the sea's flow. **37** And indeed that comes to be due to the distance of those places from the places in which the inception of the flow's and ebb's strength is.

---

[34] مضائضة. **BY** translate this as "pools," but Lane seems to connect this more with sunken places where water drains downwards rather than lakes or standing later.

Chapter III.5: On the cause of the flow and ebb [of the tide]

1 Previous people gave much attention to the cause of the flow and ebb, but disagreed over it. **2** But at this time we will omit [any] mention of their disagreement, since there is no benefit to it: I will state what agrees with the view of the philosophers on them. **3** I say that the flow and ebb come to be with the joining together of three things: one of them is [1] the condition of the place of the water, the second [2] the condition of the water, and the third [3] the Moon's moving of the water.

4 As for [1] the first, it is that the water gathers together in deep, broad, long places, its course [in them] being [for] some period of time, and in them are mountains in many different places, and what predominates over many places of its floor is hardness, and a compactness of [its] parts, with many winds gathered together in it: because more winds gather in hard floors with compacted parts and the places of mountains, than gather in soft floors.

5 And [2] the second is that many waters gather in these same areas and pause for a long time, but it is not evident in them what pours forth into them from the wadis and rivers, nor what comes out of them, because when waters stand for a long time, they become thick, salty to the taste, bitter, and other tastes, and dense vapor and winds are produced in them due to the saltiness of the water and its bitterness, and because of the vapor that rises up into it from the [sea] floors.

6 Now as for [3] the vapor, it increases in that water, while as for the winds, when they gather and multiply in that water, then the Moon elevates it, moving that water through her character, motion, and rising from the horizon, so that all of the water moves, becomes tepid and warm due to its thickness, melting, begins to move, and advances with the Moon.

7 So when the water moves by means of the Moon's moving it, and it warms up and melts, it heaves[35] and needs a place greater than [its] original place: and that heaving in the motion of the water increases, and the winds which are in the upper water of the sea move to its lower part. **8** And that motion connects with the winds which are on the floor of the sea, so that the

---

[35] تنفّس. That is, to breathe strongly. **BY** translate this as "seethe," which suggests more violence than what I take Abū Maʿshar to mean here.

winds which are in it and in the lower part of the water are raised up, so they may come out of some of the places: thus the wind is raised up by their motion and their raising up of the water to up above, and the water heaves, rises, and overflows, so that the flow [of the tide] comes to be from it. **9** And the water does not cease to rise, moving, heaving with the Moon's moving it and with her own rising up. **10** And the wind moves the water as well, raising it up, and that wind goes out gradually, and [the water] melts and heaves so long as the Moon is rising [and] going towards the Midheaven (for at that point the flow reaches its endpoint). **11** For this reason there are violent, powerful winds in the sea at the inception of the flow, and when the Moon declines from the Midheaven, the water returns by means of its own character to its place, and there is an ebbing. **12** Now when the Moon reaches the stake of the west, the flow advances until the Moon reaches the stake of the earth; then the water ebbs until the Moon reaches the horizon of the east. **13** And when the Moon appears from the horizon, the flow returns to the same way it was [before].

14 Now as for what we said about the conditions of the floor of the sea and the waters, we said that because the floor of the sea and its waters have different conditions. **15** For the places which are not deep, nor hard, nor are there mountains in them, do not have abundant vapors or winds. **16** And the places which are deep, wide, and long, and whose waters are thick, salty and bitter, are abundant in vapors and winds in those places. **17** So for this reason the inception of the flow's power, and the predominance of the water, comes to be from every deep, expansive place with compact parts or abundant mountains predominating over its [sea] floor.

18 Now when the power of the flow begins from just these same places with abundant vapor and winds (in which there is a connection of that with the water of the sea), the flow begins in all of that because of the vapor and winds which are produced from its saltiness, bitterness, and dryness, and because in the Moon is the characteristic of setting that water fully into motion, and because the whole sea gains from the power of the motion of the waters which are in those places where the inception of the flow's power is.

19 And when the floor of the sea has few mountains, or is [more] loose, the water penetrates from it into other seas and places, or that water in which the waters that flow into it or go out of it are obvious, or it is water moving subtly, shifting like wadis, rivers, and springs—so the gathering of winds is not abundant in it because it melts and the wind which is in the water heaves and goes out bit-by-bit and gradually, along with the motion of the water and its shifting. **20** And the wind which raises that water disperses and does not gather in it, so when the Moon is elevated above it and moves it, there is no flow and ebb in it, though there are winds and waves. **21** So for this reason the flow and ebb is not evident in many of the seas, nor in any of the wadis, rivers, and springs.

22 And also, when the Moon moves the thin, subtle running waters and they become tepid, that tepidness does not remain in them due to their subtleness; and when they melt, that melting does not increase except by a little bit, nor are there winds in them except for a very few.

23 Now as for the thick, salty waters, due to their saltiness and their bitterness there is dry in them, and many winds: so when they move, become tepid, and warm up, that slackness remains in them due to the thickness and the melting; and that melting increases their waters, and that is the reason for the power of the flow (as we stated).

[The Moon's motion from the west to the stake of the earth]

24 But as for the reason for the inception of the flow when the Moon passes to the west, and its lasting until the Moon reaches the stake of the earth, that is due to three things:

25 One of them is that [1] the line of the east is parallel to the line of the west, and every degree [by which] the Moon is distant from the east [when] rising to the Midheaven, is parallel to every degree from which the Moon is distanced from the west towards the stake of the earth. **26** And the distance of that degree from the west is the same as the distance of the degree parallel to it from the east. **27** Every quadrant which is from the east to the Midheaven is parallel to and resembles every quadrant which is from the west to the stake of the earth; so due to the correspondence of the quadrant which is from Ascendant to the Midheaven and the quadrant which is from the west to the stake of the earth, it is agreed that the flow and advance of the water from the east in one of them will be the same as in the other.

28 And the second thing is that [2] the ascensions of the signs in each country on the Midheaven and the stake of the earth, are the same as their ascensions in the right circle.³⁶ **29** Now as for the line of the degree of the Midheaven, it is parallel to the line of the degree of the stake of the fourth, but the line of the degree of the Ascendant is parallel to the line of the degree of the setting: so when a sign ascends in the east by certain degrees, and therefore passes to the west, upon its setting it reverts to the condition of the sign which is ascending in the east, because it sets with the same ascensions as a sign which ascends, and in the west it does the same as the sign which ascends from the east does; but it passes to the Midheaven and the stake of the earth with the same ascensions as in the right circle. **30** So because of that, when the Moon reaches the degree of the west, the flow begins just as it had begun when she passed to the degree of the east, and the flow remains so long as the Moon distances herself from the west until she reaches the stake of the earth (just as it had lasted when she distanced herself from the east until she reached the Midheaven). **31** Then the flow terminates when she reaches the stake of the earth, just as it had terminated when she reached the degree of the Midheaven, because these two stakes have the average ascensions in every country.

32 And the third thing is that [3] when the Moon is in the east and west, she is at one [and the same] distance from us, but when she advances from the east, the flow advances with her. **33** So, the more that the Moon is raised up close to our Midheaven, so does the flow advance until she reaches the Midheaven; and likewise when she advances towards us from the west, it will also be the inception of the flow, and it does not cease to be like that until she passes to the parallel of the line of the Midheaven (and it is the stake of the earth), and the flow reaches its endpoint. **34** As for the ebb, it is in the second and fourth, opposing quadrants, because one of them is parallel to the other: so when there is an ebb in one of them, there is one like it in the other, parallel quadrant.

35 And [some] people claimed that the flow and ebb come to be in sweet waters, like the waters of the city of Basra, the city of China, and many places among the estuaries of seas and islands, whose waters are sweet and there is a flow and ebb in them. **36** We say that the waters of Basra, China, and the

---

³⁶ That is, in right ascensions or RA. This is a matter of definition, because ascensional times are measured by the degrees of RA which pass the meridian circle where the Midheaven and IC are.

rest of the places whose condition is like theirs, and whose waters are sweet, are fresh drainage [channels] of rivers and wadis running towards them from other places and directions other than the sea: and they connect with the salty water of the sea so that a flow and ebb is found in these waters and what is like them due to their connection with the water of the sea. **37** And if these sweet waters did not connect with the water of the sea, a flow and ebb would not be found in them.

38 As for the flow, its water is tepid, while as for the ebb its water is cold: and that is because at the time of the flow the water leaves the depth of the sea and it is tepid, and its own motion and the Moon's moving it increases its tepidness. **39** So for this reason the water of the flow is tepid, and the more that the flow predominates and is more abundant, the more tepid it is; and indeed that is due to its abundant movement and the abundant departure of the waters which are at the bottom of the sea. **40** So when that water comes to be in the places far from the depths of the sea (like the shores, islands, wadis, drainage [channels], and standing bodies [of water]), it becomes cold and returns with that coldness to the sea; because of that the water of the ebb becomes cold.

41 And what the Moon does by her nature in the water of the sea, is the flow; but as for the ebb, it is not from the action of the Moon. **42** For indeed that action is the nature of the water, because when the Moon reaches one of the places indicative of a flow, the inception of the flow is there until the Moon reaches the limit of her indication for the flow in that place, and there the flow comes to an end. **43** But when the power of the flow reaches its endpoint at that time, the water returns through its own nature to the place from which it had come—and it is the ebb.

[Measuring the length of the ebb and flow]

44 And know that in natural composition, when the Moon is above the earth the flow and ebb each occur only one time, and the period of one of them will be equivalent to period of the other. **45** And when the Moon is below the earth, the flow and ebb will each occur another time, and the period of one of them will [also] be equivalent to the period of the other. **46** But as for the Moon's lingering above the earth and below it, they are hardly ever equivalent.[37] **47** For if her lingering above the earth was more than it is under it, the period of the flow and ebb when the Moon is above the earth will be longer than it is when she is under it. **48** And if the Moon's lingering below the earth was more than it is above it, the period of the flow and ebb which exists when she is under the earth will be longer than it is when she is above it.

49 So if you wanted to know the number of hours for the flow and ebb, and the Moon is above the earth, then understand the degree with which the Moon ascends, and the degree which sets with her, and confirm that: because sometimes the Moon in [her] ascending and setting precedes or comes after the degree which she is in by longitude, by reason of her latitude. **50** So understand that degree, and take what is between the degree of her ascending up to the degree of her setting in degrees of ascensions, and preserve that. **51** Then, make every 15° of [ascensions] be an equal hour,[38] and make what does not complete [a full] 15° be portions of an hour: what it comes to is the hours of the "natural" flow and ebb so long as the Moon is above the earth. **52** Now if you wanted to understand the hours of the flow alone or the hours of the ebb alone, then take one-half of these hours: for they are the hours of the "natural" flow or ebb (whichever one of them you wanted to know). **53** But if the indicators of the flow were strong, it increases the hours of the flow beyond this half, by the amount of the power of the water's motion; and if the indicators of the flow were weak, it will reduce the hours of the flow from this half, by the amount of the weakness of the water's motion.[39] **54** And whatever remains up to the complete [amount] of preserved hours, is the hours of the ebb.

55 And if you wanted to understand the amount of the flow and ebb while the Moon is under the earth, then take from the degree with which the Moon sets, up to the degree which she ascends with (by degrees of ascensions), and operate with it just as you operated with the Moon when she was above the earth.

---

[37] That is, the semidiurnal arcs above the horizon are equal to each other, and the seminocturnal arcs are equal to each other. But arcs between the hemispheres are rarely equal.

[38] That is, a civil hour of 60 minutes, rather than an unequal planetary hour.

[39] See III.6.

56 And know that the places on the sea have different latitudes, due to the differing latitudes of the countries: so if you wanted knowledge of the hours of the flow and ebb in one of the places on the sea, then understand the latitude of that place and its ascensions, then know the ascent of the Moon by the ascensions of that place.

57 Now as for the strength of the flow and ebb (and their weakness), and the abundance of their water (and its scarcity), and their increase and decrease, and which of them will be longer and of more duration in time, there are many ways to understand and know that which we will offer about that, if God wills.

Chapter III.6: On the strength of the flow and its weakness, and the abundance and scarcity of its water

1 We stated before this that the period of the flow which exists when the Moon is above the earth, is the same as the period of the ebb which is after it (and the period of the flow which exists when the Moon is below the earth is the same as the period of the ebb which is after it)—except that sometimes it happens that the period of the flow while the Moon is above the earth is longer than the period of the ebb which is after it (or the period of the flow while the Moon is under the earth is longer than the period of the ebb which is after it).[40] **2** And if the period of the flow increased beyond the amount which we had defined concerning the Moon's reaching any of the positions indicative of the space of time, then it will take away from the period of the ebb which is after that by approximately the same [amount] that it increased in the period of the flow. **3** And if anything decreased from the period of the flow, then it would increase by the same [amount] relative to the ebb which is after it, so that the total of them both is just as we stated.

4 Now as for our stating that there may be a lengthening of the period of the flow (and a shortening of it), or a lengthening of the period of the ebb (and a shortening of it), look: for if there were many indicators of an abundance of the water's flow, and its strength and predominance, then the flow

---

[40] That is, although her semiarcs are equal, the effect on the actual flow and ebb is not (due to factors listed below); thus their times might not be equal.

will last until the Moon withdraws from the degree of the stake defined for the flow, by about an hour (or more or a little less). **5** And indeed, that comes to be because of the strength of the water's movement and the intensity of its current, not from the indication of the Moon: so the period of the flow comes to be long for this reason. **6** And if the indicators of the flow were weak, then the water will ebb before the Moon's reaching the position defined for the flow, by about an hour (or more or less). **7** And indeed that comes to be because of the weakness of the water's motion, and the smallness of its current: so the period of the flow is shortened for this reason, not by reason of the Moon.

8 Now as for knowing the strength of the flow (and its weakness), and the abundance of its water (or its scarcity), one looks into it from eight things:

9 The first is [1] the distance of the Moon from the Sun, and her increase in glow (and her decrease in it).[41]

10 The second is [2] the increase of the Moon's equation beyond her mean, or a decrease from it.[42]

11 The third is [3] the position of the Moon in the circle of the apogee, and her distance or nearness from the earth.[43]

12 The fourth is [4] her rising or falling in [her] sphere of inclination,[44] and the direction of her latitude.[45]

13 The fifth is [5] the Moon's being in the northern or southern signs.[46]

14 The sixth is [6] the days which mariners who are in the west, and the people of Egypt and what borders on it, call the "days of the increase of water, and its decrease."[47]

15 And these six ways are from the special property of the indication of the Moon.

16 The seventh way is [7] knowing the strength of the flow and its weakness from the length of the day and night, and their shortness.[48]

---

[41] See **18-39**.
[42] See **40-44**.
[43] See **45-47**.
[44] That is, in ecliptical latitude. This is not a reference to declination.
[45] See **48-49**.
[46] See **50-52**.
[47] See **57-66**.

BOOK III: DEFINING ASTROLOGY, WEATHER, TIDES

17 The eighth is [8] knowing the winds strengthening the flow and ebb.[49]

[1: The Moon's relation to the Sun]

18 As for [1] the first way in knowing the abundance of the flow's water (or its scarcity), you should look into the conditions of the Moon, for she has four positions in which her conditions and her indication for an abundance of the flow's water (and its scarcity) are different, and that is in accordance with her condition relative to the Sun. **19** The first is [1a] the meeting of the Moon with the Sun. **20** The second is [1b] when there are 90° between the Moon and Sun, and one-half of the glow is in the body of the Moon and she is waxing in glow: and it is the first quarter.[50] **21** The third is [1c] when the Moon is in the opposition of the Sun. **22** The fourth is [1d] is when there are 90° between the Moon and Sun, and it is when remains one-half of the glow in her body and she is waning: and it is the second quarter.

23 So when [1a] the Moon joins with the Sun, the water of the flow is abundant, strong, for a long period of time, and the period of the ebb is less than that: because when the Moon joins with the Sun, her meeting with him increases the power of the Moon since the Sun also has an action in the strength of the flow. **24** So when they join together it strengthens the indication of the Moon, and her moving the water at that time is greater than it is at another time. **25** And likewise, the more the Moon joins with one of the planets indicative of the strength of the flow, that increases her power, so the motion of that flow becomes stronger due to the power of the Moon, and the water of the flow increases—except that when the Moon assembles with the Sun, it is stronger and more evident in action in the flow at that time than when she assembles with another besides him (due to the reason we stated), and because the Sun has an effect on the Moon which none of the [other] planets has like it (because of her increase in glow and decrease in it, and many of her motions are in proportion to her distance or nearness from him).

---

[48] See **67-98**.
[49] See **99-125**.
[50] Or, the first "square" (التَّرْبِيع).

26 Due to that, the more that she is at a specific distance from the Sun, there will occur at that time a change in the flow's strength or weakness; because if it was the distance of the meeting and [then] she distances herself from him, in accordance with her distancing it will decrease the strength of the flow from what it was at the meeting, and its period of time will decrease, but there will be an increase in the period of the ebb until the Moon reaches [1b] the first square of the Sun. **27** And that is when there are 90° between the Moon and the Sun, and there is one-half of the glow in the body of the Moon: for at that time the decrease of the flow will reach its endpoint due to this indication.

28 Now when the Moon passes by the square of the Sun, there will be more than one-half of the glow in the body of the Moon, and there the flow will begin to increase in the abundance of its water, its strength, and the length of its period of time. **29** And so long as the glow increases in the body of the Moon, the flow will not cease to increase in power until the Moon reaches [1c] the fullness: for at that time the water of the flow will be strong, high, abundant, and its lingering will be for a long period of time, and the flow will reach its endpoint, and the period of the ebb will be small.

30 And when the Moon passes by the opposition of the Sun and decreases in her glow, the strength of the flow will decrease and increases in weakness, and the period of its lingering will be less. **31** And the flow of the water will not cease to be like that, decreasing and weak, until the Moon reaches [1d] the second square of the Sun: and it is when there are 90° between her and the Sun and she is going towards the Sun. **32** For at that time the flow's decrease reaches its endpoint with respect to this indication; except that when the Moon is in this second square the flow will be weaker than it is when she is in the first square, because the Moon at this time is decreasing in her glow.

33 Now when the Moon passes by this position and gets near to the Sun, and there are less than 90° between her and him, the water of the flow increases and becomes strong and abundant, and its period of time will be long: and the water of the flow will not cease to be increasing, strong, and abundant so long as the Moon is going towards the Sun, until she conjoins with him. **34** For there the increase of the flow reaches its endpoint, and is strong, and its water abundant, [but] then for a second time it will reach a decrease in the flow just as we stated in the beginning.

35 Therefore, as we described, the time of the meeting and the opposition is the time of abundant water and the predominance of the flow, and the length of its period—except that the flow which is at the opposition is stronger and more abundant in water, and has a longer period of time, than the flow which is at the meeting. **36** And the limit of the flow's decrease is in the two squares, except that the water of the flow in the first square is stronger and has a longer period of time than the second square. **37** And this natural arrangement which we have stated as being in a single [lunar] month, is similar to what we saw of the arrangement of the flow and ebb which is in a single day and night. **38** And the amount of the Moon's course in them, is two flows and two ebbs: as for the time of the flow, the motion of the water is increasing and predominates in it; as for the time of the ebb, the motion of the water is weak and decreasing in it. **39** And likewise in a single month are two times in which the water of the flow is predominating, strong, with a long period of time, and [those] two [times] are the meeting and the opposition; and there are two times in which the water reaches its endpoint, is weak, decreasing, with a short period of time, and they are the two squares.

[2: Increase in the Moon's equation]

40 The second way is that [2] one erect the Moon: for if what comes out from the equation of the Moon increases beyond her mean, then the flow on those days will be strong and increasing, and the flow will not cease to increase so long as the equation of the Moon is increased beyond her mean; but if the Moon's equation is less than her mean, the water of the flow will decrease. **41** And if what comes out of her equating is neither an increase nor decrease of it, then the water of the flow will be neither increasing nor decreasing from the known limit—with respect to *this* indication.[51] **42** And if the equation which increases or decreases it from the mean of the Moon is small, the increase of the flow or decrease from it, will be small; but if it is great, that will be great.

43 And by the same way of working that we have done it with the equation of the Moon, may also be known the increase of the waters and flows

---

[51] That is, she might also be waxing or waning, or doing other things which affect the result, as described in the other items here. Each factor makes its own contribution.

(or their decrease) in the running wadis and rivers: because if the Moon's equation increases beyond her mean and that is on days of the flows of wadis and rivers, they will flow on those days; and if the Moon's equation subtracts from her mean, their waters will decrease. **44** And if there does not come out any increase beyond her mean or subtraction from it, the water of the rivers and wadis will neither increase nor decrease.

[3: The Moon's position relative to the apogee]

45 The third way is [3] the position of the Moon in the circle of the apogee, and her distance or nearness to the earth. **46** And it is that one looks at the Moon: for if she had already passed the apex of her apogee by 90° until she reaches 270°, she is falling in the circle of her apogee and the water of the flow on those days will be strong and predominate. **47** And if it was the contrary of that, and the Moon is rising in the circle of her apogee, the water of the flow will be weak, scarce—with respect to this approach.

[4: The Moon's latitude]

48 The fourth way is [4] that one look at the rising of the Moon and her falling in the circle of inclination, and the direction of her latitude. **49** For if the Moon was falling,[52] the water of the flow will be abundant and strong, while if she was rising, the water of the flow will be little and weak.

[5: The Moon in northern and southern signs]

50 The fifth way is [5] that one look at the Moon: for if she were in the northern signs (and they are from the beginning of Aries to the end of Virgo), then the flow in the northern seas will be strong and predominant, and that is because the Moon is at their zenith. **51** And if the Moon were in the southern signs, the flow in the northern seas will be weak, and that is due to the distance of the Moon from their zenith. **52** Now as for the southern seas, they are contrary to what we stated: for if the Moon was in the southern

---

[52] This seems to mean, "decreasing in latitude," so she is closer to the ecliptic, while "rising" means "increasing in latitude," so she is farther away.

signs (and they are from the beginning of Libra to the end of Pisces), then the southern seas will have a powerful flow, with much water; and if the Moon was in the northern signs, the flow will be weak and with little water in the southern seas.

53 And this is a general judgment, and it is that one look at the Moon: for if she culminated at a place on the sea in the north or south, the flow there will be strong and abundant, and especially if the Moon was increasing in her glow, already having passed the first square, and she is falling.[53] **54** And the flow which exists when the Moon is on the horizon of one of the places of the sea (until she terminates at the Midheaven of that place), will be stronger than the flow which exists when the Moon is between the west up to the fourth. **55** And the Moon's being in the watery, wet signs, or with watery planets, or with falling[54] planets (or her connection with them), will certainly increase in the power of the flow and in the water of rivers and springs. **56** But the Moon's assembling with planets rising,[55] and her connection with them, will reduce the water of the flow, and the water of the rivers and springs.

[6: Days of increase and decrease in water]

57 The sixth way is [6] the days which the mariners who are in the direction of the west, and the people of Egypt and what borders it, call the "days of the increase of water, and its decrease." **58** And that is that they used to look at the days of the Arab month (and that is 29 days and portions of a day):[56] for they divided them into four divisions, and each division was close to seven and a half days,[57] and they called each division of them by a name. **59** So from the beginning of the day from twenty-seven of the days of the

---

[53] I am not sure whether this "falling" is in latitude (**49**), or in the circle of her apogee (**46**).
[54] Again, this probably means falling either in latitude or in the circles of their apogees.
[55] Again, either in latitude or in the circles of their apogees.
[56] This is the synodic month, between successive conjunctions of the Sun and Moon. On average, it is about 29.53 days long.
[57] That is, 7.3825 days (29.53 / 4 = 7.3825). The first period must be a little shorter, as we will see below.

lunar month to the three and a half days which have elapsed of the month which follows it, they call those "days of the decrease of water." **60** And from after three and a half days from the beginning of the month until the completion of eleven days of the lunar month, they call them "days of the increase of water." **61** And from the beginning of twelve days up to the completion of eighteen and a half days, they call them days of the decrease of water. **62** And from after eighteen and a half days up to the completion of twenty-six days, they call them days of the increase of water.[58]

63 Masters of the sea among the Egyptians (and those bordering on them) claim that on these days which they call the days of the decrease of water the flow is weak and small, while the ebb is stronger; and that on the days which they call the days of the increase of water the flow of the sea is strong and abundant, and that the ebb is weaker. **64** Now, we asked several of the mariners who are in the region of the east, and those knowledgeable in the conditions of the sea, about these days, and they claim that they do *not* find that the water increases on all of these days which they call the days of the increase of water, nor do they find that the water decreases on all of the days which they call the days of the decrease of water—except they do state that on the days of the increase of water there is a day or two on which the water increases, and on the days of the decrease of water it is also like that in terms of a decrease. **65** And what we have found of the increase of water (and its increase) on these days which the Egyptians state, is an increase in the waters of wadis and rivers whose waters are from springs: so if it was these days which they call the days of the increase of water, the water heaves, elevates, and increases in these places; and on the days which they call the days of the decrease of water, the water sinks into the springs and decreases.

66 But some of the mariners who are in the region of the east claim that the water of the flow of the sea weakens and becomes scarce for ten [days] which elapse of the month, and for ten [days] remaining of it, and on the ten remaining [ones] the water of the flow is weaker than the first ten; and that is due to the decrease in the Moon's light.

---

[58] By Abū Ma'shar's counting, the first period is 7 days (**59**), and the rest are 7.5, making a total of 29.5.

[7: Length of day and night]

67 And the seventh way is [7] about the special property of the indication of the Sun for the abundance of the water of the sea's flow (or its scarcity), and its strength (or weakness), due to his supporting the Moon: because even if the Moon is special for the indication of the flow and ebb, her conditions relative to the six [other] planets and her alighting in the wet signs, and her assembling with any of the watery planets, sometimes strengthens her indication for it. **68** And we have mentioned that in what preceded.[59]

69 But as for now, we say that what is found in the eastern sea and in other seas (in which the flow and ebb is made clear), is that at some times the flow in the day is stronger than the flow in the night, and in other times the flow in the night is stronger than the flow in the day. **70** And indeed, that is a result of the Sun's being in the northern signs or in the southern signs: because when the Sun is between the beginning of Aries up to the end of Virgo, the day is longer than the night, and the flow in the day is stronger than the flow in the night; but when the Sun is between the beginning of Libra up to the end of Pisces, the night is longer than the day, and the flow in the night is stronger than the flow in the day.

71 And the longest that the night is, is when the Sun is in Sagittarius: for when the Sun passes into the beginning of Capricorn and the day begins an increase, the water of the sea's flow which is by day begins in strength, abundance, and a long period of time; and it does not cease to be like that until the Sun reaches the end of Pisces (and it is the time of the spring equinox). **72** For when it is at that time, the flow which is by day is close in strength to the flow which is by night (with respect to this indication), and the length of their periods are close to equal.

73 But when the Sun is between the beginning of Aries up to the end of Virgo, the flow which is by day is stronger than the flow which is by night at that time; and the strongest that the flow in the day is (with respect to this indication) is when the Sun is at the end of Gemini and the day reaches its endpoint in length.

74 And when the Sun passes into the end of Virgo (and it is the time of the autumnal equinox), the flow in the day is close in power to the flow in

---

[59] See **55-56**.

the night, in the abundance of the water and the length of the period of time. **75** And when the Sun passes into the three southern signs (and they are from the beginning of Libra to the end of Sagittarius), the flow in the night is stronger than the flow in the day. **76** And the strongest that the flow in the night is, and the longest in the period of time (with respect to this approach) is when the Sun is at the end of Sagittarius, when the night reaches its endpoint in length.

77 Now as for what we stated—that the flow in the day will be stronger than the flow in the night when the day is longer than the night, and that the flow in the night will be stronger than the flow in the day when the night is longer than the day—that is for two reasons. **78** One of them is due to the Sun's support for the Moon, and it is the length of the Sun's lingering above the earth; and the second is the length of the Moon's stay above the earth.

79 The first reason, which is due to the Sun's support of the Moon, is that when the day is longer than the night, the Sun's stay by day above the earth will be longer than his stay under the earth: so due to the length of his stay by day above the earth, there will be an increase in the loosening[60] of the waters which are in the upper part of the sea and in its depths. **80** So, if it was the time of the flow and the water was loosening into parts, it will be more susceptible to the action of the Moon, and the water of the flow will be more abundant, and its motion stronger. **81** For this reason the water of the flow on a long day is more powerful and abundant than the water of the flow on that night. **82** Now as for the flow which is at the time when its day is longer than the night and the Moon is between the stake of the west up to the stake of the earth, it will be weaker than the flow which is at that time while the Moon is between the east up to the Midheaven.

83 The second reason, which is by reason of the length of the Moon's stay above the earth, is that when the night is longer than the day, the Moon therefore rises by night, and especially between the beginning of the night up to half of it: so she will be in the signs of long ascensions, and her lingering above the earth will be in the eastern quadrant. **84** Because of this, the motion of the water will continue, and because of the continuing of its motion the loosening of its parts will multiply, and its being raised up from the depths of the sea to its surface, so that the water of the flow by night will be,

---

[60] تحليل. **BY** translate this as "rarefying."

at an increase of the night over the day, stronger and more abundant than the water of the flow in the day. **85** But as for when the flow at this time is by night, and the Moon is in the third quadrant (between the west up to the fourth), then the strength of the water of the flow in it will not be like the strength of the flow which exists when the Moon in it is above the earth.

86 And the more that the Moon at the time of the flow is in signs of long ascensions, its remaining in them will be prolonged, and the water of the flow at that time will be more abundant, predominant, [and] of a longer period of time. **87** So the water of the flow now becomes the strongest it [can] be, and the most predominant, for these two reasons which we have stated, when the Sun is in Sagittarius and Gemini—except that when the Sun is in Gemini, the water of the flow by day is more predominant and stronger than the flow in the night; and when the Sun is in Sagittarius, the water of the flow by night will be more predominant and stronger than the water of the flow in the day. **88** And when the Sun is at the beginning of Aries and the beginning of Libra, the flow of both the night and day are similar in power.

89 So it is consistent with this standpoint that the condition of the flow's strength and weakness, and its moderation, in a single year in which the Sun marks off twelve signs, should be similar to what we had stated about the condition of the flow in every month: because the strength of the flow which is by night while the Sun is in Sagittarius and the Moon above the earth, is similar to the strength of the flow which exists at the meeting of the Sun and Moon. **90** And the strength of the flow which is by night while the Sun is in Gemini and the Moon above the earth, is similar to the strength of the flow which exists when the Moon is in the fullness, in the opposition of the Sun. **91** And the flow which exists when the Sun is at the beginning of Aries and the beginning of Libra, is similar to the strength of the flow which exists every month when the Moon is in the square of the Sun (that is, the first square and the second one).

92 And for everything in our previous discussions mentioning the increase of the water of the flow (or its decrease) from time to time, neither that increase nor the decrease is equivalent in extent and quantity, but rather it differs: because sometimes the water of the flow will increase somewhat on some days, and it will increase after that or before it by more than that or less (and likewise, the decrease): so, understand that.

93 Each one of these seven natural, single indications which we have mentioned, has a separate indication for the abundance and scarcity of the water of the flow, its strength and weakness, and its moderation. **94** So understand this indication, for if all of these testimonies which indicate an abundance of the flow's water meet together at one time, then the flow's water will be strong, abundant, predominating, for a long period of time. **95** And if some of them meet together, it will be below the previous [case]: for insofar as the indicators of the flow are few, the flow will be weaker. **96** And if indications of the moderation of the water of the flow meet together at one time, the flow's water will be moderate. **97** And if some of the indicators indicate an increase of the flow's water, and others indicate a decrease, the flow's water will also be moderate. **98** And if the testimonies of a scarcity of the water's flow met together at one time, it indicates the extreme limit of the scarcity of the flow's water, and its weakness.

[8: Strength of wind]

99 The eighth way for the strength of the water of the flow and ebb, is from [8] the incidental indication.[61]

100 Now as for the seven natural ways, we have already stated them in what preceded, and indeed six of them were due to the special property of the Moon's indication, while the seventh is from the Sun's strengthening of her. **101** Now we will state the indication which accrues due to the strengthening of the flow and ebb, and the abundance and scarcity of their water, from the winds occurring in the atmosphere. **102** Know that the sea has two winds. **103** One of them is the special wind which comes to be in the belly of the water, and it is strengthening for the flow (and we have already mentioned this wind when we discussed the reason for the flow and ebb).[62] **104** The second is the wind which is in the atmosphere, and it is the general wind which people of both sea and land partake of in all places. **105** And it blows from different directions, such as the east, west, north, and south, and in what is between these positions which we stated. **106** So understand these winds and directions from which they blow, and understand the wind which blows from the direction where the current of the flow comes from, and the

---

[61] This refers to the strength of the wind.
[62] See III.5, **6-13**.

wind which blows from the direction where the current of the ebb comes from.

107 And know that the Moon's rising, and the motion of her sphere, is from east to west, and that the current of the water's flow is in accordance with the direction of the movement of the Moon's sphere, and that the ebb is in accordance with the direction of its current from the west to the east. **108** So the winds which blow from the direction which the Moon rises from, are strengthening for the current of the water of the flow; but the winds which blow from the direction which the Moon sets in, are strengthening for the current of the water of the ebb.

109 And in what has preceded we have already mentioned that for the flow and ebb which come to be while the Moon is in the upper half of the sphere, the time period of one of them is the same as the period of the other; and likewise when the Moon is in the lower half of the sphere, the period of one of them is the same as the period of the other (with respect to the Moon's natural indication)—except that contingencies happen to them at some times, so that the Moon may be in the upper half of the sphere or in the lower half of the sphere, and the time period of one of them is longer or shorter than the period of the other.[63]

110 And what happens to the flow in the length of its period, is of two types. **111** The first type, because of which the period of the flow is long, is that the indicators of the abundance of the water's flow, and its strength, are many: so the motion of the flow's water, and the intensity of its current, and its predominance and violence, last until the natural time has passed which the Moon indicates, and due to that the period of the flow becomes long. **112** We have already stated these indicators in what preceded. **113** The second type is that at the time of the flow there are strong, violent winds strengthening the current of the water of the flow, so due to that the period of the flow also becomes long. **114** So when these two indications come together, they will be excessive in the length of the period of the flow.

115 And as for the shortness of the period of the flow, it is of two types. **116** One of them is that the indicators of the strength of the flow's water are few, so the flow's water has little motion and a weak current, and due to the weakness of its motion the limit of the flow will be at the first natural indica-

---

[63] See III.5, **44ff**.

tion indicative of the limit of the flow or before it, by some period of time. **117** The second type is that there are violent winds opposing the current of the flow's water, so they repel it and it reduces the time of the flow down from the natural indication. **118** So when these two indications come together, they will be excessive in the shortness of the period of the flow.

119 And as for the ebb, the length of its period is of two types. **120** One of them is that the period of the flow which was before it is short, so it increases in the length of the period of the ebb, near to what was subtracted from the period of the natural flow,[64] and due to that it lengthens the period of the ebb. **121** The second type is that there are violent winds at the time of the ebb, with the direction of the ebb's current, so it strengthens that current and lengthens the period of the ebb. **122** So if the two indications came together, they would be excessive in the length of the period of the ebb.

123 And as for the shortness of the period of the ebb, that is of two types. **124** The first of them is that the period of the flow which was before it was long, so it reduces the period of the ebb, down from [its] natural limit. **125** The second is that there are violent winds at the time of the ebb, opposing its current, so the period of the ebb is short.

126 So these are eight ways of there being a long period of the flow and ebb, and a short one.

127 And this is an overall judgment: and it is that I say the flow is the beginning and it is what the Moon does by her nature, while the ebb is after the flow and it is the returning of the water to the sea through its own character. **128** So if the period of the flow is long, then the period of the ebb which is after it, will be short; and if the period of the flow is short, the period of the ebb which is after it will be long. **129** And for the winds whose blowing agrees with the current of the flow or ebb (whichever one that agrees with), that wind will increase in its power and in the length of its period; and the winds which oppose its current (whichever one it was), will weaken it.

130 And know that when the water of the flow reaches one of the drainage channels or islands, or the estuaries of the seas, sometimes all the water of the flow returns to the sea at the ebb, sometimes some of that returns, and sometimes more [of it] returns to the sea at the ebb than the water of the flow which had left the sea: because when the flow reaches some of the

---

[64] Or perhaps, "the natural period of the flow."

drainage [channels] or some of the estuaries of the seas, and the sea water is not retained in the places it passes into, the water of the flow will return just as it is to the sea. **131** But if part of it is retained in some of the places, [only] some of the water's flow will return to the sea. **132** And if, apart from the sea water there were waters of various wadis and rivers flowing into those drainage [channels] or estuaries of the seas which the water of the sea's flow reached, then the ebb will draw back with it those waters which flowed into those places, so the water of the ebb at that time will be greater, stronger, and more predominant than the water of the flow.

Chapter III.7: That the Moon is the cause of the flow and ebb, and the response to those opposing that

1 People have denied that the Moon, her rising and setting, and her reaching the positions which we have stated, are the reason for the flow and ebb. **2** They say that it is of the character of the sea [itself] that it should heave in its own right: for when the sea heaves, there is the flow, and when it does not heave, there is the ebb. **3** The rising of the Moon and her setting is indifferent in this, and the Moon is not a cause of them. **4** And they also say that if the Moon were a cause of the flow and ebb, it would be necessary that the wadis, rivers, and springs flow and ebb.

5 We argue against one claiming that, with four arguments:

6 One of them is that we say: [1] if the flow and ebb were due to the character of the sea and its heaving, the water of the flow would always be in a single, known condition, neither increasing nor decreasing; nor would it be stronger or more dominant at one time than at another, nor would the times of their inception and endpoints differ: because the action of natural things does not differ nor change from the condition which they are in.[65] **7** And we see the contrary of all of that, because sometimes we see the water of the flow at one time stronger and more dominant than at another time, and sometimes we see it weaker; and indeed the variation in the conditions of

---

[65] That is, one needs some other, external force or change, else the motion would continue unabated. Or, since natural things move precisely due to their natures, the activity would be identical every time.

the flow is in proportion to the variation in the conditions of the Moon, just as we have explained. **8** And of course we also see at some times that it begins at the start of the day, and at another time at the hour when the day has passed. **9** Then, the conditions of the inception of the flow and ebb vary, as do their limits, in proportion to the variation in the Moon's rising and setting and the rest of her conditions. **10** So, we know that the Moon is the cause of the flow and ebb, and the cause of the rest of their conditions.

11 And the second argument is that [2] things which heave[66] in their own right need a place greater than the place in which they are: so if the water of the sea heaves in its own right without the causality of the Moon, then upon its heaving it would need a place greater than the place which it is in. **12** But how could that water return to the sea at the time of the ebb when it does not have a place there?[67] **13** And why does that heaving which belongs to the sea, and the return of the water to it, occur with the elevation of the Moon and her declining and setting, when that is not in the character of the water's motion? **14** But since it is thus, the Moon is therefore a cause of the flow and ebb.

15 The third argument is that [3] we say that if the nature of water is to go down to the depth of the sea, and at the time of the flow we see it moving upwards (because it is raised up from the depth of the sea to its surface), then passing over to the shore, then some of it pushing another [part] with a powerful urging so that it is raised up—and it is not in the character of water to move upwards—then when we see it moving upwards and that motion is not in its character, we know that it has a mover, and that mover is the cause of its motion. **16** So if the Moon is not the cause of that motion, there is no escaping the fact that it has another cause besides the Moon. **17** But that is

---

[66] Remember, this verb (تنفّس) really means to "breathe," so Abū Ma'shar is speaking of the rhythmic swelling and contracting of the water.

[67] This is oddly stated, but I think that Abū Ma'shar is implying that his opponents' views lead to absurd consequences. Remember that the elements are supposed to move towards, and rest in, their "natural" places. But if water simply heaved (or flowed and ebbed) all by itself, then once the sea spills over into a new place, surely that new location would be its new place, and it would simply ebb and flow in that new place, independently of the rest of the sea. That is, it would not "return" to the sea, because that is no longer its place. (At least, I think that's what Abū Ma'shar means.) See also III.5, **41-43** and III.6, **127**.

what is *not* found: so therefore the water's motion does not have a cause apart from the Moon,[68] just as we stated in what preceded, with sufficient arguments.

18 The fourth argument is [4] in response to those who claim that if the Moon were the cause of the flow and ebb, one would find that the wadis, rivers, and springs flow and ebb. **19** We say that the special property which is in the part is not found in the whole, and the wadis, rivers, and springs are like the part, while the seas are like the whole. **20** But in the wadis, rivers, and springs (which are like the part) we do not find the special property which we find in the seas (which are like the whole), because the waters of the sea stand in place and are dense and salty, while the waters of wadis, rivers, and springs are moving, running along, subtle, and sweet. **21** So just as the special property of the wadis and rivers is contrary to the special property of the seas, so likewise the condition of one of them is contrary to the condition of the other. **22** And in what has preceded we have already stated for what reason there is no flow and ebb in running waters like wadis, rivers, and springs.[69]

Chapter III.8: On the different conditions of the seas, and the quality of the seas in which the flow and ebb is made obvious (and in which it is not obvious), and on the special property of the Sun's action in the seas

1 We have already described the flow and ebb, and their conditions; now we will describe seas in a comprehensive way, just as some of the naturalists have described it. **2** For they say that the Moon has different effects on all of the seas, and indeed it is made obvious in some rather than others due to the difference in their conditions and the conditions of their waters.

---

[68] And the Sun, as he has also stated.
[69] I believe Abū Ma'shar is referring to III.5, **19-21**.

[Types of bodies of water, and the tides in them]

3 Now as for the seas, they are of three kinds: one of them is [1] one in which there is no flow nor ebb; the second is [2] one in which a flow and ebb is not obvious; and the third is [3] one in which there is a flow and ebb.

4 So as for [1] the seas in which there is no flow and ebb, they are of three types. **5** The first type is [1a] waters which do not stand still for a long period of time, and whose water is not thick, nor does it become salty, nor do winds condense in them: because sometimes the water passes into some places for some reasons and becomes like a lake, and the water diminishes from it in the summer while increasing in it in the winter; or an increase will be obvious in it because of what flows into it from the waters of rivers and springs, and a decrease because of what goes out of it. **6** So that water, and the waters like it, do not have a flow nor ebb in it because through those motions which come to be from the increase of the water and its decrease, the winds do not gather or condense in it. **7** The second type is [1b] the seas which are distant from the orbit of the Moon and her zenith by a long way, so there is no flow nor ebb in them. **8** The third type is [1c] waters in which looseness predominates over their floor: because if their floor was loose, the water would penetrate from it to other seas, and the winds which are on their floor heave and are loose; and this mostly comes to be in the estuaries of the seas, and islands.

9 Now as for [2] the seas in which a flow and ebb is not obvious, they are of three types. **10** The first type is [2a] the sea in which the Moon is parallel to one of its banks, but not parallel to another due to the distance of the interval between the two shores,[70] and the other shore which the Moon is not parallel to borders on the land of places which are not inhabited: so a flow and ebb are not found in it. **11** And that is like the Sea of Ocean,[71] for the flow and ebb is not evident in it due to its expanse and the distance of one of the shores from the orbit of the Moon, from civilization, and the observation

---

[70] Abū Ma'shar may be referring to the curvature of the earth, even though he next mentions the absence of people on the other side.

[71] أوقيانس البحر, a transliteration of the Latin *Oceanus*. This probably refers to any large ocean which sailors had not yet fully traversed, such as the Atlantic or the southern parts of the Indian Ocean.

of people: because for the sea whose bank does border on civilization, its people will find a flow and ebb in it. **12** And if its banks do not border on civilization, they will not find them in it. **13** The second type is [2b] water whose two banks are known [and] extend to civilization, and the Moon is parallel to it or near to being parallel with it, nor does it have estuaries and islands extending water into it: so if the Moon passes into the two quadrants indicative of the flow, and she moves its water, and it moves and heaves, neither the flow nor ebb of that water will be obvious, but there will be waves and violent winds. **14** And indeed that comes to be in lakes and islands, and in the estuaries of the seas which are cut off from the sea. **15** The third type is [2c] the waters in which some of them flow into others: for if it was the time of the flow, the upper water heaves, flowing down below, and its increase is not obvious.

16 As for [3] the seas in which a flow and ebb is found, they are the seas which are close to the parallel of the Moon, and their motion is for some period of time, and their two banks border on civilization, and they have estuaries and islands extending water into them at the flow, and hardness and an abundance of mountains predominates over their floor.[72] **17** So if it was the time of the flow and their water heaved, and overflowed and was diffused beyond their banks, and reached their estuaries and islands, they would flow and ebb just as the Persian Sea, the Indian Sea, and the Sea of China flow and ebb, as well as the sea which is between Constantinople and Ifranjah[73] and other seas which have this quality.

[Review]

18 So the difference in the seas' conditions for the flow and ebb comes to be through these things, in accordance with what the predecessors stated (among those looking into the natural sciences). **19** Thus the quality of the seas which do not flow nor ebb have been made clear to us, as well as those in which no flow or ebb is obvious (and those in which the flow and ebb are obvious). **20** And it is clear to us that the sea does not heave in its own right,

---

[72] Or again, "land" (أرض). I'm not sure how much Abū Ma'shar is connecting a mountainous land with the actual floor of the sea next to it.
[73] The Mediterranean Sea.

and that the Moon is the cause of that heaving, and she is the mover of the water of the sea through her own character.

21 And we have already stated many times that the motion of earthly bodies comes to be through the heavenly bodies' moving them. **22** And an analogy to that is made obvious to us by many natural existing things which move other bodies through their own nature, at a great distance from them, without touching—just as we see the magnet-stone moving iron and drawing it to itself my means of its own character, and as we see white naphtha draw fire to itself from a great distance, and like the olive stone which draws oil to itself, and the vinegar stone which draws vinegar to itself. **23** So we see these bodies, which we have stated, act through their own character upon a body not their own, at a great distance, to draw and move upwards and downwards, and to the right and the left. **24** It is likewise in the Moon's nature to move the saltwater of the sea at her distance from it, and it is of the nature of that water to be receptive to motion from the Moon, more so than the receptivity of sweet water, [and] then to move at the time of the flow upwards from the lower parts of the sea, to its upper parts. **25** And it is also found that the Sun has different actions in the total conditions of all of the seas: in the intensity of their waves and their abundance, and stirring them up at some times of the year, and in the softness of that and its being rest in another time, in proportion to the closeness of his orbit to them or its distance from them.

[Persian and Indian Oceans]

26 And several mariners knowledgeable in their conditions have stated things we will mention about the difference of the conditions of the Persian and Indian Seas.

27 As for the Persian and Indian Seas, as a whole they are a single sea, due to the connection of one of them with the other, except that they are antithetical in their conditions: because the Persian Sea's waves are abundant and intense, and sailing it is difficult when the Indian Sea has a smooth appearance, is easy to sail, and has few waves. **28** And the Persian Sea is smooth, its waves few, and easy to sail, during the convulsion of the Indian Sea, the rocking of its waters, the clashing of its waves, its gloominess, and the difficulty of sailing it.

29 Now the moment when the Persian Sea first begins to be difficult is upon the Sun's entering Virgo, and his nearness to the autumnal equinox;

and its waves do not cease to multiply, and its waters to rock, and its surface to be unpleasant, until the Sun passes into Pisces. **30** And the most intense that the unpleasantness of its surface can be (and the abundance of its waves, and its intensity), is at the end of the season of autumn, upon the Sun being in Sagittarius. **31** Now if it was close to the spring equinox, it would begin to have few waves, and a smooth surface, and be easy to sail, until the Sun returns to Virgo. **32** And the smoothest that its surface can be, and the easiest to sail, is at the end of the season of spring, and it is upon the Sun's being in Gemini.

33 As for the Indian Sea, it is exactly contrary to this: because upon the Sun's being in Pisces and his nearness to the spring equinox, it begins in [its] gloominess and its water becomes dense, and its waves abundant, so that people do not sail it due to its gloominess and its difficulty; and it does not cease to be like that until the autumnal equinox draws near. **34** And the most intense that its gloominess and the unpleasantness of its surface can be, is upon the Sun's being in Gemini. **35** But when the Sun passes into Virgo, its gloominess becomes scarce, its waves decrease, its surface becomes smooth, and easy to sail, until the Sun passes into Pisces. **36** And the smoothest its surface can be is upon the Sun's being in Sagittarius, except that the Persian Sea [can be] sailed at all times of the year. **37** As for the Indian Sea, people do not sail it when it is stirred up due to its gloominess and the difficulty of sailing it.

38 And due to the difference in their condition, and the stirring-up of each one at a time different from the other, they are named by the nature of the season in which they are stirred up. **39** So as for the Persian Sea, it is named after the nature of black bile due to its beginning to be stirred up at the start of the season of autumn, and its difficulty, and the intensity of its strength at the end of this season, and its remaining in that condition until the end of the season of winter. **40** But as for the Indian Sea, it is named after the nature of yellow bile due to its beginning to be stirred up at the start of the season of spring, and the intensity of its strength at the end of this season, and its lasting in [that] condition until the end of the season of summer.

41 And knowledgeable mariners have defined each one of these two seas by means of a known limit among them. **42** They say that the beginning of the limit of the Persian Sea is from what borders on the east, and it is from the mouth of the "one-eyed" of the Tigris, and its end terminates at the island called Tīz, [in] Makrān.[74] **43** And from there is reckoned the beginning of the border of Sind, and its border is from what borders the west from the mouth of the "one-eyed" of the Tigris until it terminates at the Sea of Aden, and in the east of the Persian Sea from the cities of the countries of Persia, Makrān, and Kirmān, and the west of the countries of the Arabs (and they are Bahrain, Omān, Musqat, and Suqutrā),[75] until one reaches the depression[76] of Aden (and it is the end of the peninsula of the Arabs), and there is the place which is called the "Armored" (and it is a route in the sea which is taken to the Sea of Jeddah, Syria, Egypt, and Rome),[77] and from what borders the bank of the Arabs from the Persian Sea is found seed-pearls and excellent tears.[78]

44 As for the Indian Sea, its limit is from what borders on the east from the port of Tīz[79] in Makrān, and the end of it are the countries of China; and its limit from what borders on the west is the beginning of the depression of Aden, and its end the countries of the Zanj. **45** In the east of the Indian Sea, among the cities are the countries of India, Qamar, Zanj, Zānaj, and many different peoples of India. **46** All of them have rain in the summer except for the higher parts of their countries which are far from the sea, like the lands of Tibet, Kābul, and others among the cities and places there, of the steppes and deserts, and ruined places described by longitude and latitude, [which are] not inhabited. **47** But these do not have rain in the summer, though they do have snow in the winter due to the coldness of their air. **48** As for the west of the Indian Sea, if those sailing the sea cut across the sea of the depression of Aden, the first land they come to is the island called the lands of the Berbers, and they are inhabited; and in them are a type of Zanj connect-

---

[74] Tīz (تيز) was actually a port on Chabahar Bay (in modern Iran), now called Tīs, approximately 60° E 30', 25° N 30'. See LeStrange, pp. 322 (map) and 329-30.
[75] Also spelled Socotra, this is a large island in an archipelago directly off the tip of the Horn of Africa.
[76] غبّ. The port city of Aden sits in the depression of a dormant volcano.
[77] Or rather, Asia Minor and Constantinople.
[78] حبّ اللؤلؤ والقطري (القطر) الجيّد. I take this to mean small round pearls as well as tear-shaped ones. The word القطري or القطر can refer to molten metals in the form of tears or drops, too.
[79] Lit., the "island" or "peninsula" of Tīz, as above.

ed with the lands of Sudan. **49** And in that western direction are the countries of the Zanj and the Zānaj.

50 And for all of these which we have mentioned (and others of those in that western region which are in islands), there is no man among them who reaches the land and knows that they are connected with [other] lands, nor have people of the north and south of these two seas defined them for us, nor the peoples who reside in these two regions.

51 Now, one wanting [to reach] China will cut across the eastern Indian Sea and circle around it until he passes over to China.

52 And one wanting the Zanj will pass to its west until he comes to the place of the Zanj which he wants.

53 And one wanting the Zānaj will veer towards its east until he passes to Kalah, then will cross over to the lands of the Zānaj. **54** And indeed, they start out on this route because if they cut across the land of the Zanj, wanting the countries of the Zānaj, they would pass over into the gloominess in which the glow of day is not evident except for the amount of six hours every day: so due to that they head for the Indian Sea [in] the eastern direction to Kalah, then pass over to the region of the west [of] this sea until they reach the countries of the Zānaj.

55 So this is the sum of what the knowledgeable mariners have stated to us about the condition of these two seas. **56** But any sea will have a condition different from another sea at every time of the year, in accordance with its clime, latitude, and distance from the orbit of the Sun at that time—except that we do not intend to do justice here to the conditions of all of the seas. **57** Indeed, by stating the difference in the condition of these two seas, we wanted to report that just as the Sun comes to have a special property of action in each of the [two] seas (the Persian and the Indian), which is different from his action in the other, so likewise in every sea, at all times of the year, he has a special property of doing something which he does not have in other seas.

Chapter III.9: On the Moon's indication for animals, plants, and minerals, through the increase and decrease of her glow

1 In what has preceded we have already stated the special property of the Moon's indication for the flow and ebb, and the rest of their conditions, and that the Moon is the cause of the heaving of sea water, and it is not this salty sea water alone which rises or lowers with the Moon's rising and lowering, and increases and decreases through her own increase in glow and its decrease, but rather many species of many types [also do]. **2** Because we find many things that, so long as the Moon is increasing in glow, and culminating at some place, there is much increase in them; and so long as the Moon is decreasing in her glow or falling from their zenith, they do not increase except by a little bit. **3** And this is found in many species of animals, trees, herbs, and minerals.

4 As for the bodies of animals, at the time of the Moon's increase in her glow they are stronger, and heating, moistening, generation, and growth comes to be more predominant in them; but after the fullness the bodies are weaker, and the cold is more predominant over them.

5 And so long as the Moon is increasing in her glow, the temperaments which are in the bodies of men (such as blood, phlegm, and others) will be on the surfaces of the bodies and the veins, and the surface of the body increases in humidity, wetness, and a fine [appearance]. **6** And when the Moon decreases in glow, these temperaments pass into the depths of the body and veins, and the surface of the body increases in dryness: and that is evident among those knowledgeable in medicine.

7 But as for the sick, much of their conditions is known from the increase of the Moon in her glow (and her decrease in it), because the bodies of those who get sick at the beginning of the month come to be stronger in repelling illnesses and ailments, while the bodies of those who get sick at the end of the month come to be weaker in repelling ailments. **8** So due to the variation in the conditions of bodies at the time of the Moon's increase in her glow (and her decrease in it), the ailments also vary. **9** And as for the conditions of the sick day-by-day, they are understood from the motion of the Moon on every day, and from her reaching the sextile, square,[80] and opposition of her

---

[80] We should have expected Abū Ma'shar to mention the trine as well.

own place, to the right and left. **10** And the days in which the Moon is in these positions, are called the "known" days:[81] and from the condition of the Moon on these days is known the condition of the sick person.

11 As for the masters of the sea and those wanting knowledge of weather omens, they look at the meeting and fullness, and they make it be like a root; then they look at the Moon's arrival from that place to these "known" days and places which we named, and from them they understand the condition of winds, mists, rains, and heat and cold.

12 As for the hair of animals, so long as the Moon is increasing in her glow, its sprouting is quick, thick, and abundant; but when the Moon decreases, its sprouting is slow, not abundant, and not thick.

13 And the Moon has an action in a living man as well, because when a man spends too long sitting or sleeping under the Moon by night, it produces laziness and slackness in his body, and it stirs up colds and migraines in him. **14** And also, when the meat of an animal has exposure by night, it alters its smell and taste.

15 And as for animal things which are cold, wet, and white, such as milk, brain, egg whites, and other cold and wet things, the Moon has evident effects in them: because the milk products in the udder multiply and are abundant from the beginning of the month up to its half, so long as the Moon is increasing in glow; but when the glow of the Moon decreases, their abundance is diminished and does not increase. **16** And likewise, the brains in the heads of animals increase and are produced at the beginning of the month, more so than what is produced at the end of the month; and likewise egg whites, for the egg which congeals in the bellies of birds at the time of the Moon's increase in her glow, is more ample in whiteness and more abundant than one which occurs in their bellies at the end of the month. **17** Now as for the day and night, when the Moon is above the earth in the eastern quadrant or at the culmination[82] of some place, the milk products in the udders of their sheep will be abundant. and there will be an increase in them and in the brains of their animals; and if an egg were in the belly of birds at that time, its white would be more abundant than the egg white which oc-

---

[81] These are normally known as "critical" days. See also I.5, **183-84**.

[82] سمت, which normally means "azimuth," but here must refer to being on the meridian.

curs in their bellies at a different time of the day and night. **18** And if the Moon withdrew and set from them, it would subtract from everything we stated. **19** (And if a man studied that, he would find what we stated to be evident.)

20 And it is already found that for fish in the seas, wetlands, and running waters, if it was from the beginning of the month up to the fullness, they leave their hiding-spots and the depths of the wetlands and seas, and increase in their fat and size; and if it was from after the fullness up to the meeting, they enter their hiding-spots and the depths of the seas and waters, and do not become fat. **21** And as for the day and night, so long as the Moon is advancing from the east to the Midheaven, they will appear, coming out from their hiding-spots, and increase in their fat; while if the Moon withdrew, they would disappear into their hiding spots, not increase in their bodies nor become fat, unless it was [just] a little fat.

22 And likewise things that scratch the earth:[83] for their coming out from their burrows in the first half of the month is more frequent than their coming out from them in the last half. **23** And everything that stings and bites: in the first half of the month it is stronger in the activity of biting and stinging, and its seeking and eagerness [for prey], and stronger in its poison, than it is in the last half. **24** And predatory animals too: for in the first half of the month they more often seek prey than they do in the last half.

25 Now as for trees and plantings, when they are planted when the Moon is increasing in her glow, or advancing towards the Midheaven, they will take root, enlarge, develop, bear fruit, and accelerate their sprouting, development, and yield; but if the Moon was decreasing in glow or withdrawing from the Midheaven, they will not accelerate [their] sprouting, and will slow down in bearing fruit, and sometimes will dry out. **26** And many plants which are worn [as clothing] will become corrupted, like flax: for it burns and cuts it off when it is exposed to the Moon by night.

27 As for the Moon's special property for fruits, fragrant herbs, seeds, legumes, and grasses, so long as the Moon is increasing in her glow until she is full, their growth and increase will be more than their growth and increase in the last half of the month. **28** And this is evident among farmers and mas-

---

[83] خرشة الأرض. Or perhaps more broadly, "crawl" the earth: insects, reptiles, and the like.

ters of sowing. **29** But that is not [so] among scholars and those possessing knowledge from them: rather, among most of them that is found in types of fruit and legumes, like plums,[84] melons, apricots, cucumbers, watermelons, gourds, and [other] types of legumes and fruits. **30** And they also evidently perceive from the beginning of the month up to its half, that [these things] grow, increase, and are produced more so than what increases and grows from the decrease of the Moon up to the end of the month. **31** And at the time when the Moon rises and culminates by day and night, more grows and increases than grows and increases in the rest of the times of the day and night.

32 As for minerals, from the beginning of the month to the fullness they are produced and increase in the heart of their essence,[85] and in their shininess, clarity, and purity, more so than they are produced and increase in what is from the Moon's decrease up to the meeting. **33** And most of her action and appearance is in soft stones (and that is evident [and] known among the masters of minerals).

34 And the Moon has many special properties in the alteration of the bodies of animals, plants, and minerals which are found among those who inspect them, which we have not mentioned: because in this book of ours our aim has not been to report every special property of the Moon in things, but we have aimed in this place to report that the Moon has a special property in the alteration of things which other planets do not.

35 The Third Book of the *Book of Introduction* is completed.

---

[84] الخوج, which in other dialects can mean peaches (or perhaps other pitted fruits).

[85] في ذات جواهرها. This word I have translated as "essences" (جواهر), can also mean "gemstones."

BOOK IV: [THEORY OF ASTROLOGY & CLASSIFICATIONS OF THE PLANETS][1]

And in it are nine chapters

1. Chapter IV.1: On the natures of the seven planets quick in motion, according to what Ptolemy said.
2. Chapter IV.2: On the natures of the planets, and their fortunes and infortunes <and what is blended of them>,[2] according to what the generality of the masters of the stars stated.
3. Chapter IV.3: On our response to one claiming that the natures of the planets, and their fortunes and infortunes, are known from their colors.
4. Chapter IV.4: On our establishing the existence of the fortunes and infortunes, according to the teachings of philosophy.
5. Chapter IV.5: On knowing which of the planets is a fortune, and which of them an infortune.
6. Chapter IV.6: On the different conditions of the fortunes and infortunes, and the shifting of one of them over to the nature of the other.
7. Chapter IV.7: On the natures of the planets, and their shifting from nature to nature, and the strength of their nature inherent in them (and its weakness).
8. Chapter IV.8: On the masculinization of the planets, and their feminization.
9. Chapter IV.9: On the diurnal and nocturnal planets.

---

[1] Reading for the uninformative *"Book Four of the Introduction to the Science of the Judgments of the Stars."*
[2] Adding with the title below.

Chapter IV.1: On the natures of the seven planets quick in motion, according to what Ptolemy said

1 Several of the Greek kings right after Alexander the Two-Horned, son of Phillip, were each called Ptolemy (there were ten people, nine men and a woman). **2** They used to stay in Egypt, and the years of their rule were 275. **3** They were generally sages, and among them was Ptolemy the Sage, who wrote the book *Almagest*, on the explanations for the motion of the sphere, and what is in it (of the planets). **4** Now, one of them wrote a book on the judgments of the stars, and attributed it to Ptolemy, the author of the *Almagest*, so it is said that the one who wrote *The Book of Judgments*[3] was the one who wrote the *Almagest*. **5** But we do not know the truth of that from its error—except that the one who composed *The Book of Judgments* did state the natures of the planets and the explanations of them in his book.[4]

[Ptolemy's attribution of elemental natures to the planets]

6 And he began by saying that the Sun warms and dries in a maturing, unhurried way, and [the Sun] is more apparent in that and more evident in activity than the rest of the planets due to his might; and the more that he is elevated towards our zenith, we increase in warmth. **7** And he claimed that the nature of the Moon is wetness due to her sphere's nearness to the earth, and her receptiveness to the vapors which rise up from it. **8** And he claimed that the nature of Saturn is the cold and the dry, due to the distance of his sphere from the hotness of the Sun, and its distance from the wetness of the earth's vapor. **9** And he claimed that the nature of Mars is hotness and the dry, due to his color resembling fire, and his nearness to the Sun, and because [the Sun] is under him, so that [the Sun's] heat rises up towards him and warms him. **10** And he claimed that Jupiter is temperate in mixture, because his sphere is between the spheres of Saturn and Mars, and indeed for this reason his nature comes to be temperate hotness and wetness. **11** And he claimed that the nature of Venus is temperate heating and moistening: as for her heating, it is due to the nearness of her sphere to the Sun; and as for

---

[3] The *Tetrabiblos*.
[4] That is, in *Tetrabiblos* I.4.

her moistening, it is due to what affects her of the wet vapor which surrounds the earth. **12** And he claimed that the nature of Mercury is sometimes dryness, sometimes wetness: as for his dryness, it is due to his nearness to the Sun, and that he is not distant from [the] Sun by a great interval; as for his wetness, it is due to the nearness of his sphere to the circle of the Moon.

13 So, this is what Ptolemy claimed about the natures of the planets, and what he argued concerning that. **14** But now we will state what is contestable about his view:

[Abū Ma'shar's criticism of Ptolemy]

15 As for what he claimed about the Sun and his heating of things with maturation and slowness, that is found from his activity.

16 But as for his statement that the nature of the Moon is wetness due to the nearness of her circle to the earth, and her reception of the moistures which rise up from it, that it rejected among the wise because the distance which is between the surface of the earth and the closest position which the Moon is in, is approximately 128,094 miles, taking a mile as 3,000 cubits. **17** And this is made clear in the book in which the distances of the superior bodies from each other is stated.[5] **18** For the greatest the rising of the vapors can be from the surface of the earth into the atmosphere is 16 stades (according to what the Philosopher claimed), and the stade is 400 cubits: that makes 2 miles, a tenth, and a thirtieth of a mile.[6] **19** So if the highest that the vapors which rise from the earth into the atmosphere could go is 2 miles, a tenth, and a thirtieth of a mile, and closest that the distance of the Moon from the surface of the earth could be is approximately 128,094 miles, then where does the vapor of the earth reach the Moon from, so as to change her nature? **20** And also, if the Moon had received the vapors, the vapors would alter her nature; and if the vapors alter her nature, then the transformation,

---

[5] Exact source unknown, but it could be some version of Ptolemy's *Planetary Hypotheses*, which was partly translated from a later Arabic version by Goldstein in 1967.

[6] If a stade is 2/15 miles, then the height of 16 stades is 2 2/15 of a mile, or 2 miles + 1/10 + 1/30, as Abū Ma'shar says.

alteration, and corruption inherent to lower bodies (which take on vapors) would be inherent to *her*. **21** The vapors, therefore, do not reach the Moon, nor does she receive anything from them.

22 As for Mars, [the author] stated that his nature is heating, drying, burning, because his color resembles the color of fire and because the hotness of the Sun affects him (since he is above the Sun). **23** And he made the nature of the Sun be like the nature of fire, since it is in motion upwards; and indeed by his nature [the Sun] warms everything which is close to it, or his heat affects it like the activity of fire. **24** But this statement is false for those who look into the natural sciences, because they claim that the hotness which we find from the Sun is an effect of his operating on *us*: so the Sun's activity in his own sphere and among the planets is not like the activity of fire among these existing things [among us].[7] **25** For the Sun and all of the planets, there is nothing which by its *nature* is related to hotness, coldness, wetness, or dryness, because they do not consist of any of these. **26** And also due to this, they do not take on any of [these natures]: because a body does not take on anything of these natures except what it consists of, but all of the planets are contrary to this since they are simple bodies. **27** The planets, therefore, do not take on anything of these four principles, and that is not in their nature. **28** And if the planets did take on hotness from the Sun, and were warmed like bodies which we see around us, then their colors would already have changed to what is burned, or they would already have been burned up for many days and years.

29 He mentioned Venus: he claims that she is temperate in mixture, and that her nature is hotness and wetness. **30** Now as for the hotness, he states that it is due to her nearness to the Sun, while as for the wetness it is due to what affects her from the wet vapor which rises up from the earth. **31** As for what he claims about her being affected by the wet vapor which rises up from the earth, we know that the sphere of Venus is above the sphere of the Moon, and we have already made it clear that the vapor which rises up from the earth does not reach the sphere of the Moon: so where does it reach the sphere of Venus from? **32** And as for his statement that a little hotness affects her from the Sun, and that her nature is heating due to her nearness to the Sun, if the nature of the Sun was like the nature of fire, anything near to

---

[7] For one thing, the heat goes *downwards* to us.

him would be warmed by him. **33** So if Mars came to be heating [and] drying due to his nearness to the Sun, then hotness and the dry already ought to have overcome the nature of Venus, and there would be no wetness in her nature at all: because the Sun would already have dried out her wetness due to her nearness to him.[8]

34 Then he mentioned Saturn: he claimed that he was cooling [and] drying, and claimed that his cold was due to his distance from the hotness of the Sun, and his dryness was due to his distance from the wetness of the vapor of the earth. **35** In what preceded we have already shown it false that the Sun has an effect in the bodies of planets from heating, and that if a planet was far from the Sun it would become cold in its own right, and if it drew close to him it would grow warm in its own right, and that the vapor of the earth would affect the planets so that they would be wet due to the nearness to him, or be dry due to the distance from him. **36** The coldness of Saturn, therefore, is not due to his distance from the Sun, nor is he dry due to his distance from the vapor of the earth.

37 And he mentioned Jupiter: he claimed that he is temperate in mixture, because his circle is between Saturn (who cools) and Mars (who heats), and that those two collaborate and combine together in his nature, so that he comes to be temperate; and he makes the nature of Jupiter to be receptive of the hot and the cold. **38** But in what preceded we have already shown it false that Mars is hot in his own right, or Saturn cold in his own right, and that any of the planets would take on one of these four natures. **39** So Jupiter does not, therefore, take on the nature of the hot or cold, nor anything of them in his essence: not heating, cooling, the moistening, nor the drying, like the hotness, coldness, wetness, and dryness of things which are found among us.

40 As for Mercury, he stated that [Mercury] is drying at one time, and wet at another: as for his dryness, it is due to his nearness to the Sun, and as for his wetness it is due to the nearness of his sphere to the sphere of the Moon (and that the vapor of the earth affects him so as to moisten him). **41**

---

[8] Remember also that Venus is not only "near" the Sun in terms of how their concentric spheres are arranged, but because her motion closely tracks his (as does that of Mercury). The sphere of Mars is higher than the Sun's, but he spends most of the year in other parts of the zodiac. So the heating activity of the Sun would have a greater effect on Venus than it would on Mars.

Now as for what he stated about his dryness due to the nearness of his sphere to the Sun, if it were like that then Venus would necessarily have been dryer than Venus, because her sphere is closer to the Sun than Mercury's sphere is. **42** (And we have shown it false many times that the Sun heats the bodies of the planets or dries them out.) **43** But as for his statement that his wetness is due to the nearness of his sphere to the Moon, and that the vapor of the earth affects him so as to moisten him, we have already shown it false that the planets moisten one another, and that the vapors which rise up from the earth should reach the sphere of the Moon: so how is it possible that they should reach the sphere of Mercury so as to moisten him?

Chapter IV.2: On the natures of the planets, and their fortunes and infortunes, and what is blended of them, according to what the generality of the masters of the stars claimed

1 Since we wanted a statement of the natures of planets, and their fortunes and infortunes, and what is blended of them, in accordance with what the generality of the masters of the stars claimed, we begin by stating the four principles and the composite humors, and their natures and special properties, in an abbreviated way. **2** And indeed we do that because they claimed that they understood the planetary fortunes and infortunes, and what is blended of them, when they made a comparison by analogy of their natures with the natures of the four principles and the composite humors.

3 Now as for what they state about the natures of the four principles and the composite humors, they are correct in that. **4** But as for their comparison by analogy, the analogy is false because they have erred in their analogy and strayed from the path of truth.

5 The first thing they start with, is to say that the ancient scholars agreed that existing things which are below the sphere of the Moon are the four principles and what is produced from them (of the composite humors and individual beings). **6** Now as for the four principles, they are fire, air, water, and earth. **7** As for the composite humors, they are yellow bile, blood, phlegm, and black bile.

[Majority view on elements, colors, and tastes]

8 And the generality of the ancients did agree that [1] the four principles have a nature and special property, although they do not have colors nor tastes; and that [2] the colors and tastes belong to everything which is produced from them: for they claimed that fire does not actually have a color, and the color we do see it as having is based on the body which takes on the activity of the fire, and that [fire's] special property is hotness, and its activity is burning. **9** As for air, it is a body not having a color, except that it is receptive to colors; and its special property is wetness, and its activity is to cause things to sprout and bring them forth. **10** As for water, it does not actually have a color, but we see its color based on the thing in which the water is; and its special property is coldness, and its activity is nourishing things. **11** And as for earth, it does not actually have a color, but what we see of its color is based on what vapors are in it, and their alterations to it; and its special property is dryness, and its activity is to preserve things. **12** As for tastes, fire and air do not have a taste, but earth and water differ in taste because each place on earth has a taste contrary to the taste of another place; and that is in accordance with the difference of the moistures which are in it. **13** As for water, its taste is discovered in accordance with the nature of the place in which the water is: because if that place was good, the taste of the water which is in it will be sweet; and if that place was salty, the taste of that water is salty. **14** The four principles, therefore do not actually have a color nor taste, but they do have a nature and special property is in accordance with what we stated before.

Nature	Dominant principle	Special property	Humor	Taste
Fire	Hot	Burns	Yellow bile	Bitter
Air	Wet	Grows	Blood	Sweet
Water	Cold	Nourishes	Phlegm	Salty
Earth	Dry	Preserves	Black bile	Sour

Figure 22: Principles, humors, and tastes (IV.2, 8-11 and 27-30)

Book IV: Theory of Astrology, Classifying Planets 211

[Minority view on elements, colors, and tastes]

15 Now some of the ancients did agree with them in what they stated about the natures of these principles and their special properties, while they differed with them in the colors and tastes: and they claimed that some of these principles do have a color and taste, one has a color but not a taste, and one has no color nor taste but is receptive of colors and tastes. **16** As for the two principles which have colors and tastes, they are water and earth: for the color of water is the white and its taste sweetness, while the color of earth is a dusty color and dullness, and its taste bitterness. **17** And [some] people said that the taste of earth is sweetness, and argued for that by saying that the earth makes things sprout, so if its taste was bitterness, it would not make anything sprout: so this is their argument. **18** As for what has color but not taste, it is fire, and its color is the red. **19** And they argued for that [by saying] fire is what is drawn out by the striking together of two bodies, or from lightning: and they said even if the color of that fire which we see in the atmosphere differs by a small increase or small decrease from the true definition of redness which belongs to fire, in accordance with the body in which the color of fire is seen, redness is the closest of the colors to it. **20** As for what does not have a color nor taste, and is receptive of colors and tastes, it is air: because it is receptive of antithetical colors like the white and the black (and what is between them both), and taste is known by its being the medium between a thing which has a taste, and the sense of taste. **21** (We have left out information about these principles and their conditions because we are not aiming at a detailed investigation of them in this place, and if we have no need to state this in the future, we will not do so.)

[Humors, colors, tastes]

22 But as for the four composite humors, they are yellow bile, blood, phlegm, and black bile. **23** And all of the ancients agreed that each one of these four humors has a nature, special property, color, and taste. **24** As for their colors, they are perceived by vision; their tastes are perceived by the sense of taste. **25** As for their natures (which are hotness, coldness, wetness, and dryness), they claimed that they are perceived by the color, taste, or touch. **26** And as for the special properties of things, they are perceived by their actions which appear at the time when one thing gets close to another, or one of them touches another.

27 So as for yellow bile, its color is the color of fire, its taste bitterness, its nature hotness and dryness, its special property is hotness, and its activity is burning; and this matches the nature of fire and its special property. 28 As for blood, its color is redness, its taste is sweet, its nature hotness and wetness, its special property wetness, and its activity is that it causes things to sprout and brings them forth; and this matches the nature of air and its special property. 29 As for phlegm, its color is the white, its taste the salty, its nature coldness and wetness, its special property coldness, and its activity is that it nourishes things; and this matches the nature of water and its special property. 30 As for black bile, its color is dust-colored and dullness, its taste is the sour, its nature is coldness and dryness, its special property is dryness, and its activity is binding[9] things; and this matches the nature of earth and its special property.

[Planets, colors, and temperaments]

31 So this is what they stated about the natures of the principles and the humors. 32 But then they made a comparison about these things with a false analogy, in which they went astray. 33 And that is because they said all of the *planets* are receptive of colors: so when we want to know their natures, we understand that from their colors, since they are simple bodies not having tastes (because tastes belong to every body composed of the principles). 34 So since one does not need the sense of taste for knowing their natures, and they are far from us (so that we are not able to get information about their natures by touch), then indeed their natures are perceived to be the heating, cooling, moistening, or drying, in accordance with their taking on colors (based on their preceding statement that the natures of things are perceived by means of color).

35 And they said that some things are perceived by means of others, and we seek information about what is absent from us and far away by means of what we witness and what is near to us: and these humors and principles are near to us, while the planets are far from us. 36 So, we get information about the natures of the planets from the nature of the principles, humors, and colors, because these humors and the rest of the beings which are produced

---

[9] إمساك. Or, "restraining." Medically, this word also means "constipation."

from the principles, with their colors and the rest of their qualities, come to be from the powers of the planets in accordance with *their* natures and colors. **37** Thus one should seek information about their natures by means of the correspondence of their color with the color of these humors and principles. **38** So when we see the color of one of the planets matching the color of one of the four humors, we know that the nature of that planet corresponds to the nature of that humor, and to the nature of the principle corresponding to it by nature and special property. **39** And if the color of a planet was contrary to the color of the four humors, we blend its color and make its nature be in accordance with what resembles its color upon that blending.

40 They said: since the color of black bile is dust-colored and dullness, and its nature is the nature of earth (cooling, drying), and the color of Saturn is dust-colored and dullness, we know that he corresponds to them both[10] in the nature of the cold and the dry, and their special property and activity.

41 And they said that since we see the color of yellow bile resembling the color of redness and fire, and the nature of those two is heating [and] drying, and the color of Mars resembles its color, we know that he corresponds to them both[11] in the nature of hotness and the dry, and in their special property and activity.

42 As for the Sun, they said that his nature is hotness and the dry, and that is in two ways: one of them is because his color resembles the color of embers burning strongly, so we judge that his nature is hotness and the dry, just as we judged it for Mars. **43** And the second one is because the hotness is apparent from his activity, due to his warming of bodies, and his drying out the wetness which is in them.

44 As for Venus, they said that since we see color as being between whiteness and yellowness, and this color stands in contrast to the colors of these composite natures, we mix her color and attribute her nature to what resembles her color at the mixing. **45** So due to the yellowness which is in her, and its resemblance to the color of yellow bile, we attribute it to hotness; and due to the whiteness which is in her, and its resemblance to the color of phlegm, we attribute it to wetness. **46** And since the whiteness and yellowness is balanced in her, we attribute her nature to temperate hotness and

---

[10] That is, to black bile and earth.
[11] That is, to yellow bile and fire.

wetness: and this corresponds to the nature of blood and air, and to their special properties and activities.

47 As for Jupiter, they said that since we see his color resembling whiteness altering to a little yellowness, we mix it just like we mix the nature of Venus: and we said that the nature of Jupiter is temperate wetness and hotness, and this corresponds to the nature of blood and air, and to their special properties and activities.

48 As for the Moon, they said that since we see her color resembling whiteness, and we see a little dullness in her, we attribute her nature to wetness due to the whiteness which is in her, and to coldness due to the dullness which is in her. **49** So we say that the nature of the Moon is wetness and coldness, and this corresponds to the nature of phlegm and water.

50 As for Mercury, they said since we see him to be receptive of colors (because sometimes we see him green, sometimes dusty, and sometimes he is different from both of these colors), and all of this is at different periods of time, even when he is at a single elevation from the horizon, we say that Mercury has a variable nature due to his receptivity to different colors, except that have found him in these colors [inclining] towards the dust-colored (which is the color of earth), more closely [than] to the rest of the colors. **51** So we say that the nature of Mercury [inclines] to the nature of earth (which is the dry), more closely [than] to the rest of the natures.

[Fortunes and infortunes, and the blended]

52 Now, when the generality of the masters in the profession of the stars assigned the natures of the planets according to this condition of the colors, they looked at the nature of each planet. **53** And when they saw its nature to be hotness and wetness, or coldness and wetness, they said that this is the nature of generation, growth, and life: so they called it a fortune. **54** And they looked at every planet whose nature was hotness and dryness, or coldness and dryness, and said this is the nature of corruption and death: and they called it an infortune. **55** And every planet of a varied nature, they called a fortune with the fortunes, and an infortune with the infortunes.

56 So, since the nature of Saturn (according to what they claimed) was cooling [and] drying, and the nature of Mars heating [and] drying, they made them into infortunes. **57** And since the nature of Venus and Jupiter were hotness and wetness, while the nature of the Moon is coldness and wetness, the called them fortunes. **58** And as for Mercury, since he is of a varied nature, they made him be a fortune with the fortunes, and an infortune with the infortunes. **59** But as for the Sun, they found his nature to correspond to the nature of Mars in hotness and the dry, except that they found him to be a planet of the day—and the nature of the day is good fortune. **60** So, they made him be an infortune at some times, and a fortune at other times.

61 And this is what the generality of the masters of the profession of the stars claimed about the natures of the planets and their explanations, and the fortunes among them, the infortunes, and the blended.

Chapter IV.3: On our response to one claiming that the natures of the planets, and their fortunes and infortunes, are known from their colors

1 In the chapter before this one we stated what the generality of the masters of the stars claimed about the nature of the planets, and their fortunes and infortunes, and what is blended of them: and indeed, that they knew that from the colors of the planets when they compared them to the colors of the four humors and principles. **2** But we will respond to their statement[12] with four arguments.

3 The first of them is [1] that we say: The color of Saturn is different from the color of black bile as well as the color of earth, because Saturn is lead-colored, and this is different from the two colors which you compared the color of Saturn to. **4** As for Jupiter, if there is yellowness in his color, then his color should not be related to whiteness, because when the color of whiteness is mixed with one of the [other] colors, it is altered from the definition of whiteness to that color which it associates with. **5** As for Venus in particular, blueness is apparent in her color, so you should not relate her color to whiteness. **6** As for Mars, even if his nature comes to be heating due to his color's resemblance to fire, we already know that the Sun is more intense in hotness than Mars is: so the color of the Sun ought to be more intensely red than the color of Mars—but we do not see it as being like that. **7** As for Mercury, even if we did see him to be of varied color, that is not because he is

---

[12] Or more literally, "we will throw their statement back on them" (فرَددنا ذلك عليهم (قولهم).

varied in *nature*: and that is because when we look at him he is close to the horizon, so at the time of our viewing him there are various vapors arranged between us and him. **8** As for the Moon, her color should not be related to whiteness unless one lacks visual perception!

9 As for the second argument, we say that [2] one ought compare something by analogy to what is of its own category, and not to a different category: because terrestrial bodies are composed of the four principles, while the bodies of the planets are not composed of them but rather are simple bodies. **10** So one ought not to make an analogy of one to the other, nor make the nature of the upper bodies be like the nature of earthly bodies (in terms of hotness, coldness, wetness and dryness), due to an agreement in color.

11 The third argument is that [3] we say: We do not perceive the *nature* of one of the bodies which are below the sphere of the Moon, nor the bodies of the planets, by its color; we come to that by an analogy with existing things which are below the sphere of the Moon. **12** And we say: We already see bodies matching one another through color, like two bodies whose colors are whiteness, or blackness, or redness, or the rest of the colors. **13** But we see some of them contrasting with others through nature and special property: and that is that we see the color of both snow and lime as whiteness, but the nature of snow is cooling, while the nature of lime is heating; and we see both aloe flowers and pomegranate blossoms to be red, but the nature of the pomegranate blossoms is cooling, while the nature of aloe flowers is heating. **14** And many things are found to be like what we have stated; and just as the natures of these things differ from each other, so likewise do their special properties differ. **15** And if things were perceived by means of their colors, and then we saw two bodies having a single color, their natures ought not to differ—nor their special properties. **16** So in this way it is shown to be false that the nature of any existing things which are under the sphere of the Moon (or their special properties), or the natures of the planets and their special properties, should be perceived by means of their colors.

17 The fourth argument is that [4] we say: Why do you claim that Saturn and Mars are infortunes, and that (as you claim) by their nature they correspond to the nature of two of the four principles (and they are fire and earth), and to the nature of two of the four humors (and they are yellow bile and black bile), when generation, life, and growth comes to be through these two principles and humors, and everything around you which is of the nature of generation and life, is a fortune? **18** Why then do you claim that

Saturn and Mars are infortunes? **19** So, we reject what they state as being the explanation for the misfortune of Saturn and Mars.

20 And we will state the reason for the fortunes and infortunes, and their natures, if God wills.

Chapter IV.4: On our establishing the existence of the fortunes and infortunes, according to the teachings of philosophy

Fortune-infortune in astrology: how related to physics		
General statements		1-3, 18, 25
[1]-[2] Planetary systems in themselves		
[1] Nature of planet	Pertains to planet in its own system	4-6, 9
[2] Special property of planet	Difference between planets' systems	7-8
[3] What is stimulated in the world by [1]-[2]		
[3a] Particularization of species in genus	Planets' relation to us	10-18, 25
[3b] Particularization of individuals in a species[13]		
[3c] Generation and corruption of individuals		
[4] What astrology studies, to make judgments about [3b]-[3c][14]		
[4a] Motion of planet in its system (see [1])	Differences between individuals	18-25
[4b] Planets' differing motions (see [2])		
[4c] Elements' receptivity to being acted upon		

Figure 23: Reading guide to astrological theory in IV.4

---

[13] Category [3b] has to do with producing a unit or individual of a species.

[14] Category [4] is about how the individuals or units produced by the planets differ from one another.

1 The ancient sages used to judge good fortune and misfortune for all natural existents[15] which are below the sphere of the Moon, and they named them by that. **2** So as for what pertains to them in terms of agreement,[16] generation, moderation,[17] inclination, similarity, the blending of the principles and their composition in natural individuals,[18] and the endurance of individuals, and their safety and fineness, their power; and humanity, understanding, discrimination, knowledge; and the benefits of assets, rank, and might; and the good, delight, comfort, pleasure, and the rest of what belongs to this category, they used to call it "good fortune." **3** And as for what there was of corruption in formation and composition, excess, destruction, ugliness, weakness, illnesses, chronic diseases, poverty, inferiority, baseness, distresses,[19] bestiality,[20] fatigue, toil, and everything of this category, they used to call it "bad fortune."[21]

4 And in what preceded we have already stated the manner of the planets' activity (through their motions) in this terrestrial world, which is connected to them by nature.[22] **5** So now I say that we find each of the seven planets having different motions in itself, and that is due to the abundance of their spheres and the difference in the conditions of those spheres.

6 Now, [1] every planet's motion in its own right is a natural, regular motion, its motion not increasing at one time beyond its motion at another time, except that even though the motion of each one of them in itself is a regular motion, [1a] its motion on the epicycle,[23] and [1b] the motion of the epicycle on its eccentric sphere,[24] and [1c] the motion of the eccentric

---

[15] Lit., "all natural things which are found."
[16] الاتّفاق. See IV.6, **1**.
[17] Or, "temperateness" (الاعتدال).
[18] See **16** below.
[19] الغموم. This also connotes sorrows.
[20] البهيمية. That is, being like a beast in behavior and emotions.
[21] See the more astrological treatment of this in IV.6, especially **1-11**.
[22] See for example, I.5, **3-11**, and III.2, **34-35**. Abū Ma'shar will say a little more about this in **5-6, 9**, and **13** below: the planetary nature is simply to move within their own circles, but that produces a effect on us through their *relation to* us (**10-12**), since our world is connected to them by nature.
[23] Lit., "the sphere of rotation" (فلك التدوير).
[24] Lit., "the sphere departing the center" (فلك خارج المركز).

sphere in the sphere of the signs, [all] contrast with [2] the motion of others among the seven planets. **7** And they contrast with each other in [2a] the greatness and smallness of their bodies, and [2b] the difference of their colors, and [2c] the distance of their spheres from each other, and [2d] their nearness or farness from us.

8 So due to the contrast between the conditions of one and the others, we know that each planet has a [1] nature and [2] special property, which is contrary to the nature and special property of others among the planets. **9** Now as for [1] the natures of the planets, the philosophers stated that they are spherical, simple bodies, with a natural motion circling around them.[25] **10** As for [2] the special property of each of them, [they said] they understood it by means of [3] what is stimulated by the strengths of their motions, in [3a] the particularization of the different species among genera,[26] and in [3b] the natural composition of individual beings which [4] contrast with each other, and [3c] their generation and corruption.[27] **11** So they named some of these effects "good fortune," and some of them "misfortune," in the manner of our statement about that above.[28]

12 Therefore, the good fortune and misfortune which exist among us are due to the [2] special property of the planet's motions, not due to [1] their nature: because by their nature none of them is a fortune nor an infortune.[29] **13** They are designated as good fortune and misfortune by means of [3] what *manifests from* the [2] special property of the motion of each of them, within these four principles [which are] connected to them by nature. **14** Due to that, the sages said that what is *natured* is not what *natures*,[30] and we

---

[25] مستديرتها. By "them," I take him to mean that they circle around, or rotate around their *spheres*. Actually I would have expected him to say "circling around *us*" (مستديرتنا).

[26] This refers to special properties among all terrestrial classes of things (not necessarily animal species), such as certain metals within larger categories of metals.

[27] Abū Ma'shar mentions this generation and corruption again in IV.5, 3.

[28] See **1-3**.

[29] That is, by their natures they simply move in their circles (**9**).

[30] Reading الطّبائع with Lemay and **P**, which is evidently also how John understood his MS. **BY** follows other MSS by reading "natures" (الطبائع), but this does away with the active-passive distinction Abū Ma'shar is trying to draw. These terms became

seek information about what nat*ures* by means of the natur*ed*; and the individuals of the species of animals, plants, and minerals are in the [four] natures[31] [only] potentially, when they are not [actually being] natured.

15 And [3a] the particularization of the different species among the genera, and [3b] the composition of the four natures in the individuals of the species, is by means of the strengths of the motions of the planets, by the permission of God. **16** So since their motions potentially indicate [3a] the particularization of species among genera, and the agreement of the natures, and [3b] their composition in natural individual beings, they cause good and bad fortune, because humanity and bestiality are both equally in the genus and the natures by potential, neither of them having superiority over the other in that, nor is there a distinction between them in it.[32] **17** But they assume a nature[33] and are [materially] composed, and are divided between their forms and their individuality[34] by the powers of [the planets'] movements, so that humanity inclines to comfort, pleasure, understanding, thought, and the knowledge of things which are and will be, while bestiality inclines to fatigue, suffering, roughness, and slaughter.

18 So for this reason they cause good and bad fortune; and due to [the fact] that [3b] the particularizing of the individuals of different species comes from their powers, by means of the variation in their conditions, so it exists in [4] the contrast between each individual among the individual ani-

---

common in medieval Latin philosophy, and were rendered as *naturans* ("naturing," active) and *naturata* ("natured," passive).

[31] Here I believe Abū Ma'shar means "terrestrial, elemental natures." That is, combinations of elements on earth (i.e., the four natures or elemental qualities) do not form real individuals such as humans or ferns unless they have actually been *natured* by something doing the *naturing*. Until then, humans and ferns only exist potentially. This is standard Aristotelian-type thinking.

[32] For example, we are all capable of acting in contrary ways (such as humanely or in a beastly way), but that only exists as a potential. (In a similar way, "animal" is equally potentially a human or beast.) Once we do act, we cannot exhibit both contrary behaviors in the same way. So, while good and bad fortune potentially exist in everything, they become actually good or actually bad (and not both equally), once they are natured or are actively influenced to become one way or another.

[33] That is, they *become natured* (تطبّعت).

[34] Refer back to the discussion in Ch. I.4, especially **54-74**.

mals, plants, and minerals, in terms of fineness or ugliness, or strength or weakness, or excellence or badness, or the sweet-smelling or the stinking, which is harmful to an animal or beneficial to it—and the rest of the various conditions which bring good or bad fortune.

19 As for [4] the contrast between the qualities of some terrestrial individuals and others, that comes to be by one of three things. **20** The first of them is by [4a] what is found among *us*, in terms of the contrast between the planet's motion and condition in itself at one of the times, and its own motion and condition at another time. **21** The second is by [4b] the contrast between the motion of the planet and its condition at every time, and the motion of *another* planet and *its* condition. **22** The third is in terms of [4c] the receptivity of the four principles being stimulated by them at that time: because things are stimulated by the motion of the planets within these four principles, in accordance with [the planet's] condition and motion at that time, and in accordance with the receptivity of those things being acted upon by it. **23** So at a time when those things which are acted upon[35] do take on[36] a complete and congruent[37] motion and condition from the planet, that planet at that time is called a "fortune," and these things acted upon by its motion and condition are called "fortunate." **24** And at a time when these things take on from it what is contrary to completeness and agreement, the planet is called an "infortune," and those things "unfortunate."

25 So it is clear and apparent to us that among the planets of the sphere there are fortunes as well as infortunes, and that the good fortune and bad fortune from them is what comes to be in [3a] the particularization of the different species among a single genus, and from those is what comes to be in [3b] the composition of each of the individuals of a single species. **26** And what is in it of [4] the qualities which contrast with others (such as it exists in the superiority of some individuals over others), is by means of some of

---

[35] Or, "which are stimulated by" (تنفعل).

[36] Or, "receive" (يقبل): this refers to the principle of receptivity in **22**.

[37] المتّفقة. This is the same as "agreement" in **1** and **24**. By this Abū Maʿshar seems to mean that the influence harmonizes with the nature of the thing (thus promoting its own natural type, growth, and change), as opposed to clashing with it.

the special properties and conditions which pertain to *that* individual and are not in other individuals of that species.[38]

Chapter IV.5 On knowing which of the planets is a fortune, and which of them an infortune

1 In the chapter which was before this we already stated that in the sphere there are fortunes and infortunes: [now] we want to make clear which of them are fortunes, and which of them infortunes.

2 So I say that the composition of individuals comes to be through the moderation of natures, and the moderation of natures comes to be through the moderation of the time,[39] and the moderation of the time comes to be by the thing acted upon ([and] in which the moderation exists) by the strength of the motions of any of the planets. **3** For in terms of what comes from the planets, whatever it is by which we seek information about the moderation of the time, coming-into-being, and life in this world, is a fortune; and whatever it is from them by which we seek information about the excess of the time (by the hot or the cold), and corruption, destruction, and what is like that, is an infortune. **4** And in this way the ancients understood which of the planets is a fortune, which of them an infortune, and which of them blended, and which of them is heating, cooling, moistening, and drying, and which of them male and female, and which nocturnal and diurnal, and the rest of what is ascribed to them.[40] **5** And they called the planets that due to what they found in terms of the strengths of their motions in this world in the conditions of the times (as to [their] moderation and fitness, or excess and corruption)—not because in themselves they are heating, cooling, moisten-

---

[38] See also IV.5, **66ff**, and my footnote to sentences **67** and **73** there.

[39] الزمان. This word can also refer to a "season," which Abū Ma'shar will use below. But I keep it general in this paragraph, because in predictive techniques the conditions and general natures of the planets are used to describe those periods of time as well.

[40] Gender is discussed in IV.8, and sect in IV.9. According to Abū Ma'shar then, all of the elemental, gender, and sect differences are attributed to them based on the effects caused by their varied motions and natures.

ing, or drying, or diurnal or nocturnal, or anything of those things which are found below the sphere of the Moon.

[1: Planets' good and bad effects on weather]

6 As for [1] what manifests from their activities in the seasons in countries, it is of two types: one of them is [1a] what is what the planet does by itself,[41] and the second is [1b] how the Sun partners with it in its action.

7 In terms of [1a] the way that the planet [acts] by itself, it is like Saturn when he governs the indication of the year[42] without Mars or any other planet looking at him: for the cold of winter becomes excessive among the Turks and in the generality of the cold, northern cities, ruining what is in them of animals and vegetation (and [that is] more confirmed in the cold and the dry for the people of this region when he is rising up from the middle of the circle of his apogee).[43] **8** As for the countries excessive in the hot, in a year in which Saturn governs the indication for them, it decreases the hotness of their air, and cools and moistens, and individual animals and plants become strong, and it moderates their mixture (and [that is] more confirmed for the goodness of their air and its temperateness, if Saturn was declining).[44]

9 Now as for Mars, when he governs the year without Saturn or any other planet looking at him, in the season of winter it diminishes the cold in the cold, northern countries, and warms their air with an increase of the hot, and moderates the mixture of animals and plants in it (and of course it does some of that if Mars alone was in the northern signs in the season of winter). **10** But as for the southern countries, in the season of summer in that year the heat would be excessive so that it would corrupt the mixture of animals and plants, and cause destruction from the harshness of the heat (and of course their air would be altered by the heat if Mars was in the southern signs in the season of summer).

11 And because we have stated in what preceded that the shifting of the season comes to be by means of the Sun's shifting in the quarters of the cir-

---

[41] Or, is "unique" (ينفرد).
[42] That is, in a mundane chart.
[43] See IV.7 for more on this.
[44] هابط. That is, in the circle of his apogee.

cle, and that the seasons of one year differ from the seasons of another year by means of the partnership of the planets with the Sun,[45] when therefore [1b] Saturn is in one of the combinations relative to him in the winter without Mars or any other planets looking at them, it increases in the cold of winter as well as its length.[46] **12** And sometimes gales of northern winds of excessive cold will multiply, and there will be a corruption of animals and vegetation in it, and especially in the northern regions; and it is more confirmed for that if Saturn was rising.[47] **13** But if he was like that relative to the Sun in the summer, the heat of the air would decrease and it would increase in its cold, and the summer would be short; and especially if Saturn was declining [in the apogee].

14 As for Mars, if he was in one of the combinations relative to the Sun in the season of summer, without Saturn or any others looking at them, the summer would be excessive in heat, long, corrupting, and especially in the regions which are between the tropic[48] of Aries up to Cancer (and it is more confirmed for that if Mars was rising up). **15** Now if Mars was like that relative to the Sun in the season of winter, without the planets' looking at them, that winter will be warm, short, and gales of southern winds will be abundant.

16 As for Jupiter, if he mixed with the Sun in one of the seasons of the year, and none of the planets looks at them, the air of that season will be tempered by heat and wetness causing growth and generation, and gales of northern, temperate winds will multiply, strengthening for animals and vegetation. **17** And his action in the year will be likewise when he governs over it.

18 As for Venus, if she mixed with the Sun in one of the seasons of the year, and no planet is looking at them, then if that was in the winter and spring, she will balance them both out; but if it was in the summer and au-

---

[45] See I.2, **16** and **30-31**.

[46] The idea seems to be that the Sun is already causing the cold of winter, so adding Saturn to him will not moderate the *Sun*, but add more cold to the *winter* which is caused by the Sun. Likewise in **14-15**, the Sun causes the hotness of summer, so adding Mars will make the summer hotter, or moderate the coldness of the winter which is caused by the Sun.

[47] Again, in the circle of his apogee.

[48] مدار.

tumn, she will reduce their dryness. **19** And her action in the year will be likewise if she was the governor over it.

20 As for Mercury, if he mixed with the Sun in one of the seasons of the year, and no planet is looking at them, then the air of that season will have much variation, and changes by winds and part of the dry which is of the genus of wind—except that it will not reduce the nature of moderation of that season. **21** And his activity in the year will be likewise if he was the governor over it.

22 As for the Moon, in the first quarter of the [lunar] month she is heating [and] moistening, in the second quarter she is heating [and] drying, in the third quarter she is cooling [and] drying, and in the fourth quarter she is cooling [and] moistening. **23** And by her course through all of the signs in a single [lunar] month, she sets into motion the character of the seasons of the solar year, and mixes one with the other, and strengthens them, and moderates the natures so that animals and plants survive. **24** So if she was the governor over the year, or mixed with the Sun in one of the seasons, the condition of the quarters of the year (in terms of hotness and wetness, hotness and dryness, coldness and dryness, and coldness and wetness), will be as we stated about her condition in the quarters of a single month.

25 And people have said, "From the beginning of the month to the opposition, the Moon's nature is warmth and wetness, and from after the fullness to the end of the month her nature is coldness and wetness." **26** And they also said if the Moon governed over the year, then the first half of the year would be hot [and] wet, and the second half would be cooling and wet. **27** But the first statement is more correct, because the Moon's indication for altering the quarters of the months and the years is found when she is the governor over one of them or mixes with the Sun.

[2: Which planets are fortunes and infortunes, based on the elements]

28 Now [2] as for Saturn and Mars, since excessive cold and excessive heat is found from their activities in the seasons when they govern over them, and whenever these two principles are more excessive the destruction of animals comes to be (along with their excessiveness), for this reason they made them both infortunes: for even if temperateness is produced in one of the places by the activity of their cold or heat, that temperateness is not truly due to the special property of their action. **29** As for Saturn, he is harsher in unfortunateness than Mars is, because cooling and drying, and the cold and the dry, are antithetical to life. **30** And even though Mars is excessive in hotness and dryness, his harm is below the harm of Saturn because the support for living things is by means of hotness and wetness. **31** Saturn, therefore, is more unfortunate than Mars.

Fortunes	Infortunes
☉	♄
☽	♂
♃	
♀	
☿	

Figure 24: Fortunes and infortunes (IV.5)

32 As for the Sun, his special property is the action of the seasons, [elemental] compositions, and the indication of life generally, which is the genus:[49] so they made him a fortune for these three reasons.

33 As for the Moon, since she circles around all of the signs in a single [lunar] month, and sets into motion the four seasons of the year, and moderates the natures and strengthens them, and does in them what the Sun does in a single year, they made her a fortune. **34** But the Sun is stronger and more manifest in good fortune than the Moon and the rest of the planets of the circle, for reasons which we stated before.[50]

35 As for Jupiter, the special property of his activity in the seasons is tempering, and gales of northern winds which are moderating for the natures, while as for Venus the special property her activity in the seasons is tempering and moistening. **36** So, they made them both be fortunes.

37 As for Mercury, because the special property of his activity in the seasons is that he alters them with a small alteration towards winds and the dry, and he does not shift it away from the nature of temperateness, they make him be a fortune—except that due to the great variety of his condition in retrogradation and stationing, and quickness of motion, then even though [a] his activity in the seasons is to change them to winds and a little dryness, and [b] winds are quick in motion and change from condition to condition, and [c] the dry (a passive principle) takes on the variety of changes from the two active principles (just as we stated in Book II),[51] they made him be mixed with what he associates with (of the signs and planets), changing to

---

[49] That is, for living things. See I.4, **59**.
[50] Probably in **33** immediately above. Abū Ma'shar repeats this point in IV.6, **28**.
[51] See II.4, **17-24**.

their nature, shifting to *them*, receiving [and] strengthening *them*. **38** And they said: Mercury is a fortune with the fortunes and an infortune with the infortunes, male with the male ones and female with the female ones, and diurnal with the diurnal ones and nocturnal with the nocturnal ones; and in every sign and with every planet he is like the nature of that sign and planet, and carries out its activity. **39** So if Mercury was alone in the signs, and none of the planets looks at him, then his special property will appear and he will become a fortune—except that he will already have taken on the nature of the sign he is in (in terms of hotness, coldness, dryness, and wetness).

40 Now if we wanted to know the more fortunate of these three,[52] and the most powerful, we would find Venus and Mercury to be lowest. **41** The greatest distance which Venus may have from the Sun is 47° and [some] minutes, and the distance of Mercury 27° and [some] minutes. **42** And we find Mercury to be the most frequent of them in burning.[53] **43** But we find Jupiter to be high up, being distant from the Sun by 180°. **44** So we find Jupiter having two powerful special properties which Venus and Mercury do not have: as for the first, he is higher up; the second is that he distances himself from the Sun by 180°. **45** So since we find him having these two superior [qualities], we know that he is the most fortunate of the three. **46** But as for Venus, she is above Mercury, and her distance from the Sun is greater than his, and she has less burning and retrogradation than he does: so Venus comes after Jupiter in good fortune, and before Mercury.

47 So in this way we know which planet among them is a fortune, and which an infortune, and which blended: indeed, the Sun is the most fortunate of the planets, then after him the Moon, then Jupiter, then Venus, then Mercury; and Saturn is more unfortunate than Mars. **48** And each one of them has a special property in the indication of good fortune and misfortune, which does not belong to the other planets.

[3: That fortunes and infortunes take on each other's characters]

49 Many of ancients claimed that [3] they understood the fortunes and infortunes by experience, and this fortunateness and unfortunateness which

---

[52] That is: Jupiter, Venus, and Mercury.
[53] We should add "retrogradation," since Abū Ma'shar mentions that in **46**.

belongs to the planets varies: because even though Saturn and Mars are both infortunes due to their activity of excessive heat and excessive cold in some places, in other places temperateness is produced from their activity, so that they come to be in the *character* of fortunes for people whose air is temperate.[54]

50 And the fortunes, even though they effect temperateness in the seasons of the year (so that they become fortunes because of that), sometimes they come to have different conditions so that they come to be in the *character* of infortunes through those conditions of theirs: for at one time a planet will move and shift from position to position by means of its motion, and it will culminate over[55] one of the places, and rise up in one of its spheres, and decline in another, and its conditions will vary greatly [and] naturally, in the manner we stated and will state.

51 So for the fortunes as well as the infortunes, sometimes [a] each one of them will effect at a single time actions which vary in good fortune and bad fortune, due to the variation of their natural conditions which they have at one time, and sometimes [b] the fortunes perform the function of infortunes, and the infortunes perform the functions of fortunes in individuals by means of their shifting from one condition to the contrary of that condition.[56]

52 And what manifests from their activities (in terms of good fortune and bad fortune), is from the *special property* of the planet's indication, not from its *nature*.[57] **53** For if a planet had produced good or bad fortune through its nature, the indication of the Sun over things would be the same as the indication of Mars (and that is because according to the natures *attributed* to them, they are heating and drying), and a planetary fortune would always be a fortune, and an infortune always an infortune, and a fortune would not be

---

[54] See also the example of Saturn in **8** above.
[55] يسامتْ. Or, "face over against," in the sense of being at the summit of some circle.
[56] See also **56** and **64**. That is, they vary with their own category, and also can take on the stamp or character of the opposite one.
[57] Recall from IV.4, **6-8** that each planet's nature is simply to move in its circle; but each has its own special property based on the differences between the planetary systems. These special properties and differences are what influence the material world and generate conventionally good and bad things.

turned to bad fortune, nor an infortune to good fortune. **54** But it is not like that, because the Sun is a fortune and Mars an infortune; and a fortune is indeed turned to bad fortune, and an infortune is indeed turned to good fortune. **55** So the planets do not effect fortunateness and unfortunateness by their nature, but they do effect it through their special property. **56** Because of that, sometimes a planetary fortune comes to perform the function of the infortunes, and an infortune sometimes performs the function of a fortune; and sometimes a single planet at a single time, will perform different functions of good and bad fortune.

57 An analogy of that is that fire by its *nature* is heating [and] drying, but its *special property* is burning: so when it begins to manifest its special property, along with its manifesting that special property it produces many actions different from the burning.[58] **58** If it had effected the burning through its nature, *everything* heating [and] drying would burn—but many activities [like that] do not have [burning], and we find the contrary of that: because at [any] one time fire moistens, melts, warms, dissolves, gathers together, binds, and separates, although moistening, gathering, and binding are different from[59] burning. **59** And sometimes fire does do them at one time in different individuals, in accordance with those individuals' receptivity to its action, and their nearness to or distance from it.[60] **60** And sometimes it does that in a single individual, time after time.

61 And snow is likewise, for its true special property is to chill, but sometimes warming manifests from its activity: because if snow fell upon one of an animal's limbs, it would chill it and hinder the skin so that the hotness would go out from it to the outside of the body, condensing[61] the hotness in

---

[58] That is, burning is just a special property, not its only one. It will have other effects on things, depending on what *those* things are. It may just warm up a cold thing, and not burn it. See **58-59**.

[59] Or, "contrary to" (خلاف).

[60] For example, the same Sun can, at the same time, burn a California forest and give someone a nice tan, because the forest and the body are susceptible in different ways.

[61] Or, "concentrating." But cold condenses, so this seems the more appropriate way to put it.

that limb and warming it.⁶² **62** So two mutually antithetical things manifest from the activity of snow, and they are chilling and warming together at the same time: one of them [directly] from its true special property, and the second from the activity of that special property. **63** And examples of these special properties are found to belong to many bodies.

64 Now fortunateness and unfortunateness are like that, for they are [directly] due to the special property of a planet's activity, not from its nature. **65** So because of that, a single planet will come to do different things by its special property at a single time, with respect to being fortunate and being unfortunate, and sometimes it will do that in time after time.

[4: Which special properties are used in astrology]

66 Now these special properties which belong to the planets in good and bad fortune, are of two types. **67** One of them is [4a] the true special property, which does not alter the indication of the planets due to what they indicate through their different conditions, nor do astrologers use this special property: and it is that the fortunes do what is fortunate, and the infortunes do what is unfortunate, in the particularization of species from genera, and the particularization of individuals from the species, and the manner of their composition.⁶³ **68** So those activities, and the good and bad fortune which belongs to the planets in these things, never changes. **69** Because even if the different conditions of the planets (which belong to them at all times), are the cause of change from condition to condition in the mixture of sperm, planets, and minerals, there is no conversion of the species to

---

⁶² This certainly seems like a strange way to put it, since if we go outside in winter without a hat, our head does not *feel* warm. But Abū Ma'shar's point is that if heat escapes through the head, then the warmth must be concentrating there while taking it away from other parts of the body.

⁶³ This refers back to Ch. IV.4, **10-17**, items [3a], [3b], and [3c]. So for example, (**67-68**) Saturn will always generate Saturnian classes of things, and produce individuals with Saturnian features, in his typical Saturnian way, and those things are generically "unfortunate" even if they are necessary for the production of an animal or plant. But (**69-71**) Saturn's change in condition from eastern to western, or in his exaltation or fall, will not produce *non*-Saturnian things or convert an animal into a different species: it will only produce alterations and changes *within* that same thing.

something else within the powers of those differences—so that by them it [would] convert from the sperm of a man to something else, or the sperm of a horse to something else (and likewise the rest of the animals). **70** Nor do plants change over from species to species by means of the different conditions of the planets. **71** However, their conditions in themselves do change to a suitability of creating, mixing, and combining, or to their corruption, or to strength or weakness, or to the rest of the qualities.

72 And the other special property is [4b] the varying fixed one [which is] used in the art of the judgment of the stars. **73** And this is the one which a planet indicates in terms of good or bad fortune through the variation in its conditions, [in relation to] the varying qualities which belong to single individuals: such as generation or corruption, stinginess or generosity, tallness or shortness, fatness or skinniness, whiteness or blackness, wealth or poverty, and rank, authority, and might.[64] **74** For a planetary fortune does indicate misfortune in this area in some of the times, and a planetary infortune indicates good fortune in it in some of the times, in accordance with the varying conditions of the planets in the signs in which they are: such as easternization or westernization, and masculinization and feminization, and the rest of the various conditions which they have. **75** And these are the conditions which are the cause of their shifting over from good fortune to bad fortune, or from bad fortune to good fortune; but that indication which they have by that fixed condition, they have forever. **76** And an example of that is that [4a] Saturn's special property is unfortunateness, except that if by day he was above the earth, easternizing, of a suitable condition in himself and in his place within his sign, then he would be turned to the character of the fortunes, and indicate good fortune. **77** And when he is in this condition which we stated by day, then the indication of good fortune is fixed for him. **78** And the fortunes are like that when they are turned to the character of infortunes, for they indicate something of the detestable: so when they are in that condition which they have shifted to, then that special property of

---

[64] This refers back to Ch. IV.4, **18-24** and **26**. That is, the *variation in a planet's conditions* causes important *variations between individuals*, in the types of things which the planet causes. According to Ch. IV.4, this happens in three ways: (1) the planet's own variation at different times, (2) its being different from other planets, and (3) the receptivity of terrestrial things to its activity.

unfortunateness is fixed for them. **79** Thus, two special properties of the planet become fixed for it.⁶⁵

80 And thus the existence of special properties is limited to saying that when a thing exists, its special property exists along with it. **81** So if the planets exist through their natures, their special property in indicating both good fortune and misfortune always exists along with them. **82** And in everything we state in the future, when it is said that a planet indicates good fortune or bad fortune "by its nature," we mean by that what its *activity* indicates through its *special property*.

[5: Five categories of good and bad effects]

83 As for [5] the planets' actions in matters of good fortune and bad fortunes, it is of five types.

84 The first one is [5a] that good fortune and bad fortune are effected together by [the planets'] powers at a single time, in a single thing: such as their particularizing many different species from a single genus at a single time, and one of the species⁶⁶ is superior to others; or like their particularizing many individuals from a single species at a single time, and some of them are superior to others.

85 The second is [5b] that good fortune as well as bad fortune manifests for a single planet at a single time but in two different things, just as is found from the activity of Saturn if he governed the year: in one of the regions ex-

---

⁶⁵ Abū Ma'shar is not helping his explanation by this loose sense of the word "fixed." He seems to mean that a planet becomes an "accidental" or "incidental" fortune or infortune (or accidentally better or worse) due to its varying conditions: fair enough. But it's unclear whether it is "fixed" because those qualities are fixed in the thing which it produces (such as a natal Saturn permanently imprinting his qualities on a native), or because that *range of variation* is permanent for the planet itself. In the end, I suppose it amounts to the same thing.

⁶⁶ This is in the singular, which makes it seem like a portion of the single species is superior. But this does not really make sense, since only members of a single class can be superior to others. So I believe Abū Ma'shar means that some species among the *many* species of the same genera, are superior. An example of this might be that Mercury particularizes the human species from other species (I.4, **59**), which is superior to those other species.

cessive, destructive cold, and in another region temperateness. **86** And he would do that in a single day and a single night, because if he was in one of the positions of the circle, he would belong to both a people in the place of their daytime, and to others in the place of their nighttime: so for the people who are in the place of daytime he would indicate something of good fortune, and for the people who are in the place of nighttime he would indicate something of bad fortune. **87** Thus at a single time he would indicate, for one of them, something of good or bad fortune contrary to what he would indicate for the other.

88 And the third is [5c] that good fortune and bad fortune are effected by the power of the planet at two different times, through two different conditions, such as manifests from the activity of the Sun and planets: because when they incline to one of the regions, or culminate over them at one of the times of the year, their activities are manifested in that place; but when they incline away from it or turn away from culminating over it, their activity withdraws from it and their activity will be in the other region which they do culminate over or are close to.

89 The fourth is [5d] that sometimes a planetary fortune performs the function of the infortunes through its special property, and an infortune sometimes performs the function of the fortunes through its special property; and that is in two ways. **90** One of them is as we stated about excessive heat being produced by them in the seasons in one place, and temperateness in another. **91** And the second is by the difference of their conditions in their own right,[67] or in their signs.[68]

92 The fifth is [5e] that the variation in the generation of things comes to be by the difference of their motions which are found among us; and because their motions are natural, so the things which are effected by the strengths of their motions are natural. **93** (But as for the good fortune and bad fortune which is produced in those things, they are from their special property.)

---

[67] في ذاتها.
[68] For these, see especially Chs. IV.6 – IV.9.

94 And in this way, each planet comes to have five characteristics.[69] **95** For [1] the number of the planets' special properties is apparent to us, and which of them is a fortune and which an infortune, and [2] which of them blended, and that [3] sometimes there manifests for the fortunes an activity like the infortunes, and sometimes there manifests for the infortunes an activity like the fortunes, and that [4] good fortune and bad fortune are from their special properties, and that [5] the things which are effected by the strengths of their motions in this world are natural.

Chapter IV.6: On the different conditions of the fortunes and infortunes, and the shifting of one of them over to the nature of the other

General criteria for judgment	Particular conditions of planet
[1] Moderation or [3] Excess	[a] Condition in itself: elemental mixture, Solar phase, sect, etc.
[2] Similarity or [4] Contrariety	[b] Dignity in signs
	[c] Angularity and places, rulership, aspects

Figure 25: Theory of accidental fortunes and infortunes (IV.6, 1-11)

1 In what has preceded we have already stated which of the planets is a fortune, and which of them an infortune, and which is blended,[70] and that good fortune is [1] moderation and [2] similarity, and misfortune is [3] excess and [4] contrariety,[71] and that they have varying conditions[72] in fortunateness and unfortunateness: because each one of them shifts from that indication to another one by means of the variation of their conditions which they have [a] in their own right, and [b] in their positions in the signs, and [c] due to the rotation of the

---

[69] خواص. I take this to refer to the five categories he has discussed in this chapter [1]-[5], and not just the five types of activity in the last category [5a-5e].
[70] See IV.5, **37-39** and **47**.
[71] See IV.4, **1-3**.
[72] Or perhaps, "situations" or "circumstances" (الحالات). See below.

sphere[73]—except that even though they may shift from condition to condition, the misfortune of some is [nevertheless] greater than their good fortune, and the good fortune of some is greater than their misfortune.

[*General comparisons and combinations*]

2 Now as for the [1] moderation of a planet, that exists through [a] its condition in itself: such as hotness and coldness, wetness and dryness, and easternization and westernization,[74] and the diurnal and nocturnal, and the rest of the conditions which it has in its own right.

3 And as for the [2] similarity indicative of generation, that exists through [b] its place in its sign in which it has a corresponding[75] share: such as house, exaltation, bound, triplicity, and the rest of the proper shares which planets have in the signs, of what we will mention in what lies ahead.

4 So if a planetary infortune was in a condition in which [1-a] its mixture was moderated, or [2-b] its place was similar to it, it is turned to good fortune; but if it was in the contrary of what we stated, it will manifest its unfortunate nature. **5** And as for a fortune, if it was in the [1-a] suitable conditions[76] or in the [2-b] positions similar to it in suitability, it will manifest its good fortune; while if it was in the contrary of that, it will come to be in the character of the infortunes.

6 And that is just like how we see that if Saturn (with his power in what is unfortunate) was the lord of the triplicity of the Ascendant in nativities, and he was [c] in a stake, in a [a] suitable condition and [b] place, it would indicate the native's upbringing and survival; while if he was in a bad condition and place, it would indicate that the native will not be brought up. **7** (And if he was the indicator of assets or real estate and was in a bad condition and

---

[73] That is, the houses or places (especially angularity, or being in a good/bad place, or ruling a good/bad place). Abū Ma'shar does imply this sometimes (such as in **6**), but for the most part he omits [c]. See also **26, 34,** and **39**.

[74] These are relations to the Sun and not intrinsic characteristics, but they are functions of the planet's own movement in its sphere.

[75] موافق, here and throughout. This might also be understood as a "matching" or "harmonious" share or dignity.

[76] That is, the sect, solar phase, and other conditions mentioned in **2**.

place, it would indicate the wasting of assets and the destruction of real estate, and something detestable because of them both.)

8 And likewise if Jupiter was the indicator of upbringing, and he is in a [a] suitable condition, in [b-c] an excellent place, then it indicates upbringing and survival; while if he was in a bad condition and place, it would indicate ruin and corruption.[77] **9** (And if he was the indicator of assets and he is in a suitable condition, it would indicate the benefits of assets; while if he was in a bad condition, it would indicate fines and loss.)

10 So a fortune and infortune each on its own will indicate life and survival (and the benefits of assets and real estate) by means of *some* of the conditions, while at another time they would indicate death, the wasting of money, a lower price, and loss. **11** But the indication of evil comes to them at one [particular] time just as they indicate good in another time, through the difference of their conditions.[78]

[Specific conditions for each planet which shift it between good and bad fortune]

12 Now let us state the conditions of both, by which [each] shifts from one condition to another. **13** And I say that [a] the nature of the day is moderate hotness, and the nature of the night is coldness and wetness;[79] and the nature of an easternizing planet is moderate hotness and wetness, and the nature of a westernizing planet is excessive coldness—except for the Moon alone, because her nature in easternization and westernization is to the contrary, just as we stated.[80]

14 So if it was Saturn (with his power in what is unfortunate, due to his effect of excessive cold in the seasons), moderation is found from [a] his activity in hot positions [on earth], so that for their people he is in the character of the fortunes. **15** But his moderation and good fortune is likewise [a]

---

[77] Note the subtle difference in indications: Saturn in a bad condition will not indicate upbringing at all (**6**), presumably because he is naturally an infortune anyway; Jupiter in a bad condition will indicate an upbringing but characterized by ruin and corruption (**8**), presumably because he is naturally a fortune.
[78] This refers back to IV.5, **88-91**.
[79] Or more probably, *moderate* coldness and wetness.
[80] See IV.5, **22-24**.

by day due to its heat, and in the diurnal, male signs, or if in himself he was easternizing, or if he was [b] in one of the signs similar to him (like the house, exaltation, bound, or one of his shares corresponding to him): for if it was like that, it indicates good fortune. **16** And his indication for an abundance of good fortune and its power will be in proportion to what is brought together for him from among these excellent conditions; while if something of these conditions was subtracted, it subtracts from his indication of good fortune. **17** But if he was in [a] a place of the night,[81] or westernizing, or in the nocturnal, female signs, or in [b] his own fall or his unhealthiness, or in [c] the positions which are bad for him, it will manifest his nature which is corruption and misfortune; and to the extent that these bad conditions were more numerous, his indication for misfortune will be stronger. **18** And this planet's indication for misfortune is greater and more powerful than it is for good fortune, and he is the most unfortunate planet of the sphere.[82]

19 As for Mars, he is an infortune by his nature due to his indication for excessive heating, except that moderation is prepared by [a] his activity in cold places: and that is because when Mars governs the cold places by indication,[84] their air warms up and the mixture of their people

Saturn	Mars
Moderation: Hot clime, weather Diurnal chart Diurnal sign Easternizing	*Moderation:* Cold clime, weather Nocturnal chart Nocturnal sign Westernizing
Similarity: Dignity	
Place: In good place Ruling good place	

Figure 26: Infortunes as accidental fortunes (IV.6, 14-22)[83]

---

[81] I think this means either that he is contrary to the sect (i.e., in a nocturnal chart), or he is below the horizon in a diurnal chart, so in a place where night exists.

[82] See IV.5, **29-31**.

[83] I use Abū Ma'shar's terminology for this chapter, but in other places like **19-21** and IV.9, **7** he changes it slightly (viewing westernization as a type of similarity, whereas here he calls it a form of moderation).

[84] That is, in a mundane chart such as an ingress or a New or Full Moon.

becomes moderated there. **20** But if Mars was in [a] a place of the night, or was westernizing, or was in the nocturnal, female signs, or in the wet, cold signs, or in [b] the positions similar to him (such as the house and exaltation), and [c] the excellent places, it indicates moderation and a fine mixture, and he comes to be in the character of the fortunes; and to the extent that these mixed conditions are abundant for him, his indication for good fortune will be stronger. **21** But when he is in [a] a place of the day, or in the male signs, or [b] in exile[85] and fall, it manifests his unfortunate nature; and the more abundant that these conditions contrary to his moderation and similarity are, his corruption and misfortune will be harsher. **22** And this planet's indication for misfortune is greater than it is for good fortune.

23 As for Jupiter, because his nature is moderate hotness indicating generation, he is a fortune; and likewise the day, for it is hotter and more moderate and more fortunate than the night, because the day belongs to motion and life, while the night belongs to stillness and tranquility. **24** By his moderate hotness, Jupiter is adapted to[86] a moderate, hot period, so that the day comes to be more harmonious and apparent for the effects of Jupiter than the night is: so [a] by day and in diurnal signs, and in easternization, and in [b] the signs in which he has proper[87] shares, he is more apparent for good fortune; and the more numerous that these testimonies are, the stronger and more apparent his indication for good fortune will be. **25** But as for if he was in [a] a position of the night, or in the feminine signs, or in [b] positions which do not correspond to him,[88] it will subtract from his good fortune; and sometimes it will grant corrupting, disappearing fortunes, and good fortunes because of which something detestable will affect him. **26** And if, along with these bad conditions it happened that [c] he had testimony in one of the houses of the circle indicative of corruption (like the eighth house, the sixth, or twelfth), and through his conditions and place he indicated badness, then due to the corruption of his condition and his testimony in those bad houses he would come to be in the stamp of the infortunes. **27**

---

[85] I should think this would be *detriment* and fall. Being in exile is a standard Arabic term for alienation or peregrination.
[86] Or, "agrees with" or "is suitable for" (يلائم).
[87] صالحة.
[88] توافقه.

But this planet's good fortune is powerful, and his shifting over to the stamp of the infortunes is [only] a little bit.

28 As for the Sun, by his effect upon the seasons, and because compositions do not come to be except in places over which his transit is moderate,[89] and he has an indication for life generally, they made him be a fortune for these three reasons—except that at some times he does have the effect of the infortunes through an excess of heat or cold. **29** For, when he culminates over some places he scorches them and corrupts their animals and plants, just as is discovered from his effect in many places of the southern region if he culminated over them; and indeed many places are corrupted by cold when he turns away from them and does not grant them the power of his heat, so that their animals and plants are ruined there due to the harshness of the cold (and that is found in many places in the region of the north). **30** And sometimes, due to some places being in a situation of distance or closeness, he will ruin some things at some times of the year (due to his nearness to them or distance from them), but will not do that at another time. **31** And if his transit in one of the places was in moderation, their air will have a fine mixture, and their summer will not be excessive in the hot, and their winter not excessive in the cold. **32** So, they made him be an infortune by assembly and opposition,[90] a fortune when looking from the sextile and trine, and a blended condition of good fortune and bad fortune from the square. **33** They compared his assembling with planets to his culminating over the places whose animals and plants he ruins due to the harshness of the hot, and they compared his opposition to the extreme limit of his distance from the places whose animals and plants he ruins due to the harshness of the cold, and they compared his square to them to the positions in which he

---

[89] See **30-33**. This means that the combination of his declination (which is a function of the season) and the latitude of a place, make his heat moderate: such as springtime in temperate latitudes. The contrary would be something like winter in the arctic, or summer near the equator.

[90] This is by analogy with his effects in the seasons. Thus the conjunction is too close, like in the northern hemisphere if he is in northern declinations in latitudes towards the equator (too hot, like the height of summer in Mexico city); the opposition is too far away, like being in southern declinations in more northerly latitudes (too cold, like the arctic in winter). See **33** for Abū Ma'shar's version.

corrupts some of their animals at one time of the year but does not corrupt at another time, and they compared the moderation of his transit in the places in which his heat is not excessive nor his cold, to the sextile and trine. **34** And because the Sun is a diurnal planet, he indicates good fortune [a] by day, or in the male signs, or in [b] the signs in which he has testimony, or in the places which [c] he looks at moderately; but if he was in [a-b] the contrary of these conditions and signs which we stated, or he was [c] in the bad places, he indicates corruption and bad fortune. **35** And this planet's good fortune is greater, stronger, more prevalent, and more widely known, than his misfortune.

36 As for Venus, she is a fortune, wet, moderate, harmonizing with moistures. **37** So, if she was in [a] the nocturnal, feminine signs, or in the wet signs, or in [b] one of the signs similar to her, she will manifest her good fortune. **38** But if she was [a] by day, or in the diurnal signs, or in the masculine signs, or in [b] the places in which she has no share, she will take away from her good fortune. **39** And if she had [c] testimony in some of the bad houses of the circle, she indicates corruption and death. **40** (Her condition in her shifting from her nature to being unfortunate, is like the condition of Jupiter.) **41** And this planet's indication for good fortune, comfort, and having pleasure, is stronger than it is for being unfortunate.

42 As for Mercury, we have stated his nature: and indeed he is a fortune, and takes on his nature from every planet and every sign.

43 As for the Moon, she is wet, a fortune: and she comes to be a fortune through her setting the seasons of the year into motion within a single month, and her strengthening of natures; and through her wetness she is consistent with the night. **44** So, if she was in [a] the wet signs, or in the feminine, nocturnal signs, or in [b] the signs in which she has a proper[91] share, she will manifest her good fortune; and the more abundant her similarity is to the conditions which are consistent with her, so will it be greater for her good fortune (while the fewer there are, so will it be smaller for her good fortune). **45** But if she was in [a] a place of the day, or in the male, diurnal signs, or in [b] her fall or unhealthiness, it will take away from her good fortune; and sometimes it will grant corrupted fortunes when she is in a condition like this. **46** And if (in addition to these corrupting indications)

---

[91] صالح.

she had [c] a claim in one of the bad houses of the circle, then she will be turned from her good fortune to the stamp of the infortunes. **47** But because she is the greatest of the planets of the circle in wetness, and even though wetness is of the character of life and survival, [nevertheless] an abundance and an excess in any thing is of the category of corruption, and the aspect of the square and opposition is contrariety: so when at [some] time contrariety and excess come together in one of the planets, it will perform the function of the infortunes. **48** So the Moon, by the abundance of her wetness, will sometimes perform the function of the infortunes from the square and opposition (in terms of corruption and destruction). **49** And this planet's indication for good fortune is greater than it is for bad fortune.

50 So these are conditions of the planets in their own right and [in] their place, by which they confirm or weaken their indication, or increase in it, or shift from it to something else.

[Fortunes and infortunes in combination]

51 And sometimes an increase in good fortune and bad fortune is prepared for a planet due to its mixture with [another] one of the planets: because among them is what hastens the reception of the natures of those fortunes and infortunes mixing with them, as well as[92] what has trouble in receiving them.

52 So as for Saturn, he is cooling in character, viscous,[93] slow in motion, and the cold principle is active: so if he indicated something of the good or bad by one of this conditions in the root of the nativity (or at the time of inceptions), and he was strong, that thing would be lasting, fixed. **53** And if one of the planets mixed with him at some other time, so that its mixture indicated a change[94] to that indication, it would only change something small from the indication of the root.

---

[92] Shortening for readability, for "and among them is."
[93] Or more blandly, "thick" (غليظ).
[94] Or, "alteration" (تغيير). Thus if Venus combines with Saturn, it alters Saturn's indication by making it incline toward something Venusian, without actually changing the substance of what Saturn indicates. Abū Ma'shar is a bit looser with his language for Jupiter, speaking there of a "contrary" indication (**55**).

54 As for Jupiter, his nature is moderate hotness, and he is slow in motion, while hotness is an active principle: so if he indicated something in one of the inceptions and he is strong, then it will be lasting, fixed. **55** And if after that a planet mixed with him, so that it indicated the contrary of that indication, he would only take on a small change from it.

56 As for Mars, he is quick in motion, heating, drying, and hotness is an active principle (while the dry is a passive principle): so if he indicated something in one of the times and he was strong, [and] then after that one of the fortunes or infortunes mixed with him, he would take on some change from that planet—and he is quicker and greater in being receptive to changes than the two planets which are above him.

57 As for the Sun, due to his dryness and the quickness of his motion, and the difference of his conditions in the seasons, he takes on changes from every planet mixing with him, and conveys them to this world.

58 As for Venus, she is moderate, wet, and wetness is a passive principle: so she is quick to take on changes from the fortunes and infortunes, and she generally takes on the mixtures of the planets which mix with her.

59 As for Mercury, his nature is dryness, and dryness is a passive principle: so he is receptive to all changes, [and] his nature shifts to what associates with him.

60 As for the Moon, she is most indicative planet in the circle for wetness, so due to her wetness she is the quickest of them to take on changes. **61** And if she mixed with one of the planets, she would take on the nature of the planet.

62 So examine this natural, wondrous order which belongs to the planets in taking on changes: that Saturn, since he is the highest of the planets, the slowest of them in motion, and the coldest of them, comes to *not* take on changes from the planets mixing with him, except for something insignificant—and all of the planets which are lower than him are greater and quicker in receptivity to change. **63** And the Moon, who is the lowest of the planets, and the quickest of them in motion, and the most wet of them, is the greatest of the planets in receptivity to change, and the quickest of them to take on their natures.

[Being a fortune or infortune, vs. being in the stamp of one]

64 Now as for the infortunes, even though they may indicate good fortune, they are not said to *be* fortunes, but they are said to be *in the stamp of* the fortunes, in the matter which they indicate good fortune for—although success in that good fortune will come to be through difficulty and hardship, and its owner will be disturbed by it,[95] with much toil because of it, and perhaps he will not benefit at all from his good fortune, and will not delight in it, and it will [only] be enjoyable for someone else, or it will be bequeathed to another, or many troubles and calamities will afflict him because of it. **65** And as for the fortunes, even if corruption would manifest from their activity in the way that it manifests from the activity of the infortunes, they are not said to *be* infortunes in that time, but it is said that they are *in the stamp of* the infortunes in that matter which they indicate misfortune for—and along with that misfortune there will be patience, endurance, satisfaction, contentment, consolations (and part of the good fortune will tarnish him[96] from time to time).

66 As for the Head of the Moon's Dragon, it has an indication for leadership and a little good fortune, because from it the Moon begins her ascent in her circle of inclination:[97] and ascent and elevation is a good fortune. **67** And as for the Tail, its nature is misfortune because from it the Moon begins her descent in her circle of inclination, and declining[98] is a misfortune. **68** In some of the times the Head performs the function of the infortunes, and the Tail performs the function of the fortunes, for some of the reasons which we will state. **69** (And the Heads of the planets' Dragons and their Tails are [also] like that in good fortune and misfortune.)

---

[95] Reading منغصًا with Lemay and **P**, for **BY**'s مبغضًا ("be hated").

[96] ويشوبه. Another meaning of this verb is "to mix with," so **BY** reads that "a bit of good fortune will mix with it." But to me this does not make sense, since the last qualities mentioned are already good: so we already know that good things will mix with the misfortune. (Plus, the gender of the attached pronoun is wrong.) I think what Abū Ma'shar means is that some of the good fortune will even turn out bad or generate resentment.

[97] That is, of ecliptical latitude.

[98] الهبوط. This is the same verb used for a planet "in its fall" and for descending in the sphere of the apogee, as just mentioned.

Chapter IV.7: On the natures of the planets, and their shifting from nature to nature, and the strength of their nature inherent in them (and its weakness)

Planet	Apogee in 2020
♄	3° 13' ♑
♃	10° 48' ♎
♂	0° 31' ♍
☉	13° 12' ♋
♀	11° 01' ♋

Figure 27: 2020 apogees

1 None of the planets are heating or cooling in their own right, nor wet or drying, but these things are attributed to the planets due to what is found regarding their action in this world. **2** And each planet has an indication for two principles: one of them is the fixed principle which it does not shift away from but it is altered so that it increases in its power or weakness, in accordance with its place in its [own] sphere,[99] its sign, the quadrants of the circle, and the rest of its conditions. **3** As for the other principle which the planet has, sometimes it is fixed in it, and sometimes it shifts from that nature it has to another one: and indeed that is due to its rising or falling in the sphere of its apogee, or the abundance of its receptivity to changes (or its scant receptivity to them), so that the planet is referred to the nature which it takes on when its condition is different.

[Apogee and elemental principles]

4 So as for Saturn, we have already stated that what is found from his indication in this world is excessive cold, and indeed an excess of cold comes to be through the dry: so Saturn by his nature is cooling and drying. **5** Now as for his nature of cold, it is inherent to him, not shifting from him, because it is an active principle, except that sometimes it alters so that he increases in it or decreases in it. **6** But as for the nature of the dry, sometimes he shifts from it to another, because it is a passive principle; and sometimes it alters by means of an increase in it or a decrease in it, so when that alteration is abundant, it shifts to another nature.[100]

---

[99] That is, in the sphere of its apogee.
[100] Namely, to the wet: see **11** below.

7 Now if Saturn was rising from the middle of the circle of his apogee,[101] his nature is fixed in the cold and dry, and it will be likewise if he was in a cold, dry sign or quadrant, or in the rest of the cold, dry positions. 8 So if these conditions added up, he would be excessive in the cold and dry, while if they were subtracted it would be less. 9 And if he was in the hot, dry signs, the indication of his cold would be weak, while his dryness would be strong. 10 And if he was rising just as we stated, and he was in the wet signs, it would take away from the nature of his dryness; and if along with this he was in the bound of a wet planet, or in a wet quadrant, and is in a wet area relative to the Sun,[102] it would take away from his dryness. 11 But if all of these conditions came together for him at one time, and he is rising, he will shift to wetness so that he becomes cooling and wet. 12 And if Saturn was falling from the middle of the circle of his apogee, he would be cooling and wet. 13 But if along with

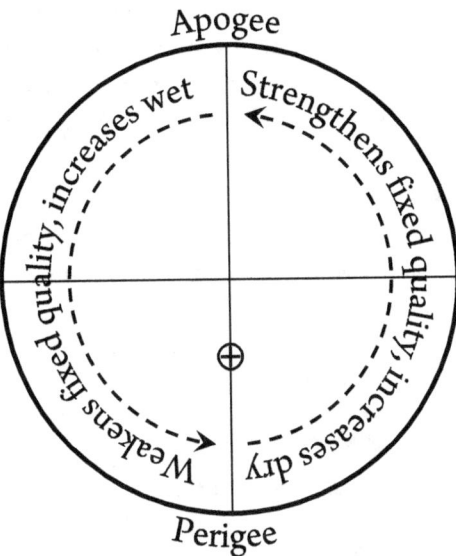

Figure 28: Alteration of qualities in circle of apogee

---

[101] See Figure 28 here. I do not think Saturn needs to be rising from the middle of his circle, as Abū Ma'shar doesn't say this for the other planets below. Instead, I think the rising and falling involves a gradual process. In the Figure here, circle of some planet's apogee is eccentric or off-center from the earth (⊕) in the direction of the apogee. The arrows show the direction of the planet's movement around the zodiac, towards and away from the apogee. For Saturn, the apogee in 2020 AD is 3° 13' Capricorn, and in much of 2020 Saturn is in late Capricorn. Thus his coldness and dryness is reinforced by his sign, even though he is moving away from the apogee, slightly weakening the strongest cold and adding a little moisture. When he enters Aquarius, the sign will weaken his cold more and add even more moisture, just as his further movement towards his perigee also indicates.

[102] See **44** below.

that he was in a wet sign, or in the bound of a wet planet, or in a wet quadrant, or his area relative to the Sun was like that, then he would increase in his wetness; and if all of these came together at one time, he would become excessive in wetness. **14** And if, at the time of his falling from the circle of his apogee, he was in the hot, dry signs, the indication of his cold would be weak, and the power of his wetness would decrease. **15** And if along with this he was in a hot, dry quadrant, or in the bound of a heating, drying planet, or his area relative to the Sun was in the same condition, it would take away from his wetness, and his dryness would be strong, and his cold weak. **16** Now if all of these conditions came together while he was falling, he would become cooling and drying.

	Fixed quality	Variable quality
♄	Cold	Dry
♃	Hot	Wet
♂	Hot	Dry
☉	Hot	Dry
♀	Hot	Wet
☿	Dry?	Cold?
☽		Varies

Figure 29: Fixed and variable qualities of planets (IV.7)

17 As for Mars, what is found from his activity at [some] time[103] is excessive heat, and indeed an excess of heat comes to be through the dry: so the nature of Mars is heating and drying. **18** And as for the hotness, it is the fixed nature for him, while the dryness sometimes shifts from him. **19** So if Mars were rising in the circle of his apogee, his nature would be fixed in hotness and dryness; and it will be likewise if he was in a hot, dry sign or quadrant. **20** Now if these conditions were abundant, he would be excessive in hotness and the dry. **21** But if he was in the cold, dry signs it takes away from his hotness, and his dry nature would be strong. **22** And if he was rising [while] in a wet sign, or in the bound of a wet planet, or in a wet quadrant, or he was in a wet area relative to the Sun, it takes away from his dryness. **23** And if these conditions of wetness came together for Mars while he was rising, he would shift to wetness so that he would become heating and wet. **24** Now if he was falling in the circle of his apogee, he would be heating and wet: so if the conditions of wetness were abundant in him and he was falling, he would be excessive in wetness. **25** But if he was falling and the conditions of hotness and the dry were dominant over him, he would be heating and drying.

---

[103] Or, "season" (الزّمان).

26 As for Jupiter, he is moderately heating and wet, just like we stated about his activity at [some] season.[104] **27** So if he was rising in the circle of his apogee, his indication for moderate hotness would be stronger; and if he was falling, his indication for moderate wetness would become strong. **28** And as for the hot or wet signs similar to him, of course they would strengthen his moderate hotness and wetness; but [in] the signs not similar to him, his moderation in hotness and wetness would be weakened and reduced.

29 As for the Sun, he is heating and drying: so if he was rising from the middle of the circle of his apogee, his nature would be fixed in hotness and the dry; while if he was falling, his nature would be heating and wet. **30** And of course the nature of the signs and quadrants of the circle will alter his nature just as we stated about the alteration of the nature of other planets.

31 As for Venus, she is moderately heating and wet, just as we stated about her activity in the seasons; and her situation in the strength of her hotness (or its weakness) is like the situation of Jupiter.

32 As for Mercury, what dominates in his nature is the dry, and he associates a little bit in the cold.[105] **33** Now if he was rising in the circle of his apogee, he would be strongly drying, and a small bit of heat would mix with him; but if he was falling, his nature would be wetness along with a little bit of the cold. **34** And of course Mercury takes on the four natures by the variety of his conditions, and likewise through his nature Mercury takes on everything he mixes with (of the natures of the planets and signs).

[Synodic cycle and elemental principles]

35 And as for the Moon, she is varying in nature, in accordance with the difference of the divisions of the month:[106] because in the first quarter of the month, her nature is heating and wet, and the nature inherent to her in this quarter is wetness. **36** Now if she was in this quarter [but] rising in the circle of her apogee, her nature would be strong in hotness, weak in wetness; and if

---

[104] See IV.5, **16-17**.
[105] See also IV.8, **8-9**.
[106] Reading الشّهر for السّنة ("the year"). But her qualities in each quarter do stand in parallel with the quarters of the year as defined by the Sun.

she was falling in it, the nature of her excessive wetness would be more dominant in her.

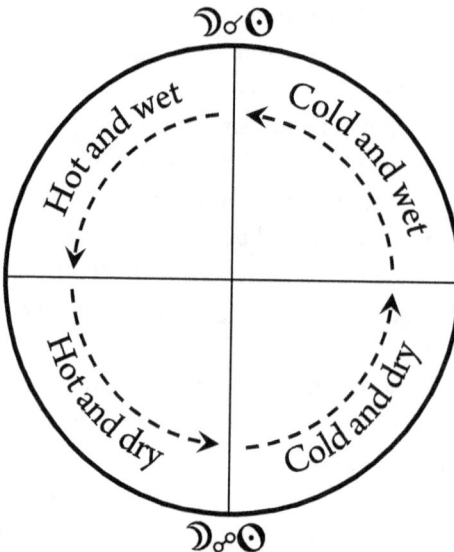

Figure 30: Alteration of qualities in Lunar phases

37 In the second quarter of the month her nature comes to be heating and drying, and the nature inherent to her in this quarter is the hotness. **38** So if she was rising in the circle of her apogee in this quarter, what is dominant in her nature is hotness as well as the dry, resembling excess; and if she was falling, her nature would be moderately heating and wet. **39** In the third quarter of the month, her nature comes to be cooling and drying, and the nature inherent to her in this quarter is the dry. **40** So if she was rising in this quarter, the nature of the dry would become strong over her and the cold would be little; and if she was falling, the nature of cold would be more dominant over her, and a part of the dry would be in her. **41** In the fourth quarter of the month her nature comes to be cooling and wet, and the nature inherent to her in this quarter is the cold. **42** So if she was rising, the nature of cold would be more dominant over her, [and] there would be a small bit of wetness in her; and if she was falling, what would dominate over her nature would be excessive wetness, with a little bit of the cold. **43** And the condition of the Moon in her place within the signs and the rest of the conditions (with respect to the alteration of her nature) is like the situation of the other planets.

BOOK IV: THEORY OF ASTROLOGY, CLASSIFYING PLANETS

44 And as for the three superior planets, from the time of their easternization from the Sun up to the first station their nature is wetness; and from the first station to their opposition to the Sun their nature is hotness; and from that time up to the second station their nature is the dry; and from the second station up to their entering under the rays, their nature is coldness.

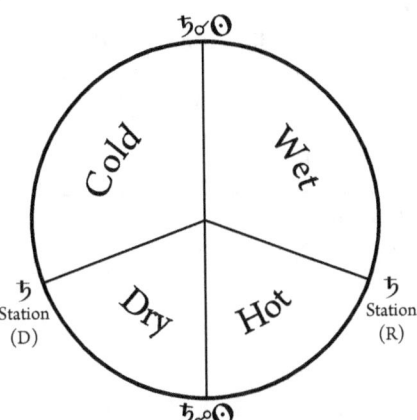

Figure 31: Superiors' phases

45 But as for Mercury and Venus, from the time of their easternization (while they are retrograde) until they go direct, their nature is wetness; and from the

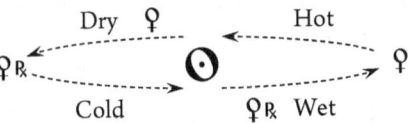

Figure 32: Inferiors' phases

time of their direct motion until they conjoin with the Sun their nature is hotness; and from their departure from the Sun and their westernization until they station, their nature is the dry; and from the time of their retrogradation until they conjoin with the Sun, their nature is the cold.

46 As for the Head, its nature is hotness; as for the Tail, its nature is coldness.

47 And of course other conditions happen to the planets so that they increase or decrease in the indication of their heat, cold, dryness, or wetness. **48** So, work with the strength of their character (or its weakness) just as we have stated.

Chapter IV.8: On the masculinization of the planets, and their feminization

1 Reproduction comes to be through the meeting of the male and the female. **2** Now as for the male, its nature is hotness, and it is active; and as for the female, its nature is wetness and it is passive. **3** And the planets have an indication for masculinization and feminization, so the hot planets are indicative of masculinization, and the wet planets are indicative of feminization.

	Planets	Why
Masculine	♃ ♂ ☉	Hot
	☊	Hot, masc
Weak masc / neutral	♄	Cold, dry
	☿	Dry[107]
Feminine	☽ ♀	Wet
	☋	Cold, fem

Figure 33: Masculine and feminine classification of planets

4 Thus Jupiter, Mars, and the Sun are male because their nature is hotness.

5 But as for Saturn, the nature inherent to him is the cold, and cold is an active principle; and his varying nature is the dry, and the dry is akin to hotness: so Saturn is indicative of masculinization for these two reasons. **6** But because his nature does not have hotness in it, his indication for masculinization is weaker than that of the indication of the [other] three planets which we stated. **7** So for this reason, in the matter of masculinization he sometimes indicates eunuchs, the effeminate, and males who do not have sex, nor are children born to them, and they do not have seed.

8 And as for Mercury, the dry is more dominant in him, and the dry is akin to hotness: so Mercury is male. **9** But because his nature does not have hotness in it, he indicates youths who have not attained puberty, and eunuchs. **10** And because the dry is a passive element, it indicates that he takes on the nature of the planets (in terms of masculinization and feminization).

11 As for Venus, she comes to be feminized due to her indication for moderate wetness.

12 As for the Moon, she comes to be feminized due to the abundance of her wetness.

13 As for the Head, its nature is hotness and masculinization; as for the Tail, its nature is coldness and feminization.

---

[107] And he participates in some coldness, according to IV.7, **32**.

14 And these things which we have stated about the masculinization of the planets and their feminization, are things which are *attributed* to the planets—except that sometimes their conditions vary, so that the male ones indicate feminization, and the female ones masculinization, due to the variation of their conditions. **15** And that is because [1] the easternizing, appearing planets (and they are the ones which arise before the Sun) are indicative of masculinization, while the westernizing ones (and they are the ones setting after the Sun) are indicative of feminization. **16** And [2] if the planets were from the Ascendant to the Midheaven, or from the setting to the stake of the earth, in these two eastern quadrants they indicate masculinization; but in the remaining two western quadrants they indicate feminization. **17** And of course [3] their conditions vary in masculinization and feminization in their positions in the signs, and the houses of the circle (and we will state those in what is to follow).

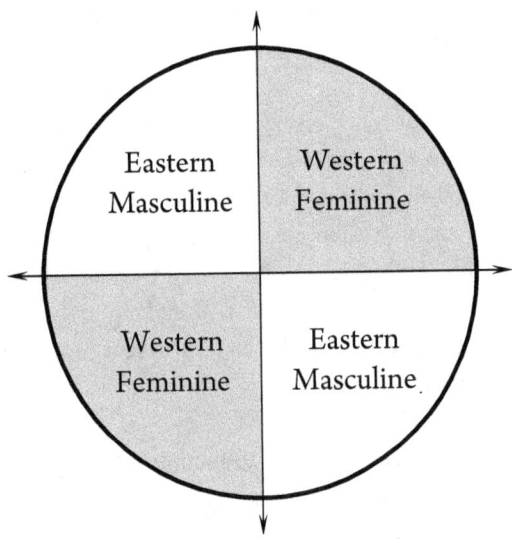

Figure 34: Masculine and feminine quadrants

Chapter IV.9: On the diurnal and nocturnal planets

1 Among the planets are diurnal ones and nocturnal ones: and they gave them these indications because they looked at the planets whose natures by day are more moderate than by night, and made them diurnal; and for the planets whose natures are more moderate by night than by day, they made them nocturnal.

2 As for Saturn, we already stated that his nature is moderated by day, so he is diurnal.

3 And as for Jupiter, due to the moderateness of his nature he comes to be diurnal, and that is because the day [itself] is more moderate than the night.[108]

4 As for Mars, his nature is excessively heating and drying, and indeed the excessiveness of his hotness and dryness is moderated by night due to the cold of the night and its wetness: so Mars is nocturnal.

5 As for the Sun, he is a diurnal planet.

6 As for Venus, she is a planet with wetness in her, and the nature of wetness harmonizes with the nature of night, so Venus is nocturnal. **7** And when she is westernizing, she has a stronger indication and is more apparent for good fortune, because the nature of westernizing is similar to the nature of night and feminization; but if she was easternizing and by day was above the earth in male signs, it subtracts from her good fortune and moderateness, because she will incline a little bit towards the nature of diurnal planets and to masculinization.

Diurnal	Nocturnal
☉	☽
♃	♀
♄	♂
☊	☋
☿	

Figure 35: Diurnal and nocturnal planets (IV.9)

8 As for Mercury, the dry is more dominant in him, and the dry is akin to hotness, and the day is hot: so when Mercury stands alone, his indication for diurnality is more dominant, and when he easternizes [the indication] is diurnal; but when he westernizes he is nocturnal. **9** And upon westernizing he is more apparent for activity and stronger than [he is] upon easternizing, because upon westernizing he is direct, while at the beginning of easternizing he is retrograde. **10** And he mixes with diurnal and nocturnal planets, and shifts to their nature when he conjoins with them or connects with them.

11 As for the Moon, she is the luminary of the night, and in her is wetness, so she is nocturnal for these two reasons.

12 As for the Head, it is diurnal; and as for the Tail, it is nocturnal (and likewise the [other] planets' Heads and their Tails).

---

[108] See IV.6, **12** and **23**.

13 And these natures of diurnality and nocturnality which belong to the planets, are inherent them: they do not deviate from them except that the planets' easternization strengthens the indication of the diurnal planets and weakens the indication of the nocturnal planets (apart from Mercury: for we have stated that when he is westernizing it is stronger for his nature, and more indicative of good fortune).[109] **14** And the planets' westernization strengthens the indication of the nocturnal planets, and weakens the indication of the diurnal planets.

15 The Fourth Book of *The Introduction* is completed.

---

[109] Remember from **8-9** that in himself Mercury is diurnal, but when westernizing he is a big stronger because he westernizes while direct.

BOOK V: [ON THE SHARES OF THE PLANETS IN THE SIGNS]
And in it are twenty-two chapters

1. Chapter V.1: On the shares of the planets in the signs.
2. Chapter V.2: On the reason for the planets' houses, according to what some of the masters of the stars claimed.
3. Chapter V.3: On the reason for the planets' houses, according to what fits with the statement of Ptolemy.
4. Chapter V.4: On the reason for the planets' houses, according to what fits with the statement of Hermes, from Agathodaimōn.
5. Chapter V.5: On the reason for the planets' exaltations, according to what some of the astrologers claimed.
6. Chapter V.6: On the reason for the planets' exaltations, according to what Ptolemy claimed.
7. Chapter V.7: On the reason for the planets' exaltations, according to what fits with the statement of Hermes.
8. Chapter V.8: On the different bounds of the planets, and their conditions.
9. Chapter V.9: On the bounds of the people of Egypt.
10. Chapter V.10: On the bounds of Ptolemy.
11. Chapter V.11: On the bounds of the Chaldeans.
12. Chapter V.12: On the bounds of Astrātū.
13. Chapter V.13: On the bounds of the Indians.
14. Chapter V.14: On the lords of the triplicities.
15. Chapter V.15: On the faces and their lords, according to what fits with the statement of the scholars of Persia, Babylon, and Egypt.
16. Chapter V.16: On the faces and their lords according to what the Indians said: and they call them the *darījān*.
17. Chapter V.17: On the *nawbahr* of the signs (and it is the ninth-part), according to what fits with the statement of the Indians.
18. Chapter V.18: On the twelfth-parts of the signs, and the lords of each degree of every sign.
19. Chapter V.19: On the male and female degrees.
20. Chapter V.20: On the bright, dark, dusky, and empty degrees.
21. Chapter V.21: On the wells of the planets in the signs.
22. Chapter V.22: On the degrees increasing in good fortune.

BOOK V: THE SHARES OF THE PLANETS IN THE SIGNS

Chapter V.1: On the shares of the planets in the signs

1 Since the twelve signs and seven planets are what are used in the indication for things generally which are quick to change, come into being, and pass away, and in what has preceded we have already stated the condition of each one of them individually in an abbreviated way, now let us begin and state the planets' partnering in the signs and their shares: such as by house, exaltation, the triplicities, bounds, faces, joy, fall, unhealthiness,[1] and the degrees indicative of excellence or badness.

2 And indeed, these shares are appointed to them in the signs in accordance with the mixing of the natures of the positions with the natures of the planets, as well as the rest of their conditions, in terms of: rising and falling,[2] and their changing from condition to condition, and their manifesting their nature and power in some positions but their weakness in another position, and their presence in some positions which resemble their nature (and do not resemble it), in terms of hotness and coldness, and dryness and wetness, and masculinization and feminization, and the diurnal and nocturnal, and good fortune and misfortune, and their culminating over some of the climes or their distance from them, and the rest of the conditions of the signs and planets, according to what each one of the positions requires due to the condition of that planet.

3 Then, they made their order be according to different conditions, because they made some of them be in the arrangement of the planets' spheres above one another (based on what nature it has),[3] and others in accordance with the agreement of the natures of those positions with the natures of the planets and their conditions (such as the agreement of the watery signs with the planets watery in nature, and the agreement of the diurnal signs with the diurnal planets), and others in accordance with the antithesis of some of them with others (like the antithesis of the hot and fiery signs and planets

---

[1] That is, "detriment."

[2] These terms (صعود وهبوط) most likely refer to rising and falling relative to the apogee, but perhaps to changes in latitude as well.

[3] على ما هو عليه في الطبيعة. This seems obscure to me, but Abū Ma'shar might be referring to Ptolemy in V.3.

with the cold and watery planets and signs), and the rest of what we said which is like that.

4 And indeed, they made it be like that so every planet in every condition would have a share in every one of the twelve signs, due to the blending of the planets' indication with the indication of the signs, in generation and corruption, and the good and the bad.

5 So for these reasons there came to be shares of the seven planets in the twelve signs.

Chapter V.2: On the reason for the planets' houses, according to what some of the masters of the stars claimed

1 All of the ancients agreed that Aries and Scorpio are the two houses of Mars, Taurus and Libra the two houses of Venus, Gemini and Virgo the two houses of Mercury, Sagittarius and Pisces the two houses of Jupiter, Capricorn and Aquarius the two houses of Saturn, Leo the house of the Sun, and Cancer the house of the Moon. **2** But as for what reason they made these signs be the houses of these planets, they disagreed about that.

3 People[4] ignorant of the qualities of the sphere as well as of natural things and their conditions, said that the planets used to move every day in accordance with their daily mean motion, and they did not have slowness nor retrogradation until they were bound to the Sun and Moon (and at the time the Sun was in 15° of Leo, and the Moon in 15° of Cancer): then the wandering[5] stars received houses in accordance with their bonds[6] in relation to the direction of the Sun and Moon.[7]

4 The bond of Mercury was 21° 30', and indeed when these degrees are added to the portions of the Sun in Leo, it comes to 6° 30' of Virgo. **5** And

---

[4] Abū Ma'shar returns to these people on the subject of exaltations, in V.5, **15ff**.
[5] Or more accurately, "wavering" (متحيّرة); but "planet" in Greek means a "wandering" star.
[6] رباط.
[7] That is to say, from which direction of the zodiac they are related to the Sun and Moon. See what follows.

when it is subtracted backwards from the portions of the Moon in Cancer, that comes to 23° 30' of Gemini.[8]

6 As for Venus, the length of her bond is 47° 11', so if these degrees are added to the portions of the Sun, and subtracted from the portions of the Moon backwards, it comes to Taurus and Libra.

7 And the length of the bond of Mars is 78°, so when these degrees are added to the portions of the Sun and subtracted from the portions of the Moon, it comes to Aries and Scorpio.

8 And the length of the bond of Jupiter is 120°, so if these degrees are added to the portions of the Sun and subtracted from the place of the Moon, it comes to Pisces and Sagittarius.

9 And the length of the bond of Saturn is 136°, so when these degrees are added to the portions of the Sun and subtracted from the portions of the Moon, it comes to Capricorn and Aquarius.

10 And they said: We added it to the portions of the Sun and subtracted it from the place of the Moon, because the Sun is diurnal and the Moon nocturnal. **11** So these people claimed that for this reason these signs were made the houses of these planets.

12 But this statement is wrong, because if by this "bond" they meant [1] the degrees of their equations, it is found that the equations of the superior planets are few, while the bonds in these degrees which they stated are many, having a great disparity with the degrees of their equations.

13 And if by this they meant [2] the degrees which, when that same [amount] is between the Sun and the five planets, they change their figures to retrogradation or direct motion, then that would have to be in accordance with the *mean* degrees in which the planets go retrograde when they are that distance from the Sun. **14** But we find the contrary of that, because Saturn does not retrograde nor go direct except when there are fewer than those degrees which they stated [as being] a little more. **15** And Mars does not retrograde nor go direct except when there are more than those degrees between him and [the Sun]. **16** And Jupiter, Venus, and Mercury sometimes go retrograde and direct when there are fewer than those degrees between them and the Sun. **17** And if they had determined the "bond" according to

---

[8] In this way, the longest extent of their "bond" comes to the signs they rule.

the extremity of their distance from the Sun,⁹ then they would have had to make the bond of all of the superior planets be 180°.

18 Also, just as they made the bond of the two inferior planets be according to their equations,¹⁰ so likewise they would have had to make the bond of the superior planets be according to their equations. **19** But instead they determined these degrees based what [they needed] to do so that they would fall into one of the [desired] positions in their houses: thus what they stated is not an explanation of the houses of the planets.

20 Now as for other people, they offered other reasons for the planets' houses, whose statements we will not mention except to say that they are nonsense and fables.

21 All of these [people] are certainly ignorant of the conditions of the planets and natural things, because the motions and condition of the sphere and the planets in it do not vary from what they ought to be: all of them are set into motion with a natural, direct motion, not increasing their motion in themselves on any day beyond their motion on another day—although what is found among *us* in the difference of their motion is due to the abundance of their circles, and the varying motion of each circle relative to the others. **22** And that is obvious and clear among those who look into the higher sciences.

23 As for Hermes and Ptolemy (the author of *The Book of Judgments*),¹¹ they both made clear the reason for the houses of the planets: and we will state that, if God wills.

Chapter V.3: On the reason for the planets' houses, according to what fits with the statement of Ptolemy¹²

1 The seven planets have an indication over things quick to change, and generation and corruption in this world. **2** But the luminaries are more uni-

---

⁹ That is, their farthest "elongation."
¹⁰ This shows that in the *zījes* of those astrologers, the amounts in **4** and **6** above played a role in their equations (as also suggested in **12**).
¹¹ That is, the *Tetrabiblos*.
¹² This chapter is an elaboration of *Tet.* I.17 (Robbins pp. 79-83).

versal in indication over things generation and corrupting, than are the others.

3 As for the Moon, she is the nearest of the planets to us, and the quickest of them in motion, and the greatest of them in terms of shifting in the signs and a difference of condition. **4** So because of that, her conditions come to resemble the conditions of things quick in generation and corruption. **5** But the planets are most apparent in their activity at the zenith, and the nearest of the signs to us in terms of the zenith are Gemini and Cancer. **6** Now as for Gemini, it is a male sign and the sign which, when the Sun is in it, he is at the endpoint of the spring season; and by its masculinization and due to its being a sign which is the end of a season when the Sun is in it, it does not fit with the nature of the Moon. **7** But as for Cancer, it is a female sign and the sign which, when the Sun enters it, it is the beginning of the summer season: it is wet in nature, and feminine, and the Moon is a female, wet planet, indicative of beginnings; Cancer is the nearest of the feminine signs to us in terms of the zenith, and the Moon the nearest of the planets to us. **8** So Cancer and the Moon coincide in wetness, femininity, the indication of beginning, and nearness to us, and for these four reasons they made Cancer be the house of the Moon.

9 As for the Sun, the air is warmed and heated by his rising, and by his presence in Cancer, Leo, and Virgo it comes to be summer, except that the most apparent the nature of the summer can be, and the hot and the dry, and the most intense, is when the Sun is in Leo: and it is a male sign, heating, drying, and by his nature the Sun is indicative of hotness and the dry, and masculinization; and Leo is the middle of the season of summer, and the Sun the middle of the seven planets. **10** So the Sun and Leo coincide in hotness, the dry, masculinity, being in the middle of the spheres and the season of summer, and for this reason Leo became the house of the Sun.

11 And another reason is that since [1] the Sun is the luminary of the day, and the Moon the luminary of the night, and [2] they follow one another in the indication of generation and corruption, and life and beginnings, and [3] from their meeting one obtains information about will come to be in the world up to their opposition (and likewise one seeks information from their opposition up to their meeting), and [4] the meeting and opposition each come to be through the quickness of the Moon's motion and her course towards the Sun, and [5] the most apparent their activity and natures can be in the indications for what occurs in this world is when they come to be in these two signs culminating above us, Cancer (the convertible, wet, feminine sign culminating above our heads, indicative of the beginning of the season) was given to the planet matching it due to the nature of wetness, femininity, the quickness of shifting from sign to sign, and the indication for beginning—and that is the Moon. **12** And the heating, drying, male, diurnal sign which follows Cancer (and it is Leo) was given to the heating, drying, male, diurnal planet matching it due to its nature, and it is the Sun.

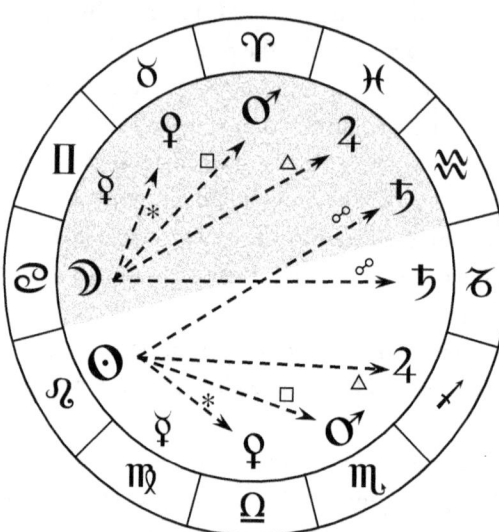

Figure 36: A *Thema Mundi* with lunar and solar halves (V.3, 13-19)

13 And since Cancer and Leo are the two houses of the luminaries, indicative of generation and growth, and these two signs belong to the season of summer, Capricorn and Aquarius were made the houses of Saturn because these two signs belong to the season of winter and the cold, and Saturn is cooling and drying, and his nature is contrary to the nature of the two luminaries [and] antithetical to them, and his sphere is the highest of the spheres. **14** Due to this it was begun with him after the luminaries and his houses were made to be antithetical to the houses of the luminaries.

15 As for Jupiter, he is indicative of moderation, and his sphere borders on the sphere of Saturn: so the two signs which border on the houses of Saturn were given to Jupiter (and they are Sagittarius and Pisces), and from the houses of the luminaries they came to be in the place of the trine and affection.

16 As for Mars, he is a heating infortune, and his sphere borders on the sphere of Jupiter: so his two houses were made to be those which border on the houses of Jupiter (and they are Scorpio and Aries), and from the houses of the luminaries they came to be in the place of a square and bad fortune.

17 As for Venus, her nature is moderation, and her sphere follows[13] the sphere of the Sun, so her two houses were made to be those bordering on the houses of Mars (and they are Libra and Taurus), and from the houses of the luminaries they came to be in the place of a sextile and affection.

18 And the two remaining signs were granted to Mercury, and they are Gemini and Virgo.

19 And because the luminaries are the most apparent of the planets in activity in this world, they gave one half of the circle to the Sun (and it is from Leo to the end of Capricorn), and the other half to the Moon (and it is from the beginning of Aquarius to the end of Cancer), so that each one of the luminaries would have a partnership with each planet in one of its two houses which are in the half of the circle attributed to that luminary.

Chapter V.4: On the reason for the planets' houses, according to what fits with the statement of Hermes, from Agathodaimōn

1 Since we[14] wanted to know the houses of the seven planets from among the twelve signs, we looked and found two different figures[15] and distances for each of the five planets, such as easternization and westernization, and retrogradation and direction; but we do not find but one figure for each of the luminaries, because the Sun does not have easternization nor westernization, and the Moon does not have retrogradation.

---

[13] يلي, which means "to border on," as I have translated it elsewhere here. But in Ptolemy the point is that she is *below* Mars (and the Sun): if we insisted in the "border" language here, we would have to put her next to the house of the Sun, which wouldn't make sense.

[14] This is probably Hermes speaking, or Abū Ma'shar speaking with the voice of Hermes, even though Abū Ma'shar refers to other parts of the *Gr. Intr.* in **9**. I believe that Abū Ma'shar's own reflections begin at **21** below.

[15] أشكال. This word, in **1-2** and Hermes's other text below in **37-43**, is the same word used in Sahl's *On Times* (Ch. 1, **6-7** and **17** and Ch. 3, **29**), both of them referring to major phases made by the planets. It suggests to me that both Abū Ma'shar and Sahl are drawing on the same Hermes text. Note that 'Umar al-Tabarī (in *TBN* III.1, in *PN2*) also cites Hermes and these phases when referring to prediction, as Sahl does.

2 Now, from what we found of the conditions of the five planets, we concluded that [1] each one of them has two houses, each house harmonizing with one of its two figures, and that [2] each one of the luminaries has a single one harmonizing with its figure, and that they are the strongest of the planets (because whatever is fixed and remains in a single figure is strongest for it, and firmer for its form, while whatever introduces change and an alteration in figures is weaker for it)—except that the ancients called the Moon the "planet of the Sun," because none of the [other] five planets needs another for its light, since it has easternization and westernization with its own light.[16] **3** But the Moon does not have light in her easternizaton, westernization, and the rest of her conditions except by means of the Sun, and she draws his light from him. **4** For matter has no foundation without form, the form manifests nothing without matter, and matter is in need of form (which is what presides over nature): and the Moon is the matter and the Sun the form, so the Moon's activity does not manifest except by means of the Sun. **5** So due to that, they called her the "planet of the Sun."

6 So wherever the Sun should have an allotment,[17] the allotment of the Moon will follow it: thus the house of the Moon is conjoined to the house of the Sun, and the exaltation of the Moon is after the exaltation of the Sun,[18] and the day of the Moon is after the day of the Sun, and the distribution[19] of the Moon is after the distribution of the Sun.[20]

7 So when these things had been prefaced to us, we began the distribution of the houses of the circle amongst the planets from the agreement[21] of natures: because each essence is strengthened due to its essentiality agreeing with what is mixing with it, and it is corrupted due to its antithesis. **8** And the indication of that is that fire has no foundation when adjacent to water, since each of them is corrupting to its associate: so as for fire, it is strengthened [by what] is suitable to fire.

---

[16] بنور نفسه. This may be the origin of later phrase, that a planet is "in its own light" (في نور نفسه) when it is away from the Sun's rays.
[17] حصّة, which is yet another word for a portion or share (i.e., a dignity).
[18] See V.7, **9**.
[19] قسمة, in the sense of "dividing the signs out" to the planets.
[20] See **9-19** below.
[21] اتّفاق.

BOOK V: THE SHARES OF THE PLANETS IN THE SIGNS

9 Now the general hotness which is in this world is from the Sun, and in Book II of this book of ours we stated that upon his being in 15° of Leo, it is the strongest it can be in hotness and the dry in this world:[22] so the most worthy of the houses of the circle for him is Leo, due each of them being adapted[23] to the other in nature; and the strongest that it[24] can be, is in 15° of it.

10 So since we knew the house of the Sun and the place of his strength within it, we began with the house of the Moon (who is conjoined to the Sun), and we named every 30° (which is the amount of a single sign) one of the "Lots." **11** Then we cast out 30° from 15° of Leo to the right side and the left, and one of the two Lots occurred in 15° of Cancer, and the other in 15° of Virgo. **12** Now we knew that the most worthy position for the Moon is the sign appropriate to her nature, the cold [and] the wet being strengthening for it: so Cancer came to be the house of the Moon, and her power came to be in 15° of it.[25]

13 And once we finished with the houses of the Sun and Moon, we looked at the sphere which follows the sphere of the Moon, and found it to be the sphere of Mercury. **14** So we cast out the two "Lots" [forwards] from 15° of Leo, and backwards from 15° of Cancer, and one of them falls in 15° of Gemini (and is the right side), while the other falls in 15° of Virgo (the left side), so that Gemini and Virgo come to be the houses of Mercury.

15 Then we found the sphere of Venus following the sphere of Mercury, so we cast out the two Lots from the houses of Mercury to the right and left, and they fell in 15° of Taurus and in the same of Libra: so they became the houses of Venus.

16 Then we found the sphere of the Sun following the sphere of Venus, but we have already made his position and houses clear.

17 Then we found the sphere of Mars following the sphere of the Sun, so we cast out the two Lots from the houses of Venus, to the right and left, and

---

[22] See II.7, **22**, also from Hermes-Agathodaimōn.
[23] Or, "fitted" (ملائمة).
[24] Or perhaps, "he" (meaning the Sun). But I think Abū Ma'shar is speaking of where their mutual fitness and adaptation is strongest.
[25] As a reminder, Ptolemy begins from the Moon, while Hermes begins from the Sun.

they fell in 15° of Scorpio and in the same of Aries: so they became the houses of Mars.

18 And we found the sphere of Jupiter following the sphere of Mars, so we cast out the two Lots from the houses of Mars, to the right and left, and one of them fell in 15° of Sagittarius, and the other in the same of Pisces: so they became the houses of Jupiter.

19 And we found the sphere of Saturn following the sphere of Jupiter, so we cast out the two Lots from the right and left side of the houses of Jupiter, and one of them fell in 15° of Capricorn, and the other in the same of Aquarius: so they became the houses of Saturn.

20 In this way Agathodaimōn divided out the houses.

[Comments by Abū Ma'shar; Rhetorius]

21 The strength of this division, and its truth, is that the two houses of Saturn (who is the most unfortunate of the planets of the circle, and the most indicative of them for corruption) is in the opposite of the houses of the luminaries (indicative of generation and growth). **22** Also, the houses of Mars (who is below [Saturn] in unfortunateness) are in the square of both of their houses (because the unfortunateness of the square is below that of the opposition). **23** And because the trine and sextile are of the distribution of the fortunes, and the trine is more powerful than the sextile, and Jupiter is more fortunate than Venus, the two houses of Jupiter came to be in trine to the houses of the luminaries, while the two houses of Venus are in sextile to their houses. **24** And we found the cord of Mercury to reach close to 30 portions, and in good fortune he is below Venus: so the two houses of Mercury border on the houses of the luminaries according to the amount of approximately one-half of the sextile.

25 But [some] people[26] appointed the houses of the planets in accordance with the natures being antithetical to[27] each other. **26** And that is because the Sun and the Moon are portrayed as being the luminaries of the

---

[26] Namely Rhetorius, Ch. 8.

[27] تضاد, one of the verb forms which officially designates the "detriment" of a planet, and the opposite of the sign it rules—especially when translating the Greek *enantiōma*, as with the version of Rhetorius here.

world, while Saturn is portrayed as darkness, and at all times darkness is the antithesis of light, and light is the antithesis of darkness: so due to that, the houses of Saturn were made to be opposite the houses of the luminaries. **27** As for Jupiter, he is an indicator of assets and immovable property, and Mercury an indicator of knowledge, explanation, and wisdom, but the seeking of knowledge puts little value in and disdains assets, and the seeking of assets disdains knowledge, because the passion for assets and wealth is the antithesis of the passion for knowledge and explanation: so the houses of one of them were made to be the antithesis of the houses of the other. **28** As for Mars, he is an indicator of war, fighting, terror, and fear, while Venus is an indicator of gentleness, passions, and pleasures, and at all times joy is the antithesis of terror, fighting, and fear: so due to that, the houses of one of them were made to be in the opposition of the houses of the other.

29 All of the ancients distributed the houses in one of these four ways which we have stated: because some of them [1] started in the distribution of houses with the luminaries, then with the sphere which follows the sphere of the Moon, then rising up until it reached the sphere of Saturn (just as Hermes reported from Agathodaimōn).[28] **30** And some of them [2] began with the luminaries and then Saturn, just as Ptolemy did.[29] **31** And some of them [3] gave to the infortunes the opposite of the houses of the luminaries as well as their squares, and to the fortunes the trine and sextile, and they made the houses of Mercury be on the two sides of the houses of the luminaries.[30] **32** And some of them [4] made it be in accordance with the natures' being antithetical to each other.[31] **33** And all of these divisions result in one [and the same] thing.

34 And due to the antithesis of the natures of those planets which we stated, the seventh from the house of each planet came to be its "unhealthiness."[32]

---

[28] In **9-19** above.
[29] See V.3, **13-14**.
[30] This seems to refer to **22-24** above.
[31] That is, Rhetorius in **25-28** above.
[32] وبال, another standard Arabic word for detriment.

[Hermes-Agathodaimōn again]

Direct motion Easternizing *Moderation* *Suitability*	Retrogradation Westernizing *Less moderation*
♄ ♒ ♃ ♐ ♂ ♏	♄ ♑ ♃ ♓ ♂ ♈
Direct motion **Westernizing** *Moderation* *Suitability*	**Retrogradation** **Easternizing** *Less moderation*
♀ ♉ ☿ ♍	♀ ♎ ☿ ♊

Figure 37: Similarity of planets' houses with their figures and moderation (V.4, 35-43)

35 And[33] since the distribution of the houses of the planets begins with the houses of the luminaries (because they are the most powerful of the planets of the circle), the Sun came to have an allotment in every male sign, and the Moon an allotment in every female sign. **36** But the five planets are not like that, because each individual planet has an allotment of the male and female in each of its two houses.

37 And[34] due to the strength of the luminaries, and that each of them has a single figure and a single house, each of them in its house came to indicate a figure of moderation, composition, and growth. **38** But as for the five planets, they are the contrary of that because each one of them has two figures and two distances: for in one of its houses it indicates the figure of direct motion, easternization, suitability, and moderation, and in the other house it indicates a figure of retrogradation, westernization, and a decrease of moderation.[35]

---

[33] I believe we resume Hermes-Agathodaimōn here, because Abū Ma'shar has finished his summary up to **33**, and I have not seen evidence that any version of "unhealthiness" was used by Greek sources (**34**). Note also that the text begins to use "allotment" for dignities again, just as Hermes-Agathodaimōn did in **6**, and in **35** repeats the method of starting with the luminaries, which was explicitly the Hermes-Agathodaimōn approach in **29**.

[34] For what follows, refer back to **1ff**.

[35] Note that Hermes-Agathodaimōn stresses how easternization and westernization work differently for the superiors and inferiors (**42-43**).

39 For Saturn in Capricorn indicates the figure of retrogradation and westernization, due to the agreement of the cold and dryness of them both;[36] but in Aquarius he indicates the figure of direct motion and easternization, due to the hotness of Aquarius and its wetness.[37]

40 Jupiter in Sagittarius indicates the figure of direct motion and easternization, but in Pisces he indicates the figure of retrogradation and westernization.

41 Mars in Scorpio indicates the figure of direct motion due to the mixture of Scorpio's wetness and its cold, and due to the hotness of Mars and his dryness; but in Aries he indicates the figure of retrogradation due to the meeting of their hotness and dryness.

42 Venus in Taurus indicates the figure of suitability and direct motion as well as westernization, because westernization is more appropriate to her; and in Libra she indicates the figure of retrogradation and the beginning of easternization.

43 And Mercury in Virgo indicates the figure of direct motion and westernization, while in Gemini he indicates the figure of retrogradation and easternization.

[Abū Ma'shar again: "The Lot of the nature of the houses"]

44 The ancients also derived a Lot for the houses of the planets, from the luminaries and their houses, and they called it the "Lot of the nature of the houses." **45** And it is that you calculate, for any time you wanted, from the degree of the Sun to 15° of Leo (by equal degrees),[38] and whatever it comes to, add to it what the Moon has traveled in her sign, cast it out from the sign of the Moon, and where the counting runs out, there is this Lot. **46** Then, at that time take from the degree of the Moon to 15° of Cancer, and whatever it comes to, add to it what the Sun has traveled in his sign, cast it out from the

---

[36] That is, Saturn and Capricorn.
[37] It would have been simpler for Hermes-Agathodaimōn to say that the planets work better in the house of their own sect (as Saturn and Aquarius are both diurnal); but he has consistently been making a naturalistic case for astrology. These signs also happen to be the signs in which the planets rejoice.
[38] That is, zodiacal degrees.

sign of the Sun, and where your calculation terminates, there is this other Lot. **47** And know that neither one of them will fall into in one of the houses of the planets without the other one falling in the other one; and if one of the two Lots falls into the house of one of the luminaries, the second Lot will fall into the house of the other luminary.

Chapter V.5: On the reason for the planets' exaltations, according to what some of the astrologers claimed

Planet	Degree	Range
♄	21st ♎	20°-20°59'
♃	15th ♋	14°-14°59'
♂	28th ♑	27°-27°59'
☉	19th ♈	18°-18°59'
♀	27th ♓	26°-26°59'
☿	15th ♍	14°-14°59'
☽	3rd ♉	2°-2°59'
☊	3rd ♊	2°-2°59'
☊	3rd ♐	2°-2°59'

Figure 38: Standard exaltation degrees (V.5)

1 The seven planets have an exaltation and fall in the twelve signs, and all of the scholars in the profession of the stars agree that:[39]

2 The exaltation of the Sun is in the 19th degree of Aries.

3 The exaltation of the Moon is in the 3rd degree of Taurus.

4 The exaltation of Jupiter is in the 15th degree of Cancer.

5 The exaltation of Mercury is in the 15th degree of Virgo.

6 The exaltation of Saturn is in the 21st degree of Libra.

7 The exaltation of Mars is in the 28th degree of Capricorn.

8 The exaltation of Venus is in the 27th degree of Pisces.

9 The exaltation of the Head is in the 3rd degree of Gemini.

10 The exaltation of the Tail is in the 3rd degree of Sagittarius.

11 And the degree of the fall of every planet is in the opposition of the sign of its exaltation, in the same degree as the exaltation.

---

[39] See also the Hermes-Agathodaimōn version in V.7. Note that not all of these degrees were agreed upon in ancient times: this includes the poem of Dorotheus, which sometimes spoke of an exaltation "around" a certain degree, and a common confusion between an ordinal degree (such as the 2nd) and the cardinal degree (2°). Also, it is only in the Persian tradition that the Nodes have exaltations.

12 But as for what reason these signs and the degrees named in them were singled out as the exaltation of each planet (rather than other degrees of that sign), that is something whose knowledge was difficult for the generality of [our] predecessors as well as later people. **13** Ptolemy did state a reason for the exaltation of the planets in the signs in an abbreviated way, but he did not state the reason for their *degrees* in the signs.[40] **14** As for Hermes, he stated a reason for the exaltation of the planets in the signs as well as their actual degrees, in a detailed way, and we will state his account in what lies ahead.[41]

[A Thema Mundi based on exaltations]

15 As for people who lay claim to explanations in the science of the profession of judgments, [but] for whom the knowledge of the nature of the higher bodies and their movements is obscure (as well as the reasons for generation and corruption), they offered a pretended reason in that, by saying that these seven planets [at Creation] were made to be in the signs of their exaltations, in the degree attributed to it as the exaltation, and from that degree they began [their] motion at the beginning of what they have traveled, and every planet travels on every day the amount of its mean motion for a day. **16** They kept traveling for a long time in that condition, [and] then were they were bound to the two luminaries (and they were in Leo and Cancer); and the length of their bonds was in the amount of the degrees which we mentioned in what preceded.[42] **17** So, the degree of the planets' exaltation came to be the position from which they begin [their] movement at the start of their being, and their houses came to be in accordance with the length of their bonds to the Sun and Moon.

18 Now as for what they stated about the reason for the houses of the planets (that they came to be according to the length of their bonds with the luminaries), we have already stated its wrongness in Chapter 2 of this Book.[43] **19** But as for what they stated about them being created in the de-

---

[40] See Ch. V.6.
[41] See Ch. V.7.
[42] See Ch. V.2, **4-9**.
[43] See Ch. V.2.

grees of their exaltations, and beginning their motion from those degrees, and having traveled in their mean motion every day, [and] then being bound to the Sun and Moon, [note that] their motion varies and retrogradation happens to them. **20** But if the Maker and Creator (may He be blessed and exalted) had brought forth these seven planets at the beginning of their being in the degrees of their exaltations in the signs, in the condition and movement which they claim, [and] then had wanted to alter their motions from what they had been, so that He bound these five to the luminaries, then why were these five singled out by retrogradation and direct motion by reason of that bond, while the Sun and Moon do not have retrogradation, and *they* both are also bound to [the *others*]?

21 And just as the planets are bodies having colors, and they are seen by their colors, so likewise their bonds ought to be bodies having visible colors.

22 Or, for what reason did the Maker (mighty and great) not assign these varying motions to them *without* binding them to [the luminaries], since just as He was able to bring them forth at the beginning, so likewise he was able to change whatever motions of theirs He willed, at whatever time He willed, without binding them to others? **23** For if He was unable to do that except by bonds, then He would be lacking in strength in that—but one cannot really believe that claim unless one is ignorant, not understanding the power of God over things (He is great and exalted beyond what the prattlers say).

24 And also, if these five planets vary their motion, and retrogradation happens to them because they are bound to the Sun and Moon, then it ought to be that, on every day, the motion of Sun and Moon is the same as [their own] mean motion, since they *do not* have retrogradation. **25** But we have found that they *do* have variation in course.

26 All that we have said is an indicator of the worthlessness of their claim, and their lying, **27** And these [people] have also lied in what they lay claim to, concerning the reason for the degree of the planets' exaltations and their houses, and the variation in their course, and their retrogradation—all of the philosophers and scholars in the profession of the stars (of the people of Persia, the Indians, and the Greeks).

[An Indian-Persian Thema Mundi]

28 But some of them[44] say that the seven planets began to move from the beginning of Aries, so that they moved in their condition which they are in now, and they erect the planets based on that. **29** And all of them agree that their motion is not changed from what it had been, and they do not diverge from their condition, nor from their motion which they remain in;[45] and indeed each one of them individually has a special property in its own right, and its [own] color and movement. **30** And the reason why each one of them is distinguished by a condition it remains in, and one different from [any] other, is that it is an effect of its motion (by which it is distinguished in terms of generation and corruption in this world), different from what is effected by the motion of other [planets].

Chapter V.6: On the reason for the planets' exaltations, according to what Ptolemy claimed

1 Ptolemy, the author of *The Book of Judgments*, said:[46] Since we have found that when the Sun is in Aries he begins the ascent towards the north and to the zenith [above] our heads,[47] and the length of the day increases over the night, and the nature of the hot increases, and when he comes to be in Libra the day decreases relative to the night, and he will descend to the

---

[44] This refers to Indian (and Persian) theories, which claimed that the planets were conjoined at 0° Aries at the time of Creation. For more, see my *AW2*.

[45] Lit., "which they do not cease to be in"; but that is perhaps too many negatives to be easily understood.

[46] Abū Ma'shar now begins to quote from Ch. I.19 of the *Tetrabiblos* (Robbins pp. 89ff).

[47] Not necessarily to the zenith (if we compare with the words of Ptolemy), but in northern declination and higher in the sky (for observers in the northern hemisphere).

south—due to that, Aries was made the exaltation of the Sun, and Libra (which is contrary to Aries, and its diametrical opposite),[48] was made his fall.

2 As for Saturn, his nature is cooling; but due to the cold of his nature he is antithetical to the heating nature of the Sun, because when the hot increases, cold decreases (and when the cold increases, hot decreases). **3** So Libra was made the exaltation of Saturn, and Aries his fall, contrary to what they assigned to the Sun.

4 Taurus was made the exaltation of the Moon because when the Sun is in Aries and the Moon is in Taurus, it is the start of the appearance of her glow (and it is also the start of the Moon's triplicity). **5** And they made her fall be Scorpio, because it is diametrically opposite her exaltation.

6 And they made Cancer be the exaltation of Jupiter, because by his nature Jupiter is indicative of the moderate winds of the north: so when he is in Cancer, there arise winds of the north which are productive of vegetation (by the permission of God), and the nature of Jupiter becomes strong. **7** And they made Capricorn be his fall, because it is diametrically opposite his exaltation.

8 And they made Capricorn be the exaltation of Mars, because Capricorn is southern, and it is diametrically opposite the exaltation of Jupiter, and because the nature of Mars is burning and southern: for when he comes to be in it, his hotness becomes strong. **9** And they made Cancer be his fall, because it is diametrically opposite his exaltation.

10 And they made Pisces be the exaltation of Venus, because the nature of Pisces is wetness, and in [Pisces] the wetness of the season of spring begins, and Venus is wet: so when she comes to be in it, her wetness becomes strong. **11** And they made Virgo be her fall, because it is diametrically opposite her exaltation.

12 And they made Virgo be the exaltation of Mercury, because Virgo is a sign in which the dryness of the season of fall begins, and the nature of Mercury [inclines] towards the dry which is <in> it, so when he comes to be in it, his dryness becomes strong. **13** And they made Pisces be his fall because it is diametrically opposite his exaltation.

---

[48] نظير here and below, which I would normally translate as "the counterpoint." But Ptolemy uses the word *diametron* ("diameter") and *antithesis* ("antithesis"), so I follow him instead of adding new vocabulary.

Chapter V.7: On the reason for the planets' exaltations, according to what fits with the statement of Hermes

[Principles used in the exaltations]

♄	21ˢᵗ ♎⁴⁹	20°-20°59'
♃	16ᵗʰ ♋	15°-15°59'
♂	28ᵗʰ ♑	27°-27°59'
☉	19ᵗʰ ♈	18°-18°59'
♀	27ᵗʰ ♓	26°-26°59'
☿	16ᵗʰ ♍	15°-15°59'
☽	3ʳᵈ ♉	2°-2°59'
☊	3ʳᵈ ♊	2°-2°59'
☊	3ʳᵈ ♐	2°-2°59'

Figure 39: Hermes's exaltation degrees (V.7)

1 For things which have an inception, at the beginning of their inception they are in [a state of] advancement and increase; at their middle they are stronger and the most robust they can be; and at their end they are retreating and weak.⁵⁰ 2 And an indicator of that, is that for everything among animals or vegetation which is natured, in its youth it is advancing and increasing, while in its middle it is the strongest it can be, and at its end it is retreating and weak. 3 So because of that, each planet is said to be advancing and increasing at the beginning of the signs, and in their middle it is the strongest it can be, and at their end it is retreating and weak. 4 And they are like that at the beginning of their easternization and direct motion,⁵¹ and its middle, and its end. 5 Thus it has become clear to us in this way that the strength of the planets is in the middles of the signs.

6 And we have already stated in Book II that Aries and Cancer are the two advancing, increasing signs (due to the increase of the day in them, and the elevation of the Sun above us), and that Libra and Capricorn are both retreating and decreasing (due to the decrease of the day in them, and the

---

⁴⁹ See **46-49** below. Despite this claim, by calculation it should occur in the 22ⁿᵈ degree, or 21° - 21° 59'.

⁵⁰ See II.3, **5ff**. The words here for "advancement" (إقبال) and "retreating" (إدبار) are the same words sometimes used by Sahl to indicate being angular or succedent, or being cadent or declining, which the astrologers also compared to the process of generation, maturing, and then declining. (But it is not always clear in Sahl whether this is by sign or quadrant division.)

⁵¹ That is, their easternization *while they are in* direct motion: this needs to be specified because Venus and Mercury are stronger when they emerge as evening planets and set after the Sun.

lowering of the Sun away from us).[52] **7** So we know that the most worthy of the places for the exaltation of the fortunes is the two increasing, advancing signs, and that the most worthy of the places for the exaltation of the infortunes is the two decreasing, retreating signs, because[53] there is no exaltation of two planets a single sign, just as there is no house belonging to two planets in a single sign.

[The exaltation signs]

8 Now since we have found that when the Sun comes to be in Aries, he begins an ascent and increase of the day over the night, we know that the most worthy of the places for the exaltation of the Sun is Aries, and in 15° of it he is the strongest he can be. **9** And in Chapter 4 of this Book[54] we have already made clear that the Moon is conjoined with the Sun, and the Moon's allotment follows the allotment of the Sun, so we know that the sign of the Moon's exaltation is Taurus, because it follows the sign of the Sun's exaltation.

10 And we have found the antithesis of brightness to be darkness, and the Sun has brightness and light, while Saturn has the indication of darkness:[55] so the most worthy of the places for Saturn's exaltation is the antithesis of the place in which the Sun is exalted—and it is Libra. **11** And the strongest he can be is in 15° of it. **12** And we have found that the place in which the decrease comes to an end, is Capricorn: so we know that the exaltation of the second infortune is in it, and his power is in 15° of it.

13 And we already know that after the two luminaries, no planet is more fortunate than Jupiter,[56] and no place is more powerful (after Aries) than

---

[52] See II.7, **5-7**.

[53] This "because" appears a bit ambitious and sudden. Hermes means that since there is only one exaltation per sign, it is not enough to pick the single most advancing and increasing sign, and put all of the exaltations of the fortunes there (and likewise for the retreating signs and infortunes). So, we have to spread them out among multiple signs that best match these concepts.

[54] See V.4, **2-6**.

[55] See V.4, **26**.

[56] See IV.5, **47**.

Cancer: so it becomes clear to us that the exaltation of Jupiter is in it, and his power is in 15° of it.

14 Now that we understand the exaltations of these five planets, and the place of their power in those signs, we want to understand the exaltation of the remaining two planets, as well as their power. **15** It has already preceded [this] statement, that a single sign is not the exaltation of two planets. **16** And we have found Venus is not distanced from the Sun by more than 47° and [some] minutes, and she is a moist, feminine planet, and we already know that Taurus is the exaltation of the Moon, and that Pisces is more appropriate for Venus (due to its wetness and feminization) than Gemini is: so the power of Venus comes to be in 15° of Pisces.[57]

17 And the power of Mercury is in 15° of Virgo, in the triplicity of Taurus: and indeed we have made him be in the triplicity of Taurus because Mercury is not distanced from the Sun by more than 27° and [some] minutes, and he is a planet in which there is dryness (of the nature of the first period of autumn), and Taurus is a sign resembling Mercury in the nature of the dry and its nearness to the exaltation of the Sun—except that Taurus has already become the exaltation of the Moon.[58] **18** So the most worthy of the signs for the exaltation of Mercury is Virgo (and the strongest he can be is in 15° of it), because it resembles him in the dry and in the nature of the beginning of the period of the autumn. **19** And indeed, the length of [Virgo's] day, and its path in the circle, is the same as the length of the day of Aries and its path:[59] so due to the agreement of [Virgo's] path with that of Aries, which is the exaltation of the Sun (and indeed [Virgo's] transit in the circle in the length of the day is one [and the same] transit), Virgo came to be closer to Aries than Taurus by means of its nature.

---

[57] The point Hermes is making is that while Gemini is within 47° of Aries (the Sun's exaltation), Gemini is less appropriate for her than Pisces, which is within the same range on the other side. He will make a similar point about Mercury below.

[58] Again, the point is that we would prefer Mercury's exaltation to be within 27° or so degrees of Aries (the Sun's exaltation), namely in Taurus. But given the rules above, that is not possible: so the next best thing would be to put him in another sign of the same triplicity. In this way his exaltation will be within 27° or so of Leo (the Sun's *house*). But in the following sentences Hermes seems to heap on more reasons which contribute little that is plausible.

[59] For signs of the same daylight, see VI.5, **6-11**.

20 And also, just as we made the exaltation of Saturn be in the sign which is the antithesis of the exaltation of the Sun (due to the contrast of one with the other), so likewise we have made the exaltation of Mercury be in the contrary of the exaltation of Venus, because in the position where Venus is humbled,[60] there is the exaltation of Mercury (due to wisdom being antithetical to pleasure and being overjoyed).

[The exaltation degrees]

21 Now since we have understood the houses in which these planets are exalted, and the power of each planet in that sign, we want to know the limit[61] of the degree of exaltation in every sign, for every planet.

22 So we return to what we had stated in Book II, that the beginning of the division is from the Sun, and from midday, and from the beginning of Aries, and from the equator,[62] and from the Midheaven:[63] because the Sun rises up upon his entering Aries,[64] and the day begins to increase, and the day is the cause of the night, and midday is the most powerful period of the day. **23** And also, the ascensions of the Ascendants of the world differ among themselves.[65]

24 Now as for the position of the equator, the ascensions of the signs in their Ascendant and Midheaven is one [and the same], and just like those degrees, so is the transit of all of the signs in the Midheaven of the world,[66] and likewise the degrees of all of the planets' exaltations are in one [and the

---

[60] Or, "abased" (يتّضع). This is an indication of the Greek origin of the Hermes text, since that is the original meaning of being in "fall" (Gr. *tapeinōma*). The Arabic هبوط does not have quite the same meaning.

[61] حدّ. Below I also translate this as "boundary." Hermes is speaking of the exact degree of the exaltation, which he sometimes wants to be just beyond or short of some other position, hence its "limit" or "boundary."

[62] Lit., the "line of equality."

[63] See II.7, **35**.

[64] That is, these signs increase in northern declination.

[65] يختلف عليهم.

[66] At the earth's equator, the length of time it takes for a sign to rise (as the Ascendant) is the same as the time it takes to pass fully across the Midheaven.

same] condition for the world. **25** So for those reasons, the beginning of the division is from the position of the right circle, and from the Midheaven.

26 And we already know that when the first minute of Aries is on the Midheaven (at the equator), the first minute of Cancer will be rising. **27** So due to that, the ancients said Cancer is the Ascendant of the world: and the most worthy of the signs to be ascending at the beginning of the world's development, is the degree of Cancer in which the exaltation of Jupiter is.

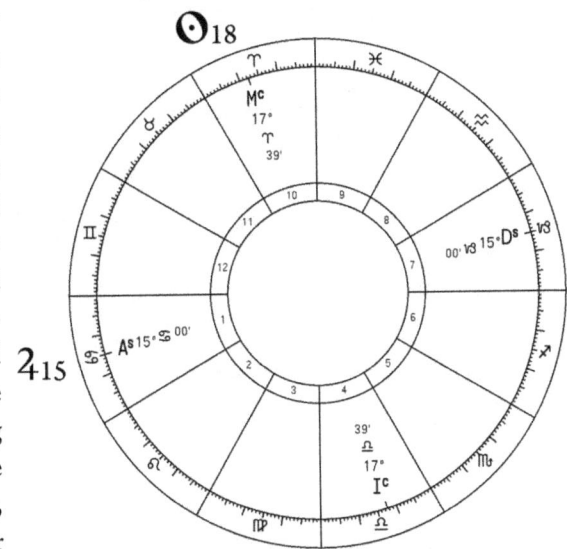

Figure 40: Exaltations of Jupiter and Sun (from Hermes, V.7, 27-30)

28 Now, if 15° of Cancer was ascending at the equator, the eighteenth degree of Aries is on the Midheaven. **29** But if the Sun was in 15° of Aries, he would be withdrawing, while if he and Jupiter were in the stakes, the Sun would be in 19° of Aries.[67] **30** So, the most worthy of the degrees and positions for the exaltation of the Sun, is the nineteenth degree of Aries.[68]

31 And we already know that, of the causes of the sphere, there is none that lacks rules[69] and organization, and among the rules of organization is that Jupiter is in the Ascendant of the world. **32** And if it were like that, he would be in parallel with[70] the degree of Mars, and each one of them would be corrupting to the nature of his associate, taking away from the utmost of

---

[67] Or rather, in the "nineteenth" degree of Aries, 18°.
[68] That is, 18°.
[69] أحكام. This usually means "judgments," but can also mean a "rule." In this context it means something like a "standard" which is rational or judged from God's perspective, so I have favored "rules."
[70] مزاويًا. That is, "opposed to," here and below.

his indication: for indeed the meaning of the degree of a planet's exaltation is the position of the extreme limit of its nature's manifestation in that sign, and its reaching the "utmost" of its indication for good fortune.

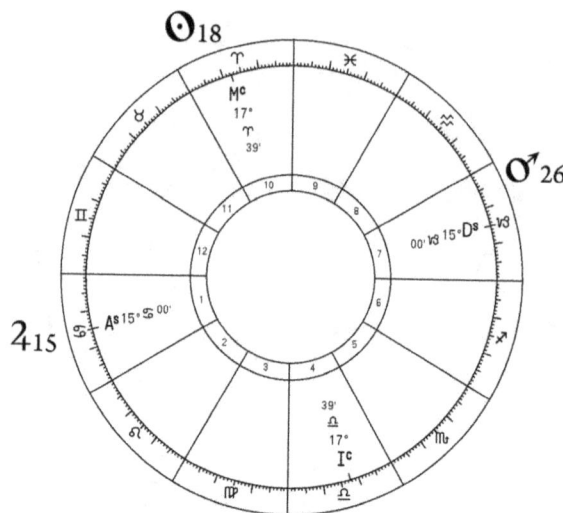

Figure 41: Exaltation of Mars (from Hermes, V.7, 35-37)

33 Now if we wanted to assign specific degrees to the distance which is between the two of them, we are informed about that by the amount of the distance of the planets from the Sun: because many of their conditions are attributed to them in accordance with their distance from him. 34 So we have found that every planet is weak when there are less than 12° between it and him, and sometimes some of them are not seen until they are distanced from him by 12°: so we call these degrees the "amount of distance."

35 Then, we add that to the place of Mars by ascensions of the right circle:[71] and it falls into the twenty-seventh degree. 36 If we had subtracted it, it would have occurred in the fourth degree of [Capricorn], in a place of withdrawal and weakness; and in addition to that he is an infortune by nature, [and would be] going into parallel with the fortune, corrupting it. 37 So we added it to him, so the degree of exaltation would be in a position in which the planet would be in a stake, advancing, strong, making his nature manifest.

---

[71] That is, in right ascension (RA).

38 As for Venus, because of the sign of her exaltation being the antithesis of the sign of Mercury's exaltation (due to the nature of the season), and her contrariety to him by indication, and the indication of each undermining the other when they are parallel to each other, we treat them just as we treated Mars, with an increase in the amount of distance beyond her place in the middle of Pisces, so that it falls into 28° of it.

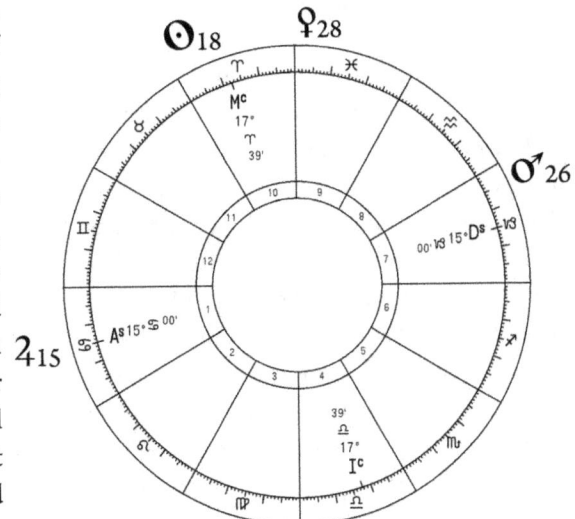

Figure 42: Exaltation of Venus (from Hermes, V.7, 38)

39 And when the infortunes are in fewer degrees than the fortunes, they are going towards them, doing violence to them, subtracting from their powers: so the most worthy of the degrees for the exaltation of Mars is the twenty-eighth degree of Capricorn, and the most worthy of the degrees for the exaltation of Venus is the twenty-seventh degree of Pisces. **40** And when Venus is like that, she would be close to the stake of the

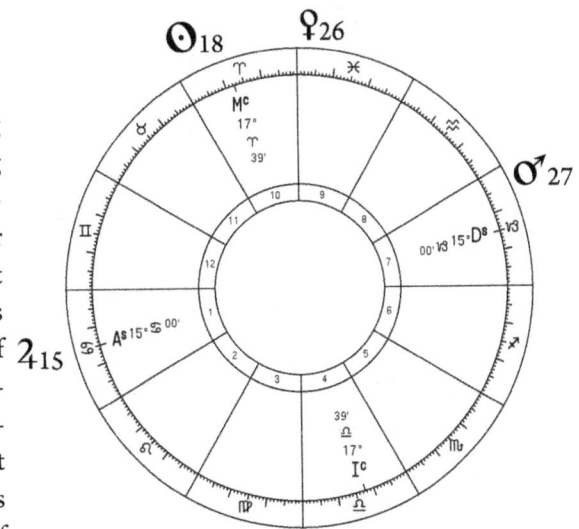

Figure 43: Mars and Venus adjusted (from Hermes, V.7, 39)

tenth, and that position harmonizes with her fortunate nature, due to its indication for good fortune. **41** But if we had subtracted the amount of those degrees from her place, she would have passed into the division[72] of the house of destruction and death, in a position contrary to her nature.

42 And as for Mercury, his exaltation is in 15° of Virgo because his house and exaltation are in one [and the same] sign. **43** Now if the exaltation of a planet was in its house, then in its middle it is the strongest it can be, and the most manifest in activity, just as we stated before—and especially if it is advancing in what follows the stake. **44** And Jupiter does not undermine him, but rather they are harmonious, blended due to Mercury's receiving the nature of [Jupiter's] good fortune, because each one of them is in the sign of his exaltation, in the same degree as the other. **45** If we had added something of the degrees to his place, he would have come closer to the parallel of Venus, and come into a place of withdrawal.

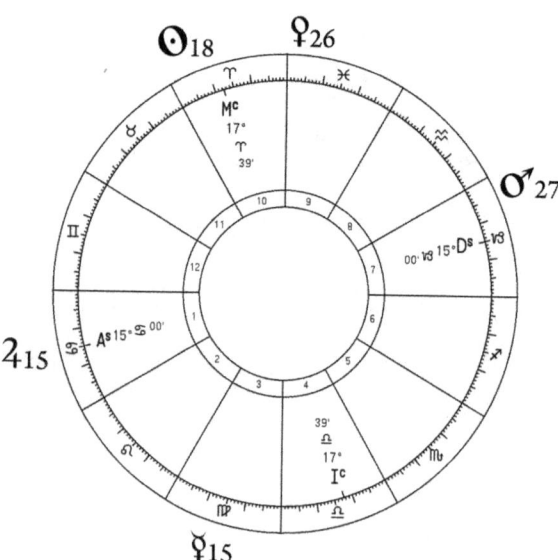

Figure 44: Exaltation of Mercury (from Hermes, V.7, 42)

46 As for Saturn, he is in the square of the degree of Jupiter, corrupting to his nature, and the square is one-half of an opposition: so we add 6° (and it is one-half of the amount of the distance) to the position of Saturn, and it comes to the twenty-first degree of Libra, so there is the degree of Saturn's exaltation. **47** Thus the degree of his exaltation comes to be in the stake of the fourth, gaining power,

---

[72] This is an indication that Hermes is using quadrant divisions: if we subtracted 12° in RA from her, it would come to 2° 10' Pisces, which is still in the ninth sign, but would be in the eighth quadrant division.

relinquishing the degree of the square of Jupiter and the parallel with the exaltation of the Sun. 48 And if we had subtracted [the amount] from him, he would have passed into a position of withdrawal, going toward the degree of them both, undermining them. 49 But if Jupiter had been parallel to Saturn, we would have added the full amount of the distance to the middle of Libra, just as we did with the others.

50 As for the Moon, she comes to be in the degree of her exaltation in accordance with her distance from the Sun and her visibility, because sometimes she is seen when she is distanced from him by less than 12° by [some] minutes, and sometimes she is seen when these degrees are completed by her and she comes to be at the boundary of the thirteenth degree.

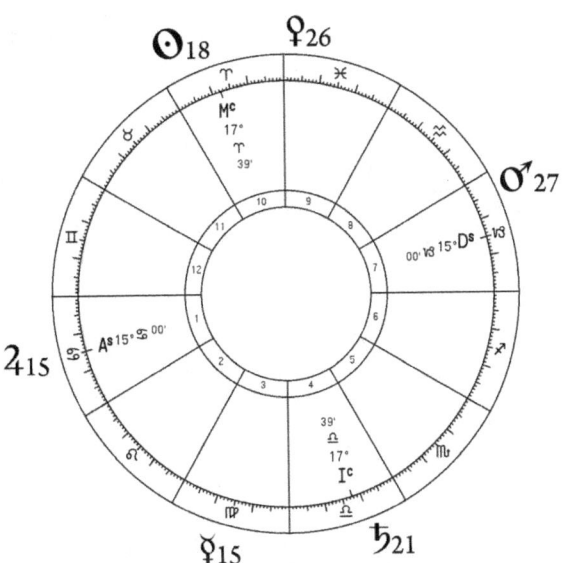

Figure 45: Exaltation of Saturn (from Hermes, V.7, 46)

51 So, the degree of her exaltation comes to be in the position which, if she were in it and the Sun was in the degree of his exaltation, she would be at the beginning of the boundary of her visibility (based on working out the visibility by ascensions of the right circle at the location of the equator): and it is the third degree of Taurus. 52 If she were in the second degree of it, she would be short of the boundary of the first degree of visibility, while if she was in the fourth degree from it, she would already have passed it.

53 And indeed, her visibility is like that when she has one-half of [her] latitude in the south, because when the planets have one-half of their latitude, they are the most balanced they can be in the condition of latitude. 54 But if you worked out her visibility in accordance with this latitude in the direction of the north, the beginning of the limit of her visibility would be at the end of Aries, and our statement was already presented before, that Tau-

rus is the exaltation of the Moon, and that a single sign is not the exaltation of two planets.[73]

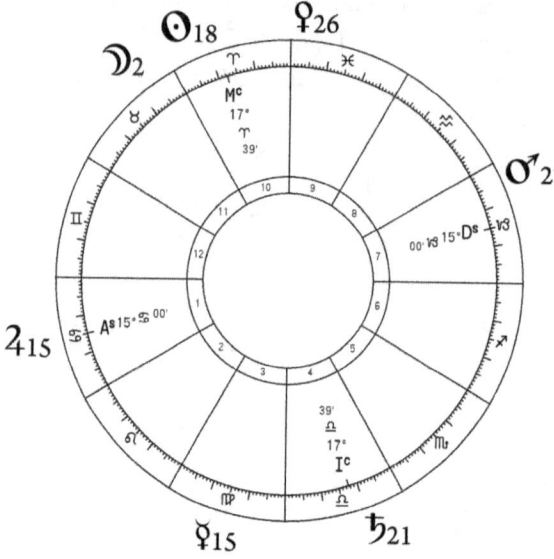

Figure 46: Exaltation of Moon (from Hermes, V.7, 51)

55 And in addition to this as well, the exaltation of the Head is in the stooped-over signs,[74] which do not resemble it.[75]

56 As for the Head, it is the position of the Moon's ascent [in latitude], and Gemini is a position of ascent: so due to their agreeing in ascent, its exaltation comes to be in it. **57** And indeed, its exaltation comes to be in the third degree of it, because when it is at this distance from the Moon, there is the amount of a single sign between them, and she will have one-half of her latitude by which she is seen in the degree of her exaltation.

58 As for the Tail, it is the position of the Moon's descent, and Sagittarius is a position of lowness,[76] so due to their agreeing in one [and the same] thing, its exaltation came to be in the third degree of it.

---

[73] See **7** and **9** above.

[74] المتطامنة. Other translations might be "low" or "quiet," but I think Hermes is referring to the "crooked" signs (of which Gemini is one).

[75] Meaning unclear. Perhaps it means that the crooked signs do not resemble the *principle* of the Head or North Node (which indicates uprightness, height, and expansion). But there is also an indication that this sentence is somehow distorted, in that the Latin manuscript **H** omits it.

[76] This is probably because it leads to the most southern declination.

59 So for these reasons, the degrees of the planets' exaltations came to be in these positions.

[Abū Ma'shar's comments, and alternatives]

60 And pertaining to the correctness of this procedure, and its truth, is that [1] the degrees of the exaltation of the superior planets occur in the stakes, and [2] the degrees of the exaltation of the inferior planets come to be in the positions harmonious with them, so that when each one of them is in that degree it is at the utmost manifestation of its nature; and [3] the degrees of the fortunes come to be before the degrees of the infortunes contrary to them, because the beginnings of generation belong to the fortunes [but] then they are followed by corruption, which is of the indications of the infortunes.

61 Now, [some] people offer an excuse for the distance of those degrees between Mars and Venus by saying: "When Jupiter is in the degree of the Ascendant of the world, he is parallel to the degree of Mars. **62** And we already know that the infortunes do violence to the fortunes, so we wanted to assign a specific limit to the distance which is between them. **63** And we are informed about that by the distance of the Moon from the Sun and her visibility, because their indication is for what occurs in this world (more manifestly so than the indication of the rest of the planets), and the abundance of changes in things happens in accordance with her distance from him. **64** And we found that the Moon's visibility is generally when she is distanced from him by 12° and she comes to be in the thirteenth: so we added 13° to the middle of Capricorn by the right circle, and [the exaltation of Mars] occurred in the twenty-eighth degree of it.

65 "And as for Venus, we worked with her just as we worked with Mars, except that we added 11° to her place, because she is seen when her distance from the Sun is less than the distance of Mars, and the amount of her body[77] is less than the amount of Mars's body, by 1°. **66** So we subtracted that single degree from the 12°, and 11° remained; and we added it to the 15° of Pisces,

---

[77] جرم. This is also known as her "orb." See VII.3, **10-11**.

and it came to the twenty-seventh degree: and there is the degree of her exaltation."[78]

Chapter V.8: On the different bounds of the planets, <and their conditions>[79]

1 We have found the bounds to be of five types. **2** As for one of them, it is [1] the bounds of the people of Egypt; the second is [2] the bounds of Ptolemy, the third [3] the bounds of the Chaldeans (and they are the people of Babylon), the fourth [4] the bounds of Astrātū, and the fifth [5] the bounds of the Indians.

3 Now as for [4] Astrātū, he divided every sign among the seven planets, and assigned the two luminaries a share in the bounds; and he argued in favor of that by saying that the planets do not have a share in the circle without the Sun and Moon also having the same.[80]

4 But as for the rest of those I mentioned, they divided a single sign among the five wandering planets, and did not assign the luminaries a share in it; and indeed they rejected a distribution of the luminaries among the bounds of the signs because they [only] partner with the planets in their houses.

5 As for some of the ancients, they claimed that the Sun has a partnership with their[81] lords in the signs which are in the half of the circle which is from the beginning of Leo to the end of Capricorn; and the Moon has a partnership with their lords in the signs which are in the other half, and it is from the beginning of Aquarius to the end of Cancer.[82]

---

[78] Abū Ma'shar does not explain why he thinks this alternative explanation is bogus, but we can guess: it must have something to do with using the number 13 for Mars instead of 12, and in the strange explanation for only using 11° for Venus—it sounds too *ad hoc*.

[79] Adding the brackets in accordance with the table of contents.

[80] See Ch. V.12.

[81] That is, the lords of the *signs*, not the bounds. Abū Ma'shar is now entertaining the views of these others who deny bounds to the luminaries.

[82] See also V.3, **19** and the Figure there.

BOOK V: THE SHARES OF THE PLANETS IN THE SIGNS

6 And some of them claimed that the Sun has a partnership with their lords in the first half of the male signs, and the Moon has a partnership in the other half of them. **7** But as for the feminine signs, from their beginning up to [the first] half of them the Moon has a partnership with their lords, while the Sun has a partnership with their lords in the last half. **8** So, since the luminaries partner with the planets in these signs in the two ways we stated, they were satisfied with this share which they have in the signs without needing to assign them a share in the bounds.

9 And as for [other] people, they said that all of the ancients gave the luminaries no share in the bounds because the natures are five: heating and drying are of the nature of Mars, heating and moistening the nature of Jupiter, cooling and drying the nature of Saturn, cooling and moistening the nature of Venus, and being blended of them is of the nature of Mercury. **10** But the nature of Venus matches the nature of the Moon in wetness and feminization, and the nature of Mars matches the nature of the Sun in hotness and masculinization, so due to the match of their natures with the natures of the luminaries,[83] they were satisfied with their share in the bounds without assigning the luminaries a share in them. **11** And they said that each one of the luminaries operates in the bound of the planet matching it by nature, similarly to[84] the operation of the planet.

12 And the most sound of the divisions is the division of those who do not assign the luminaries a share in the bounds of the signs (and it is the one on which the ancients agree); except that for each one of these, even though there is a distribution of each sign among the five planets, its author differs in the order of its planets, and the amount of degrees of each planet's bound: but the generality of them make the end of the signs be the bounds of the infortunes, because the end of the signs is of the share of retreating and weakness, just as we stated in what preceded;[85] and retreating and weakness are a misfortune, and the infortunes are more suitable for that.

13 Now as for Ptolemy, he found fault with the order of the bounds of the Egyptians and Chaldeans, as well as the amount of degrees in the bound of

---

[83] See III.1, **12** and **14**.

[84] مثل. I hesitate to translate this as the stronger "same as."

[85] This probably refers to either (or both) II.7, **1** and V.7, **1-7**, which reflect the view of Hermes-Agathodaimōn.

each planet: and he claimed that the most sound of the bounds is what he found in an ancient, effaced book, whose author is not known.[86] **14** But he abhorred that it might be attributed to himself, lest fault should adhere to the author of those bounds just like Ptolemy found fault in the bounds of others.

15 But we have found all of the ancients among the scholars of the masters of the stars to have employed the bounds of the people of Egypt in judgments, because they are more correct. **16** And, the degrees of the bounds of each planet matches its greater years.[87]

17 We will state the bounds of each one of these [sources], individually.

---

[86] *Tet.* I.21 (Robbins p. 103).

[87] This is also true of Ptolemy's bounds, as reflected in the Teubner critical edition (see V.10 below).

Chapter V.9: On the bounds of the people of Egypt[88]

♈	♃ 6 0° - 5° 59'	♀ 6 6° - 11° 59'	☿ 8 12° - 19° 59'	♂ 5 20° - 24° 59'	♄ 5 25° - 29° 59'
♉	♀ 8 0° - 7° 59'	☿ 6 8° - 13° 59'	♃ 8 14° - 21° 59'	♄ 5 22° - 26° 59'	♂ 3 27° - 29° 59'
♊	☿ 6 0° - 5° 59'	♃ 6 6° - 11° 59'	♀ 5 12° - 16° 59'	♂ 7 17° - 23° 59'	♄ 6 24° - 29° 59'
♋	♂ 7 0° - 6° 59'	♀ 6 7° - 12° 59'	☿ 6 13° - 18° 59'	♃ 7 19° - 25° 59'	♄ 4 26° - 29° 59'
♌	♃ 6 0° - 5° 59'	♀ 5 6° - 10° 59'	♄ 7 11° - 17° 59'	☿ 6 18° - 23° 59'	♂ 6 24° - 29° 59'
♍	☿ 7 0° - 6° 59'	♀ 10 7° - 16° 59'	♃ 4 17° - 20° 59'	♂ 7 21° - 27° 59'	♄ 2 28° - 29° 59'
♎	♄ 6 0° - 5° 59'	☿ 8 6° - 13° 59'	♃ 7 14° - 20° 59'	♀ 7 21° - 27° 59'	♂ 2 28° - 29° 59'
♏	♂ 7 0° - 6° 59'	♀ 4 7° - 10° 59'	☿ 8 11° - 18° 59'	♃ 5 19° - 23° 59'	♄ 6 24° - 29° 59'
♐	♃ 12 0° - 11° 59'	♀ 5 12° - 16° 59'	☿ 4 17° - 20° 59'	♄ 5 21° - 25° 59'	♂ 4 26° - 29° 59'
♑	☿ 7 0° - 6° 59'	♃ 7 7° - 13° 59'	♀ 8 14° - 21° 59'	♄ 4 22° - 25° 59'	♂ 4 26° - 29° 59'
♒	☿ 7 0° - 6° 59'	♀ 6 7° - 12° 59'	♃ 7 13° - 19° 59'	♂ 5 20° - 24° 59'	♄ 5 25° - 29° 59'
♓	♀ 12 0° - 11° 59'	♃ 4 12° - 15° 59'	☿ 3 16° - 18° 59'	♂ 9 19° - 27° 59'	♄ 2 28° - 29° 59'

Figure 47: Table of Egyptian bounds

---

[88] I have converted Abū Ma'shar's list of planets and size of the bounds into a table, and added the cardinal degrees myself (e.g., 0° - 5° 59').

Chapter V.10: On the bounds of Ptolemy

Comment by Dykes. I have put Abū Ma'shar's version of Ptolemy's bounds into tabular form, adding the cardinal degrees of their amounts (such as 0° - 5° 59'). But Abū Ma'shar's version is wrong, because the degrees for each planet do not add up to its greater planetary years. For example, Saturn should have 57°, but here he has 62°. I have highlighted where his table departs from the Hübner edition of the *Tetrabiblos*, which I provide immediately afterwards (and which does have the correct number of degrees).

♈	♃ 6 0° - 5° 59'	♀ 8 6° - 13° 59'	☿ 7 14° - 20° 59'	♂ 5 21° - 25° 59'	♄ 4 26° - 29° 59'
♉	♀ 8 0° - 7° 59'	☿ 7 8° - 14° 59'	♃ 7 15° - 21° 59'	♄ 6 22° - 27° 59'	♂ 2 28° - 29° 59'
♊	☿ 7 0° - 6° 59'	♃ 6 7° - 12° 59'	♀ 7 13° - 19° 59'	♂ 7 20° - 26° 59'	♄ 3 27° - 29° 59'
♋	♂ 6 0° - 5° 59'	♃ 7 6° - 12° 59'	☿ 7 13° - 19° 59'	♀ 6 20° - 25° 59'	♄ 4 26° - 29° 59'
♌	♄ 6 0° - 5° 59'	☿ 7 6° - 12° 59'	♀ 6 13° - 18° 59'	♂ 6 19° - 24° 59'	♃ 5 25° - 29° 59'
♍	☿ 7 0° - 6° 59'	♀ 6 7° - 12° 59'	♃ 5 13° - 17° 59'	♄ 6 18° - 23° 59'	♂ 6 24° - 29° 59'
♎	♄ 6 0° - 5° 59'	♀ 5 6° - 10° 59'	♃ 8 11° - 18° 59'	☿ 5 19° - 23° 59'	♂ 6 24° - 29° 59'
♏	♂ 6 0° - 5° 59'	♃ 8 6° - 13° 59'	♀ 6 14° - 19° 59'	☿ 6 20° - 25° 59'	♄ 4 26° - 29° 59'
♐	♃ 8 0° - 7° 59'	♀ 6 8° - 13° 59'	☿ 5 14° - 18° 59'	♄ 6 19° - 24° 59'	♂ 5 25° - 29° 59'
♑	♀ 6 0° - 5° 59'	☿ 6 6° - 11° 59'	♃ 7 12° - 18° 59'	♄ 6 19° - 24° 59'	♂ 5 25° - 29° 59'
♒	♄ 6 0° - 5° 59'	☿ 6 6° - 11° 59'	♀ 8 12° - 19° 59'	♃ 5 20° - 24° 59'	♂ 5 25° - 29° 59'
♓	♀ 8 0° - 7° 59'	♃ 6 8° - 13° 59'	☿ 6 14° - 19° 59'	♂ 5 20° - 24° 59'	♄ 5 25° - 29° 59'

Figure 48: Table of Ptolemaic bounds according to Abū Ma'shar

♈	♃ 6 0° - 5° 59'	♀ 8 6° - 13° 59'	☿ 7 14° - 20° 59'	♂ 5 21° - 25° 59'	♄ 4 26° - 29° 59'
♉	♀ 8 0° - 7° 59'	☿ 7 8° - 14° 59'	♃ 7 15° - 21° 59'	♄ 4 22° - 25° 59'	♂ 4 26° - 29° 59'
♊	☿ 7 0° - 6° 59'	♃ 6 7° - 12° 59'	♀ 7 13° - 19° 59'	♂ 6 20° - 25° 59'	♄ 4 26° - 29° 59'
♋	♂ 6 0° - 5° 59'	♃ 7 6° - 12° 59'	☿ 7 13° - 19° 59'	♀ 7 20° - 26° 59'	♄ 3 27° - 29° 59'
♌	♄ 6 0° - 5° 59'	☿ 7 6° - 12° 59'	♀ 6 13° - 18° 59'	♃ 6 19° - 24° 59'	♂ 5 25° - 29° 59'
♍	☿ 7 0° - 6° 59'	♀ 6 7° - 12° 59'	♃ 5 13° - 17° 59'	♄ 6 18° - 23° 59'	♂ 6 24° - 29° 59'
♎	♄ 6 0° - 5° 59'	♀ 5 6° - 10° 59'	♃ 8 11° - 18° 59'	☿ 5 19° - 23° 59'	♂ 6 24° - 29° 59'
♏	♂ 6 0° - 5° 59'	♃ 8 6° - 13° 59'	♀ 7 14° - 20° 59'	☿ 6 21° - 26° 59'	♄ 3 27° - 29° 59'
♐	♃ 8 0° - 7° 59'	♀ 6 8° - 13° 59'	☿ 5 14° - 18° 59'	♄ 6 19° - 24° 59'	♂ 5 25° - 29° 59'
♑	♀ 6 0° - 5° 59'	☿ 6 6° - 11° 59'	♃ 7 12° - 18° 59'	♂ 6 19° - 24° 59'	♄ 5 25° - 29° 59'
♒	♄ 6 0° - 5° 59'	☿ 6 6° - 11° 59'	♀ 8 12° - 19° 59'	♃ 5 20° - 24° 59'	♂ 5 25° - 29° 59'
♓	♀ 8 0° - 7° 59'	♃ 6 8° - 13° 59'	☿ 6 14° - 19° 59'	♂ 6 20° - 25° 59'	♄ 4 26° - 29° 59'

Figure 49: Table of Ptolemaic bounds
(Hübner critical edition of *Tetrabiblos*)

Chapter V.11: On the bounds of the Chaldeans

1 The Chaldeans were a people who used to dwell in Babylon at an early time, and in the reports circulating among nations it is said that the first one who had dwelt and lived there was Noah the Prophet (the prayer of God be upon him): and it is that when he followed after the Flood, he and those with him passed over into Babylon in order to seek warmth and heat, and they stayed there.

2 So they reproduced, and their group multiplied after Noah, and they ruled over them and built buildings there, and their dwellings came up to the Tigris and Euphrates so that they dwelt on their banks, until they reached from the Tigris to the lower Kaskar,[89] and from the Euphrates to behind Kufa. **3** Their place was the one called the Suwād today.

4 Their kings stayed in Babylon, and the name of the first of them was Tiglath-Pileser.[90] **5** And the Chaldeans were the soldiers of their kings, and they and their kings did not cease to be joined in that [same] condition until Darius I[91] killed and exterminated them.

6 And all of the Chaldeans were learned in calculating the stars and making judgments about them, making use of them and not preferring any [other] science to them. **7** And people from all climes used to follow their scholars in teaching the calculation of the stars and their judgments, and it is said that the first to teach them the stars was Abātir,[92] the son of Shem, son of Noah.

8 Now, Ptolemy and others stated that in their judgments they used to employ bounds which were contrary to the bounds of the Egyptians and contrary to the bounds of others, and they used to make a division of the

---

[89] This is a district in the eastern part of the Great Swamp along the Tigris, which contains the city of Wāsit. Wāsit is roughly equidistant between Kūfa, Basrah, and Ahwāz. See LeStrange, pp. 39 and 42.

[90] Abū Ma'shar: *Tighāth Bilīsar*. This may be Tiglath-Pileser I (r. 1114-1076 BC), who was a king of the Middle Assyrian period.

[91] Darius the Great (r. 522-486 BC) was the third of the Achaemenid Persian kings. In 522 BC, the new Babylonian king Nebuchadnezzar III revolted against the Persians, taking advantage of political turmoil and the new accession of Darius, but the revolt was quickly put down with great force.

[92] This is perhaps Shem's son Arpachshad.

bounds of the signs of each triplicity according to a single concept, and made the division of the bounds of some triplicities by day be [certain] degrees, and by night they made it be different from that. **9** And Ptolemy stated them in his *Tetrabiblos*, but then after that he stated that no mention of those bounds is found in the books of their ancients, nor did their prior ancestors who were trustworthy in knowledge mention them. **10** So, we have left off from stating them in this book of ours, because they are not bounds which are agreed upon among the ancient scholars of the stars, due to the disagreement and confusion which is in them.[93]

	8°	7°	6°	5°	4°
♈ ♌ ♐	♃ 0° - 7° 59'	♀ 8° - 14° 59'	♄ 15° - 20° 59'	☿ 21° - 25° 59'	♂ 26° - 29° 59'
♉ ♍ ♑	♀ 0° - 7° 59'	♄ 8° - 14° 59'	☿ 15° - 20° 59'	♂ 21° - 25° 59'	♃ 26° - 29° 59'
♊ ♎ ♒	♄ 0° - 7° 59'	☿ 8° - 14° 59'	♂ 15° - 20° 59'	♃ 21° - #° 59'	♀ 26° - 29° 59'
♋ ♏ ♓	♂ 0° - 7° 59'	♃ 8° - 14° 59'	♀ 15° - 20° 59'	♄ 21° - 25° 59'	☿ 26° - 29° 59'

Figure 50: Table of Chaldean bounds (*Tet.* I.21)

---

[93] Nevertheless I include them here. As Abū Ma'shar mentioned (8), these bounds are sensitive to triplicity and sect, and the luminaries have no rulership. In the fiery triplicity, the degrees are assigned first to the triplicity lord of fire—which can only be Jupiter, because the Sun plays no role. The next degrees are assigned to Venus, the triplicity lord of earth, then to the triplicity lord (or rather, lords) of air, then to the remaining lord of water. (Venus cannot act as the triplicity lord of water, because she is already used for earth.) The special wrinkle in this scheme is that the airy triplicity has two lords (Saturn, Mercury), since they are not luminaries, nor do they reappear in the other triplicities like Venus does. However, they switch by night. So by day, their order in the fiery signs would be Saturn 6°, then Mercury 5°. But by night, their order would be Mercury 6°, then Saturn 5°. Thus the amount of degrees ruled by Saturn and Mercury differ by day and night. I have highlighted Saturn and Mercury in each row of the table.

Chapter V.12: On the bounds of Astrātū

Comment by Dykes. In this scheme, the first bound lord is the lord of the sign itself, and the rest follow in Chaldean order (Saturn, Jupiter, Mars, Sun, Venus, Mercury, Moon). Both luminaries are used. The number of degrees for each planet by rank is: Venus 60, Jupiter 55, Mars 53, Mercury 51, Saturn 49, Sun 48, Moon 44.

♈	♂ 6	☉ 4	♀ 4	☿ 5	☽ 3	♄ 2	♃ 6
	0°-5°59’	6°-9°59’	10°-13°59’	14°-18°59’	19°-21°59’	22°-23°59’	24°-29°59’
♉	♀ 4	☿ 7	☽ 5	♄ 5	♃ 3	♂ 3	☉ 3
	0°-3°59’	4°-10°59’	11°-15°59’	16°-20°59’	21°-23°59’	24°-26°59’	27°-29°59’
♊	☿ 3	☽ 4	♄ 5	♃ 5	♂ 6	☉ 4	♀ 3
	0°-2°59’	3°-6°59’	7°-11°59’	12°-16°59’	17°-22°59’	23°-26°59’	27°-29°59’
♋	☽ 8	♄ 2	♃ 2	♂ 6	☉ 3	♀ 5	☿ 4
	0°-7°59’	8°-9°59’	10°-11°59’	12°-17°59’	18°-20°59’	21°-25°59’	26°-29°59’
♌	☉ 1	♀ 7	☿ 6	☽ 4	♄ 6	♃ 3	♂ 3
	0°-0°59’	1°-7°59’	8°-13°59’	14°-17°59’	18°-23°59’	24°-26°59’	27°-29°59’
♍	☿ 9	☽ 4	♄ 2	♃ 2	♂ 3	☉ 5	♀ 5
	0°-8°59’	9°-12°59’	13°-14°59’	15°-16°59’	17°-19°59’	20°-24°59’	25°-29°59’
♎	♀ 8	☿ 3	☽ 2	♄ 5	♃ 5	♂ 2	☉ 5
	0°-7°59’	8°-10°59’	11°-12°59’	13°-17°59’	18°-22°59’	23°-24°59’	25°-29°59’
♏	♂ 6	☉ 6	♀ 6	☿ 4	☽ 2	♄ 3	♃ 3
	0°-5°59’	6°-11°59’	12°-17°59’	18°-21°59’	22°-23°59’	24°-26°59’	27°-29°59’
♐	♃ 9	♂ 5	☉ 5	♀ 4	☿ 3	☽ 2	♄ 2
	0°-8°59’	9°-13°59’	14°-18°59’	19°-22°59’	23°-25°59’	26°-27°59’	28°-29°59’
♑	♄ 7	♃ 7	♂ 3	☉ 2	♀ 6	☿ 2	☽ 3
	0°-6°59’	7°-13°59’	14°-16°59’	17°-18°59’	19°-24°59’	25°-26°59’	27°-29°59’
♒	♄ 8	♃ 6	♂ 6	☉ 4	♀ 2	☿ 2	☽ 2
	0°-7°59’	8°-13°59’	14°-19°59’	20°-23°59’	24°-25°59’	26°-27°59’	28°-29°59’
♓	♃ 4	♂ 4	☉ 6	♀ 6	☿ 3	☽ 5	♄ 2
	0°-3°59’	4°-7°59’	8°-13°59’	14°-19°59’	20°-22°59’	23°-27°59’	28°-29°59’

Figure 51: Table of the bounds of Astrātū (V.12)

Chapter V.13: On the bounds of the Indians

1 The Indians assigned the bounds of the male signs in one way, and the bounds of the female signs in another way. **2** Thus Aries: from its beginning to a whole[94] five degrees, it belongs to Mars; and what is after that to a whole ten degrees belongs to Saturn; and after that to a whole eighteen degrees belongs to Jupiter; and after that to a whole twenty-five degrees belongs to Mercury, and after that to a whole thirty degrees belongs to Venus.

3 And Taurus up to a whole five degrees belongs to Venus, and after that to a whole twelve degrees belongs to Mercury, and after that to a whole twenty degrees belongs to Jupiter, and after that to a whole twenty-five degrees belongs to Saturn, and after that to a whole thirty degrees belongs to Mars.

4 And Gemini, Leo, Libra, Sagittarius, and Aquarius, are like Aries. **5** Cancer, Virgo, Scorpio, Capricorn, and Pisces are like Taurus.

♈ ♌ ♐	♂ 5	♄ 5	♃ 8	☿ 7	♀ 5
♊ ♎ ♒	0°-4°59'	5°-9°59'	10°-17°59'	18°-24°59'	25°-29°59'
♉ ♍ ♑	♀ 5	☿ 7	♃ 8	♄ 5	♂ 5
♋ ♏ ♓	0°-4°59'	5°-11°59'	12°-19°59'	20°-24°59'	25°-29°59'

Figure 52: Table of Indian bounds (V.13)

6 So this is the distribution of the bounds according to what these people said; but the most correct of these bounds, are the bounds of the people of Egypt.

Chapter V.14: On the lords of the triplicities

1 The trine is an amount consistent with the goodness of a mixture, due to its amount ranging over equal lines of the circle: for the sphere of the signs

---

[94] الكملة, which the lexicon describes as a "complement." But Abū Ma'shar means that five ordinal degrees are filled out, from 0° 00' 00" to 4° 59' 59". See the table below.

has three rings:⁹⁵ and they are the ring of Aries, the ring of Cancer, and the ring of Capricorn. 2 So due to that, the rotation of the twelve signs is divided out to the triplicities, each triplicity among them being three signs. 3 (And we have already stated another explanation for the trine⁹⁶ of the signs, in Treatise II.)⁹⁷

4 And these signs (in which one is trining the others) have lords, so that the lords of the trine of the male signs belong to male planets, and the lords of the trine of the female signs belong to female planets.⁹⁸ 5 And we begin with the planets greatest in testimony in the triplicity, and the strongest of them in domain.⁹⁹

6 Now the first of the triplicities is male signs, and they are Aries, Leo, and Sagittarius; their lords by day are the Sun, then Jupiter (and by night Jupiter, then the Sun), and the partner to them both by day and night is Saturn.

7 The second triplicity is Taurus, Virgo, and Capricorn, and they are feminine signs: their lords by day are Venus, then the Moon (and by night the Moon, then Venus), and the partner to them both by day and night is

---

⁹⁵ دوائر. These are circles of latitude: the tropic of Cancer, the tropic of Capricorn, and the equator in the middle (through 0° Aries and 0° Libra). What Abū Ma'shar (or Hermes-Agathodaimōn, see footnote below) means is that the trine (120°) is the result of dividing the circle by three, and the trine connotes temperateness. These three rings also describe the most temperate and inhabitable parts of the world, and the most favorable for life. Therefore there is a relationship between the four triplicities (groups of three signs denoted by triangles), the trine aspect, temperateness, and favorability to life. The signs at each of these four places are also the convertible signs of their own triplicities.

⁹⁶ Or, "trining" (تثليث), literally "dividing into three."

⁹⁷ This was the Hermes-Agathodaimōn explanation (II.7, **1-13**). But the astronomical explanation here does match the kind of thinking of Hermes-Agathodaimōn, since the major changes in daylight (which they described) also happen at the celestial equator and the tropics. For this reason, I believe that the present chapter also represents the Hermes-Agathodaimōn view.

⁹⁸ This is true by day, but not by night. It would be better to say that the two main triplicity lords are of the same *sect* as the signs (if we allow for the flexibility of Mercury). Thus for example, the primary lords of the watery triplicity (which are nocturnal signs) are Venus and Mars, even though Mars is male. This blurring of sect and gender is rife in the Arabic tradition.

⁹⁹ حَيِّز. Or perhaps, "the strongest of them by *sect*."

Mars—except that Mercury acts as partner to them both in Virgo especially.[100]

	Diurnal	Nocturnal	Partner
♈ ♌ ♐	☉	♃	♄
♉ ♍ ♑	♀	☽	♂ (and ☿ when in ♍)
♊ ♎ ♒	♄	☿	♃
♋ ♏ ♓	♀	♂	☽

Figure 53: Dorothean triplicity lords (V.14)

8 The third triplicity is Gemini, Libra, and Aquarius, and they are male signs: and their lords by day are Saturn, then Mercury (and by night Mercury, then Saturn), and the partner to them both by day and night is Jupiter.

9 The fourth triplicity is Cancer, Scorpio, and Pisces, and they are female signs: their lords by day are Venus, then Mars (and by night Mars, then Venus), and the partner to them both by day and night is the Moon.

Chapter V.15: On the faces and their lords, according to what fits with the statement of the scholars of Persia, Babylon, and Egypt

1 Each one of the twelve signs is divided into three divisions, each division being 10°, called a "face," and it is attributed to a planet. **2** So the first face of Aries belongs to Mars, and he is its lord; the second face of it belongs to the planet which follows Mars in his sphere; and the third face belongs to the third one from the sphere of Mars. **3** The first face of the second sign belongs to the fourth planet from the sphere of Mars—and they appointed the lords of the faces of the signs like that, in the order of the planets' spheres, each following immediately after the other. **4** And whenever one reaches the Moon, one returns to Saturn.

---

[100] This statement comes from Dorotheus (*Carmen* I.1, **5**). In other words, for any planet or point in Virgo, its triplicity lords will still be Venus and the Moon, but Mercury will be the partner rather than (or in preference to) Mars.

5 And an example of that is that from the beginning of Aries up to 10° of it is the face of Mars (and he is the lord of Aries); the second face (and it is from the eleventh degree[101] of Aries up to a whole twenty) is the face of the Sun; and the third face (and it is from the twenty-first degree up to a whole thirty degrees) is the face of Venus.

6 And from the beginning of Taurus up to the completion of ten degrees is the face of Mercury, and the second face of Taurus is the face of the Moon, and the third face the face of Saturn.

7 And the first face of Gemini belongs to Jupiter, the second face of it to Mars, and likewise the faces of the [rest of] the signs, and their lords.

	0° - 9°59'	10° - 19°59'	20° - 29°59'
♈	♂	☉	♀
♉	☿	☽	♄
♊	♃	♂	☉
♋	♀	☿	☽
♌	♄	♃	♂
♍	☉	♀	☿
♎	☽	♄	♃
♏	♂	☉	♀
♐	☿	☽	♄
♑	♃	♂	☉
♒	♀	☿	☽
♓	♄	♃	♂

Figure 54: Table of Chaldean faces (V.15)

---

[101] Reading for the incorrect "eleven degrees."

Chapter V.16: On the faces and their lords according to what the Indians said: and they call them the *darījān*

1 The Indians agree with others in the division of each sign into three divisions, in the manner of the faces; but they call each division of it a *darījān*. **2** And they call their lords the "lords of the *darījān*," except that they differ with others about their lords.

3 They make the lord of the first *darījān* be of the sign—I mean, the lord of the first face belongs to the lord of that sign—and the lord of the second *darījān* belongs to the fifth sign from it, and the lord of the third *darījān* belongs to the lord of the ninth sign from it.

4 And that is like Aries: for the first 10° of it is the *darījān* of Mars (the lord of Aries), and the

	0°- 9° 59'	10°- 19°59'	20°- 29°59'
♈	♂	☉	♃
♉	♀	☿	♄
♊	☿	♀	♄
♋	☽	♂	♃
♌	☉	♃	♂
♍	☿	♄	♀
♎	♀	♄	☿
♏	♂	♃	☽
♐	♃	♂	☉
♑	♄	♀	☿
♒	♄	☿	♀
♓	♃	☽	♂

Figure 55: Table of Indian *darījān* (V.16)

second 10° is the *darījān* of the Sun (the lord of Leo), and the third 10° is the *darījān* of Jupiter (the lord of Sagittarius).

5 Taurus: the lord of the first *darījān* of it is Venus (its lord), the lord of the second *darījān* of it is Mercury (the lord of Virgo), and the lord of the third *darījān* of it is Saturn (the lord of Capricorn).

6 Gemini: the lord of the first *darījān* of it is Mercury (its lord), the lord of the second *darījān* of it is Venus (the lord of Libra), and the lord of the third *darījān* of it is Saturn (the lord of Aquarius).

7 And the lord of the first *darījān* of Cancer is the Moon (its lord), the lord of the second *darījān* is Mars (the lord of Scorpio), and the lord of the third *darījān* is Jupiter (the lord of Pisces).

8 The lord of the first *darījān* of Leo is the Sun (its lord), the lord of the second *darījān* is Jupiter (the lord of Sagittarius), and the lord of the third *darījān* is Mars (the lord of Aries).

9 And likewise the *darījān* of every sign: the first one of it belongs to its own lord, the second to the lord of sign of the triplicity which follows it (and it is the lord of the fifth sign from it), and the third belongs to the lord of the sign of the triplicity which is after that (and it is the lord of the ninth sign).

10 And indeed they make it be according to this model because they claimed that every sign has three faces, and every triplicity three signs, so the lords of these triplicities are more appropriate to every face of them, than others are. **11** But the division by others (of those who preceded, which we stated)[102] is more sound.

Chapter V.17: On the *nawbahr* of the signs (and it is the ninth-part), according to what fits with the statement of the Indians

1 When the Indians divided the signs into three faces, and assigned the third face of each sign to the lord of the ninth sign from it (in the way we stated before this),[103] after that they divided each sign into nine ninth-parts, and assigned the lord of the ninth ninth-part of each sign to the lord of the ninth sign from it: and it is what they call a *nawbahr*. **2** So, each ninth-part comes to be 3° 20', and it is 200'.

3 And they divided each sign into nine divisions because the ninth sign relative to each sign is the end of its triplicity, and the limit[104] of its nature. **4** Thus they made the division of each sign be according to the number of signs which are between them, in succession: and there are nine, each ninth-part of them being of the nature of one of the signs. **5** And the lord of each ninth-part is the lord of that sign.

6 So the first ninth-part of Aries belongs to Mars (the lord of Aries), the second ninth-part to Venus (the lord of Taurus), and the third ninth-part to Mercury (the lord of Gemini), so that the ninth ninth-part of Aries comes to belong to Jupiter (the lord of Sagittarius).

---

[102] That is, in Ch. V.15 above.

[103] That is, in Ch. V.16 above. For more on the ninth-parts, see *PN4* III.9-III.10.

[104] نهاية.

BOOK V: THE SHARES OF THE PLANETS IN THE SIGNS

	♈ ♌ ♐	♉ ♍ ♑	♊ ♎ ♒	♋ ♏ ♓
#1: 0°00'–3°20'	♂	♄	♀	☽
#2: 3°20'–6°40'	♀	♄	♂	☉
#3: 6°40'–10°00'	☿	♃	♃	☿
#4: 10°00'–13°20'	☽	♂	♄	♀
#5: 13°20'–16°40'	☉	♀	♄	♂
#6: 16°40'–20°00'	☿	☿	♃	♃
#7: 20°00'–23°20'	♀	☽	♂	♄
#8: 23°20'–26°40'	♂	☉	♀	♄
#9: 26°40'–30°00'	♃	☿	☿	♃

Figure 56: Table of Indian ninth-parts (V.17, 1-13)

7 And the first ninth-part of Taurus comes to belong to Saturn (the lord of Capricorn), the second ninth-part to Saturn (the lord of Aquarius), the third ninth-part to Jupiter (the lord of Pisces), the fourth ninth-part to Mars (the lord of Aries), and they assigned the lords of the ninth-parts in accordance with the successive lords of the signs.

8 And there is a short way by which one may know the lords of the ninth-parts of every sign: and it is that you look at the convertible sign which is in every triplicity: for its lord is the lord of the first ninth-part belonging to the signs of that triplicity, and the lord of the second sign from it is the lord of the second ninth-part of that sign—and likewise the rest of the lords of the ninth-parts of that triplicity.

9 So Aries, Leo, and Sagittarius <are a triplicity>:[105] the lord of the first ninth-part for *each one* of them is Mars (the lord of Aries); the lord of the second ninth-part is Venus (the lord of Taurus); and the lord of the third ninth-part is Mercury (the lord of Gemini).

10 Taurus, Virgo, and Capricorn are a triplicity: so the lord of the first triplicity for each one of them is Saturn (the lord of Capricorn), and the lord of the second ninth-part is Saturn (the lord of Aquarius).

11 Gemini, Libra, and Aquarius are a triplicity: so the lord of the first ninth-part for each one of them is Venus (the lord of Libra), and the lord of the second ninth-part of them is Mars (the lord of Scorpio).

12 Cancer, Scorpio, and Pisces are a triplicity: so the lord of the first ninth-part for each one of them is the Moon (<the lord of Cancer>), and the lord of the second ninth part of them is the Sun (<the lord of Leo>).

13 And the lords of the ninth-parts are known like that to be in the succession of the lords of the signs.

[Another scheme]

14 Now, the lords of the *nawbahr* are also assigned in another way, and it is that you divide the sign into nine division (as with the first operation), then you assign the lords of the ninth-parts in the order of the spheres of the planets: so the first ninth-part of Aries is assigned to Mars, the second one of it to the Sun, the third to Venus, the fourth to Mercury, the fifth to the Moon, the sixth to Saturn, the seventh to Jupiter, the eighth to Mars, and the ninth to the Sun. **15** As for Taurus, the first *nawbahr* of it is assigned to Venus, the second to Mercury, the third to the Moon, until its nine *nawbahrs* run out. **16** Then the first one of Gemini is assigned to the Moon, the first one of Cancer to Jupiter, the first one of Leo to the Sun, the first one of Virgo to Mercury, the first one of Libra to Saturn, the first one of Scorpio to Mars, the first one of Sagittarius to Venus, the first one of Capricorn to the Moon, the first one of Aquarius to Jupiter, and the first one of Pisces to the Sun. **17** But this one is not agreed upon, while the first one is correct.

---

[105] Adding in brackets to match the parallel sentences below.

Chapter V.18: On the twelfth-parts of the signs, and the lords of each degree of every sign

1 All of the ancients (among the scholars of the stars) divided each sign into twelve divisions, so that each division is 2 ½ degrees, and is called a "twelfth-part."

2 Indeed, they did that so a single sign would have the nature of [all] twelve signs in it: for the first division of it is like the nature of the sign itself, and the nature of the second division is like the nature of the second sign from it, and the nature of the third division is like the nature of the third sign, and likewise the rest of the twelve divisions.

3 And its calculation has a short version: and it is that you see how much there is from the beginning of the sign up to the degree and minute whose twelfth-part you want to know, and you multiply it by 12, and you cast out what it amounts to from the beginning of that sign, 30 for every sign, and wherever the counting comes to an end, the nature of that degree and twelfth-part is in that sign.

	0°-2.5°	2.5°-5°	5°-7.5°	7.5°-10°	10°-12.5°	12.5°-15°	15°-17.5°	17.5°-20°	20°-22.5°	22.5°-25°	25°-27.5°	27.5°-30°
♈	♈	♉	♊	♋	♌	♍	♎	♏	♐	♑	♒	♓
♉	♉	♊	♋	♌	♍	♎	♏	♐	♑	♒	♓	♈
♊	♊	♋	♌	♍	♎	♏	♐	♑	♒	♓	♈	♉
♋	♋	♌	♍	♎	♏	♐	♑	♒	♓	♈	♉	♊
♌	♌	♍	♎	♏	♐	♑	♒	♓	♈	♉	♊	♋
♍	♍	♎	♏	♐	♑	♒	♓	♈	♉	♊	♋	♌
♎	♎	♏	♐	♑	♒	♓	♈	♉	♊	♋	♌	♍
♏	♏	♐	♑	♒	♓	♈	♉	♊	♋	♌	♍	♎
♐	♐	♑	♒	♓	♈	♉	♊	♋	♌	♍	♎	♏
♑	♑	♒	♓	♈	♉	♊	♋	♌	♍	♎	♏	♐
♒	♒	♓	♈	♉	♊	♋	♌	♍	♎	♏	♐	♑
♓	♓	♈	♉	♊	♋	♌	♍	♎	♏	♐	♑	♒

Figure 57: Table of twelfth-parts (V.18, 1-3)

4 Hermes and all of the ancients divide every sign into divisions other than these as well, and it is that they make every degree of the sign follow the nature of one of the signs. **5** So the first degree of the sign will follow its own nature, and the second degree the nature of the second sign from it, and the third degree the nature of the third sign from it, until the twelfth degree of the sign will follow the nature of the twelfth sign from it—and the thirteenth degree of that sign will follow the nature of that sign itself, and the fourteenth degree of it the nature of the second sign. **6** And they used to make each of the thirty degrees be according to the nature of one of the signs, like that. **7** And Hermes stated many judgments in his books, degree-by-degree for every sign, in different categories, in the topics of nativities and questions.

	♈	♉	♊	♋	♌	♍	♎	♏	♐	♑	♒	♓
0°	♈	♉	♊	♋	♌	♍	♎	♏	♐	♑	♒	♓
1°	♉	♊	♋	♌	♍	♎	♏	♐	♑	♒	♓	♈
2°	♊	♋	♌	♍	♎	♏	♐	♑	♒	♓	♈	♉
3°	♋	♌	♍	♎	♏	♐	♑	♒	♓	♈	♉	♊
4°	♌	♍	♎	♏	♐	♑	♒	♓	♈	♉	♊	♋
5°	♍	♎	♏	♐	♑	♒	♓	♈	♉	♊	♋	♌
6°	♎	♏	♐	♑	♒	♓	♈	♉	♊	♋	♌	♍
7°	♏	♐	♑	♒	♓	♈	♉	♊	♋	♌	♍	♎
8°	♐	♑	♒	♓	♈	♉	♊	♋	♌	♍	♎	♏
9°	♑	♒	♓	♈	♉	♊	♋	♌	♍	♎	♏	♐
10°	♒	♓	♈	♉	♊	♋	♌	♍	♎	♏	♐	♑
11°	♓	♈	♉	♊	♋	♌	♍	♎	♏	♐	♑	♒
12°	♈	♉	♊	♋	♌	♍	♎	♏	♐	♑	♒	♓
13°	♉	♊	♋	♌	♍	♎	♏	♐	♑	♒	♓	♈
14°	♊	♋	♌	♍	♎	♏	♐	♑	♒	♓	♈	♉
15°	♋	♌	♍	♎	♏	♐	♑	♒	♓	♈	♉	♊
16°	♌	♍	♎	♏	♐	♑	♒	♓	♈	♉	♊	♋
17°	♍	♎	♏	♐	♑	♒	♓	♈	♉	♊	♋	♌
18°	♎	♏	♐	♑	♒	♓	♈	♉	♊	♋	♌	♍
19°	♏	♐	♑	♒	♓	♈	♉	♊	♋	♌	♍	♎
20°	♐	♑	♒	♓	♈	♉	♊	♋	♌	♍	♎	♏
21°	♑	♒	♓	♈	♉	♊	♋	♌	♍	♎	♏	♐
22°	♒	♓	♈	♉	♊	♋	♌	♍	♎	♏	♐	♑
23°	♓	♈	♉	♊	♋	♌	♍	♎	♏	♐	♑	♒
24°	♈	♉	♊	♋	♌	♍	♎	♏	♐	♑	♒	♓
25°	♉	♊	♋	♌	♍	♎	♏	♐	♑	♒	♓	♈
26°	♊	♋	♌	♍	♎	♏	♐	♑	♒	♓	♈	♉
27°	♋	♌	♍	♎	♏	♐	♑	♒	♓	♈	♉	♊
28°	♌	♍	♎	♏	♐	♑	♒	♓	♈	♉	♊	♋
29°	♍	♎	♏	♐	♑	♒	♓	♈	♉	♊	♋	♌

Figure 58: A *monomoria* system from Hermes (V.18, 4-7)

8 (As for other people, they used to assign the lords of these degrees be in a different way, but the one which Hermes stated is more correct.)

Chapter V.19: On the male and female degrees

1 Within the twelve signs are male and female degrees: so if there was a nativity or question about males, and the planets and degree of the Ascendant occurred in male degrees, it would be stronger for them; and if there was a nativity or question about females, and the stars occurred in the female degrees, it would be stronger for them.

3 Now as for some of the ancients, they used to look at the male signs and make [them] be male from their beginning up to twelve and a half degrees, and twelve and a half degrees female, then two and a half degrees male, and two and a half female. **4** And as for the female signs, they used to make [them] be female up to twelve and a half degrees, then twelve and a half degrees male, then two and a half degrees female, then two and a half degrees male.

5 And [some] people[106] assigned the degrees of each sign (in terms of masculinization and feminization) in accordance with the nature of the twelfth-parts of the signs, and they said: As for the male signs, each one of them up to two and a half degrees from their beginning is male, following the nature of the sign itself; then two and a half degrees female, following the nature of the second sign from it; then two and a half degrees male, following the nature of the third sign from it, then female like that in this fashion, up to the end of the signs. **6** And as for the female signs, each one of them up to two and a half degrees from their beginning is female, then two and a half degrees male, then female like that.

7 So, in these three ways they stated the masculinization of the degrees of the signs, and their feminization. **8** Whenever two or three of these indica-

---

[106] That is, Vettius Valens (*Anth.* I.11), probably from the *Bizidaj*.

tions coincide[107] in masculinization or feminization for a single position, it is stronger for it.[108]

2[109]	Masc.	Fem.	Masc.	Fem.	Masc.	Fem.	Masc.
♈	7 0°-6°59'	2 7°-8°59'	6 9°-14°59'	7 15°-21°59'	8 22°-29°59'		
♉	7 0°-6°59'	8 7°-14°59'	15 15°-29°59'				
♊		6 0°-5°59'	11 6°-16°59'	6 17°-22°59'	4 23°-26°59'	3 27°-29°59'	
♋	2 0°-1°59'	5 2°-6°59'	3 7°-9°59'	2 10°-11°59'	11 12°-22°59'	4 23°-26°59'	3 27°-29°59'
♌	5 0°-4°59'	2 5°-6°59'	6 7°-12°59'	10 13°-22°59'	7 23°-29°59'		
♍		7 0°-6°59'	5 7°-11°59'	8 12°-19°59'	10 20°-29°59'		
♎	5 0°-4°59'	5 5°-9°59'	11 10°-20°59'	7 21°-27°59'	2 28°-29°59'		
♏	4 0°-3°59'	6 4°-9°59'	4 10°-13°59'	5 14°-18°59'	8 19°-26°59'	3 27°-29°59'	
♐	2 0°-1°59'	3 2°-4°59'	7 5°-11°59'	12 12°-23°59'	6 24°-29°59'		
♑	11 0°-10°59'	8 11°-18°59'	11 19°-29°59'				
♒	5 0°-4°59'	7 5°-11°59'	6 12°-17°59'	7 18°-24°59'	5 25°-29°59'		
♓	10 0°-9°59'	10 10°-19°59'	3 20°-22°59'	5 23°-27°59	2 28°-29°59'		

Figure 59: Male and female degrees (V.19)

---

[107] Lit., "meet" or "come together" (اجتمع).
[108] Note that on this topic, Abū Ma'shar does not take a stance on which one is correct, so that one might use all three and play the odds.
[109] Sentence 2 is a table constructed from the sentences in *Gr. Intr.* which for the most part simply list amounts of degrees and genders. I have listed Abū Ma'shar's degrees in boldface, and added the actual degrees and minutes below. The table is very similar to that of Firmicus Maternus in *Mathesis* IV.23.

Chapter V.20: On the bright, dark, dusky, and empty degrees

1 In this scheme the degrees of the signs are in four classes:[110] the first of them are [1] the bright degrees, the second [2] the dusky degrees (and they are also said to be those having a shadow, and smoky), the third are said to be [3] vacant (I mean, an empty void), and the fourth are said to be [4] dark.[111]

2 So when the planets occur in [1] the bright degrees, it is more powerful for them in the indication of the good, and they indicate brilliance, brightness, and good fortune.

3 And if they occur in [4] the dark degrees, they indicate difficulty, what is detestable, and a gloomy, bad matter.

[1] Bright	B	نيّرة \ مضيئة
[2] Dusky	K	قتمة
[3] Empty	E	خالية \ فارغة
[4] Dark	D	مظلمة

Figure 60: Four categories of brightness

4 And if they occur in the [2] dusky degrees (I mean, those having a shadow), or in the [3] vacant degrees, they indicate a small detestable thing.

---

[110] See Figure 60 for their abbreviations and typical Arabic words. In the large table below, the bright degrees are sometimes called "glowing" or "shining," and the empty degrees "vacant," but I will simply use the abbreviations here to make it easy to understand.

[111] To avoid confusion, the [1] bright are the best, the [2] dusky and [3] vacant in the middle, and the [4] the worst. Below he will treat them this way but put them in a different order: [1], [4], and [2]-[3].

♈	3 K	5 D	8 K	4 B	4 D	5 B	1 D
	0°-2°59'	3°-7°59'	8°-15°59'	16°-19°59'	20°-23°59'	24°-28°59'	29°-29°59'
♉	3 K	7 D	2 E	8 B	5 E	3 B	2 K
	0°-2°59'	3°-9°59'	10°-11°59'	12°-19°59'	20°-24°59'	25°-27°59'	28°-29°59'
♊	7 B	3 K	5 B	2 E	6 B	7 K	
	0°-6°59'	7°-9°59'	10°-14°59'	15°-16°59'	17°-22°59'	23°-29°59'	
♋	7 K	5 B	2 K	4 B	2 D	8 B	2 D
	0°-6°59'	7°-11°59'	12°-13°59'	14°-17°59'	18°-19°59'	20°-27°59'	28°-29°59'
♌	7 B	3 K	6 D	5 E	9 B		
	0°-6°59'	7°-9°59'	10°-15°59'	16°-20°59'	21°-29°59'		
♍	5 K	4 B	2 E	6 B	4 D	7 B	2 E
	0°-4°59'	5°-8°59'	9°-10°59'	11°-16°59'	17°-20°59'	21°-27°59'	28°-29°59'
♎	5 B	5 K	8 B	3 K	7 B	2 E	
	0°-4°59'	5°-9°59'	10°-17°59'	18°-20°59'	21°-27°59'	28°-29°59'	
♏	3 K	5 B	6 E	6 B	2 D	5 B	3 K
	0°-2°59'	3°-7°59'	8°-13°59'	14°-19°59'	20°-21°59'	22°-26°59'	27°-29°59'
♐	9 B	3 K	7 B	4 D	7 K		
	0°-8°59'	9°-11°59'	12°-18°59'	19°-22°59'	23°-29°59'		
♑	7 K	3 B	5 D	4 B	2 K	4 E	5 B
	0°-6°59'	7°-9°59'	10°-14°59'	15°-18°59'	19°-20°59'	21°-24°59'	25°-29°59'
♒	4 D	5 B	4 K	8 B	4 E	5 B	
	0°-3°59'	4°-8°59'	9°-12°59'	13°-20°59'	21°-24°59'	25°-29°59'	
♓	6 K	6 B	6 K	4 B	3 E	3 B	2 K
	0°-5°59'	6°-11°59'	12°-17°59'	18°-21°59'	22°-24°59'	25°-27°59'	28°-29°59'

Figure 61: Degrees of brightness (V.20)

Chapter V.21: On the wells of the planets in the signs

1 In the signs there are degrees called "wells," such that if one of the planets occurred in those very degrees of the signs, without being powerful,[112] the disappearance of its brilliance will not be delayed, and its indication being very weak.[113] **2** So if the fortunes occurred in them, their condition will be like what we stated about weakness, but as for the infortunes, if they occurred in them their indication will be weakened (and sometimes they will indicate incidental good fortune due to their inability to [create] misfortune, and sometimes the nature of their misfortune will be strengthened). **3** And the ancients have already stated the places in which they indicate suitability or corruption, but we will state that in its own place.[114]

4 Now as for the exact degrees of the wells in their signs, they certainly do disagree about them; but we will leave aside any mention of their disagreement about them, and will state their degrees in the signs in accordance with what the generality of the old scholars of the people of Persia and Egypt agree on.

6 So these are the degrees of these signs which we said that if the planets were in them, they are in the wells.[115]

---

[112] غير متقدّر

[113] ضعف عن, which usually means "is too weak to do X."

[114] For specific delineations, see *PN4* VIII.15.

[115] The following table represents a set of sentences in Abū Ma'shar which simply lists the ordinal degrees (for example, "the 6th, 11th, 17th," and so on). I have added columns to give the cardinal degrees and minutes which correspond to Abū Ma'shar's values.

Sign	Ordinal	Cardinal	Sign	Ordinal	Cardinal
♈	6th	05°-05°59'	♎	1st	00°-00°59'
	11th	10°-10°59'		7th	06°-06°59'
	17th	16°-16°59'		20th	19°-19°59'
	23rd	22°-22°59'		30th	29°-29°59'
	29th	28°-28°59'			
♉	5th	04°-04°59'	♏	9th	08°-08°59'
	13th	12°-12°59'		10th	09°-09°59'
	18th	17°-17°59'		17th	16°-16°59'
	24th	23°-23°59'		22nd	21°-21°59'
	25th	24°-24°59'		23rd	22°-22°59'
	26th	25°-25°59'		27th	26°-26°59'
♊	2nd	01°-01°59'	♐	7th	06°-06°59'
	12th	11°-11°59'		12th	11°-11°59'
	17th	16°-16°59'		15th	14°-14°59'
	26th	25°-25°59'		24th	23°-23°59'
	30th	29°-29°59'		27th	26°-26°59'
				30th	29°-29°59'
♋	12th	11°-11°59'	♑	2nd	01°-01°59'
	17th	16°-16°59'		7th	06°-06°59'
	23rd	22°-22°59'		17th	16°-16°59'
	26th	25°-25°59'		22nd	21°-21°59'
	30th	29°-29°59'		24th	23°-23°59'
				28th	27°-27°59'
♌	6th	05°-05°59'	♒	1st	00°-00°59'
	13th	12°-12°59'		12th	11°-11°59'
	15th	14°-14°59'		17th	16°-16°59'
	22nd	21°-21°59'		23rd	22°-22°59'
	23rd	22°-22°59'		29th	28°-28°59'
	28th	27°-27°59'			
♍	8th	7°-7°59'	♓	4th	3°-3°59'
	13th	12°-12°59'		9th	8°-8°59'
	16th	15°-15°59'		24th	23°-23°59'
	21st	20°-20°59'		27th	26°-26°59'
	25th	24°-24°59'		28th	27°-27°59'

Figure 62: The wells of the signs (V.21)

Chapter V.22: On the degrees increasing in good fortune

1 The ancients claimed that within the circle are degrees increasing in good fortune, and they said that when planets indicate the native's good fortune by means of their positions, and the Moon or the Lot of Fortune is in these degrees, or [these degrees] are exactly on the Ascendant, then they will increase in the native's good fortune. **2** And if they indicate downfall, then these will instigate some motion towards high rank and power.

4 And people said that if the Ascendant was one of these degrees which we will state [below], or the Sun by day or the Moon by night was in one of them, and they were in an excellent position of the circle, and the planets of the root of the nativity indicated good fortune, then they will make him attain nobility and the houses of kings, and he will conquer lands and cities, and possess many assets:

3		Increasing in good fortune	
	♉	15th	14°-14°59'
		27th	26°-26°59'
		30th	29°-29°59'
	♌	3rd	02°-02°59'
		5th	04°-04°59'
	♏	7th	06°-06°59'
	♒	20th	19°-19°59'

Figure 63: Degrees increasing in good fortune (V.22, 1-3)

5	Ordinal	Cardinal		Ordinal	Cardinal
♈	19th	18°-18°59'	♎	3rd	02°-02°59'
				5th	04°-04°59'
				21st	20°-20°59'
♉	3rd	02°-02°59'	♏	12th	11°-11°59'
				20th	19°-19°59'
♊	11th	10°-10°59'	♐	13th	12°-12°59'
				20th	19°-19°59'
♋	1st – 3rd	00°-02°59'	♑	12th-14th	11°-13°59'
	14th – 15th	13°-14°59'		20th	19°-19°59'
♌	5th	04°-04°59'	♒	7th	06°-06°59'
	7th	06°-06°59'		16th-17th	15°-16°59'
	17th	16°-16°59'		20th	19°-19°59'
♍	2nd	01°-01°59'	♓	12th	11°-11°59'
	12th	11°-11°59'		20th	19°-19°59'
	20th	19°-19°59'			

Figure 64: Degrees of elevation and power (V.22, 4-5)

6 Now these things above which we have stated, are[116] partnerships of the planets with the signs, and all of the ancients (among the scholars of the stars) have generally agreed about them; and along with that they have a partial partnership [deriving] from the special blending of each with the other, which we will state in its own place in each book.

7 And some of the Indians (and certain individuals among the masters of the stars) have assigned partnerships to the planets with the signs [which are] *not* the ones we have stated; but we have omitted mention of them because in this Book we are stating everything which resembles the blending of the planets' natures with the signs in the natural arrangement of [those things] which all scholars of the profession of the stars agree upon.

8 The Fifth Book is complete, praise be to God.

---

[116] Lit., "have."

BOOK VI: [ON THE CLASSIFICATIONS OF THE SIGNS]
And in it are thirty-three chapters

1. Chapter VI.1: On the natures of the signs, their conditions, and what images ascend in the faces.
2. Chapter VI.2: On the ascensions of the signs on the equator and in the seven climes, according to what Theon claimed.
3. Chapter VI.3: On the symmetry of the degrees of the circle.
4. Chapter VI.4: On the signs loving one another, hating one another, and hostile to one another, and straight and crooked in ascensions, and obedient and disobedient to one another.
5. Chapter VI.5: On the signs agreeing in the belt and ascensions, agreeing in power, and agreeing in manner.
6. Chapter VI.6: On the signs which harmonize with each other in a "natural" opposition and sextile, but do not look at each other.
7. Chapter VI.7: On the signs which harmonize with each other from the square.
8. Chapter VI.8: On the years of the signs, and their months, days, and hours.
9. Chapter VI.9: On the indications of the signs for collections of countries and locales in lands.
10. Chapter VI.10: On the signs indicating motion and rest.
11. Chapter VI.11: On the rational signs which indicate a class of people and their conditions.
12. Chapter VI.12: On the division of what belongs to each sign, in terms of the limbs of the human body.
13. Chapter VI.13: On the signs indicative of grace and beauty, and the signs indicative of generosity and liberality, and the signs which accumulate and become full, and which grant ease, and which pour forth, and which seize and take.
14. Chapter VI.14: On the signs indicative of lewdness and illnesses.
15. Chapter VI.15: On the signs indicative of women's chastity and their modesty.
16. Chapter VI.16: On the signs of many children, twins, and few children, as well as sterility.
17. Chapter VI.17: On the signs of cut limbs, and the signs of much sharpness and anger.

18 Chapter VI.18: On the signs indicative of the conditions of voices.
19 Chapter VI.19: On the signs indicative of mange, leprosy, spots, itching, ringworm, deafness, muteness, baldness, thinness of the beard, stringy hair, and an armpit which does not have hair.
20 Chapter VI.20: On the positions in the signs indicative of defects in the eye.
21 Chapter VI.21: On the signs indicative of culture, beguiling speech, deception, cunning, the signs of anxiety, and the dark signs.
22 Chapter VI.22: On the signs indicating types of birds, and everything having four feet, and predatory animals and venomous things, things scratching the earth, and animals of the water.
23 Chapter VI.23: On the signs indicative of trees and vegetation.
24 Chapter VI.24: On the signs indicative of types of waters, and the signs indicative of what is worked by fire.
25 Chapter VI.25: On the directions of the signs.
26 Chapter VI.26: On the stakes of the circle and their quadrants, and the twelve houses, the sum of their indications, and the reason for that, and the houses of the planets' joys.
27 Chapter VI.27: On the quadrants of the circle being attributed to what is bodily and spiritual, and other things.
28 Chapter VI.28: On the blending of the natures of the stakes of the Ascendant.
29 Chapter VI.29: On the colors of the quadrants of the circle, and the twelve houses.
30 Chapter VI.30: On the rising quadrants of the circles, and those falling, and the tall and the short.
31 Chapter VI.31: On the distribution of the four natures, to things.
32 Chapter VI.32: On explaining the quarters of a single day and single night, and their twenty-four hours.
33 Chapter VI.33: On the lords of the days and hours.

Chapter VI.1: On the natures of the signs, their conditions, and what images ascend in the faces

1 In Book II we stated the natures of the individual signs, and in Book V we stated the planets' collaboration in the signs; in this Book we want to state the special property of the signs' indication as a whole as well as their degrees, so far as they are appropriate for this Book. **2** Now as for this chapter, we will state what images ascend in their faces.

3 When the generality of the masters of the stars read the account of what images ascend in each of the faces of the signs in some of the books of the ancients, they believed it was a thing with no meaning, because they had not found an account of their indications in most of the books, nor did they know what each of their images indicates. **4** But Hermes, Ptolemy, Dorotheus, Teucer, Antiochus, and other scholars of their regions, as well as the scholars of India, have already stated the special property of the indications of those images and things in special books, according to what occurs in this world.

5 Now as for some of their indications, they are similar to their physical shape, name, or situation;[1] as for others, their indication is far from that. **6** But those learned in the profession of the stars (and the knowledge of the nature of both higher and earthly things) understand them. **7** And we will state those indications in books where a mention of them is needed.

8 In their mentioning these images in the manner they did, the ancients did not have in mind that there would [actually] be images like them in the circle (marked out by lines, a shape, and body), so that each image would ascend with that form in every face of the signs. **9** But for every position in the circle, and every face of the signs, they found a special property in the indication of things coming to be in this world. **10** And they found the generality of people believing that no degree of the circle has, in its own right, a special property in indicating something, unless there were images in it (so that those images would indicate those things by means of their special property). **11** So the ancients related the indications of the positions of the circle, and the faces of the signs, to images and things, [only] claiming that

---

[1] This probably means that a star in Pegasus, or part of Pegasus ascending in the chart, indicates horses.

they arose in the faces of the signs so that they[2] would be closer to the understanding of one looking at them. **12** And they named those images by different names, and assigned a condition[3] to each one of them different from the condition of another. **13** As for some of those images and their condition, they are close to the name and condition of existing things, and so they assigned them those remarkable names and conditions so there would be a connection between the names of the images of the circle (and their conditions), and the names of these things found among us (and their conditions).

14 But some of the scholars of the people of one region, do disagree with other scholars of the people of another region, in the constitution of those images, forms, and conditions, and we have found that to be in three types: and we have already stated them in this book of ours.[4] **15** There are individuals among the ancients who state that in the circle there are other images and things contrary to what we have explained, and they discuss them much in the manner of riddles; but we will leave that aside because it has little resemblance to this book of ours. **16** Here, with respect to the constitution of the images and things which ascend in the faces of the signs, we have stated what resembles [the project of] this book, in terms of what the scholars of the judgments of the stars have agreed upon in every period.

17 The first thing we will start with, is stating the images which the ancients of the people of Persia, the Babylonians, and Egypt agreed upon. **18** Then after that, we have stated what the people of India agree on; then after that the 48 images which the Sages Aratus and Ptolemy mentioned.

19 Each image among those they mentioned is comprised of several stars, and we have found that since the time of Ptolemy up to this one, the stars have moved many degrees: and through the withdrawing of the stars from their positions, the images have ceased to be parallel to the faces which they

---

[2] That is, the scholars' views and artificial shapes. So, according to Abū Ma'shar the beings depicted in the constellations are convenient shorthand and devices for remembering what the stars themselves are indicating.

[3] In the rest of this paragraph we can see that Abū Ma'shar's fetishization of the word "condition" (حال) gets in the way of clear exposition.

[4] Reference uncertain, as he only mentioned some of the names and groups in **4**. In **17-18** he will list them explicitly.

BOOK VI: ON THE CLASSIFICATIONS OF THE SIGNS

had been in at the time of Ptolemy. **20** So we have stated for the images what corresponds to their ascending with the faces of the signs in *our* time, and that is 1,160 of Alexander.[5] **21** But as more years pass by, one must correct the ascension of the images which Ptolemy stated within the faces of the signs, for that period.

22 Now as for the images which the people of India mentioned, and the people of Persia, Egypt, and others, they ascend in the faces of the signs but do not withdraw from their positions, because they claim that the indications of those images and things are of the special property of the indication of those faces.[6] **23** But the names of those images and things in them follow the meaning borrowed [from the faces]. **24** And as for some of these images which they stated, they ascend in one full face, while some of them ascend in two faces or many faces.

[Aries 1]

25 ARIES. As for Aries, its nature is fiery, yellow bile, its taste bitter, upright in shape, having two colors and facing two directions, the day increasing beyond 12 hours, decreasing in ascensions from 30.

26 In the first face of it ascends a woman called Athena (the Glowing, the Bright), and the tail of the Sea Fish (and it is called the Aqār,[7] and it is also called Cetus), and the beginning of the Triangle, and the head of the

---

[5] That is, about 830 AD. But see my Introduction about the dating of the book.

[6] I think this simply means that they have a sidereal zodiac, so there is no need to precess—which means the stars themselves bear the special property, not a tropically-calculated section of the ecliptic.

[7] الأقار. This unknown word is the spelling preferred by **BY**, and an Arabic root matching **BY**'s preference (قور) connotes something hollowed out (like the belly of a hungry fish?) or cutting a hole in something. That sounds like one of the alternative Greek names of Cetus, which had to do with blowing or spouting (from the Gr. *prēthein*: see Allen, p. 161). On the other hand, it looks like Arabic MS **C** had الأفارق, and the Latin **J** had the similar *alifcar*. That Arabic root فقر can connote the spine or vertebrae, which suggests a sea-monster with a notable spine. A third possibility is that it is a bad transliteration for the Greek *ichthus*, "fish."

Tā'mūr[8] (and it is a Bull Stag, and the image of its head is the head of a dog),[9] in its left hand is a lamp and in its right hand a key.

27 The Indians claim that in this face ascends a black man with red eyes, mighty in body and strong in heart, mighty in his soul, a large white garment on him which he has cinched about his waist with a cord; and he is angry, standing on his feet, and he is vigilant, a guardian.

28 And as one of the 48 images (according to what agrees with the statement of Ptolemy),[10] there ascends the back of the Woman on the Throne, and her rear, knee and left hand; and there ascends the middle of the back of the Woman who sees no husband, up to the rear, thighs, and parts of the hem [of her dress]; and there ascends the Second Fish, and some of the flaxen[11] thread; and the following part of the belly of Cetus.

[Aries 2]

29 In the second face of Aries ascends Andromeda, and the middle of that Sea Fish (and it is the 'Aqār), and the middle of the Triangle, and the middle of the Tā'mūr (and it is the Bull-Stag),[12] and half of a Snake, and a field for

---

[8] تَأمُور. This and its variant yā'mūr (يأمور) indicate a certain beast (probably mythical), similar to a mountain goat (Lane, p. 99a). A related word similar in sound (mentioned in the same entry by Lane), is yahmūr (يحمور), which is an oryx (a large, horned antelope). What seems to have happened is as follows. Teucer lists two animals, a Baboon or Dog-headed animal, and a Cat (Gr. ailouros) whose head appears here. Somehow, this Tomcat was converted into the mountain-goat beast (Ar. tā'mūr, yā'mūr), which sounds like an oryx (Ar. yahmūr), and so Abū Ma'shar converts it back into something familiar by calling it by the somewhat ungrammatical Arabic name of "bull stag" (ثور أيّل). But in the meantime, the Tomcat and the Baboon had collapsed into the same animal: hence Abū Ma'shar also says that this tomcat-mountain-goat-oryx-bull-stag is also the Dog-headed animal. But see also **156**, where Teucer does actually speak of a Stag, making the confusion more complicated.
[9] This is Teucer's *Cynocephalus*, "The Dog-head."
[10] For all of the Arabic names of the Ptolemaic constellations, see Ch. II.1 and its diagrams.
[11] Or, "linen" (كتان). That is, the fishing line of the constellation. See also **31**.
[12] Again, this is Teucer's Tomcat combined with his Dog-headed animal, in **26** above.

sowing, and a Sea Ship, and a Horseman with a lance in his hand, and a Woman combing her head,[13] and Armor made of iron, and the Head of the Ghoul,[14] and the scimitar[15] of Perseus (that is the sword of Perseus)—and Perseus is the one bearing the Head of the Ghoul, and in Arabic it is called the Mongoose,[16] and in Persian *Fīlsūs*.[17]

30 The Indians claim that in this face ascends a woman with a garment on her and a red cloth, having a single foot, her image resembling the image of a horse; in her soul she would go and seek clothes, ornaments, and children.

31 And according to what agrees with the statement of Ptolemy, in this face there arises the thigh of the Woman on the throne, and her two lower legs, and her feet; and the head of Perseus, and part of his right palm, and the remainder of the hem of the Woman who sees no husband, and her feet; and the Triangle; and the head of Aries and its two horns; and the remainder of the flaxen thread which is in the curve, and the chest of Cetus.

[Aries 3]

32 In the third face of Aries ascends a male youth called Cassius,[18] and he is sitting upon a throne with a spread on it, with him two statues;[19] and after the throne ascends Perseus (that is, *Fīlsūs*), tilting [his head] down, calling upon God. 33 And there ascends the chest of the Fish as well as its head

---

[13] That is, Cassiopeia.
[14] That is, Algol, β Perseus.
[15] أرفاء, a transliteration of the Gr. *harpē*, "scimitar."
[16] النَّمس, apparently referring to Perseus itself in an older Arabic form. But this noun also means "the stink" or "the corruption," which could likewise be a designation for Algol as an evil star.
[17] This is more likely *firsūs*, as a transliteration of Perseus: see **32**.
[18] قاسيوس. This seems rather to be Cassiopeia.
[19] معه تمثالين, although this is not the proper dual ending. This could also be read as "sculpted images." But the normal image of Cassiopeia does not have two separate bodies like this (which we would expect to be indicated by stars). See however **37**, where Orion has two lamps (fixed stars).

(and it is the Aqār),[20] and the following part of that Triangle, and the tail of the Tā'mūr (and it is the Bull-Stag),[21] and the second half of the Snake.

34 The Indians claim that in this face ascends a man of reddish color, with red hair, and he is angry, being hindered, in his hand a bracelet of wood and a rod, and on him red clothing, precise in the arts of iron, wanting to do good but not being able to: and indeed he wants the good because it is the face of Jupiter (as the Indians claim),[22] but he cannot because it is the house of Mars.

35 And according to what agrees with the statement of Ptolemy, in this face there arises the chest of Perseus, and his left palm (in which the head [of the Ghoul] is), and the tuft [of hair] which is in the head of Aries, and the body of Aries, and the head of Cetus and its two forelegs.[23]

[Taurus 1]

36 TAURUS. As for Taurus, its nature is earthy, black bile, its taste sour,[24] the day increasing beyond hours of equality, deficient in form, *nīmjird* (that is, as though a half),[25] terrestrial,[26] turning[27] with a hump.[28]

---

[20] Or rather, Cetus: see **26** and my footnote there.
[21] Again, this is the tail of the Cat, which Abū Ma'shar source has combined with other things (see above).
[22] See V.16, **4**.
[23] Or rather, its front fins.
[24] حامض. Or, "acidic," especially with a citrus taste. Compare with two other views in IV.2, **16-17**.
[25] The Persian prefix *nīm* means "half," or something in two parts. Only the front half of the animal appears in the image. See also **120** and **132**.
[26] أرض, referring to the lower parts of an animal near the ground, but also productive of vegetation. This matches the Greek Teucer, both in "terrestrial" and in terms of "wealth-bringing."
[27] مدوّرة. Or perhaps, "rotated," referring to its *shape*. See also Capricorn in **132**.
[28] مدوّرة بناتئ. Taurus has only the front half of the animal, and its rises from the hump on its back. Nevertheless something is strange about the wording here, including the feminine ending on مدوّرة. But if this were an attached male pronoun, it would mean something like "turning it with a hump." I do note that **45** below uses

37 In the first face of it ascends the sword-wielding Giant,[29] in his left hand a sword, and in his right hand his scabbard and staff,[30] and he is girded with a sword, and on his shoulders two lamps[31] talking to him and calling him by his name. **38** And there ascends the Mighty Ship, and above it the Wild Beast, and in it a naked man sitting, and under the Ship one-half of the body of a Dead Woman. **39** And there ascends a man [with his head] turned downwards, and the head of a dog (and it is the image called *Saksar* in Persian,[32] and its meaning is that the image of its head is the head of a dog), so the head of that image ascends.

40 The Indians claim that in this face ascends a woman with much hair on her head, beautiful and curly, resembling a noble woman; she has a child, and on her are clothes, some of which have been touched by burning fire; and she is concerned about seeking clothing and ornaments for her child.

41 And according to what agrees with the statement of Ptolemy, in this face there arises the middle of Perseus and his rear, and the Head in his left hand, and the rear of Aries and its buttocks, and the place which is at the cut of Taurus, and the jaws of Cetus, and the curve which is in the River, and the spout of water at the end of the River.

[Taurus 2]

42 In the second face of Taurus ascends a Ship, and a naked man rushing towards that Ship, raising his hands, in his hand a key; and the remaining half of that Dead Woman, and the middle of the body whose head resembles the head of a Dog, and in its right hand a staff, and a bare idol, and a turban,[33] and in his left hand a key, and he is beckoning with this right and left hands.

---

an entirely different word for "hump" (سنام), so something else might be going on here.
[29] That is, Orion.
[30] Or, "mace" (عصّاه).
[31] The stars Betelgeuse and Bellatrix.
[32] Ar. سكسر (from the Pers. سگسر), "dog-head."
[33] مندیل; or, some kind of cloth. But I think this is probably مندل, which refers to a skrying mirror or magic mirror.

43 The Indians claim that in this face ascends a man whose face and body resembles a lamb, and he has a woman with a form just like a bull, and his fingers are like goatish cloven hooves;[34] and that man is strong in his body, with much hotness in his stomach and body, a glutton, not letting up in his heating; on him is a shabby garment; he is concerned about the real estate of a residence and lands, and building, and moving cattle out for plowing and tilling. **44** And there ascends a spiritual image turned upside down, in its right hand a rod, [and] raising up the left hand.

45 And according to what agrees with the statement of Ptolemy, in this face there arises the two knees of Perseus, and his lower legs, and the following foot, and the back of Taurus and its hump, and the root of its foreleg, and the tender parts of its belly, and its right hoof; and the beginning of the River, and some of its middle until close to its end.

[Taurus 3]

46 In the third face of Taurus there arises the following part of the body of the one whose head resembles the head of the dog, and a standing[35] man holding a Snake, and two wheels upon which a young man is sitting,[36] with two horses drawing them, and a Driver and Goat, with the Driver holding it in his left hand.

47 The Indians claim that in this face ascends a man with intensely white teeth and long legs, his teeth sticking out from his lips, red in color as well as his hair, his body resembling the body of an elephant and a lion; confused in reason, meditating on evil, sitting on a carpet, on him is velvet covered with black sable. **48** And there ascends a northern Horse, Dog, and a resting Calf.

49 And according to what agrees with the statement of Ptolemy, in this face there arises the right foot of Perseus, and the shoulder of the One clutching the reins, and the left hand, and the tip of his lowest parts, and his left leg, and the nape of the neck of Taurus, and its head, and its two knees, and its left hoof, and the root of its horn; and the tip of the garment which is

---

[34] These images are obviously versions of the Ram (Aries) and the Bull (Taurus).

[35] Reading قائم with the sense of the Latin **H**, for the nonsensical نائم ("sleeping," or "lying down").

[36] This is evidently the Charioteer Auriga on the chariot.

BOOK VI: ON THE CLASSIFICATIONS OF THE SIGNS

in the hand of the Giant, and the beginnings of the River, and the curve which is in the river.

[Gemini 1]

50 GEMINI. As for Gemini, its nature is the nature of blood, its taste sweet, and it is of the color of the sky, upright in shape, facing many directions.[37]

51 In the first face of Gemini ascends the tail of the image whose head resembles the head of a dog, and a man with a rod in his hand, and with him ascends two wheels from the direction of the south, with two horses on them, a sitting man driving them, and the head of a Snake having a horn.

52 The Indians claim that in this face ascends a beautiful woman, righteous, standing upright in the air, concerned about seeking ornaments and a child, knowledgeable about sewing and wondrous arts which resemble that; and there ascends with her the mirror of those who polish.

53 And according to what agrees with the statement of Ptolemy, in this face there arises the head of the One clutching the reins, and what is at [his] elbow, and what is in his right knee, and his right foot (and it participates in the tip of the horn of Taurus); and the other, southern horn of Taurus, and the left shoulder of the Giant, and his left foot, and the head of the Hare, and its forelegs.

[Gemini 2]

54 In the second face of Gemini ascends a man, [and] with him a *mizmār*[38] of gold which he blows on; and 'Irqlās (and people called him Hercules, and he is the Kneeler upon his Knee), and the Snake climbing on a tree, fleeing from 'Irqlās, and the middle of the Serpent having a horn, and a Jackal having a mark upon its foreleg.

55 The Indians claim that in this face ascends a man in the image of the *zanj*[39] but the color of a white animal,[40] and he has bound his head in a head-

---

[37] Lit., "of many faces."
[38] This is a woodwind instrument resembling an oboe.
[39] This is a general term for black Africans on the eastern side of the continent.

band of metal;⁴¹ and he wears weapons, and on his head a helmet of iron, and on that helmet a crown of silk brocade, and in his hand a bow and arrows, and he loves entertainment and joking around. 56 And with him ascends a garden with many fragrant herbs, and a cithara (and it is a *sanj*)⁴² which he plucks, and he sings and takes herbs from the garden.

57 And according to what agrees with the statement of Ptolemy, in this face there arises the right palm of the One clutching the reins, and one of the two following hooves of Taurus, and the hand of the Giant, and his shoulder, head, chest, belt, knee, and foot; and the chest of the Hare and its rear.

[Gemini 3]

58 In the third face of Gemini ascends Apollo, and on his head fragrant leaves,⁴³ and with him a cithara⁴⁴ (and it is a *sanj* having⁴⁵ strings), and a *mizmār* of gold. 59 And there ascends the Barking Dog,⁴⁶ and the Dolphin (and it is one of the animals of the sea), and a Lynx, and the Tailor's shears, and the first half of the Lesser Bear, and the tail of the Snake having a horn, curled around the root of the Ear of grain.

60 The Indians claim that in this face ascends a man seeking weapons to wear, and with him a bow and quiver, and in his hand arrows, clothing, and many ornaments; and in his soul he composes songs and writes them down, and [he enjoys] delights, entertainment, and fun of various types.

---

⁴⁰ العنقاء, following Lane's discussion of white stallions and white birds (or animals with a white patch). In context this sounds like an albino African.

⁴¹ And especially, lead (رصاص).

⁴² Lane (p. 1731c) explains this as a kind of instrument with metal cymbals, but that it was also the Arabized transliteration of a Persian stringed instrument.

⁴³ I have decided to follow Latin **H** in reading ريحان for this uncertain word, especially since Apollo was associated with crowns of bay laurel leaves. **BY** speculate إيجانة, which they translate as "stone jug," which I cannot make sense of.

⁴⁴ Reading as كثار. Apollo's special instrument was the cithara, a stringed instrument which the modern "guitar" comes from. I read this for **BY**'s speculative كنّار, and other variations found in Lemay, as this is the obvious answer which Abū Ma'shar goes on to explain in the parentheses.

⁴⁵ Reading ذو with Lemay, for **BY**'s و ("and").

⁴⁶ This is another version of the Howling Dog, Bootes.

61 And according to what agrees with the statement of Ptolemy, in this face there arises the shoulder of the following Twin, and his hand and rear, and his right foot; and the thighs of the preceding Twin and his feet; and the tail of the Hare; and the mouth of the Dog, its forelegs, and its right leg; and the first oar of the Ship, and the tip of the second oar.

[Cancer 1]

62 CANCER. As for Cancer, its nature is watery, phlegmatic, and its taste salty.

63 In the first face of it ascends the last half of the Lesser Bear, and the whole image called the Satyr turning around towards its back, and it is close to a Muse[47] who plucks the cithara (and it is the *sanj*) and plays [the *mizmār*], and in his[48] hand is an amulet of iron, whose head is brass; and the first of the three Virgin Maidens,[49] and the head of the Scarab, and the tail of the Wall-gecko.

64 The Indians claim that in this face ascends a young man with a handsome image, on him a cloth and ornaments, and some crookedness in his face and fingers,[50] his body resembling the body of a horse and an elephant; and he has white legs, and on his body hang types of fruits, and the leaves of trees, and his home is in a jungle where sandalwood grows.

65 And according to what agrees with the statement of Ptolemy, in this face there arises the face of the Greater Bear, and the head of the preceding and following Twins, and the rear of the preceding Twin and his hand, and the Lesser Dog, and the remainder of the Greater Dog, and the stern of the Ship, and the root of the oar.

---

[47] موسى, which is a man's name in Arabic but here is the transliteration of the Greek *Mousa*, "Muse," a female deity. Thus later in the sentence Abū Ma'shar speaks of something in "his" (the Muse's) hand.

[48] Abū Ma'shar probably says "his" because *Mūsā* is a male name in Arabic; he does not realize that this is a transliteration of the Greek *Mousa*, "Muse."

[49] That is, the Graces (Teucer).

[50] The word for "crookedness" (عوج) shares the same root as the word for "ivory" (عاج), which is a curved, white substance from an elephant; and note that he resembles an elephant and has white legs. This kind of connection suggests that there is much more going on with these Indian faces than meets the eye.

[Cancer 2]

66 In the second face of Cancer ascends the second of the Virgin Maidens, and the likeness of a Cloud,[51] and preceding half of a Dog, and half of the two ears of a Donkey, and the northern Donkey, and the middle of the Scarab, and the middle of the Wall-gecko.

67 The Indians claim that in this face ascends a young woman pretty to look at, on her head a crown of lotuses[52] and red fragrant herbs, and in her hand a rod of wood, and she cries out from her love of drinking and singing, and prostrating herself in the houses of worship.

68 And according to what agrees with the statement of Ptolemy, in this face there arises the head of the Greater Bear, and the following side of Cancer, and the stern of the Ship.

[Cancer 3]

69 In the third face of Cancer ascends the third of the Virgin Maidens, and she varies between advancing and retreating; and the following half of the Dog, and the second half of the ears of the Donkey, and the second, Southern Donkey, and the end of the Scarab, and the head of the Wall-gecko.

70 The Indians claim that in this face ascends a man whose foot resembles the foot of a turtle, and the color of his foot is like the color of the *kushut*,[53] a *jubbah*[54] spread over his body, and on him ornaments of gold, and in his soul he would board a ship and sail the sea so as to import gold and silver, making ornaments for women out of them.

71 And according to what agrees with the statement of Ptolemy, in this face there arises the root of the neck of the Greater Bear, and its preceding right foreleg; and the two claws of Cancer, and its Manger; and the head of

---

[51] That is, the nebula Praesepe, called the "Manger."

[52] نيلوفر, which might be Egyptian white lotuses, or "blue lotuses" (see Lane p. 2871).

[53] الكشوت. In Persian is a word كشتو, meaning "half-ripened grapes," which might be relevant here.

[54] جبّة. This is normally a cotton or woolen garment, perhaps quilted; but it can also mean a coat of mail.

the Serpent; and the sail of the Ship, and that [portion of] its body which borders on that.

[Leo 1]

72 LEO. As for Leo, its nature is fiery, yellow bile, and its taste bitter.

73 In the first face of it ascends a Jackal[55] and a Dog shooting with a bow, and the image of a Lion, and half of a Ship with its sailor in it, and the head of Hydra (and it is a black water snake), and the head of a Horse, and the head of a Donkey.

74 The Indians claim that in this face ascends a tree with mighty roots, on its branches a dog, a jackal, and a vulture; and a man on whom is fancy[56] [but] soiled clothing, and he is preoccupied with sorrow over his parents. **75** And with him ascends the master of the Horse looking in the direction of the north, his image resembling the image of a jackal.[57] **76** And with it ascends an arrowhead and arrow, and the head of a dog, and something resembling a dog.

77 And according to what agrees with the statement of Ptolemy, in this face there arises the neck of the Greater Bear, and its following left leg; and the top of Leo and its forelegs; and the neck of the Serpent; and the middle of the Ship.

[Leo 2]

78 In the second face of Leo ascends an Idol raising its hand up above, crying out at the top of its voice, and with him are the Cymbals of dancers made of copper, and [singing] different songs; and there ascends a drinking Vessel,[58] a Cup, Glass, and Reed-flutes of gazelle horns, and a Duck, a Pig,

---

[55] Reading ذنب with Lemay. **BY** read ذنب, "tail," which would read "a tail and a dog," which does not make sense to me. See also **74**.
[56] مرتفع. This word means things of high rank or eminence.
[57] Or wolf, reading ذنب with **BY**. But some MSS read دبّ, "bear."
[58] تغار من شراب. But I have been unable to identify in any lexicon the key word for "vessel" here (تغار), nor does it seem to appear in **BY**'s index. Nevertheless it is clearly the Mixing-bowl or Crater.

and a Bear⁵⁹ with an upright hand, and the remaining half of the Ship, and the neck of the Hydra (that is, the black watery snake), and the middle of the Horse, and the middle of the Donkey.

79 The Indians claim that in this face ascends a man who is haughty about small things,⁶⁰ on his head a crown of white fragrant herbs, and in his hand a bow; he takes from robbers, [being] malicious, irascible, in the harshness of his anger he resembles the lion, wrapping himself in a garment of the color of a lion.

80 And according to what agrees with the statement of Ptolemy, in this face there arises the shoulders of the Greater Bear, and its preceding right foot; and the neck of Leo and the root of its foreleg; and the middle of the Serpent; and the beginning of the Ship.

[Leo 3]

81 In the third face of Leo ascends a youth [who is] a driver of riding animals, and in his hand a whip (and Teucer calls the whip a "hammer"),⁶¹ and he pulls a cart in which there is a man sitting, and a small youth following him, in his left hand a garment and a vessel.⁶² **82** And there ascends a Raven, and the middle of the black water Snake, and the following part of the Horse, and the following part of the Donkey.

83 The Indians claim that in this face ascends a man whose image is like the image of the *zanj*,⁶³ ugly, revolting, with much toil, harsh anxiety, in his mouth is fruit and meat, and in his hand a jug.

84 And according to what agrees with the statement of Ptolemy, in this face there arises the chest of the Greater Bear, and the middle of Leo, and some of the Serpent.

---

⁵⁹ Reading دبّ with **BY**, but other MSS read ذئب ("jackal").

⁶⁰ أنفه إلى الدقّة ما هو, a difficult phrase. I think this might mean he is narrow-minded and petty. It might also mean he is disdainful (أنف) of details (دقّة), but the arrogance is definitely implied.

⁶¹ According to the Teucer in Rhetorius, the Charioteer holds a wheel (*trochos*), although we might rather expect him to be holding a whip.

⁶² Again, تغار (see **78** above).

⁶³ That is, black Africans of the eastern part of the continent.

BOOK VI: ON THE CLASSIFICATIONS OF THE SIGNS

[Virgo 1]

85 VIRGO. As for Virgo, it possesses two bodies, and has three images.[64]

86 In the first face of it ascends a Maiden whom Teucer calls a *dōshīzah*[65] (and it is a virgin), pretty and clean, with long hair, a beautiful face, in her hand two ears of grain, and she is sitting upon a throne with a spread upon it. **87** And she is nursing a small boy, feeding him broth in a place called an "atrium" (and some nations call that boy 'Īsū', and the meaning of that is Jesus).[66] **88** And there ascends with it a man sitting upon that throne, and there ascends with it the star of the Ear of grain,[67] and the following parts of the Water Snake, and the head of the Raven, and the head of the Lion.

89 The Indians claim that in this face ascends a young virgin woman, on her an old garment and clothing, in her hand precious things,[68] and her hand is in suspense;[69] and she is standing in the middle of fine, fragrant herbs, wanting to reach the houses of her fathers and her friends, so as to seek clothes and ornaments.

90 And according to what agrees with the statement of Ptolemy, in this face there arises the tip of the tail of the Sea Dragon; and the following part of the tail of the Bear, and its following leg; and the rear of Leo, its two legs, and tail; and the Cup which is in the Serpent; and part of the trunk of the Serpent.

---

[64] Teucer: "three-faced." But I am not sure why, although Teucer implies two possibilities: the woman nursing a child (or Isis-Horus), and the woman holding the ear of grain. Virgo is also depicted with wings, reflecting her imagery as the Greek goddess of Justice or *Dikē*.

[65] Reading دوشیزه with the Persian spelling, for دوشیبه.

[66] 'Īsā. Note that while the iconography of mother and child is similar to Mary and Jesus, there is also an odd linguistic overlap because the form of the Greek Isis used here is *Isin*.

[67] That is, Spica.

[68] Reading tentatively for وجوه.

[69] ویدها معلّقة. According to Lane (p. 2137), this verb is especially applied to women whose status is left in suspense because their husbands are absent but not dead or divorced. Note her old clothes, but the valuables (if that is correct) in her hand, and wanting to gain clothes and ornaments: she seems to be in transition and doing neither one thing nor the other.

[Virgo 2]

91 In the second face of Virgo ascends a Muse, and he[70] plucks the cithara (and it is a *sanj*), and plays [the *mizmār*], and there ascends a man accompanied by a tuft of hair,[71] and half of an image called by the Romans "Bootes" (and in Persian *al-Nābīnā*), and he is a man whose head is like the head of a Bull, half of him ascending from it, and in his hand half of a naked man; and there ascends half of the piece of wood on whose head is iron by which one plows the earth,[72] and the tail of the black water Snake, and the middle of the Raven,[73] and the middle of the Lion.

92 The Indians claim that in this face ascends a black man, hair sprouting forth on his whole body, and on him are three garments: one of them leather, the second silk, and the third a red garment; and in his hand an inkwell, and he loves to look at accounts, expenditures, and all assets which are demanded or paid out.[74]

93 And according to what agrees with the statement of Ptolemy, in this face there arises some of the tail of the Sea Dragon; and the rear of the Greater Bear; and the tip of the Lock of hair; and the head of Virgo, and her left shoulder; and the head of the Raven, and its beak and wing; and the tail of the Centaur.

[Virgo 3]

94 In the third face of Virgo ascends the other half of Bootes (or *al-Nābīnā*), and the remaining half of the naked man, and the other half of the piece of wood whose head is iron, and the tail of the Raven, and the tail of the Lion, and the Ear of grain, and two Bulls, and half of a male shepherd.

95 The Indians claim that in this face ascends a deaf woman, clean, white, mighty in her soul, wearing a garment dyed and washed [but] not dried;

---

[70] Again, Abū Ma'shar believes this is a proper male name, not the transliteration of the Greek for "Muse." See **63**.

[71] This must be Coma Berenices.

[72] That is, half of a plow. But apparently in the image of Abū Ma'shar, this was a hand-held device more like a hoe.

[73] غداف, not the usual غراب.

[74] يرجع ويردّ.

white leprosy on her body;⁷⁵ and she is concerned with reaching the houses of worship so as to pray in them.

96 And according to what agrees with the statement of Ptolemy, in this face there arises some of the tail of the Sea Dragon; and the root of the tail of the Greater Bear, and the remainder of the Lock of hair; and the right shoulder of Virgo, and some of her chest; and the chest of the Raven, and the side of the following wing; and the rear of the Centaur, and the thigh of its following leg.

[Libra 1]

97 LIBRA. As for Libra, it is an airy sign, sanguine, balanced, decreasing in the day, increasing in ascensions, having two colors and two aspects, upright in form.

98 In the first face of it ascends a man resembling an angry man,⁷⁶ in his left hand a Balance, and in his right hand a weight; and there ascends written books, and three boys (all of them called *qurtūmā*),⁷⁷ and right after them there ascends a Muse, and he is sitting on a mat,⁷⁸ plucking the cithara (and it is the *sanj*), and he is singing and playing [the *mizmār*]; and there ascends the head of the Sea Dragon,⁷⁹ and the first portion of the Lake which the Romans call the Acherousian Lake (that is, "golden"),⁸⁰ and some of the Persians called it the Greater Zāb;⁸¹ and there ascends a portion of the Ship.

---

⁷⁵ I follow **BY**, but there are other readings, such as "but not dried by her; white leprosy on her hand."

⁷⁶ This might refer to Hades (in Teucer), but the rest of this description with his weight and balance, belongs to the Indian image below.

⁷⁷ قرطوما, meaning uncertain. But it sounds like three stars close together.

⁷⁸ فرش. But **BY** read فرس, "horse."

⁷⁹ That is, Draco.

⁸⁰ Not really, but the Arabic translator must have confused this prefix with the Greek *chrys-* (meaning "golden"). This lake was the name of a swamp which connected to the Underworld.

⁸¹ This river runs through Turkey and Iraq, and joins with the Tigris River south of Mosul.

99 The Indians claim that in this face ascends a man with a *qafīz*[82] and a balance in his hand, and he is sitting in a shop in the market, and he is concerned about dry measures, weighing, and buying and selling, being knowledgeable about that.

100 And according to what agrees with the statement of Ptolemy, in this face there arises the middle of the tail of the Greater Bear; and the middle of the trunk of Virgo, and her left palm in which the Ear of grain is; and the tail of the Raven; and some of the tail of the Serpent; and the right shoulder of the Centaur; and some of the trunk of the Horse from the end parts of its rear, and the soft parts of its belly.

[Libra 2]

101 In the second face of Libra ascends a man driving [animals] (and the Persians call him *Būdāsif*,[83] while the Romans call him *'Inīchus*),[84] and in his cart is a man sitting, in his hand a whip, and a red basket belonging to a merchant man, [and] in it are an exquisite sword, silk brocade, a scabbard, an apothecary's bag, and tailors' tools,[85] and a tent in which there are masters of perfumes, and a man sitting upon a bed, and around him are aides. **102** And there ascends a small boy, and the middle of the Ship, and the preceding portion of the Centaur above the Ship, and the middle of the Sea Dragon, and the middle of the Acherousian Lake (that is, the golden one, and the Persians call it the Greater Zāb),[86] and there ascends a spring of water.

103 The Indians claim that in this face ascends a man whose image is like the image of the Sea Dragon, of the color of a vulture, naked, thirsty,[87] with

---

[82] This is a weight for dry measuring.

[83] But in the first face of Scorpio Abū Ma'shar says this is the name of the Centaur (**111**). See also Burāq in **155**.

[84] This is a transliteration of the Gr. *Hēniochos*, "Charioteer." The rest of this sentence is not in Teucer, and probably comes from an Indian source.

[85] صفت or صفة. This word has to do with things that are matched or set into rows, so I believe it refers to the standard patterns and forms which a tailor uses to measure and cut cloth.

[86] See footnotes to **98**.

[87] عطشان. Or, "desiring."

weak hands, wanting to fly into the air, his concern being for women and children.

104 And according to what agrees with the statement of Ptolemy, in this face there arises some of the tail of the Sea Dragon; and the tip of the tail of the Greater Bear; and the lower left leg of the trunk of the Howling Dog;[88] and the hem of Virgo; and the head of the Centaur, and its shoulders[89] and chest.

[Libra 3]

105 And in the third face of Libra ascend the following part of the Sea Dragon, and the complete Ship, and the end of the Centaur, and the complete Lake of gold, and the brain of the head, and the summit of the direction of the brain,[90] and a naked man called Ariadne,[91] reclining and putting his left hand on his head, it being already supported by his right hand.[92] **106** And there ascends the Crown of Ariadne, and it is above the head of the [animal] driver, both of their heads having two crooked horns, one of them above the other, they being called "Ballista" and Adonis. **107** And there ascends another part they call "heaven."

108 The Indians claim that in this face ascends a man whose face resembles the face of a horse, on him is a scabbard and in his hand a bow, and arrows already nocked[93] in the bow, and he is in a thicket wanting to hunt, and sits alone, meditating on things.

109 And according to what agrees with the statement of Ptolemy, in this face there arises some of the tail of the Sea Dragon, and its foreleg, arm, right

---

[88] That is, Bootes.
[89] This dual is from **BY**, but the MSS have only one shoulder.
[90] These must be the "two heads" mentioned by Teucer.
[91] That is, the Cretan princess. **BY** prefer the spelling وارتدي, *Wārtadī*, but the manuscripts do not all agree and only the name Ariadne appears here in Teucer. Anyway, the next sentence accurately follows the Greek in speaking of the crown of Ariadne.
[92] Reading قد عمد with Lemay for **BY**'s في عنقه ("on his neck"), especially because their reading does not make sense of the following prepositional phrase بها ("by it," referring to the hand).
[93] Lit., "plucked out" (نزع), but they cannot be simply plucked out of a quiver and in the bow without being nocked.

knee, and right side; and the extremity of the hem of Virgo, and her two feet; and the left foreleg of the Centaur, and the leg of the Predatory Beast.[94]

[Scorpio 1]

110 SCORPIO. As for Scorpio, its nature is watery, phlegmatic.

111 And in the first face of it ascends the following part of the male horse called the Centaur (and it is also called *Budāsif*),[95] and there ascends the following part[96] of the Bull, and the Cavalry archer, in his hand a staff, and something called a *sanjah*.[97]

112 The Indians claim that in this face ascends a woman with a fine physique, red in body, harmonious in all of her affairs, concerned with eating food, a scarcity of bread, and seeking assets and contention in the land so that she might remain on it.[98]

113 And according to what agrees with the statement of Ptolemy, in this face there arises the root of the foreleg of the Lesser Bear; and some of the tail of the Serpent; and the head of the Howling Dog, as well as his right arm; and the chest of Libra and its shoulders; and the tip of the left, northern pan;[99] and the foreleg of the Predatory Animal, and its rear and tail; and the preceding foot of the Centaur.

---

[94] السبع. That is, Lupus the Wolf.
[95] This might be an Arabic transliteration for Bucephalus, the famous horse of Alexander the Great.
[96] Or rather, the leading parts.
[97] الصنجة. According to Lane, the proper singular for this is سنجة, referring to either a weight used in a balance scale, or the steelyard used for hanging the pans. Since the first face of Scorpio (which contains the claws) were originally the pans of Libra, this attribution makes sense (although it does not appear in Teucer).
[98] Or, "until" she remains on it (حتّى).
[99] Reading كفّة with Lemay. **BY** incorrectly read فكّة, which they interpret as the star Alphecca (in Corona Borealis).

[Scorpio 2]

114 And in the second face of Scorpio ascends Asclepius (and he is a naked man), and the middle of the Centaur (and he is the male horse), and the middle of the Bull.

115 The Indians claim that in this face ascends a foreign woman away from her country, pretty in the face, naked, having no clothes, ornaments, assets, nor anything, binding her leg with a snake, and she is in the sea, wanting to come to land.

116 And according to what agrees with the statement of Ptolemy, in this face there arises the root of the foreleg of the Lesser Bear; and some of the tail of the Sea Dragon; and the staff of the Howling Dog; and the Northern Crown; and the head of the Snake-Charmer; and the thighs of Libra and its two feet; and the crown of Scorpio; and the back of the Predatory Animal.

[Scorpio 3]

117 And in the third face of Scorpio ascends the preceding parts of the male horse (and it is the Centaur), and it is mighty in form, bearing a hare already biting into it,[100] and the preceding parts of the Bull, and the preceding parts of the female dog turning [her] back,[101] and she has a collar she pulls on; and 'Inīchus[102] (that is, the one holding onto the reins), and in his hand are two snakes.

118 The Indians claim that in this face ascends a dog, jackal, and wild boar, and a powerful tiger with white fur, and types of prey, the dwelling place of all of them in a jungle of sandalwood, looking at each other, and each of them afraid of the other.

---

[100] **BY** treat this as though the hare is biting the Centaur, but since I don't think any biting is traditionally involved in the constellation, it could be either way.

[101] صارف. **BY** plausibly read this as though she is in heat, but the verb is masculine singular so the meaning is unclear. In the first face of Sagittarius, Teucer calls this the "Dog turned away." But it is unclear why Abū Ma'shar's source makes it feminine. In **122** below, the author intentionally uses the pronoun "he," and the dog turns its back toward its tail, so it is not in heat.

[102] Or rather, Ophiuchus (Teucer). But Abū Ma'shar reads this as though it is the Charioteer, as in **101**.

119 And according to what agrees with the statement of Ptolemy, in this face there arises the chest of the Lesser Bear, and the curve which is in the trunk of the Sea Dragon; and the foot of the Kneeler upon his bent knee, and his shoulder and right arm; and the right arm of the Snake-charmer; and the belly of Scorpio and the joint[103] of its body;[104] and the head of the Brazier in which there is fire.

[Sagittarius 1]

120 SAGITTARIUS. As for Sagittarius, it has two bodies and two natures, not complete, *nīmjird* (that is, cut into two halves).[105]

121 In the first face of it ascends the image of a spiritual, naked man, the head turned downwards, called the Suffering One, on his head a raven pecking with its beak on the head of the Suffering One. **122** And there ascends the body of the female dog turning [her] back, and it is turning its head downwards to its tail; and the head of the Falcon.

123 The Indians claim that in this face ascends a naked man, from his head to the middle of his back in the image of a man, and following that in the image of a horse; and in his hand is a bow, and arrows nocked in the bow, and he is crying out, wanting to go to the place of people grouped together,[106] and he takes the furnishings of groups of people in order to keep them for himself.

124 And according to what agrees with the statement of Ptolemy, in this face there arises the neck of the Lesser Bear; and some of the trunk of the Sea Dragon; and the rear of the Kneeler upon his knee; and the spine of his back, his head, and hands; and the right shoulder of the Snake-charmer, his rear, left thigh and left foot; and the sting of Scorpio and what borders on it (of the joints); and the main body of the Brazier.

---

[103] Lit., "knot" (عقد).

[104] Reading "body" (جسد) with **BY** for Lemay's "sting" (حمة), as the sting is designated by another word in the next face.

[105] For this concept of being in two halves, see also **36** and **132**.

[106] الزمزمة. This word also refers to the distant rumbling of thunder or a lion's roar, and I wonder if this originally played a role in the meaning of the image, it being confused with the sense of "groups of people." See also VI.9, **20**.

[Sagittarius 2]

125 In the second face of Sagittarius ascends *Kiyāphiyūs* (or Cepheus), putting his left hand on his mouth, holding onto the horn of Capricorn with his right, and extending his right one to the Wild Beast (that is, the Wild Dog). **126** And there ascends the head of that Wild Beast, and half of Adonis (that is, half of the Hare), and the head of the Lion, and the middle of the body of the Suffering One, and half of Argo (and it is the Ship), and the first half of the Dolphin, and the middle of the Falcon.

127 The Indians claim that in this face ascends a sitting woman, powerful in beauty, with much hair, a dress on her, and earrings, and between her hands[107] an open basket with ornaments in it.

128 And according to what agrees with the statement of Ptolemy, in this face there arises the chest of the Lesser Bear; and some of the trunk of the Sea Dragon, and some of its head; and the left knee of the Kneeler, his foot, and left arm; and the head of the Snake-charmer, his left shoulder, and left palm; and some of the body of the Snake; and the tip of the upper curve of the Bow [of Sagittarius], and the position of the grip of the hand, the arrow and arrowhead, the lower curve; and some of the Southern Crown.

[Sagittarius 3]

129 In the third face of Sagittarius ascends the Dog having the hand of Cepheus in its mouth, and the whole body of Arūnis (the Hare), and the rest of the body of the Lion, and the rest of the body of the Suffering One upside down, and the remaining half of the Ship, and what remains of the Dolphin, and the tail of the Falcon, and half of the Greater Arcturus (the Greater Bear, and they are the great Daughters of the Bier); and the Sea Dragon and the Snake are hideous to look at, very twisted.

130 The Indians claim that in this face ascends a man whose color is the color of gold, on him earrings, and in his hand two bracelets of wood, he being wrapped in a garment of inner tree bark, sitting upon a fine bed.

131 And according to what agrees with the statement of Ptolemy, in this face there arises the middle of the trunk of the Lesser Bear; and some of the

---

[107] Or more idiomatically, "in front of her" (بين يديها).

trunk of the Sea Dragon, and its top; and some of the main body of the Lyre[108] (and it is a turtle, and also called the Falling Vulture); and the root of the tail of the Snake of the Snake-charmer; and the head of the Archer, and his preceding shoulder and leg; and the Southern Crown.

[Capricorn 1]

132 CAPRICORN. As for Capricorn, it is earthy, dusty, pertaining to tilling, *nīmjird* (that is, turned[109] in shape),[110] not finished, upright, having two essences and two natures.

133 And in the first face of it ascends a half of the Greater Bear, and the watery Woman called Nereis[111] (and she is like a man who dwells in the sea), and there ascends the Lyre (and it is a *sanj*) which that woman plucks, and the head of the Great Fish, and the preceding part of the Bad Spring of water,[112] and the preceding part of the foul Predatory Beast whose body resembles the body of an ape, and its head the head of a dog (called *Saksar* in Persian).[113]

134 The Indians claim that in this face ascends a man black in color, angry, his body like the body of a wild boar, hair on his whole body, with long teeth, and sharp, like a length of wood and the sharpness of thorns; and with him a fetter for cattle and riding animals, and a fishhook with which he hunts for fish.

---

[108] Spelled in the MSS as لوزا (Lūzā).

[109] مدوّر, as with Taurus in **36**, which could also mean "rotated." However, I believe the problem lies in the text and it should be something like "half," as with Taurus (**36**) and Sagittarius (**120**). Teucer makes Capricorn double-formed, half-voiced, half-finished (as here), and mutilated. So, the original translator might have been trying to capture several things with this, and didn't succeed.

[110] See also **36** and **120**.

[111] The name of a nymph.

[112] That is, Teucer's "Ominous One." I believe that Abū Ma'shar's source is trying to say "The Evil Eye," since "eye" and "spring" are the same word in Arabic. It may be confused because this part of the zodiac has more water creatures, so the meaning has shifted to being an evil spring of water.

[113] See **39**.

135 And according to what agrees with the statement of Ptolemy, in this face there arises the middle of the trunk of the Lesser Bear; and some of the trunk of the Sea Dragon, and its neck; and the whole trunk of the Lyre[114] (and it is the turtle, and it is also called the Falling Vulture), and the tip of its tail, and some of its wing; and that which is in the Lock of the Archer's hair,[115] and in the trunk of his horse.

[Capricorn 2]

136 And in the second face of Capricorn ascends a woman called in Roman *Bāwānū*[116] (and in Persian 'Īzād, and she is also called Hīlāniyāt),[117] and she is sitting upon a bed; and there ascends a Tree vine, and the middle of the Great Fish, and the middle of the Bad Spring,[118] and the middle of the foul Predatory Beast (that is, the one called *Saksar* in Persian), and there ascends half of the Wheel.

137 The Indians claim that in this face ascends a woman with black clothes on her, and a wrapping garment,[119] and equipment [used] for a calf [but] burned by fire, and she is working the iron[120] for it; and there arises a weasel and a work horse.

138 And according to what agrees with the statement of Ptolemy, in this face there arises the following part of the Lesser Bear; and some of the trunk of the Sea Dragon (of what borders on its middle), and some of what borders on its chest; and the right wing of the Hen, its neck, head, and beak; and

---

[114] Spelled in the MSS as لوزا (Lūzā).
[115] This may be the cape in the Greek version. See also **138** below.
[116] There are variant spellings, but this is the Greek Eileithua, a Greek goddess of childbirth associated with Poseidon.
[117] This transliteration was probably *Hīlāthiyāt*, to match *Eileithua*.
[118] Again, this could be translated as "evil eye," which would be closer to Teucer's "Ominous One." See my comment to the first face in **133**.
[119] كساء. The descriptions often tell us the color or composition, but it is missing here. One of the Latin MS has "woolen," but that could simply be generic.
[120] تعمل له الحديد. Or, "the sharp knife" (الحديد). **BY** follow some MSS with تعمل آلة الحديد, which they translate as "making an iron tool." But for the tool to be *made of* iron, it would be من حديد.

the main body of the Arrow[121] (which is called "the gift");[122] and the trunk of the Flying Vulture; and the horn of Capricorn and its top; and the tip of the Archer's lock of hair (which is called "the spear").[123]

[Capricorn 3]

139 In the third face of Capricorn ascends the tail of the Great Fish, and the following part of the Bad Spring, and the following part of the foul Predatory Beast (that is, the ape whose head is the head of a dog), and the remaining half of the Wheel. **140** And there ascends something spiritual called "Satan" straight in stature, with no head, and it bears its own head in its hand.

141 The Indians claim that in this face ascends a woman pretty to look at, with black eyes, a delicate hand, doing many works; she is concerned with obtaining types of iron ornaments for herself.

142 And according to what agrees with the statement of Ptolemy, in this face there arises the rear of the Lesser Bear; and the curve which is in the trunk of the Sea Dragon, and the following part of the trunk of the Hen, its right leg, knees, and left wing; the Dolphin; and the arm of the Water-bearer; and the middle of the trunk of Capricorn; and the tail of the Southern Fish.

[Aquarius 1]

143 AQUARIUS. As for Aquarius, it is an airy, sanguine sign.

144 And in the first face of it ascends Eridanus (and it is a river which the Jar holds), and the head of the one gripping the Horse (and Teucer calls it the Māhījīr),[124] and the head of the Father of Centaurus (and it is called

---

[121] That is, the constellation Sagitta, not the arrow of the Archer Sagittarius.

[122] النَّوْل, which **BY** translate using the less common "loom."

[123] الطِّرادَة, which has to do with hunting but according to Lane there is some disagreement about exactly what it means.

[124] I'm not sure what Greek term this could be transliterating; it might actually be Persian.

'Asfiyār),[125] and he is raising his left hand up above; and the head of the Ibis (and it is a bird with a black head, hunting fish from the water).

145 The Indians claim that in this face ascends a man whose image is the image of the *zanj*,[126] in the form of a vulture, with him is velvet, and a carpet, and he is concerned with repairing a vessel of brass and wood, so that he may pour oil, wine, and water into it.

146 And according to what agrees with the statement of Ptolemy, in this face there arises the root of the tail of the Lesser Bear; and the leg of Cepheus and his right hand; and the left leg of the Hen, and the tip of its left wing; and the head of the first Horse; and the head of the Water-bearer and his right shoulder; and the rear of Capricorn and its tail; and the following part of the body of the Southern Fish.

[Aquarius 2]

147 In the second face of Aquarius ascends the middle of the body of the one which grips the Horse, having taken his horse with his left[127] [hand], and with his right hand a wild boar, already trampling it with his foot; and in his hand two Snakes, and the middle of the Father of the Centaur, and the wing of the Ibis bird which hunts fish from the water; and there ascends the Sea Dragon.

148 The Indians claim that in this face ascends a man with a long beard, his head and image like the *zanj*,[128] resembling a horseman; and in his hand a bow and arrows, and a bag with sapphires, pearls, gold, chrysolite, and the rest of the costly jewels.

149 And according to what agrees with the statement of Ptolemy, in this face there arises the middle of the tail of the Lesser Bear; and the thigh of Cepheus, his rear, and right shoulder; and the trunk of the second Horse, and its head; and the vessel which is in the hand of the Water-bearer (and it

---

[125] This seems to be a transliteration of Teucer's Greek *hippokratoros*, "the one controlling the horse"; Arabic has no *p*, so just use an *f* or *b* instead. Note that Abū Ma'shar's source has turned a single figure controlling a horse, into two.

[126] This is a general term for black Africans on the eastern side of the continent.

[127] Lit., "northern."

[128] This is a general term for black Africans on the eastern side of the continent.

is the beginning of the bucket of Aquarius), and the rear of the Water-bearer, and his thighs; and the middle of the body of the Southern Fish.

[Aquarius 3]

150 In the third face of Aquarius ascends the Great Bird (and it is the Great Hen, and it is called the tail of the Hen, and also called "Cygnus"),[129] and the following part of the Father of the Centaur; and there arises the Jackal seizing the hand of the Father of the Centaur, and it is biting him. **151** And with the hand of the Father of the Centaur ascends the Bad Spring, and there ascends the whole Bird which is called the Ibis.

152 The Indians claim that in this face ascends a man black in color, angry and wicked, hair in his ear, and on his head a crown of tree leaves, fruits, and paint, and he deals in types of iron goods, passing them on from one place to another.

153 And according to what agrees with the statement of Ptolemy, in this face there arises middle of the tail of the Lesser Bear; and the thigh of Cepheus, his left shoulder, and head; and the root of the foreleg of the Horse, and its withers;[130] and some of the main body of the bucket of Aquarius, and the right lower leg of the Water-bearer, and his left foot; and the end of the Water-bearer's bucket, and the spout of water which is the head of the Southern Fish.

[Pisces 1]

154 PISCES: As for Pisces, it is a watery sign.

155 In the first face of it ascends half of the Horse having two wings (in Roman it is called Pegasus, and Teucer calls it Burāq).[131] **156** And there ascends the head of the Bull Stag (and it is called the Tā'mūr),[132] with two

---

[129] ققنس, qiqnus.

[130] This is the top of the horse's back between the shoulder blades.

[131] Probably not Teucer, but in Islamic tradition Burāq is the flying horse which bore Muhammad to heaven on his "night journey." See also Budāsif in **101** and **111**.

[132] The Teucer material corresponding to this now does talk about a Stag (see below), so the confusion of animals I noted in **26** was even more complicated.

snakes in its nostrils (and Teucer claimed it is head of a Scorpion having two snakes in its mouth),[133] and the beginning of the stream which is called the Nile,[134] and the tail of the *Qurqurdīlūs* (and it is a crocodile, and it is called the "burned path").

157 The Indians claim that in this face ascends a man with fine garments on him, and with him a poker of iron with which he works in fire, and in his hand three fishes which he has put down in front of him, and with him ornaments; and he is walking towards his home.

158 And according to what agrees with the statement of Ptolemy, in this face there arises the tip of the tail of the Lesser Bear; and the left arm of Cepheus; and the belly of the second Horse, and the beginning of the first Fish, and some of the bucket of Aquarius.

[Pisces 2]

159 And in the second face of Pisces ascends the middle of the Bull Stag in whose nostrils are two snakes (and Teucer claimed that it is the middle of the Scorpion with two snakes in its mouth), and the middle of the River Nile, and the middle of the *Qurqurdīlūs* (and it is a crocodile, and it is called the "burned path"), and the first half of the Kneeler upon his Knee.

160 The Indians claim that in this face ascends a woman with a pretty face, a white body, in a ship on the sea, her chest tied to its rudder;[135] and with her are her family and acquaintances, and she wishes to depart for land.

161 And according to what agrees with the statement of Ptolemy, in this face there arises the tip of the tail of the Lesser Bear, and the lower leg of Cepheus, and his foot; and the hand of the Woman on the throne, grasping the throne; and the shoulder of the Woman who does not see a husband;

---

[133] Actually no, this time Teucer really does refer to a Stag.

[134] نيلوس, *Nīlūs*. This appears to be a simple transposition, because the Greek has *Linos*, the name of a mythical minstrel. If so, then it is fortuitous because of the other water creatures or rivers in this part of the sky. On the other hand, maybe the mistake is in the Greek tradition, because it sure would make sense for the Crocodile to be swimming in the Nile.

[135] This sounds more like the figurehead on the bow.

and the head of the Woman taking part in the following portion of the Horse;[136] and the following part of the first Fish; and the tail of Cetus.

[Pisces 3]

162 And in the third face of Pisces ascends the following part of the Tā'mūr (or the Bull Stag). **163** And Teucer claimed that it is the following part of the Scorpion, and the end of the River Nile, and the head of the *Qurqurdīlūs*, twisting around towards his back fighting his opponents, and guiding them in front of him,[137] and the second half of the Kneeler upon his Knee.

164 The Indians claim that in this face ascends a naked man stretching out his leg and sticking a lance in his belly, and he is seated in the desert, crying out in fear of robbers and fire.

165 And according to what agrees with the statement of Ptolemy, in this face there arises the tip of the tail of the Lesser Bear; and the middle of the back of the Woman on the throne; and the chest of the Woman who does not see a husband; and part of the flaxen thread; and the following parts of Cetus.

Chapter VI.2: On the ascensions of the signs on the equator and in the seven climes, according to what Theon claimed

1 At the equator, the ascension of the twelve signs from the east, and their position in the middle of [its] heaven is in one state; and for every four signs, the degrees of ascensions of each one of them there is the same as the others.[138] **2** But as for the rest of the seven climes, the ascensions of each of a pair of[139] signs from the east have the same number of degrees, although each of the signs marks the middle of the heaven in all of the climes with the

---

[136] According to **BY**, this is Andromeda.
[137] This is an idiom, for the more literal "between its hands" (بين يديه). But perhaps the constellation really does have something between its hands.
[138] See **6-8**.
[139] Lit., "each of two."

same ascensions in the right circle. **3** And between the middle of each of two climes there is a distance of one-half of a civil hour.[140]

4 And we will now state the ascensions of the right circle and the seven climes; and [although] some people among the ancients already stated the ascensions of the signs in a different way than how we will state them, we have omitted their version because it is not correct. **5** Here we will state the ascensions of the seven climes according to the way that Theon gave them.[141]

6 As for Aries and Pisces and Virgo and Libra, each of them ascends in 27° 50' at the equator. **7** Taurus, Aquarius, Leo, and Scorpio each ascend in 29° 54' at the equator. **8** Gemini, Cancer, Capricorn, and Sagittarius each ascend in 32° 16' at the equator.

9 The first clime is Ethiopia:[142] its latitude is from 1° 00' to 20° 13', and its ascensions are produced for a latitude of 16° 27'. **10** The hours of the longest day for a place which has these ascensions, is 13 hours. **11** And this clime belongs to Saturn.

12	AT
♈ ♎	24° 20'
♉ ♏	27° 04'
♊ ♐	31° 06'
♋ ♑	33° 26'
♌ ♒	32° 44'
♍ ♓	31° 20'

Figure 65: AT, Clime 1

---

[140] Lit., of an "equal" hour (ساعة مستوية).
[141] These values match the *Almagest* II.8. See also Appendix A with a modern ascensional times table, and my recalculation of Ptolemy's latitudes at the end of this chapter.
[142] In *Almagest* II.8, this is the clime of Meroe.

13 The second clime is Aswān:[143] its latitude is between 20° 13' and 27° 12', and its ascensions are produced for the latitude of 23° 56'. **14** The hours of the longest day for a place which has these ascensions, is 13 ½ hours. **15** The Persians claimed that this clime belongs to Jupiter, while the Romans claimed it belongs to the Sun.

16	AT
♈ ♎	22° 37'
♉ ♏	25° 38'
♊ ♐	30° 30'
♋ ♑	34° 02'
♌ ♒	34° 10'
♍ ♓	33° 03'

Figure 66: AT, Clime 2

17 The third clime is Alexandria:[144] its latitude is between 27° 12' and 33° 49', and the ascensions are worked for the latitude of 30° 22'. **18** The hours of the longest day for a place which has these ascensions, is 14 hours. **19** The Persians claimed that this clime belongs to Mars, while the Romans claimed it belongs to Mercury.

20	AT
♈ ♎	20° 13'
♉ ♏	24° 12'
♊ ♐	29° 55'
♋ ♑	34° 37'
♌ ♒	35° 36'
♍ ♓	34° 47'

Figure 67: AT, Clime 3

21 The latitude of the fourth clime[145] is between 33° 49' and 38° 23', and its ascensions are produced for the latitude of 36° 06'. **22** The hours of the longest day for a place which has these ascensions is 14 ½ hours. **23** The Persians claimed that this clime belongs to the Sun, while the Romans claimed it belongs to Jupiter.

24	AT
♈ ♎	19° 12'
♉ ♏	22° 46'
♊ ♐	29° 17'
♋ ♑	35° 15'
♌ ♒	37° 03'
♍ ♓	36° 27'

Figure 68: AT, Clime 4

---

[143] This is the modernized spelling; the Arabic transliterates the original Greek (Gr. Soēnē).
[144] In the *Almagest*, "Lower Egypt."
[145] In the *Almagest*, Rhodes.

25 The latitude of the fifth clime[146] is between 38° 23' and 42° 58', and its ascensions are produced for the latitude of 40° 56'. **26** The hours of the longest day for a place which has these ascensions is 15 hours. **27** The Persians and Romans claimed that this clime belongs to Venus.

28	AT
♈ ♎	17° 32'
♉ ♏	21° 19'
♊ ♐	28° 39'
♋ ♑	35° 53'
♌ ♒	38° 31'
♍ ♓	38° 06'

Figure 69: AT, Clime 5

29 The latitude of the sixth clime[147] is between 42° 58' and 47° 02', and its ascensions are produced for the latitude of 45° 01'. **30** The hours of the longest day for a place which has these ascensions is 15 ½ hours. **31** The Persians claimed that this clime belongs to Mercury, while the Romans claimed it belongs to the Moon.

32	AT
♈ ♎	15° 55'
♉ ♏	19° 52'
♊ ♐	27° 58'
♋ ♑	36° 34'
♌ ♒	39° 57'
♍ ♓	39° 49'

Figure 70: AT, Clime 6

---

[146] In the *Almagest*, the Hellespont.
[147] In the *Almagest*, the "Middle of Pontus." Pontus was a region of land on the southern edge of the Black Sea (the northern edge of modern Turkey), but Ptolemy's latitude corresponds more to the peninsula of land jutting out into the Black Sea, whose eastern edge encloses the Sea of Azov. Ptolemy probably means this, as the southern edge of the Black Sea (historical Pontus) is only at about 40°-41° N.

36	AT
♈ ♎	14° 20'
♉ ♏	18° 23'
♊ ♐	27° 17'
♋ ♑	37° 15'
♌ ♒	41° 25'
♍ ♓	41° 20'

Figure 71: AT, Clime 7

33 The latitude of the seventh clime[148] is between 47° 02' and 63° 00', and its ascensions are calculated for the latitude of 48° 32'. **34** The hours of the longest day for a place which has these ascensions is 16 hours. **35** The Persians claimed that this clime belongs to the Moon, while the Romans claimed it belongs to Mars.[149]

Clime	Longest Daylight Hours	City Or Region	Ptolemy's Place Latitude	Correct Place Latitude	Correct Clime Latitude
(Equ.)	12		0°		0°
1	13	Meroë	16° 27'	16° 56'	16° 45'
2	13 ½	Syēnē	23° 51'	24° 05'	24° 15'
3	14	Lower Egypt	30° 22'	Varies[150]	31°
4	14 ½	Rhodes	36°	36° 10'	36° 30'
5	15	Hellespont	40° 56'	40° 13'	41° 30'
6	15 ½	Mid-Pontus	45° 01'	45° 00'?	45° 35'
7	16	Borysthenes	48° 32'	46° 30'	49° 10'

Figure 72: Seven climes in the *Almagest*, with modern latitudes[151]

---

[148] In the *Almagest*, the "Mouths of Borysthenes." Even if the shape and location of the delta has changed somewhat over time, Ptolemy's latitude is still far too high.

[149] I have reversed these, since the text claims Mars for the Persians, and the Moon for the Romans. But this is not possible, given their schemes. The Persians are clearly assigning the planets in Chaldean order, which means they must assign the Moon to this clime; and only Mars is missing from the Roman scheme, so he must also go here.

[150] The Nile Delta covers a large area, so Ptolemy's latitude is good enough.

[151] The *Almagest* presented eleven climes, but astrologers regularized it to seven (in association with the seven planets).

Chapter VI.3: On the symmetry of the degrees of the circle

1 The symmetry of the degrees of the signs is in accordance with the relationships of figures,[152] and the counting out of one in relation to others.[153] **2** A geometrical affinity is like the affinity of one of the figures to another, or the affinity of part of a figure to the whole of that figure. **3** But a numerical affinity is that some portions of one of the numbers are countable into the whole of that number, just as 3 is a part of 9, and 3 is countable into 9 three times, so that 3 and 9 each have an affinity with the other.[154]

[Geometrical affinities]

4 When the ancients[155] spoke of "degrees of the exact aspects of the signs," they meant the affinity of one with the other, in three coinciding things:

5 One of them is [1] if some number of degrees of the circle is countable into all of the degrees of the circle.[156]

---

[152] This refers to Abū Ma'shar's geometrical and shape-based approach in **2** and **4-16**.
[153] This refers to Abū Ma'shar's numerical and ratio-based approach in **3** and **17-25**.
[154] This seems to mean the following: three is really three units (i.e., three "ones"). But three units can also be grouped together as a set, and if *three* of those *sets* are added together, it makes nine. Thus each unit in 3 corresponds to one of the sets of 3 in the number 9. If so, then there is a numerical affinity between 3 and 9. Likewise, there would be a numerical affinity between 4 and 16. But Abū Ma'shar is not really interested in the concept of squaring numbers here, just in pointing out 1-1 relationships between units and the same number of sets of those same number of units: 1-3, 1-3, and 1-3. I think the reason he includes this numerical affinity here, is because it allows him to show that the ratios used to convert aspects into each other, come from grouping the units of degrees within them in similar ways.
[155] That is, Ptolemy in *Tet.* I.13 (Robbins pp. 73-75).
[156] Operationally, this means "divides into 360°, without remainder." Thus 90° individual degrees is divisible into 360° individual degrees without remainder. (All of the exact aspects below also happen to count into 360° in accordance with one of the special ratios in **17-24**, which is important.)

6 The second is [2] if the number those degrees corresponds to[157] an [integer] number of signs, and the number of those signs counts into all of the signs.[158]

7 And the third is [3] if that number of degrees of the circle encompasses arcs (within the range of the circle of signs), [such that] [3a] the figures whose arcs you are working with have equal sides and angles, proportionate to each other, and [3b] for each figure among them there is a relationship equivalent to[159] the whole range.

8 So, by the coinciding of these three things, any degree of the circle has a relationship to another (I mean, an aspect to it), and that is in seven ways: the opposition, two trines, two squares, and two sextiles. **9** As for the opposition, it is when the distance of one of the degrees from the other is 180°. **10** As for the trine, it is when the distance of one of the degrees from the other is 120°. **11** As for the square, it is when the distance of one of the degrees from the other is 90°. **12** As for the sextile, it is when the distance of one of the degrees from the other is 60°.

13 In each one of these numbers, which is the amount of an exact aspect, are brought together the three relationships which we stated, because:
- [1] 180° counts into 360° twice;
- [2] but it has 6 of the signs, and 6 counts into the 12 signs twice;
- [3a] and it encompasses two equivalent, <right>[160] angles,
- [3b] and the circle is divided into two figures of equivalent sides and angles, both with an affinity to the whole range.

---

[157] موافقًا. That is, "is equivalent to": such as 90° being equivalent to or "fits into" 3 signs.

[158] That is, the size of the aspect is an integer number of signs, and that integer number is a factor of 12. Thus, 90° is equivalent to 3 signs, and 12 is divisible by 3 without remainder.

[159] In the examples below, Abū Ma'shar instead uses the phrase "an affinity to" (مناسبة).

[160] I have added this because Abū Ma'shar points out this function of the right angle in all of the other examples below.

Book VI: On the Classifications of the Signs

14 As for 120,
- [1] it counts into the degrees of the circle three times;
- [2] and it has four of the signs, and the four counts into all the signs three times;
- [3b] and the range of the circle is divided by three equivalent, proportional figures, each figure with an affinity to the whole range;
- [3a] and its angles (which are about the center) are a right angle plus one-third.

15 As for 90,
- [1] it counts into the degrees of the circle four times;
- [2] but it has three of the signs, and the three count into all of the signs, four times;
- [3b] and the range of the circle is divided by four equivalent, proportional figures, each figure having an affinity to the whole range;
- [3a] and its angles (which are about the center) are right [angles].

16 As for 60,
- [1] it counts into all of the degrees of the circle six times;
- [2] but it has two of the signs, and the two count into all of the signs six times;
- [3b] and they divide the range of the circle by six equivalent, proportional figures, each figure having an affinity to the whole range;
- [3a] and its angles (which are about the center) encompass two-thirds of a right angle.

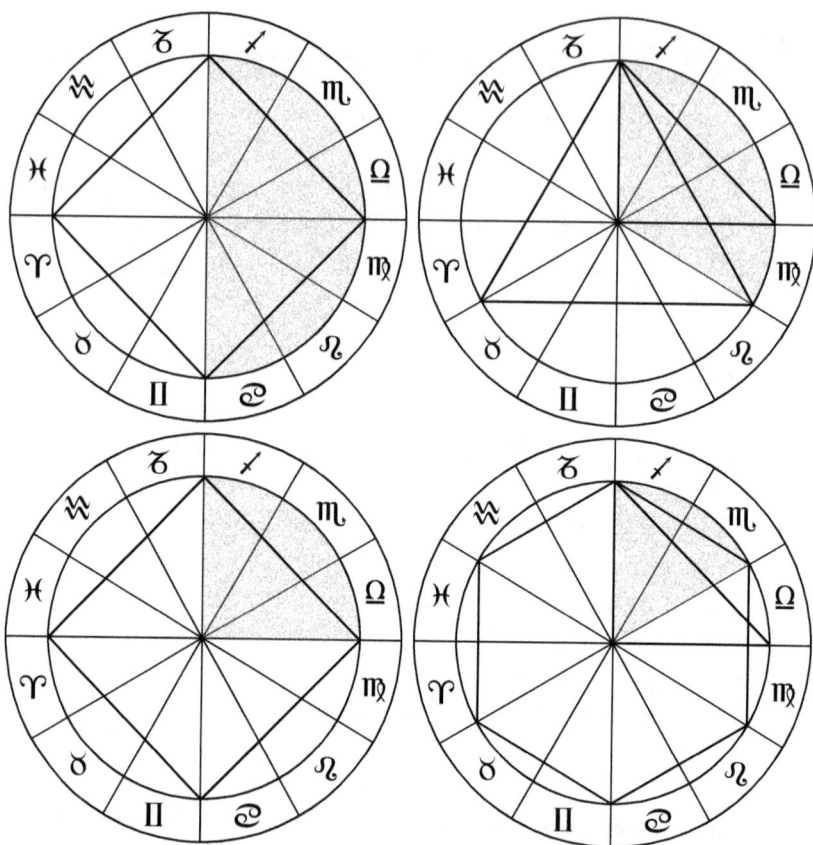

Figure 73: Geometrical affinities (VI.3, 4-16)

[Mathematical affinities]

17 Now as for the philosophers who dealt with numbers,[161] they used to call the half and the third "the mighty calculations,"[162] and they said from them both, and from the doubling of one of them,[163] and from the relation-

---

[161] Or more literally, the "enumerating philosophers."
[162] That is, a "superparticular," corresponding to Ptolemy's *megistōn* ("great, mighty").
[163] This half, one-third, and doubling corresponds to **18-21**.

ship of one to the other by the amount of the half and the third,[164] there is an affinity of the degrees of the circle which are in an exact aspect.

17	Relationships: 1/2, 1/3, doubling, and relation of 1/2 to 1/3	
18	Divide circle by 1/2 (= ☍)	360° → 1/2 → 180°
19	Divide each 1/2 by 1/2 (= □)	180° → 1/2 → 90°
20	Divide ☍ by 1/3 (= ✶)	180° → 1/3 → 60°
21	Multiply ✶ by 2 (= △)	120° → 1/2 → 60° 60° → 2 → 120°
22	☍ = △ + 1/2 △	120° → 3/2 → 180°
23	△ = □ + 1/3 □	90° → 4/3 → 120°
24	□ = ✶ + 1/2 ✶	60° → 3/2 → 90°

Figure 74: Summary of harmonies (VI.3, 17-24)

18 So they said that the aspect of the opposition is from two equivalent angles, and when one amount of the two halves of the circle inherently has some relationship, the other half inherently has the same thing. **19** Then, they divided each one of the two [halves] into two halves, so that each division came to 90°: and it is the aspect of the square. **20** Then they divided the half[165] into three divisions, and each third came to 60°: and it is the aspect of the sextile. **21** Then they doubled the degrees of the sextile, so it came to be 120°, and it is the aspect of the trine.

22 So[166] in the 180, the part in it is 120, plus half of that. **23** And in the 120 is 90 plus one-third of that. **24** And in the 90 is 60 and one-half of that.

---

[164] This is the superparticular relationship of 3/2 and 4/3, described in **22-24**.
[165] That is, each 180°.
[166] Sentences **22-25** describe how the aspects are superparticulars (which means that the denominator, *as well as one of its factors*, added together, make the numerator). Thus in 3/2, the numerator 3 is the sum of 2 (the denominator) and one of its own factors (namely, 1). In music, which Ptolemy says is most important here, the factors must be 2 or 3 (as mentioned above). But a more colloquial way of putting it is that each aspect can be converted into the others or is a function of the others. Thus we can convert the square into a trine by adding its own 1/3, or the opposition by doubling it, or the sextile by subtracting its own 1/3. Likewise you can convert an

25 Thus in the relationship of one to the other, it was found [that] in the greater number which precedes its partner[167] there is the same [amount] as the lesser[168] plus one-half of it,[169] or the same [amount] as it plus one-third of it: so because of that they adopted these amounts as the exact aspects.

[Other views]

26 Now as for other people, they said that the ancients understood the aspect from the conditions of the planets. **27** As for the opposition, it comes from the complete light in the body of the Moon, because the Moon does not cease to increase in light until she comes to be in the opposition of the Sun; and when she withdraws from that place she decreases in her glow. **28** As for the square, they understood it from the conditions of the planets relative to their apogees, because at every 90° by which the planet distances itself from the apex of its apogee, its condition in its motion changes. **29** As for the trine, they understood it from the two superiors,[170] because if there were approximately 120° between one of them and the Sun, they go retrograde if they were direct, and go direct if they were retrograde. **30** As for the sextile, it is the amount matching one-half the diameter of the circle,[171] and the amount of the distance of the two houses of Venus from the two houses of

---

opposition into a trine by subtracting its own 1/3, or a square by halving. (A sextile is one-half of a sextile, so maybe that's how he gets the trine, by that extra step.) But you can't do this with the quintile (72): adding its own 1/3 is 96; subtracting 1/3 is 48; doubling it is 144. So ultimately, this is what he means by there being a proportion *among* aspects. It's not just about being able to divide 360° by any number at all.

[167] This "greater" number which "precedes" the other, is the numerator. So in the fraction 3/2, 3 is the "greater number" which precedes the "lesser number" 2.

[168] That is, the denominator.

[169] This is equivalent to 3/2 of the lesser number.

[170] That is, Saturn and Jupiter.

[171] That is, the radius. If you draw a circle with a compass, by definition the distance between the two legs of the compass is the radius, or one-half the diameter. Place the fixed point of the compass on the circumference, and cut off a section of the circumference with the moving or drawing point: it will mark a point 60° away, the sextile.

the luminaries. **31** So, for the reasons we stated, they knew the aspect of the planets.

32 Now when something of some sign ascends, the affinity of that ascending degree and its aspect in the several signs[172] will be withdrawing from the degrees which we had stated. **33** And that is because if the Ascendant was the first degree of Aries, its sextile would fall at the beginning of Gemini, and its square at the beginning of Cancer, and its trine at the beginning of Leo (and its aspect will be likewise in the other direction). **34** And the more that the degrees of the ascent of Aries increase in the way we stated, the degrees of its aspect to the signs which it looks at will increase.[173] **35** But Aries does look at Gemini and Aquarius with a sextile aspect, and at Cancer and Capricorn with a square aspect, and at Leo and Sagittarius with a trine aspect, and at Libra with the aspect of opposition. **36** And the amount of each sign's exact aspect to the other signs, follows this situation.[174]

[Ptolemy again]

37 And all of the ancients[175] called the aspect of the trine and sextile the "finest amounts," and the most indicative of them for harmony and affection, due to the fact that they begin from harmonious signs and terminate in the same: because if they begin with the masculine they finish at the masculine,

---

[172] في عدد البروج.

[173] This is awkwardly put, because instead of speaking of fixed relationships between zodiacal degrees (which has been the subject so far), Abū Ma'shar now turns to the aspects of points associated with the zodiac (here, the Ascendant). He seems to mean the following. Let 1° Aries be rising: its exact sextile aspect will fall into 1° Gemini. But as the heavens turn, 2° Aries will be on the horizon, so the exact aspect from the Ascendant will "increase" to 2° Gemini. But then the original degrees of 1° Aries and Gemini will be in a constant state of "withdrawing" from the Ascendant and *its* sextile, even though those degrees within the zodiac are still in a sextile relationship to each other (**35-36**). To my mind this whole paragraph is unnecessarily confusing and should have been omitted, unless it plays some role in response to **26-31**.

[174] Note well: there are no "out-of-sign" aspects.

[175] Again, Ptolemy. But he does not call the aspects the "finest" or "worst," as Abū Ma'shar does here.

and if they begin with the feminine they finish at the same. **38** As for the square and opposition, they called them the "worst[176] amounts," due to the difference of their signs in the beginning and the endpoint.

39 And the most powerful symmetry of degrees of the circle is the opposition, then after that the square, then the trine; as for the sextile, it is below them all in power.[177]

[Rejecting other "harmonics"]

40 Now [some] people have rejected what we stated at first about the amounts of the aspecting of the degrees of the signs, and they said: "By the degrees of the exact aspects, the ancients meant [1] those which count into all of the degrees of the circle.[178] **41** So it must be that among the exact aspects there is a division by five, eight, nine, ten, and others, because one-fifth of the degrees of the circle is 72, and they count into all of the degrees of the circle, five times; and one-eighth <counts into> of all of the degrees of the circle, as well as one-ninth and one-tenth: each one of them counts into all of the degrees of the circle a different [amount] of times, according to the relationship of each of them to the other."[179]

42 But we say: By the exact aspects they did not simply mean [1] the amount of degrees which count into the degrees of the circle, but they determined it by the coinciding of [1-3] those three things in one [and the same] position.[180] **43** For if one of the relationships was found for one [aspect], but the same thing is not found to have[181] the remaining two

---

[176] Reading أسوأ with the sense of the Latin **H**, for the Arabic استواء ("equality").

[177] Abū Ma'shar is here linking "symmetry" (تناظر) with the power of the aspect itself.

[178] This is criterion [1] as described in **5**.

[179] By the "relationship of each of them with the other," I think these objectors mean that if we divide the circle by 5 (the quintile) we get 72, and these are "related" because their product is 360 (5 x 72 = 360). But that is not the full set of relationships which Abū Ma'shar means, as he will now explain.

[180] That, is the three mathematical relationships described in **4-7**, and explained by the passages after that.

[181] Lit., "in," or "to be in."

BOOK VI: ON THE CLASSIFICATIONS OF THE SIGNS   355

[relationships], they did not grant it a relationship[182] in the degrees of the circle. **44** So even if one-fifth of those degrees, and the rest of what you stated about the parts, do [1] count into all of the degrees of the circle several times, the number twelve does not have [2] the same parts as it, [which are] countable into it: because if one of the numbers was divided by one of [those] parts, a fraction would occur in it when it is tried.[183] **45** So the philosophers and masters of counting do not reckon [something] as a "part" belonging to the whole of that number, but they [only] reckon [something] as its parts [if it is] a number in which there is no fraction upon testing it out.

46 For this reason, they did not grant a relationship[184] between degrees of the circle except for the range of numbers and ways which we stated before.

Chapter VI.4: On the signs loving one another, hating one another, and hostile to one another, and straight[185] and crooked in ascensions, and obedient and disobedient to one another

1 Among the signs are those [1] loving one another, hating one another, and hostile to one another. **2** And among them what is [2] straight in ascensions and crooked in ascensions. **3** And among them what is [3] obedient to another and not that.

---

[182] Here Abū Ma'shar should have said "affinity" (مناسبة) instead of "relationship" (نسبة).

[183] For example, suppose we wanted the quintile (an amount of 72°), which is based on the number 5. The number 5 does go into 360° without remainder, namely 72. But neither 5 nor 72 comprise an integer number of signs which divides into 12. This is another way of saying that we cannot use doubling, halving, or thirds, to convert these other so-called aspects or "harmonics" into the other aspects. Despite their name, these other divisions do not actually allow a *harmonization between* aspects, or if they do it requires many operations. But the numbers 2 and 3, which are factors of 12, do allow direct relationships and conversions between the classical aspects. (And if any kind of division of 360 was allowed, we could make 1° aspects on the theory that 360 is divisible by 1).

[184] Again, Abū Ma'shar should have said "affinity" (مناسبة) instead of "relationship" (نسبة).

[185] Omitting an extra "in ascensions," to match the title in the table of contents.

4 Now as for [1] the signs loving one another, they are those which look at each other from the trine and sextile. **5** The signs hating one another are those looking at each other from the square. **6** Those hostile to one another are those looking at each other from the opposition.

7 As for those [2] straight in ascension, they are those which rise in an upright fashion, and the ascensions of each one of them is greater than 30°: and they are from the beginning of Cancer to the end of Sagittarius. **8** The signs crooked in ascension are those which rise in a slanted fashion, and the ascensions of each one of them is less than 30°: and they are from the beginning of Capricorn to the end of Gemini.

9 Now [3] the signs which are crooked in ascension are obedient to those straight in ascensions, and they indicate agreement and love—and the most indicative of that is when they look at each other with an aspect of affection. **10** And that is like Gemini, for it is obedient to Leo (and Leo is to Gemini),[186] and Taurus to Cancer (and Cancer to Taurus); and Taurus and Capricorn to Virgo (and Virgo to them both), and Scorpio to Pisces (and Pisces to Scorpio), and Sagittarius to Aquarius (and Aquarius to Sagittarius), and Capricorn to Scorpio (and Scorpio to Capricorn). **11** But as for Aries to Libra, and Capricorn to Cancer, it is the contrary of affection because even though one of them is obedient to its associate, they look at each other from the opposition.

---

[186] Abū Ma'shar has omitted all instances of "commanding," which should be in the parentheses here. Thus Gemini is obedient by affection to Leo, because Gemini is crooked and sextiles Leo. But Leo *commands* Gemini with affection, because Leo is straight. This version of the commanding and obeying signs is one of five I have found in the traditional literature: there was no clear and agreed-upon definition. His "Persian" version mentioned below in **12** and again in VI.5, **6-11**, is the fifth version, in which the signs obey each other but apparently none commands.

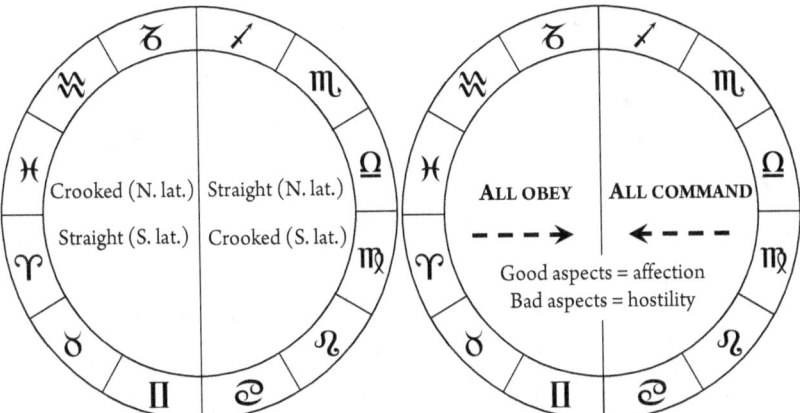

Figure 75: Straight and crooked signs (VI.4, 7-8)

Figure 76: Abū Ma'shar's commanding and obeying signs (VI.4, 9-11)

12 And the obedient signs are also named in another manner: and they are the "equal[187] signs, agreeing in power," those for which the hours of the day of one, are the same as the hours of the day of the other (and we will state that, if God wills).[188]

Chapter VI.5: On the signs agreeing in the belt and ascensions, agreeing in power, and agreeing in manner[189]

1 We have already mentioned the signs' looking at each other, but for each of the signs are found other relationships to each other apart from looking, all of them indicating agreement and affection: and they are in three ways.

---

[187] المقتدرة, which normally means simply that something is powerful or possesses power. But it does also mean to be equivalent in power, and is how Abū Ma'shar describes the Persian version in the next chapter (VI.5, **6-11**).
[188] See the next chapter, VI.5, **6-11**.
[189] الطريقة, referring to a way of being or condition—probably because they are ruled by the same planet (see below). These are normally called "agreeing in the *path*," but that word is the masculine form, الطريق.

[1: Agreeing in the belt and ascensions]

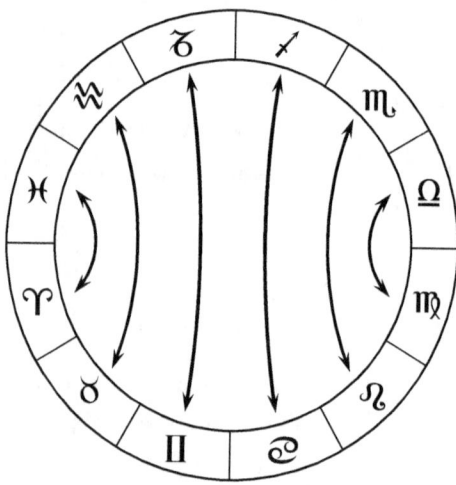

Figure 77: Signs agreeing in the belt and ascensions (VI.5, 2-5)

2 As for the first of them, it is that [1] two signs will agree [by] partaking in the belt: and it is that the distance of each one of them in its own direction of the belt of the equatorial sphere is equivalent,[190] and the ascensions of one of the two signs is the same as the ascensions of the other. 3 And that is like Aries with Pisces, Taurus with Aquarius, Gemini with Capricorn, Cancer with Sagittarius, Leo with Scorpio, and Virgo with Libra: for these signs agree with each other in ascensions.

4 Now as for [the first] one of the two signs, it begins the agreement of its ascensions with the other from the beginning of the sign, but the second one begins it from the end of the sign: because the ascensions of the first degree of Aries agree with the ascensions of the last degree of Pisces, and the ascensions of 10° Aries agree with the ascensions of 20° Pisces, and the ascensions of the end of Aries are the same as the ascensions of the beginning of Pisces. 5 And the ascensions of the beginning of Taurus are the same as the ascensions of the end of Aquarius, and the ascensions of the end of Taurus the same as the ascensions of the beginning of Aquarius—and analogously until the ascensions of the beginning of Virgo are the same as the ascensions of the end of Libra, and the ascensions of 10° Virgo are the same as the ascensions of 20° of Libra, and the ascensions of the last degree of Virgo are the same as the ascensions of the first degree of Libra.

---

[190] That is, their declinations will be equal, but in opposite directions: thus the northern declination of any degree in Aries, will correspond to the southern declination of any degree in Pisces.

BOOK VI: ON THE CLASSIFICATIONS OF THE SIGNS   359

[*2: Agreeing in power*]

6 And as for [2] the second [way], it is the signs "agreeing in power."[191] **7** (The people of Persia call every pair of signs among them "equal in power," and also call them "obeying *each other*.")[192] **8** And they are the signs which, when the Sun is in one of them, the hours of its day are equivalent to the hours of the day of the other sign.[193] **9** And that is like Cancer and Gemini, Taurus and Leo, Aries and Virgo, Pisces and Libra, Aquarius and Scorpio, and Capricorn and Sagittarius, for the hours of the day of one of the two signs is equivalent to the hours of the day of the other sign.

10 And one begins with one of them from the beginning of the sign, and with the second one from the end of the sign: like the hours of the day of the 30th degree of Gemini, for it is the same as the hours of the day of the 1st degree of Cancer; and the hours of the day of the 29th degree of Gemini is the same as the hours of the day of the 2nd degree of Cancer, and the hours of 10° of Gemini the same as the hours of 20° of Cancer, and the hours of the day of the beginning of Gemini

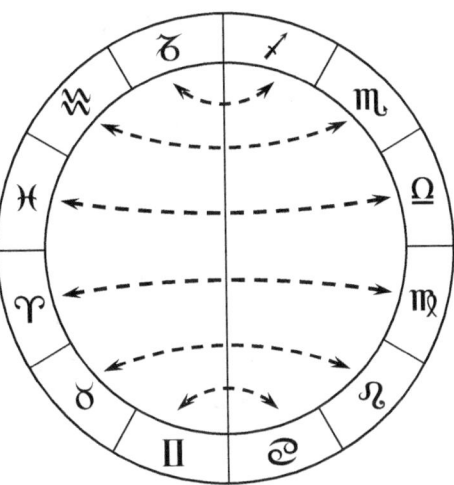

Figure 78: Signs agreeing in power, Persian signs obeying each other, antiscial signs (VI.5, 6-9)

---

[191] See the previous chapter, VI.4, **12**.
[192] See my footnote to VI.4, **12**, where they can also be said to "possess power," but are being treated in one meaning of the verb as being "equal in power." Since they are equal in power (due to the equality of daylight), there is no commanding relationship between them. This is different from the obeying-commanding relationships in VI.4, **9-11**, because the straight and crooked signs are *not* equal with respect to ascensions.
[193] These are also the signs and degrees which have an "antiscial" relationship with each other.

the same as the hours of the day of the end of Cancer, and the hours of the day of the last degree of Taurus the same as the hours of the day of the first degree of Leo. **11** And [it is] in this way until the hours of the day of the 30th degree of Virgo are the same as the hours of the 1st degree of Aries, and the hours of 20° of Libra the same as the hours of 10° of Pisces, and the hours of the end of Libra the same as the hours of the beginning of Pisces, and the hours of the beginning of Scorpio the same as the hours of the end of Aquarius, and the hours of the beginning of Sagittarius the same as the hours of the end of Capricorn, and the hours of the beginning of Sagittarius the same as the hours of the beginning of Capricorn.

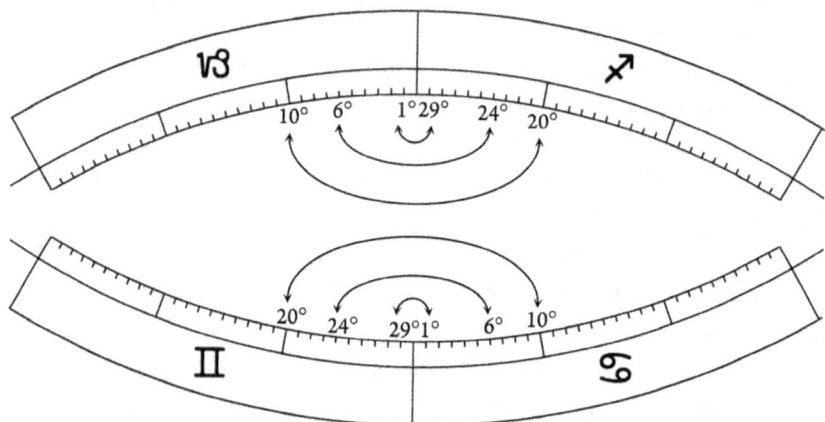

Figure 79: Detail of signs agreeing in power, Persian signs obeying each other, or antiscial signs (VI.5, 10-11)

BOOK VI: ON THE CLASSIFICATIONS OF THE SIGNS

[3: Agreeing in manner]

12 As for [3] the third [way], it is the signs "agreeing in manner": and it is that two signs belong to a single planet. **13** That is like Aries and Scorpio being the two houses of Mars,[194] and Taurus and Libra the two houses of Venus, and Gemini and Virgo the two houses of Mercury, and Sagittarius and Pisces being the two houses of Jupiter, and Capricorn and Aquarius being the two houses of Saturn: for each one of the pair in these signs is in the "manner" of its associate.[195]

14 Cancer and Leo are the two houses of the luminaries, and they are also in a single "manner," because each one of them acts as proxy for[196] its associate.[197]

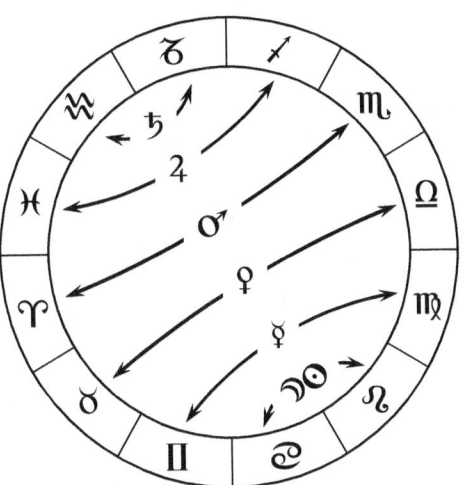

Figure 80: Signs agreeing in manner (VI.5, 12-14)

---

[194] In the next chapter, Abū Ma'shar will say that their aversion and distance from one another puts them in a "natural" opposition, but because they are in the same manner or are ruled by the same lord, they can still harmonize. The same goes for Taurus-Libra, which are in aversion and far away.

[195] صاحبه, which is also the usual word for its "lord," referring to the planet ruling each pair. Abū Ma'shar probably used this word intentionally, to suggest that they are of the same "manner" because they have the same lord.

[196] ينوب. Or, it can "substitute" for it. The verb here (ناب) is the root of one of the words for sect, the "shift" (نوبة). Abū Ma'shar is evidently referring to the fact that the Sun and Moon alternate roles as the sect light, alternating and substituting for each other by night and day.

[197] Again, صاحبه.

Chapter VI.6: On the signs which harmonize with each other in a "natural" opposition and sextile, but do not look at each other[198]

1 We have stated before this that the aspect of the opposition is one of antithesis and hostility, and indeed one must speak of antithesis and hostility in some oppositions—but not in all of them, because sometimes one of the signs is far from the other and they do *not* look at each other, so one of the two is said to be in the opposition of the other "by nature" (due to their agreement in [1] ascensions, [2] power, or [3] manner).[199] **2** And they indicate harmonization and affection due to their agreement in what we stated before. **3** And among them are also found signs not looking at each other due to their nearness to each other, and that is called a "natural" sextile: and it indicates harmony as well.

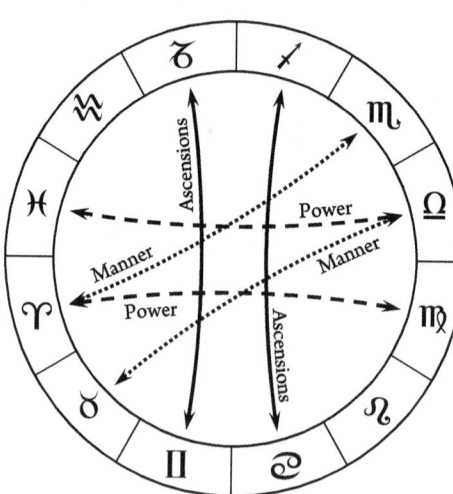

Figure 81: Signs in aversion but with "natural" opposition (VI.6, 1-2, 4)

4 Now as for the signs in which one of them does not look at its associate due to the distance which is between them, [so that] it was said that one of them is in a "natural opposition" from the other but indicates agreement and affection, they are some of the signs agreeing in [1] ascensions [but] one of them is distant from its associate (like Gemini and Capricorn, Cancer and Sagittarius); or those agreeing in [2] power [but] one of them is far from the other (like Aries

---

[198] That is, these are all of the signs which can harmonize despite being in aversion to each other.

[199] That is to say, signs in aversion *can* harmonize if they have any of the relationships from Ch. IV.5 above: the same ascensions (VI.5, **2-5**), the same power (VI.5, **6-11**), and the same manner (VI.5, **12-14**). We have already seen several instances of this in Ch. VI.5.

Book VI: On the Classifications of the Signs

and Virgo, and Libra and Pisces); or those agreeing in [3] manner [but] what is between them is distant (like Aries and Scorpio, and Taurus and Libra).

5 And as for the signs in which one of them does not look at the other due to their nearness to each other, they are called a "natural sextile" and indicate affection and harmony: and they are some of the signs agreeing in [1] ascensions [but] one of them is close to the other (like Aries and Pisces, and Virgo and Libra), or the signs agreeing in [2] power [but] one of them is close to its associate (like Gemini and Cancer, and Sagittarius and Capricorn), or those agreeing in [3] manner [but] one of them is close to its associate (like Capricorn and Aquarius).[200]

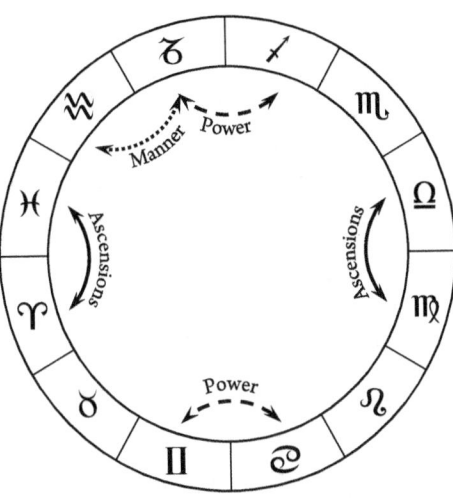

Figure 82: Signs in aversion but with "natural" sextile (VI.6, 1-3, 5)

---

[200] To be consistent, Abū Ma'shar should have added Cancer-Leo as being [3] in the same manner, as he pointed out in VI.5, **14**.

Chapter VI.7: On the signs which harmonize with each other from the square

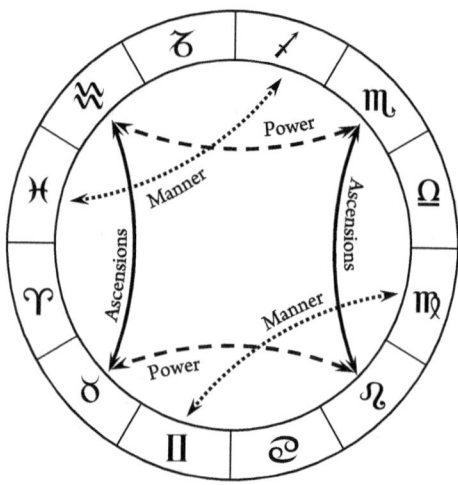

Figure 83: Signs harmonizing by square (VI.7)

1 We have already made clear in what preceded that the squares of the signs indicate conflict and hostility, but one must not say this for all squares, because among the squares are what indicates harmony and affection.[201] 2 And indeed, that comes to be through their [1] agreement in ascensions (like Taurus and Aquarius, and Leo and Scorpio), or by their agreement in [2] the length and decrease of the hours of the day (like Taurus and Leo, and Aquarius and Scorpio), and by their agreement in [3] manner (like Gemini and Virgo, and Sagittarius and Pisces).

3 So, these squares are indicative of harmonization. 4 But as for the rest of them, they are indicative of conflict and hostility.

---

[201] Unlike the signs in aversion which can harmonize (IV.6), these signs already see each other by a square, but Abū Ma'shar wants to use the same categories from IV.5 to harmonize these squares.

BOOK VI: ON THE CLASSIFICATIONS OF THE SIGNS   365

Chapter VI.8: On the years of the signs, and their months, days, and hours

1 The years of the signs, as well as their months, days, and hours, are derived in two ways.

2 The first way is [1] that you make the degrees of the signs' ascensions in the clime which you want, be: for each degree a year, and every 5' a month, up to what you want in terms of days and hours.[202]

3 The second way is [2] that you make the years of each sign, and its months, be the same as the lesser years of its lord.[203] **4** But as for their days and hours, one derives [that] for each sign with two different methods.[204] **5** The first method is [2a] that you multiply the lesser years of the lord of that sign by 12, so that it becomes months; then you double those months, then after that one adds to them the same number as the lesser years of that planet, and divide the sum by 10: what comes out is the days, but what remains is the portions of tenths of a day. **6** So the sum is the days of that sign and the portions of a day.[205]

---

[202] These are *not* the values which appear in the table below, but are the usual way of converting ascensional times (AT) into a 360-day year (somewhat imprecise as to the calendar, since there are only 360 ascensions total). For example, let the AT of some degree in the zodiac at some latitude be 1.27 AT. This is 1.27 years. Multiply the .27 by 12 (months) to get 3.24 months. Multiply the .24 by 30 (days) to get 7.2 days. Multiply the .2 by 24 (hours) to get 4.8 hours. Multiply the .8 by 60 (minutes) to get 48 minutes. Thus, 1.27 AT is worth 1y 3m 7d 4h 48m (although the months are 30 days apiece). I suppose one could also convert this into a proper tropical period by multiplying the .27 by 365.2422, to omit the months and jump immediately to an exact number of days: 1y 98d 14h 46m.

[203] These are the two shaded columns on the left, below, labeled *Method 2*: thus since the lesser years of Mars are 15, his signs have 15 years and 15 months. The (450d) means that 15 months of 30 days apiece are 450 days.

[204] The table below which illustrates this, can be generated directly from Valens, *Anth.* IV.10. This shows that that portion of Valens was available to the Persians and to Abū Ma'shar, through the *Bizidaj*.

[205] This is the middle shaded column below, labeled *Method 2a*. Let us use Aries. The lesser years of Mars are 15: multiply by 12 (=180), double it (= 360), add the integer number of 15 lesser years (= 375), then divide by 10 (= 37.5). This is equivalent to 37 days, 12 hours. Note that part of this procedure is redundant, and

7 The second method[206] is that [2b] the lesser years of the planet are taken and made into months, <then that is multiplied by 12>,[207] then one casts out one-half, then from the remaining one-half are cast out the equivalent number of the planet's lesser years, then one divides the remainder by 24 hours:[208] what comes out is the days, and what remains are the hours. **8** So the sum is the days and hours of that sign, by the second method.[209]

---

part is for convenience. For one thing, we could have skipped all of this and simply divided the number of days in the entire period by 12: 450d / 12 = 37.5. (But perhaps the method is complicated because one wants to show how the lesser years can be part of the calculation.) But even if we start Abū Ma'shar's way, instead of multiplying the months by 12 and doubling it, we could simply have multiplied by 24. Finally, after the complicated adding and dividing by 10, he says that the remainder tells us the "portions of tenths" of a day. This is not really helpful and probably refers to a table that astrologers would have used for convenience: if our result is 37.5, the "5" means "five tenths" of a day, which is the same as one-half of a day, or 12 hours. With a modern calculator this is unnecessary.

[206] This Method 2b is incomplete as it appears in Abū Ma'shar, and I have added a missing instruction in the text. The results are equivalent to dividing the total number of days in the months, by 144. Again, Aries: if we divide the total days (450) by 144, we get 3.125, which is the 3 days and 3 hours we find in the columns on the right. This also means that Method 2b is somehow related to Method 2a. For as I stated above, Method 2a is the result of dividing the total days by 12, and Method 2b is the same as dividing Method 2a by 12. For Aries, if we divide the 450 days by 12 we get 37.5, which is the same as Method 2a. But if we divide 37.5 by 12 we get 3.125, which is Method 2b. But Method 2b must have some other rationale, because why should there be two versions of the days, if one is just a derivative of the other? I suspect that it has something to do with diurnal rotation, which is why Abū Ma'shar has us divide by 24 in sentence 7: the whole circle rotates once in 24 hours, at 15 AT per hour.

[207] This is the missing instruction: note that we also did this at the beginning of Method 2a in sentence **5**. The fact that no MSS contain it, suggests to me that it was originally explained in the *Bizidaj* (or perhaps in al-Andarzaghar) but that Abū Ma'shar omitted it by accident: thus, no later scribe was able to replicate it.

[208] These don't have to be 24 *hours*, unless this method is somehow based on diurnal rotation. Only the number 24 is necessary.

[209] Take Aries again. The months are still 15, as before. Multiply 15 by 12 (= 180), divide in half (= 90), subtract the integer number of 15 lesser years (= 75), and divide by 24 (= 3.125). This result is 3 days, 3 hours. Again, part of this is redundant:

BOOK VI: ON THE CLASSIFICATIONS OF THE SIGNS 367

9 And we will state that, if God wills:[210]

10	Years (Method 2)	Months (Method 2)	Days, hours (Method 2a)	Days (Method 2b)	Hours (Method 2b)
♈	15	15 (450d)	37 ½	3	3
♉	8	8 (240d)	20	1	16
♊	20	20 (600d)	50	4	4
♋	25	25 (750d)	62 ½	5	5
♌	19	19 (570d)	47 ½	3	23
♍	20	20 (600d)	20	4	4
♎	8	8 (240d)	8	1	16
♏	15	15 (450d)	15	3	3
♐	12	12 (360d)	12	2	12
♑	27	27 (810d)	27	5	15
♒	30	30 (900d)	30	6	6
♓	12	12 (360d)	12	2	12

Figure 84: Planetary years and months, from Valens (VI.8)

Chapter VI.9: On the indications of the signs for collections of countries, and locales in lands

1 In this chapter we want to state what the signs indicate, as a summary of[211] countries and locales in lands. **2** But as for a detailed examination of what the signs indicate in terms of climes, their countries, and every place in a land, we will state that separately from this book.

---

multiplying by 12 and dividing in half is the same as multiplying by 6. Now we can see that it is necessarily true that directly dividing the total days by 144 is equivalent to this roundabout Method 2b. Let m be the integer number of months. It is necessarily true that: $30m/144 = ((12m/2) - m)/24$. In the case of Aries or Mars, m is 15: $30(15)/144 = 3.125$. But $((12(15)/2) - 15)/24$ is also 3.125.

[210] What follows in the Arabic text is a list of signs and numbers, so I have converted them into a table and called it sentence **10**.
[211] Lit., "of the sums/collections of."

3 ARIES: Among countries it has Babylon, Persia, Azerbaijān, and Palestine. **4** And among locales it has deserts,²¹² sheep pastures, villages, places in which one works with fire, a robbers' lair, and houses roofed with wood.

5 TAURUS: Among countries it has the Sūwād, Māhīn, Hamadhān, and the Kurds who are in the mountains.²¹³ **6** And among locales it has lands with few waters [but] in which one sows, all healthy arable land, and every place close to the mountains, orchards, gardens, trees, waters, and the places of elephants and cattle.

7 GEMINI: Among countries it has Jurjān, Armenia, Azerbaijān, Jīlān, Burjān, Mūqān, Egypt, and the communities of Barqah; and it has a share in Isfahān and Kirmān. **8** And among locales it has the mountains, cultivated lands, compacted sandy lands, hills, places of hunters, those who play backgammon, entertainers, and singers.

9 CANCER: Among countries it has Lesser Armenia, what is in the rear of Mūqān, Numidia (and it is a portion of Ifrīqīyah), eastern Khurāsān, China, and Marw al-Rūd; and it has a share in Balkh and Azerbaijān. **10** And among locales it has wetlands, jungles, coasts, the banks of rivers, river bluffs, and the places of trees.

11 LEO: Among countries it has the Turks up to the end of the inhabited world which borders on it, Sogdiana, Abarshahr, and Tūs. **12** And among locales it has waterless deserts, wadis with difficult paths, lands having gravel, every land with predatory animals, the palaces of kings, castles, mountains and hills, the elevated [portion] of places, forts, and impenetrable fortifications.

13 VIRGO: Among countries it has Jaramāqah, al-Shām, the Euphrates, al-Jazīrah; and among the communities of Persia what borders on Kirmān. **14** And among locales it has every land on which one sows, the dwelling places of women, entertainers,²¹⁴ singers, and promenades.

15 LIBRA: Among countries it has al-Rūm²¹⁵ and what is between its borders up to Ifrīqīyah and what is around it, Upper Egypt up to the borders of

---

²¹² الصّحارى. Or, steppes and other sandy-type land.

²¹³ الجبال, which can also indicate specifically a mountainous region in western Iran.

²¹⁴ Or perhaps, the places of entertainments (الملهين). Note that both signs ruled by Gemini have this signification.

²¹⁵ That is, "the Romans" or the Byzantine Empire.

Ethiopia, Barqah, Kirmān, Sijistān, Kābul, Tukhāristān, Balkh, and Herat. **16** And among locales it has [land] on which one sows among the tops of mountains, and every land on which there are date palms, and a place of hunting and falcons, every lookout post[216] and path, an elevated place looking down, and it has vast expanses and deserts.

17 SCORPIO: Among countries it has the land of the Hijāz, the nomadic desert of the Arabs and its regions up to Yemen, and it has Tangiers, Qūmis, Rayy, and it has a share in Sogdiana. **18** And among locales it has the places of vines and mulberries, and things in gardens which resemble that, and every rotting, dirty place, prisons, places of anxiety and sorrow, ruins, and the burrows of scorpions.

19 SAGITTARIUS: Among countries it has al-Jibāl,[217] Rayy, and Isfahān. **20** And among locales it has gardens and every place one irrigates time after time, and it indicates the places of the Herpads[218] and rolling thunder,[219] and the place of the rest of the religions, the smooth desert, and the places of riding animals, oxen, and young calves.

21 CAPRICORN: Among countries it has Ethiopia, Makrān, Sind, the river Makrān,[220] the coast of the sea which borders on those regions,[221] Omān, the two seas[222] up to Hind and its borders up to China; and it has the Ahwāz, and the eastern border of the land of al-Rūm.[223] **22** And among locales in lands it has castles, gates, gardens, and every irrigated place, and it has wadis, waterwheels, rivers, irrigation canals, ancient cisterns, every river bluff on which there are trees, and a shore at which ships are housed for the night,[224]

---

[216] This can include places of ambush.
[217] الجبال, a mountainous region in western Iran. But this can also simply mean "mountains." See **5** above.
[218] These are low-level Zoroastrian priests who tend the sacred fires.
[219] الزمزمة. Or, "the lion's roar." See the footnote to VI.1, **123**.
[220] According to **BY**, this is the Indus river. But according to LeStrange p. 331, the Indus was called the Mihrān. The province of Makrān is mainly desert. Nevertheless Abū Ma'shar probably does mean the Indus.
[221] This is most likely the Gulf of Oman.
[222] البحرين, Bahrain.
[223] The Byzantine Empire.
[224] Reading مبيت with **N** for Lemay's and **BY**'s منبت, "planted" (but which **BY** translates as "made").

the places of dogs, foxes, wild animals, predatory beasts, the settlements[225] of strangers,[226] lodgers, and slaves, and the places in which fire was already kindled.

23 AQUARIUS: Among countries it has the Sūwād up to the region of al-Jibāl,[227] Kūfa and its region, the rear of the Ḥijāz, the land of the Copts in Egypt, the west of the land of Sind, and it has a share in the land of Persia.[228] **24** And among locales it has places of waters, flowing rivers, seas, canals and what is in them, everything dug out by pickaxes, every place irrigated by water, places in which there are aquatic birds (and other birds), every place in which there are vines, or in which one sells wine, or whores take lodgings, and every mountainous, wild land.

25 PISCES: Among countries it has Tabaristān, the northern region of the land of Jurjān, and it has a share in the land of al-Rūm up to the land of al-Shām, al-Jazīrah, Egypt, Alexandria, what is around Egypt, and the Red Sea (I mean, the Sea of Yemen), and the east of the land of Hind. **26** And among locales it has what is close to the seas and their shores, lakes, jungles, the coasts of seas, fish,[229] the places of angels and worshipers, and a place of weeping and sorrow.

---

[225] مناظل. Or, stopping-points.

[226] Or, "foreigners" (الغرباء).

[227] الجبال, a mountainous region in western Iran. But this can also simply mean "mountains." See **5** and **19** above.

[228] Or perhaps more narrowly, the region of Fārs (الفارس).

[229] السمك. However, with different voweling this can mean an interior, upper place of a place, near the roof (from the verb سمك, to raise something up high). This could be relevant because the next clause refers to angels and worshippers. One can imagine this referring to a steeple, dome, or similar structure in a place of worship.

Chapter VI.10: On the signs indicating motion and rest

1 Aries, Taurus, and Gemini: when their lords coincide with them[230] (and they are Mars, Venus, and Mercury), they are set in motion.

2 Cancer, Leo and Virgo: when their lords coincide with them (and they are the Moon, the Sun, and Mercury), they are at rest.

3 Libra, Scorpio, Sagittarius: when their lords coincide with them (and they are Venus, Mars, and Jupiter), they are set in motion.

4 Capricorn, Aquarius, and Pisces: when their lords coincide with them (and they are Saturn and Jupiter), they are at rest.

Chapter VI.11: On the rational signs which indicate a class of people and their conditions

1 The rational[231] signs which indicate a class of people and their conditions, are: Gemini, Virgo, Libra, Aquarius, and the first half of Sagittarius.

2 Now as for Gemini, it belongs to the mighty; Virgo, Libra, and Sagittarius belong to those in the middle; and Aquarius belongs to the underclass.

3 And the signs indicate the conditions of people in another way, and that is because Aries and its triplicities are of the

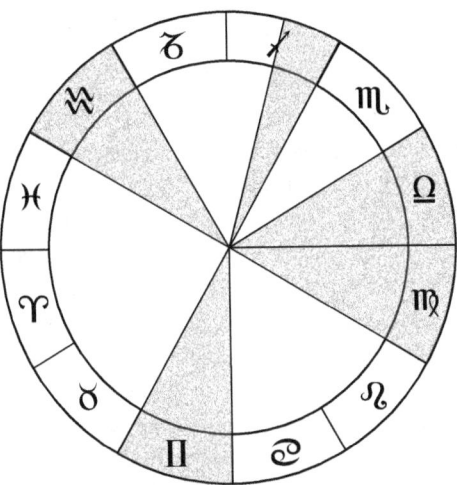

Figure 85: Rational signs (VI.11)

---

[230] Lit., "in them." Abū Ma'shar is sometimes picky about pointing out that planets are not really "in" the signs, but revolve parallel to them, so they only correspond to or coincide with them.

[231] This can also mean "speaking" (الناطقة), but could be confused with the "voiced" signs in VI.18 below.

signs of kings; Gemini and its triplicities are of the signs of nobles and the mighty; Taurus and its triplicities are of the signs of those in the middle; and Cancer and its triplicities are of the signs of the underclass.

Chapter VI.12: On the division of what belongs to each sign, in terms of the limbs of the human body

1 Aries has: the head, face, the pupil of the eye, and the innards,[232] and what emerges in them and in the eyes and ears, in terms of ailments.

2 Taurus has: the neck and its vertebrae,[233] the throat, and what emerges in them in terms of ailments and their illnesses, like scrofula,[234] abscesses,[235] a rotting of the nose,[236] curvature of the back,[237] and pain in the eye.[238]

3 Gemini has: the shoulders, upper arms, the hands, and the shoulder-blades.

---

[232] المصارين, which normally means "guts" or "intestines." But surely Abū Ma'shar means something different, so I have chosen the more neutral "innards," referring to the inner parts of the eye and head.

[233] خرزته. I am not fully confident about this word. **BY** read "Adam's apple," presumably treating it as the singularizable collective noun meaning a "bead"; Hava says that the phrase خرزة الرّقبة ("bead of the neck") does refer to an Adam's apple. But Hava also says that خرز الظّهر ("beads of the spine") refers to vertebrae. To me it seems redundant to speak of both the Adam's apple (here) and the throat (the next word). It makes more sense to speak of the neck as a whole, the bones in back, and the insides: see also later in the sentence, where curvature of the spine is specifically mentioned. Another possibility is that it means something like the "nodules" of the neck, namely the lymph nodes: this is where scrofula originates (mentioned later in the sentence).

[234] This is a bacterial infection of the lymph nodes in the neck, causing visible eruptions and growths.

[235] الخراج. Or any kind of "eruption" in the skin, including tumors.

[236] الخياشيم. This is especially of the inner part of the nose, going back into the sinuses.

[237] حدبة الظهر. Or more colloquially, being a "hunchback." This must be kyphosis, an extreme rounding of the upper back and spine (ظهر especially refers to vertebrae)

[238] In several of the signs here, eyes are mentioned because their *constellations* contain fixed stars which indicate harm to the eyes (see Ch. VI.20). This shows that the tropical signs were not fully detached from the constellations at this time.

4 Cancer has: the chest, the female breasts, the heart, stomach, the rib structure,[239] spleen, the lung and its illnesses, and everything emerging in the eye (of sluggishness[240] and amaurosis),[241] and in hidden places of the chest.

5 Leo has: the upper stomach, the heart, sinews,[242] the side, bone, the two halves of the back,[243] the back,[244] and the ailments which appear in them.

6 Virgo has: the belly and the hidden places in it, such as the intestines, guts, the diaphragm, and other things.

7 Libra has: the lower stomach, the navel and below it to the external genitalia, the loins,[245] the two hip-joints,[246] the buttocks, and waist.[247]

8 Scorpio has: the penis, testicles, rump, bladder, ovaries,[248] perineum, the vulva of women and the inner part.[249] **9** And its illnesses are like difficult urination, scrotal hernia, hemorrhoids (and the flow of blood from them), cancer, and a film[250] in the eyes.

---

[239] الأضلاع.

[240] الثقل. Or, "thickness, heaviness." Maybe this refers to what we call a "lazy eye"?

[241] الكمنة. Amaurosis is a blotting or blacking out of the eyesight, due to poor blood flow.

[242] العصب. This verb also connotes "nerves," just as we use a string or cord metaphor when we say a "nervous" person is "high-strung."

[243] المتنان. This refers to something like "core strength," especially due to the muscles which keep one's middle strong and erect.

[244] This is especially the vertebrae (see above).

[245] الصّلب. This can also mean "backbone," so it might include the muscles and vertebrae in the lower back, connecting with the pelvis. The word fundamentally refers to rigidity and strength.

[246] الوركان. Or rather, the extreme upper thighs which lead into the hip-joints. This can also be translated as "haunch" or "hip," but is clearly lower than the waist or haunch at the end of this sentence.

[247] الخصارة. Or, the waist and upper hips. This word comes from a verb which means "to clasp around the waist," so it's probably the upper hips and lower waist where one's hands would touch. It can mean "haunch" or "hip," but must be higher up than the hip-joints just mentioned.

[248] الأنثيان. Wehr has "testicles," but the root of this verb means "to be feminine." So I take it to mean the ovaries.

[249] المخّ. This can also refer to "marrow," because the word refers to soft innards.

[250] الغشاوة.

10 Sagittarius has: the upper legs, birthmarks and markings, and things growing on the limbs (like digits),[251] and an added appendage.[252] 11 And its illnesses are like blindness and being one-eyed, and it indicates baldness, falling from raised places, and misfortunes from riding animals and predatory animals, lameness, dislocation, amputation, and what is like that.

12 Capricorn has: the knees and their sinews. 13 Its illnesses are like amaurosis in the eyes.

14 Aquarius has: the two lower legs to the bottom of the ankles and their sinews. 15 Its illnesses are like jaundice, black bile, fracture, amputation, and pains in the veins.[253]

16 Pisces has: the feet, their extremities, and their nerves.[254] 17 Its illnesses are like nerve pain, gout, and numbness.

Chapter VI.13: On the signs indicative of grace and beauty, and the signs indicative of generosity and liberality, and the signs which accumulate and become full, and which grant ease, and which pour forth, and which seize and take

1 The[255] signs indicative of grace, beauty, and cleanliness when they are ascending, or the lord of the Ascendant or the Moon is in them, or the victor over the Ascendant, are: Gemini, Virgo, Libra, Scorpio,[256] Sagittarius, and Pisces. 2 And these signs which we stated also indicate the generosity of soul and its liberality, and a capacity for spending.

---

[251] This would include extra toes (أصابع).

[252] I think this comes from the fact that the human part of Sagittarius is added to the horse body. But Abū Ma'shar might also mean an appendage or limb is abnormally "growing" (زائد).

[253] This probably refers to varicose veins.

[254] Again, this could mean "sinews."

[255] This paragraph corresponds to Sahl, *Nativities* Ch. 1.38, **21**. Note that Abū Ma'shar's text now corrects the Sahl MSS by reading "grace" (صباح) for "yelling" (صياح). His use of "beauty" then makes more sense than Sahl's "lying."

[256] We would expect Taurus instead of Scorpio, in which case these would be all of the signs ruled by Mercury, Venus, and Jupiter. But Sahl also has Scorpio.

3 As[257] for the signs which accumulate and become full, they are Aries and its triplicities. **4** The signs which grant much ease[258] are Taurus and its triplicities. **5** The signs which pour forth and empty out are Gemini and its triplicities. **6** And the ones which seize and take are Cancer and its triplicities.

7 And if the signs pouring forth [and] emptying out[259] were in a bad place due to the rotation of the sphere, and the infortunes were in them, they indicate an abundance of spending, the corruption of the way of life, and its restriction, and the disappearance of assets from him when he has gotten them, and sometimes he will be not be blessed with good fortune and assets at all. **8** And if they were in a suitable condition due to the rotation of the sphere (except that the infortunes were in them), they indicate that his condition of capacity[260] and ease is more than the first [situation]. **9** And if they were in a suitable condition due to the rotation of the sphere [but] made fortunate, they indicate thrift and expansion in the way of life, and the matter of uprightness in prosperity.[261]

10 And if the signs granting ease[262] were in a suitable condition due to the rotation of the sphere and the fortunes' alighting in them, they indicate the benefits of many assets; but if they were the contrary of that, they indicate calamities because of assets.

11 As for the signs which take,[263] if they were corrupted they indicate poverty and suffering.[264]

12 As for the signs which accumulate and become full,[265] if they were in a suitable condition, made fortunate, they indicate a carefree way of life, ease, and good fortune. **13** But if an infortune was in them and it is in a bad posi-

---

[257] This paragraph corresponds to Sahl, *Nativities* Ch. 1.38, **42-45**.
[258] اليسار. I have relied more on the meaning of the root here; but this could also be "prosperity."
[259] That is, the airy signs in **5**.
[260] السَّعَة. Or, "plenty, abundance."
[261] This is the same word as that used for "ease" in **4**.
[262] That is, the earthy signs in **4**.
[263] That is, the watery signs in **6**.
[264] الشَّقَاء. Or, "wretchedness."
[265] That is, the fiery signs in **3**.

tion in the circle, it indicates poverty. **14** And if, along with the infortunes' being in them, it was in an excellent position, and the infortune had a claim, it would indicate benefit and advantages which are not much.²⁶⁶

Chapter VI.14: On the signs indicative of lewdness and illnesses

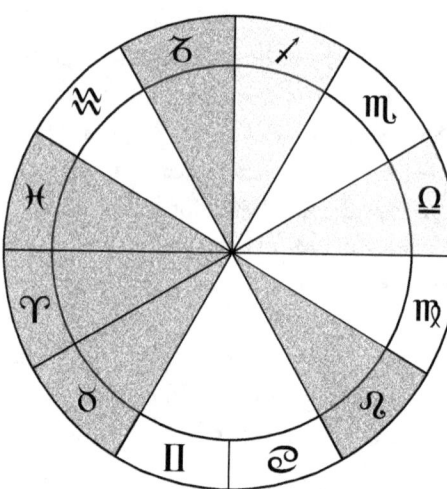

Figure 86: **Signs of lewdness and illness (VI.14)**

1 The signs which indicate lewdness²⁶⁷ and illnesses are Aries, Taurus, Leo, Capricorn, and Pisces.

2 But as for Libra and Sagittarius, they both indicate that except that they are below the [others] in strength.

3 Within the signs there are also degrees indicating lewdness, an excess of sexual intercourse, and illnesses through the planets' mixing with them, [but] we will state them in another book.

---

²⁶⁶ ليست بالكثير. Or perhaps, "which do not [involve] having a lot."
²⁶⁷ Or, "lechery" (الشّبق). Compare Rhetorius Chs. 5 and 76, and *Carmen* II.7, **5**.

Chapter VI.15: On the signs indicative of women's chastity and their modesty

1 The signs indicative of women's chastity and their modesty are Taurus, Leo,[268] Scorpio, and Aquarius.

2 The signs indicative of their looseness and corruption are Aries, Cancer, Libra, and Capricorn.

3 And the signs indicative of being in the middle, and moderation in their modesty, are Gemini, Virgo, Sagittarius, and Pisces.

Chapter VI.16: On the signs of many children, twins, and few children, as well as sterility

1 The signs of many children are Cancer, Scorpio, Pisces, and the last half of Capricorn.[269]

2 The signs of twins are the last half of Capricorn, and those having two bodies;[270] but as for those having two colors[271] and faces[272] (such as Aries and Libra), sometimes they indicate twins as well.

3 The signs of few children are Aries, Taurus, Libra, Sagittarius, and Aquarius.

---

[268] Note that these were also signs of lewdness or lechery in VI.14. But because they are fixed signs, some classified them as more modest and morally firm. See for example Sahl, *Questions* 7.1, **29-33**.

[269] That is, the fish-tail half.

[270] That is, all of the common or mutable or double-bodied signs. However, Gemini and Virgo are classified as sterile below. But this is not so much of a contradiction, because the signs are modified by planets in them: so fertile planets such as the Moon, Venus, and Jupiter in these signs would be able to produce, and might produce twins. The categories here are abstract and need to be filled out by concrete chart conditions and rules.

[271] I am not sure why Abū Ma'shar says they have two colors.

[272] I am not sure what this means. This word (وجه) can also refer to "directions." Libra has two pans, and the Ram looks in the direction opposite where his body is facing, but that does not seem like enough to justify the category.

4 The signs of sterility are Gemini, Leo, Virgo, and the beginning of Taurus; and sometimes Aquarius and the beginning of Capricorn[273] indicate sterility as well.

Chapter VI.17: On the signs of cut limbs, and the signs of much sharpness and anger

1 The signs of cut limbs are Aries, Taurus, Leo, and Pisces.
2 The signs of much sharpness and anger are Aries, Leo, and Scorpio.

Chapter VI.18: On the signs indicative of the conditions of voices

1 Those voiced signs with a strong voice are Gemini, Virgo, and Libra.
2 Those moderate in voice (I mean which have half a voice) are Aries, Taurus, Leo, and Sagittarius.
3 Those weak in voice are Capricorn, Aquarius.
4 And those not having a voice are Cancer and its triplicities.
5 So if Mercury was in a sign not having a voice, nor does he look at one with a suitable aspect, and he is made unfortunate, the native's tongue will be corrupted, or else his hearing, and perhaps he will be deaf and mute.

---

[273] That is, the goat-horned half.

Chapter VI.19: On the signs indicative of mange,[274] leprosy, spots, itching, ringworm, deafness, muteness, baldness, thinness of the beard, stringy hair,[275] and an armpit[276] which does not have hair

1 The signs indicative of these things we stated are five: and they are Aries, Cancer, Scorpio, Capricorn, and Pisces. 2 For if the Moon, Lot of Fortune, or Lot of the Invisible was in one of them, made unfortunate, it indicates that one of these ailments will afflict the native.

3 (And we know that that will afflict him from the book in which nativities are stated.)[277]

4 And if one of these indicators were in these signs, and Jupiter was in the twelfth from the Ascendant, then the native will be bald; and likewise if the Moon was in them while she is under the rays.

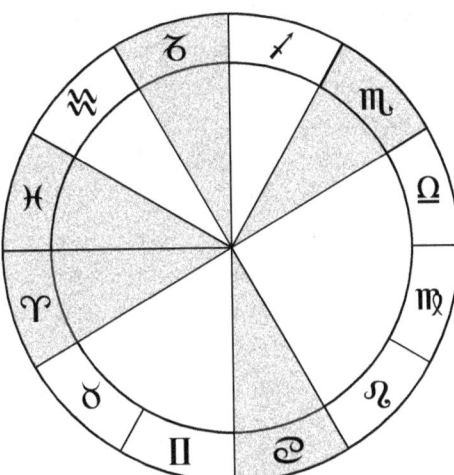

Figure 87: Signs of skin diseases and little hair (VI.19)

---

[274] الجرب. Or, "scabies."
[275] Reading السباط with Lemay and Sahl's *Nativities* Ch. 1.38, 30, for **BY**'s attempted correction, السناطة ("lacking sideburns").
[276] Reading الإبط with Lemay and Sahl's *Nativities* Ch. 1.38, 30 for **BY**'s الأثط (unknown, but **BY** reads as "one who has no beard").
[277] I am not sure if Abū Ma'shar is referring to one of his own books on nativities, or someone else's. But this passage is based on Rhetorius Ch. 3.

Chapter VI.20: On the positions in the signs indicative of defects in the eye

1 The positions in the signs which indicate an ailment of the eyes, are [1] the position of the Pleiades in Taurus, [2] the position of the nebula in Cancer, Scorpio (the position of [3] its leg and the position of [4] its stinger),[278] Sagittarius (the position of [5] the arrows), and Capricorn (the position of [6] the spines). **2** And the position of [7] the pour of water[279] from Aquarius also indicates an eruption in the eyes. **3** But as for Libra and Leo, they both sometimes corrupt the vision as well.[280]

4 Now as for [1] the Pleiades, they are from 13° 36' Taurus to 14° 30'; their latitude in the north is from 3° to 5°.

5 As for [2] the nebula which is in Cancer,[281] it is in it at 21° 08'; its latitude in the north is 40'.

6 As for [3-4] the leg of the Scorpion, there are two (and both of them are in Scorpio): one of them is in it at 20°, and the other in it at 21° 10'; their latitude in the south[282] is 6°.[283]

---

[278] Abū Ma'shar has done something wrong here. It is customary to make the star or stars in and around the stinger harm the eyes. But Abū Ma'shar has first added a leg as [3], and then in **6** below he ignores the stinger altogether and instead uses both of the stars which are only in the last leg (*Almagest* VIII.1, p. 372, stars #10 and #11). As for the stinger which he should have included, there are two possibilities. The first is the pair of stars which are actually in the sting, Shaula (#20, λ Scorpio) and Lesath (#21, υ Scorpio). The second is a nebula just to the rear of the sting, which Abū Ma'shar later identifies as a "cutter" in *PN4* IX.8, **46** (Ptolemy's #22, now called G Scorpio and CGlo 6441).

[279] This is most likely the Pitcher itself: see **9** below.

[280] The reference to Leo is undoubtedly to Coma Berenice, specifically the nebulous mass identified in Ptolemy as his Leo star #33 (modern designation 15(c) Com.). There are also degrees in Libra attributed to Rhetorius by Arabic sources (but which are not in the Greek Rhetorius), as well as in the *Bizidaj*: for both, see Sahl, *Nativities* Ch. 6.2, **68** and **70**.

[281] This is Praesepe.

[282] Correcting for "north."

[283] These are Ptolemy's stars #10 (13(c2) Scorpio) and #11 (d Scorpio, or BSC 6070). But as I mentioned above, this is an error: Abū Ma'shar should have used the

Harming eyes	Identification in *Almagest* VIII.1
[1] Pleiades (♉)	#30-#33, but esp. η (Alcyone)
[2] Praesepe (♋)	#1: M44 or MCG 2632
[3] Shaula & Lesath? (♏)	#20: λ Scorpio (Shaula) #21: υ Scorpio (Lesath)
[4] Nebula by sting? (♏)	#22: G Sco + Cglo 6441?
[5] al-Nasl (♐)	#1: γ Sagittarius
[6] Spines of ♑	#9-#10: τ, υ Capricorn; or #21-#22: ε, κ Capricorn
[7] Pour of ♒	#9 - #12: γ, ζ, η, π Aquarius

Figure 88: Stars harming eyes (VI.20), corrected by Dykes

7 The place of [5] the arrows in Sagittarius is 15° 20', its latitude in the south 6° 20'.[284]

8 The [6] spines of Capricorn are 22°, its latitude in the north 39° 15'.[285]

9 The [7] pour of water of Aquarius is four stars,[286] and they are from 20° 10' Aquarius to 24° 20' of it; its latitude in the north is from 8° 10' to 10° 20'.

10 And these positions which we have stated are their degrees in longitude and latitude in *our* time period; but their positions must be searched out and measured for every time period, because they move and withdraw from these degrees which we have stated.

---

two stars in the stinger, Shaula (#20, λ Scorpio) and Lesath (#21, υ Scorpio). Again, he might have included the cluster (Ptolemy's #22). See footnote above.

[284] This is al-Nasl, γ Sagittarius, on the point of the arrow (*Almagest* VIII.1, #1).

[285] Ptolemy identifies two stars in the "southern spine" of Capricorn, which are ε or κ Capricorn (*Almagest* VIII.1, #21 and #22). But these are between 23° and 25°, so with Abū Ma'shar's added precession they could not be 22°, as he has it here. However, there are two other stars in the neck (#9 and #10), τ and υ Capricorn, which Ptolemy lists as 11° 40' and 11° 50'. We would only have to add a precession of 10° 10' or 10° 20' to get Abū Ma'shar's value, so these seem more likely. Of course the latitude given by Abū Ma'shar is totally unusable.

[286] These are the four stars which are in the Water-Bearer's right forearm, hand, and two to the south of this forming the pitcher (*Almagest* VIII.1, #9 - #12): γ, ζ, η, and π Aquarius.

11 And in the signs are positions and degrees indicative of illnesses, corruption of the eye, and calamities we will state in their own place, if God wills.[287]

Chapter VI.21: On the signs indicative of culture, beguiling speech, deception, cunning, the signs of anxiety, and the dark signs

1 The signs indicative of culture, deception, beguiling speech, and cunning, are Leo, Sagittarius, Capricorn, and Pisces.[288]

2 The signs of anxiety are Leo, Scorpio, and Capricorn.[289]

3 The signs of anxiety are also the "dark signs,"[290] and there is a little darkness in Virgo and Libra [also].[291]

Chapter VI.22: On the signs indicating types of birds, and everything having four feet, and predatory animals and venomous things, things scratching the earth,[292] and animals of the water

1 As for Gemini, Virgo, Sagittarius, and Pisces, they indicate types of birds; and the second and third faces of Capricorn also indicate types of birds, because the Flying Vulture[293] and the tail of the Hen[294] are there.

---

[287] See the listing of other degrees of chronic illness and harm to the eye, from al-Andarzaghar, Rhetorius, the *Bizidaj*, and Nawbakht, in Sahl, *Nativities* Ch. 6.2, **48-75**. In terms of calamities, he may be referring to his list of "cutters," which are in PN4 IX.8, **33-50**.

[288] Reading "Pisces" with **BY** for Lemay's preference for **P**: "Scorpio."

[289] Sahl omits Capricorn in his *Nativities* Ch. 1.38, **6**.

[290] Or, "gloomy" (المظلمة).

[291] There might be a mixup here. In Sahl's *Nativities* Ch. 1.38, **7-8**, the "powerful" signs are Taurus, Leo, and Virgo; the signs of darkness are Libra and Capricorn. So maybe the juxtaposition of these sentences in a common source led Abū Ma'shar to confuse the categories.

[292] خرشة الأرض, which **BY** translates as "insects" (but that would be the similar word خشرة). I take this to denote all manner of creeping and crawling things.

[293] The constellation Aquila, "the Eagle."

2 Aries, Taurus, Leo, and the last half of Sagittarius are the signs having four feet; and the first half of Capricorn sometimes indicates what is like that.

3 Aries and Taurus belong to everything having a cloven hoof, Leo to everything having canine teeth and talons, and the last half of Sagittarius to everything having hooves.

4 As for Leo, Scorpio, Sagittarius, and Pisces, they are the signs of predatory animals.

5 Cancer, Scorpio, Sagittarius, and Capricorn are the signs of venomous things, snakes, scorpions, and what scratches the earth.

6 As for the watery signs, they indicate animals of the water.

Chapter VI.23: On the signs indicative of trees and vegetation

1 As for the signs of tall trees, they are Gemini, Leo, Libra, and Aquarius.

2 The signs of trees which are below that are Cancer, Scorpio, and the last half of Pisces.

3 The signs of vegetation are Taurus and its triplicities, for Taurus belongs to planted crops,[295] Virgo to seeds,[296] and Capricorn to grass.[297]

Chapter VI.24: On the signs indicative of types of waters, and the signs indicative of what is worked by fire

1 The watery signs are Cancer and its triplicities: so as for Cancer, it belongs to rain, Scorpio to flowing water (and Aquarius indicates the same as well, due to the river in which it is),[298] and Pisces belongs to still[299] water.

---

[294] The constellation Cygnus, "the Swan."
[295] الغرس.
[296] Reading البذور with Lemay and **P** for **BY**'s البذر ("sowing").
[297] Or, "pasture" (كلاء).
[298] This is the river which pours out from the Pitcher in Aquarius, into the mouth of Pisces.
[299] Or, "stagnant, sluggish" (الرّاكد).

2 As for the signs which indicate everything worked by fire, they are Aries, Leo, Scorpio, and Aquarius.

Chapter VI.25: On the directions of the signs

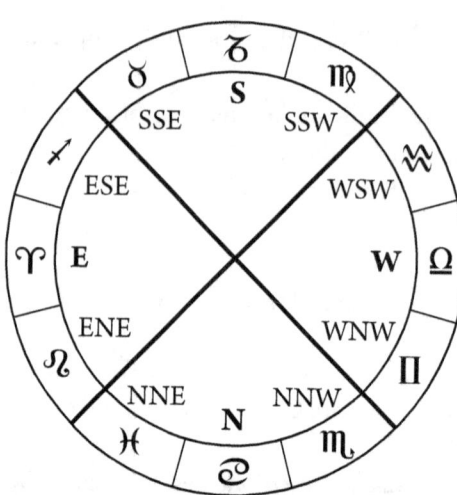

Figure 89: Terrestrial directions by sign (VI.25)

1 Aries, Leo, and Sagittarius are eastern. **2** But Aries is the heart[300] of the east, and its wind is the east wind; Leo is to the left of the east, and its wind is slanted between the east and north; Sagittarius is to the right of the east, and its wind is slanted between the east and south.

3 Taurus, Virgo, and Capricorn are southern. **4** But Capricorn is the heart of the south, and its wind is the south wind; Taurus is to the left of the south, and its wind is slanted between the south and the east; Virgo is to the right of the south, and its wind is slanted between the south and the west.

5 Gemini, Libra, and Aquarius are western. **6** But Libra is the heart of the west, and its wind is the west wind; Aquarius is to the left of the west, and its wind is slanted between the west and the south; Gemini is to the right of the west, and its wind is slanted between the west and the north.

7 Cancer, Scorpio, and Pisces are northern. **8** But Cancer is the heart of the north, and its wind is the north wind; Scorpio is to the left of the north, and its wind is slanted between the north and west; Pisces is to the right of the north, and its wind is slanted between the north and west.

---

[300] That is, the "center" of the east, or due east.

Chapter VI.26: On the stakes of the circle and their quadrants, and the twelve houses, the sum of their indications, and the reason for that, and the houses of the planets' joys

1 Since we have finished stating the natures of the signs and their conditions, and the special property of their comprehensive indications of things,³⁰¹ [now] we begin to state the stakes of the circle and their quadrants, and the twelve houses.

[The four quadrants; houses as quadrant divisions]

2 Because the highest sphere rotates the sphere of the signs and the rest of the spheres from east to west by one rotation in a day and night, and at any time one of the degrees of the sphere of signs will be on the horizon of the east, and one of them on the very degree of the Midheaven, and one of them precisely on the setting horizon, and one of them in the very degree of the fourth, and from each position to the next is a quarter of the circle,³⁰² and every quarter is divided into three divisions, and each of the divisions is called a "house,"³⁰³ at all times the circle will have four quadrants in accord-

---

³⁰¹ جوامع الأشياء. That is, they gather many things together by indicating them in a concise way. This could also be understood as, "their indications for collections of things."

³⁰² The word for "quarter" and "quadrant" is the same in Arabic (ربع). I begin with "quarter" here, because Abū Ma'shar is speaking about the *division* of the horizonal system into four parts or quarters. But by the end of this sentence I switch to "quadrant," to refer to each division as a unit with its own astrological properties. This will help distinguish it from the seasonal quarters of the zodiac.

³⁰³ Note that Abū Ma'shar never questions why this is called a "house," especially since he routinely refers to the signs as the "houses" of the planets. We can see that a conceptual split is taking place, in which the signs are the houses of the planets, but then it is taken for granted that these divisions are houses. Nevertheless he is very aware that two house systems exist, as I show extensively in *PN4* and we can see below in VIII.3, **14-15**.

ance with the seasons of the year,[304] and twelve houses according to the number of the signs.

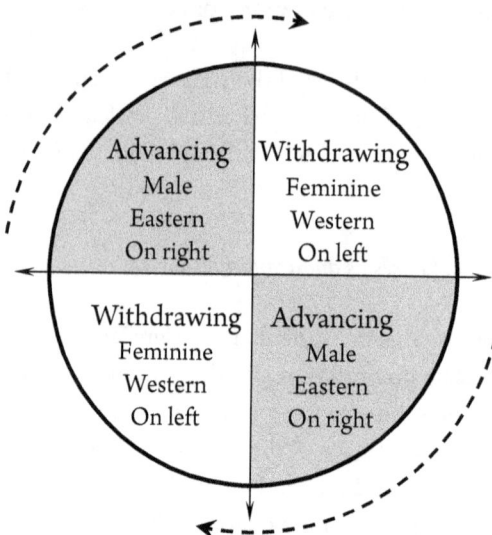

Figure 90: Advancing and withdrawing quadrants (VI.26, 3)

3 Now the two quadrants which are from the Ascendant to the Mid-heaven, and from the setting to the fourth, are called "advancing, male, eastern, on the right," while the two quadrants which are from the tenth to the setting and from the fourth to the Ascendant are called "withdrawing, feminine, western, on the left." **4** (But what is above the earth is also called "right," and underneath the earth "left.")

---

[304] فصول السّنة. I would expect this to be "the parts of the day," since Abū Ma'shar has been speaking of diurnal rotation.

5 And the house which is at the beginning of a quadrant is called a "stake," and the house which follows it is called "what follows the stake," and the third house from it is called "withdrawing from the stake."[305]

6 And the first of the houses of the circle is the house whose beginning rises from the horizon of the east, and the one after it is the second, then the third, then the fourth— and likewise the rest of the houses of the circle are each called by the name of the number which follows that, up to the twelfth house.

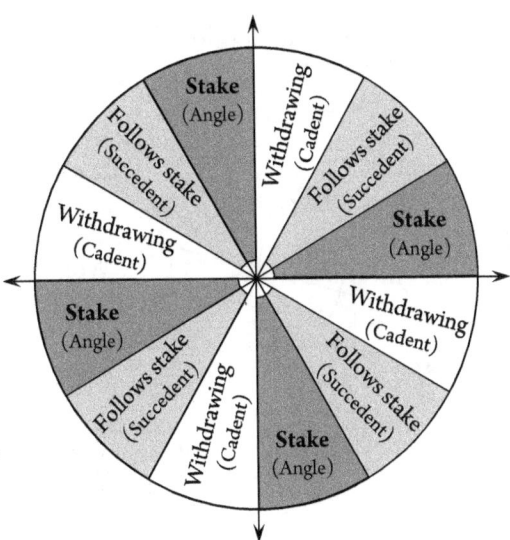

Figure 91: Quadrant divisions by angularity (VI.26, 5)

[*Names and significations of the houses*]

7 And every one of these twelve houses is called by a name particular to it, and is attributed to existing things.

8 So the first house is called "the Ascendant," and it indicates bodies, life, and the conditions of every inception and motion.[306]

9 The second house is called the "house of assets," and it indicates the collecting of assets and amassing them, and the causes of [one's] means of subsistence[307] and their conditions, and taking and giving.

---

[305] This is because it withdraws from the *next* stake. The more proper way to do this would be to group the divisions into triads centered around the stake: that way the division to the right is withdrawing away from it, and the one on the left is what follows the stake because it is coming up to it.

[306] Or, "impulse, undertaking" (حركة).

[307] Or, "way of living, lifestyle" (معاش), with financial overtones.

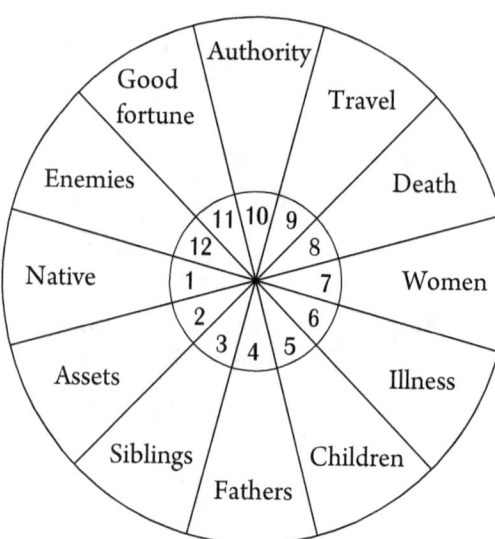

Figure 92: Basic topical meanings of the twelve places or houses (VI.26)

10 The third house is called the "house of siblings," and it indicates the conditions of brothers and sisters, relatives, relations by marriage, reflection,[308] opinion, religion, understanding,[309] contentions in religions, books, reports,[310] messengers, travel, women, and dreams.

11 The fourth is called the "house of fathers," and it indicates the conditions of fathers, roots,[311] and race; lands, villages, cities, building, waters, and everything concealed, hidden, or what is under the earth, and buried treasure; and the outcome, death, and what is after death (in terms of what happens to the conditions of the dead man, such as burial, exhumation, being robbed, burning, or being thrown from some place, and other things pertaining to his situation).

12 The fifth is called the "house of children," and it indicates children, messengers[312] and gifts, charitable giving, hope, seeking women, making

---

[308] الحلم. This can also mean a "dream," but more in the sense of musing and dreaming about the future. I assume that Abū Ma'shar intends this meaning here because he has paired it with "opinion." At the end he will use the plural, and by that he intends normal dreams (and perhaps prophetic dreams).
[309] الفقه. Or, "instruction," especially in religious law.
[310] الأخبار. This includes "rumors."
[311] الأصل. Or, one's "origin."
[312] In later English-language astrology this is usually rendered as "legates."

friends[313] as well as friends, cities and the conditions of their people, and the produce[314] of landed estates.

13 The sixth is called the "house of illness," and it indicates illnesses and what resembles them, chronic illness, slaves and servant-girls, a price reduction,[315] oppression,[316] and migration from place to place.

14 The seventh is called the "house of women," and it indicates women, and marriage and its causes; contentions and antitheses;[317] travel; and destruction and its cause.

15 The eighth is called the "house of death," and it indicates death, killing, inheritances, lethal poisons, fear about everything already destroyed and gone astray,[318] things entrusted for safekeeping,[319] idleness, negligence, and confusion.[320]

16 The ninth is called the "house of travel," and it indicates travels, roads, absence from the homeland;[321] the matter of divinity,[322] prophethood, reli-

---

[313] المصادقة. This also connotes approval and assenting to things.

[314] الغلّات. That is, what they "yield"; this can also mean the revenues generated from the yield.

[315] الوضيعة. Or, something sold at a loss. It can also mean something deposited for safekeeping, but that seems too honorable for the typical significations of the sixth.

[316] الظلم. Or, "injustice, wrong."

[317] Or, "oppositions" (الأضداد).

[318] It is hard to tell whether this refers more to fear, or to something destroyed (i.e., "dead"), or the principle of idleness, because fear about something already gone is idle or useless. Perhaps Abū Ma'shar means it as a combination of all three.

[319] الودائة, a different word than in the sixth house (see footnote). We might think that this belongs to the category of "other people's wealth," and that might be so. But it also fits under the category of "idleness," because wealth that is only being stored is not doing anything productive.

[320] الخبل. Or, "insanity."

[321] الغربة. Or more drastically, "exile." But I would expect another house like the twelfth to indicate that, since the ninth is configured to the Ascendant and so implies the ability to return home.

[322] الرّبوبية. Lit., "lordship."

gion,³²³ and all houses of worship; philosophy, foreknowledge, the science of the stars, and soothsaying;³²⁴ books, messengers, reports,³²⁵ and visions.³²⁶

17 The tenth is called the "house of authority," and it indicates high rank, the king, the government authority, the ruler, the judge, and nobility; reputation and fame;³²⁷ trade professions and works; and mothers.

18 The eleventh is called the "house of good fortune," and it indicates hope,³²⁸ good fortune, friends, praiseworthy action, commendation, children, and helpers.

19 The twelfth is called the "house of enemies," and it indicates enemies, suffering, sorrow, distresses, envy, slander, cunning, stratagems, toil, trouble, and riding animals.

20 So, these are the names of the twelve houses, and these things are attributed to them.

[Reasons for the house significations]

21 Now as for why these things are attributed to these houses, and why they are named that way, the masters of this art stated that these things are attributed to them and named by them in accordance with [1] the order of the planets' spheres, and their [2] indications, [3] natures, and [4] conditions.³²⁹

---

³²³ الدّين. This word for religion has a special sense of being bound and committed to something higher, with a sense of obligation; contrast this with debate and contention between religions in the third house.

³²⁴ الكهانة. Or, "divination."

³²⁵ الأخبار. Or, "rumors."

³²⁶ الرّؤيا. Or, "dreams."

³²⁷ These two words are interesting: "reputation" (الذِّكر) means that people are "talking about" you; "fame" (الصّوت, lit. "voice") means you have influence because your "voice" is heard.

³²⁸ الرّجاء. Or, "expectation."

³²⁹ Generally, [1]-[2] are found in **22-46**. Abū Ma'shar seems to quickly deal with [3] in **48-50**, and [4] in **51-54**. The planetary scheme described here sounds good at first, but begins to break down noticeably in the eighth through twelfth places. Compare **39-46** below, with the planetary explanations and significations in **62-64**.

22 So as for the first house, they called it "ascendant" due to its ascending from the horizon of the east.[330] **23** And indeed those indications which we mentioned come to belong to it because they resemble its indications by means of the indication of Saturn: for he is the highest of the seven planets, and the first of them, and he has an indication for darkness,[331] absence,[332] and the inception of the falling of the

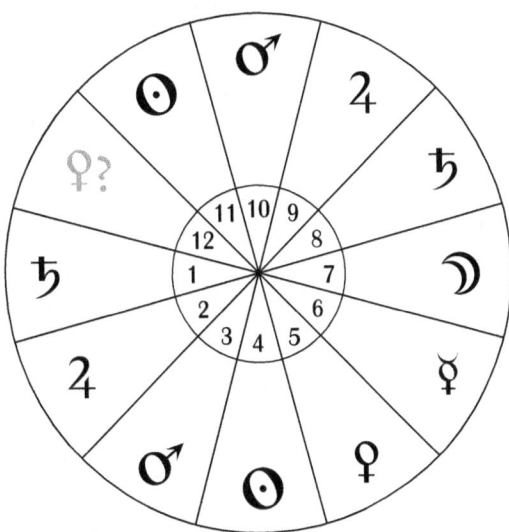

Figure 93: A planetary scheme to explain topical place meanings (VI.26)

sperm,[333] and bodies so long as they are in the womb—and the Ascendant is the first of the twelve houses, and all of its degrees are under the earth in the position which is attributed to darkness and absence. **24** So due to the agreement of one with the other in the indication of being first and the rest of what we stated, they gave the Ascendant the indication over the falling of the sperm, and bodies and their conditions. **25** And because the ascending degree goes out from under the earth and absence to the horizon of the east and appearance, and the native certainly appears from the belly of his mother into this world, the conditions of the degree of the Ascendant resemble the conditions of the native, and more deservedly so the indication over

---

[330] This sentence reveals the tension between whole signs and quadrant houses. Quadrant divisions do not actually rise up *from* the horizon: by definition the first house is *below* the horizon (see also **24**). Only signs ascend from the horizon, and things in them remain in those signs as they rise up.

[331] الظلمة. Or, "gloominess": that, perhaps not total darkness, but something like it.

[332] الغيبة. Also, "invisibility."

[333] I.e., at conception.

bodies and their conditions, than do the rest of the degrees of the house of the Ascendant and [the other] positions of the circle.

26 And because the native's leaving the belly of his mother into this world is the second condition, and his [physical] form's survival in that condition of his comes to be through food, the means of subsistence, and assets, and indeed Jupiter is in the second sphere from Saturn, Jupiter came to have the indication over food, the means of subsistence, and assets by which [the native's] survival in the second condition comes to be, and the second house came to have the signification over these things; and because these things are brought together by means of assets, they gave this name principally to it. **27** So due to that, the second house is called the "house of assets."

28 As for Mars, he is in the third sphere, and he and Saturn resemble each other, are similar to each other, and are akin to each other in bad fortune; and brothers are sisters are like that, as well as relatives and in-laws, for they are related as kin due to the mother and father. **29** So Mars came to have the indication over brothers and sisters, relatives, and in-laws, and the third house came to have the indications of these same things as well. **30** And because brothers and sisters are closer in paternal kinship than the rest of what we stated, the third house is called the "house of brothers and sisters."

31 As for the Sun, he is in the fourth sphere, and he associates with the Moon and interacts closely with her in every month, so they likened that to the association of a man with a woman at the beginning of childbearing; and because the Sun is male and the Moon female, the Sun came to have the indication for fathers, grandfathers, races,[334] and origins, while the Moon has the indication for mothers and women. **32** So the fourth house came to have the indication for the same thing that the Sun does; and because paternity brings together everything we stated, the fourth house is called the "house of fathers."

33 As for Venus, she is in the fifth sphere, and she is a partner with Jupiter and his co-distributor in good fortune. **34** And Jupiter has the indication over food, the means of subsistence, and assets, but what follows upon this in good fortune is women, sexual intercourse, children, delight, and entertainment: so she came to have the indication for women, sexual intercourse, and children, and the fifth house came to have the indication over the same as

---

[334] الأجناس. Or, "nations." This is meant in the sense of ethnic and regional identities.

that. **35** And because children come to be through the joining together of everything we stated, the fifth house is called the "house of children."

36 As for Mercury, he is in the sixth sphere, and he is on a short leash, close to the Sun, with much retrogradation, burning, and hiddenness. **37** In the abundance of his burning, retrogradation, and nearness to the Sun he resembles a sick person, and[335] those with weak bodies who have no strength; and in the abundance of his motion and the variation of his conditions he resembles servants and wretches: so he came to have the indication over ailing, illness, suffering, and slavery; and the sixth house came to have the indication over that same thing.

38 As for the Moon, she is in the seventh sphere and has many meetings and oppositions with [the Sun], so she came to have the indication over women, marriage, making friends and seeking things from people,[336] and the seventh house came to have the indication over that same thing.

39 As for the eighth house, its indication is related to the indication which Saturn has before the native's leaving the belly of the mother, and to his undermining, corrupting, destructive, lethal nature: so the eighth house is called the "house of death."[337]

40 As for the ninth house, it is called the "house of travel," migration, religion, and charitable actions due to its returning to Jupiter, indicative of the second condition: because upon the native's leaving the belly of his mother he will shift from place to place, and from condition to condition, and from the nature of Saturn to the nature of Jupiter, so due to that he indicates travel.[338] **41** And just as Jupiter is a fortune, and among the good fortune of the world he indicates assets, wealth, and riches (as we stated before), and an-

---

[335] Reading the rest of this sentence with Lemay, as **BY** contains some kind of transcription error: numerous clauses are out of place and then end abruptly.

[336] المطالبة. The usual meaning of this noun is "making demands," but this verb is used for "demand" in the sense of economics as well, viz., *seeking* goods (طلب). Also, the Moon is a general significator in elections or inceptions. So, a milder form of this verb is more appropriate.

[337] Note that there's no rationale for combining the two sets of significations: what is the connection between lethality, and being protected in the womb?

[338] This seems like quite a stretch as an explanation.

other good fortune comes to be through religion,[339] due to that he indicates religion, and this house came to have the same indication as that. **42** And also, due to the fact that Jupiter and Venus are the two fortunes, and good fortunes are of two kinds (one of them the good fortune of earthly things and the second one the fortune of the hereafter), and the good fortune of the hereafter is superior to the good fortune of earthly things, and indeed [the good fortune of the hereafter] is sought by means of religion, and Jupiter is more fortunate than Venus—due to that it came to have the indication over religion by which the good fortunes of the hereafter are sought, which are the superior ones. **43** And Venus came to have the indication over the good fortunes of earthly things, among entertainments, delight, and joy.[340]

44 As for the tenth house, it is called the "house of authority" due to its returning to Mars, indicative of seeking authority, leadership, subjugation, might, wars, and fighting.

45 As for the eleventh house, it is called the "house of good fortune" due to its returning to the Sun, indicative of good fortune, splendor, and hope.

46 As for the twelfth house, it is called the "house of enemies" because it withdraws from the Ascendant and does not look at it, and when the stake of the Ascendant indicates something, what withdraws from it indicates the contrary of it.[341]

47 The masters of the stars claimed that for these reasons they attributed these things to these houses.

48 Now, other things among the indications of a planet are attributed to every house among them, which is given to that house based on its nature. **49** And that is like the eighth house, because it indicates inheritances and ancient things, and distresses and anxieties, and negligence,[342] and losing one's faculty of reason—and other things similar to what Saturn indicates.

---

[339] But good fortune arrives by sorts of paths: family ties are a form of benefit and good fortune, as are romantic relationships, friends, and so on.

[340] However, following this logic, Venus should have been a better model for the earthly fortune and needs of the second house.

[341] Note that Abū Ma'shar quietly ends his discussion without mentioning that the planetary model requires Venus to supply the significations there. This is the final indication that the model has broken down and the Chaldean order of the planets is not the explanation for the house meanings.

[342] Or, "idleness" (الكسل).

50 And [it is] like the ninth house, because it indicates many things of those indicated by Jupiter, of the matter of religions, piety, charitable action, and virtue.

51 And sometimes the indication of one of the houses is in accordance with its situation relative to the circle and its characteristic, and sometimes one of them is in accordance with what the seventh [house from] it indicates. **52** And that is like the third house: because it indicates travel and reports, and messengers, religion, the sciences, and virtue due to its withdrawing, and because it is the opposite of the ninth. **53** And the fourth house is the same: for it indicates immovable property, lands, and cities by its special property and its situation relative to the stakes of the circle; and the fifth house, because it indicates messengers,[343] and the sixth house sometimes indicates riding animals [like the twelfth], and the twelfth house sometimes indicates illness [like the sixth]. **54** And each one of them is like that because they have indications over many things of different types.

55 Now as for other people, they said that these indications which we stated did not come to these houses for these reasons, but the special property of each house is to indicate these things, just as the special property of each planet has an indication over different things. **56** But everything they say eventually amounts to the same thing.[344]

---

[343] Something has gone wrong with the text, because we should expect Abū Ma'shar to say something about the tenth (as the opposite of the fourth) and the eleventh (as the opposite of the fifth).

[344] Lit., the same "meaning" (المعنى).

[The joys of the planets, and their explanations]

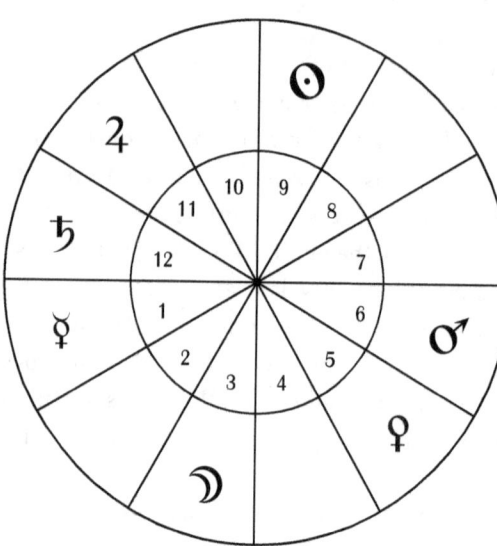

Figure 94: Planetary joys in the places (VI.26)

57 Each planet has a joy in one of these houses, in accordance with the harmonization of its indications, with the indications of the planets. **58** Thus Mercury rejoices in the Ascendant, because the Ascendant indicates beginnings, youth, and impulse: and Mercury indicates the rational soul, speech, discussion, and children and youth.³⁴⁵ **59** The Moon rejoices in the third, because the third house indicates travel and transferring, the postal service, messengers, and reports; and likewise the Moon indicates what is like³⁴⁶ that through her essence. **60** Venus rejoices in the fifth, because the fifth house indicates children and women: and Venus indicates what is like that through her essence. **61** Mars rejoices in the sixth, because the sixth indicates illness, slaves, and evil: and Mars indicates what is like that. **62** The Sun rejoices in the ninth, because the ninth house indicates divinity, religions, worship, and the good: and the Sun indicates what is like that. **63** Jupiter rejoices in the eleventh, because the eleventh house indicates the good, good fortune, wealth, hope, and friends: and Jupiter indicates what

---

³⁴⁵ The idea is that the faculty of reason begins in childhood; note that the second Age of Man according to Ptolemy is the age of Mercury. However, in practical delineation one begins with the topic of nourishment and upbringing, which is indicated by the Ascendant and the Moon (just as the Ptolemaic Ages begin with the Moon). This is an indirect indication that some of Abū Ma'shar's discussions are later attempts to explain the tradition.

³⁴⁶ مثل ذلك, here and below. I have often translated this as "the same" (which it can mean), but here Abū Ma'shar seems to veer towards "the similar."

is like that. **64** Saturn rejoices in the twelfth house, because the twelfth house indicates suffering, anxiety, distress, and enemies: and Saturn indicates what is like that.

Chapter VI.27: On the quadrants of the circle being attributed to what is bodily and spiritual, and other things

1 Among the signs are what is body but not spirit, and what is spirit but not body, and what is spirit as well as body, and what is neither spirit nor body. **2** And indeed that is known from their situation relative to the quadrants of the circle.

3 For what is between the Ascendant and the Midheaven[347] is spirit but not body: and indeed it comes to be like that because it appears from the earth to the place of light, advancement, increase, and speed. **4** And what is between the Midheaven and the seventh is neither spirit nor body: and for that reason the house of travel and death is put there, since travel and death and the bound[348] of the setting [means] disap-

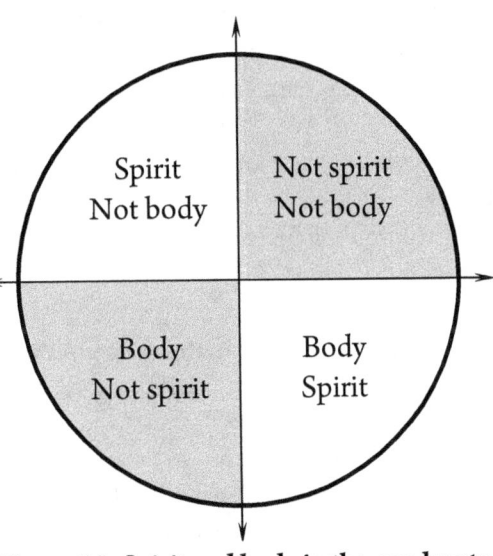

Figure 95: Spirit and body in the quadrants (VI.27)

---

[347] That is, the axial degrees themselves.

[348] ‮حد‬. Or perhaps, "boundary." The Descendant or western horizon is used in Ptolemy's longevity techniques, the seventh indicates the destination for travel, and Rhetorius Ch. 77 (Holden pp. 75-76) refers to Critodemus on the lord of the bound of the Descendant indicating death.

pearance, transition,³⁴⁹ and emptiness of place. **5** And what is between the Ascendant and the stake of the earth is body but not spirit, because it is in the dark, and in the opposition of the ninth, the eighth, and the setting. **6** And what is between the stake of the earth and the setting is body as well as spirit, due to its opposition to the eastern quadrant.

Chapter VI.28: On the blending of the natures of the stakes of the Ascendant³⁵⁰

1 The twelve signs are characterized by the four natures, and indeed they were characterized by that because every individual is brought forth into being from these four natures, by means of the indications of the signs. **2** So when the native's Ascendant is one of the signs, you will find the signs indicative of the four natures in its stakes, but they mix with one another. **3** And that is like fiery Aries, if it was ascending: earthy Capricorn would be on the Midheaven, and airy Libra in the stake of the seventh, and watery Cancer in the stake of the earth.

4 And you will find the stakes of every sign like that if you count them.³⁵¹

Chapter VI.29: On the colors of the quadrants of the circle, and the twelve houses

1 Each Ascendant is red in color from its degree up to the stake of the earth, and from the stake of the earth to the west it is black in color, and from the stake of the west to the Midheaven it is green in color, and from the Midheaven to the Ascendant it is white in color.

---

³⁴⁹ Or, "change of place" (انتقال).
³⁵⁰ This is the original title as shown in the table of contents, but the title in the body of the text reads "the stakes of the *circle*." I follow the table of contents and **2**, which make it clear that these are the stakes of the Ascendant.
³⁵¹ This is an idealized scheme, since of course the MC and IC will often be on other signs. It would make a big difference if one took the signs which are actually on the MC/IC axis, if one is using this to determine something of the native's humoral mixture.

Book VI: On the Classifications of the Signs

2 And among the signs, the Ascendant is a little dust-colored, and the second and twelfth green, the third and eleventh yellow, the fourth and tenth red, the fifth and ninth white, the sixth and eighth black, and the seventh dark[352] (according to the color of the hour in which the Sun sets).

Chapter VI.30: On the rising quadrants of the circles, and those falling, and the tall and the short

1 The half of the circle from the Midheaven up to the Ascendant, to the end of the third house, is said to be "rising," and other half from the ninth to the setting to the beginning of the fourth house is said to be "falling."

2 And from the Ascendant to what follows the stake of the earth, up to the setting, indicates what is short, while from the seventh to the Midheaven to the Ascendant, indicates the tall.

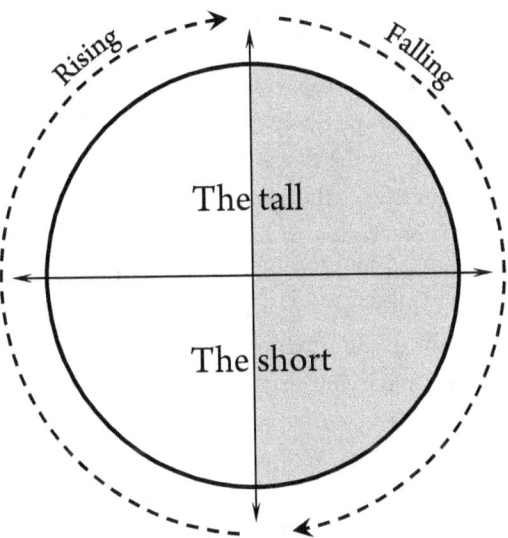

Figure 96: Rising-falling and tall-short hemispheres (VI.30)

Chapter VI.31: On the distribution of the four natures, to things

1 The natures are four, and the directions four, the winds four, the seasons four, and the signs are divided into four divisions, and the circle divided into four divisions, and the day and night are each [divided into] four divisions, and the years of a man [into] four conditions.

---

[352] Or, "gloomy" (مظلم).

2 Now the first of the natures is the nature of blood: it is hot and wet; among the directions it has the east; of winds, the east wind (and it is from the front);[353] of seasons, the spring; of signs, Aries, Taurus, and Gemini; of the quadrants of the circle, from the Ascendant up to the Midheaven; of the day and night, the first quarter; and of the ages of man, childhood.

3 Then the second nature, and it is yellow bile: it is hot and dry; among the directions it has the south; of winds, the south wind; of seasons, the summer; of the signs, Cancer, Leo, and Virgo; of the quadrants of the circle, from the Midheaven up to the degree of the setting; of the day and night, the second quarter; and of the ages of man, youth.

4 Then the third nature, and it is black bile: it is cold and dry; among the directions it has the west; of winds, the west wind; of seasons, the autumn; of the signs, Libra, Scorpio, Sagittarius; of the quadrants of the circle, from the setting up to the degree of the stake of the earth; of the day and night, the third quarter; of the ages of man, maturity.

5 Then the fourth nature, phlegm: it is cold and wet; of the directions it has the north; of the winds, the north wind; of seasons, the winter; of the signs, Capricorn, Aquarius, and Pisces; of the quadrants of the circle, from the stake of the earth up to the Ascendant; of the day and night, the fourth quarter; and of the ages of man, old age.

Chapter VI.32: On explaining the quarters of a single day and single night, and their twenty-four hours

1 When we want knowledge of the sections of a single day and night, we need to determine them both together, and determine a single year as well: because days and nights are parts of the year. **2** So, when we understand the

---

[353] القبول, lit., "reception," or to receive someone face-to-face. This is evidently an old name for the east wind which is different from the special name just used (الصّبا). I translate it this way because Abū Ma'shar uses names for the other winds which in Arabic show spatial direction if one faces east. The name here refers to being face-to-face (just as one faces east), the south wind means "on the right" (التيمّن), the west wind refers to "turning your back" to something (الدبور), and the north wind refers to something "on the left" (الشمال).

determination of the year and its sections, the division of a single day and single night will become clear for us, because when something attaches to the whole, the same thing attaches to the part.[354]

3 Now as for a single day and single night, it is from the time of the Sun's rising from the eastern horizon, and the turning of the highest sphere around us, up to when it returns him to it. **4** And a single year is from the beginning of the Sun's motion from one of the positions in the circle, and his marking off the twelve signs, and his return to the position in which he had been: and that is according to the nature of the four principles, which are air, fire, earth, and water. **5** And just as the four principles are, so are the four sections of the year (and they are spring, summer, autumn, and winter): for the spring is hot and wet, according to the nature of air; and summer is hot and dry, according to the nature of fire; and autumn is cold and dry, according to the nature of earth; and winter is cold and wet, according to the nature of water.

6 And just as each one of these four principles has a beginning, middle, and end, so likewise each one of the sections of the year has a beginning, middle, and end: thus each section of the year has three conditions, and there are four sections. **7** So when we multiply the conditions of the time of the first section (and there are three) by the four sections of the year, that comes to twelve, each one of them being called a "month." **8** Thus a single year becomes twelve months, every three months according to the nature of one of the sections of the year.

9 And just as days and nights are parts of the year, and the year has four sections, so likewise a single day and single night have four sections: and the nature of each section of the day and night is like the nature of each section of the year.

10 And just as each section of the year has three conditions, so likewise each section of the day and night has three conditions.

11 And just as each condition of the sections of the year is called a "month," so likewise each condition of the sections of a single day and single night is called an "hour."

12 And just as the conditions of the sections of a single year are twelve months, so likewise the conditions of the sections of a single day and a single

---

[354] Of course this is not necessarily true: in logic this is considered the "fallacy of division."

night are [each] twelve hours: thus the sum of the hours of a day and night are twenty-four, each three hours according to the nature of one of the sections. **13** Thus the first quarter of the day and night (and it is three hours) matches the nature of air and the spring, and it is heating and wet. **14** The second quarter of the day and night matches the nature of fire and the summer, and it is heating and drying. **15** The third quarter of the day and night matches the nature of earth and autumn, and it is cooling and drying. **16** And the fourth quarter of the day and night matches the nature of water and the winter, and it is cooling and wet.

Chapter VI.33: On the lords of the days and hours

1 In the chapter which was before this one we stated the sections of a single day and single night, and for what reason they made the day and night be twenty-four hours. **2** Now we will state the lords of the days and hours.

3 As for the lords of the days and hours, one begins them from the first day.[355] **4** They made it belong to the diurnal planet which is the Sun, and that is because the Sun is the planet by whose rising the day comes to be, and by his setting the night comes to be: so, they began with him and made him be the lord of the day which is called by the name "the one" (and it is Sunday),[356] and made him be the lord of the first hour of it. **5** Then they made the second hour from it belong to Venus, because her sphere follows the sphere of the Sun, and they made the lords of the hours be in this manner, in the order of planets in their spheres, until they returned to the Sun. **6** And whenever the counting reached him, they would begin with him and do it just like the first time, until the lords of the twenty-four hours completed the amount of a single day and a single night.

7 Then they looked at the planet which the counting had reached at the twenty-fifth count, and made it be the lord of the day which followed, and made it be the lord of the first hour of that day, as well. **8** Then they made the planet which followed it in the sphere be the lord of the second hour—and they did it like that with the days. **9** So the first hour of Sunday belongs

---

[355] In Arabic, "the first day" is the name for Sunday.
[356] See **22**.

to the Sun (who is the lord of the day), and the second hour to Venus, the third to Mercury, the fourth to the Moon, the fifth to Saturn, the sixth to Jupiter, the seventh to Mars, the eighth to the Sun, the ninth to Venus, the tenth to Mercury, the eleventh to the Moon, and the twelfth to Saturn. **10** [But then] the first hour of the night belongs to Jupiter, the second to Mars, the third to the Sun—and they worked like that in the twenty-four hours so that the twenty-fourth hour of Sunday belongs to Mercury.

11 [Then] the counting for the twenty-fifth time reaches the Moon, so they made her be the lord of Monday, and the lord of the first hour of it as well. **12** And they made the second hour belong to Saturn, and likewise all of the hours, so that the twenty-fourth hour of Monday belongs to Jupiter. **13** And after that the counting reaches Mars, so they made him become the lord of Tuesday and the lord of its first hour. **14** And the lords of the days are known by that, so that the lord of Wednesday is Mercury, the lord of Thursday Jupiter, the lord of Friday Venus, and the lord of Saturday Saturn. **15** The last of the hours of Saturday, upon the completion of twenty-four hours, belongs to Mars, then the hours of the beginning of Sunday start from the Sun, just as was done at first. **16** So as for the number of the hours of the seven days, they are 168, and each of the seven planets has twenty-four hours every week, the amount of the number of hours in a day and night.

17 And know that the beginning of the hours of the day are from the inception of the Sun's rising from the eastern horizon, while the beginning of the hours of the night are from the disappearance of the Sun's body from the horizon of the west.[357]

---

[357] We could call this the "true" beginning and end of day: so long as any part of the Sun's disk is still above the horizon, it is still daytime. Most people assume that day begins and ends when the center of his disk is on the horizon.

	Sunday	Monday	Tuesday	Wed.	Thursday	Friday	Saturday
	Diurnal hours: from sunrise						
1	☉	☽	♂	☿	♃	♀	♄
2	♀	♄	☉	☽	♂	☿	♃
3	☿	♃	♀	♄	☉	☽	♂
4	☽	♂	☿	♃	♀	♄	☉
5	♄	☉	☽	♂	☿	♃	♀
6	♃	♀	♄	☉	☽	♂	☿
7	♂	☿	♃	♀	♄	☉	☽
8	☉	☽	♂	☿	♃	♀	♄
9	♀	♄	☉	☽	♂	☿	♃
10	☿	♃	♀	♄	☉	☽	♂
11	☽	♂	☿	♃	♀	♄	☉
12	♄	☉	☽	♂	☿	♃	♀
	Nocturnal hours: from sunset						
1	♃	♀	♄	☉	☽	♂	☿
2	♂	☿	♃	♀	♄	☉	☽
3	☉	☽	♂	☿	♃	♀	♄
4	♀	♄	☉	☽	♂	☿	♃
5	☿	♃	♀	♄	☉	☽	♂
6	☽	♂	☿	♃	♀	♄	☉
7	♄	☉	☽	♂	☿	♃	♀
8	♃	♀	♄	☉	☽	♂	☿
9	♂	☿	♃	♀	♄	☉	☽
10	☉	☽	♂	☿	♃	♀	♄
11	♀	♄	☉	☽	♂	☿	♃
12	☿	♃	♀	♄	☉	☽	♂

Figure 97: Planetary hours and days

18 Now as for their beginning the days from Sunday, they did that for two reasons. **19** One of them is because [when] the masters of the art of the stars from Persia and India worked with the days of the world, they begin them from Sunday: the Sun was rising from the horizon of the east of the inhabited world in the first minute of Aries at the start of that day, and it is the place which is called *Kankriz*.³⁵⁸ **20** And from that time and day they reckoned the mean [positions] of the planets, and from it they counted the chronologies of their ancient years. **21** We calculate *Kankriz* as being six hours from the middle of the earth, and 108° from ancient Babylon of Iraq (which was at the outlet of the Euphrates), and it is 7 1/5 equal hours.

22 And the second reason is that all nations, despite the difference of their years and the incompatibility of their religions, called the first day by a single name which is the beginning of the numbers,³⁵⁹ and after it they called [the next day] by the second number, and it is Monday.³⁶⁰ **23** And likewise for the rest of the days, they named them according to the order of the natural numbers (which are one, two, three, four, and five).³⁶¹ **24** So for these reasons they began the lords of the days and their hours, from Sunday.

25 The Sixth Book is completed, with praise to God, His superiority, and His strength!³⁶²

---

[358] كنكرز or كنكدر. **BY** follow Lemay and Nallino in suggesting that this word should be "Kangdez" (from Pahlavi).
[359] In Arabic, "the first day" means "Sunday."
[360] Likewise, "the second day" means "Monday."
[361] Again, in English this is Sunday, Monday, Tuesday, Wednesday, Thursday.
[362] **BY** note that many manuscripts end with the following: "It always begins with Sunday because God (be He exalted) began the creation on it." See also **19** above.

BOOK VII: [ON THE CONDITIONS OF THE PLANETS, & THEIR SPECIAL INDICATIONS FOR THINGS][1]

And in it are nine chapters

1. Chapter VII.1: On the conditions of the planets in themselves.
2. Chapter VII.2: On the conditions of the planets relative to the Sun, in front of him and behind him.
3. Chapter VII.3: On the conditions of the planets in the quadrants of the circle and their houses, and the range of the power of their bodies.[2]
4. Chapter VII.4: On the planets' assembling with each other, and the mixture of their qualities, and which of them is stronger, and which weaker.
5. Chapter VII.5: On the planets' looking at each other, and their connection and separation, and the rest of their similar conditions which follow upon that.
6. Chapter VII.6: On the planets' good fortune, strength, weakness, and misfortune, and the corruption of the Moon.
7. Chapter VII.7: On the casting of the planets' rays, according to the work of Ptolemy.
8. Chapter VII.8: On knowing the years of the planets' *fardārs*, and their mighty, greater, middle, and lesser years.
9. Chapter VII.9: On the natures of the seven planets, and their special indications for existing things.

---

[1] Reading with **P**, for "Book Seven of the Introduction to the Science of the Judgments of the stars."

[2] أجرام. That is, their "orbs."

Chapter VII.1: On the conditions of the planets in themselves

1 In what has preceded we have stated the natures of the planets (the heating, cooling, moistening and drying), and their special property in fortunateness and unfortunateness, and maleness and femaleness, and diurnality and nocturnality, and other things besides this.[3] **2** But in this Book we will state their conditions and their special indications over things since each one of them in itself has different conditions, and it is that:

3 It is rising in its apogee or falling in it, or it is in the middle zone of this circle.[4]

4 Or, it is increasing in motion, light, and might, or is decreasing in it, or is average in motion, light, and size.[5]

5 Or, it is adding in number or subtracting in it.[6]

6 Or, it is increasing in calculation or decreasing in it, or it is in its middle path.[7]

7 Or, it is increasing in travel or decreasing in it, or it is in its mean motion.[8]

8 Or, it is northern (rising or falling), or southern (rising or falling), or it has much latitude or little latitude, or it has no latitude.[9]

9 Or, it is in its domain or in the contrary of its domain.[10]

---

[3] See especially IV.4-IV.9.
[4] See **10-13** below.
[5] See **14-22**.
[6] See **23-25**.
[7] See **26-28** below.
[8] See **29-33** below.
[9] See **34-36** below.
[10] See **37-39**.

[*Rising and falling in the apogee*]

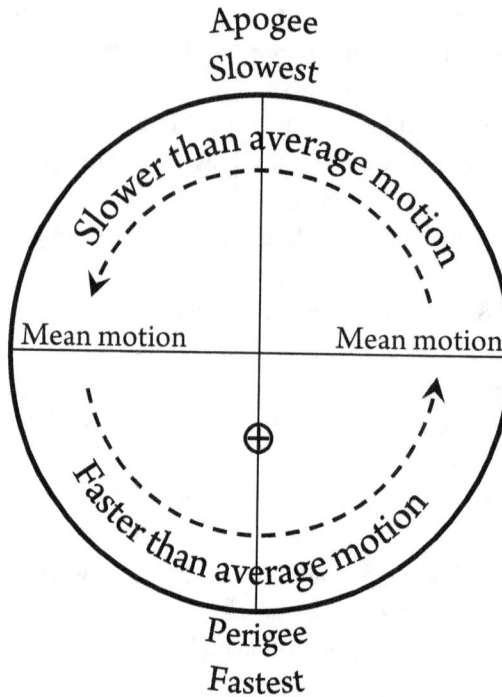

Figure 98: Speed relative to apogee (VII.1, 10-13)

10 So as for the planets' rising in the apogee, if the corrected[11] planet is at the top of its apogee, or between it and [the apogee] are less than 90° to the right or left, then it is rising in the zone of the circle of its apogee [and] decreasing in motion (and the slowest it can be in motion is if it was exactly at the top of its apogee). **11** And if there were exactly 90° between it and the top of its apogee on both sides at the same time, then it is in the middle zone of the circle of the apogee, and it is even in motion.[12] **12** But if it goes past the top of its apogee by 90° until it reaches exactly 270°, then it is falling from the middle of the circle of its apogee [and] increasing in motion (and the most it can be in motion is if it was in the opposition of its apogee). **13** And upon its actually being in the apex of the circle of the apogee, or in its exact opposition, the planet will not have an equation in the circle of its apogee.

---

[11] المقوّم. This is the true position of the planet after the corrections have been applied to the mean position.

[12] معتدل السّير.

BOOK VII: CONDITIONS & INDICATIONS OF THE PLANETS

[Increasing in motion, light, and size]

14 Now as for a planet's increase in light and size, that is said because sometimes a planet is seen to be small in its body, sometimes it is seen to be big, and sometimes it is seen to be average in body; and indeed one sees [it] in this condition in accordance with its closeness and distance relative to the earth, not that in itself it is [really] small or big.[13] **15** So if a planet was in the middle zone of the circle of the apogee, it would be average in light and size. **16** And the most average it can be in its body is when, in addition to what we said, it is in the middle zone of its epicycle as well. **17** And if it was rising from the middle zone of the circle of the apogee, it is decreasing in light, with little size. **18** And the least it can be in light, might, and <greatest in> distance from the earth, is when it is at the utmost elevation in the circle of its apogee (and that happens to be when it is also at the apex of its epicycle). **19** And if it was falling down from the middle zone of the circle of the apogee, it is increasing in light and size. **20** And if it was in the opposition of the apex of the circle of the apogee, it will be the most increased it can be in light and might. **21** And the most it can be in light, the most sizeable in body, and closeness to the earth, is if in addition to this it is in the perigee of its epicycle.

22 And the three superior planets are also said to be increasing in light (and decreasing in it) in the manner that is said about the Moon: because when they go past the Sun until they oppose him, they are said to be increasing in light; but after that until their meeting with him, they are said to be decreasing in light (except that the first [way] which we stated previously is the one agreed upon [by all]).

[Adding and subtracting in number]

23 As[14] for adding in number and subtracting in it (or neither adding nor subtracting), that is known from the two columns of the number of the plan-

---

[13] For the following, refer to the diagram of the apogee and perigee in Figure 98 above.

[14] This has to do with how a planet's position in its system relates to the corrections or equations which must be applied to it. It does not have direct astrological import.

ets' equation in the accepted[15] *zījes*. **24** The first of the two columns is from a single degree increasing up to 180, and the other decreases from 360 to 180: so if the number sought for equation is found in the first column it is said to be adding in number; and if it was in the second column it is said to be subtracting in number. **25** And if it was exactly 180, then it is neither adding nor subtracting.

[Increasing and decreasing in calculation]

26 And[16] as for increasing in calculation, it is that one adds what comes out from its equation to its mean [position] at the end of the operation, while decreasing is what is subtracted from it. **27** But as for its being in the middle path, it is when it does not have an equation added to its mean [position], nor subtracted from it: and if it was like that, then the planet in the circle of inclination is in the path of the Sun, with him to the minute or in the minute exactly opposing him. **28** But as for Venus, when the correction[17] of the Sun is subtracted from her mean so that nothing remains or exactly 180° remains, then she is with the Sun in a single minute and has no equation.

[Increasing and decreasing in rate of motion]

29 As for increasing in its rate of movement (with respect to the five planets), it is that it travels more than its mean motion; and decreasing in its travel is that it travels less than its mean motion (and it will be in its average travel if its motion is like its average travel).[18] **30** But as for Venus and Mercury, their mean motion in one day at a [particular] time is not like their mean travel for the day. **31** And indeed, the conditions of the motion for each of them is known by looking [at this]: if the motion of one of them on

---

[15] محلولة.

[16] This concept plays a role in whether the planets' longitudes are ahead of or behind their expected mean positions, and refers to how one uses the older astronomical tables.

[17] تقويم.

[18] This has astrological meaning, in that planets which are moving faster than average may indicate things which are accomplished more quickly and directly; if slower than average, more slowly and with delays.

any of the days is more than the motion of the Sun on that day, then it is quick in motion, increasing in it; and if it was less than his motion, then it is slow in motion, decreasing in it; and if it was exactly like the Sun's motion, then it is in its mean rate of motion).

32 And know that when the five planets are determined by the *zīj* of the Persians and the Indians,[19] so that one of the two[20] is in the first or fourth sector,[21] it is slow in course: and one uses the quick *kardajas* for it.[22] **33** And if it was in the second or third sector, it is quick in motion, and one uses the slow *kardajas* for it.

[Rising and falling in latitude]

34 Now as for a northern planet, that is when it goes beyond the Head of its own Dragon until it reaches its own Tail; but as for a southern one, it is when it goes beyond the Tail of its Dragon until it reaches its Head. **35** And if it was exactly 90° from the Head or Tail of its own Dragon, then it is the greatest it can be in latitude in that direction: and the closer it gets to either one, the less it is for its latitude. **36** And if it was with them, it will not have latitude.

[Domain]

37 As for "domain,"[23] it is that a male[24] planet by day is above the earth (and by night below the earth), in a male sign; but if it was female, then by

---

[19] This would be the *Zīj al-Shāh* and the *Sindhind*, respectively.

[20] Abū Maʿshar seems to mean "*the position of the planet* in one of the two *zījes*." I am not currently sure how likely it is that the two *zījes* would disagree on the planetary position.

[21] Reading منطقة ("zone, region") as the astronomically more common, and related word نطاق.

[22] The *kardajas* have to do with the numerical intervals between the rows in astronomical tables.

[23] حيّز, often transliterated as *haiz* or *hayyiz* in Latin. It is often used to mean simply "sect," but in this case it is a special sect-related condition. See also VII.6, **13**.

[24] Instead of "male" and "female," Abū Maʿshar should probably be saying "diurnal" and "nocturnal." Either way, Mars will stand out because he is a male, nocturnal

day it is below the earth (and by night above the earth), in a female sign—except for Mars alone, because he is contrary to what we said. **38** So if a planet was in this condition, it is in its domain, and it is strong in nature, indicative of balance[25] and suitability. **39** But if any of what I said is taken away, it takes away from the nature of balance; and if it was contrary to all of this, it is in the contrary of its domain, and indicates corruption and the contrary of balance.

Chapter VII.2: On the conditions of the planets relative to the Sun, in front of him and behind him

1 The planets have different conditions relative to the Sun, in accordance with their nearness to him or their distance from him.

["On the right" and "on the left" of the Sun]

2 Now as for Saturn, Jupiter, and Mars, from the time of their separation from the Sun until they oppose him to the minute, they are "on the right side" of him; and from the time of their opposition until they conjoin with him, they are "on the left side" of him.

3 But as for Venus and Mercury, from [the time] of their separation from the Sun and they are retrograde in the region[26] of the east until they go direct, become quick, overtake the Sun, and conjoin with him, they are "on the right side" of him; and after their separation from him and they are moving direct towards the region[27] of the west, until they station in the west and return, and the Sun overtakes them and they meet with him, they are "on the left side" of him.

---

planet: so either he must be in a different hemisphere (diurnal/nocturnal) or in differently-gendered sign (male-female).

[25] الاعتدال. Or perhaps, "moderation."

[26] ناحية

[27] ناحية

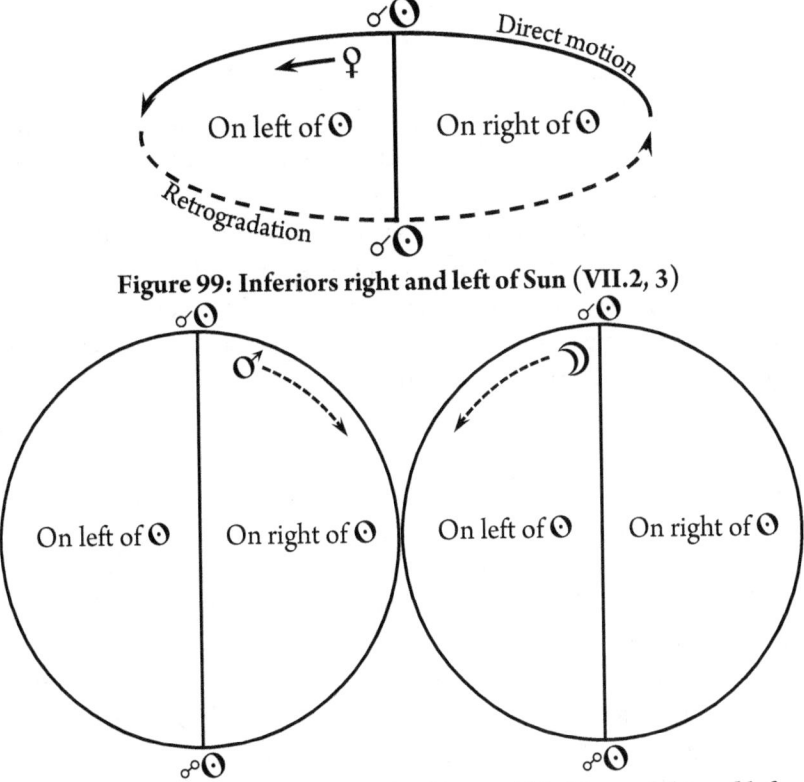

Figure 99: Inferiors right and left of Sun (VII.2, 3)

Figure 100: Superiors right and left of Sun (VII.2, 2)

Figure 101: Moon right and left of Sun (VII.2, 4)

4 And as for the Moon, from the time of her separation from him until she opposes him, she is "on the left side" of him, and when she passes beyond his opposition until she conjoins with him, she is "on the right side" of him.

5 But, they do [all] have different conditions relative to him:

[The three superiors]

6 So as for the three superiors, they have seventeen conditions from him.

7 As for the first, it is the meeting of the planets with the Sun in one minute: and if the planet was before the exact meeting or after it by [up to] 16', it is said to be "in the heart."²⁸ **8** And it is made to have these minutes because the extent of the sphere of the Sun is approximately 32', so that makes two halves (and the most that the extent of the sphere of the Sun reaches is close to 34'). **9** So when there is less than one-half of the extent of his sphere between the planets and [the center of] the Sun (or [that] same [amount]),²⁹ in one of the two directions at that time, they are in the heart, indicative of good fortune.

10 Now when the Sun is distant from them by more than one-half of those minutes (in the direction in which they are), the planets come to the second condition, and they are said to be "under the rays of the Sun, burned in the east." **11** Now as for Saturn and Jupiter, they are both burned until the Sun is distant from them within 6°, while Mars is like that until the Sun is distant from him within 10°.

12 When these three planets come to the completion of these degrees, then they have already gone past burning and shift over to the third condition, and they are said to be simply "under the rays," and from there they begin in [their] advancement towards easternization, and they are suitable for granting their greater years as well as spear-bearing. **13** And they do not cease to be in their condition until there come to be 15° between Saturn and Jupiter, and the Sun—and 18° between Mars and [the Sun]. **14** And when they reach the completion of these degrees, they have completed their three conditions, and after that they are called "easternizing, strong in easternization." **15** And from the time of their separation from the Sun until they come to have these degrees in these three conditions, they are said by the Persians to be [at] "the day-limit."³⁰ **16** And even though we have called these planets "easternizing" at this time, we don't mean by it that they are [actually] *seen* in

---

²⁸ صميمي, the source of the Latin transliteration *cazimi*. This also has connotations of being sincere, deep, true, and so on.

²⁹ أو مثله. That is, at exactly half (16') and not just less than half.

³⁰ *Kinārrūziyah* (كناروزية). This translation comes from **BY** in their Glossary.

the east, because sometimes one of them will be seen in some climes before it is distant from the Sun by the range of these degrees, and sometimes one will be seen at this time, and sometimes one will be seen after that: but we do mean by their easternization that they have separated from the power of the Sun's body.

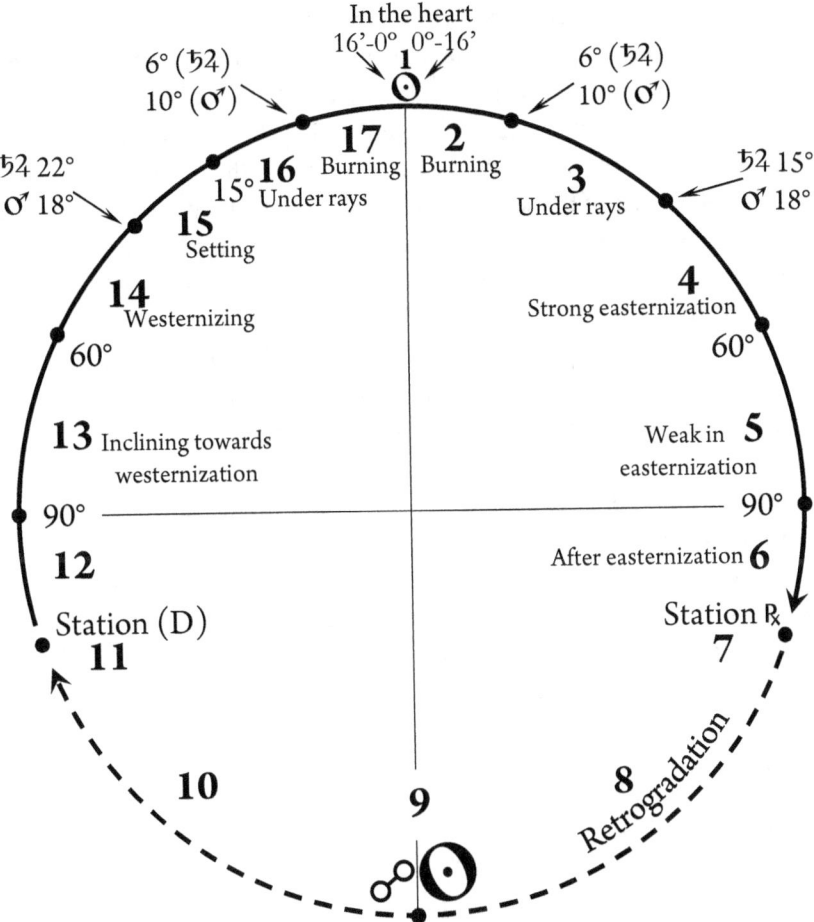

Figure 102: Synodic cycle of superiors (VII.2, 6-34)

17 And when they come to the degrees which we have stated, they shift over to the fourth condition, and are said have "proper,[31] strong easternization [that is] manifest and visible," and they do not cease to be in that condition of theirs until there are 60° between them and the Sun (and that is the amount of the sextile). **18** And until the time when there is that range of degrees between them, it is the most powerful it could be in easternization, spear-bearing, and being on the right side[32] of the Sun.

19 Now when they have gone past these degrees they shift over to the fifth condition, and it is called "weak in easternization," and their right-siding for the Sun is weak, as well as their spear-bearing. **20** And they do not cease to be like that until there come to be 90° between them and the Sun (the amount of degrees of the square). **21** Then after that they are not said to be "easternizing," because when the Sun rises and there are more than the amount of these degrees between him and these planets, they withdraw towards the western quadrant.[33]

22 And when they pass beyond these degrees, they shift over to the sixth condition, and are said to be "after easternization" until they station.

23 And as long as they are in the first station, they are in the seventh condition.

24 And when they go retrograde, they are in the eighth condition until the opposition.

25 And when they oppose the Sun, they are in the ninth condition (and when the three superior planets are in the opposition of the Sun, the people of Persia call it the "night-limit"[34] of the opposition).

26 Then after that, so long as it is retrograde it is in the tenth condition.

27 And when it stations towards direct motion, then it is in the eleventh condition.

---

[31] نفس.

[32] التّيامن, which also means to bring luck. All three meanings are connected here: being on the right side, bringing luck, and spear-bearing for the Sun. In Sahl I translate this as "right-siding" when it refers to spear-bearing.

[33] This is an idealized situation, because the zodiacal distance between the Ascendant and Midheaven is rarely exactly 90°. Abū Ma'shar is making an analogy between the horizon and meridian, and the Ascendant and Midheaven.

[34] *Kinārshabī* (كنارشبي). This translation is from **BY** in their Glossary.

28 And when it goes direct, it is in the twelfth condition, until there are 90° between it and [the Sun].

29 And when it comes to be in the amount of these degrees, it shifts over to the thirteenth condition, and is called "inclining towards westernization," because at the disappearing of the Sun [below the western horizon] it will withdraw from the Midheaven towards the region[35] of the west.

30 And it will not cease to be in its condition until there are 60° between it and [the Sun], and then after that it will shift over to the fourteenth condition, and is called "westernizing," and does not cease to be like that until there are 22° between Saturn and Jupiter and [the Sun] in the west (and 18° between Mars and [the Sun]).

31 And when they come to have these degrees, they shift over to the fifteenth condition, and are said to be "in the degrees of setting" until there come to be 15° between them and the Sun.

32 And when they come to these degrees they shift over to the sixteenth condition, and are called "under the rays," and they not suitable for granting their greater years. **33** And from this condition to their conjunction with the Sun it is called by the Persians the "night-limit"[36] of westernization.

34 And they do not cease to be called simply "under the rays" until there are 6° between Saturn and Jupiter and [the Sun], and 10° between Mars and him, and there they shift over to the seventeenth condition, and are called "burned under the rays"; and they do not cease to be in that condition until they come to the limit which is called "in the heart."

[Inferior planets]

35 And as for Venus and Mercury, they have sixteen conditions relative to the Sun.

36 The first is that they are with the Sun, and between them (on the side[37] in which they are) is the amount of minutes by which they are called "in the heart."[38]

---

[35] ناحية.
[36] *Kinārshabī* (كنارشبي).
[37] ناحية.
[38] See **7-9** above.

37 And when they go beyond those minutes into the east, they shift over to the second condition, and are called "burned" until there comes to be up to[39] 7° between them and the Sun. **38** Now as for Venus in particular, sometimes she will be seen in the east or west while she is [still] with the Sun in 1', and indeed it is like that when she is at the utmost of her latitude (and that is because her greatest latitude is 8° 56', according to what Ptolemy claimed).[40] **39** So when Venus is in this condition of great latitude and visibility, she is not called "burned," but rather she is called "appearing" until her latitude is below 7° and she nears the Sun a little bit[41] by latitude: then perhaps she will not be seen, and is called "burned" at that time.

40 Now when they are distant from [the Sun] at a full 7° in longitude, then they have passed beyond burning and are said to be "under the rays," and they come to the beginning of their advancement towards easternization, and are fit to grant the greater years and spear-bearing, until there are up to[42] 12° between them and the Sun.

41 And when these degrees are completed for them, they shift over to the fourth condition, and it is the condition of "strong easternization," and they do not cease to be in their condition until they station.

42 And when they station, they are in the fifth condition.

43 And when they go direct in the east, they are in the sixth condition, until they speed up and come near to the Sun.

44 And when there are 12° between them and [the Sun] in the east, they shift over to the seventh condition, and are said to be simply "under the rays" until there are 6°[43] between them and [the Sun].

45 Then they shift there to the eighth condition, and are called "burned under the rays" until they come to be in the heart.

46 And when they are in the heart of the Sun they shift over to the ninth condition.

---

[39] That is, "just under" (دون).

[40] In other words, by longitude she is still "conjoined" with or "in the heart" with the Sun; but in actual spatial terms she is so far from him in latitude that she can be seen.

[41] Adding / reading قليلاً with Lemay.

[42] That is, "just under" (دون).

[43] To me it seems this should be 7° as in **40**, but this is what the text says.

47 And when they go beyond those given minutes into the west, they shift over to the tenth condition, and in that condition they are said to be "burned" until there come to be 7° between them and the Sun in the west.

48 Then, at that [time] they are shifted into the eleventh condition, and are said to be "under the rays" until there come to be 15° between them and [the Sun].

49 And when they pass beyond these degrees they shift over to the twelfth condition, so long as they are moving direct in the west.

50 And when they station, they come to be in the thirteenth condition.

51 And when they go retrograde, they come to be in the fourteenth condition until they come near to the Sun and there are 15° between them and him.

52 Then they shift there to the fifteenth condition and are said to be "under the rays" until there come to be 7° between them and him.

53 Then they shift there to the sixteenth condition and are said to be "burned" until they come to the first condition of being in the heart.

54 And these two planets, after they separate from the Sun and they are easternizing retrograde, they are said [by the Persians] to be at "the day-limit"[44] of easternization and retrogradation, until they are distant from [the Sun] by 12°. **55** And when they station and get close to the Sun on this side and they are faster in motion than he is, and there come to be 12° and less between them and him, until they conjoin with him and they are direct, it is called "the day-limit"[45] of easternization and direct motion. **56** And when they pass by the Sun to the west and are direct, they are said to be at "the night-limit"[46] of westernization and direct motion until there come to be 15° between them and him. **57** And when they station and retrograde in the west and the Sun overtakes them, and there are 15° and less between them and him, until they conjoin with him they are said to be at "the night-limit"[47] of westernization and retrogradation.

---

[44] *Kinārrūziyah* (كناررروزية). This translation comes from **BY**'s Glossary.
[45] *Kinārrūziyah* (كناررروزية). This translation comes from **BY**'s Glossary.
[46] *Kinārshabiyah* (كنارشبية). This translation comes from **BY**'s Glossary.
[47] *Kinārshabiyah* (كنارشبية). This translation comes from **BY**'s Glossary.

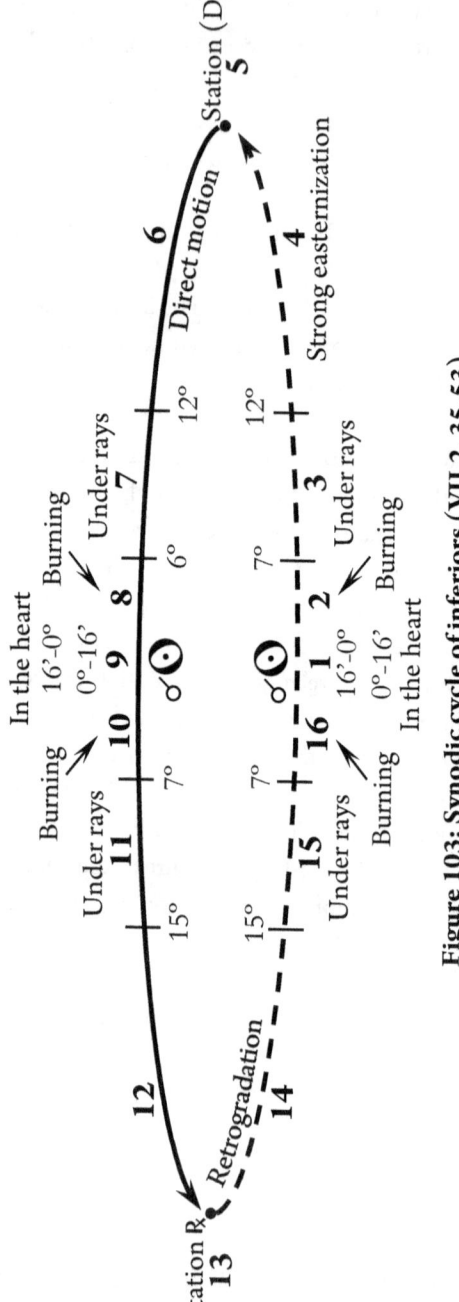

Figure 103: Synodic cycle of inferiors (VII.2, 35-53)

[Conditions of the Moon]

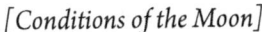

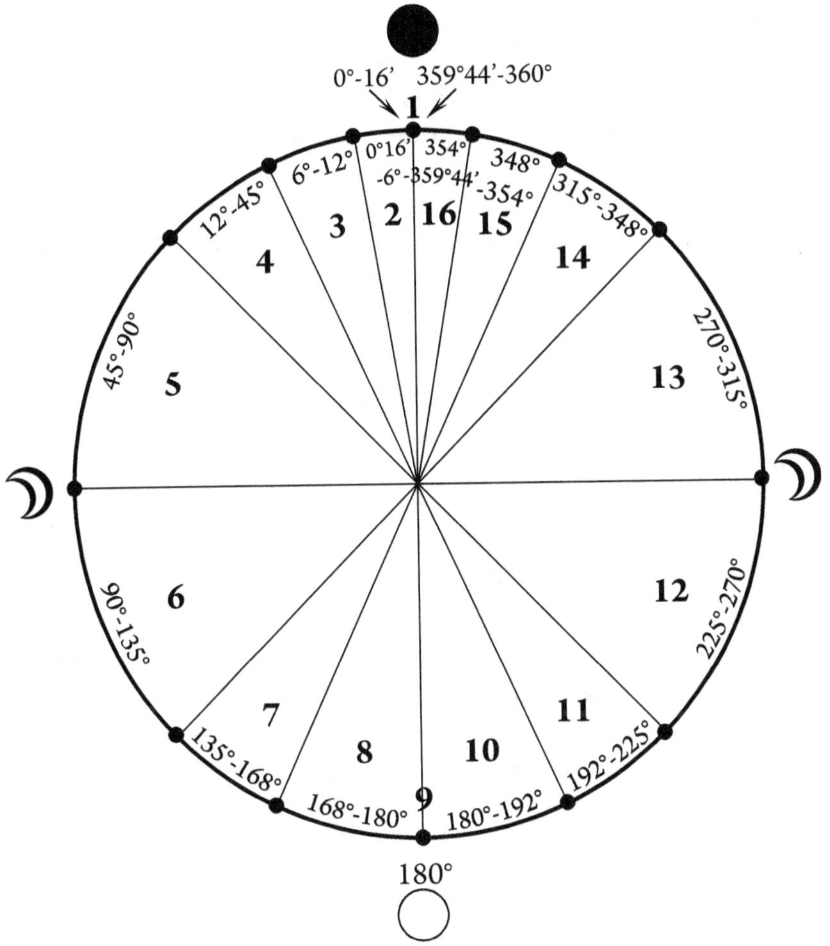

Figure 104: Synodic cycle of Moon (VII.2, 58-74)

58 And as for the Moon, she has sixteen conditions relative to the Sun.

59 Now as for the first, it is when she is with him, preceding him or lagging behind him by the range of those minutes in which we stated that if there was that much[48] between a planet and [the Sun], it is said to be "in the heart."[49]

60 And when she passes beyond them to the west, she shifts over to the second condition and is said to be "burned," and she is in her condition until there come to be 6° between her and him: because the closest she can be to the Sun when she is seen on the equator in the signs of longest ascension,[50] is when the full amount of these degrees is between her and him; and she is not seen among them[51] when in less than those degrees.

61 And when she passes beyond these degrees she shifts over to the third condition, and is said to be "under the rays" until she is distant from him in the west by 12°.

62 And when she passes beyond these degrees she shifts over to the fourth condition, and will be in her condition until she is distant from him by 45°: and that is where one-fourth of [her] glow comes to be in her body.

63 And when she passes beyond these degrees she shifts over to the fifth condition, until there come to be 90° between her and him.

64 And when she passes beyond these degrees she shifts over to the sixth condition, until there come to be 135° between her and him, and it is where three-quarters of the glow comes to be in her body.

65 Now when she passes beyond these degrees she shifts over to the seventh condition, until she falls short of the opposition by 12°.

66 Now when these degrees are between her and his opposition, she shifts over to the eighth condition until she opposes him.

67 And when she opposes him she shifts into the ninth condition.

---

[48] Lit., "a like amount" (مثلها).

[49] See **7-9**.

[50] Abū Ma'shar adds the word "there" (هناك) at this point, but I am not sure what role it plays.

[51] عندهم. Meaning uncertain: usually a plural inanimate noun like "signs" or "degrees" takes the feminine singular, but this is the masculine plural. Abū Ma'shar might be referring to the Persians, whom he has previously mentioned. In that case, this rule about the distance of the Sun is based on what is visible at the latitude of Persian astrologers, and might not be applicable at other climes. This may also relate to the view of Hermes about the visibility of the Moon when determining the degree of her exaltation, in V.7, **50-54**. In that case, the "them" in this sentence would refer to a specific people, perhaps living on the equator.

Book VII: Conditions & Indications of the Planets

68 And when she passes beyond his opposition she shifts over to the tenth condition, and will be in her condition until she is distant from his opposition by 12°.

69 And when she passes beyond them she shifts over to the eleventh condition, and will be in her condition until one-fourth of the glow is subtracted from her body: and it is where she is distant from his opposition by 45°.

70 And when she passes beyond them she shifts over to the twelfth condition, until she is distant from his opposition by 90°, and one-half of the glow remains in her body.

71 And when she passes beyond them she shifts over to the thirteenth condition, until there are 45° between her and him, and one-fourth of the glow remains in her body.

72 And when she passes beyond them she shifts over to the fourteenth condition, and does not cease to be in her condition until there are 12° between her and him in the east.

73 And when she is that many degrees from him she shifts over to the fifteenth condition, and comes to be under the rays: and she does not cease to be in her condition until there are 6° between her and him.

74 And when these degrees are between them both, she shifts over to the sixteenth condition, and is said to be burned; and she does not cease to be in her condition until the amount of those minutes which are called "in the heart" are between her and him.

75 And every one of these conditions has indications for things which we will mention in our book, in the places where mention of them is needed.

Chapter VII.3: On the conditions of the planets in the quadrants of the circle and their houses, and the range of the power of their bodies

1 The planets have four conditions relative to the quadrants of the circle and the twelve houses:

2 The first is if one is in the advancing and withdrawing quadrants of the circle.[52]

3 The second is if it is in one of the houses of the circle which are the stakes.[53]

4 The third is if it is in a house which follows a stake.

5 The fourth is if it is in the withdrawing houses.

Degrees on both sides	
☉	15°
☽	12°
♄ ♃	9°
♂	8°
☿ ♀	7°

Figure 105: Bodies or orbs of planets

6 And when any planet is in a position in the signs, its body has the power of a given number of degrees preceding it and following it. **7** The power of the Sun's body is 15° in front of him, and the same behind him. **8** The power of the Moon's body is 12° in front of her, and the same behind her. **9** The power of the each of the bodies of Saturn and Jupiter is 9° in front of him, and the same behind him. **10** The power of the body of Mars is 8° in front of him, and the same behind him. **11** The power of each of the bodies of Venus and Mercury is 7° in front of them, and the same behind them.

---

[52] See VI.26, **3**.
[53] See VI.26, **5**, for this and the next two sentences.

Chapter VII.4: On the planets' assembling with each other, and the mixture of their qualities, and which of them is stronger, and which weaker

1 Each of the seven planets has an assembly with another one at some time, and it has an aspect to certain signs far away from it.

2 Now as for their assembly, it will be of one of them with another in their sign in which they are—and sometimes they also assemble with one of the fixed stars, or one of the nebulae, or the Head or Tail of its own Dragon, or the Head or Tail of another's Dragon, or [a planet] will assemble with the rays of one of the planets, or one of the Lots, or the twelfth-parts.[54]

3 And a planet is said to be assembling with something of what we state, if they were both in a single sign;[55] and it is stronger for the indication of their assembly if there were 15° and less between one of them and the other, [whether] in front of it or behind it.[56]

4 And the bodies of the seven planets have a range of power in their places, which we have already stated in the chapter which was before this.[57]

5 So if, upon the assembling of two planets, the amount of one-half of the body of each of them in degrees was between the one and the other (or less than that, [whether] preceding it or behind it), it is more apparent for the indication of the assembling of one with the other. **6** But if one of them is within the degrees of the strength of the body of the other, while the other is *not* merging with the degrees of strength of the body of the planet assembling with it, it will be weaker for their indication. **7** And that is like Saturn and the Moon: if they were in a single sign, and the distance between them both was within 12° in front of them or behind, Saturn would be in the power of the body of the Moon, while the Moon would not be in the power of the body of Saturn, until there is a little under 9° between them. **8** But if each of them *was* in the power of the body of its associate, the indication of their

---

[54] See **15-16**.
[55] See also **13-14**, and VII.5, **10-14**, and **22-23**: there are no proper "out-of-sign" conjunctions.
[56] In Hellenistic astrology, merely being in the same sign is sometimes called "co-present."
[57] See VII.3, **6-11**.

assembly would become strong—and if in addition they were in a single bound, it is more powerful in indication.

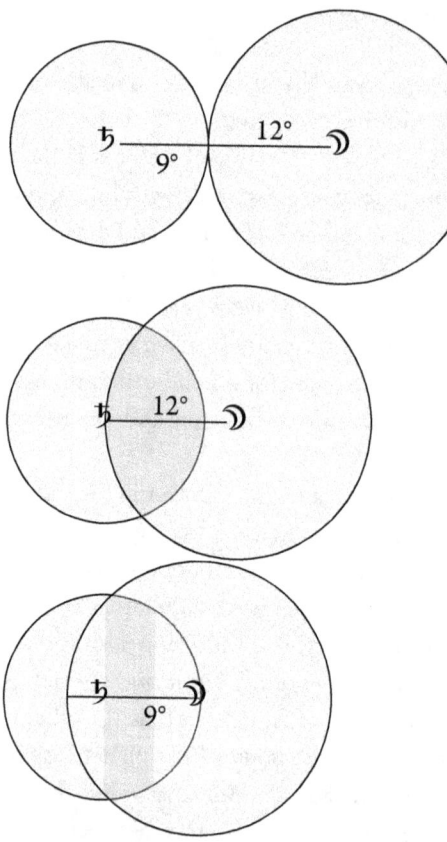

Figure 106: Assembling with planets' bodies or orbs (VII.4, 5-8)

9 And the more that one of them gets closer to its associate, they are both more increased in power in the indication of what they indicate. 10 And when they encounter each other's bodies, they come to be in the peak of their indication for good or evil.

11 But when one of them departs from its associate, their indication is weakened: and the more that they distance themselves, they will be like that in the weakness of the indication, until one of them goes out of the sign in which the other is. 12 So if between them there was the amount of one-half the body of each of them, and one of them is *going towards* the other, then it is more powerful for their indication than if that amount of degrees was between them but one of them had already *departed* from the other.

13 And when the two planets are in two different signs, and each one of them is in the power of the body of the other by the amount of degrees, then they are *not* said to be "united,"[58] because of the difference of their signs; but rather it is said that one of them is "in the power" of the other's body. 14 But due to the merging of the power of their bodies they will have an indication

---

[58] مقترنان. That is, it is not a proper assembly or conjunction.

over a small matter, as compared with what they would indicate in a [proper] assembly.

15 Now as for the fixed stars, the ancients did not assign the range of a body to them: so if one of the seven planets assembles with one of the fixed stars, so that between them was the range of one-half (or less) of the body of that planet which is of the seven, then the fixed star will be in the power of the planet's body. **16** And their condition in the power of their bodies will be in this manner if they assemble with one of the nebulae, or the Heads of the Dragons or their Tails, or the rest of what we have mentioned.[59]

[Planetary conjunctions are only apparent]

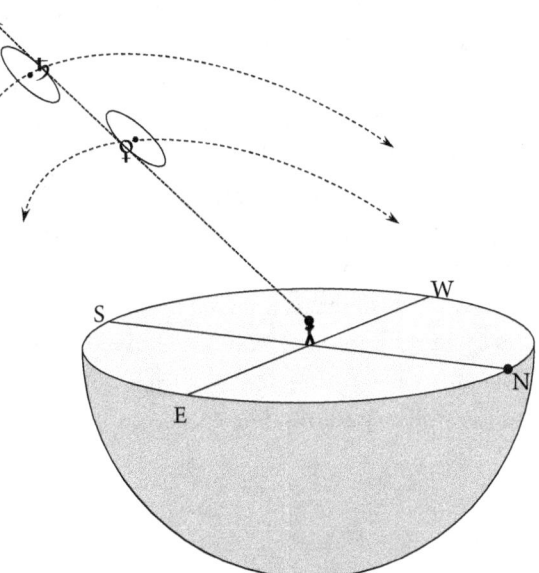

Figure 107: Planets visually united (VII.4, 17-20)

17 Now, people have thought that when two planets unite, they are [actually] joining with their bodies in a single position of the sphere—but it is not like that. **18** For really, the meaning of "uniting" is one of them being "set over against" the other,[60] since one of them is higher than its associate, and its sphere is different from the sphere of the other. **19** So, one of them will be set over against its associate and they will be in parallel to a single position in the circle of signs, and are both moved along in a single path, so that someone looking at them both will [only] see them as being united

---

[59] For more on this, see **43** below.
[60] المسامتة.

due to their distance from the earth, and the great distance in height between one of them and its associate. **20** For this reason we have said that the meaning of "uniting" is being "set over against" [each other].[61]

[Whether conjunctions cancel out their qualities]

21 And people have [also] claimed that when two planets unite it nullifies the natural indication which each of them indicates by itself, and that from their uniting would occur an indication for *another* thing different from their two natures.

22 And they protest concerning that by saying that when any two things which exist among us meet and combine, from their blending would occur a third thing apart from them both: but they would both act through their natures in the blending, not individually. **23** And that is like water and wine, for upon their meeting and mixing, the nature and essence of each is corrupted and a third thing blended of both comes to be, different from them in essence and nature. **24** And many existing things are in this condition.[62]

25 But we say that for the two things, even if they combine and one of them corrupts the essence of the other upon [their] blending, there will [still] be found in them the quality of each of them in their blending, in the manner in which that is found in them individually: and that is because when a man drinks water and wine blended together, the wine will intoxicate him through its hot nature and its own special property, and the water mixed with it will hydrate the body. **26** And an example of that is also found in

---

[61] In Figure 107, an observer on earth at his local horizon looks into the heavens and sees Venus and Saturn *apparently* united at exactly the same point. But from the perspective of the diagram, we can see that they are not actually united in space, and are in different parts of their own planetary systems and epicycles. But viewed from earth, they do appear to be united "in" a particular degree.

[62] The point of contention seems to be that since material bodies combine like this, and planets are also bodies (or have material influences), then a conjunction would nullify the distinct qualities of each planet: a Moon-Saturn conjunction would be neither Lunar nor Saturnian, but something else. So, we need to explain how planets can combine without this happening.

drugs that are combined with one another, such as theriac:[63] because it dissolves the colic[64] due to the hot, dissolving medicine which is in it, but it retains difference[65] due to the binding,[66] retentive medicine in it.[67]

27 And we also say that the mixing of bodies with each other is due to these lower, fluid bodies,[68] because when two of them meet and combine, one of them corrupts the other and so nullifies the essence of each of them, and from them occurs a third thing apart from them. **28** But as for higher bodies,[69] it is contrary to that: because when [two of them] unite, they do not combine their essences together, nor does one of them corrupt the other, but rather in their own bodies and natures they would [still] be in their own [respective] condition, though indeed their *qualities* would be combined when one of them is parallel to the other and they are moved in a single path.[70] **29** So due to the survival of their natures in their own [respective] conditions, the indication of each one will be manifest at the assembly just as it appears separately; but due to the mixing of their qualities and their

---

[63] This was a complicated mixture of substances (with many different recipes) often thought to be a panacea; it sometimes even included small amounts of poison. So, Abū Ma'shar is talking about medicines that even have *contrary* qualities: this is why he says it "retains difference," later in the sentence.

[64] This refers especially to painful gas and constipation.

[65] الاختلاف. Or perhaps better, "distinctness."

[66] Reading المحدّرة with Lemay (a rare use of this verb which connotes thickening and twisting). But **BY** read المخدّرة, "numbing." I think my reading makes Abū Ma'shar's point, that the same medicine can have contrary qualities (loosening and expelling, binding and retaining).

[67] Abū Ma'shar's response is that each of the two material things still retains something of its nature: thus, *if* celestial bodies worked in the same way, in a Moon-Saturn conjunction there would still be something Lunar and Saturnian at work. (But he will point out in **28** that the analogy between material things and the planets is imprecise.)

[68] That is, material things on earth.

[69] That is, the planets.

[70] To me this sounds like light shining through two colored filters: the effect may be a third, mixed color, but the filters remain as they are. But this also explains why Abū Ma'shar needed to preface this passage with sentences **17-20**, because they show that unlike lower, material bodies which actually combine, the uniting of celestial bodies is only apparent.

being moved in our[71] path, a third thing will occur from the indication due to them.[72]

30 And in accordance with the nearness of one of them to the other (or its distance from it), and their places in relation to the nature of their sign, and their condition relative to the houses of the circle, and the planets' looking at them, many different things will occur in the world at any time (from the indication of their assembly), which are contrary to what occurs at another time. **31** And the more planets which mutually assemble with each other, the more numerous are the things which are stimulated by them. **32** And the ancients have made clear the indications of the assembly of the planets with each other, in their books.[73]

[Assessing the mixture and power of a conjunction]

33 Upon their assembly with each other, the planets have two conditions: one of them is [1] the mixing of the qualities of one with the other, and the second is [2] the power of one over the other.[74]

34 Now as for [1] mixing their qualities, it is through what is ascribed to their natures (of heat, cold, dryness, and wetness), and that is known by five things.[75] **35** The first of them is [1a] by the special property of their natures. **36** The second is [1b] by their rising or falling in the circle of the apogee. **37** The third is [1c] by their place in relation to the nature of their sign. **38** The fourth is [1d] by their condition relative to the Sun. **39** The fifth is [1e] by

---

[71] سمتنا, emphasizing that conjunctions happen from *our* perspective. This reinforces my metaphor of two colored filters which are only seen as mixed from a particular perspective.

[72] Or, "a third thing will occur *to* them," which seems more awkward. Thus, even if some material bodies do corrupt each other's natures when combined, *planets* continue to retain their own essences and effect them—but the *qualities* (which derive from their activity) may be altered.

[73] Abū Ma'shar may be thinking of Dorotheus in *Carmen* II.14-II.23, but similar lists are also in Firmicus Maternus (*Mathesis* VI) and Valens (*Anth.* I.19-I.20).

[74] That is, certain conditions like easternization plus the planetary special properties will tell us what principles are being mixed (like hot and cold). Other conditions tell us which of these are more powerful.

[75] For the following, see especially Ch. IV.7, which describes these for all planets.

their condition in the quadrants of the circle.⁷⁶ **40** And we have already mentioned that in Book IV of this book of ours, and in other places.⁷⁷

41 And as for their [2] power [over one another] upon assembling, that is through the conditions of each one of the two in the circle of the apogee and the circle of inclination,⁷⁸ at its rising or falling in both of them: because [2a] the closer of the two to the apex of the circle of its apogee is stronger in influence over the one farther from [its own] apex, and [2b] the northern rising one with much latitude is stronger than the northern rising one with less latitude than it, and [2c] the northern rising one is stronger than the northern falling one, and [2d] the northern one is stronger than the southern one, and [2e] the southern rising one is stronger than the southern falling one, and [2f] the southern one with less latitude is stronger than the southern one with more latitude. **42** And this strength and weakness belongs to the seven planets relative to each other.

43 But as for when one of them⁷⁹ assembles with one of the fixed stars or one of the nebulae, the Lots, or the rest of what we mentioned before, one looks at the condition of that planet (which is of the seven) in itself, and its strength or weakness, and what it indicates through its assembly with that thing: because the fixed stars, Lots, and the rest of what we mentioned do not have a circle of the apogee nor a circle of inclination.

[Interlude and analysis: Mars and Saturn in conjunction]

44 Now the ancients did say that when Saturn and Mars unite, they indicate good fortune because each of them balances out the nature of his associate⁸⁰—and this statement of theirs is correct, except that it needs clarification. **45** And that is because each of them has two natures: one of the two

---

⁷⁶ See IV.8. See also VII.6, **28-29** and **45-46**.
⁷⁷ Again, see especially IV.6 and IV.7.
⁷⁸ المائل, referring to ecliptical latitude (not declination). So, the relative strength of planets is a matter of position in latitude and relative to their apogees.
⁷⁹ Reading the plural (since we are now speaking about all of the planets), for the dual ("one of the two").
⁸⁰ See for example *Carmen* II.18, **2** (which does not spell it out exactly), and especially *Mathesis* VI.22.

natures inheres in it, and the other nature sometimes shifts from it to its contrary.[81] **46** So the nature of Saturn is cooling and drying, but sometimes it will shift from the dry so that it becomes cooling and moistening. **47** The nature of Mars is heating and drying, and sometimes it will shift from the drying so that it becomes hot and wet.[82]

48 And in Book IV of this book of ours we have already stated when the nature of each one of the two becomes strong or weak, and when they shift from nature to nature: and indeed that comes from their conditions in the circle of their apogees, and from their positions in the signs, and from their area[83] relative to the Sun, and their positions in the quadrants of the circle.[84]

49 So if their uniting was in the fiery signs (and they are Aries and its triplicities), then the heat of Mars is strengthened, and his wetness[85] decreased, while the coldness of Saturn is also decreased as well as his wetness, while he increases in in his dryness. **50** But as for their uniting in the earthy signs (and they are Taurus and its triplicities), the dryness of Mars is strengthened and his wetness decreased, while the coldness of Saturn is strengthened, as well as his dryness. **51** As for their meeting in the airy signs (and they are Gemini and its triplicities), their moderation and mixture is strengthened, as well as their wetness.[86] **52** And as for their uniting in the watery signs (and they are Cancer and its triplicities), the heat of Mars is decreased as well as his dryness (and it will be changed to wetness), and there will be an increase in the coldness of Saturn as well as his wetness.

---

[81] See IV.7, **2-3**.

[82] Again, this means his inherent quality is hot, and secondarily drying.

[83] أفقهما.

[84] Again, see IV.7. Abū Ma'shar just mentioned these above in **34-39**, and will now review it below.

[85] Or rather, any wetness he happens to be producing at the time. The awkwardness here is that Mars is naturally heating and drying, which means his normal energy is *actually* drying and only *potentially* moistening. So if we say that being in Aries decreases his wetness, we imply that he was already actually moistening, which he is not assumed to do. But I am quibbling here: the point is that the hot and dry signs will produce more heating and drying, reducing any wetness.

[86] See also **60** below. In the airy signs, Saturn's cold will be moderated (but not changed) by the heat, while being moistened a bit; Mars will be strengthened in the hot by the heat, and also moistened a bit (which moderates the hot).

53 And their condition relative to the Sun is like that, since the nature of each is strengthened or weakened due to the fact that from the time of the Sun's departing from them until their first station, the nature of them both is changed to wetness, just as they are changed when they are in Gemini and its triplicities. **54** And from their first station to their opposition to the Sun the nature of them both is changed to heat, just as they are changed when they are in Aries and its triplicities. **55** And after their opposition up to the second station the nature of them both is changed to the dry, just as they are changed when they are in Taurus and its triplicities. **56** And after the second station up to their meeting with him, the nature of them both is changed to the cold, just as they are changed when they are in Cancer and its triplicities.[87]

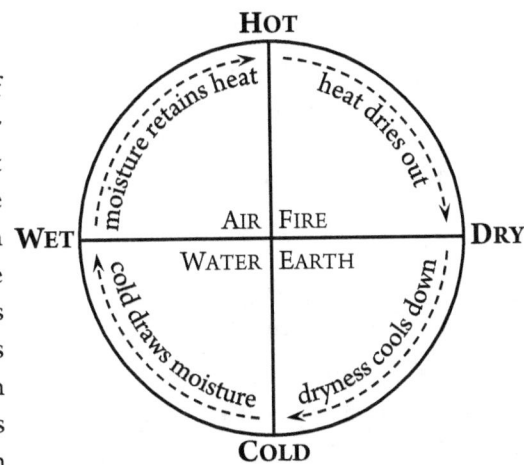

Figure 108: Cycle of simple principles

57 And of course one of their natures will also be changed from condition to condition in accordance with the nature of their sign, and their condition in the quadrants of the circle, in the rest of the ways which we mentioned previously.

58 So examine that for them both at their uniting, because when they unite and combine in *two* qualities, and their power is moderated, they indicate the utmost of their indication for good fortune; and if at their uniting they combine in a *single* quality, the indication of their good fortune is decreased as compared with the first [combination].

---

[87] See the Figure associated with IV.7, **44**.

59 So as for their mixing in two qualities,[88] it is in three ways: the first is if Mars is hot and wet while Saturn is cold and dry; the second is if Mars is hot and dry while Saturn is cold and wet; the third is if Mars is hot and wet while Saturn is cold and wet. 60 For if they were in one of these three conditions, then they would be combining in two qualities, and would indicate harmony, the good, and good fortune: because if they were both wet,[89] that wetness takes away from the heat of Mars and the coldness of Saturn, and they will come to be in the nature of moderation, and indicate good fortune. 61 And the mixing of the quality of the other two types is in this manner.[90]

62 But as for their mixing in a single quality, that is if Mars is hot and dry, and Saturn cold and dry. 63 Now if they mutually assemble in this condition, their mixing will be by a single quality and they will have less moderation and

♂-♄ mixing in two qualities: moderation			
♂	H	W	Will always mix by primary quality (H-C), since they always differ from each other.
♄	C	D	
♂	H	D	
♄	C	W	
♂	H	W	Will mix by secondary quality *if* at least one has been altered.
♄	C	W	
♂-♄ mixing in one quality: less moderation, harshness			
♂	H	D	Only mix by primary quality (H-C), since they are naturally both D.
♄	C	D	

Figure 109: Mars-Saturn conjunctions (VII.4, 59-64)

---

[88] See Figure 109. Because their primary qualities (heat and cold) are opposed, they will always have a combination in one quality. The mixture by a second quality will involve one of them being wet, or else both of them being wet (so as to change that quality in both of them). Nevertheless, note that this does not always make intuitive sense: Saturn-Mars conjunctions in Cancer should be more moderated, because in watery signs Mars would be H-W and Saturn C-W, the third type of mixture in two qualities. Yet in some mundane astrology this is said to be particularly bad. The answer may be suggested in **77** below: being in fall or detriment corrupts their strength, and in the case of government and politics a disintegrating or weak government and military can bring disaster, whether or not there is moderation.
[89] This is the third type listed in **59**.
[90] See also **108-09**.

mixing: because if they both came to be drying, that increases the dry in the heat of Mars, strengthens the cold of Saturn, and decreases their moderation, and they would indicate little good.[91] **64** And for everything which Saturn and Mars indicate by their meeting (in terms of good fortune and the good) in the inception of works, things sought,[92] nativities, and the revolutions of years, due to their unfortunate natures they will indicate that it will be with toil, exertion, and trouble, and they will tarnish that with injury, and something detestable, and will burden the soul and body with burning shocks—but if the fortunes aid them at the time of the indication,[93] they will liberate [the native] from [the misfortunes] after that (and if not, his destruction will be in it).

[Conjunctions with the Sun]

65 And addition to knowing the blending of their qualities upon their uniting, one ought to know the stronger of the two from the way we stated,[94] because its nature and action will be stronger and more apparent.

66 Now as for the Sun, upon his assembly with the planets he has a condition different from the condition of the planets' assembly with each other: because for all of them, when they go under his rays, he burns them and weakens their power. **67** The most intense harm for the planets by burning is that of the Moon and Venus, because they are both cooling and moistening: so when they enter into burning, the Sun dissolves them[95] by means of his heat, dries out their wetness, and damages them in accordance with the hostility of the Sun's essence towards their essence. **68** But as for Saturn and Jupiter, burning is less harmful to them because they both harmonize with the Sun in one of their characteristics: Jupiter harmonizes with [the Sun]

---

[91] Nevertheless they will (allegedly) signify *some* good, because the heat of Mars will counteract the coldness of Saturn.

[92] That is, in questions or horary.

[93] That is, in real time. An example would be if a natal Saturn-Mars conjunction becomes activated for age 44, and at the solar revolution of that year Jupiter and Venus closely aspect Saturn's and Mars's natal or revolutionary positions (or better yet, both).

[94] See **41-42**.

[95] That is, he dissolves their coldness.

through heat, and Saturn through the dry.⁹⁶ **69** And the harm for Mars and Mercury, when they are direct while being burned, is the least harmful of all of them,⁹⁷ because they are both of the essence of the Sun: and an essence does not damage its own essence, nor does it corrupt it.

70 And for these reasons some of them will come to be stronger than others while burning, and some of them will mix with the Sun (and he will mix with them through his nature as well), and some of them will make him fortunate, and some of them make him unfortunate.

71 For if Mars and Saturn came to be under the rays of the Sun, and he burned them, they would also make him somewhat unfortunate due to their meeting with him—except that what would affect them from the corruption of burning by the Sun would be greater than what would affect him from their misfortune. **72** And the misfortune of the Sun from Mars when [Mars] is under his rays, is greater than [the Sun's misfortune] from Saturn, because sometimes the Sun will mix with [Saturn] in two qualities, and sometimes he will mix with [Saturn] in a single quality—but [the Sun's] condition with Mars is not like that.⁹⁸

73 As for which of the two qualities [the Sun and Saturn] combine in, the activity in it is like the activity of Saturn and Mars when they unite:⁹⁹ because the Sun is heating and drying, and sometimes he is heating and moistening, while Saturn is cooling and drying, and sometimes he is cooling and moistening. **74** (And the shifting of each one from one nature to another is known from the four ways which we mentioned above.)¹⁰⁰ **75** So if the Sun assembled with Saturn and they combined in two qualities, what affects Saturn from the corruption of being burned by [the Sun], and what affects the

---

⁹⁶ In this case, the Sun is normally a moderating H-D, while Jupiter is a moderating H-W: so they should combine in a more moderating way. Saturn is an excessive C-D, so if he is burned we might expect the Sun's heat to moderate his cold; but one might also think that their combined Ds would intensify and cause problems.

⁹⁷ Lit., "below all of their harm."

⁹⁸ Since both the Sun and Mars are H-D, they can only mix in one quality: the secondary one (D), when one or both of them is more W. But Saturn is naturally C-D, which means he can mix in one quality (the primary one, which is always different), or in both (when one or both is more W).

⁹⁹ See **59-61** above.

¹⁰⁰ See **34-39** above, but more specifically in **48-64**.

Sun from the misfortune of Saturn, will be little. **76** But if they combined in a *single* quality,[101] the condition of corruption for each one of them from his associate will be greater than the first [way], except that the Sun will be stronger than Saturn. **77** And if in addition to the burning Saturn met with the corruption of his own position due to his sign (such as [being in] fall, and what is like that), and a bad condition relative to [his] position in the circle, and he mixed with the Sun in a single quality, he would be excessive in corruption, and weak.[102]

78 But as for Mars, if he was under the rays of the Sun, [the Sun] will burn him, except that he will make [the Sun] more unfortunate than the misfortune of Saturn towards [the Sun] will, because sometimes Mars will mix with [the Sun] in a single quality while being burned,[103] and sometimes he will not mix with him in any of the qualities:[104] but when they *do* combine it will be less for the misfortune of both.[105] **79** For indeed their combination will be when they are both heating and moistening, or one of them is heating and moistening; but if they were both heating and drying they will not combine, and it will be greater for the corruption of each of them from its associate (except that what affects Mars from the corruption of burning by the Sun is greater than what affects [the Sun] from [Mars's] misfortune).

80 Now as for Mercury, what affects him from the corruption of burning by the Sun is less than what affects other planets, and that is due to his nearness to [the Sun], and due to the reason which we stated before.[106] **81** And that is when he is direct: but when he is retrograde, what he gets from the harm of being burned is greater. **82** And if he was made unfortunate during the time of his being under the rays, he will grant to the Sun a portion of his misfortune; but if he was made fortunate, he will grant [the Sun] something

---

[101] That is, if they were both D.
[102] An example might be a Sun-Saturn conjunction in Aries, which is the fall of Saturn and exaltation of the Sun, and in which case they are both D (due to Aries being H-D).
[103] For example, if they combined while Mars is easternizing (which makes him more W): then the Sun would be H-D, and Mars H-W.
[104] For example, if they combined in Aries: then they would both be fully H-D, since Aries is H-D.
[105] Reading the dual with **BY**.
[106] Perhaps this refers to **69**.

of his good fortune: because Mercury accepts the natures of the fortunes and infortunes, and will pass them on to [the Sun].

83 As for Jupiter, Venus, and the Moon when they assemble with the Sun and he burns them, if any of them is strong in the way we discussed concerning their strength,[107] what affects it from the corruption of burning will be less. **84** But these three planets will make the Sun a little bit fortunate if they were under his rays, even if the Sun burns them and corrupts them.

85 And for all planets, if they were with the Sun "in the heart" in the manner we stated before,[108] then in many matters it indicates good fortune: and that is because when they and the Sun are moved [together] above us in one path, the Sun will convey to us the nature of the planets indicative of generation and good fortune,[109] through his own good fortune.

[Other conjunctions]

86 As for the Moon, when she assembles with Saturn and Mars they will make her unfortunate, except that in general her misfortune from Saturn is said to be harsher than that from Mars. **87** But if it was in the first half of the [lunar] month her nature is heating: so should she mix with the cold of Saturn with her heating nature, her misfortune from Saturn will be less; and she [should] not mix with the heat of Mars, for her misfortune from him would be harsher. **88** And if it was in the last half of the [lunar] month, cold will predominate in her and her cold will mix with the heat of Mars so that her misfortune from him will be less, while she [should] not mix with the coldness of Saturn, for her misfortune from him will be harsher. **89** And if the Moon is made strong through one of the strengths which we mentioned,[110] what affects her from their misfortune will be less; but if one of them was

---

[107] Perhaps referring to the apogee and latitude, in **41-42**.

[108] See VII.2, 7.

[109] I read this as though it is the planets which indicate generation and good fortune (which these planets do). But this could also be read as: he conveys *the nature that indicates generation and good fortune*. That is, even if these planets are harmed by burning, he will convey only the portion which indicates generation and good fortune.

[110] See **41** above.

stronger than the Moon, the misfortune which affects her from it will be greater and harsher.

90 As for Saturn and Jupiter, when they unite the nature of the stronger one of them will be more apparent.

91 And one looks like that with the uniting of Venus and Mars, and the assembling of the rest of the planets with each other.

92 And if several of the planets united, the strongest of them will be more apparent in activity.

[Types of mixing, and Saturn-Mars again]

93 And people have claimed that since Saturn and Mars are each an infortune by itself, through its own nature, then if they united they would not indicate good fortune, but rather they would indicate an excess of misfortune. **94** And they argued about that by saying, "If two things were of one type and a single nature, and they came together, it would be stronger for the nature of that thing: because when fire is added to fire that is like it, it is not changed from its nature but rather the activity from them which agrees with burning[111] will be stronger.[112] **95** Likewise, if firmness[113] was joined to a firmness like it, it would not be changed from its nature, but rather what is found concerning the action of its nature upon their being joined, would be stronger and more apparent. **96** And these two planets are like that: if each of them is an infortune by itself, then if they united they would not indicate good fortune (which is contrary to their natures), but rather they would indicate an excess of misfortune and corruption."

---

[111] يكون فعل ما يجتمع منها على الاحتراق أقوى, an awkward phrase. But perhaps Abū Ma'shar is reminding us that there are other fiery activities, like drying.

[112] This argument relies on two things: a close analogy between material bodies and the celestial bodies, and that planets actually change their "natures" like material bodies do when blended. Abū Ma'shar will deny both (see also **28-29** above), and has already argued in IV.5, **80-82** that planets' true natures are not directly known by us: instead we can only speak of the effects of their special properties.

[113] الصّبر. This can also refer to aloe wood, so Abū Ma'shar is thinking of something hard like wood.

Bodies	Components	Mixture	Example
Rigid	Big parts	[1] Fastening ترکیب	Chair
Rigid	Small parts	[2] Heterogeneous mixture اختلاط	Mixed grains
Fluid	Same kind	[3] Aggregate اجتماع	Water-water
Fluid	Resisting kinds	[4a] Blend (by analogy) امتزاج	Water-oil
Fluid	Contrary kinds	[4b] Blend (true) امتزاج	Water-wine

- True blending so as to produce a 3rd thing requires contraries which corrupt and change each other.
- Planets aren't rigid, so they don't fasten or make a heterogeneous mixture. They don't aggregate to make more of the same, or resist each other to blend analogously, nor blend truly.
- Planets are only analogous to material things. Each retains its *nature*, and they only combine *qualities*.

Figure 110: Argument against planets mixing like material bodies (VII.4, 97-109)

97 But we say that, in [relation to] this topic, the conditions of bodies existing among us[114] are of four types: one of them is [1] fastening,[115] the second a [2] heterogeneous mixture, the third [3] aggregating,[116] and the fourth [4] blending.[117] **98** And bodies are either rigid or fluid.[118]

---

[114] That is, on earth.

[115] التّرکیب. This word is used in construction, and refers to things which are externally fitted with, attached to, or inserted into one another. In previous Books I have translated it more loosely as "composition," but this is the more precise term. The Greek equivalent in the Stoics and Alexander of Aphrodisias is "juxtaposition."

[116] الاجتماع. Aggregation produces more of the same thing, like adding water to water.

[117] الامتزاج. For Abū Ma'shar, true blending requires some kind of corruption: see **106**.

99 Now as for the rigid ones, if their parts were big, and some of them were [1] fastened to others, things of varied shapes would come from them: such as if wood was fastened to wood, a door or chair or something else would come to be from it. **100** And as for those with small parts, if some of them came together with others through their own natural shape, they would be called a [2] heterogeneous mixture: and that is like wheat and barley, and what is like that.

101 As for fluid bodies, either two things of a single kind would come together (like water with water, and wine with wine), so that they are said to [3] aggregate, or, if one would resist[119] the other (like oil and water), they would be said to [4] blend [but only] by analogy.[120] **102** But if one of them was contrary to[121] the other, and the parts of one were introduced into the other, and one of them would corrupt the other, then from their blending would occur a third thing different from them both: and that comes to be in both fluid and rigid bodies. **103** As for the fluid bodies, that is like the example of water and milk, water and wine, and what is like that: and they are said to be *truly* blending. **104** As for rigid bodies, that is like the heterogeneous

---

[118] A lot of what Abū Ma'shar is talking about, is a function of (1) how big or small the parts are, so it's partly related to our perception; and (2) how the substances interact with each other. As he says about the example of flour and medicines in **104**, when the two flours are ground finely, they look like one thing and as bread will have one overall flavor; multiple medicines ground in the same pill will look like a single substance and give you an overall effect, even though the substances themselves are not changing ("corrupting") each other. Well-balanced incenses can be like this, too.

[119] Or more literally, "stand in the way of," "stand on" (يقف على).

[120] It is only by analogy, because Abū Ma'shar says true blending involves an interactive corruption or chemical change between the two contrary substances (**102**).

[121] This "contrariness" allows them to change (or "corrupt") each other so as to make a third substance, which makes it different from the resistance just mentioned about oil and water. But as we can see, Abū Ma'shar seems to be using some of the terms loosely, because he admits in **104** that what *looks* like blending and the production of a third thing in the case of blended flours and medicines, is only apparent: it is really a case of heterogeneous mixing.

mixing of wheat flour and barley flour, or the heterogeneous mixing of medicines with each other, when they are ground [together].[122]

105 And the blending[123] of things with each other is different from the aggregation of one with the other, because when something is [only] brought into a relation with something like it, they are said to be [only] aggregating, not blending. **106** Indeed, a [4b] true blending[124] happens by something coming together with its contrary,[125] and one of them corrupting the nature of the other.

107 Now if two planets united, their condition would not be like [1-2] the condition of rigid bodies, nor would they [3] aggregate so as to become one thing (like water with water, and fire with fire, and firmness with firmness), nor would one of them [4a] resist the other (like oil and water), nor would they be [4b] blended in their *being*[126] so that one of them would corrupt the other (like water and wine)—but rather, through the being and nature of each in its own condition, one of them would mix with its associate in the *quality* which is contrary to the quality of the other planet. **108** So, Saturn and Mars differ in *quality*, and they come to be infortunes through what is attributed to each of them due to the excessive quality in corruption. **109** If they are united in two qualities, their differing quality will be combined, and one of them will weaken the corrupting power of the quality which belongs to the other, so that the excessiveness of their quality (which is indicative of badness) will disappear from them both, and they will come to be of[127] the character of fortunes.[128]

---

[122] In this case, the "blending" is only apparent: it is a function of the fact that we can't tell the two flours apart by sight or taste. Thus Abū Ma'shar has said it was an example of blending, but because the bodies are rigid they are really only heterogeneously mixed.

[123] ممازجة, which is Form 3 of this verb ("combining, mixing") and not the Form 8 he has been using for this technical discussion ("blending"). I translate it as though it is Form 8.

[124] Again, Abū Ma'shar uses Form 3 (see above), but I translate it as Form 8.

[125] مخالفه. This could be understood more loosely as "what is different from it."

[126] بذاتهما. Or, "essence," or "in their own right."

[127] Or, "they will result in" (يصيران). But remember, they only have the "stamp" or "character" (طبع) of fortunes, they are not actually fortunes.

Chapter VII.5: On the planets' looking at each other, and their connection and separation, and the rest of their similar conditions which follow upon that

1 In this chapter we want to state the twenty-one conditions which belong to the planets, and they are:

[1] Looking
[2] Connection
[3] Separation
[4] Emptiness of course
[5] Wildness[129]
[6] Transfer
[7] Collection
[8] Reflection of light
[9] Blocking
[10] Handing over nature
[11] Handing over power
[12] Handing over two natures
[13] Handing over management
[14] Returning
[15] Revoking
[16] Resistance
[17] Escape
[18] Cutting the light
[19] Favor
[20] Recompense
[21] Reception.

---

[128] That is, each by itself is highly or excessively corrupting (**108**). But when they mix in two qualities, this mixture will moderate the harsh excessiveness and so they will have the *character* or stamp of fortunes.

[129] Or, "the wild" (الوحشي).

2 Now, the **LOOKING**[130] of every planet is to the given signs, and there are seven signs: the third sign from it, and the fourth, fifth, seventh, ninth, tenth, and eleventh. **3** And it looks at every degree of the sign as well as everything which is in it (of planets, Lots, and other things). **4** And the strongest thing there is in its looking at every one of the degrees of these signs, is the degree which is related most closely by number to the degree of its own sign (such as 60°, 90°, 120°, and 180°), in degrees of equality;[131] and if the aspect was far from these degrees, its aspect will be weaker.

5 And its looking at the eleventh sign, and the third from it, is the aspect of the sextile;[132] and at the tenth and fourth sign from it is the aspect of the square; and at the ninth and fifth sign from it is the aspect of the trine, and at the seventh [sign] is the aspect of opposition.

6 Now as for the ninth, tenth, and eleventh signs, it looks at them from its right, while as for the third, fourth, and fifth signs, it looks at them from its left. **7** So the aspect of the seven planets to the signs, and everything in them, and their looking at each other, is in these ways.[133]

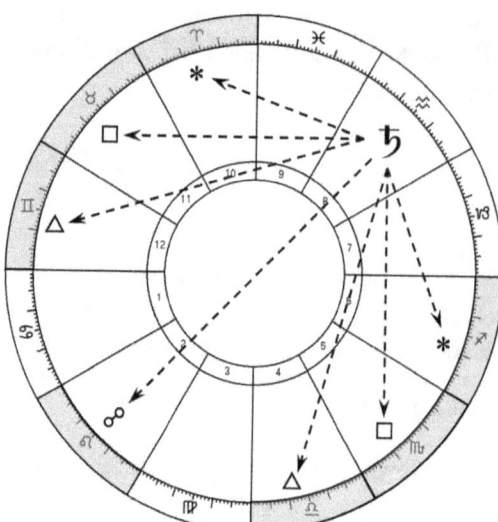

Figure 111: Saturn looking at signs (VII.5, 2-7)

---

[130] Or, "aspect" (النَظر). This is fundamentally by whole signs.
[131] That is, zodiacal degrees. I have added the degree symbol to the preceding numbers even though Abū Ma'shar does not actually say "degrees," because it is implied.
[132] Or more literally, "looking by sextile," and so on with the rest.
[133] Or, "in these directions" (على هذه الأنحاء).

BOOK VII: CONDITIONS & INDICATIONS OF THE PLANETS

8 And the signs which they do not look at,[134] are four: and they are the second from it, and the sixth, eighth, and twelfth: the number of degrees in these four signs is 120°, the degrees equivalent to[135] the number of the degrees in the trine.

9 Now as for the [2] CONNECTION of one with another, the light one connects with one which is slower than it, and this is in eight ways: one of them is the connection by assembly,[136] and seven are a connection by looking.[137]

[Connecting by body: the conjunction or assembly]

10 So as for the connection by assembly, it is that two planets are direct in motion, in a single sign, and the one of them light in motion is in fewer degrees than the slow one. **11** So as long as the one light in motion is below the slow one [in degrees], it is

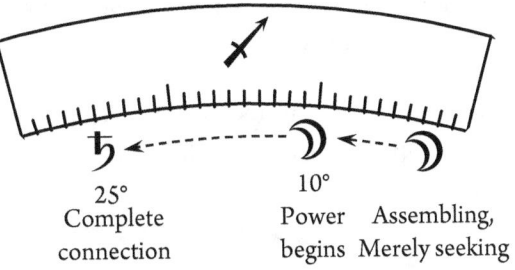

Figure 112: Assembling in same sign (VII.5, 10-13)

"going towards" the connection with it by assembly; and when it comes to be with it in a single degree and minute, then it has completed its connec-

---

[134] These are signs "in aversion" to a place. In Figure 111, the signs in aversion to Aquarius (where Saturn is) are Pisces, Cancer, Virgo, and Capricorn.
[135] Or, "in accordance with" (على قدر).
[136] مقارنة. See **10-24**. For many years I have translated this word as "assembly," although in Latin and later English astrology this came to be "conjunction" (Lat. *coniunctio*). "Conjunction" is a valid translation, but it connotes something more exact and close by degree. The Arabic describes a greater variety of ways in which planets can be physically together, from simply being in the same sign (which in Greek is called "co-presence"), to being within about 15° degrees of each other (see **12**), to being joined exactly. So I am going to stick with "assembly," but on occasion when it really seems appropriate I use "conjunction."
[137] See **25-33**.

tion. **12** And the beginning of the power of the connection by assembly, and mixing the nature of the connecting one with the connected one, is when there are 15° between them; and the more that one of them gets near its associate the stronger it is, until they are united. **13** And this is when they are in a single sign.[138]

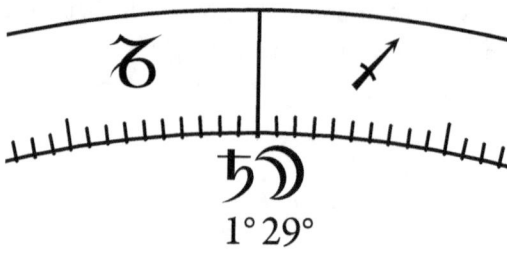

Figure 113: Mixing natures across signs (VII.5, 14, 23, 32)

14 But if they were in two different signs, and there were few degrees between them, that is not counted as a "connection by assembly," but they are both "mixing their natures" in a weak way.[139]

15 Now if one planet assembled with several planets in varying degrees, and it is lighter than them, then it will connect with the nearest one ([that is], the one nearest it).

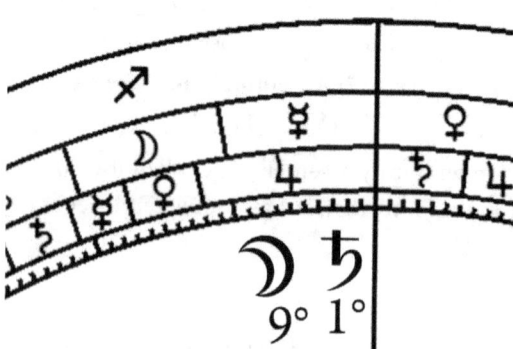

Figure 114: Moon separating, still strongly in nature of Saturn (VII.5, 18)

16 And if the light one passed by the slow one by one minute or by less than that, then it has already [3] SEPARATED from it. **17** And if one planet separated from another by assembly, and it is not connecting with <another> planet, then one of them will be "in the nature" of its partner so long

---

[138] See VII.4, **3**.

[139] Note well: there are no "out-of-sign" conjunctions (and likewise no out-of-sign aspects). See also VII.4, **3** and **13-14**, and VII.5, **22-23**. Ch. VI.3 also discusses the exact aspects.

as it is in the sign in which they united.[140] **18** And the strongest that the mixture of their natures could be, is if they were both in one bound, and not distant from each other by the amount of one-half of the body of the one in fewer degrees.[141] **19** So if one of them left the bound in which they were united, it is weaker for their mixture; and if in addition they were distant from each other by more than the amount of one-half of their bodies, it is weaker for the mixture of their natures. **20** And if, upon its separation from it, *another* planet encounters it before it leaves the bound in which they had both united, or before it is distant from the first planet by the amount of one-half of the body of the one in fewer degrees, then the light planet will be in the nature of *two* planets: the one it separates from and the one it connects with.[142] **21** And when it has separated from the second planet by body, its condition with it will be like its condition with the first planet it had separated from.

22 And if a number of planets united, and they were in a single degree and minute, or they were assembled by degree, then some of them will share in the natures of others; and each one of them will remain in the power of the nature of the other one until it is distant from it by the amount of one-half of its body.

23 And if their uniting was at the end of a sign, then the power of one-half of their two bodies will be in the sign which follows them;[143] and when the light one of the two changes over to the next sign, then it will remain "in the

---

[140] That is, it will carry the management until something else happens: another connection, or a change of sign.

[141] In Figure 114, the Moon has separated from Saturn. But because she is still in the same bound (i.e., Jupiter's), and because she is not separated by more than one-half of Saturn's body or orb (i.e., 9°), she is still "strongly" in the nature of Saturn until she leaves the bound or separates by more than 9°, and especially if something else happens to her.

[142] That is, until it completes the connection with the second planet: see **34-37**.

[143] In Figure 115, the Moon and Saturn have completed their connection at 29° Sagittarius. The power of their bodies extend into Capricorn: Saturn extends 9°, to 8° Capricorn; the Moon extends 12°, to 11° Capricorn.

nature" of its associate until it is distant from it by the amount of one-half of its body—except that this way of mixing their natures is weak.[144]

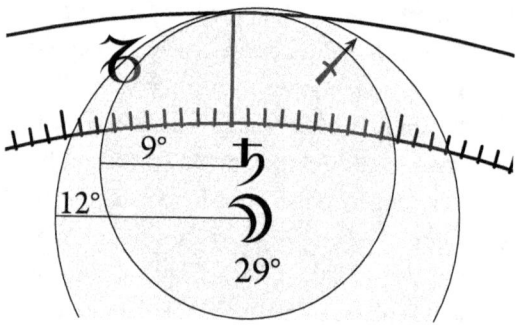

Figure 115: Assembly at end of sign, bodies extend into next sign (VII.5, 23)

24 And sometimes at the assembly both of the two planets will be retrograde, or one of them will be retrograde and the other direct: the connection of one of them with the other, and its separation from it, will be by retrogradation.

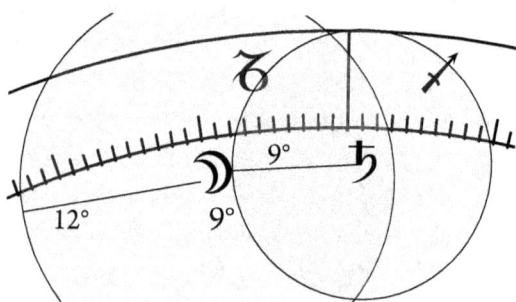

Figure 116: Moon leaving the nature of Saturn (VIII.5, 23)

---

[144] In Figure 116, the Moon has passed over to 9° Capricorn, beyond the power of Saturn's body: so even if we allow that Saturn is mixing with her nature (since her orb still covers him), she no longer mixes directly with his. This is a weak mixture.

[Connecting by looking or aspect]

25 And as for the connection by aspect in longitude, it is that the planets are in the signs which see each other from the sextiles, squares, trines, or opposition. **26** And if they were like that, then the one quick in motion goes to the connection of the slow one, until the quick one comes to be, in *its* sign, in the same degree and minute as the slow planet is in *its* sign: and when it comes to be like that, it has completed its connection.[145]

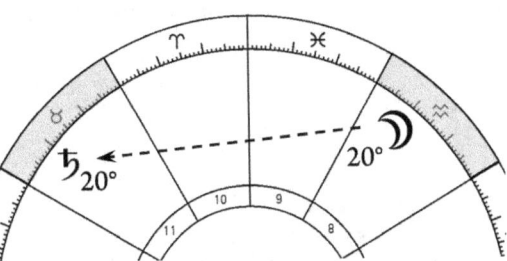

Figure 117: Square connection from signs which see each other (VII.5, 25-26)

27 And the beginning of the power of the connection by aspect is when there are 12° between the two planets: and the more that one of them comes near its associate by [an exact] aspect, it is stronger for it.

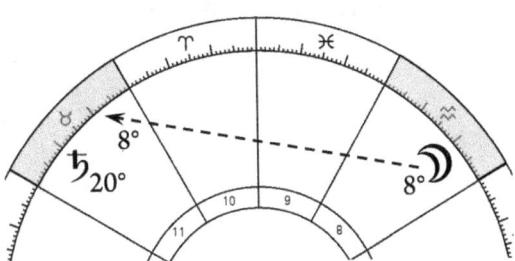

Figure 118: The power of the square connection begins (VII.5, 27)

---

[145] In Figure 117, the Moon and Saturn are in signs which see each other by square. The Moon completes a square connection by degree when she moves into the exact degree and minute in her sign, as Saturn is in his sign (20°). Note that this means there are no "out-of-sign" aspects, because the signs themselves form the basis for the aspects. For example, if the Moon were at 27° Aquarius and cast an exact sextile into 27° Aries, and Saturn were at 1° Taurus, modern astrologers would consider this an "out-of-sign" sextile. But because he is in Taurus, which sees Aquarius from a square, he can *only* have a square connection with her. See also **32-33** below.

28 And sometimes a planet will be going to the connection of a planet by assembly or aspect, but will not catch up to it in its sign before they are both changed over to the sign which follows them.[146]

[*Multiple planets*]

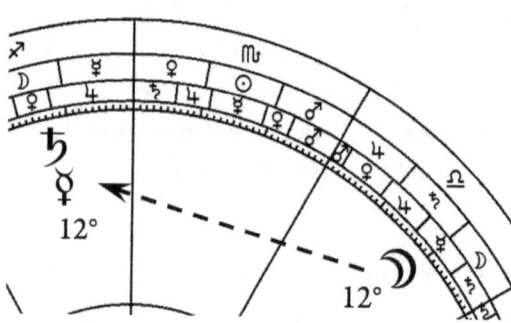

Figure 119: Moon connects with Saturn first (VII.5, 29)

29 And when two planets are in a single degree and minute, and [another] planet connects with them both, then its connection with them both is considered to be first of all with the planet which has more shares in the sign handing over (of the house, exaltation, bound, triplicity, or face), but then after that its connection will be with the other planet.[147]

---

[146] See the related condition "Escape," in **119** below. Note that aspect rays are not given specific "orbs," because they are not bodies with a glow of power around them (unlike planets). The distance of 12° may be analogous to the Moon's own body, as the 15° distance for an assembly may be analogous to the Sun's body.

[147] In Figure 119, the Moon hands over her management by a sextile connection to Mercury and Saturn, who are conjoined exactly. Saturn has more dignities in the place where the Moon is (exaltation, face, triplicity), than Mercury does (bound, triplicity). Therefore, she connects with Saturn "first." The source of this interest is probably elections and questions, because we want to know whether the Moon connects with the planet we want, or is being blocked from doing so. In **93** below, just this sort of blocking scenario is considered: so if we wanted her to connect with Saturn in this chart, she would be doing it. Note that this rule is also an example of reception (**129-30**).

30 And if two planets connected with some [other] planet from a single degree and minute, then that one of the two which has more claims in the sign of the planet accepting their connection will be considered the first one in connection with it.[148] **31** (And the lord of the bound will take precedence over the rest of the claimants, when their claims are equal.)

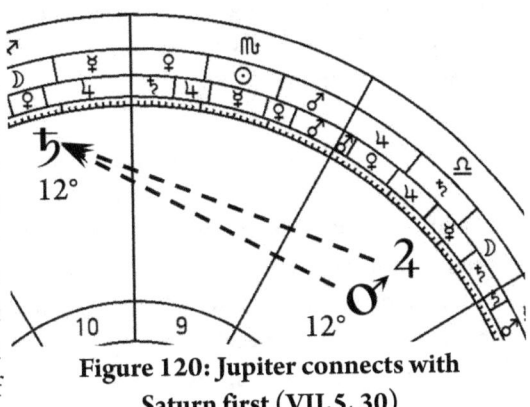

Figure 120: Jupiter connects with Saturn first (VII.5, 30)

[No out-of-sign aspects]

32 And if the light planet was at the end of the sign, empty in course, with the power of one-half of its body having already gone to the next sign from it, and the rays of some other slow planet are at the beginning of that sign (which the light one is being changed into), and they are not looking at each other, then the mixture of their natures will be small, and the light one will not

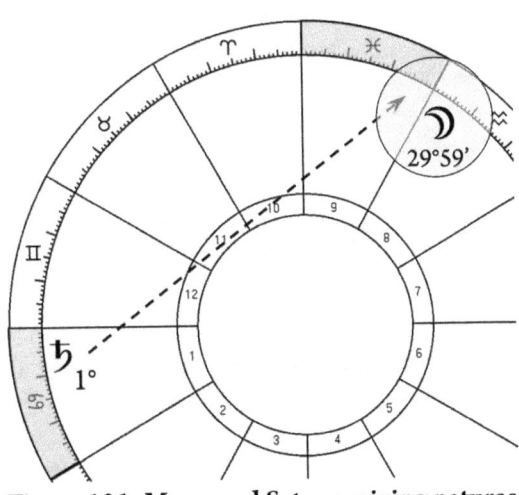

Figure 121: Moon and Saturn mixing natures until sign changes (VII.5, 32-33)

---

[148] In Figure 120, Mars and Jupiter are conjoined exactly, and both are faster than, and handing over management to, Saturn. Jupiter has more dignities in Saturn's position than Mars does, so Jupiter connects with Saturn "first." Again, this is an example of reception (**129-30**).

be reckoned as connecting with the slow one until it is changed over to the other sign. **33** But upon its changing over and looking at it, the light one will be connecting with the slow one.[149]

[Separating and connecting with a new planet]

34 And[150] in all of this, when one of them goes beyond its associate by 1' or less, then it has already separated from it—except that they will both be blending in nature. **35** And if the light one does not encounter the body of a planet or its light [by aspect] in that sign, then the one of them will remain in the light of the other so long as the quick one is in that sign it is in. **36** (And the strongest blending of their two natures upon separating is before it separates from it by a complete degree). **37** But if the light one *does* encounter a planet in that sign (by its body or its light), then upon completing its connection with the other one it will depart from the nature of the planet which it has separated from by looking, and will be in the nature of the planet it connects with: because the condition of the connection by assembly is different from the condition of the connection by looking.

[Connection by latitude]

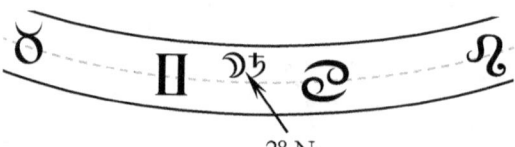

Figure 122: Connection in latitude by assembly (VII.5, 39)

38 Now as for the connection of the planets with each other by latitude, it is in three ways. **39** One of them is a connection by assembly, and it is that the two planets are united and

---

[149] In Figure 121, the Moon is about to change signs, and the power of her body or orb is in the next sign. Saturn cannot see her yet because their signs are in aversion (**32**), so they can only weakly mix their natures. But when she moves into Pisces, she will connect properly with him by trine (**33**).

[150] The next few sentences seem to combine the scenario just described (**32-33**) with doctrine that connecting by body is more powerful than connecting by ray (**93-94** below). The point is that when a planet separates and then connects with something else, that new planet's influence will take over.

Book VII: Conditions & Indications of the Planets 453

their latitude is the same, on one side [of the ecliptic], and one of them eclipses the other.

40 The second way is a connection by opposition, and it is that the two planets are opposing each other and one of them is rising up in the north, and the other coming down in the north (or one of them is rising up in the south and the other is coming down in it), and the degrees of their latitude are the same.

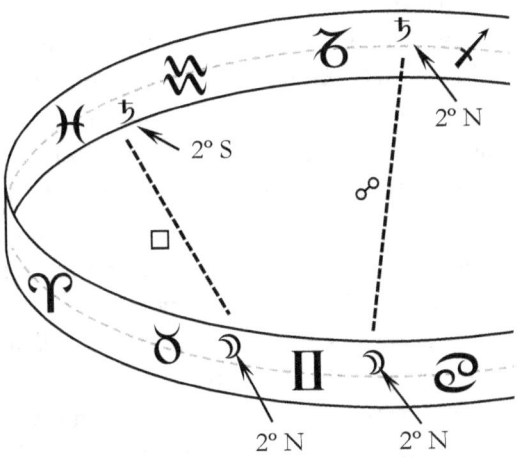

Figure 123: Connection in latitude by opposition (VII.5, 40-41)

41 The third type of connection by latitude is that the two planets are looking at each other from the six directions (and they are the two sextiles, squares, and trines), and one of them is rising up in the north and the other coming down in the south, or one of them is rising up in the south and the other coming down in the north.

42 And in these three ways one looks at the one with fewest degrees of latitude: when it has reached the more distant degrees of its latitude which overtake the degrees of latitude of the other planet with greater latitude (whether it is heavier or lighter than it), then it connects with it by latitude. **43** For when its latitude comes to be the same as the latitude of that planet, then its connection with it is complete. **44** But when its latitude increases beyond that, then it has separated from it in latitude, except that the one of them will remain in the power of the nature of its associate (on the side of its connection with it by latitude), so long as the two planets are on the [same] side [in] which the one of them connected with its associate. **45** For when the two sides become different or one of them begins to rise up and the other to come down, then the one of them has already departed from the power of the nature of the other in latitude.

46 And the connection of the planets in latitude has another type: and it is that one looks at the two planets: for when they look at each other so that the northern one of them is adding in the degrees of its latitude beyond the place in which it is, and the southern one is decreasing in the degrees of its latitude, in the direction of its place,[151] then one sees how many degrees are between them in longitude after that. **47** For if there are less than 60° (or 90°, or 120°, or 180°) between the light one and heavy one, then the light one connects with the heavy one. **48** But if the same[152] [amount] of degrees which we mentioned concerning this were between them, then its connection with it is already completed. **49** And if there were more than that between them, then it has already separated from it.[153]

50 And sometimes there is a connection of a planet with one planet in longitude, and with another planet by latitude. **51** And because of this Dorotheus said:[154] If a slave ran away and there was a connection of the Moon with Mars in longitude, but with Jupiter in latitude (or with Jupiter in longitude and with Mars in latitude), then due to the connection with Mars in one of the ways it indicates finding the runaway; and due to her connection with Jupiter in the other way it indicates that his master will be pleased with him,[155] and he will escape punishment.

52 And the most firm connection and separation is if it was with the lord of its bound, house, exaltation, triplicity, or face; and stronger than that is if it

---

[151] Or more literally, "is subtracting the degrees of its latitude in its region from its place." I think this simply means that the planet with northern latitude is becoming more northern, and the planet with southern latitude is also heading north towards it, so that its own degrees in southern latitude are becoming fewer.

[152] مثل. Or rather, the "exact" same amount.

[153] The idea here seems to be that the absolute number of degrees between them is like a fudge factor, so that the amount of latitude can be added to their longitude in a way similar to a normal aspect.

[154] See *Carmen* V.37, **31-32**. 'Umar's version has the Moon connecting with Mars in latitude but Jupiter connecting with *Mars* by longitude, although later in the sentence it does have Jupiter looking at the Moon. Abū Ma'shar's reading is neater, but neither agrees with the Greek prose version in Heph. III.47, **23-24**. There, Hephaistion has a totally different scenario involving (for example) the Moon post-ascending Mars while Mars sets, and Jupiter looking at her.

[155] يرضى عنه. This does not seem psychologically correct, nor does Hephaistion or 'Umar's Dorotheus say that. **BY** read this as Form IV ("reconciled with"), but the preposition ى and shows that it is Form I.

happened to be a connection by longitude and latitude at the same time with a single planet, for in that case their indication will not diverge.

[Connection by signs with equal ascensions]

53 And[156] another type of connection and separation [even][157] *without* the planets' looking at each other is said to be a "natural connection and separation," and indeed the scholars among the astrologers used them in the special characteristics pertaining to[158] the conditions of nativities and questions. **54** As for the everyday[159] ones among them, they used to reject the understanding of it due to their coarseness and its difficulty for them, and so because they didn't understand it, they threw out the use of it. **55** But the ancients among the people of Persia, Babylon, and the Egyptians certainly mentioned it in their famous books known as the *Bizidajāt*,[160] and others—and it is of two types:

56 One of them is from the nature of the degrees of the signs corresponding in ascensions, such as Aries and Pisces, Taurus and Aquarius, Gemini and Capricorn, Cancer and Sagittarius, Leo and Scorpio, and Virgo and Libra. **57** So when a planet is in the first degree of Aries, then it is in the nature of a planet which is at the last degree of Pisces, and is connecting with it by a "natural connection." **58** And if a planet in Aries was in less than 10°, then it goes to the connection with the nature of the degree of the planet which is in Pisces, in 20°, until the 10° are completed for it: for there it completes its connection with the nature of the degree of the planet which is in Pisces in 20°, due to the correspondence of their degrees in ascension. **59** And if it was in Aries in 11°, then it has already separated from the nature of the planet

---

[156] For this subsection, see VI.5, **2-4** and its Figure.
[157] I add this because some of the signs of equal ascensions below do look at each other.
[158] في خواصّ من.
[159] Lit. "public" (الجمهور), but reading more as a contrast with "scholars."
[160] That is, the "Anthologies" (Pers.). This may refer to the book attributed to Buzurjmihr, which at least contained material by Valens and Dorotheus (as can be seen in *ASB1*).

which is in that degree,[161] and its connection will be with the nature of the degree of the planet which is in Pisces in less than 20°, until the planet which is at the end of Aries is in the nature of the planet which is at the beginning of Pisces.

60 And the one at the beginning of Taurus is in the nature of the degree of the planet which is at the end of Aquarius.

61 And the planet which is at the beginning of Gemini is in the nature of the degree of the planet which is at the end of Capricorn. **62** And the planet which is in 12° of Gemini is in the nature of the degree of the planet which is in 18° of Capricorn: so when it passes beyond 12° of Gemini, then it has separated from it and comes to be in the nature of the planet which is in less than 18° of Capricorn. **63** And the planet which is at the end of Gemini is in the nature of the degree of the planet which is at the beginning of Capricorn.

64 And the planet which is in the first degree of Cancer is in the nature of the degree of the planet which is in the last degree of Sagittarius, due to their correspondence in ascensions. **65** So when it comes to be in more degrees of Cancer, then it comes to be in the nature of the planet which is in less than 29° of Sagittarius, until the planet which is at the end of Cancer is in the nature of the planet which is at the beginning of Sagittarius.

66 And the planet which is at the beginning of Virgo is in the nature of the degree of the planet which is at the end of Libra, and the planet which is at the end of Virgo is in the nature of the degree of the planet which is at the beginning of Libra: and that is due to the correspondence of the ascensions of these degrees to each other.

[Connection by antiscia or signs "agreeing in power"]

67 And the second type is from the degrees of the signs corresponding in the hours of the day:[162]

68 For the planet which is in the last degree of Gemini is in the power of the degree of the planet which is in the first degree of Cancer, and the planet which is in 12° of Gemini is in the power of the degree of the planet which is

---

[161] Namely, the one in 20° Pisces.

[162] These are the degrees of antiscia, or "agreeing in power." See the Figure for VI.5, **6-11**.

in 18° of Cancer, and the planet which is at the beginning of Gemini is in the power of the degree of the planet which is at the end of Cancer. **69** And the planet which is at the beginning of Leo is in the power of the degree of the planet which is at the end of Taurus. **70** And the planet which is at the end of Aries is in the power of the degree of the planet which is at the beginning of Virgo, until the planet which is at the beginning of Aries is in the power of the degree of the planet which is at the end of Virgo. **71** And the planet which is at the beginning of Libra is in the power of the degree of the planet which is at the end of Pisces. **72** And the planet which is at the end of Libra is in the power of the degree of the planet which is at the beginning of Pisces. **73** And the planet which is at the beginning of Sagittarius is in the power of the degree of the planet which is at the end of Capricorn. **74** And the planet which is at the end of Sagittarius is in the power of the degree of the planet which is at the beginning of Capricorn. **75** And indeed it comes to be like that due to the correspondence of every degree of them with the others in the length of the hours of the day.

[Connection by "natural" aspects from aversion]

76 And the connection of the planet which is in Gemini with the degree of the planet which is in Capricorn, or the one which is in Sagittarius with the one in Cancer, or the one in Aries with the one in Virgo, or the one in Libra with the one in Pisces, is called a "natural connection by opposition."[163]

77 And the connection of the one in Gemini with the one in Cancer (or the one in Virgo with the one in Libra, or the one in Sagittarius with the one in Capricorn, or the one in Pisces with the degree of the planet which is in Aries), is called the "natural connection by sextile."[164]

---

[163] See the Figure for VI.6, **4**. Abū Ma'shar omits here the Aries-Scorpio and Taurus-Libra connection, which is by "agreeing in manner."
[164] See the Figure for VI.6, **5**. Abū Ma'shar omits here the Aquarius-Capricorn connection, which is by "agreeing in manner."

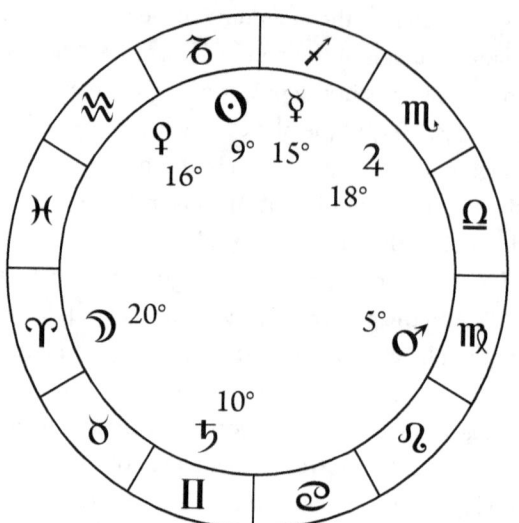

78 [4] EMPTINESS OF COURSE is that a planet separates from the connection of a planet (by assembly or looking), and will not connect with a planet so long as it is in its [current] sign.[165]

Figure 124: Emptiness of course (VII.5, 78)

---

[165] In Figure 124, the Moon has separated from several exact connections, and will not connect with any other planet by body or ray, so long as she is in Aries.

79 [5] WILDNESS is if a planet is in a sign such that absolutely no planet looks at it: so if it was like that, it is called "wild."[166] **80** And that happens mostly to the Moon, even though her connection is made with the lords of the bounds in which she is: so for as long as she is in the bound of a planet, she is counted as being connected with the lord of that bound. **81** So when she goes out of it into another bound, then she has separated from it and connected with the lord of the bound which she has shifted into.

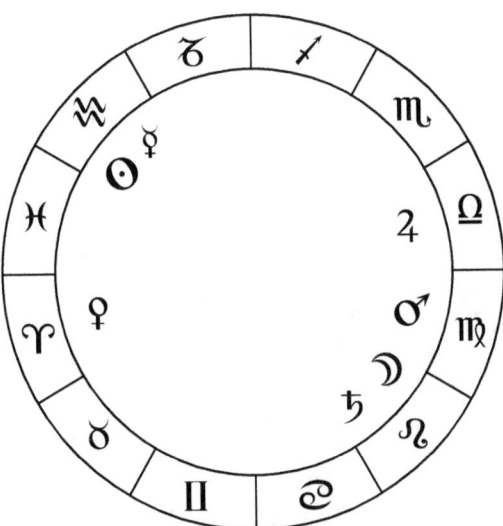

Figure 125: Wild Mars (VII.5, 79)

82 And sometimes this type of connection and separation is used for a planet empty in course.

---

[166] In Figure 125, Mars is wild because he is in aversion to all other planets: thus, no planet looks at him.

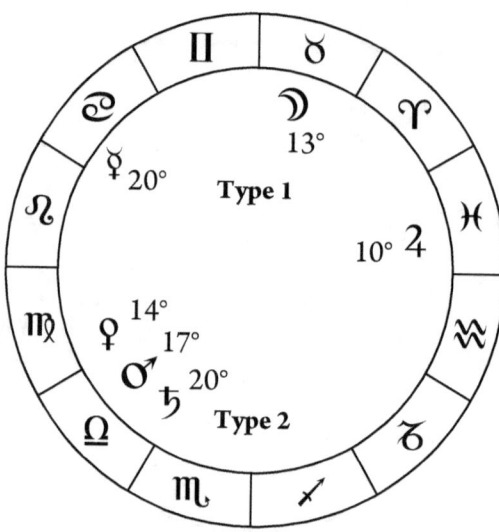

Figure 126: Transfer (VII.5, 83-85)

83 [6] TRANSFER is of two types.

84 One of them is that the light planet separates from the slow one, and then connects with another so that it transfers the nature of the one it is separating from, to the one it connects with.[167]

85 And the second is that a light planet connects with a planet slower than itself, and that slow one connects with [yet] another planet, so that the slow planet shifts the nature of the light planet over to the [third] planet which it connects with.[168]

---

[167] In Figure 126, suppose we want Mercury and Jupiter to connect (Type 1). They see each other by trine, but Mercury has already separated by degree. However, the Moon sees them both, separating from Jupiter and connecting with Mercury, transferring the light from Jupiter to Mercury. Thus, the Moon is saving a connection that is failing due to the separating Mercury.

[168] In this same Figure, Venus is connecting with Mars, but he is already connecting with Saturn, so he transfers the management of Venus over to Saturn (Type 2). Unlike Type 1, Saturn is not separating from anyone, and Mars is acting as intermediary for a Venus-Saturn connection which is already underway.

86 [7] COLLECTION is if two planets (or more than that) connect with a single planet, so that it collects their light, and takes up their natures.[169]

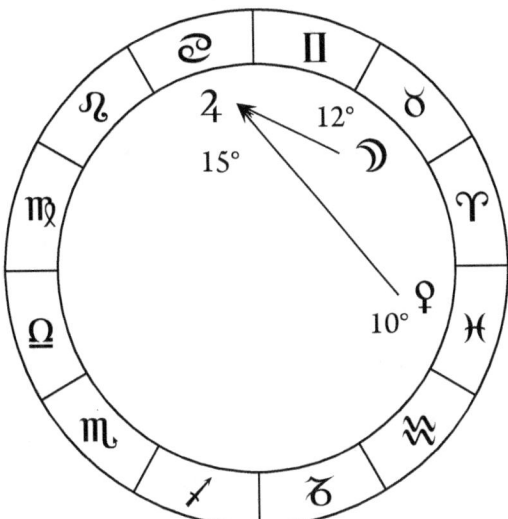

Figure 127: Collection (VII.5, 86)

---

[169] In Figure 127 we might want the Moon and Venus to connect, but the Moon is already separating from the sextile of Venus. However, they both connect with Jupiter, a slower planet in a later degree. He collects their light and joins their management through his own activity and significations.

87 [8] REFLECTION OF LIGHT is of two types.

88 One of them is that a planet (or two planets) one seeks a signification from is not connecting with its associate, nor are they looking at each other, but they *are* both looking at [another] planet (or connecting with it), so that the planet which is being looked at or connected with sees one of the places of the circle, and reflects the light of the two to that place which it looks at.[170]

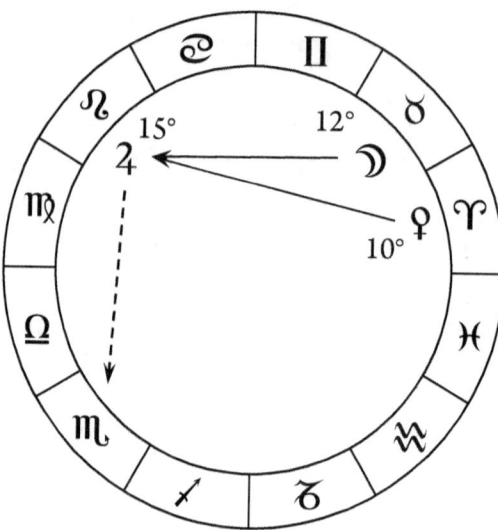

Figure 128: Reflection as collection from aversion (VII.5, 87-88)

---

[170] This kind of reflection is meant to act as collection (**86**), but for two planets in aversion. In the figure for collection above, Venus and the Moon could see each other, their only problem was that they were separating. But in Figure 128 they are in aversion: they both connect with Jupiter, who collects their light. He then acts as a reflection point, and moves their light on to some other place which is relevant to the question. So if this were a horary chart about making money in a job, Venus and the Moon indicate the querent and the job. But they do not see each other. However, Jupiter in the eleventh collects their light and reflects it on to the second house (Scorpio), bringing them together with the money.

89 And the second type is that the lord of the Ascendant and [the lord of] the sought matter are not looking at each other, or they are both separating, but a planet transfers between them both so that it reflects the light of one of them to the other.[171]

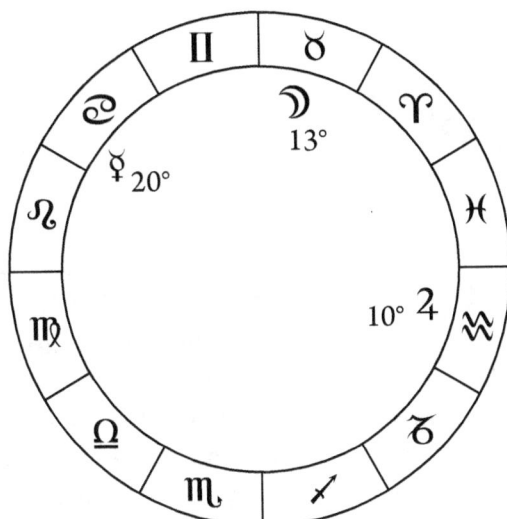

Figure 129: Reflection as transfer from aversion (VII.5, 89)

---

[171] This kind of reflection is a transfer of light (**83-85**), but for two planets in aversion. Compare this with transfer Type 1 (**84**): there, Jupiter and Mercury could see each other but Mercury was already separating. Now Mercury and Jupiter are in aversion, so they need another planet (here, the Moon) to reflect the light from Jupiter over to Mercury and complete the connection.

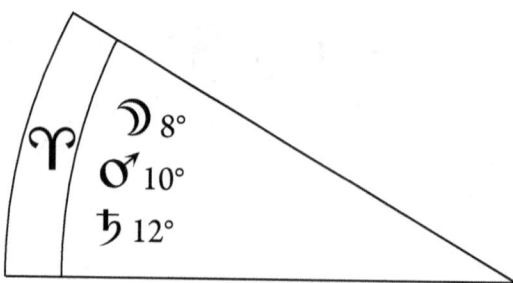

Figure 130: Blocking #1 (VII.5, 91-92)

90 [9] BLOCKING is of two types.

91 The first of them is by assembly,[172] and it is that three planets are in a single sign, in different degrees, and the heavy one has more degrees than [the other] two, so that the middle one blocks the one with the fewest degrees from connecting with the [first] heavy one, until it passes by it. **92** And[173] that is like if Saturn was in Aries, in 20°, and in it Mercury in 15°, and [also] in it Venus in 20°: so Mercury has blocked Venus from connecting with Saturn until he passes by [Saturn], and then after that will be the connection of Venus with Saturn.

---

[172] This version of blocking is the same as Sahl's Blocking #1 ("Intervention"), in *Introduction* Ch. 3, **35-37**.

[173] I have not used Abū Ma'shar's example for the Figure here, because the degrees are too close and the example inverts the role of Mercury and Venus. Instead, I have used Sahl's example in Figure 130. In Abū Ma'shar's version, Venus should be blocking Mercury, and after she passes by Saturn, Mercury will connect with Saturn. But Abū Ma'shar states it the other way around. Instead, in the Sahl version here the Moon wants to connect with Saturn, but she is blocked by the body of Mars. (Sahl's example is not the best either, because the Moon moves so quickly, she will pass by both of them before Mars fully connects with Saturn.) At first glance, this is the same as Transfer #2 (see **845** above), but it seems to me that the difference lies in what we want the planets to do. In a horary chart, if we wanted the Moon to connect with Mars, the connection would successfully complete but Mars would also be transferring and diverting the matter on to Saturn (which could be good or bad depending on the question). But if we wanted the Moon to connect with *Saturn*, then Mars is standing in the way and blocking (or in Sahl's language, "intervening" in) the matter, preventing it from occurring straightforwardly.

93 And the second type of blocking is from the manner of looking:[174] and it is that two planets are in a single sign, and the light one is connecting with the heavy one, and another, [third] planet connects with that heavy one by looking, <but by degree it is less than the light one which is uniting>:[175] thus the one with it in its sign blocks the one looking, and spoils its connection when the degrees of them both are the same.[176]

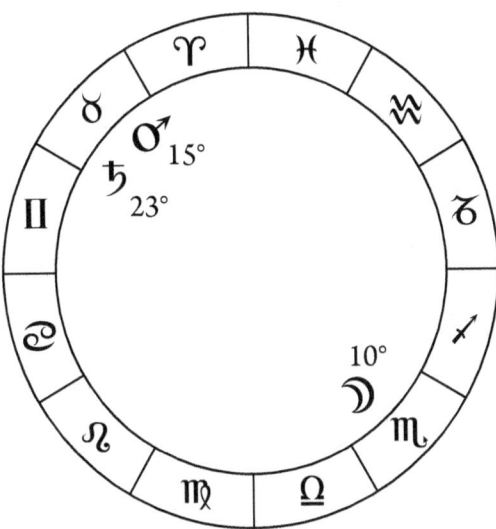

Figure 131: Blocking #2 (VII.5, 93-94)

94 But as for when the degrees of the one looking are closer to the connection [of the heavy one] than the degrees of the one joining [by body], the connection belongs to the one looking, because it connects with it before the one joining with it [by body].[177]

---

[174] This version of blocking is the same as Sahl's Blocking #3 ("Nullification"), in *Introduction* Ch. 3, **38-48**.

[175] I have added the material in brackets from Sahl's sentence **38** because it is key to understanding this type of blocking. See also **29** above, which anticipates this scenario.

[176] Again, I use the example from Sahl. Mars is the "light" planet, and seeks to connect with Saturn by body in the same sign. The Moon also wants to connect with Saturn, but is sending a ray from the opposition and is in fewer degrees than Mars. Thus Mars blocks her connection with his body. But Sahl adds another point (in his **44-48**), namely that a connection by body is more powerful than, and will block, a connection by aspect.

[177] This simply means that when the Moon's ray passes by Mars and no other planet blocks her, she will be able to connect with Saturn: this is what Sahl says in his **40**).

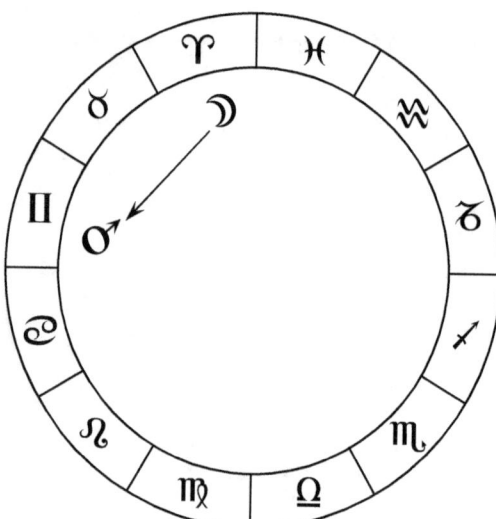

Figure 132: Handing over nature
(VII.5, 95)

95 [**10**] **HANDING OVER NATURE** is if a planet connects with the lord of the sign in which it is (or with the lord of its exaltation, the lord of its bound, the lord of its triplicity, or the lord of its face), so that it hands over the nature of that planet to it.[178]

---

[178] That is, it is handing over *the lord's own nature*, to the lord. In Figure 132 the Moon in Aries is handing over Mars's own nature back to him, because she is in his sign. The practical application of this is unclear, except perhaps that Mars's activity will be more hot and dry, or more powerful. This is an example of reception (**129**), but with a focus on *what* is being handed over rather than who is doing it.

96 [11] Handing over power is if a planet is in its own house (or exaltation, bound, triplicity, or face), and connects with another planet, so that it hands over *its own power* to it.[179]

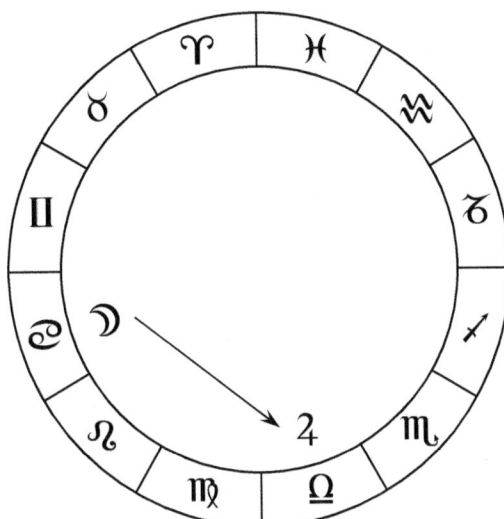

Figure 133: Handing over power (VII.5, 96)

---

[179] In Figure 133, the Moon in Cancer hands over her own power to Jupiter. My guess is that this means that whatever Jupiter is doing will have increased authority and power, because the Moon is fully behind and supporting his operation.

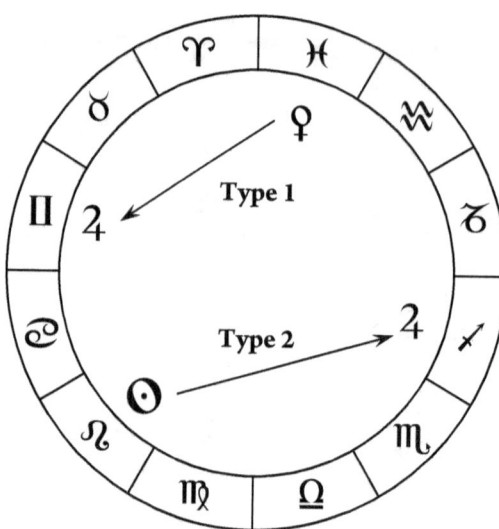

Figure 134: Handing over two natures (VII.5, 97-100)

97 [12] HANDING OVER TWO NATURES is of two types.

98 One of them is if a planet is in a sign in which it has a claim, and it connects with another one also having a claim in it. 99 And that is like Venus, if she connected with Jupiter from Pisces.[180]

100 And the second type is if a planet connects with a planet which is of its sect,[181] such as the connection of a diurnal planet with a diurnal one, and they are both in the place of a diurnal one; and [the connection of] a nocturnal one with a nocturnal one, and they are both in the place of a nocturnal one.[182]

---

[180] See Figure 134. Because Venus is in her own exaltation, she hands over power (**96**) to Jupiter; but because he is the lord of her sign, she is also handing over his nature (**95**).

[181] من حيّزه. Or, "of its *domain*."

[182] This seems to be a way of constructing the opposite of "counteraction," a negative condition where planets of one sect are in signs ruled by planets of the other sect, or similar situations. See Schmidt 2009, pp. 243-46.

101 [13] HANDING OVER MANAGEMENT is if a planet connects with a planet (of whatever type the connection is),[183] so that it hands over its own management to it. **102** Now if that was from a sextile or trine, and there was reception between them, that handing over is from harmony;[184] and from the assembly, if there was a blending between them, it is also harmony. **103** But if it was the contrary of what we stated, the handing over of management is not from harmony.[185]

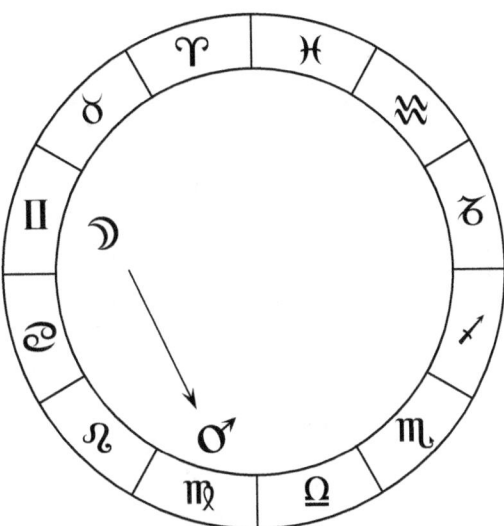

Figure 135: Handing over management (VII.5, 101-02)

---

[183] That is, no matter whether it is a conjunction or some other aspect. Compare this successful handing over, with the next category, in which the management is rejected and returned.

[184] مُلاءَمة. This can also mean "appropriateness" and "suitability."

[185] In Figure 135, I have made the Moon in Gemini hand over her management to Mars in Virgo, which is a handing-over without harmony due to the square (**103**).

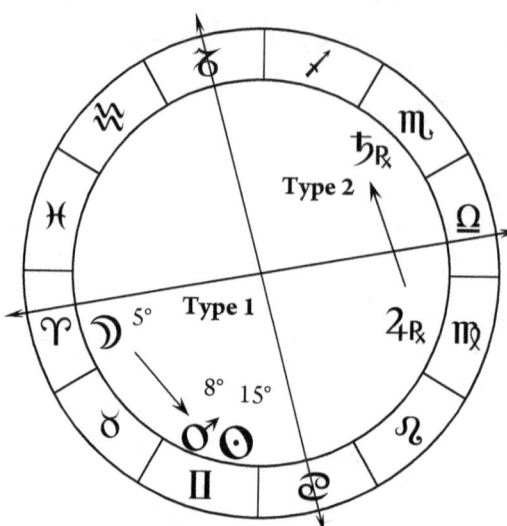

Figure 136: Returning with suitability and corruption (VII.5, 104-14)

104 [14] RETURNING[186] is of two types.

105 One of them is if a planet connects with a planet under the rays of the Sun, so that it is not able to hold onto what it accepts from it, and throws it back onto it.[187]

106 And the second one is if a planet connects with a retrograde planet, so that due to its retrogradation it returns to it what it accepted from it.[188]

107 And sometimes its returning is with suitability,[189] and sometimes corruption. **108** Now as for its returning with suitability, it is of three types. **109** One of them is if the one being handed over to receives the one handing over. **110** The second is if the one handing over is direct in motion, and the one being handed over to is burned or retrograde, with both of them being in a stake or what follows a stake. **111** And the third is if the retrograde [or] burned planet accepting [the management] is falling, and the planet handing over is in a stake or what follows a stake. **112** So if they were both like that, and the falling, burned, or retrograde one accepted the management, it will corrupt the sought matter—but when one accepting [the management] returns [it] to the one

---

[186] Or perhaps, "rejection" (الرَّدّ).
[187] In Figure 136, the Moon connects by sextile with Mars, who is burned under the Sun's rays and returns the management to her (**105**); but because he receives her and she is advancing or angular, it is returned with suitability or fitness (**109, 111**).
[188] In the Figure, Jupiter is connecting with Saturn, who is retrograde and so must return the management (**106**). But because Jupiter himself is both falling (or cadent) and retrograde, it is returned with corruption (**114**).
[189] Or, "fitness" (صلاح).

handing over, and the one handing over is in an excellent position, it will improve the sought matter after the corruption.

113 And as for its returning with corruption, it is of two types. **114** One of them is if the one handing over is falling, or[190] retrograde, or burned, <and> the one being handed over to is in a stake or what follows a stake: for when it returns to the one handing over what it had accepted from it (due to its [own] condition of retrogradation or burning), and does not take it on, the sought matter will be corrupted after [its] moving forward.[191] **115** And the second one is if the one handing over and the one accepting are both falling or burned,[192] so that it returns to it what it had accepted from it, due to the condition of its retrogradation or being under the rays: and its management is already corrupted, and the one handing over will not be able to take it up. **116** And that is when it indicates that the sought matter has neither a beginning nor end.[193]

117 [15] REVOKING is if a planet is connecting with a planet, but before it reaches it, it retrogrades away from it,[194] and its connection is nullified.[195]

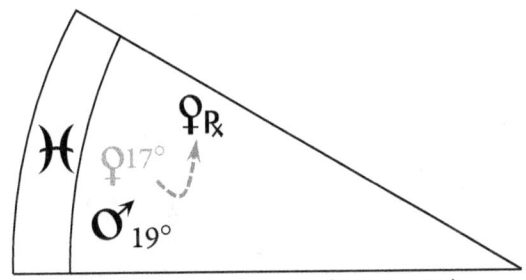

Figure 137: Revoking (VII.5, 117)

---

[190] Reading for "and."
[191] الاستقامة. Or, its being "set aright." Thus, events proceed as though normal, but then they are corrupted.
[192] Or probably, retrograde: see later in the sentence.
[193] This phrase shows that Abū Ma'shar is either reading Sahl (*Introduction* Ch. 3, **65**), or Sahl's source.
[194] That is, it turns retrograde.
[195] لطبيل. This is the same *word* which Sahl uses for his third type of blocking (*Introduction* Ch. 3, **38-44**), but it is not the same scenario.

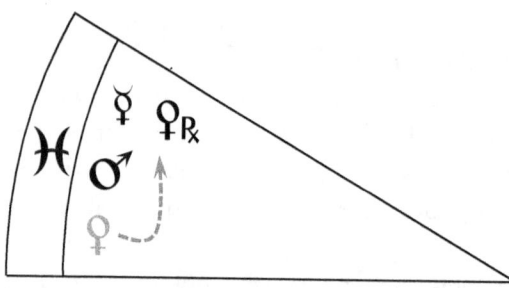

Figure 138: Resistance (VII.5, 118)

118 [16] RESISTANCE[196] is if there was a light planet in many degrees, and another planet heavier than it in fewer degrees, and a third planet lighter than that light one wanting a connection with the heavy one, so that the light one in more degrees goes retrograde and connects with the heavy one through its retrogradation—and then goes past it and there is a connection of that third one (which is lighter than the light one) with this retrograde one (which is heavier than it), not with the heavy one.

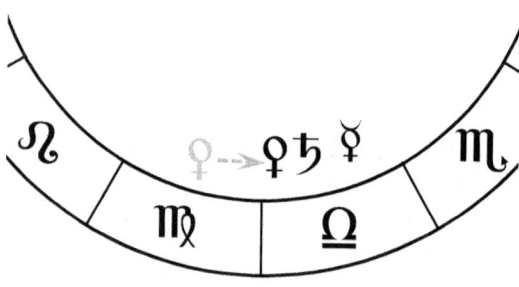

Figure 139: Escape (VII.5, 119)

119 [17] ESCAPE is if a planet is going towards the connection of a planet, but before it reaches it, the one it is connecting with shifts over to the next sign, and when the one handing over changes [to that next sign] there is one of the planets closer to it than [the first one], so its connection is with the other planet, and its connection with the first one is nullified.[197]

---

[196] الاعتراض, which also connotes "obstruction." In Figure 138, Mercury wants to connect with Mars. But Venus, who is in a later degree, suddenly goes retrograde, passes by Mars, and connects with Mercury, resisting and obstructing his attempt to connect with Mars.

[197] For "nullified," see the footnote for **117** above. In Figure 139, Venus in Virgo had wanted to connect with Mercury, who was at the end of the sign. But before she could complete the connection, Mercury passed into Libra (and went past Saturn). By the time Venus passes into Libra, she encounters the body of Saturn and connects with him, letting Mercury escape.

120 [18] CUTTING OF LIGHT is of three types.

121 One of them is if a planet wants a connection with a planet heavier than itself, and in the second sign from the light one is a planet, but before the light one reaches the connection with the heavy one, the planet which is in the

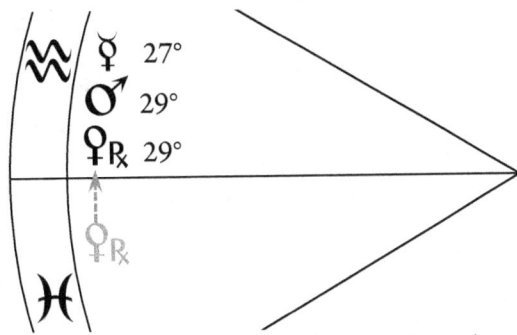

Figure 140: Cutting #1 (VII.5, 121-22)

second [sign] from it goes retrograde and enters its sign, and conjoins[198] with it, so it cuts off its light from that planet which had wanted a connection with it.[199] **122** And if that connection had indicated the completion of something, but then the condition of these two planets was like this (in terms of cutting the light of one of them from its associate), then it indicates that it prepares for the owner of the sought matter a man whom he was not paying attention to, so that he will corrupt his sought matter or cut him off from success in it.

123 And the second one is if a light planet is connecting with a planet heavier than itself, and that planet hands over to a heavy planet, but before the light one reaches the degree of the planet which is heavier than itself, that

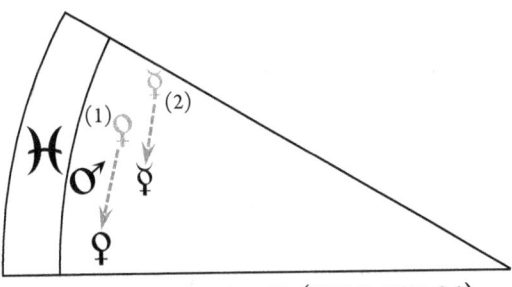

Figure 141: Cutting #2 (VII.5, 123-24)

---

[198] I take this to be a stronger sense of conjoining (i.e., by degree), rather than the looser "assembling."

[199] This is essentially resistance (**118**) or obstruction from the next sign. In Figure 140, Mercury wants to connect with Mars. But suddenly a third planet, Venus, retrogrades from the next sign and connects with Mars first. She will then connect with Mercury. It's hard to tell from the text which connection cuts off Mercury's light, but in the end I suppose it doesn't matter: Venus is interrupting the flow of events.

planet connects with the heavy planet and goes past it, so there is a connection of the light one with the heavy one, while it nullifies[200] its connection with the first one.[201] **124** And this indicates that the man will find, in his searching for the matter, something that is of the indication of the nature of that planet, and he will be eager for it, but when he is on the verge of achieving it, it will escape him and something else will happen to him.

125 And the third type is if a planet connects with a [different] planet apart from the lord of the sought matter, or a [different] planet connects with it, so that it transfers its light to the one other than the lord of the sought matter.[202]

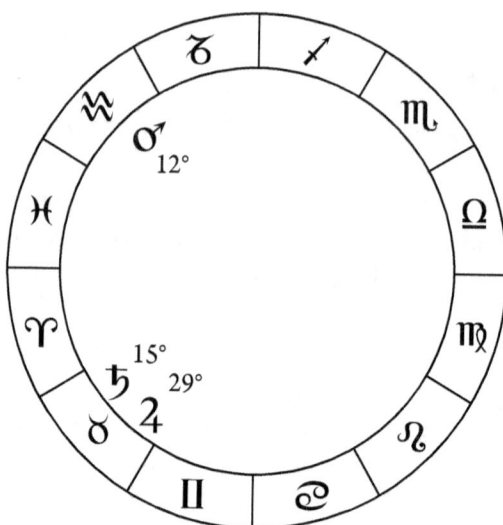

Figure 142: Cutting #3 (VII.5, 125)

---

[200] See footnote for **117** above for this word.

[201] This is a bit complicated. In Figure 141, Mercury wants to connect with Venus. But before he can do that, she connects with Mars and then continues on (1). Then Mercury is left with the conjunction of Mars (2), which was not what he wanted.

[202] In Figure 142, Mars wants to connect with Jupiter by square. But he connects with Saturn first, who cuts off his light from reaching Jupiter. At first glance this looks like Blocking #2 (**93**), which would make this cutting of the light redundant. But in Blocking #2, the two planets in the same sign must be connecting with each other, making their connection more important (especially since a connection by body outweighs one by aspect). Here, I have made Jupiter separate from Saturn so that it is not exactly the same scenario. It's possible that Cutting #3 is not really a distinct category but a variation on blocking, just as Handing over nature (**95**) is another way of talking about Reception (**129-30**).

126 [19] **Favor and** [20] **Recompense** is if there was a planet in its own well[203] or fall, and a planet connects with it (or it connects with a planet) which is friendly towards it, or one of the lords of its triplicities, or [one of] the claimants in its sign, or the one handing over or the one accepting has testimony in its own sign: for it will pluck it out and pull it out from its well or fall. **127** And [the first planet] will not cease to have favor

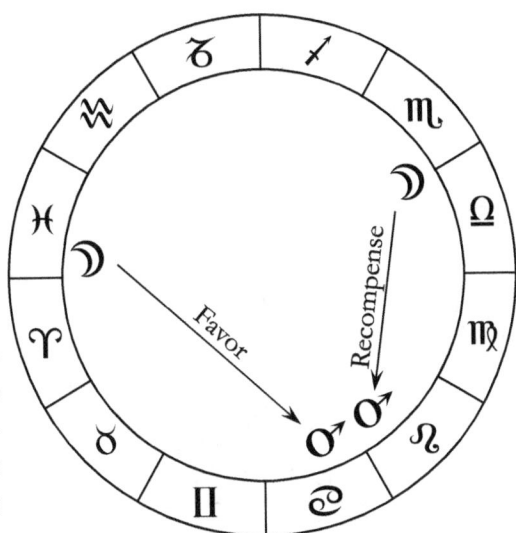

Figure 143: Favor and recompense (VII.5, 126-28)

for it[204] until the planet which had bestowed the favor on it falls into its own well or fall, and the other [planet] connects with it (or it connects with [the other]), and pulls it out of its well or fall: so it lives up to the favor which it had bestowed upon it, and compensates it for that.[205] **128** And sometimes the lord of the exaltation of the sign of the planet is called the "lord of its favor."

---

[203] For the wells, see Ch. V.21.
[204] Or feel devotion for it, or in other words "owe it a favor."
[205] In Figure 143, Mars is in his fall, and the lord of his sign (the Moon) connects with him, plucking him out of his fallen condition. Then a few weeks later, the Moon finds herself in her fall (Scorpio), and she connects with her lord Mars, who has passed into Aries. He pays back the favor by helping her. Both of these cases are instances of reception (**129-30**). However, note that these particular scenarios are also what Sahl would call "non-reception" (*Introduction* Ch. 3, **58-62**). Normally, a planet would not appreciate being connected to by the lord of its own fall—but perhaps the idea is that one should take help where one can get it, even if it involves a favor to be repaid. Since Abū Ma'shar allows other types of planet-dignity relationships here, other scenarios would not include non-reception.

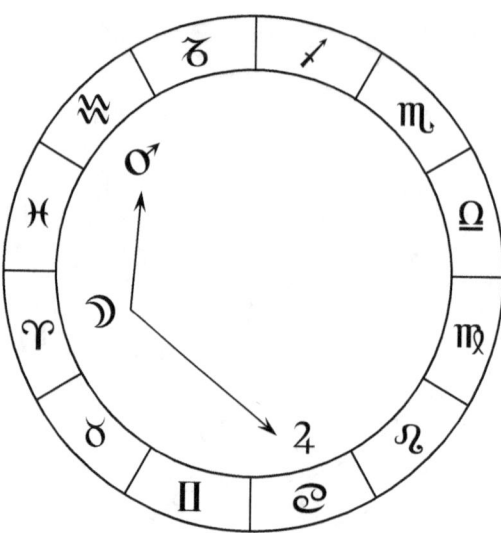

Figure 144: Reception (VII.5, 129-30)

129 [21] Reception is if a planet connects with a planet from the house of the one it connects with (or from its exaltation, bound, triplicity, or face), so that [its lord] receives it. **130** Or, a planet connects with a planet, and the one accepting the connection is in the house of the one handing over (or in the rest of its shares which we mentioned before).[206] **131** And the strongest of them is the lord of the house or exaltation. **132** But if the connection is with the lord of the bound, the lord of the triplicity, or the lord of the face alone, it is weak unless it brings together the bound and triplicity, or the bound and face, or the triplicity and face: for that will be a complete reception.[207] **133** And these claimaints also receive by looking (without a connection),[208] except that reception by connection is more powerful.

---

[206] This was also called "handing over nature" in **95**. In Figure 144, the Moon in Aries is connecting by sextile with Mars, the lord of the sign where she is (**129**), so he receives her into his house. The Moon also connects by square with Jupiter, who is in her house, so she receives Jupiter (**130**). The reason for this second type is that some planets are too slow to connect with their own lords on any regular basis: if the received planet always had to be the lighter planet and connect with its own lord, then Jupiter could only be received by Saturn while in Capricorn and Aquarius, and Saturn could never be received because he is too slow to connect with anyone (unless by retrogradation).

[207] According to Sahl in his *Introduction* Ch. 3, **54-55**, this statement about the lesser dignities is the view of Māshā'allāh.

[208] That is, there can be reception by whole-sign aspect alone.

134 And[209] if one of the two planets was in the trine of the other (or in its sextile), or in two signs of equal ascensions, or in two signs whose length of the day is one [and the same], or in two signs belonging to one [and the same] planet,[210] then one of the two will "receive" its associate due to the agreement of the nature of these signs with each other. **135** And the fortunes receive[211] each other due to the moderation of their natures, while Mars and Saturn each receive the other from the assembly, sextile, and trine.

136 And of reception, there is the [1] strong, the [2] middling, and [3] [what is] below that. **137** Now as for [1] strong reception, the majority of that belongs to the Moon relative to the Sun, because he receives her[212] from all signs, since her glow is from him—except that his reception of her from the opposition is detestable. **138** But if her connection with him is from a sign in which he has a claim, that is two receptions: a reception by nature, and a reception by sign.[213] **139** And if Mercury received a planet from out of[214] Virgo, that is also a strong reception. **140** And a [2] middling reception is the planets' reception of each other from the house, exaltation, bound, triplicity, or face.[215] **141** (But if two met [together] from this,[216] or each one

---

[209] In this paragraph, Abū Ma'shar turns to a more general sense of the Arabic word "reception" (قبول) which is *not* based on dignities: namely, that one planet will "accept" the management of another if they are in harmonious signs.

[210] These are the categories of signs which allow harmonization in Chs. VI.5-VI.6.

[211] Again, this should be read in the sense of "accept," here and with the infortunes later in the sentence.

[212] I would have expected Abū Ma'shar to say "she receives him," in the sense of taking on and reflecting his light.

[213] The "reception by nature" means it is due to her receiving a glow from him; "reception by sign" is the normal reception mentioned above in **129-30**.

[214] Reading more strongly than simply "from," since Abū Ma'shar seems to mean that the other planet is *in* Virgo: then Mercury would receive it by both house and exaltation.

[215] This is the normal reception in **129-32**.

[216] Abū Ma'shar seems to mean that one planet receives the other from two of the *dignities*. Remember that if one planet receives another by house or exaltation, it is a "complete" reception; but according to the statement here that is only average in the scheme of things. It takes two dignities or a mutual reception to be both complete and strong. (But this might be Abū Ma'shar quibbling over details.)

of them received its associate,²¹⁷ it is a strong reception.) **142** But as for the rest of what we mentioned,²¹⁸ it is [3] below that.

Chapter VII.6: On the planets' good fortune, strength, weakness, and misfortune, and the corruption of the Moon

1 As for the GOOD FORTUNE of the planets, it is that:

2 They are in the inspection²¹⁹ of the fortunes from the sextile, square, or trine, or are assembled with them.

3 Or the infortunes are falling away from²²⁰ them.

4 Or they are separating from a fortune and connecting with a fortune.

5 Or they are enclosed²²¹ between two fortunes.

6 Or [they are] in the heart.

7 Or [they are] in the inspection of the Sun from the trine or sextile.

8 Or [they are] in the inspection of the Moon while the Moon is made fortunate.

9 Or they are quick in motion, increasing in light and number.

10 Or they are in their *ḥalb*²²² (that is, in their houses, exaltations, bounds, triplicities, faces, or joys).

11 Or they are in the bright degrees.

12 Or they are received.

13 Or they are in their domains (I mean, that a male one is in a male sign or male degrees, by day above the earth and by night below the

---

²¹⁷ That is, mutual reception.

²¹⁸ Such as "reception" by signs of equal daylight, in **134**.

²¹⁹ مناظرة. In VI.3, Abū Ma'shar makes it clear this is by an exact aspect by degree (or perhaps very close to being exact?).

²²⁰ That is, "in aversion to."

²²¹ Or, "besieged." See **56-62**, especially **62**.

²²² حلب. Meaning uncertain. Here, Abū Ma'shar uses it as a synonym for "dignity" or "share," but in al-Qabīsī this is a sect-related rejoicing condition: that diurnal planets are above the earth in the day but below it by night, or that nocturnal planets are below the earth by day but above it by night. See al-Qabīsī I.78, or *ITA* III.2.

earth, or it is female, in a female sign or female degrees, by day below the earth and by night above the earth).²²³

14 And if the luminaries were in the shares of the two fortunes, for it is as though [the luminaries] are in their own shares (and likewise, if the two fortunes were in the shares of the luminaries).

15 And these good fortunes are of three types: [1] doubled good fortune, [2] being [merely] fortunate, and [3] [what is] less than that. **16** As for [1] doubled good fortune, it is if a single planet happens to have two of these claims (or more than that): and that is like Mercury if he was in Virgo, for he would have an indication over two good fortunes: the good fortune of the house, and the good fortune of exaltation. **17** Now if in addition he was in his bound, he would have an indication over three good fortunes. **18** And if the Ascendant was Virgo, he would have four good fortunes: the good fortune of the house, exaltation, bound, and joy.

19 As for [2] being [merely] fortunate, it is if a planet was in that house of its own in which its nature is moderated and agrees with it: such as Saturn in Aquarius, Jupiter in Sagittarius, Mars in Scorpio, Venus in Taurus, and the Sun and Moon in their own houses.²²⁴

20 And what is [3] below that in the indication of suitability, is if a planet is in that one of its two houses which is contrary to that: such as Saturn in Capricorn, Jupiter in Pisces, Mars in Aries, Venus in Libra, and Mercury in Gemini.²²⁵

---

²²³ See also VII.1, **37-39**.

²²⁴ These are also known as the planets' joys by sign. In all of these cases, the signs match the sect of the planet: Sagittarius is the diurnal house of the diurnal planet Jupiter, and so on. We might have expected Abū Ma'shar to list Mercury in Virgo here, since he has Mercury in Gemini in the next sentence; but he has already mentioned Mercury in Virgo as being even better in **17-19**. For the Hermes view of this, see Ch. V.4, **35-43** and the Figure there.

²²⁵ Again, see the view of Hermes in Ch. V.4, **35-43** and the associated Figure.

[The strength of the planets]

21 And the STRENGTH of the planets is:
22 If they are rising up in the north or are northern.[226]
23 Or they are rising up in the circle of their apogee.
24 Or they are in the second station.
25 Or [they are] going out of the rays of the Sun.
26 Or in a stake or what follows a stake.
27 Or the three superiors are eastern relative to the Sun (and if they look at him from the sextile it is stronger for them).[227]
28 And if <the superiors> are in the two male quadrants (and if the Sun was in these two quadrants or in the male signs, then he is also strong, unless he is in Libra).[228]
29 And concerning the strength of the three inferiors, it is if they are western or in the feminine quadrants.

[The weakness of the planets]

30 And concerning the WEAKNESS of the planets and their indication for the decrease of good fortune, it is if:
31 They are slow in course.
32 Or [they are] in the first station.
33 Or [they are] retrograde (and the more harmful retrogradation is the retrogradation of the two inferior planets—and especially if in addition to their retrogradation they are burned).
34 Or a planet is under the rays of the Sun.
35 Or [they are] in the dark degrees.
36 Or the male ones are in a female sign, or in the female degrees by day, under the earth, and by night above the earth (and if they were

---

[226] This is in ecliptical latitude.
[227] See VII.2, **17**.
[228] See IV.8, **16** for this and the next sentence.

BOOK VII: CONDITIONS & INDICATIONS OF THE PLANETS

the female ones, in a male sign or in the male degrees, by night under the earth and by day above the earth).[229]

37 Or it is in the sign of its fall.

38 Or [it is] going down in the south or is southern.[230]

39 Or [it is] falling from the stake or [from] what follows it.[231]

40 Or it is in the burned path (and that is Libra and Scorpio)—and harsher than that is if it was from 19° Libra up to 3° Scorpio, because those are the fall of the luminaries.

41 Or if it is in the opposition of its own house,[232] for at that time it will be hostile to its house, and in its "unhealthiness."

42 And if it connects with a planet [that is] retrograde, corrupted, in its own fall, or falling or withdrawing.

43 Or it is not received.

44 Or it is in exile[233] (and harsher than that is if it was empty [in course], with no fortune looking at it or planet being favorable to it).

45 Or if the three superior planets were western relative to the Sun, or they were in the feminine quadrants (and the weakness of the Sun is if he is in the feminine signs or in these two quadrants as well, unless he is in the ninth: for it is his joy).

46 And concerning the weakness of the three inferior planets, it is if they are at the beginning of their easternization, or they are in the two masculine quadrants.

---

[229] This is the contrary to **13** above, which was called a form of "good fortune"—we would therefore expect this condition to fall into the category of "bad fortune," not weakness.

[230] That is, in ecliptical latitude. But we should also include falling in the apogee, to parallel **23** above.

[231] That is, dynamically cadent; we would have expected him to use the term "withdrawing" here (زائلة), which suggests that he may mean a cadent whole sign instead.

[232] That is, in its detriment.

[233] That is, peregrine or alien.

[The misfortune of the planets]

47 The MISFORTUNE of the planets is if:

48 They are in the assembly of the infortunes, or in their opposition, square, trine, or sextile, and there are less than the bound of [a single] planet between them and the infortunes.

49 Or they are in the bounds of the infortunes, or in their houses.

50 Or one of the infortunes is elevated above them from the tenth or eleventh from their place[234] (and it is bad for that in all of this if the infortunes were not receptive of them).[235]

51 Or it is assembling with the Sun, or squaring or opposing him.

52 Or they are with the Heads of their own Dragons, or with their Tails, or they are with the Head or Tail [of the Moon's Dragon], and between them are 12° or less than that, because they will be in their Nodes.[236] **53** And the most harmful they can be for the Sun is if there were 4° between him and them (in front of him or behind), and the most harmful they can be for the Moon is if there were 12° between her and one of them, behind her or in front of her. **54** And some of the ancients claimed that the Head's nature is that of increase (so if the fortunes were with it, it increases in their good fortune, while if the infortunes were with it, it increases in their misfortune); and [they said] that the nature of the Tail is decrease (so if the fortunes were with it, it takes away from their good fortune, while if the infortunes were with it, it takes away from their misfortune). **55** And due to that, the generality of them said that the Head is a fortune with the fortunes, but an infortune with the infortunes; and the Tail is a fortune with the infortunes (because it takes away from their evil), but an infortune with the fortunes (because it takes away from their good fortune).

---

[234] This is "overcoming."

[235] غير قابل لها. I believe this simply means that "the infortunes do not receive them."

[236] Lit., "knots" (عقدتيهما).

56 And another misfortune is called "enclosure,"²³⁷ and it is of two types. **57** One of them is if a planet is in a sign, and with it in its sign is an infortune or its rays in front of it, and an infortune or its rays behind it—or, the planet is separating from an infortune by assembly or aspect, and connecting with the other infortune, in that [same] situation.²³⁸

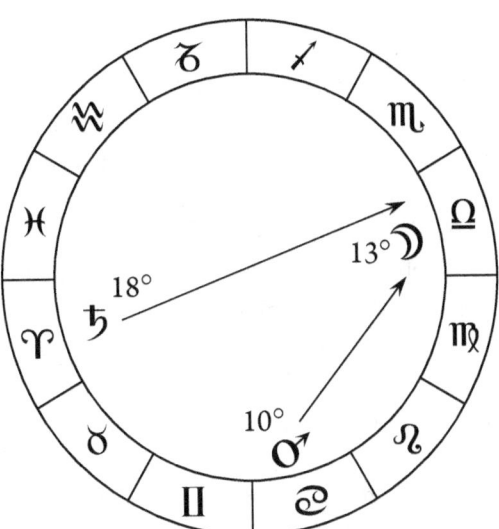

Figure 145: Enclosure or besieging by degree (VII.6, 56-57)

58 And the second type of enclosure is if a planet is in a sign, and an infortune is in the second sign from it (by its body or rays), and the other infortune or its rays is in the twelfth sign from it. **59** Now if it was not a planet in [the sign] but the situation of the Ascendant (or the rest of the signs) was like that, then the Ascendant or that sign will be enclosed.

60 And in both types,²³⁹ if the Sun or one of the fortunes looked at the enclosed planet, and there was less than 7° between the planet and those rays, then it indicates the dissolving of that misfortune. **61** And if the enclosed thing was itself a sign,²⁴⁰ and the fortunes or Sun looked at it, they will dissolve that misfortune.

62 But if the planet or sign was enclosed by the fortunes, then that is of superior good fortune.

---

²³⁷ Or, "besieging" (حصار).
²³⁸ Normally, the rays or bodies of the enclosing planets must be 7° or less on either side of the enclosed planet. See **60**, in which other planets can break the enclosure if they cast rays into this interval.
²³⁹ Actually this only refers to the degree-based type of enclosure, in **56**.
²⁴⁰ Such as the Ascendant: see **59**.

[The corruption of the Moon]

63 And the CORRUPTION OF THE MOON is in 11 ways:

64 One of them is if she is eclipsed, and harsher than that is if she is being eclipsed in the sign which she was in at the root of the nativity of a man, or in its trine or square.[241]

65 The second is if she was under the rays of the Sun, and there are 12° between her and his body in the front or in the rear.[242]

66 The third is if these same degrees were between her and the minute of his opposition, [whether she is] going towards his opposition or flowing away from it.[243]

67 The fourth is if she was with the infortunes or they were looking at her.

68 The fifth is if she was in the twelfth-part of Saturn or Mars.

69 The sixth is if she was with the Head or Tail, and there are 12° between her and one of them.

70 The seventh is if she was southern or going down in the south.[244]

71 The eighth is if she was in the burned path, and that is Libra and Scorpio.[245]

72 The ninth is if she was at the end of the signs, because at that time she will be in the bounds of the infortunes.

73 The tenth is if she was slow in motion, and it is when she goes at less than her mean motion.

74 And the eleventh is if she was in the ninth house from the Ascendant.[246]

---

[241] Cf. *Carmen* V.6, **3**, which however does not mention the square. (Nor does Hephaistion's version of Dorotheus in Heph. III.1, **3**.)

[242] See VII.2, **60-61** and **72-74**.

[243] See VII.2, **65-68**.

[244] That is, in ecliptical latitude.

[245] See also above, **40**.

[246] This would put her in the opposite of her joy, but offhand I'm not aware of this being a standardly-recognized concept.

Chapter VII.7: On the casting of the planets' rays, according to the work of Ptolemy

1 All of the masters of the stars have mentioned the casting of the planets' rays,[247] although many of them have differed from the others. **2** And we will state their disagreement about it in another book besides this one, but as for *this* book of ours we will state what Ptolemy (the author of the *Book of Judgments*)[248] said. **3** He said: If you wanted to know the casting of the planets' rays, then look at the planet to see in which of the quadrants of the circle it is.

4 For if the planet was between the Midheaven and the Ascendant, then take the right circle[249] of the degree of the Midheaven, and preserve it; then take the right circle of the degree of the planet, and preserve it. **5** Then, subtract the right circle of the degree of the Midheaven from the right circle of the degree of the planet, and divide what remains by the portions of the hours[250] of the degree of the planet: what comes out are the hours and minutes, and it is the distance of the planet from the Midheaven.

6 And if the planet was between the Ascendant and the stake of the earth, then take the right circle of the portion of the Midheaven, and the right circle of the degree of the planet, then subtract the right circle of the Midheaven from the right circle of the planet, and preserve what remains. **7** Then, take the portions of hours of the degree of the planet, multiply them by 6, and subtract them from what was preserved. **8** Divide what remains by the portions of the hours of the degree of the opposition of the planet, and what comes out are the hours and minutes, and it is the distance of the planet from the Ascendant.

9 And if the planet was between the stake of the earth and the setting, then take the right circle of the stake of the earth and the right circle of the degree of the planet, then subtract the right circle of the stake of the earth from the right circle of the degree of the planet. **10** Divide what remains by

---

[247] This is normally called "primary directions" in English-language astrology.
[248] That is, *Tetrabiblos* III.10 (Robbins pp. 291-95). But the method here is explained somewhat differently.
[249] Or rather, the right ascension.
[250] Or, the "hourly times" (Gr. *hōriaioi chronoi*), in *Tet.* III.10. This refers to special tables in the *Almagest*.

the portions of the hours of the degree of the opposition of the planet, and what comes out are the hours and minutes, and it is the distance of the planet from the stake of the earth.

11 And if the planet was between the stake of the setting and the Midheaven, then take the right circle of the stake of the earth and the right circle of the degree of the planet, then subtract the right circle of the stake of the earth from the right circle of the degree of the planet, and preserve what remains. **12** Then, take the portions of the hours of the degree of the opposition of the planet, and multiply them by 6, and subtract them from what was preserved. **13** Divide what remains by the portions of the hours of the degree of the planet, and what comes out is the distance of the planet from the stake of the setting.

14 Now if you knew the distances of the planets from the four stakes, and you wanted the casting of the rays of the sextile of a planet (or its square, or trine) towards the left, then *add* 60° to the right circle of the degree of the planet for the left sextile (and 90° for its square, and 120° for its trine), and enter what it amounts to into the [table of the] ascensions of the right circle, and take what is opposite it (of the degrees of equality of the sign in which it occurs),[251] and preserve it.

15 Then, take the ascensions of the degree of the planet, and also add to them 60° for its left sextile (and 90° for its square, and 120° for its trine), and enter what it amounts to into the arguments of the ascensions of that city which you want, and see what is opposite whichever portion occurs in the signs. **16** For if the ascensions of the right circle and the ascensions of the city[252] both occur opposite to[253] one [and the same] portion and minute, then the rays of the planet are in that degree and minute. **17** But if they differ, then understand which of them is increased over the other, and take the excess which is between them, divide it by 6, and multiply what comes out as its 1/6 by the hours of the planet's distance from the stakes. **18** Add the result to that one of the two positions which is nearest the planet by degrees of equality: if the ascensions were closer, then [add] to that; and if the right

---

[251] This refers to old tables in which the ascensions and zodiacal degrees are converted into their opposites.
[252] This refers to oblique ascensions.
[253] That is, they are equivalent to.

circle was closer to it, then [add] to that. **19** And whatever it comes to is the rays of the planet.

20 Now as for the right sextile, square, and trine, *subtract* from the ascensions of the right circle of the degree of the planet, and from the ascensions of its degree in the city for the sextile, square, and trine, the same degrees which we stated, and work with that and the hours of distance just as we said. **21** And whatever comes out, add it to the more *distant* of the two places from the planet by degrees of equality: and whatever it comes to is the rays of the planet. **22** But as for the opposition, [a planet] casts its ray into the opposition of its sign, in the same degree and minute.

Chapter VII.8: On knowing the years of the planets' *fardārs*, and their mighty, greater, middle, and lesser years

1 The planets have recognized numbers, some of them called *fardārs* and some of them years, and we will state them here by way of an abbreviated report.

	Fardārs	Lesser	Middle	Greater	Mighty
♄	11	30	43 ½	57	265
♃	12	12	45 ½	79	427
♂	7	15	40 ½	66	284
☉	10	19	39 ½	120	1461
♀	8	8	45	82	1151
☿	13	20	48	76	480
☽	9	25	39 ½	108	520
☊	3				
☋	2				

Figure 146: Planetary years

2 But as for the reasons for them, we have stated them in the book in which it is necessary to mention them.

3 So, the *fardār* of the Sun is 10 years, the *fardār* of Venus 8 years, Mercury has 13 years, the Moon 9 years, Saturn 11 years, Jupiter 12 years, Mars 7 years, the Head 3 years, and the Tail 2 years: that is 75 years.

4 But as for their [planetary] years, they are of four kinds: the mighty, greater, middle, and lesser years:

5 As for their mighty ones, the Sun has 1,461 years, Venus 1,151 years, Mercury 480 years, the Moon 520 years, Saturn 265 years, Jupiter 427 years, and Mars 284 years.

6 As for their greater years, the Sun has 120 years, Venus 82 years, Mercury 76 years, the Moon 108 years, Saturn 57 years, Jupiter 79 years, and Mars 66 years.

7 As for their middle years, the Sun has 39 ½ years, Venus 45 years, Mercury 48 years, the Moon 39 ½ years, Saturn 43 ½ years, Jupiter 45 ½ years, and Mars 40 ½ years.

8 As for their lesser years, the Sun has 19 years, Venus 8 years, Mercury 20 years, the Moon 25 years, Saturn 30 years, Jupiter 12 years, and Mars 15 years.

Chapter VII.9: On the natures of the seven planets, and their special indications for existing things

1 In this chapter we want to state the natures of the seven planets, and especially their indication for existing things. **2** And not everything we state in this chapter (of the indication of each planet) will be gathered together within a single man, but sometimes many things of them will be gathered together in him, according to the condition of the planet in itself and its condition in the houses of the circle.

Saturn:

3 As for Saturn, his nature is cooling, drying, black bile, dark, harsh in coarseness; but sometimes it is cooling [and] wet, heavy, stinking air.[254]

4 And he is of much eating, sincere in [his] affection, and indicates works of moisture, plowing, farming, the masters of villages, the cultivation of lands, building, waters and rivers, the appraising of things, the apportioning of lands, wealth and an abundance of assets, those working[255] with their hands, and avarice, harsh poverty, lowly people, travel on the seas, a long absence from the homeland, and distant, bad journeys, and delusion, malice,

---

[254] Or perhaps, "of heavy, stinking air."
[255] Or more literally, "those who perform their craft" (الصنّاع). This includes skilled laborers, but is not the same as doing fine and delicate work with the hands, which is a Mercurial signification (see **30** below).

resentment, cunning, stratagems, deception, treachery, harm, anguish,[256] solitude and little company with people, putting on airs,[257] lack of restraint,[258] haughtiness, conceit, boasting,[259] those who enslave the people,[260] managers for the Sultan, and every work [done] with evil, coercion, injustice, and anger; and fighters, chains, confinement, the stocks, and imposing restrictions;[261] and sincerity of speech, deliberateness, being unhurried, understanding, tested actions,[262] examination, stubbornness, much thought, profundity, insistence, sticking to a single path, hardly ever getting angry (but if he did get angry he would not [be able to] control himself), not loving the good for anyone.

5 And he indicates old men, and the weighty (among people),[263] fear, hardships, anxieties, sorrows, dejection, confusion,[264] complications, difficulty, adversity, restriction, the ancestors, the dead, inheritances, lamentation, orphanhood, old things, grandfathers, fathers, older brothers, slaves, stable workers, misers, people who have a bad reputation, disgraced people, robbers, gravediggers, *murdaqshes*,[265] body-snatchers, tanners, people who make things faulty,[266] sorcerers, masters of social unrest, the riffraff, eunuchs, long thought but little speech, the knowledge of secrets (and no one knows what is in his soul, nor does he disclose it to [anyone]), being acquainted with every abstruse matter, and it indicates leading an ascetic life and the devout people[267] of religious communities.

---

[256] More literally, "contraction" (الانقباض) as when one shrinks inside.
[257] Or, "being overbearing, pride," etc. (التكبّر).
[258] Or, "independence" (الحرّية).
[259] Or, "pride" (الفخر).
[260] المستعبدين للنّاس, although this verb does not normally take the preposition ل.
[261] Or more concretely, "shackling" (التّقييد).
[262] Or, "experiences" or even "tribulations" (التّجارب).
[263] Not "fat," but people with importance.
[264] Or, "perplexity" (الحيرة).
[265] The Latin edition of John explains this as "those who steal the clothes of the dead." It probably comes from Pahlavi.
[266] Or, "who find fault in things" (يعيّبون الأشياء).
[267] نسّاك, which can also refer to recluses and hermits.

Jupiter:

6 As for Jupiter, his nature is heating, wet, airy, temperate.

7 And he indicates the soul which nourishes, life, animal bodies, children, the children of children, embryos, scholars, legal experts, making judgments[268] between people, acting justly, verification, understanding, sages, the interpretation of dreams, sincerity, truth, religion, worship, modesty, piety, reverence, being god-fearing, unification,[269] insight into religion, uprightness, endurance, and [such a man] will be praised and have a good reputation.

8 And he indicates suffering,[270] zeal, and sometimes recklessness and haste will befall him, and endangering himself after [his] being unhurried and the endurance.

9 And he indicates prosperity, success, defeat for all who resist him, dignity, leadership, authority, kings, the nobles and the mighty, the greatness of [one's] good luck, comfort[271] and delight, a desire for assets and collecting them as well as exploiting them for profit, riches and the goodness of [one's] condition in luxury[272] and wealth, and his spirit will be lucky in every matter, and [his] character good, [and it indicates] charitable giving, generosity, granting, being open-handed (as well as boasting [about it]), being unrestrained [in his] soul, sincerity of affection, a love of leadership over the people of cities, and a love of those having importance as well as great people, and an inclination towards them,[273] and assisting the people in things.

10 And he indicates the love of building, and magnificent dwellings filled with people, insight into things, fidelity in [one's] commitments, fulfilling what one is entrusted with, being indulgent, fun, jokes, beauty,[274] adorn-

---

[268] Reading القضاء with Lemay for **BY**'s "judges" (القضاة).
[269] In a religious sense, being a monotheist or declaring that God is One (التّوحيد).
[270] الاحتمال, which also connotes endurance and tolerance.
[271] Reading الرّخاء with **BY** for الرّجاء, "hope."
[272] Reading for **BY**'s "*and* luxury."
[273] Reading إليهم with **BY** for Lemay's عليهم, which would mean being hostile to them.
[274] البهاء, in the sense of something magnificent and brilliant, not so much fine art.

ment, coquettishness, joy, laughter, an abundance of speech, eloquence[275] of the tongue; everyone who meets with him will delight in him, and he indicates an abundance of sexual intercourse, love of the good and hatred of evil, making peace between people, commanding what is beneficial and forbidding what is detestable.

Mars:

11 As for Mars, his nature is heating, drying, fiery, yellow bile, and his taste bitter.

12 And he indicates youth, strength, mental sharpness, heat, fires, conflagration, every matter occurring suddenly, a king who has power and valor, cavalrymen, chief commanders, soldiers, the companions of the Sultan, oppression, coercion, war, killing, fighting, courage, hardiness,[276] seeking glory, renown, and rank; the instruments of war, those entrusted with mobilizing wars, seeking retaliation, provoking discord,[277] those craving groups and splitting apart,[278] warring with one another, becoming a thief,[279] digging,[280] stealing, highway robbery, haughtiness, risk-taking, anger, regarding forbidden things as permissible, punishment, fetters, beating, imprisonment, restriction, running away, desertion, capture, prisoners, fear, conflict,[281] injustice, anger, fury,[282] recklessness, harshness, coarseness of heart, foolishness, stubbornness, with scarce examination, haste, quickness in things, daring, bad in expression, ugliness of speech (and its coarseness and

---

[275] Lit. "sharpness" (ذرابة). In a good sense it means eloquence (as I take it here), or perhaps sharpness of wit; but in a bad sense it can mean foul or bad speech.

[276] Literally this is "flogging" (الجلد), but in its adjectival form it means someone who is tough and hardy (i.e., who can endure flogging).

[277] الفتن, which has special connotations for social unrest and disagreement among groups.

[278] للجماعات والتّفرّق. But since these roots also commonly refer to sexual intercourse and divorce, I have the feeling Abū Ma'shar means something more like: "craving a lot of sex but then going one's own way."

[279] Or, "acting stealthily" (التّلصّص).

[280] That is, boring or digging through walls in order to break into a place.

[281] Or, a "lawsuit" or "contention" (الخصومة).

[282] Or more simply, "sharpness" (الحدّة).

harshness), indecency of the tongue, revealing love and affection, glad tidings, extravagance in speech, [using] wiles in answering quickly [but with] repentance in it [afterwards], a scarcity of piety and scarcity of fidelity but an abundance of lying, slander, and debauchery; swearing false oaths, deception, cunning, bad works, a scarcity of good, the undermining of suitable things, an abundance of thought[283] in matters, whims, independence[284] of opinion from situation to situation but quickly going back, an insolent look, little shame, an abundance of trouble and exertion, travels, exile, isolation, being a bad neighbor, fornication, ugly sexual intercourse, jokes, liveliness, the movement which happens at the time of a woman giving birth, the labor pains of a pregnant woman, the death of women in pregnancy, the cutting of a child in the womb, and the miscarriage of a fetus.

13 And he indicates middle brothers, the management of riding animals, veterinary science, the protection of sheep, the treatment of wounds, the craft of iron and working with it, the circumcision of boys, the desecration[285] of tombs, and the robbing of the dead.

The Sun:

14 As for the Sun, his nature is heating [and] drying.

15 And he indicates the animal soul, light and glowing, the intellect, knowledge, understanding, and the middle of the lifespan.

16 And he indicates kings, leaders, commanders,[286] rulership, nobility, crowds of people, power, a struggle to overcome, fame, brilliance,[287] arrogance, an overbearing attitude, vanity,[288] self-importance,[289] a good reputation, a desire for leadership and assets, and a powerful love of gold.

---

[283] الفكرة. This should probably be understood as "bad thoughts" or "worries," unless Abū Ma'shar means thinking about doing bad things.

[284] تصرّف, which also has connotations of arbitrary action or diversion.

[285] Specifically, "excavating" or digging them out (نبش).

[286] Or, "generals" (القوّاد).

[287] Or, "beauty" (البهاء).

[288] الزّهو, but in a positive sense this can mean "splendor" or "beauty."

[289] Or, "conceit," "boasting" (الصّلف).

17 And he indicates an abundance of speech, a love of cleanliness, and treats badly those who meet with him and get close to him with extreme insult,[290] and the people most on the brink of that are those closest to him by place, while the most fortunate of them are those far from him; one who assembles with him will not have renown, nor will any vestige of him be seen: he[291] will be put aright and corrupted, benefited and harmed, be fortunate and made unfortunate, raised up at one time and falling at another.

18 And he indicates the matter of religion and the hereafter, judges, sages, fathers, middle brothers, the multitude,[292] and pure clarity[293] in which there is nothing, and [such a man] mixes with the people, yielding to them [and] granting whatever things are asked about, having power over[294] evildoers and the lords of disobedience.

---

[290] At this point there is great interpretive overlap between the Sun and planets near him, and a Solar man (such as a king) and people near him. It is sometimes difficult to be near powerful people.

[291] Following Lemay and **C** by treating this as the person near the Solar man (or the planet near the Sun). **BY** and other MSS read this as being the Sun (or the Solar man). The point is that people or planets near the Solar man/Sun are overshadowed by him and their fortunes change with him.

[292] Reading بوشة with Lemay as an unattested variation of بوش, which can also indicate the entirety of the household (and fits with the family members here). **BY** follow other MSS by reading بيوسة, "dryness." This could also be a misspelling of the Persian باشا, which indicates a governor, lord, or vizier.

[293] Reading الصّفو الخالي, for الصّفر الخالي ("empty zero," "empty yellow"). The root/word صفو means something which has been purified and clarified. **BY** read "empty zero," which to my mind is redundant and made even more so by the following phrase about there being "nothing" in it. (But more than that, the zero had only recently been introduced in Arabic and it's highly unlikely that it would have been incorporated suddenly into astrology.) Nevertheless I feel something is wrong here, because neither the zero nor "clarity" fits well in this list of people. Perhaps Abū Ma'shar is using some obscure (or badly copied) words to describe someone who is purified because he is free of any personal agenda and is willing to take on the requests of others to combat evil (see end of sentence). Note the similarity between this and the Moon in **33** and **35**, which suggests a kind of universal quality which can take many other things on.

[294] Or, "having influence over" (قوي على).

Venus:

19 As for Venus, her nature is cooling, wet, phlegmatic, temperate, a fortune.

20 She indicates women, the mother, younger sisters, cleanliness, clothing, ornaments,[295] gold and silver, graciousness towards[296] close friends,[297] conceit, vanity, haughtiness, boasting, the love of wealth[298] and entertainment, laughter, adornment, joy, delight, dancing, playing horns, plucking the strings of the *oud*, weddings, perfume and good-smelling things, gentleness in composing melodies, playing backgammon and chess, idleness, casting off [restraint],[299] going too far [in what is bad],[300] buffoonery, occupying oneself with men and children in fornication, and every male or female fornicator,[301] or male or female singer, or one playing types of instruments; and much swearing of oaths (and lying), wine, honey, drinking sweet intoxicants,[302] having sex in various ways, as well as intercourse in the rear and lesbianism.

21 And she indicates a love for children and a love of people, and showing love towards them, tranquility towards everyone, tolerance,[303] generosity, kindliness, liberality, freedom, a good character, beauty and handsomeness, ingratiation, reception, brightness, splendor, pleasantness of speech, the feminine,[304] flirtation, passion, ridicule, wishing good health,[305] strength of the body (but weakness of the soul), much flesh in bodies, an abundance of

---

[295] Reading الحلى with **BY** for الحليّ, "jewelry."
[296] على, although this verb usually takes the preposition ل.
[297] الإخوان, which can also mean "brothers" but usually has a broader sense of friendship and camaraderie.
[298] الغناء, which can also mean "singing" when differently voweled.
[299] الخلع. This can also refer to certain Islamic divorces in which there is an exchange of money to finalize it: so perhaps, "easy divorce"?
[300] الفتك.
[301] Or, "adulterer...adulteress" (زانٍ...زانية).
[302] This mainly refers to wines made from raisins and dates.
[303] التحمّل, which really means to take on burdens and endure them.
[304] Or more literally, "feminization" (التأنيث).
[305] التمرىء, according to **BY** and their translation. But I do not find this in Lane's lexicon. Grammatically it looks like the unattested Form 2 of the verb (مرأ \ مرؤ), and if so it should be التمريء, and probably means "*instilling* good health."

craving for everything, joy in everything, making demands for every thing (being eager for it).

22 And she indicates [different] types of clean, admirable crafts and works, stringing garlands and decorating them, wearing crowns, dyes and dyers, sewing, houses of worship, virtue, adhering to religion, performing devotions, justice, fairness, scales and measuring, a love of markets and being in them, business, and selling good-smelling things.

Mercury:

23 As for Mercury, his nature inclines to the natures of the planets and signs he mixes with, [although] an equal balance of dryness and coldness is in him.

24 And he indicates childhood,[306] younger brothers, and an affection for male and female servants (as well as wanting a lot of them).[307]

25 And he indicates divinity, revelation to prophets, reason, logic, speech, reports, rumors and heeding them, science, belief, a good education, intelligence, cleverness, debate, the humanities,[308] philosophy, foreknowledge, calculation, surveying, the measurements of [both] higher and earthly things, the science of the stars, prediction,[309] tracking [signs],[310] augury,[311] omens, augury by birds, skill in matters, wisdom, obscure books, linguistic style, eloquence, pleasantness of speech and its quickness of exposition,[312] occupying oneself with the sciences, a craving for leadership and fame in them, reputation and praise because of them, and competition in them, in all things.

---

[306] Or, "youthfulness" (الحداثة).
[307] الاستكثار منهم.
[308] This also has connotations of culture and refinement (الآداب).
[309] الكهانة. Or, prophecy, fortune-telling, etc.
[310] العيافة.
[311] الزَّجر, which is normally done by birds but includes other types of divination by changes of movement; augury by birds follows below.
[312] Reading somewhat awkwardly for وسرعته الإبانة له.

26 And he indicates writing poetry, writers,[313] government agencies, the land-tax,[314] injustices, slander, lying, falsehood, forged books, and an awareness of hidden secrets.

27 And he indicates a scarcity of joy and the corruption of assets.

28 He indicates assets, distribution, markets, businesses, buying and selling, taking and giving, partnership, disavowal,[315] theft, lawsuits, cunning, deception, shrewdness, resentment, lying, deep thought, no one knows what is in his soul, and he does not reveal it to [anyone].

29 And he indicates wrestlers, enmity, serious damage from enemies, much fear of them, slaves, servants, quickness in works, crooked morals, fickleness,[316] charm, pleasantness in speech, bringing something about,[317] encouragement, obedience, endurance, sympathy, mercy, compassion, tranquility, a dignified manner, refraining from evil, beauty of religion, obedience to God, invoking rights, preserving his brethren; cowardly, timid, fearful, a beautiful voice and knowledge of melodies.

30 And he indicates skillfulness[318] of the hand, and different crafts, and proficiency in everything he undertakes, and a yearning for every consummate and complete work.

31 And he indicates cupping, and one working with razors and combs.

32 And he indicates springs of water, rivers, irrigation canals, prisons, the dead, and proficiency with[319] riding animals.

---

[313] الكِتّاب. This especially means the secretarial, accounting, and similar bureaucratic administration in the 'Abbāsid empire.

[314] The land-tax (and calculating it properly) was a key source of imperial income in the 'Abbāsid Caliphate.

[315] This should probably be read as "partnership *and* disavowal," to show Mercury's two-sided nature (which continues in the next set of words).

[316] التَلَوّن, lit. "colorful," "variegated." This connotes someone very interesting and "colorful" but superficial and not consistent.

[317] الجلب. Or, "acquisition." With different voweling it could be "clamor."

[318] This connotes fine, delicate work (رفق الكفّ), not so much that of the laborer or craftsman, which is a Saturnian signification (see **4** above).

[319] Reading الحذق with **BY** for Lemay's الجلب ("mange in").

BOOK VII: CONDITIONS & INDICATIONS OF THE PLANETS   497

The Moon:

33 And as for the Moon, she is the luminary of the night, and her nature is cooling, wet, phlegmatic (and in her is incidental heat, because her glow is from the Sun), and she is light,[320] suitable in every affair, craving joy and beauty of character, and being praised.

34 And she indicates the inception of all works, and kings, the nobles, good fortune in [one's] way of life, success in the things one wants, decency in religion, the higher sciences, wonders and sorcerers,[321] an abundance of thought about things, and premonition;[322] engineering,[323] the science of lands and waters (and their assessment), calculation and accounting,[324] and the weakness of reason.[325]

35 And she indicates women who have nobility, and marriage, every pregnant woman, upbringing and its conditions, mothers, maternal aunts, wet-nurses, and older sisters; and messengers, the postal service, reports, runaways, and lying and slander; [such a man is][326] a king with kings, a slave with slaves, and with every man he is like his nature; very forgetful, cowardly, without guile,[327] cheerful towards people, honored among them, [but then] cast out from them, not concealing his secret.

---

[320] That is, in the sense of being mobile, as opposed to the heavy, slow planets.
[321] Or more specifically, "enchanters" (سحرة).
[322] Or, "talking oneself into things" (حديث النفس). One could take this either way, because it matches both the mystical meanings just mentioned, as well as thinking "too much" about things.
[323] Specifically, using measures and proportions for underground water channels (الهندسة): so, a combination of architecture, geometry, and engineering.
[324] Reading المحاسبات with **BY** for Lemay's المساحة ("surveying"), which is also reasonable given the other indications.
[325] This seems very strange: perhaps the idea is that practical measurement and accounting is different from more abstract reasoning.
[326] Here the signification of the Moon and people signified by her overlap, since the Moon bears the light of all other planets. Note the similarity between this and the Sun in **18**, which suggests a kind of universal quality which can take many other things on.
[327] Or, "sincere" (سليم القلب). This idiom literally means "free of heart" or "flawless of heart."

36 And she indicates an abundance of illnesses, concerns with the mending[328] of bodies, shaving the hair, and an abundance[329] of food, [but] little sexual intercourse.

37 The Seventh Book is completed, with praise to God and His help!

---

[328] Or, "restoring, improvement" (إصلاح).
[329] This word also connotes luxury and great capacity (السَعة).

BOOK VIII: [ON LOTS][1]
And in it are nine chapters

1 Chapter VIII.1: On the reason for deriving the Lots.
2 Chapter VIII.2: On the classification of the Lots, and their names.
3 Chapter VIII.3: On the Lots of the seven planets.
4 Chapter VIII.4: On the Lots of the twelve houses.
5 Chapter VIII.5: On stating the Lots which are not mentioned with the seven planets, nor with the Lots of the twelve houses.
6 Chapter VIII.6: On stating all of the Lots in an abbreviated way.
7 Chapter VIII.7: On the Lots' coinciding in a single position.
8 Chapter VIII.8: On knowing the indicators of the Lots in their entirety.
9 Chapter VIII.9: On knowing the positions of any of the indicators relative to one another.

Chapter VIII.1: On the reason for deriving the Lots

1 The ancients among the masters of the profession of the stars universally mentioned the Lots, and we have not seen any of those who have preceded (of the people of this profession) who did not mention their power in the inception of works and their outcomes, in nativities and the revolutions of their years, and the revolutions of the years of the world. **2** And it got to the point in the practice of some of them that if one wanted to look into some specific matter (like assets, siblings, children, or of the rest of the matters), he would not look at that house nor at its lord, nor at the conditions of the rest of the planets relating to them,[2] but he would look at the Lot of that matter, and at its position, and the lord of *its* house, and would make a judgment about everything he wanted to from that very meaning.[3]

---

[1] Reading for the uninformative: "Book VIII of the *Book of the Introduction to the Science of the Judgments of the Stars.*"
[2] منها.
[3] See Firmicus Maternus (*Mathesis* VI.32, 4-7), which does do this.

3 But as for Hermes, and all of the predecessors of the people of Persia, the Babylonians, and the Greeks, they used to look at the house to which that thing belongs, and its lord, and the planet indicative of it by its nature,[4] and the Lot attributed to that topic, and its position in the signs, and the situation of its lord relative to it, and the assembling of the planets with the Lot (and their looking at it), and directing it[5] and making the rounds[6] in the twelve signs, so that they would judge in accordance with what it indicated. **4** And we have found what they did in that, to be correct.

5 But as for the reason for deriving the Lots, there is evident proof among those who understand the indications of the planets, and that is in two ways. **6** One of them is that when the planets get close to each other, and when they assemble with one another, or one of them is distanced from its associate by the amount of 1° (or less or more), a mixture and an indication over good or bad accrues to it from that, differently from what it would have indicated at another time. **7** And this is most evident in two planets which indicate a single thing by a natural indication: and that is like the Sun and Saturn, which both indicate the condition of the father: so that one needs to know the distance between them both at all times, in order to know the indication of the two indicators from that, and their strength and weakness at that time. **8** And for this reason they derived the Lots.

9 And the second way is that the things which the stars indicate are known by and derived from bringing together two or three indicators over a single thing. **10** But sometimes what is indicated by these indicators is in doubt, because sometimes a single matter will have two indicators, one of them nocturnal and the other diurnal; or one of them will be stronger in indication than the other one; or one of them will be an indicator over the beginning, and the other an indicator over [its] completion: so their indication is in doubt.[7] **11** So because of that they needed to derive and employ

---

[4] That is, the natural significator (such as Venus for love).
[5] That is, by primary directions.
[6] الانتقال. That is, by profecting it.
[7] For example, suppose that the natural significator (such as Venus) is in a poor condition, but the lord of the associated house (such as the seventh) is in a good one: in that case, the result would be ambiguous. But it is even more ambiguous if

Lots, so that they would look at the Lot, to see which of the indicators it was more inclined to, and they would judge based on that.[8]

12 Now as for the determination of the Lot, that is knowing the distance which is between the two indicators which are indicative of a single thing by a natural indication, and [then] its occurring in a specific position of the circle.[9] **13** And due to this way by which we determine the Lot, it is made clear to us that the position of the Lot is not known except by means of three indicators: two of them natural [and] fixed in indication, and the third a changing one. **14** As for the two natural indicators of fixed indication, they point out the interval which is between them, because by their natures they are partners in the indication of that thing: and the one which one begins from (by day or by night) is the first indicator, and the other one is the second indicator. **15** And as for the third, changing indicator, the degrees are projected from that. **16** So because of that they said, "Take what is between such-and-such a planet, to such-and-such a planet, in equal[10] signs, degrees, and minutes, and cast it out from the degree of the Ascendant (or from other places, or from one of the planets), thirty [degrees] per sign, and wherever it falls, there is the Lot by degree and minute."

17 And they cast out the distance which was between the two indicators from the Ascendant, due to two things. **18** The first of them is that the proper judgment of things in good and evil is known when one knows where that indicator is, relative to the Ascendant: so since this distance which is between the two indicators bears an indication, one needs to cast that out from the Ascendant in order to know where it is relative to it. **19** And the second thing is because the Ascendant is an indicator of bodies and inceptions, so because of that it is cast out from the Ascendant. **20** (But as for their casting

---

one does not have any clear conceptual distinction between houses, natural significators, and Lots—and already in late antiquity that seems to have been the case.

[8] This shows that by the 9th Century, the independent rationale of Lots was lost: instead, they mixed everything together like in a stew, and saw which flavor predominated, instead of understanding what the Lots mean by themselves.

[9] This is like measuring the distance between the Sun and Saturn for the father, as mentioned in **7**.

[10] "Equal" degrees are zodiacal degrees (as opposed to ascensional degrees).

that out from one of the houses of the circle, or from one of the planets, it is because that house or that planet is of the category of that Lot.)[11]

21 And because the Ascendant and the houses of the circle (from which the distance between the two natural indicators is cast out), are changing all of the time, the third indicator is called the "changing indication."[12]

22 Now as for their using equal degrees with the Lots, they did that because the planets circle around on the axis of the circle of signs, and they move in the circle of signs, and likewise the Ascendant is reckoned by the degrees of the circle of signs: and the degrees of the circle of signs are the degrees of equality (because when speaking one says the planets are "in" such-and-such sign, "in" such a degree, and the Ascendant "is" such-and-such degree of that sign). **23** And all of this is in degrees of equality, which pertains to the degrees of the circle of signs. **24** And because of that, they used degrees of equality for the Lots.

25 But as for the degrees of ascensions, that pertains to the degrees of the sphere surrounding the circle of signs,[13] and it turns the circle of the signs as well as the rest of the spheres. **26** And between the axis of the surrounding sphere and the axis of the circle of signs, are 23° 51', according to what Ptolemy claimed.[14]

Chapter VIII.2: On the classification of the Lots, and their names

1 In the chapter which was before this one, we stated the reason for deriving the Lots; but now we will state the classification of the Lots, and their names. **2** Know that the authenticated Lots which the ancients of the people of Persia, Babylon, and Egypt used, are according to what we have found in their books: and there are 97 Lots, in three categories. **3** The first category is the Lots of the seven planets, the second category is the Lots of the twelve houses, and the third category is the Lots which belong to the remaining

---

[11] For a worked example using the Lot of assets, see VIII.4, **39-43**.
[12] Or rather, changing *indicator*.
[13] That is, the sphere with the celestial equator.
[14] See *Almagest* I.12 (Toomer p. 63, n. 75). This is the obliquity of the ecliptic. The value in 2020 is 23° 26'.

things not mentioned in the twelve houses—and indeed, they are Lots which are needed on occasion in nativities, the revolutions of years, questions, and inceptions.

[The first category: Lots of the planets]

4 Now as for the number of Lots in the first category, there are 7: a Lot for each of the stars quick in motion, and each Lot is named after its planet. **5** And all of the ancient scholars of the masters of the profession of the stars, agree in the manner of their derivation.[15] **6** But as for the modern ones (from whom the much of the planets' natures is concealed), they disagree with the ancients in the derivation of the Lots of these seven planets—but we will state that in its own place.

[The second category: Lots of the houses]

7 And as for the number of Lots in the second category (and they are the well-known Lots used in the twelve houses, which the ancients agree on), there are 80 Lots.
8 Of them, the Ascendant has 3:[16] [8] the Lot of life, [9] the Lot of the support of the Ascendant,[17] [10] the Lot of logic and reason.
9 The second house has 3 Lots: [11] the Lot of assets, [12] the Lot of loaning, and [13] the Lot of found wealth.[18]
10 The third house has 3 Lots: [14] the Lot of siblings, [15] the Lot of the number of siblings, and [16] the Lot of the death of siblings.
11 The fourth house has 8 Lots: [17] the Lot of fathers, [18] the Lot of the death of fathers, [19] the Lot of grandfathers, [20] the Lot of lineage,[19]

---

[15] This is not true, as the reader will soon see. But Abū Ma'shar may be assuming that his preferred formulas are all from the most ancient scholars, and those who disagree came later.

[16] In what follows I number each of the Lots consecutively in brackets, so the reader can track each one. Abū Ma'shar tediously repeats himself in each paragraph ("the first of them is... and the second of them is...").

[17] In Greek this is the Lot of *Basis*, which is a kind of support. See below.

[18] اللقطة, quite literally things that are picked up, especially property lost by someone else.

[21] the Lot of immovable properties and estates according to Hermes, [22] the Lot of immovable properties according to some of the Persians, [23] the Lot of agriculture, and [24] the Lot of the outcomes of affairs.

12 The fifth house has 5 Lots: [25] the Lot of children, [26] the Lot which indicates the time in which there will be children, and their number, [27] the Lot of male children, [28] the Lot of female children, and [29] the Lot by which the one born (or the one asked about, or the fetus) is known to be male or female.

13 The sixth house has 4 Lots: [30] the Lot of illness, defects, and chronic illness according to Hermes, [31] the Lot of illnesses according to some of the ancients, [32] the Lot of slaves, and [33] the Lot of prisoners.

14 The seventh house has 16 Lots: [34] the Lot of men's marriage according to Hermes, [35] the Lot of men's marriage according to Valens, [36] the Lot of men's cunning and deception towards women, [37] the Lot of men's intercourse with women, [38] the Lot of men's debauchery and fornication, [39] the Lot of women's marriage according to Hermes, [40] the Lot of women's marriage according to Valens, [41] the Lot of women's cunning and deception towards men, [42] the Lot of women's intercourse, [43] the Lot of women's debauchery and their indecency, [44] the Lot of a woman's abstinence,[20] [45] the Lot of men's and women's marriage according to Hermes, [46] the Lot of the time of marriage according to Hermes, [47] the Lot of marriage's stratagem[21] and its facilitation, [48] the Lot of in-laws,[22] [49] the Lot of contentions and contenders.[23]

15 The eighth house has 5 Lots: [50] the Lot of death, [51] the Lot of the killing planet, [52] the Lot of the year in which death and want is feared for the native, [53] the Lot of the burdensome place, [54] the Lot of entanglement and hardship.

---

[19] الخيم.

[20] عفاف, which can also indicate being pure and modest.

[21] حيلة. Or, "expediency." **BY** read "arrangement," but the word connotes more craftiness and need.

[22] أختان. This normally means "sons-in-law" (as **BY** have it) or "bridegrooms," but the description of the Lot is broader than that.

[23] Or, "lawsuits and litigators."

16 The ninth house has 7 Lots: [55] the Lot of travel, [56] the Lot of traveling by water, [57] the Lot of piety, [58] the Lot of reason and depth of thought, [59] the Lot of knowledge and meditation,[24] [60] the Lot of tales[25] and the knowledge of people's reports and superstitions, and [61] the Lot of a report, as to whether it is true or false.

17 The tenth house has 12 Lots: [62] the Lot of the native's exaltation (and one for whom they have doubts about whether he belongs to his father or not), [63] the Lot of rulership and authority,[26] [64] the Lot of managers, viziers, and authorities, [65] the Lot of authority, aid, and conquering, [66] the Lot of those who are suddenly elevated, [67] the Lot of those honored and known among the people, [68] the Lot of soldiers and conscription,[27] [69] the Lot of authority and which work the native does, [70] the Lot of those who work with their own hands, and businesses, [71] the Lot of businesses, buying, and selling, [72] the Lot of a work and matter which there is no escaping having to deal with it, [73] the Lot of the mother.

18 The eleventh house has 11 Lots: [74] the Lot of nobility, [75] the Lot of ingratiating oneself among the people, [76] the Lot of being known among the people and respected among them, [77] the Lot of success, [78] the Lot of passions and eagerness for worldly things, [79] the Lot of hope, [80] the Lot of friends, [81] the Lot of compulsion, [82] the Lot of plenty and an abundance of good in the home, [83] the Lot of the soul's freedom, [84] the Lot of the praised and commended.

19 The twelfth house has 3 Lots: [85] the Lot of enemies according to some of the ancients, [86] the Lot of enemies according to Hermes, [87] the Lot of suffering.

20 So these are the Lots of the twelve houses, and there are 80 Lots; and many of the ancients did disagree on the derivation of some of them, but we will discuss that in its own place.

---

[24] الحلم. Or perhaps, "discernment."

[25] الأحاديث. This can also refer to gossip, but for this plural it makes more sense to say "tales."

[26] الملك والسلطان. Or, "the king and the Sultan."

[27] Really, this means any "obligation" (الشرط), but when paired with soldiers we are clearly speaking of conscription and drafting soldiers.

[*The third category: Lots of other topics*]

21 Now as for the Lots of the third category, there are 10 Lots: [88] the Lot of the releaser, [89] the Lot of the exhaustion of bodies, [90] the Lot of horsemanship and courage, [91] the Lot of risk-taking, [92] the Lot of cunning and deception, [93] the Lot of an occasion[28] of need and desire, [94] the Lot of necessity and the hindering of needs according to the Egyptians, [95] the Lot of necessity according to the Persians, [96] the Lot of punishment, and [97] the Lot of the work of truth.[29] **22** And [this category] has a singular specialness because its indication is not attributed to any of the twelve houses.

23 So, these are the 97 Lots. **24** As for the reason for any of these Lots' derivations, it is evident [and] the generality of the masters of the profession of the stars know it; but some of them do not know the reason for the derivation except those skilled scholars in the profession of the judgments of the stars. **25** And we have mentioned many reasons for the Lots, and explained something of the manner of their derivation, <so that> if one of the scholars in the profession of the stars would understand that, [and] then he wanted to derive something of the Lots for one of the matters for which the ancients did not derive a Lot, he would be able to do that. **26** But for now we will discuss the Lots of the seven planets.

Chapter VIII.3: On the Lots of the seven planets

1 In the chapter which was before this we discussed the classification of the Lots; now we will state the Lots of the seven planets, and a summary of their individual indicators.

2 Know that a single Lot is only derived from two indicators, which indicate a single thing in a natural way. **3** So if there were two planets equal in indication over a single thing, and they both agreed in sect[30] except that one of them was stronger by sect in one of the times than the other one is, we

---

[28] موضع. Or more simply, "place."
[29] عمل الحقّ.
[30] الحيّز, the usual word for "domain," here and below.

would begin in *that* time with the one that is stronger by sect. **4** And that is like the Sun and Saturn, for they are equal in [their] indication for the condition of fathers, and agree in sect because they are both diurnal—except that by day the Sun is more powerful, so we would begin the derivation of the Lot of the father by day with the Sun.

Indicators	How to calculate
Equal indication, same sect	Start with stronger by sect
Equal indication, different sect	Start with planet of sect
Differing in indication	Start with stronger, no reversal
Lord and sign	Start with lord, no reversal

Figure 147: Four classes of Lot calculation

5 But if there was an agreement in the equality of the indication just as we stated, but one of them was diurnal and the other nocturnal, begin by day with the diurnal one, and by night with the nocturnal one. **6** And that is like the Sun and Moon, because they are both equal in the indication of good fortune, except that one of them is diurnal and the other nocturnal: so we would begin the derivation of the Lot of Fortune by day from the Sun (the diurnal one), and by night from the Moon (the nocturnal one).

7 And if one of them was stronger in the *indication* than the other one is,[31] then we would begin by day *and* by night from the stronger one.

8 And if the indication belonged to a sign and its lord equally, one would begin for the most part with the lord of the sign [and count] up to the degree of that sign,[32] because the indication of the sign is made strong by means of the planet, and in the material object;[33] but sometimes one might begin with the sign *if* it was stronger in indication.

---

[31] Abū Ma'shar might have in mind Lots which are not reversed by night, so that one always begins with one that indicates more strongly.

[32] But see **14-15** below.

[33] وفي الشيء المادّي. This seems to mean that the sign does not have motive power on its own: it is active through its lord, and is primarily present in material objects as an elemental mixture and quality.

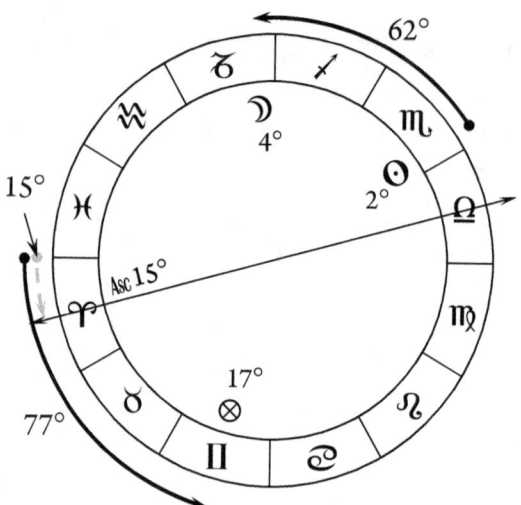

Figure 148: Projecting from beginning of rising sign

9 Then, the Ascendant collaborates with it—or one of the [other] positions of the circle, or one of the wandering stars[34] chosen in accordance with what is needed.[35] **10** And due to this, the ancients said the distance between the two indicators is taken by degrees of equality, then it is added on top of what has ascended from the beginning of the sign of the Ascendant up to the minute of the Ascendant (by equal degrees), then that is cast out from the beginning of the sign of the Ascendant. **11** But if it was cast out from something other than the Ascendant, then there is added to the distance between the two indicators, from the beginning of the sign of that indicator, up to the position in which it is (by degrees of equality), then that is projected from the beginning of *its* sign, 30° for every sign.[36] **12** And where it comes to an end, there is that Lot, with its degree and minute. **13** And everything which is taken by degrees in the use of the Lots, is in equal degrees.

14 And know that sometimes in the work of Lots one needs to take from the lord of one of the houses up to that house, but that house by *counting* is one of the signs, and by *equation*[37] is withdrawing towards another house, so

---

[34] That is, the planets.
[35] That is, the distance between the first two indicators is sometimes cast out from the Ascendant, sometimes from another position, sometimes from a third planet.
[36] So if the distance should be projected from Saturn (as in [50] the Lot of death), then one would add the degrees that Saturn has already traveled in his sign, to the distance between the two indicators, and cast the whole amount out from the beginning of Saturn's sign.
[37] بالسواء. That is, by calculation of a cusp.

that it ought to be taken from the lord of the sign by equation, to that degree in which the calculation occurs. **15** And an example of that[38] is if the Ascendant was Cancer by degree, in the fourth clime, and the house of assets by counting was Leo, but by calculation it was Cancer, [in] a given degree: so it ought to be taken from the *Moon*, who is the lord of Cancer, up to that given degree of it, and one would *not* focus on the Sun and Leo.

The Lot of the Moon: [The Lot of Fortune]

17 As for [1] the first of the Lots, it is derived from the Sun and Moon: and that is because the Sun has the greatest glow of the planets of the circle, and he is the luminary of the day and a fortune, and the day comes to be through his rising, and he is indicative of natural life, victory, might, kings and authority, governorships, commanding and prohibiting, and types of assets and jewels, and every precious, costly thing (and indeed the people's good fortune is by means of might, rulership, and authority, and assets of different kinds), and religion. **18** As for the Moon, she is the luminary of the night and a fortune, and she is the indicator of bodies, plants, and generally what happens in this world.

19 So since the Sun is the luminary of the day and the Moon the luminary of the night, they began this Lot by day from the diurnal fortune (which is the Sun) up to the fortune of the night (which is the Moon) by degrees of equality, and by night from the Moon (the nocturnal one) to the Sun (the diurnal one). **20** Then they added on top of that what had arisen from the beginning of the sign of the Ascendant up to the degree of the Ascendant [itself] by equal degrees, and then cast that out from the beginning of the sign of the Ascendant, 30 [degrees] for every sign, and where the calculation came to an end in them, they said there was this Lot. **21** And if the two luminaries were both in one [and the same] minute, then the Lot would be the minute of the Ascendant [itself].

22 This Lot is called the "Lot of Fortune," and it indicates things that are like what the luminaries indicate, and especially the indication for the soul and its good fortune, and its powers, and life, bodies, assets, benefits, good fortune, wealth and poverty, gold and silver, cheapness and expensiveness, a

---

[38] This is [11] the Lot of assets.

reputation of value and praise, and the elevation of the native, authority, governorship, kings, might, high rank, good and evil, the witness and the absent person, the apparent and the hidden, and the inner conscience,[39] and the inception of works and things sought. **23** And this Lot has precedence over the [other] Lots in the way that the Sun has precedence in glow over the [other] planets; and it is the highest, most noble of the Lots.

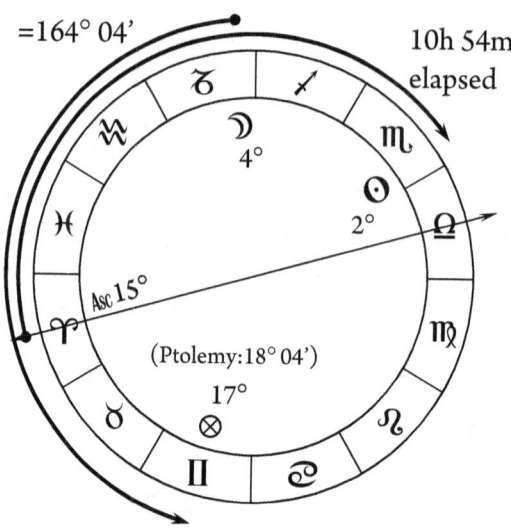

Figure 149: Ptolemy's theory of the Lot of Fortune (*Tet.* III.10; *Gr. Intr.* VIII.3, **25**)

24 And just as there is none more glowing among the planets of the circle, nor more brilliant nor better known than [these] two, and in their conditions they stand apart from the rest of the planets, so likewise if they were suitable by condition and place, and they alone possessed the indication of good fortune (like rulership, authority, and assets), so will [those things] be famous, reputed, precious, costly, with none obtaining them except for those who are special among the people, unique in their conditions above the conditions of others—and they are those who have the two luminaries and the Lot of Fortune in the excellent, praised positions in their nativities.[40]

25 And this Lot is said to be the "Lot of the Moon" and her "Ascendant":[41] and it becomes the Ascendant of the Moon and her Lot because they claimed that when one multiplies what has transpired of the hours of the day

---

[39] الضّمير, the word which means what is in the "heart" of a person. This refers to the practice of "thought-interpretation," used in conjunction with horary charts.

[40] See VIII.8, **15-36**, which expands on the importance of the indicators being in a good condition, to help the Lot.

[41] See *Tet.* III.10 (Robbins p. 275-77).

by the portions of its hours, then cast that out from the position of the Moon by degrees of equality, it will fall on the position of the Lot of Fortune. **26** And we have put this to the test, and found it [to be so], though sometimes it falls close to that place.⁴²

The Lot of the Sun: [the Lot of the Invisible]⁴³

28 Since no changes of increase and decrease in themselves are apparent to us in any of the planets (as do appear to us from the nocturnal luminary, which is the Moon), nor do the planets of the circle have any special indication over generation and development (as she does), they began [2] the Lot of the Invisible by day from her up to the Sun in degrees of equality, and by night from the Sun to the Moon. **29** And to what was brought together is added what had ascended from the beginning of the sign of the Ascendant to the degree and minute of the Ascendant in degrees of equality, and it is cast out from the beginning of the sign of the Ascendant (for every sign 30 [degrees]), and where the calculation comes to an end, there is this Lot.

30 This Lot is called the "Lot of the Invisible," and it comes after the Lot of Fortune: its characteristic indication is for the body and soul and their conditions, and religion and prophethood,⁴⁴ and piety⁴⁵ and devotion, and secrets, thought, the inner conscience, and hidden, concealed things, things

---

⁴² In other words, the length of the day determines the zodiacal interval from the Moon; or, diurnal motion determines the zodiacal interval. Figure 149 illustrates Ptolemy's approach, which is: length of daylight / 180° = hours of daylight elapsed / interval. The length of the day is 11h 58m 15s, and the hours of daylight elapsed is 10h 54m 39s. By calculation this shows that the interval to project from the Moon is 164° 04', which as Abū Ma'shar says is only "close to" the correct amount of 163°. Of course Ptolemy could claim that his method is the true one because it combines both diurnal and zodiacal motion; but the results also depend on how one measures the length of the day.

⁴³ الغيب, which can also mean "the absent," "the hidden" and especially "the supernatural": that is, the Lot of Spirit or *Daimōn*.

⁴⁴ النبوة, but perhaps this should be النُّبُوءة ("prophecy").

⁴⁵ النسك, which has special connotations for asceticism and withdrawal (which makes an appropriate contrast to the worldliness of Fortune).

which are absent, praise and commendation, the sense of honor, respect, and heat and cold.[46]

31 And this Lot and the Lot of Fortune are the most excellent of all the Lots, and the clearest in indication over every absent or present thing, and the inception of works and things sought, the revolutions of the years of the world, and nativities. **32** By day the Lot of Fortune is more evident in indication, and after that the Lot of the Invisible; while by night the Lot of the Invisible is more evident in indication, and after that the Lot of Fortune.

33 And since the seasons are altered by the transferring of the luminaries and the rest of the wandering stars from sign to sign, and alterations take place in this world in terms of moderation, heat, and cold, and the rest of the types of interchanges[47] by which the life of animal beings comes to be (or, their destruction), and the Lots are derived from these two luminaries and the rest of the planets, these two Lots and the rest of the Lots have, by their shifting from sign to sign, an indication over good and evil, and abundance and restriction, in nativities, the revolutions of years, inceptions, and questions.

34 And these two Lots (which are the Lot of Fortune and the Lot of the Invisible) indicate similarly to what the two luminaries do. **35** But [some] people among the masters of the stars have disagreed with others about the name of these two Lots, [some] of them calling the Lot of Fortune "Lot of the Sun," and the Lot of the Invisible the "Lot of the Moon."

The Lot of Saturn: "The burdensome"[48]

37 Since Saturn indicates everything which goes astray, falls, is stolen, and runs away, and he indicates lands, building, repairs, waters, confinement,

---

[46] الحرّ والبرد. But "heat" in Arabic is also used to refer to being free, active, and open, while "cold" connotes being still and emotionally calm or cold. So Abū Ma'shar or his source might also be implying the human's inner sense of motivation and tendency to act—which is also appropriate because the Lot of Spirit in Hellenistic astrology is especially associated with choice and action (as opposed to bodies and being the passive recipient of events, as with the Lot of Fortune).

[47] التغابير.

[48] الثقيل, which usually means just "heavy."

prisons, and chains, and indicates depth of thought, the sciences, matters of religion[49] and piety,[50] and success in [recovering] what has been lost and stolen, and being freed from prison and fetters, and the possession of real estate and waters, and putting the situations of religion and the sciences into use (and depth of thought is a good fortune), they said [3] the Lot of Saturn ("the burdensome") is taken by day from the degree of Saturn to the degree of the Lot of Fortune, and by night the contrary, and to it is added the degrees of the Ascendant, and it is projected from the beginning of the Ascendant, and where the calculation comes to an end, there is this Lot.

38 And its indication is for preservation, depth of thought, religion, piety, and leading an ascetic life in religion, and everything which has gone astray, was stolen, ran away, or fell into a well or the sea, or has died, and the condition of the dead, and how the death will be, and the conditions of lands and their sowing, and building and repairs, and difficult straits, greed and stinginess, good praise and bad, evil, old age, and burdens, and every thing which is in fetters or prison, and its rescue from those fetters and prison.

The Lot of Jupiter, comprising prosperity and aid

40 Since the indicator of victory, prosperity, aid, and praised outcomes is Jupiter, and all of these are good fortunes, they said [4] the Lot of Jupiter (comprising prosperity and aid) is taken by day from the Lot of the Invisible (indicative of good fortune) to Jupiter (indicative of prosperity and aid), and by night the contrary, and to it is added the degrees of the Ascendant, and it is cast out from the Ascendant: so where the calculation comes to an end, there is this Lot.

41 And its indication is for might, victory, aid, prosperity, generosity, praised outcomes, uprightness, and seeking religion and everything pertain-

---

[49] الدين. In Islamic thought, this word for religion specifically relates to teachings, rules, and laws that govern one's life; so it is also appropriate that Abū Ma'shar connects it here with Saturn, as he does with the religious law and lawgiver in the *Book of Religions and Dynasties*.

[50] النسك. This word also connotes asceticism and worldly withdrawal, which is appropriate for Saturn.

ing to its conditions, making oaths to God and putting effort into[51] actions in obedience to God, and the love of goodness, the seeking of justice, and [legal] decisions among the people, and the building of mosques, knowledge and scholars, and elevating the importance of sages, hope, and everything a man obtains pertaining to good deeds,[52] and the partnership of people with each other.

The Lot of Mars, comprising courage

43 Since the indication of daring and risk-taking belong to the nocturnal Mars, and these are among the good fortunes of the soul and its strengths, and the Lot of Fortune is indicative of the powers of the soul, and its conditions and good fortunes, they said [5] the Lot of Mars (comprising courage and risk-taking) is taken by day from Mars to the degree of the Lot of Fortune, and by night the reverse, and to it is added the degrees of the Ascendant, and it is cast out from the Ascendant, and wherever it comes to an end, there is the Lot.

44 And it indicates management, valor, risk-taking, courage, strength, daring, and severity, rudeness, coarseness, crossing the line,[53] haste, killing, robbery, foul works, debauchery, cunning, and deception.

The Lot of Venus, comprising love and familiarity[54]

46 Since the harmony of people with each other, and their mixing [with each other] is through love, familiarity,[55] and fondness; and pairing, all

---

[51] الاجتهاد, which can also mean "forming legal judgments in," another Jupiterian signification.

[52] الخيرات. This can also mean "resources," but good deeds seems to fit better in this part of the sentence.

[53] الجسارة, which is usually translated more metaphorically as "insolence," being "intrepid," "reckless," and so on.

[54] الألفة, which generally means to be on intimate terms with people (but is not necessarily erotic). This is the Valens Lot of *Erōs*, by day from Fortune to Spirit (reversed by night), and projected from the Ascendant, as Abū Ma'shar correctly has it in **47**.

spouses,[56] sex, uniting, marriage, harmonizations, amusement, and rapture is attributed to Venus (and she is indicative of that as well as affection, love, and the rest of what we stated about the indications of Venus with respect to delights and joy, all of which are good fortunes), they calculated the Lot of Venus from the Lots[57] of the two luminaries indicative of good fortune. **47** And they said [6] the Lot of Venus (which comprises love and familiarity) is taken by day from the Lot of Fortune to the Lot of the Invisible, and by night the reverse, and to it is added what has arisen from the beginning of the sign of the Ascendant, and it is cast out from the beginning of the Ascendant, and where the calculation comes to an end, there is the Lot.

48 And it indicates passion, a desire for intercourse, affection, and seeking what the soul is fond of and delights in, and love is strengthened by it, and all matters of sex and spouses, and familiarity, amusement, pleasure, and pleasantness.[58]

The Lot of Mercury, comprising stratagems[59]

50 [7] The Lot of Mercury (and it is the Lot of poverty and few stratagems) is taken by day from the Lot of the Invisible to the Lot of Fortune (and by night the contrary), and to it is added what has ascended from the beginning of the sign of the Ascendant, and it is cast out from the Ascendant, and where the calculation comes to an end, there is this Lot.

51 And it indicates poverty, fighting, fear, hatred, and an abundance of conflict, enemies, anger, and conflict in a time of anger, and business, buying

---

[55] Reading الألفة with about half of the MSS, for **BY**'s المقة ("tender love"), especially since without this word we could not directly justify the name of the Lot.

[56] Or perhaps, "couples" (الأزواج).

[57] Reading for the singular "Lot."

[58] For some interpretation, see also VIII.7, **5-7**.

[59] الحيلة, which is a singular but would not read well in English. This word refers to any kind of means or strategies to accomplish something, and by the connection to poverty below Abū Ma'shar or his source is suggesting a connection between poverty, and the cleverness necessary to get what one needs (including by deception and conflict). At any rate, this is the Valens version of the Lot of Necessity, from Spirit to Fortune (reversed by night), and projected from the Ascendant.

and selling, cunning, stratagems,⁶⁰ writing, calculation, and the seeking of different sciences as well as the stars.

52 So this is how the Lots of the seven planets are derived, according to what Hermes and the predecessors[61] among the scholars of the stars stated, and this is the summary of their indications. **53** As for the rest of the things they indicate from an examination of their blending with other planets and Lots, we will state that in different places insofar as it is needed.

[Alternative view of planetary Lots]

54 But some of those who are very ignorant about the natures of the planets have said—concerning the Lots of the five wandering stars—that one takes by day and night what is between the Sun up to the Moon, and [that] is cast out from the position of *that planet* whose Lot one wants to derive: and wherever it comes to an end, there is the Lot of that wandering star. **55** So as for the Lot of the Sun (and it is [2] the Lot of the Invisible), they said it is taken by day and night from the Moon to the Sun, and is cast out from the place of the Sun, so wherever it comes to an end, there is the Lot of the Sun. **56** And as for the Lot of the Moon (and it is the Lot of Fortune), they say it is taken by day and night from the Sun to the Moon, and then that is cast out from the position of the Moon, so wherever it comes to an end, there is the Lot of the Moon. **57** But this is not correct, because what we stated at the beginning about the derivation of these Lots is that it is derived from the *natural indicators*: and this is what Hermes and the predecessors among the scholars of the stars agree on (and it is preferable), [so this other view] does not harmonize with the ancients in terms of truth and correctness.

---

[60] The rest of the sentence now seems to veer in the direction of general Mercurial significations.

[61] Abū Ma'shar does not say "his" (i.e., Hermes's) predecessors, but just "the" predecessors.

Chapter VIII.4: On the Lots of the twelve houses

1 In the chapter which was before this we stated the Lots of the seven planets; now we will state the Lots of the twelve houses, and the manner of deriving them, and what is disputed in it, and which of them is correct, and a summary of their individual indications. **2** Many of the masters of the stars, when they found two Lots for a single topic in any of the houses of the circle, and one of the two was in conflict with its associated one in derivation, it appeared obscure to them so they did not know which of the two was more correct—but we will comment on that and make it clear in this book of ours.

3 And when we studied the conditions of the Lots, we found many Lots which were derived without valid grounds, so we have not stated them in this book. **4** But we have stated the most valid Lots, and the most correct of them in derivation: and they are the Lots which Hermes and the predecessors among the people of Persia derived, because they derived the Lots from indicators such that two of them partook in the indication of a single thing.

5 But when they looked at the twelve houses, they found that for some of the matters which are attributed to these houses (and they do indicate different conditions), many indicators indicate them, [which] they share [together] in the indication. **6** Thus they were unable to derive a single Lot for it which would fully cover the indication of the conditions of everything in it, so they derived several Lots for that very same thing, which one could consult for its conditions. **7** And [so] for every Lot, even though it indicates the category of that thing, its special property for indicating something of that topic would not belong to other Lots of that house. **8** And that is like death: for its indicators are many, and its conditions varying, because among people one will die from a long illness, another will die from an acute illness, one will be killed, another drown, and the rest of the different situations of death; so because of the abundance of indicators and the difference of their conditions, they derived four Lots for it so they could investigate the indication of its conditions from them.[62] **9** And it is like the house of authority: for its conditions differ for many of the indicators, so they derived eight Lots for

---

[62] So, [50] the Lot of death is general for death, while [51] the Lot of the killing planet suggests violence to the body, and [52] the Lot of the year in which death and want are feared, is about dire circumstances and calamity.

authority, each one of them having a special characteristic in the indication of that very same thing in the topic of power, rank, and authority, which does not belong to the other Lots like it.

10 And know that each of the houses of the circle is given out to different things, just as the fourth sign is given out to fathers, real estate, and outcomes, and the fifth sign to children, messengers, and gifts, and likewise the rest of the twelve houses, each house among them having indications over specific things attributed to it: and many of those things have Lots. **11** But sometimes one of the signs has an indication over something, and that thing does *not* have a Lot attributed to it: just as the ancients did not derive a Lot called the "Lot of gifts," or one called "the Lot of messengers," even though gifts and messengers have an indication in the fifth sign.

12 And indeed here we will proceed directly to stating the well-known Lots belonging to the indications of the twelve houses, [for] each house what is attributed to it (among the obvious indications). **13** And we have looked at each house and will make comments about the reasons for deriving many of the Lots which are in that house. **14** But we have left out comments about the reason for deriving some of them, because we know that there will be enough for those having understanding and management, in what we make clear and explain: for when the knowledgeable man understands the reason for any of the Lots of the houses of the circle, the reason for the rest of the Lots of that house will be evident to him.

The Ascendant: it has three Lots

16 The first of them is [8] the LOT OF LIFE. **17** We begin now with the derivation of the Lot of the Ascendant (and it is the Lot of life) from two planets, which are Saturn and Jupiter: because they are the highest of the planets and the most sluggish in course, and they are both indicators of the length of lifespans, survival, and lasting things.[63] **18** And due to that they were made the two indicators of the Lot of life; and the Ascendant partners

---

[63] This could be one reason why Saturn-Jupiter conjunctions are used so much in Persian mundane astrology.

with them both for the reason which preceded, [in] our statement about that. **19** And they began by day from the diurnal fortune, so this Lot by day is taken from Jupiter to Saturn (and by night the reverse), and to it is added what has arisen of the sign of the Ascendant, then it is cast out from the beginning of the Ascendant, and where it terminates, there is the Lot of life. **20** It is a Lot of the Ascendant, and this Lot indicates natural life and the conditions of bodies as well as the means of subsistence.[64] **21** So if it was in a suitable condition, it indicates the long length of the lifespan, the safety of the body, and the delight of the soul; but if it was corrupted, it indicates the shortness of the lifespan, an abundance of illnesses, and the distress of the soul.[65]

22 The second is [9] the LOT OF FIRMNESS AND SURVIVAL,[66] and it is the Lot of the Ascendant's "support."[67] **23** Since firmness and survival in this world are among the most excellent fortunes of worldly existence,[68] and indeed that is by means of the indications of the most powerful fortunes among the higher bodies, and the most powerful of the fortunes are the Sun and Moon, and their Lots are indicative of good fortune, spirit,[69] and the body (similar to what the two luminaries indicate), and firmness and survival in this world is by means of a mixture of spirit and body (and change, corruption, and passing away is from their corruption)—due to that they calculated this Lot from them both, and said the Lot of firmness and survival

---

[64] Or, "livelihood" or "way of life" (المعاش). Sahl has this Lot in his *Nativities* Ch. 2.15, **17-23**, and it is probably the same as Dorotheus's undefined Lot of livelihood (المعيشة) in *Carmen* I.29, **29**. However, Rhetorius, who often relies on Dorotheus, has his own Lot of livelihood which he defines in the same way as Abū Ma'shar's [11] Lot of assets in the second house (see **39-41** below, and Rhetorius Ch. 57, in Holden p. 58). So the authenticity of this calculation (insofar as it comes from Dorotheus) is still unclear.

[65] See also VIII.7, **10-11**.

[66] Or, "fixity, endurance" and "remaining." In VIII.2, **8** it is called the Lot of the support of the Ascendant.

[67] Again, this shows the close relation to the Greek Lot of *Basis* (*basis*, "ground, step, pedestal"). See VIII.3, **46-47**.

[68] الدنيا. This particularly means the world "down below," from the verb دنا: see how Abū Ma'shar contrasts this with the "higher" bodies later in the sentence.

[69] الرّوح. Or, "soul."

(and it is the Lot of the Ascendant's support, and the splendor of the native, and his beauty) is taken by day from the Lot of Fortune to the Lot of the Invisible, and by night the contrary, and it is added to what the degrees of the Ascendant come to, and it is cast out from the beginning of the sign of the Ascendant. **24** And this Lot matches [6] the Lot of Venus.

25 And it indicates the native's appearance, his resemblance to the fathers and mothers, and the fitness of the body, and his safety at the time of childbirth, and travel. **26** So if this Lot and its lord were in a suitable condition, the native will have a handsome appearance and body, with complete limbs, good joints, balanced fetal development,[70] undamaged extremities, a healthy body, benefiting in his travels for his whole life, and acquiring many benefits in it. **27** And if it was corrupted, it indicates the disgusting quality of the body and fetal development, and the ugliness of the appearance and the body, and an abundance of illnesses. **28** And if it was inclining towards the indicator of fathers, the native will resemble the father and the people of the father's house; but if it was inclining towards the indicator of the mother, the native will resemble the mother and the people of her house.

29 And if you wanted to know whether something would last and survive or not, [then] if you knew the nativity of a man and the revolution of his year, or a [you had] question about the firmness of something unknown (or its ceasing to be), then look at this Lot: for if it was in the inspection[71] of its claim,[72] or with the lords of the stakes, or with the lord of the Ascendant, advancing, then it indicates the firmness of that thing, and its lasting and survival. **30** But if it was withdrawing, it indicates its ceasing to be and corruption. **31** But if at the time of its advancement it was made unfortunate, the firmness of that thing will be with something detestable, and distress; and if it was made fortunate, it firmness will be with good fortune. **32** And if at the time of its withdrawing the Lot was made fortunate, he will have good

---

[70] سوي الخلقة. But one might also take this to be the native's natural constitution and build (since that is what will be evident *after* birth).

[71] مناظرة. Remember that in VI.3 this word was understood to mean an "exact aspect" by degree.

[72] مزاعمته, which means a "claim" (i.e., a dignity), but here clearly should be "claimant" (مزاعمه) or "lord."

fortune after the withdrawing of that thing from him; and if it was made unfortunate, something detestable will find him after its withdrawing.

33 The third is [10] the LOT OF LOGIC AND REASON. **34** Since Mercury is indicative of logic, thought, discrimination, and speech, and Mars is the indicator of fervor and movement,[73] they calculated the Lot of logic and reason by day from Mercury to Mars (and by night the contrary), and cast it out from the Ascendant. **35** And this Lot indicates articulated speech, logic, discrimination, knowledge, and reason. **36** So if this Lot or its lord was with the lord of the Ascendant, or[74] was in a sign in which the lord of the Ascendant has testimony, and Mercury looked at them both with strength, then he will possess articulated speech, discrimination, and knowledge. **37** And if Mars looked at the lord of the Lot and the Ascendant,[75] he will be clever, on fire,[76] sharp, [but] careless.[77]

The second house: it has three Lots

39 The first one is [11] the LOT OF ASSETS.[78] **40** Since the indicator of the native's assets is the second and its lord, they derived the Lot of assets from them both, and said the Lot of assets is taken by day and night from the lord of the house of assets to the degree of the house of assets by equation,[79] and to it is added the degrees of the Ascendant, and it is cast out from the Ascendant. **41** And this Lot indicates benefits, the means of subsistence,[80] and the nourishment which the body[81] subsists on for his whole lifespan. **42** So if it was in a suitable place, it indicates a suitable condition in assets, nourishment, and the means of subsistence; but if it was corrupted, it indicates a

---

[73] This also has connotations of action and motivation (الحركة).

[74] Reading "or" for "and."

[75] Or perhaps, "and *the lord of* the Ascendant," as with Mercury.

[76] متوقّدًا. Metaphorically this means to have a lively and impulsive mind.

[77] Reading غافلًا with Lemay and **P**. **BY** follow other MSS and read عاقلًا, "intelligent." To me it makes more sense to follow the more Martial signification of carelessness.

[78] See *Carmen* I.29, **17**.

[79] بالسواء. That is, the second house as determined by cusps rather than sign. See VIII.3, **14**.

[80] المعاش. See footnote to **20**.

[81] Reading the singular, for "bodies."

bad condition in what we stated. **43** Now as for the rest of the other types of good fortunes which are obvious from the assets which are stored away and one gets rich by, the rest of the indicators of assets and good fortune indicate those.

44 The second one is [12] the LOT OF LOANING, taken by day and night from Saturn to Mercury and cast out from the Ascendant. **45** If this Lot was made unfortunate, and[82] it or its lord had an indication in assets, then much of his assets will disappear because of loans and debts; but if the Lot was made fortunate, it indicates the contrary of that.

46 The third is [13] the LOT OF FOUND WEALTH, taken by day from Mercury to Venus (and by night the contrary), and it is cast out from the Ascendant. **47** And this Lot indicates the condition of found wealth which a man finds on the road or in any [other] places, and it indicates what falls from him or which he forgets in a place. **48** So if the claimants[83] of the Lot, or the Sun or Moon, were with this Lot, or they are looking at it with an aspect of affection, and the Lot was in a stake,[84] then he will know the owner of the found object[85] or it will pass to its owner. **49** And if something fell from the man or he forgot it in a place, and the condition of the Lots' indicators was just as we stated, then the owner will discover the found object. **50** And if the indicators of the Lot were in a suitable condition, in their own positions in the root of the nativity, then he will benefit from things he finds on roads, and will be happy with them. **51** But if it was the contrary of everything we said, then to the contrary.

The third house: it has three Lots

53 The first of them is [14] the LOT OF SIBLINGS.[86] **54** Since the sphere of Saturn and the sphere of Jupiter follow one another and they are of a single

---

[82] Reading with **BY** for Lemay's "or."

[83] That is, its lords.

[84] In inceptions for lost items, the luminaries and the angles indicate recovering the object.

[85] This could possibly be read as, "the owner of the found object will be aware of it."

[86] Or more simply, "brothers" (الإخوة). But Abū Ma'shar is careful to include sisters below, so I have chosen a more neutral word. See *Carmen* I.21, **1**.

nature insofar as they are two superior planets, and Saturn indicates kinships[87] while Jupiter indicates the generation of children and growth, and brothers and sisters each follow one another, and they are of a single nature by the humanity which is in them, and there are no brothers or sisters except in the kinship which is due to generation and growth, Hermes and all of the predecessors among the scholars said that the Lot of siblings is taken by day and night from Saturn to Jupiter by degrees of equality, and to it is added what has arisen of the sign of the Ascendant, and it is cast out from the Ascendant.

55 Now Zādānfarrūkh [al-Andarzaghar] said (and he relates this from Valens) that the Lot of siblings is taken by day and night from Mercury to Jupiter, and to it is added the degrees of the Ascendant,[88] and it is cast out from the Ascendant. **56** But what Hermes said is correct, because Saturn and Jupiter are more indicative of siblings due to the closeness of their spheres, their mixing, and their indication for siblings and childbirth; and [indeed] the ancients in some times called Saturn the "brother of Jupiter," and in some places they called Jupiter the "son of Saturn."

57 And the Lot which Hermes mentioned, as well as the lord of its house, indicates the condition of the siblings and their harmony, affection, and their emigration and travels.

58 Then look: for if the Lot and its lord occurred in a sign of many children, then they will be many; and if they occurred in a sign of few children, they will be few. **59** Now if you wanted to know how many their number will be, then take what is between the Lot up to the lord of its house (or what is between the lord of its house up to it), and make it be one for each sign between them (and if it was a sign having two bodies, then double the number

---

[87] الأرحام. This could be understood as "wombs," but so far as I know Saturn does not actually indicate wombs. Nevertheless Saturn is used in most of the standard family Lots: father, siblings, children, and marriage.

[88] Abū Ma'shar must be referring to the passage in *BA* III.3.2, **4** (and in Sahl's *Nativities* Ch. 3.11, **3**). But al-Andarzaghar has made an error, as this is Dorotheus's Lot of the *number of* siblings (*Carmen* I.23, **1**). Valens does not have a separate Mercury-Jupiter Lot. I suspect that al-Andarzaghar might have confused Dorotheus with Valens due to the *Bizidaj*.

of that sign itself). **60** And if there was a planet in what is between the Lot and the lord of its house, then take one for that as well.

61 The second is [15] the LOT OF THE NUMBER OF SIBLINGS.[89] **62** The Lot by which the number of the siblings is known, is taken by day and night from Mercury to Saturn, and to it is added the degrees of the Ascendant, and it is cast out from the Ascendant. **63** And if this Lot and the first one which is according to Hermes, and the lords of their two houses, occur in a sign of many children, then the brothers and sisters will be many, so that their number will [even] surpass the number of the signs and planets (and sometimes their number will reach the lesser, middle, or greater years of the planets); and the planets looking at them add their years to them. **64** But if the two Lots and their lords occurred in signs of few children, then they will be few. **65** (And you will know the signs of few children or many, from the Book in which the natures of the signs are.)[90]

66 The third is [16] the LOT OF THE DEATH OF SIBLINGS. **67** The Lot of the death of brothers and sisters is taken by day from the Sun to the degree of the Midheaven by degrees of equality (and by night the contrary), and to it are added the degrees of the Ascendant, and it is cast out from the Ascendant; and where it falls, there is the Lot. **68** This Lot indicates the reason for the death of the brothers and sisters: and when this Lot terminates at the indicators of the brothers and sisters by the turning of the signs (a year for every sign),[91] or the direction of degrees (a year for each degree), or the indicators of the brothers and sisters terminate at [this Lot] in the manner we stated, something detestable will affect the brothers and sisters.

The fourth house: it has eight Lots

70 The first of them is [17] the LOT OF FATHERS. **71** Since the father is prior to the child, and Saturn has an indication for what precedes, and masculinization and such, so that he has an indication for the causes by which fatherhood comes to be (and indeed the father is the cause of every child), and the planet indicative of the causes of the life of a living being is the Sun,

---

[89] Cf. *Carmen* I.23, **1**, which uses Mercury-Jupiter, not Mercury-Saturn.
[90] See Ch. VI.16.
[91] That is, by profection.

for this reason Saturn and the Sun came to be the two indicators of the father. **72** And due to that they said the Lot of fathers is taken by day from the Sun to Saturn (and by night the contrary), and to it are added the degrees of the Ascendant, and it is cast out from the Ascendant. **73** But if Saturn was under the rays, it is taken by day from the Sun to Jupiter (and by night from Jupiter to the Sun), and to it are added the degrees of the Ascendant, and it is cast out from the Ascendant: and wherever it comes to an end, there is the Lot of the father.

74 And some of the people[92] said if Saturn was under the rays, then the Lot of fathers is taken by day from Mars to Jupiter (and by night the contrary), and it is cast out from the Ascendant. **75** But what Hermes said is more correct, because Jupiter is more indicative for fathers than Mars is; moreover, if Saturn's indication was nullified by his being under the Sun's rays, the indication of the Sun would still stand, so if Saturn was under the rays it would be necessary for it to be taken by day from the Sun to Jupiter (and by night the contrary), and that be cast out from the Ascendant, just as Hermes said.[93]

76 And this Lot indicates the condition of the father, and his nobility and class, and the lord of the house of the Lot indicates the father's good fortune in his assets (or his suffering). **77** So if the Lot was in an excellent condition relative to the circle, the father will be noble, while if it was the contrary, then the contrary of it; and if its lord was in an excellent condition, he will be lucky,[94] while if it was in a bad condition and place, he will suffer. **78** But if it was made fortunate, it indicates the long length of his lifespan; while if it was made unfortunate, it indicates the shortness of his lifespan. **79** And this Lot

---

[92] Namely, Dorotheus in *Carmen* I.14, **5** (confirmed in Paul Ch. 23). But Dorotheus does not mention the reversal, and it seems wrong to begin with a nocturnal planet (Mars) by day. It should probably be reversed in any event, but I should think that by day it is from Jupiter to Mars. However, see [49] the Lot of contentions and contenders in **219-23** below, which is calculated in the same way: does this imply that if one must use this Mars-Jupiter Lot, the relationship with the father will have more contention?

[93] The obvious flaw in this logic is that being under the rays should nullify Jupiter's indication as well.

[94] Or more broadly, "happy" (سعيد).

and its lord both indicate the authority, rank, and power belonging to the native.[95]

80 The second one is [18] the LOT OF THE DEATH OF FATHERS. **81** The Lot of the death of fathers is taken by day from Saturn to Jupiter (and by night the contrary), and to it are added the degrees of the Ascendant, and it is cast out from the Ascendant. **82** And this Lot indicates the reason for the death of the fathers. **83** Moreover, when the year terminates at[96] this Lot or at its lord, they indicate a calamity for the father, and it indicates likewise when one of them terminates at the indicators of the father.

84 The third is [19] the LOT OF GRANDFATHERS. **85** The Lot of grandfathers is taken by day from the lord of the house of the Sun to Saturn (and by night the contrary), and it is cast out from the Ascendant, and wherever it comes to an end, there is this Lot. **86** Now if the Sun was in his own house, then take by day from the first degree of Leo to Saturn (and by night the contrary), and cast it out from the Ascendant. **87** And if the Sun was in the house of Saturn, then take by day from the Sun to Saturn (and by night the contrary), and cast it out from the Ascendant—and do not pay attention to whether Saturn is under the rays or appearing. **88** And this Lot and its lord both indicate the conditions of grandfathers, so that when it connects with the infortunes, a calamity will afflict the grandfathers; and whenever it connects with the fortunes, good will affect them, as well as good fortune and abundance in assets.

89 The fourth is [20] the LOT OF LINEAGE, and it is the Lot of origin and noble descent. **90** It is taken by day from Saturn to Mars (and by night the contrary), and to it is added what Mercury has traveled in his sign, and it is cast out from the beginning of the sign of Mercury: and wherever it runs out, there is this Lot. **91** So look: for if this Lot was in a stake, with one of its claimants looking at it, or the Sun or the lord of the Midheaven or one of the lords of the stakes was looking at it with an aspect of affection, then the native will have a noble origin and respected descent, not defamed in his origin nor descent. **92** And if this Lot was falling, assembled with the infortunes, or its claimants and the lords of the stakes were not looking at it, then he will be ignoble, disreputable in origin and descent.

---

[95] See [65] the Lot of authority, aid, and conquering, in **287-91**.
[96] That is, by profection.

BOOK VIII: LOTS

93 The fifth is [21] the LOT OF IMMOVABLE PROPERTIES AND ESTATES according to Hermes. **94** The Lot of immovable property and estates is taken by day and night from Saturn to the Moon, and to it are added the degrees of the Ascendant, and it is cast out from the Ascendant, and wherever it terminates, there is this Lot. **95** And this Lot is equivalent to [69] the Lot of authority and which work the native does. **96** And if this Lot and its lord were in a suitable condition and place, then he will have immovable property and estates, and be happy because of them and because of plowing and planting, and he will acquire assets because of them; but if they were in a bad condition and place, it indicates distresses, calamities, and detestable things because of immovable properties.

97 The sixth is [22] the LOT OF IMMOVABLE PROPERTIES according to some of the Persians. **98** The Lot of immovable property is taken by day from Mercury to Jupiter (and by night the contrary), and it is cast out from the Ascendant. **99** And one looks in the matters of estates and immovable property from this Lot in the way one looks at the Lot before it.[97]

100 The seventh is [23] the LOT OF AGRICULTURE. **101** The Lot of agriculture and cultivation is taken by day and night from Venus to Saturn, and it is cast out from the Ascendant, and where it comes to an end, there is this Lot. **102** So look at this Lot and its lord: for if they were made fortunate he will benefit from plowing, cultivation, and planting; and if they were made unfortunate he will not be blessed well by them, and something detestable as well as loss will affect him because of it.

103 The eighth is [24] the LOT OF THE OUTCOMES OF AFFAIRS. **104** The Lot of the outcomes of affairs is taken by day and night from Saturn to the lord of the house of the meeting (if the native was conjunctional) or to the lord of the opposition (if the native was oppositional), and to it is added the degrees of the Ascendant, and it is cast out from the Ascendant. **105** Now if this Lot and the lord of its house were in the signs of straight ascension or made fortunate,[98] then the outcomes of his affairs will be excellent; and if they were in the signs of crooked ascension or made unfortunate, the outcomes of his affairs will be bad. **106** And if they differed, so that one of them

---

[97] That is, [21].

[98] Grammatically this means the *signs* are made fortunate; but the Lot and its lord would be indirectly benefited by the sign.

was in a straight sign and the other in a crooked sign, then there will be disagreement and confusion in the outcomes of his affairs, but then after that the affair will revert to what is indicated by the sign which the lord of the house of the Lot is in.

The fifth house: and it has five Lots

108 The first of them is [25] the LOT OF CHILDREN. **109** The Lot of children according to what Hermes and all of the ancients claimed, is taken by day from Jupiter to Saturn (and by night the contrary), and to it are added the degrees of the Ascendant, and it is cast out from the Ascendant, and wherever it comes to an end, there is the Lot of children. **110** And this Lot matches [8] the Lot of life—but by night, the Lot of children and [14] the Lot of siblings coincide in the same position.

111 Now, Theophilus claimed that the Lot of children is taken by day *and* night from Jupiter to Saturn,[99] but the first Lot which Hermes and all of the ancients stated, is more correct.

112 And this Lot is consulted for whether or not the man will have children: so if this Lot and its lord were in a fertile sign, he will have many children; and if it was in a sterile sign, he will not have children; but if it was in a sign of few children, he will have few children. **113** And if this Lot does indicate the producing of children and it was made fortunate, they will survive; but if it was made unfortunate, it indicates the death of the children. **114** And it also indicates the rest of the conditions of children generally, how their relationship with the father is, in terms of harmony and disagreement, and affection and hatred. **115** And what is between this Lot up to its lord is taken (or what is between its lord to it), in terms of signs, and a child is appointed for every sign: now if between them there was a sign having two bodies, then double the number of that sign; and if there was a planet between them, reckon a single child for it.[100]

---

[99] This is not true—or at least, Theophilus makes no mention of day or night versions in his *On Various Inceptions* Ch. 5.4, **15**. This is one indication that Abū Ma'shar takes an author's silence on the matter, as evidence that it is not reversed.
[100] See also VIII.7, **10**.

116 The second Lot is the one which indicates [26] THE TIME WHEN THERE WILL BE CHILDREN, AND THEIR NUMBER.[101] **117** Since Jupiter is the indicator of the start of producing children, as well as temperate wetness and growth, and Mars has the indication of heat, motion, passion, eagerness, cohabitation, and the natural sexual intercourse[102] which is in men, and they have found that no children come to be except by cohabitation and the sexual union of men with women, and by means of innate heat mixing with moderate wetness, they said the Lot by which children are judged for them, and their number, and whether they would be male or female, is taken by day and night from Mars to Jupiter, and to it is added the degrees of the Ascendant, and it is cast out from the Ascendant, and where it comes to an end, there is the Lot. **118** So look: for if [25] the first Lot which Hermes mentioned, and the rest of the indicators of children, indicate that the native will have children, then this indicates their number. **119** And in addition, when Jupiter comes to this Lot by assembly or looks at it with strength, then children will come to be in that time (after the man has attained puberty). **120** Now if it was in a male sign the majority of his children will be male, while if it was in a female sign, the majority of them will be female. **121** And if the indicators indicated many children for the native, then look at this Lot and the lord of its house, to see in which sign it is: for it indicates that he will have children according to the number of the lesser, middle, or greater years of the lord of the Lot (and sometimes they added to it the number of the years of those looking at it).

122 The third is [27] the LOT OF MALE CHILDREN. **123** Since the Moon indicates childhood and the youngest[103] age, and Jupiter indicates generation, growth, one's constitution, and male children, they calculated the Lot of male children from them both, and said the Lot of male children is taken by day and night from the Moon to Jupiter, and to it are added the degrees of the Ascendant, and it is cast out from the Ascendant.

124 But some of the Persians said that the Lot of male children is taken by day from the Moon to Saturn, and by night the contrary, and it is cast out

---

[101] See *Carmen* II.11, **2**.
[102] More literally, "sex" or "marriage," but here I believe it refers to something like common-law marriage.
[103] Lit., "young."

from the Ascendant. **125** And Theophilus claimed that it is taken by day and night from the Moon to Saturn, and it is cast out from the Ascendant. **126** And some of the Persians as well as Theophilus said that one should have recourse to these two Lots which they stated, for the native's good fortune, just as one has recourse to the Lot of Fortune (and they were correct that this Lot has an indication for good fortune). **127** But the correct way to derive the Lot of male children is what Hermes said (and it is taken from the Moon to Jupiter), because Jupiter is more indicative of male children than Saturn is.

128 And it indicates the conditions of male children in terms of good and evil, and excellence and badness, and might and authority, and marriage, and the rest of their conditions and fluctuations. **129** And when this Lot and its lord are both in a suitable condition and place, the male children will have might, authority, and good fortunes; and when they are in a bad condition, it indicates the contrary of that. **130** And whenever this Lot is made unfortunate,[104] it indicates that the male children will have disaster and something detestable.

131 The fourth is [28] the LOT OF FEMALE CHILDREN. **132** Since the Moon has the indication of youth and feminization, and Venus has the indication of coldness and wetness, and female children, Hermes said the Lot of female children is taken by day and night from Moon to Venus, and to it are added the degrees of the Ascendant, and it is cast out from the Ascendant.

133 And Theophilus said it is taken by day from the Moon to Venus and by night the contrary, and it is cast out from the Ascendant. **134** But the one which Hermes said is more correct because each of the two planets is nocturnal, but the Moon's indication by day and night for female children is stronger than Venus's: so one ought to begin with [the Moon] <by day and night>.

135 And this Lot indicates the conditions of female children, and their marriages, and their fluctuations in their conditions: so if it was in a suitable condition they will come to praise and good fortune, and they will benefit from marriage; and if it was the contrary of that, then to the contrary. **136** And whenever this Lot is made unfortunate, the female children will have

---

[104] Reading ينحس for the obviously erroneous يحسن ("in a good state"), also in parallel with **136** below.

what is detestable. **137** And if the man had male and female children, and you wanted to know which of them will be will be more illustrious in power or more fortunate,[105] then look at [27-28] these two Lots (which are the Lots of male and female children), to see which of them is more excellent in position, and more suitable in condition, and the fortunes look at more powerfully. **138** So if the Lot of male children was more suitable in condition, then report that the male children will be more fortunate than the female ones; but if the Lot of female children is more excellent in condition, then report that the female children will be in a better condition than the male ones.

139 The fifth is [29] the LOT BY WHICH A NATIVE, SOMEONE ASKED ABOUT, AND A FETUS, IS KNOWN TO BE MALE OR FEMALE, taken by day from the lord of the house of the Moon to the Moon (and by night the contrary), and it is cast out from the Ascendant. **140** So if it occurred in a male sign, then the native or one asked about, or fetus, will be male; and if it occurred in a female sign, it is female.

The sixth house: and it has four Lots

142 The first of them is [30] the LOT OF ILLNESS, DEFECTS, AND CHRONIC ILLNESS ACCORDING TO HERMES. **143** Since pains, emaciation, and chronic illness are from an excess of heat, dryness, cold, and wetness, and from their dominating and gaining superiority, and heat and dryness belong to Mars, and wetness and cold belong to Saturn, for this reason they attributed all ailments and illnesses to these two planets, and said the Lot of illness, defects, and chronic illness is taken by day from Saturn to Mars (and by night the contrary), and it is cast out from the Ascendant. **144** And if this Lot and its lord were both in a bad condition or made unfortunate, then it indicates difficult illnesses, long-lasting emaciation, and chronic illness; and if they were both made fortunate, it indicates safety.

145 The second is [31] the LOT OF ILLNESSES ACCORDING TO SOME OF THE ANCIENTS, taken by day and night from Mercury to Mars, and it is cast out from the Ascendant. **146** And this Lot indicates illnesses which are *not* enduring, so whenever this Lot and its lord are corrupted, they both indicate

---

[105] Or perhaps, "happier" (أسعد).

an abundance of disturbance in the body, and short-term illnesses; and if it was the contrary, then to the contrary.

147 The third is [32] the LOT OF SLAVES. **148** Since servant-girls, slaves, servants, one's entourage, couriers, messengers, and quick affairs are from the indication of these two quick, light planets (which are Mercury and the Moon), they attributed all of what pertains to this category, to them both. **149** Hermes and the ancients said that the Lot of slaves is taken by day and night from Mercury to the Moon, and it is cast out from the Ascendant, and wherever it comes to an end, there is this Lot. **150** So if this Lot and its lord are both made fortunate, he will have good from slaves; and if they were both made unfortunate, he will have something detestable from them. **151** Now if the Lot was in an excellent condition but its lord in a bad condition, good will find him from the slaves but then after that harm from them will find him; and if it was to the contrary, then the contrary. **152** And if this Lot was in a sign of many children, he will have many servants and an entourage, and followers and dependents; and if it was to the contrary, then the contrary.[106]

153 But Theophilus said this Lot is taken to the contrary by night. **154** And Zādānfarrūkh [al-Andarzaghar] and others besides him claimed that the Lot of slaves is taken by day from Mercury to the Lot of Fortune (and by night the contrary), and it is cast out from the Ascendant,[107] but the first one which Hermes stated, is more correct.

155 The fourth is [33] the LOT OF PRISONERS. **156** The Lot of prisoners and fetters is taken by day from the lord of the house of the Sun to the Sun, and by night from the lord of the house of the Moon to the Moon, and is cast from the Ascendant, and wherever it comes to an end, there is this Lot. **157** So if this Lot occurred in an excellent position, with the fortunes, then it re-

---

[106] See also VIII.7, **8-9**.

[107] Abū Ma'shar is referring to the passage in BA III.11.1, **2**, which entertains and then rejects the Mercury-Fortune version. (Sahl's *Nativities* Ch. 6.10, **20** omits this calculation, presumably because al-Andarzaghar has rejected it.) This is the Hermetic Lot of Necessity, attributed to Mercury (see Paul of Alexandria Ch. 22). It is somewhat related to the topic of slaves because it signifies imprisonments, subordination, and other "constraining circumstances which happen to men as their lot at birth."

leases and sets free prisoners, the fettered, and the shackled; and if it occurred in a bad position, with the infortunes, their death and destruction will be in it.[108] **158** And if the Sun by day was in his own house (or the Moon by night in her house), then that one of the two will be the indicator:[109] then, look at that one of the two from which one derives the information, to see in which position of the circle it is, and from whom it is separating, or with whom it is connecting, and work with it in accordance with that.

The seventh house: it has sixteen Lots

160 The first of them is [34] the LOT OF MEN'S MARRIAGE ACCORDING TO HERMES.[110] **161** Since Saturn has the indication of what has precedence, and masculinization,[111] and Venus has the indication of feminization, and every male precedes the female by the nature of masculinization and action, Hermes calculated the Lot of partners for men by day and night from Saturn to Venus, and added to it the degrees of the Ascendant, and projected it from the Ascendant. **162** [Some] people said it is taken to the contrary by night and cast out from the Ascendant, but the statement of Hermes is more correct.

163 And this Lot which Hermes stated, as well as its lord, indicate the condition of the marriage of men, so if they were both in a suitable condition they indicate a suitable marriage, and good fortune and benefit because of it, and it indicates that he will marry a beautiful, appropriate woman. **164** But if they were corrupted, they indicate a corrupted marriage and calamities because of marriage and women, and he will marry corrupted women. **165** And whenever Jupiter reaches this Lot[112] or looks at it with strength, then he will marry at that time. **166** And if this Lot was with the lord of its house, or the Sun and Moon looked at the Lot and at the lord of its house with strength, then he will marry his relatives.

---

[108] That is, in their prison or shackles.
[109] I take this to mean that the sect light itself will be the indicator.
[110] See *Carmen* II.2, **2**.
[111] But see **54** and its footnote: it's more likely that Saturn is used because he indicates bonds of kinship (in this case, through marriage due to Venus).
[112] That is, by transit.

167 The second is [35] the LOT OF MEN'S MARRIAGE ACCORDING TO VALENS. **168** Another Lot belongs to men's marriage, from what Valens said: it is taken by day and night from the Sun to Venus, and to what is gathered together are added the degrees of the Ascendant, and it is cast out from the Ascendant, and wherever it runs out, there is this Lot.

169 The third is [36] the LOT OF MEN'S CUNNING AND DECEPTION TOWARDS WOMEN. **170** The Lot of men's cunning and deception towards women is like [35] the Lot of men's marriage according to Valens.

171 The fourth is [37] the LOT OF MEN'S INTERCOURSE WITH WOMEN. **172** The Lot of men's intercourse with women is like [35] the Lot of men's marriage according to Valens.

173 The fifth is [38] the LOT OF MEN'S DEBAUCHERY AND THEIR FORNICATION. **174** The Lot of men's debauchery is like [35] the Lot of men's marriage according to Valens.

175 So look at it:[113] for if it was in an excellent place, his marriage will be praised; but if it was in a bad place, his marriage will be blamed. **176** And in the indication of [36] the Lot of men's cunning and deception towards women, it indicates that if the position of this Lot was excellent, or it was in the sign of stratagems and cunning,[114] then the man will deceive whatever woman he wants to; and if it was corrupt, he will not be able to deceive any woman.[115] **177** And in the indication of [37] the Lot of men's intercourse with women, if this Lot was in a sign of sexual intercourse,[116] made unfortunate, the man will have much sex, be debauched, a fornicator; and if it was in a sign of sex [but] made fortunate, he will have much sex in praiseworthy ways. **178** And in the indication of [38] the Lot of men's debauchery and fornication, if the lord of [34] the Lot of men's wedding which Hermes stated, occurred along with [35] this Lot which Valens stated, and the lord of

---

[113] That is, at [35] the Valens Lot (from Sun to Venus). Lots [35]-[38] are all the same Lot.

[114] The twelfth sign is the place of cunning and stratagems (Ch. VI.26, **19**), but in Ch. VI.21 the individual signs of cunning are Leo, Sagittarius, Capricorn, and Pisces.

[115] Note that while this is all the same Lot, the significations are now contradictory: an excellent condition for [35] is a good marriage, but for [36] it's deception, and [37] it's praiseworthy.

[116] This is perhaps the signs of lewdness and the like, in Ch. VI.14.

this Lot [of Valens] is looking at the Lot of men's wedding [of Hermes], then he will fornicate with a woman before he marries her, but then her power[117] will rise after that, even though he is an adulterer.

179 The sixth is [39] the LOT OF WOMEN'S MARRIAGE ACCORDING TO HERMES. **180** As for the explanation of women's marriage, it is like the explanation of men's marriage, except that for women's marriage Hermes used to calculate by day and night from Venus to Saturn, and to it he adds the degrees of the Ascendant, and casts it out from the Ascendant. **181** And this Lot matches [23] the Lot of agriculture. **182** So if this Lot and its lord were both in a suitable condition, they indicate women's good fortune in marriage; and if they were both corrupted they indicate their grief, and calamities will afflict them because of marriage, and the woman will be debauched.

183 The seventh is [40] the LOT OF WOMEN'S MARRIAGE ACCORDING TO VALENS. **184** Another Lot for women's marriage from what Valens stated, is taken by day and night from the Moon to Mars, and to it are added the degrees of the Ascendant, and it is cast out from the Ascendant. **185** And some of the Persians said it is taken the contrary way by night, but the first one which Valens stated is more correct.

186 The eighth is [41] the LOT OF WOMEN'S CUNNING AND DECEPTION [TOWARDS MEN]. **187** The Lot of women's cunning and deception towards men is like [40] the Lot of women's marriage according to Valens.

188 The ninth is [42] the LOT OF WOMEN'S INTERCOURSE. **189** The Lot of women's intercourse is like [40] the Lot of women's marriage according to Valens.

190 The tenth is [43] the LOT OF WOMEN'S DEBAUCHERY AND THEIR INDECENCY. **191** The Lot of women's debauchery and their indecency is like [40] the Lot of women's marriage according to Valens.

192 And if this Lot[118] and its lord were both in a suitable condition, the woman will be praiseworthy due to her marriage; and if they were in a bad condition, the woman will be blameworthy due to her marriage, and distresses and calamities will afflict her because of husbands. **193** And in the

---

[117] أمرها. Or, "authority."

[118] Again, this is the [40] Valens Lot (from Moon to Mars), as Lots [40]-[43] are all the same Lot.

indication of [41] women's cunning and deception towards men, if the position of this Lot was excellent, and it was in the signs of cunning and stratagems,[119] in an excellent position, the woman will deceive whatever man she wants to. **194** And if it was not in the sign of stratagems or it was in a bad condition, the woman will not be able to deceive any man. **195** And in the indication of [42] the Lot of their intercourse and sex, if it was in a sign of sexual intercourse,[120] made unfortunate, then she will be a whore, an adulteress, corrupted, debauched; but if it was made fortunate, in a sign of sex, she will have much passion for sex in ways that are good. **196** And in the indication of [43] women's debauchery and indecency, if <the lord of the>[121] [39] Lot of women's marriage which Hermes stated was with [40] this Lot which Valens stated, or the lord of [40] this Lot was with [39] the Lot of marriage, then she will commit adultery with men, but then marry them after that.

197 The eleventh is [44] the LOT OF A WOMAN'S ABSTINENCE. **198** The Lot of a woman's abstinence is taken by day and night from the Moon to Venus, and cast out from the Ascendant, and wherever it falls, there is this Lot. **199** And this Lot matches [28] the Lot of female children. **200** So look at it, for if it was in a fixed sign, in the inspection of its claimants, or one of the fortunes looks at it, then the woman will be abstinent. **201** And if it was in a sign having two bodies and the fortunes looked at it, she will also be abstinent except that she will be passionate for sex in ways that are good. **202** And if it was in a convertible sign, in the inspection of the fortunes, she will be eager for sex. **203** And if the infortunes which do *not* have a share in it looked at it, and it is in a convertible sign, then she will have a powerful passion for sex, bearing herself in a detestable way because of it, and perhaps she will be an adulteress.

204 The twelfth is [45] the LOT OF MEN'S AND WOMEN'S MARRIAGE ACCORDING TO HERMES. **205** The Lot of the marriage of men and women is taken by day and night from Venus to the degree and minute of the stake of wedding, and it is cast out from the Ascendant. **206** So if this Lot was assembling with an infortune or looked at it, then both [the man and woman] will be disgraced in their marriage; and if its lord was in a bad position and

---

[119] See footnote to **176** above.
[120] See footnote to **177** above.
[121] Adding in accordance with the parallel Lot for men above (**178**).

Venus was made unfortunate by Saturn or under the rays of the Sun, he will never marry.

207 The thirteenth is [46] the LOT OF THE TIME OF MARRIAGE ACCORDING TO HERMES. **208** The Lot which Hermes stated for the time of marriage is taken by day and night from the Sun to the Moon, and to it are added the degrees of the Ascendant,[122] and it is cast out from the Ascendant. **209** So when Jupiter reaches this Lot or looks at it with strength, then the man will get married in that time to a beautiful, neat woman, radiant and pleasant; and indeed he used this Lot when the root of a man's nativity had already indicated that he would marry. **210** And the explanation for that is that, of the two luminaries, one of them is hot, male, and the other wet, female, and all birth in this world comes about by the coming together of heat and maleness with wetness and femaleness: so for this reason they calculated the Lot of the time of marriage from the two luminaries.

211 The fourteenth is [47] the LOT OF THE MARRIAGE'S STRATAGEMS[123] AND ITS FACILITATION. **212** The Lot of the marriage's stratagems and its facilitation is taken by day and night from the Sun to the Moon, and cast out from Venus, and wherever it comes to an end, there is this Lot. **213** So look at this Lot: for if it was in a suitable condition, made fortunate, in the sign of stratagems, the beginning of his marriage will be in stratagems, ease, and pleasant circumstances, and every artful stratagem he employs because of marriage, will be completed. **214** And if it was in a bad condition, made unfortunate, his marriage will be with difficulty, trouble, and nothing of his strategy because of it will be completed.

215 The fifteenth is [48] the LOT OF IN-LAWS.[124] **216** The Lot of in-laws is taken by day and night from Saturn to Venus, and to it are added the degrees of the Ascendant, and it is cast out from the Ascendant. **217** And this Lot matches [34] the Lot of men's marriage which Hermes stated. **218** So

---

[122] This should be projected from Venus, as *Carmen* II.6, **1** and *BA* III.7.1, **21** have it.

[123] حيلة. **BY** translate this as the more neutral "arrangement," but the Arabic really does imply crafty planning. The title of the Lot must reflect the—often cynical and financially-driven—practices of arranged marriage. In such an environment, finding a wife really does take stratagems and life planning.

[124] الأختان. This can also be understood as "sons-in-law," or "brothers-in-law," but Abū Ma'shar seems to mean it more broadly.

look at this Lot: for if it was made fortunate, in harmony with the lord of its house, he will be in harmony with his in-laws and the people of his women's house; and if it was made unfortunate, he will be hostile to them.

219 The sixteenth is [49] the LOT OF CONTENTIONS AND CONTENDERS. **220** The Lot of contentions and contenders is taken by day from Mars to Jupiter (and by night the contrary),[125] and is cast out from the Ascendant. **221** So if this Lot occurred in the Ascendant or with its lord,[126] or in one of the stakes, then the native will have many contentions, being burdened by them. **222** And if it was made unfortunate, something detestable will afflict him because of them, while if it was made fortunate, good will find him because of them. **223** And if this Lot occurred with the lord of the seventh, [and] in the Ascendant, then the native will be of those who contend in the presence of Sultans, sages, and judges.

The eighth house: it has five Lots

225 The first of them is [50] the LOT OF DEATH.[127] **226** Since the Moon is the indicator of bodies, and the eighth house is an indicator of death and ruin, and Saturn is an indicator of passing away, perdition, destruction, distress, sorrow, weeping, mourning, and worry, Hermes granted these three indicators the indication of death, and said the Lot of death is taken by day and night from the degree of the Moon to the degree of the eighth house by equation,[128] and to it is added what Saturn has traveled in his sign, and it is cast out from the beginning of Saturn's sign, and wherever it comes to an end, there is this Lot. **227** So if this Lot and its lord are both made unfortunate and the fortunes do not look at them, the owner [of the chart] will be killed in an ugly way; but if the fortunes did look at it,[129] then it is the contrary of that.

---

[125] This matches the alternative Lot of fathers according to Dorotheus and others (see **74**), although Dorotheus does not mention the nocturnal reversal. Does this imply that if you have to use this Lot, there will be more contention between father and children?

[126] That is, with the lord of the Ascendant.

[127] See *Carmen* IV.3, **16**.

[128] بالسواء. That is, by quadrant house cusps. See VIII.3, **14**.

[129] Or perhaps, "them."

228 And some of the Persians said regarding the Lot of death that it is taken by day from Mars to Saturn (and by night the contrary), and it is cast out from the Ascendant; but the first Lot which Hermes stated is more correct, because he derived it from the indicators which indicate death in a natural way.

229 The second is [51] the LOT OF THE KILLING PLANET.[130] **230** Since the lord of the Ascendant indicates the soul, and the Moon indicates the body, and when the soul and body are mixed in a temperate way they will remain harmonized for a long time (and when they differ, the body is destroyed), they said the Lot of the killing planet is taken by day from the degree of the lord of the Ascendant to the degree of the Moon (and by night the contrary), and it is cast out from the Ascendant, and where it runs out, there is this Lot. **231** So if the Moon alone looked at the lord of this Lot, and the Moon is in a sign of cut limbs,[131] made unfortunate, then he will be killed in captivity; but if she is not made unfortunate, then one of his limbs will be cut. **232** And if the lord of this Lot, and the lord of the eighth, were each making the other[132] unfortunate, he will be killed in captivity.

233 The third is [52] the LOT OF THE YEAR IN WHICH DEATH AND WANT IS FEARED FOR THE NATIVE. **234** Since Saturn is the indicator of cold, death, passing away, and calamities, and likewise the degree of the meeting and opposition, they calculated the Lot of calamity from these two positions, and said the Lot of the year in which death, calamity, want, harm, and hardship are feared for the native, is taken by day and night from Saturn to the lord of the house of the meeting (or to <the lord of> the house of the opposition) which was before the native's birth, and to it are added the degrees of the Ascendant, and it is cast out from the Ascendant, and wherever it reaches, there is this Lot. **235** And this Lot matches [24] the Lot of the outcome. **236** So if this Lot and its Lord were with the lord of the Ascendant, made unfortunate, then the native will have many illnesses and calamities in his body and assets, and frequently he will come to the brink of the destruction of the body and the disappearance of his assets. **237** And whenever the year termi-

---

[130] See Rhetorius Ch. 77 (Holden p. 125). Abū Ma'shar repeats this Lot as [91] below in VIII.5, **14-16**, which I believe to be in error there.
[131] See Ch. VI.17.
[132] Lit., "making its associate unfortunate."

nates at it or reaches this Lot by turning (a year for every sign), or by direction to the Ascendant or to its lord, then calamities from illnesses and ailments will afflict the native in his body, and restriction and something detestable will afflict him, and damage in his assets, and in other things besides assets, and fear for himself will strike him from different directions.

238 The fourth is [53] the LOT OF THE BURDENSOME PLACE. **239** The Lot of the burdensome place is taken by day from Saturn to Mars (and by night the contrary), and to it is added what Mercury has traveled in his sign, and it is cast out from the beginning of the sign of Mercury, and wherever the counting runs out, there is this Lot. **240** And this Lot matches [20] the Lot of lineage. **241** So if this Lot was with the lord of the Ascendant, both being made unfortunate, the native will have an inseparable[133] ailment in <the limb> which is indicated by the sign in which the Lot is, and the things he needs and seeks will come slowly to him, and his affairs will be confused. **242** And if the year from the Ascendant terminated at this Lot (or this Lot terminated at the Ascendant or its lord) by turning a year for every sign,[134] or by direction, it indicates that the native's needs will be impractical for him, and his works will be slow for him, and distresses and calamities will afflict him, and something he begins in that year will be small (if not[135] hesitation and delay in it). **243** And whenever the year terminates at this Lot, an ailment will afflict him in the place indicated by the sign in which the Lot is; and if the infortunes looked at the Lot, adversities and ruin will afflict him.

244 The fifth is [54] the LOT OF ENTANGLEMENT AND HARDSHIP. **245** The Lot of entanglement and hardship is taken by day from Saturn to Mercury (and by night the contrary), and it is cast out from the Ascendant. **246** So if this Lot and its lord were both made unfortunate, and then the year terminated at them (or at one of them), by turning a year for every sign[136] or by directing degree-by-degree, hardship and distresses will afflict the native, and something detestable will find him which he will not free himself from in that year, or his release from it will be difficult (and the more that he frees himself from one detestable thing, he will fall into another). **247** But if the

---

[133] Or, "unavoidable" (لازمة).
[134] That is, by profection.
[135] لا. This could also be read as "apart from" or "except for."
[136] That is, by profection.

fortunes looked at it from a strong position, some of that will be dissolved. **248** And if the lord of the Ascendant was with this Lot in the root of the nativity, both of them being made unfortunate, then for the native's whole life he will be in hardship and detestable things; and to the extent he does something, he will be entangled in it and something detestable will afflict him because of it.

The ninth house: it has seven Lots

250 The first of them is [55] the LOT OF TRAVEL. **251** The Lot of travel is taken by day and night from the lord of the ninth house[137] to the degree of the house of the ninth by equation,[138] and it is cast out from the Ascendant. **252** And this Lot and its lord indicate the native's travel and [his] condition in it.

253 The second is [56] the LOT OF TRAVEL BY WATER, taken by day from Saturn to 15° Cancer (and by night the contrary), and it is cast out from the Ascendant. **254** So if this Lot occurred with the fortunes in watery signs, then he will see good, benefit, profit, and safety in his traveling by water and his involvement with that; and if it was the contrary, then to the contrary. **255** Now if Saturn was in the fifteenth degree[139] of Cancer, then that degree in which Saturn is, as well as the degree of the Ascendant, will both be the indicators: so look at them both, and at their conditions, and the planets' aspects to them, then act according to what you see.

256 The third is [57] the LOT OF PIETY,[140] taken by day from the Moon to Mercury (and by night the contrary), and it is cast out from the Ascendant. **257** So if this Lot and its lord occurred with the lord of the Ascendant or with the indicators of the Ascendant, the native will be pious [and] decent.[141] **258** And likewise, if the indicators of the Lot were looking at it and at the

---

[137] Following **BY** and the abbreviated formula in VIII.6, **75**; most MSS read "sign." Abū Ma'shar means the lord of the sign where the ninth cusp is, as he is about to state.

[138] بالسّواء. That is, quadrant house cusps. See VIII.3, **14**.

[139] Or rather, 15°.

[140] الورع.

[141] عفيف. This word has connotations of purity and abstinence, as well.

lord of the Ascendant, then he will have piety; but if it was the contrary of that (or the Lot was made unfortunate), then the contrary.

259 The fourth is [58] the LOT OF REASON AND DEPTH OF THOUGHT. **260** The Lot of reason and depth of thought is taken by day from Saturn to the Moon (and by night the contrary), and cast out from the Ascendant. **261** And this Lot indicates reason, thought, and depth of thought, and examining things, and discussing and making inquiries into recondite matters, and discovering sciences, and praiseworthy ideas, and especially if Saturn by day was above the earth, easternizing, looking at the Lot and receiving it, or the Moon was looking at it from an excellent position.[142]

262 The fifth is [59] the LOT OF KNOWLEDGE[143] AND MEDITATION. **263** Since confirming [things], philosophy, deep penetration into matters, and a detailed examination in speech and long thought belong to Saturn, while reason, science, and knowledge belong to Jupiter, and to Mercury belong writing, science, and culture, as well as the testing of things, they calculated the Lot of knowledge from these three planets which we mentioned, and said the Lot of knowledge and meditation is taken by day from Saturn to Jupiter (and by night the contrary), and it is cast out from Mercury. **264** And this Lot indicates knowledge, meditation, deliberateness, and patience: so if this Lot was in the inspection of Saturn and Jupiter, received by them both (or one of them), and it was in the inspection of the lord of the Ascendant, then he will be a companion of patience and deliberateness, endurance, reason, and meditation. **265** And if Mercury looked at it he will be a companion of knowledge, testing matters, and discussing and making inquiries into recondite matters, and applying principles.[144]

266 The sixth is [60] the LOT OF TALES AND THE KNOWLEDGE OF PEOPLE'S REPORTS AND SUPERSTITIONS. **267** The Lot of tales and the knowledge of people's reports and superstitions is taken by day from the Sun to Jupiter (and by night the contrary), and it is cast out from the Ascendant.

---

[142] See also VIII.7, **12**.

[143] العلم, which can also mean "science" (and is translated as such in a few places below). This paragraph also uses معرفة, which can variously mean "knowledge" and "information." But I am not sure that Abū Ma'shar is using these words in a very precise way.

[144] Or, "models" or "proverbs" (الأمثال).

268 And this Lot matches [17] the Lot of fathers if Saturn was under the rays.[145] **269** So if this Lot occurred in a stake, in the inspection of Mercury or Venus, and the lord of the Ascendant looked at it, then the native will be a preserver of old tales and people's reports, and he will be a master of superstitions, witticisms, and amusing tales which one laughs at and is amazed by; and if it was the contrary of that, then the contrary.

270 The seventh is [61] the LOT OF A REPORT, AS TO WHETHER IT IS TRUE OR FALSE. **271** The Lot of a report, as to whether it is true or false, is taken by day and night from Mercury to the Moon, and it is cast out from the Ascendant. **272** And this Lot matches [32] the Lot of slaves. **273** So if this Lot was in a stake or in a fixed sign, or in a sign of straight ascensions, then the report is true; but if the contrary, then the contrary.[146]

The tenth house: it has twelve Lots

275 The first of them is [62] the LOT OF THE NATIVE'S EXALTATION[147] AND ONE FOR WHOM ONE HAS DOUBTS WHETHER HE BELONGS TO HIS FATHER OR NOT. **276** Since the Sun is of the sect[148] of the day, and by day he is the indicator of the native's lifespan and survival,[149] and life and the soul, and power, rank, might, authority, and victory, and the Moon is nocturnal and by night is the indicator of the same things the Sun is by day, the Lot of the native's exaltation is calculated from them both, and from their degrees in which they are exalted. **277** And they said the Lot of exaltation is taken by day from the Sun to the degree of his exaltation (which is the completion of[150] 19° of Aries), and by night from the degree of the Moon to the completion of 3° of Taurus, and to it is added what has arisen of the Ascendant, and it is cast out from the Ascendant, and wherever it comes to an end, there is

---

[145] Or rather, the Persian variation (**73**).

[146] See also VIII.7, **8-9**.

[147] شرف. In this context I would normally translate this as "nobility," but this is the Hellenistic Lot of "exaltation" (the same word, in Arabic). So I have used "exaltation" to retain the connection with the ancient sources.

[148] حيّز.

[149] That is, he is the default longevity releaser.

[150] Or perhaps, "a full" (تمام) indicating exactly 19°.

the Lot of the native's exaltation. **278** So look at this Lot: for if it occurred in the Midheaven or with planets in an excellent condition and place, the native will come to exaltation, power, and the loftiness and levels of kings; and if he was of those who are permitted to be a king, he will be successful in rulership.[151] **279** And if the Sun by day was in the nineteenth degree of Aries, or the Moon by night was in the third degree of Taurus, then the indication would belong to their degree as well as to the degree of the Ascendant. **280** And if the indicators of this Lot were looking at it or were with it, in one of the excellent combinations, then the native will belong to his [generally] recognized father; and if it was the contrary of that, then to another besides his [recognized] father.

281 The second is [63] the LOT OF RULERSHIP AND AUTHORITY. **282** The Lot of rulership and authority is taken by day from Mars to the Moon (and by night the contrary), and it is cast out from the Ascendant. **283** So if this Lot and its lord were both in a suitable condition, mixing with the lord of the tenth and the Ascendant, its owner will be a king <or> chief, or he will be with kings who receive his speech and will pay attention to him.

284 The third is [64] the LOT OF MANAGERS, VIZIERS, AND AUTHORITIES. **285** Since the indicator of taking and giving, writing, and enduring in matters,[152] and government ministry, command and prohibition, books and letters, calculation, the land-tax, levying taxes, cleverness, the mind, and making distinctions, is Mercury, and causing fear and intimidation, alarm, and beating belong to Mars, they calculated the Lot of authority and managers from them both, and said the Lot of authority and managers is taken by day from Mercury to Mars (and by night the contrary), and it is cast out from the Ascendant. **286** And if this Lot and its lord were both in a suitable condition and place, with the lord of the Ascendant, the native will be clever, intelligent, sensible, reasonable, a manager, and he will be a master of the government administration, writing for kings, levying the land-tax, and [raising] money for the greatest king, and he will be allowed [the power of]

---

[151] Or perhaps, "he will be victorious over the king" (ظفر بالملك).

[152] البقاء في الأشياء. This probably means that when things are written down, they endure and persist. But given some of the negative connotations of this Lot (and the heavy-handed power used by historical viziers), this may refer to the fact that government officials are hard to get rid of, and their bad policies difficult to reverse.

command and prohibition in the provinces, and will be among those who raise people up to the pinnacle of elevation and put down others, and at his hands both good things and mistreatment will pass to the people.

287 The fourth is [65] the LOT OF AUTHORITY, AID, AND CONQUERING. **288** The Lot of authority is taken by day from the Sun to Saturn (and by night the contrary); and if Saturn was under the rays, then take by day from the Sun to Jupiter (and by night the contrary), and it is cast out from the Ascendant. **289** And this Lot matches [17] the Lot of fathers if Saturn was under the rays. **290** And it indicates authority for the native, as well as rank, might, and power; so if it was mixed with the lord of the Midheaven and the lord of the Ascendant, then he will gain authority, power, and rank. **291** And if it was in a sign in which the lord of the Ascendant had testimony, it indicates that he will be victorious over everyone he contends with.

292 The fifth is [66] the LOT OF THOSE WHO ARE SUDDENLY ELEVATED. **293** The Lot of those who are suddenly elevated is taken by day from Saturn to the Lot of Fortune (and by night the contrary), and it is cast out from the Ascendant. **294** And this Lot matches [3] the Lot of Saturn (which is the Lot of fetters).[153] **295** So if the position of this Lot was excellent relative to the Ascendant and the fortunes, its owner will be elevated suddenly; and if he had power, then he will increase in his power by surprise, and will have authority suddenly. **296** And indeed, you should look at this Lot if you knew that the man would be elevated and gain authority. **297** But if this Lot was made unfortunate, the native will be afflicted suddenly by evil and something detestable.

298 The sixth is [67] the LOT OF THOSE HONORED AND KNOWN AMONG THE PEOPLE. **299** The Lot of those honored and known among the people, and who have rank, is taken by day and night from Mercury to the Sun, and it is cast out from the Ascendant. **300** And if this Lot and its lord were both in a suitable condition, its owner will be honored, respected, powerful, having rank among authorities and kings.[154] **301** And if it was with a planet

---

[153] Or rather, "the burdensome."
[154] The construction of this Lot seems to be both astronomical and sociological. Astronomically, Mercury closely circles the Sun, and fans and devotees are closely attached to a celebrity's fame. (Or, news and rumors [Mercury] closely surround the celebrity of a famous person [Sun]). Sociologically and philosophically, fame is

having powerful testimony in the Midheaven, the people will attribute leadership to him in the way that they attribute [it] to the chiefs of tribes, cities, and what is like these things among leaders.

302 The seventh is [68] the LOT OF SOLDIERS AND CONSCRIPTION. **303** The Lot of soldiering and conscription is taken by day from Mars to Saturn (and by night the contrary), and it is cast out from the Ascendant. **304** And if this Lot and its lord were both mixed with the lord of the Ascendant, then its owner will be an adherent of the Sultan, and will be among the soldiers and conscripts.

305 The eighth is [69] the LOT OF AUTHORITY AND WHICH WORK THE NATIVE DOES. **306** Since toil, exertion, need, poverty, and all trades and professions such as builders, blacksmiths, weavers, street sweepers, and fatiguing works belong to Saturn (who indicates suffering) and to the Moon (who indicates toil and fatigue due to the quickness of her course), and [since] Saturn is also an indicator of kings and the Moon the indicator of the common people, they calculated the Lot of authority and trades from them both, and said the Lot of authority and which work the native does is taken by day and night from Saturn to the Moon, and it is cast out from the Ascendant. **307** And this Lot indicates authority, rank, power, and which work the native does, and which trade he applies his hand to, and whether or not he will earn money and be blessed by works of authority and trades. **308** So if this Lot and its lord were both in a suitable condition, he will have authority and power. **309** And if it was in Gemini and Virgo, or in the signs having devices[155] in the trades, he will show facility[156] in manual works which kings need for their clothing and splendor, and he will be with kings because of his easy manner and skill in the trades. **310** And if it was mixed with the indicators of assets, he will profit from his trades even if he does not have power;

---

also "Mercurial" (fleeting), and like Icarus flying too close to the Sun, one may be destroyed by it. Note that this Lot could only fall in the twelfth, rising, or second signs.

[155] الحيل, which connotes mental cleverness and tricks.

[156] Reading مترفقًا with Lemay, which is also matched by its verbal noun later in the sentence ("easy manner"). **BY** read this first instance as مترفعًا, which means to take pride in, but is not followed grammatically by the preposition ب as the text reads.

and if it they were to the contrary of what we said, he will be a poor, deprived artisan, earning his daily bread.

311 The ninth is [70] the LOT OF THOSE WHO WORK WITH THEIR OWN HANDS, AND BUSINESSES. **312** The Lot of those who work with their own hands, and businesses, is taken by day from Mercury to Venus (and by night the contrary), and it is cast out from the Ascendant. **313** And this Lot matches [13] the Lot of found wealth. **314** And this Lot and its lord indicate the masters of trades who apply themselves to fine, brilliant works, like goldsmithing and everything one applies gold and silver to, and furnishings and garments [done] by hand, or one applying himself to buying and selling these things, and dealers in slave girls, and masters of gemstones, and the types of businesses which are of the character of Mercury and Venus. **315** So if this Lot and its lord were mixed with the lord of the Ascendant, its owner will show easy facility,[157] having a light hand, doing fine, exotic works by hand which kings are in need of.

316 The tenth is [71] the LOT OF BUSINESSES, BUYING, AND SELLING. **317** The Lot of business according to what some of the Persians said, is taken by day from the Lot of the Invisible to the Lot of Fortune (and by night the contrary), and it is cast out from the Ascendant. **318** And this Lot matches [7] the Lot of Mercury.

319 And if these two Lots which belong to business[158] were both in the inspection of Mercury, being received, the native will be perceptive in businesses, buying, and selling; and if they were both made fortunate, he will benefit by that, and gain profit and superiority because of it (but if the contrary, then to the contrary).

320 The eleventh is [72] the LOT OF A WORK AND MATTER WHICH THERE IS NO ESCAPING HAVING TO DEAL WITH IT. **321** The Lot of a work and matter which there is no escaping having to deal with it, is taken by day from the Sun to Jupiter (and by night the contrary), and it is cast out from the Ascendant. **322** And this Lot matches [17] the Lot of fathers if Saturn was under the rays. **323** So if this Lot was with the lord of the Ascendant, the

---

[157] Again, this can mean having a good attitude, etc.: see footnote to **309**.
[158] That is, [70] and [71].

native will be preoccupied in his works, and he will be annoyed by[159] everything [else] he needs to do until he does it and is finished with it. **324** And if some work came to a man which he could not escape having to deal with it, then look at this Lot: for if it was with the fortunes, it indicates that he will benefit by expediting that work; but if it was with the infortunes, something detestable will afflict him because of expediting that work.

325 The twelfth is [73] the LOT OF THE MOTHER, taken by day from Venus to the Moon (and by night the contrary), and it is cast out from the Ascendant. **326** And this Lot indicates the conditions of mothers. **327** And indeed, we have put the Lot of the mother in the tenth sign, because the tenth sign indicates the conditions of mothers due to its opposition to the house of fathers.

The eleventh house: it has eleven Lots

329 The first of them is [74] the LOT OF NOBILITY. **330** Since the Lot of Fortune and the Lot of the Invisible are the most noble of the Lots, and they are both indicative of nobility and elevation, the Lot of nobility is calculated from them both: and they said the Lot of nobility is taken by day from the Lot of Fortune to the Lot of the Invisible (and by night the contrary), and it is cast out from the Ascendant. **331** And this Lot matches [9] the Lot of firmness and survival, and [6] the Lot of Venus.[160] **332** And if this Lot (which is the Lot of nobility) was with the fortunes in a suitable place, received, and especially if it was in the tenth or eleventh, falling away from the infortunes, the native will have nobility and will be happy, lasting in good fortune, praised, mild-tempered, and he will be among those whom the people look to due to his good fortune and rank, and they will be proud of him and associate themselves with him,[161] and he will be like a leader of tribes,

---

[159] يضيق الصّدر. This is how the idiom reads in Wehr, and based on the next sentence Abū Ma'shar seems to mean that it will always be on his mind, it will keep bothering him until he simply does it. Literally it means that his "concern will be narrowed" (implying great focus of mind, or that he will only be able to focus on it).

[160] It also matches [75] the Lot of being loved among the people.

[161] Or more literally, they will trace their names and lineages back to him (ينتسبون إليه).

and his name will remain for ages and many years, and he will have trust, and in everything he does he will see affection and delight.

333 The second is [75] the LOT OF BEING LOVED[162] AMONG THE PEOPLE. **334** The Lot of a man who is loved among the people (or hated) is taken by day from the Lot of Fortune to the Lot of the Invisible (and by night the contrary), and it is cast out from the Ascendant. **335** And this Lot matches [6] the Lot of Venus.[163] **336** So if this Lot occurred with the fortunes, or the fortunes were the lords of its house, or the lords of its exaltation, or the lords of its triplicity, then he will be loved among the people, endeared to them, charming in their eyes; but if it occurred with the infortunes which do *not* have a share in it, then he will be detested among the people, burdensome to them.

337 The third is [76] the LOT OF BEING KNOWN AMONG THE PEOPLE AND RESPECTED AMONG THEM. **338** The Lot of being known among the people, respected, [and] being concerned with their needs, is taken by day from the Lot of Fortune to the Sun (and by night the contrary), and it is cast out from the Ascendant, and wherever it comes to an end, there is this Lot. **339** So if this Lot was advancing with the Sun, Jupiter, and the rest of the fortunes, or they looked at it and at the lord of the Ascendant from affection, then kings as well as the common people will respect the native, and he will be prominent among them, and he will be concerned with the needs of the people, make an effort in them, and will fulfill many needs with his own hands.

340 The fourth is [77] the LOT OF SUCCESS. **341** The Lot of success is taken by day from the Lot of Fortune to Jupiter (and by night the contrary), and it is cast out from the Ascendant, and where it falls, there is the Lot. **342** So if this Lot was with the lord of the Ascendant or was looking at it, and it is not made unfortunate, then the native will be successful in his needs and affairs, generally victorious in the things he wants, and his needs will be fulfilled for him, and the accomplishment of the people's needs will be prepared at his hands, in accordance with what he wants. **343** And if the fortunes looked at it, something he wants will be reduced but it will [still] be

---

[162] المحبّب. Or perhaps, "evoking love" among the people.
[163] It also matches [9] the Lot of firmness and survival, and [74] the Lot of nobility just mentioned.

easy for him; and perhaps he will seek something so that he is victorious in more than[164] what he wants, in easy ways. **344** And if this Lot was not with the lord of the Ascendant, nor in its inspection, and the infortunes looked at it, then it is to the contrary.

345 The fifth is [78] the LOT OF PASSIONS AND EAGERNESS FOR WORLDLY THINGS.[165] **346** The Lot of passions and eagerness for worldly things is taken by day from the Lot of Fortune to the Lot of the invisible (and by night the contrary), and it is cast out from the Ascendant. **347** And this Lot matches [6] the Lot of Venus.[166] **348** So look, for if the position of this Lot was excellent, then the native will conquer his passions; and if its position was corrupted, his passions will conquer him, and he will be eager for the world and its pleasures, and he will ruin his assets out of love for them.

349 The sixth is [79] the LOT OF HOPE. **350** The Lot of hope is taken by day from Saturn to Venus (and by night the contrary), and it is cast out from the Ascendant. **351** And of course people have claimed that the Lot of hope is derived like [34] the Lot of men's marriage according to Hermes is; but they are in error.[167] **352** And if this Lot (which is the Lot of hope) and its lord were in an excellent position, made fortunate, he will be successful in everything he hopes for or expects; and if it was in a bad condition and place, he will not be successful.

353 The seventh is [80] the LOT OF FRIENDS. **354** Since Mercury has a varied indication, because at some times he indicates masculinization and at others feminization, and sometimes good and sometimes bad, and he always inclines towards the strongest of the natures and the most dominant of them, and the Moon resembles him due to the quickness of her motion, and likewise a man has different conditions with friends and brethren, they make them the two indicators of this Lot, and said the Lot of friends and brethren is taken by day and night from the Moon to Mercury, and it is cast out from the Ascendant. **355** So if this Lot and its lord were both in a suitable condi-

---

[164] أكثر ممّا. This could also be read as "most of."
[165] This is the Lot of Erōs according to Valens.
[166] It also matches [9], [74], and [75].
[167] This is because Abū Ma'shar denies in **162** that [34] should be reversed at night, as these other people think it should.

tion and place, in convertible signs, he will have many brethren and friends; and if they were made fortunate he will benefit from them and they will benefit from them, and each will have good from the other. **356** And if they were both received, he will be praised among them, dear to them. **357** And some of the masters of the stars claimed that [7] the Lot of Mercury indicates the whole of the condition of friends, but that is not correct because the Lot of Mercury has [only] a partial indication for friends.[168]

358 The eighth is [81] the LOT OF COMPULSION.[169] **359** The Lot of compulsion is taken by day and night from the Lot of the Invisible to Mercury, and is cast out from the Ascendant, and where it comes to an end, there is this Lot. **360** And it indicates the affection of two friends, or the affection of a man and his woman, and that is because you should look: for if this Lot in the nativity of each one of the two was in[170] the fall of the other or its un-

---

[168] According to VIII.3, **51** as well as the Greek description in Paul Ch. 23, it is quite the opposite: Lot [7] has to do with enemies and trouble, not friends. But see [81] below, which also uses Mercury and deals with attraction and friends.

[169] الاضطرار. Or, "coercion, necessity." At this point I think something has gone wrong in Abū Ma'shar's sources. In Paul's account of the seven Hermetic Lots, there is indeed a Lot of necessity (which is an alternative translation for "compulsion"), but it is a *Fortune*-Mercury Lot and does not have these connotations. However, there is also a Lot of *Erōs* or love, which is a Spirit-*Venus* Lot, and has roughly the same meaning as given here: friendship, favor, attraction. So I believe that the correct Lot which goes here is the Hermetic Lot of *Erōs*, from Spirit to Venus by day (and reversed by night), with the same interpretation as given in **360**. I suspect that the culprit in this mixup of names and formulas is al-Andarzaghar or his source material: see my footnotes and references in Sahl's *Nativities* Ch. 11, **5**.

[170] At this point, Lemay inserts a reconstruction of what he believes ought to belong here: "...the Ascendant of the other, or in its exaltation, or in two harmonious signs, then they will love each other; and if each one of them was in...". Now, I happen to think this is a good way to look at it, and Lemay's instincts were correct. But we now know from the Arabic account of al-Andarzaghar (in Sahl's *Nativities* Ch. 11.4, **18-20**), that al-Andarzaghar (the likely author and confuser of this material), did not have a positive interpretation here, but reads similarly to how Abū Ma'shar has it. So Abū Ma'shar seems to be correct in giving this negative interpretation to what is possibly the wrong Lot, which he gets from al-Andarzaghar.

healthiness,[171] or they were in two antithetical[172] signs, then they will be hostile to each other.

361 The ninth is [82] the LOT OF PLENTY AND AN ABUNDANCE OF GOOD IN THE HOME, taken by day and night from the Moon to Mercury, and it is cast out from the Ascendant. **362** And this Lot matches [80] the Lot of friends. **363** So if this Lot or its lord were in a combination with the Lot of Fortune and the lord of the Ascendant, then the native will have a spacious home, having plenty, generous with food; and if it was the contrary, then to the contrary.

364 The tenth is [83] the LOT OF THE SOUL'S FREEDOM. **365** The Lot of the soul's freedom is taken by day from Mercury to the Sun (and by night the contrary), and it is cast out from the Ascendant. **366** So if it occurred with the fortunes (and especially with Jupiter) or Jupiter or the Sun looked at it with an aspect of affection, he will be free of soul, at ease, cheerful, smiling, tolerant; and likewise if this Lot or its lord occurred in the signs of freedom.[173] **367** But if they occurred with the infortunes or in the signs contrary to freedom, then the contrary of that.[174]

368 The eleventh is [84] the LOT OF THE PRAISED AND COMMENDED. **369** The Lot of the praised and commended is taken by day from Jupiter to Venus (and by night the contrary), and it is cast out from the Ascendant. **370** So if the fortunes (and especially Jupiter) looked at this Lot or at its lord or they were with them, then the native will be praised, commended for his exploits and good deeds, and he will be well spoken of. **371** But if the fortunes looked at it, he will not be thanked nor commended for his good

---

[171] That is, its detriment (وبال).

[172] متضاذَين. This does not match a specific category of sign in the rest of the *Gr. Intr.* But it's worth pointing out that this is not how the Arabic al-Andarzaghar has it in Sahl. In Sahl, each native's Lot of necessity is in the exact same sign (such as each being in Virgo), or they are in the signs of a single planet (such as Gemini and Virgo), or else they are in "each other's" signs. In this last category, perhaps he means that their lords are in each other's signs. For example, let one native have this Lot in Virgo, but its lord Mercury is in Scorpio; the other native has the Lot in Scorpio, but its lord Mars in Virgo.

[173] These are probably the fiery signs, or at least Leo and Sagittarius.

[174] **BY**: "in the contrary signs, then the contrary."

deeds; and perhaps he will treat a man well but that good deed will lead to blame and he will be criticized.

The twelfth house: it has three Lots

373 The first of them is [85] the LOT OF ENEMIES ACCORDING TO SOME OF THE ANCIENTS, taken by day and night from Saturn to Mars, and cast out from the Ascendant.

374 The second is [86] the LOT OF ENEMIES ACCORDING TO HERMES. **375** And Hermes claimed concerning the Lot of enemies that it is taken by day and night from the lord of the house of enemies to the degree of the house of enemies, and it is cast out from the Ascendant. **376** And one uses both of these Lots: so if they were both in the square or opposition of the lord of their own houses or the lord of the Ascendant, then the native will have many enemies; and if it was the contrary of that, then the contrary.

377 The third is [87] the LOT OF SUFFERING. **378** The Lot of suffering is taken by day and night from the Lot of the Invisible to the Lot of Fortune, and is cast out from the Ascendant. **379** And this Lot matches [7] the Lot of Mercury,[175] and indicates the suffering of the native as well as his good fortune. **380** So, if this Lot was with the lord of the Ascendant or was mixed with it in one of the bad aspects, the native will suffer for his whole life, not benefiting by, nor being prepared for, nor enjoying, his assets or his good fortune.

---

[175] At least, it matches it by day. Abū Ma'shar reverses [7] the Lot of Mercury by night.

Chapter VIII.5: On stating the Lots which are not mentioned along with the seven planets nor with <the Lots of> the twelve houses (And they are used in nativities and on many occasions along with those Lots which we mentioned above)

And their number is ten

1 The first is [88] the LOT OF THE RELEASER.[176] **2** Look, for if the native was conjunctional, then take from the degree and minute of the meeting which was before the native's birth up to the Moon (and if the native was oppositional, take from the degree and minute of the opposition which was before the native's birth up to the Moon), and cast it out from the Ascendant. **3** And this Lot is directed just as one directs the releasers, degree by degree, and it is turned[177] in the signs, sign by sign: so when it terminates at the infortunes, it indicates calamity. **4** Now sometimes, many of the scholars of the stars would find a man whom a bad calamity had afflicted in one of the times, but they would not find any of the releasers having reaching the positions of the infortunes at that time, nor would that calamity have an obvious indication in the revolution of that year, so they were not aware of the reason for it. **5** And indeed that was concealed from them because they did not direct this Lot—but if they had directed it, they would have discovered that it

---

[176] The original version of this Lot comes from Nechepsō, and is explained differently by Valens in *Anth.* III.7. In Valens, if the nativity is conjunctional, count from the prenatal conjunction to the natal Moon, and project from the Ascendant. If it is preventional or oppositional, count from the natal Moon to the *next* conjunction, and *subtract* from the Ascendant. (For preventional births, this is identical to counting from the next conjunction to the natal Moon, and adding it to the Ascendant—so we are always counting from a conjunction.) The principle here seems to be that the conjunction of the Sun and Moon is akin to the Ascendant, which is where spirit (analogous to the Sun) meets matter (analogous to the Moon): thus, we must always measure in relation to the conjunction, not the opposition. Now as for what we do next, Valens has two conflicting instructions. First, he says that the lord of the bound of the Lot will act as the longevity releaser—not the degree of the Lot. But in his first chart example, he does exactly what Abū Ma'shar instructs: we direct the degree of the Lot to the rays of the infortunes.

[177] Reading يدار with Lemay (and the sense of the Latin) for **BY**'s يزاد ("is increased"). "Turning" is a synonym for profection.

was at the time when this Lot had terminated at one of the positions indicating calamity, since this [Lot], in the direction of degrees and the turning of signs, makes clear the indication for things which is close to what the rest of the releasers indicate.

6 The second is [89] the LOT OF THE EXHAUSTION OF BODIES. **7** The Lot of the exhaustion of bodies (that is, one whose body is worn out) is taken by day from the Lot of Fortune to Mars, and by night the contrary, and it is cast out from the Ascendant. **8** And if this Lot was with the lord of the Ascendant, or with a planet having a claim in either the Ascendant or the house-master,[178] and the planet was in its *halb*[179] or a wet sign, the native will be thick in body, with powerful extremities and limbs. **9** But if it was the contrary of that, and it was with Mercury or Mars, or they governed over it, he will have an emaciated[180] body.

10 The third is [90] the LOT OF HORSEMANSHIP AND COURAGE. **11** The Lot of horsemanship and courage is taken by day from Saturn to the Moon (and by night the contrary), and it is cast out from the Ascendant.[181] **12** And this Lot matches [58] the Lot of reason and depth of thought, as well as [69]

---

[178] I am not sure if this means the planet is one of the *candidates* for being the house-master, or whether it rules some dignity where the house-master actually is. I believe it is the latter.

[179] Reading في حلبه with **BY** for Lemay's في حلّته, which could mean "in its station." But this is not the usual word for a station.

[180] نحيف.

[181] This is the Dorothean Lot of expedition (explained with quotations from Dorotheus in Heph. II.19). However, the interpretation here is totally different, and shows that Abū Ma'shar was probably drawing in part on Theophilus's *Labors* Ch. 23. There, Theophilus does accurately restate the basics of the Dorothean interpretation (that the Lot should be in the signs of Mars or Saturn). But then Theophilus says that the expedition will be on horseback if the Lot or Mars were in Aries, Taurus, Leo, or Sagittarius. Abū Ma'shar seems to be doing a version of this, even apparently drawing on Theophilus's Ch. 23, **8**, which says that the expedition will be remarkable if Jupiter and Mars are configured with each other, and pivotal. Sahl likewise must be referring to this Lot in his *Nativities* Ch. 10.3, **1-3**, which uses different language but does refer to the Mars-Jupiter aspect and being in Sagittarius (or a sign of riding animals, as Abū Ma'shar has it).

the Lot of authority and which work the native does.[182] **13** Now if this Lot (which is the Lot of horsemanship) was in the sextile of Mars or Jupiter, in the signs of riding animals, it indicates that its owner will be courageous, a knight, dealing with riding animals and their activity, and be a friend of civilization, and he will sport with lances and swords.[183]

14 The fourth is [91] the LOT OF RISK-TAKING, HARDSHIP, AND FIGHTING. **15** The Lot of risk-taking is taken by day from the lord of the Ascendant to the Moon (and by night the contrary), and it is cast out from the Ascendant. **16** And if this Lot was in the sextile of Mars or Jupiter, or in the houses of the infortunes [but] received, in powerful signs, it indicates that its owner will be a risk-taker, a warrior, hard in his body, a killer.[184]

17 The fifth is [92] the LOT OF CUNNING, DECEPTION, AND STRATAGEMS. **18** Since the indicator of cunning, deception, and stratagems, as well as outwitting,[185] malice, misdeeds,[186] slyness, and what resembles that category, is Mercury, and indeed all of these things are of the condition of the soul—and the indication for the conditions of the soul belongs to the Lot of the Invisible—they calculated this Lot from them both, and said the Lot of cunning, deception, and stratagems is taken by day from Mercury to the Lot of the Invisible (and by night the contrary), and it is cast out from the Ascendant. **19** So if this Lot and its lord were in a mixture with the lord of the Ascendant, the native will be malicious, a master of deception, cunning, stratagems, misdeeds, and slyness. **20** But if it was made fortunate, he will benefit for these reasons; while if it was made unfortunate, something detestable will find him because of them. **21** And if Mercury was with Mars or in his mixture, and he had an indication in the Lot, then its owner will be

---

[182] But Abū Ma'shar thinks that [69] should not be reversed at night.

[183] See also VIII.7, **12**.

[184] Reading قَتَّالًا, شديدًا بدنه with **BY** for Lemay's قتالًا في يديه تحرّى, شديدًا, which has the sense that he is "harsh, pursuing fighting with his own hands." Notice that in Rhetorius, this Lot describes harm *to* the native, not that the native himself will be violent. Abū Ma'shar correctly reflects Rhetorius in [51] the Lot of the killing planet.

[185] Reading الإرب with Lane's meaning, for **BY**'s الأرب. As a verbal noun, the latter means "desire" or "purpose."

[186] الجريزة. The root of this noun is a verb which means to be barren or a wasteland, and by extension to be so angry or vindictive that one wants to lay waste to one's enemy.

of those who open doors and locks by means of picking [them],[187] stratagems, and robbery.

22 The sixth is [93] the LOT OF AN OCCASION OF NEED[188] AND DESIRE. **23** Since the corruption of all things sought, and their hindrance, is from the two infortunes, and Mercury has a partnership in things sought, so that if the two infortunes are suitable and not making the sought matter unfortunate, it indicates its fulfillment (while if the two infortunes do undermine the sought matters then the matters are corrupted and delayed), for this reason they calculated this Lot from them, and said the Lot of an occasion of need and desire is taken by day and night from Saturn to Mars, and to it are added the degrees of Mercury, and it is cast out from Mercury, and wherever it comes to an end, there is this Lot. **24** And if this Lot was safe from the two infortunes (safe from Mars by day, and from Saturn by night), then it indicates the fulfilling of the needs; and if it was corrupted by them, it indicates that the needs will not be completed nor fulfilled. **25** And this Lot is used for abstract needs whose category one is not aware of. **26** But if one *did* know the category of the sought matter, whether it was assets, marriage, authority, or something besides that, one looks for that matter from its place [in the chart]; but one may turn to this Lot for help, along with that indicator.

27 The seventh is [94] the LOT OF NECESSITY[189] AND THE HINDERING OF NEEDS ACCORDING TO THE EGYPTIANS. **28** The Lot of necessity and the hindering of needs according to the Egyptians is taken by day and night from Mars to the degree of siblings,[190] and it is cast out from the Ascendant.

29 The eighth is [95] the LOT OF NECESSITY ACCORDING TO THE PERSIANS. **30** The Lot of necessity and the hindering of needs is taken by

---

[187] بالعلاج. That is, by "manipulating" the mechanism.

[188] In this paragraph, "need" and "the sought matter" is the same word: we seek what we need. In Latin-derived horary astrology this is the "quaesited" (*quaesitum*).

[189] الضرورة. This word has to do with distress and being forced into action by circumstances, and is a different form of the verb which was used to mean "compulsion" in [81] the Lot of compulsion (VIII.4, **358-60**).

[190] Or rather, to the degree "of the house" of siblings.

day and night from [6] the Lot of love and familiarity to Mercury,[191] and it is cast out from the Ascendant.

31 And one should apply these two Lots, and then look: for if they were with the infortunes (and especially with Saturn), or it[192] or its lord was with the lord of the Ascendant, then the native will be slack, lazy, barely able to motivate himself in anything which he needs, unless his need for it is unbearable or someone else induces him to do it and forces him to do it, whether he wants to or refuses to. **32** And sometimes he will be convinced with less than full consent due to the necessity, and the occasion of the need, and fear of [the opportunity] slipping away. **33** And if the lord of this Lot made the indicators of assets unfortunate, then his assets will be corrupted or calamities will afflict him in them.

34 The ninth is [96] the LOT OF PUNISHMENT,[193] taken by day from Mars to the Sun (and by night the contrary), and it is cast out from the Ascendant, and wherever it falls, there is this Lot. **35** So if this Lot was in one of the stakes or what follows it, with its claim[194] or with the lord of the Ascendant, then its owner will be a master of punishment and payback; and if it was the contrary of this, then to the contrary.

---

[191] This sounds like counting from Valens's *Erōs* to Mercury, but I think this is part of the general mixup in much of the Persian and Arabic material between the two different versions of *Erōs* and Necessity. The originator of this instruction probably meant this to be a Mercury-Fortune Lot, as is the Hermetic Lot of Necessity in Paul's Ch. 23, and as I suggested for Lot [81] in VIII.4, **358**.

[192] Abū Ma'shar now switches to the singular, showing that the Lots do not always have to be used in tandem.

[193] الجزاء. See also "payback" (المكافأة) below. These can mean "repayment" and "reward," respectively (which is how **BY** understand it). But because of the role of Mars, I feel that Abū Ma'shar really means paying someone back for *injustice*: so I have chosen "punishment" and "payback," respectively.

[194] مزاعمته, indicating a dignity. But as in a few other places, I believe Abū Ma'shar means "claimant" (مزاعمه), one of its lords. That is, I believe Abū Ma'shar wants the Lot to be (1) in a stake or what follows it, and (2) with its own lord or the lord of the Ascendant. See **40** below, where it seems a different Lot and its lord ("claim") are both withdrawing.

36 The tenth is [97] the LOT OF THE WORK OF TRUTH,[195] taken by day from Mercury to Mars (and by night the contrary), and it is cast out from the Ascendant, and wherever it comes to an end, there is this Lot. 37 And this Lot matches [10] the Lot of logic and reason. 38 So if this Lot was advancing, made fortunate, its owner will aspire to the truth, applying it, and having correctness and benefit prepared for him in it. 39 And if it was advancing but made unfortunate, then he will apply the truth but something detestable will afflict him because of it. 40 And if it was withdrawing with its claim,[196] or it was in a convertible sign, he will be knowledgeable about the truth, but not apply it.

41 And these are the famous, well-known Lots which the ancients stated, and they are used in nativities, and on many occasions pertaining to the revolutions of years, inceptions, and questions, each Lot on an occasion for which it is needed. 42 And know that for many matters among the indications of the twelve houses, and questions, inceptions, and the revolutions of years, there are Lots which we have not mentioned here, because examples of them will need to be stated in other places and books.[197]

43 But as for as for what we have stated about the indicators of the Lots in this book, it is by way of summary, not a detailed examination, because the positions of these Lots in the signs where they are, and the planets' assembling with them and their aspect to them, changes much of their indications for good or evil. 44 And we will discuss their indications in detail, in their positions in the signs in each book, in accordance with the need for it, if God wills.

---

[195] عمل الحقّ. **BY** translate this as "right action."
[196] See note to **35** above. I believe Abū Ma'shar means that both the Lot and its lord are withdrawing.
[197] This would include certain mundane Lots, mentioned in the *Book of Religions and Dynasties* (BRD), also known as *On the Great Conjunctions*.

Chapter VIII.6: On stating all of the Lots in an abbreviated way
And there are 97 Lots

1 In the chapters which have preceded we have stated the explanations for the Lots which belong to the seven planets, the twelve houses, and others (of those which are put to use in nativities, and on many occasions in questions), and we have mentioned what they have disagreed on concerning their derivation, as well as a summary of their indications (of those which suffice for this book). **2** But now we will state all of the Lots in an abbreviated way so that it might be easier for one wanting to derive them and put them down in nativities and questions. **3** And we will begin with the Lots of the seven planets, then state the Lots of the twelve houses (and which of the other Lots corresponds to them by position).[198] **4** Then after that we will state the Lots which are not of the category of the twelve houses.

5 And everything we state in this chapter concerning the derivation of the Lots, are the Lots which our predecessors (among the scholars of the stars) agreed on and saw as being correct—but we will leave off anything else about the Lots in which they disagreed, and which was stated by people who do not understand the natures of the planets.

The Lots of the planets (and their number is 7):

7 [1] The Lot of Fortune is taken by day from the Sun to the Moon by degrees of equality (and by night from the Moon to the Sun), and to it is added what has arisen of the sign of the Ascendant, and it is cast out from the beginning of the sign of the Ascendant: so where it comes to an end, there is the Lot of Fortune. **8** So if the luminaries were in a single minute, then the Lot of Fortune will be in the minute of the Ascendant.

9 [2] To the Sun belongs the Lot of the Invisible and of religion, taken by day from the Moon to the Sun (and by night from the Sun to the Moon), and to it is added the degrees of the Ascendant, and it is cast out from the Ascendant.

---

[198] That is, which Lots are calculated in the same way but for different houses and purposes.

10 [6] To Venus belongs the Lot of love and familiarity, taken by day from the Lot of Fortune to the Lot of the Invisible (and by night the contrary), and it is added to the degrees of the Ascendant, and cast out from the Ascendant.

11 [7] To Mercury belongs the Lot of poverty and few stratagems, taken by day from the Lot of the Invisible to the Lot of Fortune (and by night the contrary), and it is cast out from the Ascendant.

12 [5] To Mars belongs the Lot of courage and risk-taking, taken by day from Mars to the degree of the Lot of Fortune (and by night the contrary), and it is cast out from the Ascendant.

13 [4] To Jupiter belongs the Lot of prosperity, aid, and victory, taken by day from the Lot of the Invisible to Jupiter (and by night the contrary), and it is cast out from the Ascendant.

14 [3] To Saturn belongs the Lot of fetters and prison, and whether one would be rescued from it or not, taken by day from Saturn to the degree of the Lot of Fortune (and by night the contrary), and it is cast out from the Ascendant.

The Lots of the twelve houses (and their number is 80):

16 *The Ascendant: it has 3 Lots*

17 [8] The Lot of life is taken by day from Jupiter to Saturn (and by night the contrary), and it is added to the degrees of the Ascendant and cast out from the Ascendant.

18 [9] The Lot of the support of the Ascendant,[199] and the native's splendor and beauty, is taken by day from the Lot of Fortune to the Lot of the Invisible (and by night the contrary), and to it is added the degrees of the Ascendant, and it is cast out from the Ascendant. **19** And this Lot corresponds to [6] the Lot of Venus.

20 [10] The Lot of logic and reason is taken by day from Mercury to Mars (and by night the contrary), and it is cast out from the Ascendant.

---

[199] In VIII.4, **22**, the Lot of firmness and survival.

The house of assets: it has 3 Lots

22 [11] The Lot of assets is taken by day and night from the lord of the house of assets to the degree and minute of the house of assets by equation, and to it is added the degrees of the Ascendant, and it is cast out from the Ascendant.

23 [12] The Lot of loaning is taken by day and night from Saturn to Mercury, and it is cast out from the Ascendant.

24 [13] The Lot of found wealth is taken by day from Mercury to Venus (and by night the contrary), and it is cast out from the Ascendant.

The house of siblings: it has 3 Lots

26 [14] The Lot of siblings is taken by day and night from Saturn to Jupiter, and to it is added the degrees of the Ascendant, and it is cast out from the Ascendant.

27 [15] The Lot of the number of siblings is taken by day and night from Mercury to Saturn, and to it is added the degrees of the Ascendant, and it is cast out from the Ascendant.

28 [16] The Lot of the death of siblings is taken by day from the Sun to the degree of the Midheaven (and by night the contrary), and to it is added the degrees of the Ascendant, and it is cast out from the Ascendant.

The house of fathers: it has 8 Lots

30 [17] The Lot of fathers is taken by day from the Sun to Saturn (and by night the contrary), and to it is added the degrees of the Ascendant, and it is cast out from the Ascendant. **31** But if Saturn was under the rays, it is taken by day from the Sun to Jupiter (and by night from Jupiter to the Sun), and to it is added the degrees of the Ascendant, and it is cast out from the Ascendant.[200]

32 [18] The Lot of the death of fathers is taken by day from Saturn to Jupiter (and by night the contrary), and to it is added the degrees of the Ascendant, and it is cast out from the Ascendant.

33 [19] The Lot of grandfathers is taken by day from the lord of the house of the Sun to Saturn (and by night the contrary), and it is cast out from the Ascendant: where it comes to an end, there is the Lot of grandfa-

---

[200] But see the alternative from Dorotheus in VIII.4, **74** above, and *Carmen* I.14, **5**.

thers. **34** But if the Sun was in his own house or in one of the houses of Saturn, then take by day from the Sun to Saturn (and by night the contrary),[201] and it is cast out from the Ascendant—and do not pay attention to whether Saturn is under the rays or appearing.

35 [20] The Lot of lineage (and it is the Lot of origin and noble descent) is taken by day from Saturn to Mars (and by night the contrary), and it is added to what Mercury has traveled in his sign, and it is cast out from the beginning of the sign of Mercury.

36 [21] The Lot of immovable properties and estates according to Hermes, is taken by day <and night>[202] from Saturn to the Moon, and to it is added the degrees of the Ascendant, and it is cast out from the Ascendant.

37 [22] The Lot of immovable properties according to some of the Persians is taken by day from Mercury to Jupiter (and by night the contrary), and it is cast out from the Ascendant.

38 [23] The Lot of agriculture and cultivation is taken by day and night from Venus to Saturn, and it is cast out from the Ascendant: where it comes to an end, there is this Lot.

39 [24] The Lot of the outcomes of affairs is taken by day and night from Saturn to the lord of the house of the meeting (if the native was conjunctional) or to the lord of the house of the opposition (if the native was oppositional), and to it is added the degrees of the Ascendant, and it is cast out from the Ascendant.

The house of children: it has 5 Lots

41 [25] The Lot of children is taken by day from Jupiter to Saturn (and by night the contrary), and to it is added the degrees of the Ascendant, and it is cast out from the Ascendant.

42 [26] The Lot which indicates the time in which there will be children, and their number, is taken by day and night from Mars to Jupiter, and to it is added the degrees of the Ascendant, and it is cast out from the Ascendant.

---

[201] This is not correct: the instruction is different when the Sun is in Leo (see VIII.4, **86-87**).

[202] Adding with VIII.4, **94**.

43 [27] The Lot of male children is taken by day and night from the Moon to Jupiter, and to it is added the degrees of the Ascendant, and it is cast out from the Ascendant.

44 [28] The Lot of female children is taken by day and night from the Moon to Venus, and to it is added the degrees of the Ascendant, and it is cast out from the Ascendant.

45 [29] The Lot by which the one born (or the one asked about, or the fetus) is known to be male or female, is taken by day from the lord of the house of the Moon to the Moon (and by night the contrary), and it is cast out from the Ascendant.

The house of illnesses: it has 4 Lots

47 [30] The Lot of illness, defects, and chronic illness according to Hermes, is taken by day from Saturn to Mars (and by night the contrary), and it is cast out from the Ascendant.

48 [31] The Lot of illnesses according to some of the ancients is taken by day and night from Mercury to Mars, and is cast out from the Ascendant.

49 [32] The Lot of slaves is taken by day and night from Mercury to the Moon, and it is cast out from the Ascendant.

50 [33] The Lot of prisoners and fetters is taken by day from the lord of the house of the Sun to the Sun, and by night from the lord of the house of the Moon to the Moon, and it is cast out from the Ascendant.

The house of women: it has 16 Lots

52 [34] The Lot of men's marriage according to Hermes is taken by day and night from Saturn to Venus, and to it is added the degrees of the Ascendant, and it is cast out from the Ascendant.

53 [35] The Lot of men's marriage according to Valens is taken by day and night from the Sun to Venus, and to it is added the degrees of the Ascendant, and it is cast out from the Ascendant.

54 [36] The Lot of men's cunning and deception towards women is like [35] the Lot of men's marriage according to Valens.

55 [37] The Lot of men's intercourse with women is like [35] the Lot of men's marriage according to Valens.

56 [38] The Lot of men's debauchery and fornication is like [35] the Lot of men's marriage according to Valens.

57 [39] The Lot of women's marriage according to Hermes is taken by day and night from Venus to Saturn, and to it is added the degrees of the Ascendant, and it is cast out from the Ascendant.

58 [40] The Lot of women's marriage according to Valens is taken by day and night from the Moon to Mars, and to it is added the degrees of the Ascendant, and it is cast out from the Ascendant.

59 [41] The Lot of women's cunning and deception towards men is like [40] the Lot of women's marriage according to Valens.

60 [42] The Lot of women's intercourse is like [40] the Lot of women's marriage according to Valens.

61 [43] The Lot of women's debauchery and their indecency is like [40] the Lot of women's marriage according to Valens.

62 [44] The Lot of a woman's abstinence is taken by day and night from the Moon to Venus, and it is cast out from the Ascendant.

63 [45] The Lot of men's and women's marriage according to Hermes is taken by day and night from Venus to the degree and minute of the stake of wedding, and it is cast out from the Ascendant.

64 [46] The Lot of the time of marriage according to Hermes is taken by day and night from the Sun to the Moon, and to it is added the degrees of the Ascendant,[203] and it is cast out from the Ascendant.

65 [47] The Lot of marriage's stratagem and its facilitation is taken by day and night from the Sun to the Moon, and is cast out from Venus.

66 [48] The Lot of in-laws is taken by day and night from Saturn to Venus, and to it is added the degrees of the Ascendant, and it is cast out from the Ascendant.

67 [49] The Lot of contentions and contenders is taken by day from Mars to Jupiter (and by night the contrary), and it is cast out from the Ascendant.

---

[203] This should be projected from Venus, as *Carmen* II.6, **1** and *BA* III.7.1, **21** have it.

The house of death: it has 5 Lots

69 [50] The Lot of death is taken by day and night from the degree of the Moon to the degree of the eighth house by equation, and it is added to what Saturn has traveled in his sign, and it is cast out from the beginning of Saturn's sign.

70 [51] The Lot of the killing planet is taken by day from the degree of the lord of the Ascendant to the degree of the Moon (and by night the contrary), and it is cast out from the Ascendant.

71 [52] The Lot of the year in which death and want is feared for the native, is taken by day and night from Saturn to the lord of the house of the meeting (or to the lord of house of the opposition) which was before the native's birth, and to it is added the degrees of the Ascendant, and it is cast out from the Ascendant.

72 [53] The Lot of the burdensome place is taken by day from Saturn to Mars (and by night the contrary), and to it is added what Mercury has traveled in his sign, and it is cast out from the beginning of Mercury's sign.

73 [54] The Lot of entanglement and hardship is taken by day from Saturn to Mercury (and by night the contrary), and it is cast out from the Ascendant.

The house of travel: it has 7 Lots

75 [55] The Lot of travel is taken by day and night from the lord of the ninth house to the degree of the ninth house by equation, and it is cast out from the Ascendant.

76 [56] The Lot of traveling by water is taken by day from Saturn to 15° Cancer (and by night from 15° Cancer to Saturn), and it is cast out from the Ascendant.

77 [57] The Lot of piety is taken by day from the Moon to Mercury (and by night the contrary), and it is cast out from the Ascendant.

78 [58] The Lot of reason and depth of thought is taken by day from Saturn to the Moon (and by night the contrary), and it is cast out from the Ascendant.

79 [59] The Lot of knowledge and meditation is taken by day from Saturn to Jupiter (and by night the contrary), and it is cast out from Mercury.[204]

---

[204] Reading "Mercury" with VIII.4, **263**, for "the Ascendant."

80 [60] The Lot of tales and the knowledge of people's reports and superstitions is taken by day from the Sun to Jupiter (and by night the contrary), and it is cast out from the Ascendant.

81 [61] The Lot of a report, as to whether it is true or false, is taken by day and night from Mercury to the Moon, and it is cast out from the Ascendant.

The house of authority: it has 12 Lots

83 [62] The Lot of the native's exaltation is taken by day from the Sun to the degree of his exaltation (which is the completion of 19° of Aries), and by night from the degree of the Moon to 3° Taurus, and to it is added the degrees of the Ascendant, and it is cast out from the Ascendant.

84 [63] The Lot of rulership and authority is taken by day from Mars to the Moon (and by night the contrary), and it is cast out from the Ascendant.

85 [64] The Lot of authority and managers is taken by day from Mercury to Mars (and by night the contrary), and it is cast out from the Ascendant).

86 [65] The Lot of authority, aid, and conquering, is taken by day from the Sun to Saturn, and by night the contrary (but if Saturn was under the rays, then take by day from the Sun to Jupiter and by night the contrary); and it is cast out from the Ascendant.

87 [66] The Lot of those who are suddenly elevated is taken by day from Saturn to the Lot of Fortune (and by night the contrary), and it is cast out from the Ascendant.

88 [67] The Lot of those honored and known among the people is taken by day and night from Mercury to the Sun, and it is cast out from the Ascendant.

89 [68] The Lot of soldiering and conscription is taken by day from Mars to Saturn (and by night the contrary), and it is cast out from the Ascendant.

90 [69] The Lot of authority and which work the native does, is taken by day and night from Saturn to the Moon, and it is cast out from the Ascendant.

91 [70] The Lot of those who work with their own hands, and businesses, is taken by day from Mercury to Venus, and by night the contrary, and it is cast out from the Ascendant.

92 [71] The Lot of business is taken by day from the Lot of the Invisible to the Lot of Fortune (and by night the contrary), and it is cast out from the Ascendant.

93 [72] The Lot of a work and matter which there is no escaping having to deal with it, is taken by day from the Sun to Jupiter (and by night the contrary), and it is cast out from the Ascendant.

94 [73] The Lot of the mother is taken by day from Venus to the Moon (and by night the contrary), and it is cast out from the Ascendant.

The house of friends: it has 11 Lots

96 [74] The Lot of nobility is taken by day from the Lot of Fortune to the Lot of the Invisible (and by night the contrary), and it is cast out from the Ascendant.

97 [75] The Lot of being loved among the people is taken by day from the Lot of Fortune to the Lot of the Invisible (and by night the contrary), and it is cast out from the Ascendant.

98 [76] The Lot of being known among the people and respected among them is taken by day from the Lot of Fortune to the Sun (and by night the contrary), and it is cast out from the Ascendant.

99 [77] The Lot of success is taken by day from the Lot of Fortune to Jupiter (and by night the contrary), and it is cast out from the Ascendant.

100 [78] The Lot of passions and eagerness [for worldly things] is taken by day from the Lot of Fortune to the Lot of the Invisible (and by night the contrary), and it is cast out from the Ascendant.

101 [79] The Lot of hope is taken by day from Saturn to Venus (and by night the contrary), and it is cast out from the Ascendant.

102 [80] The Lot of friends is taken by day and night from the Moon to Mercury, and it is cast out from the Ascendant.

103 [81] The Lot of compulsion is taken by day and night from the Lot of the Invisible to Mercury, and it is cast out from the Ascendant.

104 [82] The Lot of plenty and an abundance of good in the home is taken by day and night from the Moon to Mercury, and it is cast out from the Ascendant.

105 [83] The Lot of the soul's freedom is taken by day from Mercury to the Sun (and by night the contrary), and it is cast out from the Ascendant.

106 [84] The Lot of the praised and commended is taken by day from Jupiter to Venus (and by night the contrary), and it is cast out from the Ascendant.

BOOK VIII: LOTS

The house of enemies: it has 3 Lots

108 [85] The Lot of enemies according to some of the ancients is taken by day and night from Saturn to Mars, and it is cast out from the Ascendant.

109 [86] The Lot of enemies according to Hermes is taken by day and night from the lord of the house of enemies to the degree of the house of enemies,[205] and it is cast out from the Ascendant.

110 [87] The Lot of suffering is taken by day and night from the Lot of the Invisible to the Lot of Fortune, and it is cast out from the Ascendant.

The Lots which were not mentioned with the seven planets nor in the twelve houses: and their number is 10

112 [88] The Lot of the releaser.[206] **113** Look: for if the native was conjunctional, then take from the degree and minute of the meeting which was before the native's birth, to the Moon (and if the native was oppositional, then take from the degree and minute of the opposition which was before the native's birth, to the Moon), and cast it out from the Ascendant.

114 [89] The Lot of the exhaustion of bodies is taken by day from the Lot of Fortune to Mars (and by night the contrary), and it is cast out from the Ascendant.

115 [90] The Lot of horsemanship and courage is taken by day from Saturn to the Moon (and by night the contrary), and it is cast out from the Ascendant.

116 [91] The Lot of risk-taking, hardship, and fighting, is taken by day from the lord of the Ascendant to the Moon (and by night the contrary), and it is cast out from the Ascendant.

117 [92] The Lot of cunning, deception, and stratagems is taken by day from Mercury to the Lot of the Invisible (and by night the contrary), and it is cast out from the Ascendant.

---

[205] Reading with the previous version of the formula for the clearly erroneous "Ascendant."

[206] See the footnote to VIII.5, **1** for the Valens calculation of this Lot.

118 [93] The Lot of an occasion of need and desire is taken by day and night from Saturn to Mars, and to it are added the degrees of Mercury,[207] and it is cast out from Mercury.

119 [94] The Lot of necessity and the hindering of needs according to the Egyptians is taken by day and night from Mars to the degree of the house of siblings, and it is cast out from the Ascendant.

120 [95] The Lot of necessity and the hindering of needs according to the Persians is taken by night and day from the Lot of familiarity and love to Mercury, and it is cast out from the Ascendant.

121 [96] The Lot of punishment is taken by day from Mars to the Sun (and by night the contrary), and it is cast out from the Ascendant.

122 [97] The Lot of the work of truth is taken by day from Mercury to Mars (and by night the contrary), and it is cast out from the Ascendant.

Chapter VIII.7: On the Lots' coinciding in a single position

1 Know that sometimes several Lots will coincide in a single degree, and that is in two ways. **2** The first way is that there are two Lots (or three) for different topics, but they coincide in [the formula of their] derivation, so that they both occur in a single minute. **3** The second way is that the Lots differ in derivation, but despite the difference in their derivation several of them coincide in a single degree. **4** So examine that, because even if they coincide in their position, the judgment about them [may be] different.

5 So as for the first way, in which their derivation coincides and they occur in a single minute, that is like [6] the Lot of Venus, for it is derived like [9] the Lot of the support of the Ascendant is derived: so they will occur in a single minute. **6** Now if Venus was with this Lot, then for the topic of [9] the Lot of the support of the Ascendant it will indicate the completeness of [his] limbs, and the safety of the body at the time of childbirth (for the native will resemble women), and the native's good fortune in travel. **7** But in the case of Venus being with [6] her own Lot, it indicates the native's desire for in-

---

[207] Reading Mercury here and at the end of the sentence with VIII.5, **23**, for "the Ascendant."

tercourse and affection, and searching for what the soul loves, and delighting in its pleasures.

8 And it is like [32] the Lot of slaves, for it is taken by day and night from Mercury to the Moon, and what is brought together is cast out from the Ascendant; but [61] the Lot of a report (as to whether it is true or false) is derived like that: so that the Lot of slaves and the Lot of distinguishing the truth[208] of a report from its lies will be in a single minute. **9** So, if Saturn was with the Lot and he was withdrawing [and] retrograde, then in the topic of [32] slaves it indicates their running away (but his getting control over them after that); and in the topic of [61] the Lot of distinguishing the truth of a report from its lies, it indicates its falsity.

10 And it is like [25] the Lot of children, which is taken by day from Jupiter to Saturn, thus matching [8] the Lot of life: so if Saturn was with this Lot and he was making it unfortunate, then in the topic of [25] the Lot of children it indicates their illness or ruin, while in the topic of [8] the Lot of life it indicates for the owner of the nativity, the disturbance of the body, and the victory of bad thoughts over him, and duress and spiritual fear. **11** And so the judgment about them differs, but its indication in badness for [25] the children is greater than it is for [8] the owner of the nativity, because this Lot is more all-encompassing in the indication for children.

12 And it is like [90] the Lot of horsemanship, taken by day from Saturn to the Moon, and by night the contrary, and cast out from the Ascendant, for [58] the Lot of reason and depth of thought is derived like that—except that the kind of examination in them differs: because if Saturn was with this Lot, then in the topic of [90] the Lot of horsemanship it indicates endurance in it *even if* he shrinks away from it; but in the topic of [58] the Lot of reason and depth of thought it indicates that its owner will have deep thought and recondite thinking.

13 So examine the examples of these Lots, for even if they coincide in [their] derivation and the position in which they occur, the judgment about one of the two may be contrary to the judgment about the other: and that is due to the difference of their categories.

---

[208] صدق.

Chapter VIII.8: On knowing of the indicators of the Lots in their entirety

1 In the chapters which preceded, we stated the explanations for the Lots and the manner of their derivation and strength, and what the ancients said about their indications individually. **2** But we left off looking at what the lord of the house of the Lot indicates (and [the lord of] its exaltation, bound, triplicity, and face), and who among the planets is assembling with it or who is looking at it, and where its position in the circle is, because each one of these indications has a particular character, and we will discuss them in every place where a mention of it is needed, in our books. **3** Now we will state their indicators generally.

4 So when you want knowledge of that, look at the Lot to see in which sign it occurs, then look at it: for sometimes it has one indicator, sometimes two indicators, and sometimes it has three indicators. **5** But a single Lot will not have more than three indicators, all told.

6 Now as for a Lot which has a single indicators, that is like [55] the Lot of travel if it occurred in the house of travel: for it will have one indicator, and that is the lord of the house of travel.[209] **7** And it is like [11] the Lot of assets if it occurred in the house of assets, for it will have a single indicator, and that is the lord of the house of assets. **8** And whenever it is like that with the Lots, they will have a single indicator.

9 As for a Lot which has two indicators, that is like [55] the Lot of travel if it occurred in something other than the house of travel, or [11] the Lot of assets if it occurred in something other than the house of assets, so that it will have two indicators: one of them is the lord of the house of assets, and the second the lord of the house in which the Lot is. **10** And indeed it will come to have two indicators, because you are taking [the distance] from a planet to its house. **11** So if it fell into the house of [that] planet, then it alone will be its indicator; but if it does not fall into its house, [the Lot] will come to have two indicators: one of them the planet from which the derivation of the Lot was begun, and the second the planet in whose house the Lot occurs.

---

[209] This Lot is calculated from the lord of the ninth, to the ninth: therefore, if the Lot also happens to fall in the ninth, it will be fully ruled by a single planet.

12 And a single Lot may have two indicators apart from this way as well, and that is like [1] the Lot of Fortune or [2] the Lot of the Invisible (or other Lots), because you are taking from one of the two planets to the other: so that if it occurred in the house of one of them, it will have two indicators, and they are the two planets from which you took from one of them to the other. **13** But the primary one of the two indicators for a Lot is the planet in whose house the Lot occurred.[210]

14 But if the Lot did not fall into the houses of the two planets, it will have three indicators: two of them are the two planets which you took from one of them to the other, and the third is the planet in whose house the Lot occurs.

[Strengthening the Lots]

15 And know that the Lot which has a single indicator,[211] is strengthened if its indicator looks at it.

16 The Lot which has two indicators[212] is strengthened if both of its two indicators looked at it (and the strongest of the two indicators is the lord of the house of the Lot).

17 And the Lot which has three indicators[213] is the strongest it could be if all of its indicators looked at it—and if the three indicators looked at the Lot, then the Lot's the power will be complete, and all of them will be equal in the indication.

18 But if some of the indicators looked at the Lot, and some did not look, the Lot will be decreased in strength from [that] complete indication. **19** And if some of them were retrograde or in their fall, it indicates the weakness of the Lot's indication. **20** And if none of the indicators of the Lots were looking at the Lot, the Lot will be weak and its indication will not be manifest, but everything of its indication will be [in] thought and ideas, and spiritual things, and scarcely anything of what it does indicate will be com-

---

[210] For example, if the Lot of Fortune was in Cancer, then the Moon would be the primary indicator, because she is used in the calculation and also rules the Lot.
[211] See **6-7** above.
[212] See **9-13** above.
[213] See **14** above.

pleted. **21** And if the indicators of the Lot looked at the Lot with an aspect of affection, he will see what he loves because of that thing which the Lot indicates; but if they looked at it with an aspect of hostility, something detestable will afflict him from the category of that thing.

22 And if a planet similar to the Lot's nature looked at it without the indicators looking at the Lot, it indicates the generation of some of that thing, but it will be little, or will be not be in the manner which he had envisaged, unless the planet had testimony in the Lot.[214] **23** And an example of that is if you wanted knowledge of assets, and you proceeded in accordance with [11] the Lot of assets, and you found the indicators of the Lot not looking at it—but Jupiter, who has an indication for assets by his nature, is looking at the Lot of assets. **24** Or, you wanted knowledge of marriage, and you proceeded with the Lot of marriage, but the indicators of the Lot are not looking at it—but Venus, who has an indication for marriage through her nature, is looking at the Lot.[215] **25** Or, you wanted knowledge of slaves, and you proceeded in accordance with [32] the Lot of slaves, but you found the indicators of the Lot not looking at it—but Mercury, who has an indication for slaves through his nature, is looking at the Lot.[216] **26** So if it were like this, then look: for if the one looking was a fortune by its nature, received, and it was in a stake, then it indicates the generation of that matter, even if it is small or something below the thing which you had hoped for; and it will be with the assistance of a man.

27 Now if the planet which looks at the Lot is in a house in which it has a claim, that will be from a direction he hoped for, or with the assistance of his acquaintance; but if it was in an alien sign, that will be from a direction he was not aware of or it will be with the assistance of a man he does not know. **28** And all of this is if the planet looking at the Lot, which indicates suitability and completion, was a fortune.

---

[214] That is, it has some signification for the *topic of* the Lot: see the following examples.

[215] This is a bad example because all of the normal Lots for marriage use Venus in the calculation, so she would already be one of the indicators. But [40] the Lot of women's marriage according to Valens does not use Venus, so perhaps Abū Ma'shar means that one.

[216] Again, this is a bad example: see the previous footnote.

29 But if the planet looking at the Lot was an infortune, or not receiving the Lot,[217] or it was withdrawing or corrupted, there will be movements in it, and reports,[218] but nothing which the Lot indicates will be completed. **30** Then look at the infortune: for if it was in a stake or in what follows a stake, and it is direct in motion, its corruption will be after it is thought to be completed. **31** If that infortune was Saturn and he is retrograde, then that corruption will be due to an enemy; but if it was Mars it will be due to a contention; and if Mercury was made unfortunate and he indicates the corruption, that corruption will be due to business and books. **32** And if the Moon was indicating the suitability or corruption, then look at her: for if she was increasing,[219] then that will be due to reports[220] or an increase in the matter; but if the Moon was decreasing, then due to decrease. **33** And if it was Venus, then due to women. **34** If it was the Sun, then due to the Sultan,[221] kings, and great men. **35** And if it was Jupiter, then due to religion, abstention [from things], the pious,[222] judges, and people involved in what is among them. **36** And if the Tail was assembling with the Lot, then due to the underclass; and if the Head was assembling with the Lot, then due to leaders.

Chapter VIII.9: On knowing the positions of \<any of\> the indicators relative to each other

1 Know that each Lot is derived from several indicators, the first indicator being the planet which one begins with, the second the planet to which one takes it, the third the position from which one casts out from, and the fourth the place of the Lot. **2** So if the place of three of these indicators is known

---

[217] I am not sure what Abū Ma'shar means by this, as Lots are not received. But perhaps he simply means its lord is in aversion to it.
[218] Or perhaps, "rumors" (الأخبار).
[219] That is, "waxing" (and "waning" in the next clause).
[220] Or, "rumors" (الأخبار).
[221] Or more generally, the "authorities."
[222] النسّاك, which also connotes recluses and hermits.

and one unknown, it is possible to know the position of the unknown indicator.²²³

3 Now if the position of the Lot and the two [planetary] indicators is known, and you wanted to know the degree of the Ascendant, then take from the first indicator to the second indicator by equal degrees, and cast out what is gathered together from the degree in which the Lot is, [but] from the end of the sign towards its beginning,²²⁴ and wherever the calculation runs out, there is the degree of the Ascendant.

4 And if three positions were known and the position of the first indicator was unknown, then take from the third indicator to the Lot (in the successive order of signs), cast out what is brought together from the degree of the second indicator, from the end of the sign towards its beginning, and wherever it runs out, there is the degree of the first indicator.

5 And if the second indicator was unknown, then take from the degree of the third indicator to the degree of the fourth indicator, and add to it what the first indicator has traveled in its sign, then cast it out from the degree of the first indicator forward, from the beginning of the sign toward its end, 30° for every sign, and wherever it comes to an end, there is the degree of the second indicator.

---

²²³ This can be useful in reconstructing charts from old manuscripts.
²²⁴ That is, backwards.

6 And an example of that is that the Sun was in Aries, in 17°, and he is the first indicator. **7** The Moon is in 20° Leo, and is the second indicator. **8** The Ascendant is 15° Gemini, and is the third indicator. **9** And the Lot of Fortune is in Libra, in 18°, and is the fourth indicator.

10 So [suppose] we know the position of three indicators but are ignorant of the degree of the Ascendant, and we want knowledge of it: we take

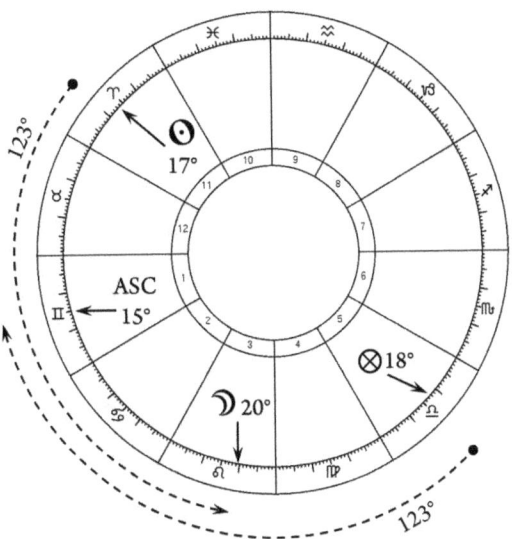

Figure 150: Relations between four Lot positions (VIII.9, 10)

from the Sun to the Moon by equal degrees, and that is four signs and 3°. **11** So we cast it out backwards from the degree of the Lot, and it runs out in Gemini, in 15°: so we know that the Ascendant was Gemini, in that number of degrees.

12 And if the unknown one had been the degree of the Sun, we would have taken from the degree of the Ascendant to the Lot (and it is four signs and 3°), then cast that out from the position of the Moon (from the end of the sign towards its beginning), and indeed the calculation would have run out in Aries, in 17°—and so we would know that the Sun was in Aries, in that same degree.

13 And if the degree of the Moon had been the unknown one, we would have taken from the Ascendant to the Lot (and it would be four signs and 3°), then add on top of it what the Sun had traveled in his own sign, then cast it out from the beginning of Sun's sign forward, and the calculation would run out in Leo, in 20°, and we would know that the Moon was there.

14 The *Book of Introduction* authored by Abū Ma'shar the astrologer, is ended; and praise be to God, the Lord of the Worlds, and the prayers of God be upon Muhammad the Prophet and upon his family, in much peace.

Appendix A: Ascensional Times

This updated table was calculated by Microsoft Excel based on equations in Peter Duffett-Smith's *Practical Astronomy with Your Calculator* (Cambridge University Press, 3rd edition 1988). It uses an obliquity of the ecliptic value of 23° 26' (mid-late 20th Cent.).

Ascensional times (AT) are given by sign and degrees, in the northern (N) and southern (S) hemispheres. They can be used for the maturation of planets in the signs, or for calculating distributions of the Ascendant (both natally and in the SR). For example:

- Let a native be born in the northern hemisphere, at 37° N. The AT of both Cancer and Sagittarius is 35.19568. Dividing this by 30° shows that each degree is worth 1.17319 AT. If the Ascendant was in Cancer, one could direct it at the rate of 1.17319 years or days per degree, until one reaches Leo and discovers the new rate.

- Let a native be born in the southern hemisphere, at 42° S. The AT of both Aries and Pisces is 38.43781. Dividing this by 30° shows that each degree is worth 1.28126 AT. If the Ascendant was in Aries, one could direct it at the rate of 1.28126 years or days per degree, until one reaches Taurus and discovers the new rate.

The AT for individual degrees is approximate, because the heavens are curved: in reality the degrees at one end of a sign will be slightly different from those at the other end. There will be some distortion especially around the end of Sagittarius and the end of Gemini, where the signs change ascension.

N:/S:	♈-♓ / ♍-♎	Yrs/1°	♉-♒ / ♌-♏	Yrs/1°	♊-♑ / ♋-♐	Yrs/1°	♌-♏ / ♉-♒	Yrs/1°	♍-♎ / ♈-♓	Yrs/1°
0°	27.91162	0.93039	29.90829	0.99694	32.18009	1.07267	29.90829	0.99694	27.91162	0.93039
5°	26.89452	0.89648	29.08617	0.96954	31.84612	1.06154	30.73040	1.02435	28.92872	0.96429
10°	25.86140	0.86205	28.24975	0.94166	31.50572	1.05019	31.56682	1.05223	29.96183	0.99873
15°	24.79521	0.82651	27.38365	0.91279	31.15193	1.03840	32.43293	1.08110	31.02803	1.03427
20°	23.67666	0.78922	26.47016	0.88234	30.77655	1.02588	33.34642	1.11155	32.14658	1.07155
21°	23.44473	0.78149	26.27996	0.87600	30.69802	1.02327	33.53662	1.11789	32.37851	1.07928
22°	23.20959	0.77365	26.08681	0.86956	30.61814	1.02060	33.72976	1.12433	32.61365	1.08712
23°	22.97103	0.76570	25.89051	0.86302	30.53679	1.01789	33.92606	1.13087	32.85220	1.09507
24°	22.72883	0.75763	25.69084	0.85636	30.45386	1.01513	34.12573	1.13752	33.09441	1.10315
25°	22.48273	0.74942	25.48756	0.84959	30.36925	1.01231	34.32902	1.14430	33.34050	1.11135
26°	22.23250	0.74108	25.28041	0.84268	30.28282	1.00943	34.53616	1.15121	33.59074	1.11969
27°	21.97785	0.73260	25.06914	0.83564	30.19444	1.00648	34.74744	1.15825	33.84539	1.12818
28°	21.71851	0.72395	24.85345	0.82845	30.10397	1.00347	34.96312	1.16544	34.10472	1.13682
29°	21.45419	0.71514	24.63305	0.82110	30.01124	1.00037	35.18353	1.17278	34.36905	1.14564
30°	21.18455	0.70615	24.40760	0.81359	29.91610	0.99720	35.40897	1.18030	34.63868	1.15462
31°	20.90927	0.69698	24.17676	0.80589	29.81835	0.99394	35.63981	1.18799	34.91396	1.16380
32°	20.62799	0.68760	23.94015	0.79800	29.71779	0.99059	35.87643	1.19588	35.19524	1.17317
33°	20.34032	0.67801	23.69736	0.78991	29.61421	0.98714	36.11921	1.20397	35.48291	1.18276
34°	20.04586	0.66820	23.44795	0.78160	29.50737	0.98358	36.36862	1.21229	35.77738	1.19258
35°	19.74416	0.65814	23.19145	0.77305	29.39701	0.97990	36.62512	1.22084	36.07907	1.20264
36°	19.43477	0.64783	22.92733	0.76424	29.28283	0.97609	36.88924	1.22964	36.38847	1.21295
37°	19.11716	0.63724	22.65503	0.75517	29.16451	0.97215	37.16154	1.23872	36.70608	1.22354
38°	18.79080	0.62636	22.37394	0.74580	29.04170	0.96806	37.44264	1.24809	37.03243	1.23441

APPENDIX A: TABLE OF ASCENSIONAL TIMES

39°	18.45511	0.61517	22.08336	0.73611	28.91400	0.96380	35.44619	1.18154	37.73321	1.25777	37.36813	1.24560
40°	18.10945	0.60365	21.78257	0.72609	28.78096	0.95937	35.57922	1.18597	38.03400	1.26780	37.71379	1.25713
41°	17.75314	0.59177	21.47073	0.71569	28.64210	0.95474	35.71809	1.19060	38.34584	1.27819	38.07010	1.26900
42°	17.38543	0.57951	21.14695	0.70490	28.49684	0.94989	35.86335	1.19544	38.66962	1.28899	38.43781	1.28126
43°	17.00551	0.56685	20.81021	0.69367	28.34456	0.94482	36.01563	1.20052	39.00636	1.30021	38.81772	1.29392
44°	16.61252	0.55375	20.45939	0.68198	28.18451	0.93948	36.17568	1.20586	39.35718	1.31191	39.21072	1.30702
45°	16.20548	0.54018	20.09324	0.66977	28.01588	0.93386	36.34431	1.21148	39.72333	1.32411	39.61776	1.32059
46°	15.78334	0.52611	19.71035	0.65701	27.83771	0.92792	36.52248	1.21742	40.10622	1.33687	40.03989	1.33466
47°	15.34496	0.51150	19.30913	0.64364	27.64887	0.92163	36.71132	1.22371	40.50744	1.35025	40.47828	1.34928
48°	14.88906	0.49630	18.88779	0.62959	27.44809	0.91494	36.91210	1.23040	40.92878	1.36429	40.93418	1.36447
49°	14.41424	0.48047	18.44429	0.61481	27.23381	0.90779	37.12637	1.23755	41.37229	1.37908	41.40899	1.38030
50°	13.91896	0.46397	17.97627	0.59921	27.00425	0.90014	37.35594	1.24520	41.84031	1.39468	41.90428	1.39681
51°	13.40150	0.44672	17.48105	0.58270	26.75721	0.89191	37.60297	1.25343	42.33553	1.41118	42.42174	1.41406
52°	12.85994	0.42866	16.95549	0.56518	26.49008	0.88300	37.87011	1.26234	42.86108	1.42870	42.96330	1.43211
53°	12.29215	0.40974	16.39597	0.54653	26.19962	0.87332	38.16057	1.27202	43.42061	1.44735	43.53109	1.45104
54°	11.69574	0.38986	15.79818	0.52661	25.88184	0.86273	38.47835	1.28261	44.01840	1.46728	44.12750	1.47092
55°	11.06802	0.36893	15.15703	0.50523	25.53169	0.85106	38.82849	1.29428	44.65954	1.48865	44.75522	1.49184
56°	10.40595	0.34687	14.46644	0.48221	25.14271	0.83809	39.21748	1.30725	45.35013	1.51167	45.41729	1.51391
57°	9.70609	0.32354	13.71902	0.45730	24.70643	0.82355	39.65376	1.32179	46.09756	1.53659	46.11715	1.53724
58°	8.96449	0.29882	12.90569	0.43019	24.21150	0.80705	40.14869	1.33829	46.91089	1.56370	46.85874	1.56196
59°	8.17667	0.27256	12.01517	0.40051	23.64228	0.78808	40.71790	1.35726	47.80140	1.59338	47.64656	1.58822
60°	7.33745	0.24458	11.03320	0.36777	22.97641	0.76588	41.38378	1.37946	48.78337	1.62611	48.48579	1.61619
61°	6.44080	0.21469	9.94132	0.33138	22.18049	0.73935	42.17970	1.40599	49.87525	1.66251	49.38244	1.64608
62°	5.47973	0.18266	8.71516	0.29051	21.20170	0.70672	43.15849	1.43862	51.10142	1.70338	50.34350	1.67812
63°	4.44602	0.14820	7.32152	0.24405	19.94967	0.66499	44.41052	1.48035	52.49505	1.74983	51.37722	1.71257
64°	3.32989	0.11100	5.71355	0.19045	18.25095	0.60837	46.10924	1.53697	54.10303	1.80343	52.49334	1.74978
65°	2.11972	0.07066	3.82180	0.12739	15.70264	0.52342	48.65755	1.62192	55.99478	1.86649	53.70352	1.79012
66°	0.80141	0.02671	1.53651	0.05122	10.88222	0.36274	53.47797	1.78260	58.28006	1.94267	55.02182	1.83406

Appendix B: Table of Lots

The following table organizes Abū Ma'shar's Lots from Book VIII, according to their diurnal formula and the point they are projected from. It is designed to let the reader compare the interpretations and find common themes. Where Abū Ma'shar indicates an alternative calculation for the same Lot, I list it as [XX-alt].

From	To	Project	Lot #
♄	♃	ASC	[8] [14] [18]
♄	♃	☿	[59]
♄	♂	ASC	[30] [85]
♄	♂	☿	[20] [53] [93]
♄	☉		
♄	♀	ASC	[34] [48] [79]
♄	☿	ASC	[12] [54]
♄	☽	ASC	[21] [58] [69] [90]
♄	⊗	ASC	[3] [66]
♄	☌☍	ASC	[24]
♄	Lord ☌☍	ASC	[24] [52]
♄	15° ♋	ASC	[56]
♃	♄	ASC	[25]
♃	♂		
♃	☉		
♃	♀	ASC	[84]
♃	☿		
♃	☽		
♂	♄	ASC	[50-alt] [68]
♂	♃	ASC	[17-alt2] [26] [49]
♂	☉	ASC	[96]
♂	♀		
♂	☿		
♂	☽	ASC	[63]
♂	⊗	ASC	[5]
♂	3rd	ASC	[94]
☉	♄	ASC	[17] [65]

APPENDIX B: TABLE OF LOTS

☉	♃	ASC	[17-alt1] [60] [65-alt] [72]
☉	♂		
☉	♀	ASC	[35] [36] [37] [38]
☉	☿		
☉	☽	ASC	[1] [46]
☉	☽	♀	[47]
☉	MC	ASC	[16]
☉	19° ♈	ASC	[62]
Lord ☉	♄	ASC	[19]
Lord ☉	☉	ASC	[32]
♀	♄	ASC	[23] [39]
♀	♃		
♀	♂		
♀	☉		
♀	☿		
♀	☽	ASC	[73]
♀	DESC	ASC	[45]
☿	♄		[15]
☿	♃	ASC	[14-alt] [22]
☿	♂	ASC	[10] [31] [64] [97]
☿	☉	ASC	[67] [83]
☿	♀	ASC	[13] [70]
☿	☽	ASC	[32] [61]
☿	⊗	ASC	[32-alt]
☿	φ	ASC	[92]
☽	♄	ASC	[27-alt]
☽	♃	ASC	[27]
☽	♂	ASC	[40] [41] [42] [43]
☽	☉	ASC	[2]
☽	♀	ASC	[28] [44]
☽	☿	ASC	[57] [80] [82]
☽	8th	♄	[50]
☽	3° ♉	ASC	[62]
Lord ☽	☽	ASC	[29] [32]
⊗	♃	ASC	[77]
⊗	♂	ASC	[89]

⊗	☉	ASC	[76]
⊗	♀	ASC	[6] [9] [74] [75] [78]
♀	♃	ASC	[4]
♀	☿	ASC	[81]
♀	⊗	ASC	[7] [71] [87]
[6]	☿	ASC	[95]
☌☍	☽	ASC	[88]
Lord 1st	☽	ASC	[51] [91]
Lord 2nd	2nd	ASC	[11]
Lord 9th	9th	ASC	[55]
Lord 12th	12th	ASC	[86]

Bibliography

Abū Ma'šar, *The Great Introduction to Astrology* (2 vols), trans. and ed. Keiji Yamamoto and Charles Burnett (Leiden: Brill NV, 2019)

Abū Ma'shar, *Persian Nativities IV: On the Revolutions of the Years of Nativities*, Benjamin N. Dykes trans. and ed. (Minneapolis, MN: The Cazimi Press, 2019)

Al-Battānī, *Zīj al-Sābi'*, trans. Nallino, Karl A. (Milan: Minerva G.M.B.H., 1903)

Al-Bīrūnī, Muhammad bin Ahmad, *The Book of Instruction in the Elements of the Art of Astrology*, trans. R. Ramsay Wright (London: Luzac & Co., 1934)

Al-Bīrūnī, Muhammad bin Ahmad, *Al-Bīrūnī on Transits*, trans. Mohammad Saffouri and Adnan Ifram, commentary by E.S. Kennedy (Beirut: American University of Beirut, 1959)

Al-Bīrūnī, Muhammad bin Ahmad, *The Chronology of Ancient Nations* (Lahore: Hijra International Publishers, 1983)

Al-Hashīmī, *The Book of Reasons Behind Astronomical Tables*, trans. and ed. Fuad I. Haddad, E.S. Kennedy, and David Pingree (Delmar, NY: Scholars' Facsimiles and Reprints, 1981)

Allen, Richard Hinckley, *Star Names: Their Lore and Meaning* (New York: Dover Publications Inc., 1963)

Al-Qabīsī, *The Introduction to Astrology*, eds. Charles Burnett, Keiji Yamamoto, Michio Yano (London and Turin: The Warburg Institute, 2004)

Al-Tabārī, 'Umar, *Three Books on Nativities*, in Dykes 2010 (*Persian Nativities II*)

Aristotle, *The Complete Works of Aristotle* vols. I-II, ed. Jonathan Barnes (Princeton, NJ: Princeton University Press, 1984)

ibn Bishr, Sahl, trans. and ed. Benjamin N. Dykes, *The Astrology of Sahl b. Bishr Volume I: Principles, Elections, Questions, Nativities* (Minneapolis, MN: The Cazimi Press, 2019)

Boll, Franz, *Sphaera* (Leipzig: B. G. Teubner, 1903)

Copenhaver, Brian P., *Hermetica* (Cambridge: Cambridge University Press, 1992)

Dorotheus of Sidon, *Carmen Astrologicum*, trans. and ed. Benjamin N. Dykes, 2nd Edition (Minneapolis, MN: The Cazimi Press, 2019)

Dykes, Benjamin trans. and ed., *Introductions to Traditional Astrology: Abū Ma'shar & al-Qabīsī* (Minneapolis, MN: The Cazimi Press, 2010)

Dykes, Benjamin, trans. and ed., *Astrology of the World I: The Ptolemaic Inheritance* (Minneapolis, MN: The Cazimi Press, 2013)

Dykes, Benjamin, trans. and ed., *Astrology of the World II: Revolutions & History* (Minneapolis, MN: The Cazimi Press, 2014)

Dykes, Benjamin, trans. and ed., *Persian Nativities I: Māshā'allāh & Abū 'Alī* (Minneapolis, MN: The Cazimi Press, 2009)

Dykes, Benjamin, trans. and ed., *Persian Nativities II: 'Umar al-Tabarī & Abū Bakr* (Minneapolis, MN: The Cazimi Press, 2010)

Firmicus Maternus, *Mathesis*, trans. and ed. Benjamin N. Dykes (forthcoming)

Goldstein, Bernard R., "The Arabic Version of Ptolemy's *The Planetary Hypotheses*," *Transactions of the American Philosophical Society*, Vol. 7, Part 4 (1967), pp. 3-55.

Gundel, Wilhelm, *Dekane und Dekansternbilder* (Glückstadt and Hamburg: J. J. Augustin, 1935)

Gutas, Dimitri, *Greek Thought, Arabic Culture* (New York: Routledge, 1998)

Hava, J.G., *Arabic-English Dictionary for Advanced Learners* (New Delhi: Goodword Books, 2011)

Hephaistio of Thebes, *Apotelesmatics* vols. I-II, trans. and ed. Robert H. Schmidt (Cumberland, MD: The Golden Hind Press, 1994 and 1998)

Hephaistion of Thebes, *Apotelesmatics Book III: On Inceptions*, trans. Eduardo Gramaglia and ed. Benjamin N. Dykes (Minneapolis, MN: The Cazimi Press, 2013)

Hippocrates, *On Airs, Waters and Places*, trans. Francis Adams (The Dodo Press, 2009)

King, David A. and Julio Samsó, "Astronomical Handbooks and Tables from the Islamic World (750-1900): an Interim Report," in *Suhayl* Vol. 2 (2001), pp. 9-105.

Lane, Edward, *An Arabic-English Lexicon* (Beirut: Librairie du Liban, 1968)

Le Strange, Guy, *The Lands of the Eastern Caliphate* (London: Frank Cass & Co. Ltd., 1966)

Lemay, Richard, *Abū Ma'shar and Latin Aristotelianism in the Twelfth Century* (Beirut: American University of Beirut, 1962)

Lemay, Richard, *Abū Ma'shar al-Balhi: Liber Introductorii Maioris ad Scientiam Judiciorum Astrorum*, Vols. I-IX (Naples: Istituto Universitario Orientale, 1995)

Paul of Alexandria, *Late Classical Astrology: Paulus Alexandrinus and Olympiodorus*, trans. Dorian Gieseler Greenbaum, ed. Robert Hand (Reston, VA: ARHAT Publications, 2001)

Piperakis, Spyros, "Decanal Iconography and Natural Materials in the *Sacred Book of Hermes to Asclepius*," in *Greek, Roman, and Byzantine Studies* Vol. 57 (2017), pp. 136-61.

Porphyry of Tyre, *Introduction [Isagoge]*, trans. and ed. Jonathan Barnes (Oxford: Clarendon Press, 2003)

Ptolemy, Claudius, *Apotelesmatika*, ed. Wolfgang Hübner (Stuttgart: B.G. Teubner Verlag, 1998)

Ptolemy, Claudius, *Ptolemy's Almagest*, trans. and ed. G.J. Toomer (Princeton, NJ: Princeton University Press, 1998)

Ptolemy, Claudius, *Tetrabiblos*, trans. F.E. Robbins (Cambridge and London: Harvard University Press, 1940)

Rhetorius of Egypt, *Astrological Compendium*, trans. and ed. James H. Holden (Tempe, AZ: American Federation of Astrologers, Inc., 2009)

Schmidt, Robert trans. and Robert Hand ed., *Dorotheus, Orpheus, Anubio, & Pseudo-Valens: Teachings on Transits* (Berkeley Springs, WV: The Golden Hind Press, 1995)

Schmidt, Robert E., trans. and ed. *Definitions and Foundations* (Cumberland, MD: The Golden Hind Press, 2009)

Sezgin, Fuat, *Geschichte des Arabischen Schrifttums* vol. 7 (Leiden: E.J. Brill, 1979)

Theophilus of Edessa, trans. Eduardo Gramaglia and ed. Benjamin Dykes, *Astrological Works of Theophilus of Edessa* (Minneapolis, MN: The Cazimi Press, 2017)

Valens, Vettius, *The Anthology*, vols. I-VII, ed. Robert Hand, trans. Robert Schmidt (Berkeley Springs, WV: The Golden Hind Press, 1993-2001)

Glossary

This Glossary contains astrological terms from all branches of traditional astrology, from all of my translations. Most entries also provide the Greek, Latin, and Arabic source words. Boldface terms in the definitions and descriptions indicate that the Glossary also contains that word.

- **Absent from** (Ar. غائب عن). See **Aversion**.
- **Accident** (Lat. *accidens*, Ar. حادث, عرض). An event which "befalls" or "happens" to someone, though not necessarily something bad.
- **Adding in course.** See **Course**.
- **Advancement, advancing** (إقبال \ مقبل; Lat. *accedens*). Refers to being (1) dynamically **angular** or **succeedent**, i.e. moving by **primary motion** toward an **axial** degree. (But occasionally might refer to angular or succeedent **whole signs**). Its two antonyms are **retreat/retreating**, and **withdrawal/withdrawing**. It can also refer to (2) the **eastern quadrants**.
- **Advantageous places.** One of two schemes of **houses** which indicate affairs/planets which are more busy or good in the context of the chart. The seven-place scheme according to Timaeus and reported in *Carmen* includes only certain signs which **look at** the **Ascendant** by **whole-sign**, and suggests that these places are advantageous for the *native* because they look at the Ascendant. The eight-place scheme according to Nechepsō lists all of the **angular** and **succeedent** places, suggesting places which are stimulating and advantageous for a planet *in itself*.
- **Ages of Man** (Ar. أسنان الإنسان). Ptolemy's division of a typical human life span into periods ruled by planets as **time lords**.
- **Agreeing signs.** Groups of signs which share some kind of harmonious quality. Sometimes planets are said to agree with one another, although this meaning must be taken in context.
- *Alcochoden.* Latin transliteration for *kadkhudhāh*, the **House-master**.
- **Alien** (Lat. *alienus*, Ar. غريب). Lit., "a stranger, foreigner." When a planet is not in one of its five **dignities**. In later astrology in English this is often called "peregrine," from Lat. *peregrinus* ("foreigner, pilgrim").
- *Almuten.* A Latin transliteration for Ar. *mubtazz*: see **Victor**.
- **Angles, succeedents, cadents.** A division of houses into three groups which show how powerfully and directly a planet acts. The angles are the 1st, 10th, 7th and 4th; the succeedents are the 2nd, 11th, 8th and 5th; the cadents

are the 12th, 9th, 6th and 3rd. But the exact regions in question will depend upon whether and how one uses **whole-sign** and **quadrant houses**, especially since traditional texts refer to an angle or pivot (Gr. *kentron*, Ar. وتد) as either (1) equivalent to the **whole-sign** angles from the **Ascendant**, or (2) the **axial degrees** of the **Ascendant-Midheaven** themselves, or (3) **quadrant houses** (and their associated strengths) as measured from the degrees of the axes.

- **Antiscia** (sing. *antiscion*), Greek for "throwing shadows." Refers to a degree mirrored across an axis drawn from 0° Capricorn to 0° Cancer. For example, 10° Cancer has 20° Gemini as its antiscion.

- **Apogee of eccentric/deferent** (Ar. أوج). The point on a planet's **deferent circle** that is farthest away from the earth; as seen from earth, it points to some degree of the zodiac.

- **Applying, application** (Lat. *applicatio*). When a planet is in a state of **connection**, moving so as to make the connection exact. Planets **assembled** together or **looked at** by sign, but not yet connecting by the relevant degrees, are only "wanting" to be connected.

- **Apsides, apsidal line.** In geocentric astronomy, the line passing through the center of the earth, which points at one end to the **apogee** of a planet's **deferent**, and at the other end to its **perigee**.

- **Arisings** (Lat. *orientia*). See **Ascensions**.

- **Ascendant.** Usually the entire rising sign, but often specified as the exact degree on the horizon (the **axial degree**). In **quadrant houses**, a space following the exact rising degree up to the cusp of the 2nd house.

- **Ascensions** (Ar. مطالع, Lat. *ascensiones*). Degrees on the celestial **equator**, measured in terms of how many degrees pass the **meridian** as an entire sign or **bound** (or other spans of zodiacal degrees) passes across the horizon. They are often used in the predictive technique of ascensional times, sometimes as an approximation of primary **directions**.

- **Aspect** (Lat. *aspectus*, Ar. نظر). For the verb, see **look at**. As a noun, a **configuration** between two things (such as two planets or a planet and a sign): see **sextile**, **trine**, **square**, and **opposition**. See also **Connection** and **Assembly**

- **Assembly** (Lat. *conventus*, Ar. مقارنة). When two or more planets are in the same sign, and more intensely if within 15°. (It is occasionally used in Arabic to indicate the conjunction of the Sun and Moon at the New Moon, but the more common word for that is **meeting**).

- **Aversion.** Being in the second, sixth, eighth, or twelfth sign from a place, as a planet in Gemini is in the twelfth from, and therefore in aversion to, Cancer. Such places are not **configured** and so cannot **look at** or see each other by the classical scheme of **aspects**.
- **Axial degree, axis.** The degree of the **zodiac** which the horizon or **meridian**: the **Ascendant, Midheaven, Descendant,** and *Imum Caeli/IC*.
- **Ayanamsha.** In sidereal astrology, a point or degree which acts as the beginning of the zodiac. The **equinoctial point** acts as the ayanamsha in the tropical **zodiac**.
- *Azamene*. Equivalent to **Chronic illness**.
- **Bad ones.** See **Fortune/Infortune**.
- **Barring.** See **Blocking**.
- **Bearing** (Lat. *habitudo*). Hugo's term for any of the many possible planetary conditions and relationships.
- **Benefic:** see **Fortune/Infortune**.
- **Benevolent.** See **Fortune/Infortune**.
- **Besieging** (Lat. *obsido*). Equivalent to **Enclosure**.
- **Bicorporeal signs.** Equivalent to "common" signs. See **Quadruplicity**.
- **Blocking** (Lat. *prohibitio*, Ar. منع), sometimes called "prohibition." When a planet blocks another planet from completing a **connection**, either through its own body or **ray**. This may happen in several ways: see Sahl's *Introduction* Ch. 3, **31-48**.
- **Body** (Lat. *corpus*, Ar. جرم). Normally, a planet considered by itself, in the degree where it is located. But in **aspect** theory, also equivalent to an **orb**.
- **Bodyguarding.** See **Spear-bearing**.
- **Bound, bounds** (Gr. *horion*, Lat. *terminus*, Ar. حدّ). Unequal divisions of the zodiac in each sign, each bound being ruled by one of the five non-**luminaries**. Sometimes called "terms," they are one of the five classical **dignities**.
- **Bright, smoky, empty, dark degrees.** Certain degrees of the zodiac said to affect how conspicuous or obscure the significations of planets or the Ascendant are.
- **Burned up, burning** (Lat. *combustus, combustio*; Ar. محترق, احتراق). Normally, when a planet is between about 1° and 7.5° away from the Sun. See also **In the heart**.
- **Burnt path** (Lat. *via combusta*). A span of degrees in Libra and Scorpio in which a planet (especially the Moon) is considered to be harmed or less

able to effect its significations. Some astrologers identify it as between 15° Libra and 15° Scorpio; others between the exact degree of the **fall** of the Sun in 19° Libra and the exact degree of the fall of the Moon in 3° Scorpio.
- *Bust*. Certain hours measured from the New Moon, in which it is considered favorable or unfavorable to undertake an action or perform an **election**.
- **Busy places**. Equivalent to the **Advantageous places**.
- **Cadent** (Lat. *cadens*, "falling"; Ar. ساقط). Typically, when a planet is one of the following **whole sign** or **quadrant houses** (called "cadent/falling" from the **angles**): 3rd, 6th, 9th, 12th. But see also **falling away from**, which is equivalent to **Aversion**.
- **Cardinal**. Equivalent to "movable" or "convertible" signs. See **Quadruplicity**.
- **Cardine**. Equivalent to **Angle**.
- **Cazimi**: see **In the heart**.
- **Centers of the Moon**. Also called the "posts" or "foundations" of the Moon. Angular distances between the Sun and Moon throughout the lunar month, indicating possible times of weather changes and rain.
- **Choice**. See **Election**.
- **Choleric**. See **Humor**.
- **Chronic illness (degrees of)**. Sometimes called the "azamene" degrees, which are especially said to indicate chronic illness, due to their association with certain fixed stars.
- **Claim** (Ar. مزاعمة). See **Dignity**.
- **Cleansed** (Ar. نقي, Lat. *mundus*). Ideally, when a planet is in **aversion** to the **infortunes** (but certainly not in an **assembly**, **square**, or **opposition** to them.
- **Clothed**. Equivalent to one planet being in an **assembly** or **aspect** with another, and therefore partaking in (being "clothed in") the other planet's characteristics.
- **Collection** (Lat. *collectio*, Ar. جمع). When two planets **aspecting** each other but not in an applying **connection**, each **apply to** a third planet.
- **Combust** (Lat. *combustus*). See **Burned up**.
- **Commanding/obeying**. A division of the signs into those which command or obey each other (used sometimes in **synastry**).
- **Common signs**. See **Quadruplicity**.

- **Complexion.** Primarily, a mixture of elements and their qualities so as to indicate or produce some effect. Secondarily it refers to planetary combinations, following the naturalistic theory that planets have elemental qualities with causal power, which can interact with each other.
- **Confer.** See **Handing over**.
- **Configuration.** A geometrical relationship, figure, or **aspect** between signs, which allows things to **look at** each other or **connect**.
- **Configured.** To be in an **aspect** by **whole-sign** (though not necessarily **connecting** by degree).
- **Conjunction** (Lat. *conjunctio*, Ar. قران). As a relationship of planets, normally equivalent to **assembly** and **connecting** by body. In mundane astrology it refers to the **mean** conjunction (normally, of Saturn and Jupiter).
- **Conjunction/prevention.** The position of the New (conjunction) or Full (prevention) Moon most immediately prior to a **nativity** or other chart. For the prevention, some astrologers use the degree of the Moon, others the degree of the luminary which was above the earth at the time of the prevention.
- **Connection** (Lat. *continuatio*, Ar. اتّصال). When a planet **applies** to another planet (by body in the same sign, or by **ray** in **configured** signs), within a particular number of degrees up to exactness.
- **Conquer** (Lat. *vinco*). Normally, the equivalent of being a **victor**, which comes from the same Latin verb.
- **Convertible** (Lat. *conversivus*, Ar. منقلب). See **Quadruplicity**. But sometimes planets (especially Mercury) are called convertible because their **gender** is affected by their placement in the chart.
- **Convey.** See **Handing over**.
- **Corruption.** Normally, the harming of a planet, such as being in a **square** with an **infortune**. But sometimes, equivalent to **Detriment**.
- **Counsel** (Lat. *consilium*). See **Management**.
- **Counting** (Ar. عدد). In the context of **house** theory, it refers to **whole-sign** houses (namely, assigning the house numbers by counting each sign); it is opposed to **quadrant houses** (by **division** or **equation**).
- **Course, increasing/decreasing in.** For practical purposes, this means a planet is quicker than average in motion. But in geometric astronomy, it refers to what **sector** of the **deferent** the center of a planet's **epicycle** is. (The planet's position within the four sectors of the epicycle itself will also

affect its apparent speed.) In the two sectors that are closest to the planet's **perigee**, the planet will apparently be moving faster; in the two sectors closest to the **apogee**, it will apparently be moving slower.

- **Crooked/straight.** A division of the signs into those which rise quickly and are more parallel to the horizon (crooked), and those which arise more slowly and closer to a right angle from the horizon (straight or direct). In the northern hemisphere, the signs from Capricorn to Gemini are crooked (but in the southern one, straight); those from Cancer to Sagittarius are straight (but in the southern one, crooked).
- **Crossing over** (Gr. *parallagē*). When a planet begins to **separate** from an exact **connection**. See also **Right/left**.
- **Cusp** (Lat. *cuspis*). In **quadrant houses**, the degree which marks the division between one house and another.
- **Cutter, killer, destroyer** (Ar. قاطع, قاتل). A planet or point which ends the life when the **releaser** meets it by distribution.
- **Cutting of light** (Ar. قطع النّور). Any of several ways in which a **connection** is prevented, such as by **blocking**.
- *Darījān.* An alternative **face** system attributed to the Indians.
- **Dastūriyyah** (دستوريّة). See **Spear-bearing**.
- **Decan** (Lat. *decanus*). A division of the **zodiac** into 36 divisions or **faces** of 10° each.
- **Decimation.** A form of **overcoming**, specifically from the superior **square** (i.e., the tenth sign from something else).
- **Declination.** The equivalent on the celestial **equator**, of geographical latitude. The signs of northern declination (Aries through Virgo) stretch northward of the **ecliptic**, while those of southern declination (Libra through Pisces) stretch southward.
- **Decline, declining** (Gr. *apoklima*, Ar. حدر, سقط). Equivalent to **cadence** or **falling** by whole sign, but perhaps in some Arabic texts referring rather to cadence by **quadrant house** divisions.
- **Decreasing in number.** See **Increasing/decreasing in number**.
- **Deferent.** The large circle which is off-center or **eccentric** to the earth, on which a planet's system rotates.
- **Degrees of equality** (سواء), **equal degrees.** Degrees of the zodiac, as opposed to degrees of **ascensions** or measured on the celestial **equator**.
- **Descension** (Lat. *descensio*). Equivalent to **fall**.

- **Detriment** (Lat. *detrimentum*, Ar. ضدّ, وبال). The sign opposite a planet's **domicile**. For example, Libra is the detriment of Mars.
- **Dexter.** "Right": see **Right/left**.
- **Diameter.** Equivalent to **Opposition**.
- **Dignity** (Lat. *dignitas*, Ar. مزاعمة, نصيب, حظّ). Any of (typically) five ways of assigning rulership or responsibility to a planet (or sometimes, to a **Node**) over some portion of the zodiac. They are often listed in the following order: **domicile, exaltation, triplicity, bound, face/decan**. The opposite of domicile is **detriment**, the opposite of exaltation is **fall**.
- **Directions, directing** (Ar. تسيير, Lat. *directio*). A predictive technique in which a point in the chart (the significator) is considered as stationary, and other planets and their **connections** by degree (or even the **bounds**) are sent forth (**promittors**) as though by **primary motion** until they come to the significator. The degrees between the significator and promittor are converted into years of life. This is the method used in **distributions**. An astronomically less accurate version is done by **ascensions**. Some astrologers also allow "converse" directions, in which points may be directed contrary to primary motion.
- **Disregard.** Equivalent to **Separation**.
- **Distribution** (Lat. *partitio, divisio*; Ar. قسمة). The primary **direction** of a **releaser** (often the degree of the **Ascendant**) through the **bounds**. The bound **lord** of the distribution is the **distributor**, and any body or **ray** which the **releaser** encounters is the **partner**.
- **Distributor** (Lat. *divisor*, Ar. قاسم). The **bound lord** of a directed **releaser**. See **Distribution**.
- **Diurnal.** See **Sect**.
- **Division** (Ar. تسويّة, قسمة). In the context of **house** theory, it refers to any **quadrant house** system, as these are derived by dividing each of the the **quarters** by three. Synonymous with houses by **equation**, and opposed to **whole-sign** houses by **counting**.
- **Domain** (حيّز). Sometimes, a synonym for **sect**. But also used for a specific sect and **gender**-based planetary condition, in which a planet is in a sign of its own gender and also in its preferred hemisphere relative to the Sun (for example, Jupiter being in a male sign and above or below the horizon, wherever the Sun is).

- **Domicile.** One of the five **dignities**. A sign of the **zodiac**, insofar as it is owned or managed by one of the planets. For example, Aries is the domicile of Mars, and so Mars is its domicile **lord**.
- **Doryphory** (Gr. *doruphoria*). Equivalent to **Spear-bearing**.
- **Double-bodied.** Equivalent to the common signs. See **Quadruplicity**.
- **Dragon:** see **Node**.
- **Drawn back** (Lat. *reductus*). Equivalent to being **cadent** from an **angle**.
- **Dodecametorion.** Equivalent to **Twelfth-part**.
- **Duodecima.** Equivalent to **Twelfth-part**.
- **Dustoria** (Lat. transliteration of Ar. *dastūriyyah*). See **Spear-bearing**.
- **East** (Lat. *oriens*). The **Ascendant**.
- **Eastern** (Lat. *orientalis*, Ar. شرقيّ) and **western** (Lat. *occidentalis*, Ar. غربيّ). Four primary meanings: (1) when a planet rises before the Sun or Moon in an earlier zodiacal degree (eastern), or setting after it in a later degree (western); (2) to be outside the **Sun's rays** and visible (eastern) or under them and invisible (western). See also **Easternize, easternization**. (3) When a planet is in an eastern/diurnal or western/nocturnal **quadrant** of the chart: the eastern quadrants are from the horizon/Ascendant to the **meridian**/Midheaven, and from the Descendant to the IC; the western quadrants are the opposite. (4) In an eastern or western quadrant relative to the Sun: eastern is to be in the 90° span of the zodiac which precede the Sun, and the opposite 90°; the other two are western.
- **Easternize, easternization** (شرّق \ تشريق), and **westernize, westernization** (غرّب \ تغريب). Two meanings: (1) when a planet is coming out of or going under the **Sun's rays**, with different distances for different planets (normally around 15° from the Sun); (2) when a planet is close enough to the Sun that *within 7 or 9 days* it will come out of our go under the rays. **Superior planets** easternize and westernize when rising before or setting after the Sun, respectively. The **inferior planets** Venus and Mercury are ambiguous, since each can come out of or go under the rays on either side. See **Eastern and western**.
- **Eccentric.** As an adjective, it describes circles that are "off-center" to the earth; it is also a synonym for the **deferent circle**, the larger circle in a planetary model (which is likewise eccentric or off-center).
- **Ecliptic.** The path defined by the Sun's motion through the **zodiac**, defined as having 0° ecliptical latitude. In tropical astrology, the ecliptic (and

therefore the zodiacal signs) begins at the intersection of the ecliptic and the celestial **equator** (the **equinoctial point**).

- **Election** (Lat. *electio*, Ar. اختيار). Literally, "choice": the deliberate choosing of an appropriate time to undertake an action (called an **inception**), or avoid something unwanted.
- **Element** (Lat. *elementum*, Ar. أصل, طبيعة). One of the four basic bodies or qualities (fire, air, water, earth) describing how matter and energy operate, and used to describe the significations and operations of planets and signs. They are usually described by pairs of four other basic qualities (hot, cold, wet, dry). For example, Aries is a fiery sign, and hot and dry; Mercury is typically treated as cold and dry (earthy).
- **Emptiness in course** (Lat. *vacuum cursu*, Ar. خلاء السّير, Gr. *kenodromia*). Medievally, when a planet does not complete a **connection** for as long as it is in its current sign. In Hellenistic astrology, when a planet does not complete a connection within the next 30°.
- **Enclosure** (Gr. *perischesis, emperischesis*; Lat. *obsido*; Ar. احتوى, حصر, ضغط). When a planet has the rays or bodies of the **infortunes** (or alternatively, the **fortunes**) on either side of it, by degree or sign.
- **Epicycle.** A circle on the **deferent**, on which a planet turns.
- **Equant.** In Ptolemaic astronomy, a mathematical point in outer space from which measurements are made. At the equant, planetary motion is seen as virtually constant and unchanging in speed.
- **Equation, Equate.** (1) In astronomical theory, a correction that is made to the **mean motion/position** of a planet, in order to convert its idealized or **mean** position to its **true motion/position**. Equations are found in a table of equations calculated individually for each planet. (2) In **house** theory, it refers to any **quadrant house** system, where house divisions are derived by exact calculation or equation (Ar. التّسوية); synonymous with house division by **division**, and **whole-sign** houses by **counting**.
- **Equation of the center (planetary theory).** The angular difference between where the center of a planet's **epicycle** is, as seen from the **equant** (also known as its **mean position**), and its **true position** as seen from earth.
- **Equation of the center (solar theory).** The angular difference between the **mean Sun** (where we expect it to be) and the **true Sun** (where we observe it to be).

- **Equator (celestial).** The projection of the earth's equator into space, forming a great circle. Its equivalent of latitude is called **declination**, while its equivalent of longitude is called **right ascension** (and is measured from the beginning of Aries, from the intersection of it and the **ecliptic**).
- **Equinoctial point, equinox.** The point where the circles of the **ecliptic** and celestial **equator** cross, which defines the beginning of spring (and 0° Aries, in the tropical **zodiac**) or beginning of autumn (and 0° Libra).
- **Escape** (Ar. فوت, Lat. *frustratio, evasio*). When a planet wants to **connect** with a second one, but the second one moves into the next sign before it is completed, and the first planet makes a **connection** with a different, unrelated one instead.
- **Essence** (Lat. *substantia*, Ar. جوهر). Deriving ultimately from Aristotelian philosophy, the fundamental nature or character of a planet or sign, which allows it to indicate or cause certain phenomena (such as the essence of Mars being responsible for indicating fire, iron, war, *etc.*). This word has often been translated as "substance," which is a less accurate term.
- **Essential/accidental.** A common way of distinguishing a planet's conditions, usually according to **dignity** (essential) and some other condition such as its **configurations** or **connections** or rulership (accidental).
- **Exaltation** (Lat. *exaltatio*, Ar. شرف). One of the five **dignities**. A sign in which a planet (or sometimes, a **Node**) signifies its matter in a particularly authoritative and refined way. The exaltation is sometimes identified with a particular degree in that sign.
- **Excellent place** (Ar. مكان جيّد). Includes several of the **advantageous places**, among which the Ascendant, Midheaven, and eleventh are consistently mentioned. (These may be the only excellent places.)
- **Exile** (Ar. غربة) In Arabic astrology, an **alien** (or "peregrine") planet. But in some later Latin astrology (Lat. *exilium*), it denotes being in **detriment**.
- **Face** (Lat. *facies*, Ar. وجه). One of the five **dignities**. The **zodiac** is divided into 36 faces of 10° each, starting with the beginning of Aries. Each division is equivalent to a **decan**.
- **Facing** (Ar. مواجهه). See **Proper face**.
- **Fall** (Gr. *hupsōma*, Ar. هبوط, Lat. *casus, descensio*). The sign opposite a planet's **exaltation**; sometimes called "descension."
- **Falling** (Lat. *cadens*, Ar. ساقط). Several uses. (1) Refers to being **cadent**, but sometimes ambiguous as to whether dynamically by **quadrant division** or by **whole sign** (which is also called **declining**). When understood

dynamically, it is equivalent to **retreating** and **withdrawing**. (2) A planet coming down from its **apogee** (sometimes with Ar. هبط).
- **Fall away from** (Ar. سقط عن). See **Aversion**.
- **Familiar** (Lat. *familiaris*). A hard-to-define term which suggests a sense of belonging and close relationship. (1) Sometimes it is contrasted with being **alien**, suggesting that a familiar planet is one which is a **lord** over a degree or **place** (that is, it has a **dignity** in it): for a dignity suggests belonging. (2) At other times, it refers to a familiar **configuration** or **connection** (and probably the **sextile** or **trine** in particular): all of the family houses in a chart have a **whole-sign** aspect to the **Ascendant**.
- *Firdāriyyah*. See *fardār*.
- **Feminine**. See **Gender**.
- **Feral** (Ar. وحشيّ, Lat. *feralis*). Equivalent to **Wildness**.
- **Figure** (Lat. *figura*). One of several polygons implied by a **configuration**. For example, a planet in Aries and one in Capricorn do not actually form a **square**, but they imply one because Aries and Capricorn, together with Libra and Cancer, form a square amongst themselves.
- *Fardār, firdāriyyah* (Ar. فردار, فردارية). A **time lord** method in which planets rule different periods of life, with each period broken down into sub-periods (there are also mundane versions).
- **Firm**. In terms of signs, the **fixed** signs: see **Quadruplicity**. For houses, equivalent to the **Angles**.
- **Fixed**. See **Quadruplicity**.
- **Fixing** (Gr. *pēxis*). See **Root**.
- **Flow away** (Lat. *defluo*, Ar. انصبّ). See **Separation**.
- **Foreign** (Lat. *extraneus*, Ar. غريب). Usually equivalent to **Peregrine**.
- **Fortunate, made fortunate** (Lat. *fortunatus*, Ar. مسعود). A planet whose condition is made better, often by a **trine** or **sextile** from a **fortune**.
- **Fortune/Infortune** (Ar. سعد \ نحس, Lat. *fortuna / infortuna*). A division of the planets into groups that cause or signify typically "good" things (Jupiter, Venus, usually the Sun and Moon) or "bad" things (Mars, Saturn). Mercury is considered variable.
- **Foundation of the lifespan** (Ar. أصل العمر). The expected longevity shown by the **house-master**.
- **Foundations of the Moon**. See **Centers of the Moon**.
- **Free** (Ar. بري, Lat. *liber*). Sometimes, being **cleansed** of the **infortunes**; at other times, being out of the **Sun's rays**.

- **Gender.** The division of signs, degrees, planets and hours into masculine and feminine groups.
- **Glow** (Ar. ضوء). This has three primary meanings: (1) a planet in "its own glow" is of the **sect** of the chart, or in some sect-related rejoicing condition; (2) the Moon increases and decreases in her light or glow by waxing and waning; (3) a planet can be "in its own glow" when it is out of the **Sun's rays** so as to be visible.
- **Good ones.** See **Fortune/Infortune.**
- **Good places.** Equivalent to **Advantageous places.**
- **Governor** (Ar. المستولي \ الوالي). Normally a generic term referring to a **victor** over a place, such as the Ptolemaic victor (by rulership and **aspect**). Sometimes used to denote the **house-master** or a **time lord.**
- **Greater, middle, lesser years.** See **Planetary years.**
- **Halb** (Ar. حلب). Probably Pahlavi for **sect**, but normally describes a special sect-related rejoicing condition. For **diurnal** planets, when they are in the same hemisphere as the Sun (upper or lower); for **nocturnal** planets, when they are in the hemisphere opposite the Sun. For example, if Saturn during the day is above the earth (where the Sun by definition also is).
- **Handing over** (دفع إلى) When a planet applies by **connection** to another, it hands over its **management.**
- **Harm.** A broad category of conditions by which a planet may be made **unfortunate.**
- **Hayyiz.** (Ar. حيّز). Arabic for **domain**, technically equivalent to *halb*, except that the planet is also in a sign of its own **gender**. But sometimes this term simply means **sect**.
- **Head (of the Dragon).** See **Node.**
- **Hexagon.** See **Sextile.**
- **Hīlāj** (Ar. هيلاج, from the Pahlavi for "releaser"). Equivalent to **releaser.**
- **Hold onto.** Hugo's synonym for a planet being in or **transiting** a **sign.**
- **Honor guard, paying honor** (تكرمة). A synonym for **Spear-bearing.**
- **Horary astrology.** A late historical designation for **questions.**
- **Hours (planetary).** The assigning of rulership over hours of the day and night to planets. The hours of daylight (and night, respectively) are divided by 12, and each period is ruled first by the planet ruling that day, then the rest in descending planetary order. For example, on Sunday the Sun rules the first planetary "hour" from daybreak, then Venus, then Mercury, the Moon, Saturn, and so on.

- **House** (Gr. *oikos*, Lat. *domus*, Ar. بيت). A twelve-fold spatial division of a chart, in which each house signifies one or more areas of life. Two basic schemes are (1) **whole-sign** houses, in which the **signs** are equivalent to the houses, and (2) **quadrant houses**. But in the context of dignities and rulerships, "house" is the equivalent of **domicile**: so, Aries is the house of Mars.
- **House-master** (Gr. *oikodespotēs*, Ar. كدخذاه). Often called the *alcochoden* in Latin, from the Arabic transliteration of a Persian word (*kadkhudhāh*). One of the **lords** of the longevity **releaser**, preferably the **bound lord**. But the Greek word is also used in a general way to mean simply any **lord**, or even a **victor**.
- **Humor** (Lat. *humor*, Ar. خلط). Any one of four mixtures or substances in the body (according to traditional medicine), the balance between which determines one's health and **temperament** (outlook and energy level). Choler or yellow bile is associated with fire and the choleric temperament; blood is associated with air and the sanguine temperament; phlegm is associated with water and the phlegmatic temperament; black bile is associated with earth and the melancholic temperament.
- **Hundred, Hundreds** (الألف). A Persian mundane **time lord**, which rules the world for a period of 100 years.
- *Hyleg*. See *Hīlāj* and **Releaser**.
- **IC**. See *Imum Caeli*.
- **Imum Caeli** (Lat. "lowest part of heaven"). The **axial degree** or degree of the zodiac on which the lower half of the **meridian** circle falls; in **quadrant house** systems, it marks the beginning of the fourth **house**.
- **In the heart**. Often called *cazimi* in English texts, from the Ar. كصميمي. A planet is in the heart of the Sun when it is either in the same degree as the Sun (according to Sahl b. Bishr and Rhetorius), or within 16' of longitude from him.
- **Inception** (Lat. *inceptio*, Ar. ابتداء). See **Election**.
- **Increaser, decreaser** (Ar. زائد, ناقص). A planet which natally connects by body or ray to the **house-master**, and increases or decreases the **foundation of the lifespan**.
- **Increasing/decreasing in calculation**. A planet is increasing in calculation when its **equation** is added to the **mean motion/position**, because the **true motion/position** is farther ahead in the zodiac than the mean one. It is decreasing in calculation when the equation is subtracted.

- **Increasing/decreasing in number.** When the daily speed of a planet (or at least the speed of the center of its **epicycle**) is seen to speed up (or slow down). When moving from its **perigee** to its **apogee**, it slows down or decreases in number, because it is moving farther away from the earth; when moving from the apogee to the perigee, it speeds up or increases in number because it is coming closer to the earth.
- **Indicator.** A generic term synonymous with **significator**. See also **namūdār**.
- **Indicator of the lifespan** (Ar. دليل العمر). The **house-master**.
- **Inferior** (Lat. *inferior*, Ar. سفليّ). The planets lower than the Sun: Venus, Mercury, and sometimes the Moon.
- **Infortunes.** See **Fortune/Infortune**.
- **Inspection** (مناظرة). An **aspect**, but in Abū Ma'shar's *Gr. Intr.* (and perhaps in all others), it specifically means an exact (or very close) degree-based **connection** from another sign. It seems to be equivalent to the Greek *katopteuō*, "scrutinize."
- **Intercepted** signs. In **quadrant houses**, a sign which does not have a **cusp** on it, but is wholly contained by two cusps: one in the sign before it, and one in the sign after it.
- **'Ittisāl** (Ar. اتّصال). Equivalent to **Connection**.
- **Jārbakhtār** (Ar. جاربختار, from the Pahlavi for "distributor of time"). Equivalent to **Distributor**; see **Distribution**.
- **Joy** (Lat. *gaudium*, Ar. فرح). Signs or hosues in which the planets are said to "rejoice" in acting or signifying their natures.
- **Kadkhudhāh** (كدخذاه). An Arabic transliteration from Pahlavi or Middle Persian for the **House-master**, often called the *alcochoden* in Latin transliteration.
- **Kardaja** (Ar. كردجة, from Sansk. *kramajyā*). The numerical interval used in rows of an astronomical table, when entering an **argument** and then finding the result in the relevant column (and therefore sometimes seems to refer to portions of the astronomical circles themselves). Ptolemy's tables often used intervals of 6°, while Indian tables often used 3° 45', which is 1/24 of 90°.
- **Kasmīmī** (Ar. كصميمي). See **In the heart**.
- **Kingdom.** See **Exaltation**.

- **Largesse and recompense** (Ar. نعمة والمكافاة). A reciprocal relation in which one planet is rescued from being in its own **fall** or a **well**, and then returns the favor when the other planet is in its fall or well.
- **Leader** (Lat. *dux*). Equivalent to a **significator** for some topic. The Arabic word for "significator" means to indicate something by pointing the way toward something: thus the significator for a topic or matter "leads" the astrologer to some answer. Used by some less popular Latin translators (such as Hugo of Santalla and Hermann of Carinthia).
- **Linger in** (Lat. *commoror*). Hugo's synonym for a planet being in or **transiting** through a **sign**.
- **Lodging-place** (Lat. *hospitium*). Hugo's synonym for a **house**, particularly the **sign** which occupies a house.
- **Look at** (Lat. *aspicio*, Ar. نظر). Two things may look at each other if they are in signs which are **configured** or in **aspect** to each other by a **sextile, square, trine,** or **opposition**. See also **Whole signs**. Places and planets which cannot see or look at each other, are in **aversion**.
- **Look down upon** (Ar. أشرف). A synonym for **overcoming**, and in particular **decimation**.
- **Lord of the year.** Usually, the **domicile lord** of a **profection**, namely where the profection **terminates**. But in mundane astrology it can also refer to a kind of **victor**, the planet in the chart which is the most powerful and sums up the meaning of the year.
- **Lord.** A designation for the planet which has a particular **dignity**, but when used alone it usually means the **domicile** lord. For example, Mars is the lord of Aries.
- **Lord of the orb.** See **Orb**.
- **Lord of the question.** See **Owner**.
- **Lord of the year.** In mundane ingress charts, the planet that is the **victor** over the chart, indicating the general meanings of the year. But in **profections**, the lord of the sign of the **terminal point**.
- **Lot** (Gr. *klēros*, Lat. *pars, sors*, Ar. سهم, قرعة). Sometimes called "Parts" (and falsely called "Arabic Parts"). A place (often treated as equivalent to an entire sign) expressing a ratio derived from the position of three other parts of a chart. Normally, the distance between two places is measured in zodiacal order from one to the other, and this distance is projected forward from some other place (usually the Ascendant): where the counting stops, is the Lot. The Lot of Fortune is the most famous Lot.

- **Lucky/unlucky.** See **Fortune/Infortune.**
- **Luminary** (Lat. *luminarium*, Ar. نيّر). The Sun or Moon.
- **Lunation.** See **Conjunction/prevention.**
- **Malefic.** See **Fortune/Infortune.**
- **Malevolent.** See **Fortune/Infortune.**
- **Management** (Ar. تدبير). A generic term referring to how a planet "manages" a topic by signifying it. Typically, planets **hand over** and "accept" management to and from each other, simply by **applying** to one another.
- **Manager** (Ar. المدبّر). Sometimes, the planetary **partner** in **distributions**; sometimes a term for the longevity **releaser**. But also a generic name for planets which have any kind of **management**.
- **Masculine.** See **Gender.**
- **Maximum equation.** In solar theory, the greatest angular amount of the **equation of the center**, which occurs when the **mean Sun** is perpendicular to the **apsidal line.**
- **Mean motion/position.** The motion or position of a planet as measured from the **equant**, namely assuming a constant rate of speed. To be contrasted with **True motion/position.**
- **Mean Sun.** A fictitious point which revolves around the earth in exactly one year, in a line parallel with the **true Sun**. The mean Sun represents where we would expect the Sun to be, if it traveled in a perfect circle around the earth. It coincides with the true Sun at the Sun's **apogee** and **perigee**.
- **Meeting** (Ar. اجتماع). The **conjunction** of the Sun and Moon at the New Moon, which makes it a **connection** by body. See **Conjunction/prevention.**
- **Melancholic.** See **Humor.**
- **Meridian.** The great circle which has its center at the middle of the earth, and points north-south relative to the horizon. The degree which intersects the **ecliptic** (or **axial degree**) is called the degree of the **Midheaven** or *Imum Caeli/IC.*
- **Midheaven.** Either the tenth sign from the **Ascendant**, or the **axial degree** on which the celestial **meridian** falls.
- **Minister.** A synonym for **Governor.**
- **Movable signs.** See **Quadruplicity.**
- *Mubtazz* (Ar. مبتزّ). See **Victor.**
- **Mutable signs.** Equivalent to "common" signs. See **Quadruplicity.**

- **Namūdār.** (Ar. نمودار) Persian for "indicator," a special way of determining the moment of conception or the nativity (if they are known only approximately).
- **Native** (Lat. *natus*, Ar. مولد, مولود). The person whose birth chart it is.
- **Nativity.** Technically, a birth itself, but used by astrologers to describe the chart cast for the moment of a birth.
- **Ninth-part** (Ar. نهبهر, Lat. *novenarium*). Divisions of each sign into 9 equal parts of 3° 20' apiece, each ruled by a planet. Used predictively by some astrologers as part of the suite of **revolution** techniques.
- **Nobility.** Equivalent to **Exaltation**.
- **Nocturnal.** See **Sect**.
- **Node** (Lat. *nodus*, Ar. عقدة), lit. "knot." The point on the ecliptic where a planet passes into northward latitude (its North Node or Head of the Dragon) or into southern latitude (its South Node or Tail of the Dragon). Normally only the Moon's Nodes are considered.
- **Northern/southern.** Either planets in northern or southern latitude in the **zodiac** relative to the ecliptic, or in northern or southern **declination** relative to the celestial **equator**.
- **Not-reception** (Ar. غير مقبول). When an **applying** planet is in the **fall** of the planet being applied to, or applies from a place in which the other planet has no **dignity**.
- **Number** (Ar. عدد). For house theory, see **counting**. For its use in calculating planetary positions, see **Increasing/decreasing in number**.
- **Oblique ascensions.** The **ascensions** used in making predictions by ascensional times or primary **directions**.
- **Obstruction.** See **Resistance**.
- **Occidental, occidentality.** See **Eastern and western**.
- **Opening of the portals/doors.** Times of likely weather changes and rain, determined by certain **transits**.
- **Opposition** (Lat. *oppositio, oppositum*; Ar. استقبال, مقابلة. A **configuration** or **aspect** either by **whole sign** or degree, in which the signs have a 180° relation to each other: for example, a planet in Aries is opposed to one in Libra.
- **Optimal place** (Lat. *optimus*). See **Excellent place**.
- **Orb** (Ar. دور, Lat. *orbis*), **lord of the orb**. Denotes a natal **time lord** technique; this same word is the basis of **Turn** (a mundane technique), and sometimes **Turning** (see **Profections**).

- **Orbs/bodies** (Lat. *orbis*, Ar. جرم). A space of power or influence on each side of a planet's **body** or position, used to determine the intensity of interaction between different planets.
- **Oriental, orientality.** See **Eastern and western.**
- **Overcoming.** When a planet is in the eleventh, tenth, or ninth sign from another planet (i.e., in a superior **sextile**, **square**, or **trine**); being in the tenth sign is considered **decimation**, a more domineering or even harmful position.
- **Overlord** (Ar. المسلّط). Refers to a **victor** over a place, but often used to designate the primary **triplicity lord**.
- **Own light** (Ar. ضوء, Lat. *lumen suum*). See **Glow**.
- **Owner** (صاحب). The person who "owns" or is the subject of a chart: the **native** is the owner of a nativity, the **querent** is the owner of the question chart, etc.
- **Part.** See **Lot**.
- **Partner** (Ar. شريك, Lat. *particeps*). The body or **ray** of any planet which a **directed releaser** encounters while being **distributed** through the **bounds**.
- **Peregrine** (Lat. *peregrinus*, Ar. غريب), lit. "a stranger, foreigner." See **Alien**.
- **Perigee (of eccentric/deferent).** The point on a planet's **deferent circle** that is closest to the earth; as seen from earth, it points to some degree of the zodiac. It is opposite the **apogee**.
- **Perverse** (Lat. *perversus*). Hugo's occasional term for (1) the **infortunes**, and (2) **places** in **aversion** to the **Ascendant** by **whole-sign**: definitely the twelfth and sixth, probably the eighth, and possibly the second.
- **Phlegmatic.** See **Humor**.
- **Pitted degrees.** Equivalent to **Welled degrees.**
- **Pivot** (Lat. *cardo*). Equivalent to **Angle**.
- **Place** (Gr. *topos*, Lat. *locus*, Ar. مكان). Equivalent to a **house**, and more often (and more anciently) a **whole-sign** house, namely a **sign**.
- **Planetary years.** Periods of years (or, other units of time) which the planets signify according to various conditions.
- **Portion** (Ar. جزء, Lat. *pars, portio*). Normally, refers to either (1) a specific zodiacal degree, especially the degree of the Ascendant or the degree where a **ray** falls, or (2) the degrees within a particular **bound**: especially, the bound in which the Ascendant falls.
- **Possess.** Hugo's synonym for a planet being in or **transiting** a **sign**.

- **Post** (Ar. مرکز). A **stake** or **angle**. (The Arabic verb is virtually equivalent to Ar. *watada*, used for a stake.) Sometimes translated as **center**, as in the centers of the Moon.
- **Posts of the Moon**. See **Centers of the Moon**.
- **Prevention**. See **Conjunction/prevention**.
- **Predominator** (Gr. *epikratētōr*). See **Victor**.
- **Primary directions**. See **Directions**.
- **Primary motion**. The clockwise or east-to-west motion of the heavens. See **secondary motion**.
- **Profection** (Lat. *profectio*, "advancement, setting out"). A predictive technique in which some part of a chart (usually the **Ascendant**) is advanced by an entire sign or in 30° increments for each year of life.
- **Prohibition**. Equivalent to **Blocking**.
- **Promittor** (lit., something "sent forward"). A point which is **directed** by **primary motion** to a **significator**, or to which a significator is **released** or directed (depending on how one views the mechanics of directions).
- **Proper face** (Gr. *idioprosōpos*). A relationship between a planet and a **luminary**, so that the **signs** the occupy have the same relationship as the **domiciles** they rule. For example, Leo (ruled by the Sun) is two signs to the **right** of Libra (ruled by Venus): so whenever Venus is **western** and two signs away from the Sun, she will be in the proper face of the Sun.
- **Pushing**. See **Handing over**.
- **Qāsim/qismah** (Ar. قاسم, قسمة) See **distributor** and **distribution**.
- **Quadrant**. A division of the heavens into four parts, defined by the circles of the horizon and **meridian**, marked out by the **axial degrees** of the **Ascendant-Descendant**, and **Midheaven-IC**.
- **Quadrant houses**. A division of the heavens or local space into twelve spaces which overlap the **whole signs**, and are assigned topics of life and ways of measuring strength (such as Porphyry, Alchabitius Semi-Arc, or Regiomontanus houses). For example, if the degree of the **Midheaven** fell into the eleventh sign, the space between the Midheaven and the Ascendant would be divided into sections that overlap with, and are not coincident with the signs.
- **Quadruplicity**. A "fourfold" group of signs indicating certain shared patterns of behavior. The movable (or cardinal or convertible) signs are those through which new states of being are quickly formed (including the seasons): Aries, Cancer, Libra, Capricorn. The fixed (sometimes "firm") signs

are those through which matters are fixed and lasting in their character: Taurus, Leo, Scorpio, Aquarius. The common (or mutable or bicorporeal) signs are those which make a transition and partake both of quick change and fixed qualities: Gemini, Virgo, Sagittarius, Pisces.
- **Quaesited/quesited**. In **horary** astrology, the matter asked about.
- **Querent**. In **horary** astrology, the person asking the question (or the person on behalf of whom one asks).
- **Questions**. The branch of astrology dealing with inquiries about individual matters, for which a chart is cast.
- **Radical** (Lat. *radicalis*). See **Root**.
- **Radix** (Lat. *radix*). See **Root**.
- **Ray, raying** (Lat. *radius, radiatio*; Ar. شعاع). An imaginary line which represents an exact **aspect** cast from a planet to the corresponding degree in another sign, such as if a planet is in 15° Gemini and casts a **square** ray to 15° Virgo. See also **Sun's rays**.
- **Receive, reception** (Lat. *recipio*, Ar. قبل). What one planet does when another planet **hands over** or **applies** to it, and especially when they are related by **dignity**, or by a **trine** or **sextile** from an **agreeing** sign of various types. For example, if the Moon applies to Mars, Mars will accept her application; and if he rules the sign in which she is, he will receive her (an intensified condition).
- **Reflection** (Ar. رد, Lat. *redditus*). When two planets are in **aversion** to each other, but a third planet either **collects** or **transfers** their light. If it collects, it reflects the light elsewhere.
- **Refrenation**. See **Revoking**.
- **Regard** (Lat. *respectus*). Equivalent to **looking at** or an **aspect**.
- **Releaser** (Ar. هيلاج). The point which is the focus of a **direction**, often one of a standard set of five (the luminaries, **Ascendant**, **Lot** of Fortune, and the prenatal **lunation**. In determining longevity, it is the **victor** among a set of possible points, which often includes the five just mentioned.
- **Remote** (Lat. *remotus*, prob. a translation of Ar. زائل). Equivalent to **cadent**: see **Angle**. But see also *Judges* §7.73, where al-Ṭabarī (or Hugo) distinguishes being **cadent** from being **remote**, probably translating the Ar. زائل and ساقط (**withdrawing** and **falling**).
- **Render**. When a planet **hands over** to another planet or place.

- **Resistance** (Ar. اعتراض). When one planet is moving towards a second (wanting to be **connected** to it), but a third one in a later degrees goes **retrograde**, connects with the second one, and then with the first one.
- **Retreat, retreating** (Ar. إدبار \ مدبر). Refers to being (2) dynamically **cadent**, i.e. moving by **primary motion** away from an **axial** degree. (But occasionally might refer to being cadent by **whole signs**.) A near synonym to **withdrawal**. Its antonym is **Advancement**. It may also refer to (2) the **western** quadrants.
- **Retrograde, retrogradation** (Lat. *retrogradus*, Ar. راجع). When a planet seems to move backwards in its **secondary motion**.
- **Return, Solar/Lunar.** Equivalent to **Revolution**.
- **Returning** (Ar. ردّ, Lat. *redditus, reditio*). What a **burned** or **retrograde** planet does when another planet **hands over** to it.
- **Revoking** (Ar. انتكاث, Lat. *refrenatio*). When a planet making an applying **connection** stations and turns **retrograde**, not completing the connection.
- **Revolution** (Lat. *revolutio*, Ar. تحويل). Sometimes called the "cycle" or "transfer" or "change-over" of a year. Technically, the **transiting** position of planets and the **Ascendant** at the moment the Sun returns to a particular place in the zodiac: in the case of nativities, when he returns to his exact natal position; in mundane astrology, usually when he makes his ingress into 0° Aries. But the revolution is also understood to involve an entire suite of predictive techniques, including **distribution**, **profections**, and *fardārs*.
- **Right ascensions.** Degrees on the celestial **equator** (its equivalent of geographical longitude), particularly those which move across the **meridian** when calculating arcs for **ascensions** and **directions**.
- **Right/left.** Right (or "dexter") degrees and **configurations** or **aspects** are those earlier in the zodiac relative to a planet or sign, up to the **opposition**; left (or "sinister") degrees and configurations are those later in the zodiac. For example, if a planet is in Capricorn, its right aspects will be towards Scorpio, Libra, and Virgo; its left aspects will be towards Pisces, Aries, and Taurus.
- **Right-siding, being on the right, right-sidedness** (تنامن \ ميمنة). A synonym for **Spear-bearing**.
- **Root** (Gr. *pēxis*, Lat. *radix*, Ar. أصل). A chart used as a basis for another chart; a root particularly describes something considered to have concrete

being of its own. For example, a **nativity** acts as a root for an **election**, so that when planning an election one must make it harmonize with the nativity. A horary or **question** chart is considered "radical" or "rooted" if it fits certain criteria, such as harmonizing with the **querent's nativity**.

- **Safe** (Ar. سليم). When a planet is not being harmed, particularly by an **assembly** or **square** or **opposition** with the **infortunes**. See **Cleansed**.
- **Sālkhuday / sālkhudāh** (Ar. سالخداه \ سالخدى, from Pahlavi, "lord of the year"). Equivalent to the **lord of the year** in a **profection**.
- **Sanguine**. See **Humor**.
- **Scorched** (Lat. *adustus*). See **Burned up**.
- **Secondary motion**. The motion of planets forward in the zodiac, rather than the **primary motion** of the heavens around the earth.
- **Sect** (Gr. *hairēsis*). A division of charts, planets, and signs into "diurnal/day" and "nocturnal/night." For similar terms, see **Glow, Share**, and **Domain**.
- **Sector** (Ar. نطاق). A division of the **deferent** circle or **epicycle** into four parts, used to determine the position, speed, visibility, and other features of a planet.
- **See**. See **Look at**.
- **Seeing, hearing, listening signs**. A way of associating signs similar to **commanding/obeying**.
- **Separation** (Lat. *separatio*, Ar. انصراف). When planets have completed a **connection** by **assembly** or **aspect**, and move away from one another.
- **Sextile** (Lat. *sextilis*, Ar. تسديس). A **configuration** or **aspect** either by **whole sign** or degree, in which the signs have a 60° relation to each other: for example, Aries and Gemini.
- **Share** (Ar. حظ, but sometimes نصيب, or حصّة, "allotment, share"). Often equivalent to **dignity**, but sometimes used to mean **sect** (where it is synonymous with and perhaps confused with **domain** (Ar. حيّز).
- **Shift**. (1) Equivalent to **sect** (Ar. نوبة), referring not only to the alternation between day and night, but also to the period of night or day itself. The Sun is the lord of the diurnal shift or sect, and the Moon is the lord of the nocturnal shift or sect. (2) In mundane astrology, it refers to the shift (Ar. انتقال, Lat. *mutatio*) of the Saturn-Jupiter conjunctions from one **triplicity** to another about every 200 (tropical zodiac) or 220 (sidereal zodiac) years.

- **Sign.** One of the twelve 30° divisions of the **ecliptic** or **zodiac**, named after the constellations which they used to be roughly congruent to.
- **Significator** (Lat. *significator*, Ar. دليل). Either (1) a planet or point in a chart which indicates or signifies something for a topic (either through its own character, or house position, or rulerships, *etc.*), or (2) the stationary point in primary **directions**.
- **Significator of the king.** In mundane ingress charts, the **victor** planet which indicates the king or government.
- **Sinister.** "Left": see **Right/left**.
- **Slavery.** In Hugo of Santalla's Latin, equivalent to **Fall**.
- **Sought matter, sought thing** (Ar. حاجة). See **Quaesited**.
- **Sovereignty** (Lat. *regnum*). In Hugo of Santalla's Latin, equivalent to **Exaltation**.
- **Spear-bearing** (Ar. دستوريّة, Lat. *dustoria*, Gr. *doruphoria*). A special configuration in a chart showing eminence and prosperity, of which there were several types and definitions. Spear-bearing requires that there be a royal planet (usually, a **luminary**), which is accompanied by a spear-bearing planet.
- **Square.** A **configuration** or **aspect** either by **whole sign** or degree, in which the signs have a 90° relation to each other: for example, Aries and Cancer.
- **Stake** (Ar. وتد). Equivalent to **Angle**.
- **Sublunar world.** The world of the four **elements** below the sphere of the Moon, in classical cosmology.
- **Substance** (Lat. *substantia*). Sometimes, indicating the real **essence** of a planet or sign. But often it refers to financial assets (perhaps because coins are physical objects indicating real value).
- **Succeedent.** See **Angle**.
- **Suitable, suitability** (Ar. صالح \ صلاح). For **places** of the chart, equivalent to the schemes of **advantageous places**. Otherwise, a general term for the good or bad condition of a planet.
- **Sun's rays** (or Sun's beams). In earlier astrology, equivalent to a regularized distance of 15° away from the Sun, so that a planet under the rays is not visible at dawn or dusk. But a later distinction was made between being **burned up** (about 1° - 7.5° away from the Sun) and merely being under the rays (about 7.5° - 15° away).

- **Superior** (Lat. *superior*, Ar. علويّ). The planets higher than the Sun: Saturn, Jupiter, Mars.
- **Supremacy** (Lat. *regnum*). Hugo's word for **exaltation**, sometimes used in translations by Dykes instead of the slightly more accurate Latin **sovereignty**.
- **Synastry.** The comparison of two or more charts to determine compatibility, usually in romantic relationships or friendships.
- **Tail (of the Dragon).** See **Node**.
- *Tasyir* (Ar. تسيير, "dispatching, sending out"). Equivalent to primary **directions**.
- **Temperament** (Lat. *temperamentum*, Ar. مزاج). The particular mixture (sometimes, "complexion") of **elements** or **humors** which determines a person's or planet's typical behavior, outlook, energy level, and health.
- **Terminal point, termination, terminate** (Ar. انتهاء). The sign or degree which a **profection** comes to, at a particular day or time.
- **Testimony** (Lat. *testimonium*, Ar. شهادة). From Arabic astrology onwards, a little-defined term which can mean (1) the planets which have **dignity** in a place or degree, or (2) the number of dignities a planet has in its own place (or as compared with other planets), or (3) a planet's **assembly** or **aspect** to a place of interest, or (4) generally *any* way in which planets may make themselves relevant to the inquiry at hand. For example, a planet which is the **exalted** lord of the **Ascendant** but also **looks at** it, maby be said to present two testimonies supporting its relevance to an inquiry about the Ascendant.
- **Tetragon.** See **Square**.
- **Thought-interpretation.** The practice of identifying a theme or topic in a **querent's** mind, often using a **victor**, before answering the specific **question**. Called the "extraction of the heart" in Arabic (استخراج الضمير), it was sometimes used to identify an object in the hand prior to a consultation.
- **Thousand, Thousands** (المائة). A Persian mundane **time lord**, which rules the world for a period of 1000 years.
- **Time lord.** A planet or sign ruling over some period of time according to one of the classical predictive techniques. For example, the **lord of the year** in nativities is the time lord over a **profection**.
- **Transfer** (Lat. *translatio*, Ar. نقل) When one planet **separates** from one planet, and **connects** to another. Not to be confused with a **shift** of triplic-

ities in Saturn-Jupiter conjunctions, or annual **revolutions**, either mundane or natal.

- **Transit** (Lat. *transio*, Ar. مرّ). The passing of one planet across a planet or point (by body or **aspect** by exact degree), or even through a particular sign.
- **Translation** (Lat. *translatio*). Equivalent to **Transfer**.
- **Traverse** (Lat. *discurro*). Hugo's synonym for a planet being in or **transiting** through a **sign**.
- **Triangle**. Normally, equivalent to **trine**, but sometimes **triplicity**.
- **Trigon**. Normally, equivalent to **trine**, but sometimes **triplicity**.
- **Trine** (Lat. *trinus*, Ar. تثليث). A **configuration** or **aspect** either by **whole sign** or degree, in which the signs have a 120° relation to each other: for example, Aries and Leo.
- **Triplicity** (Ar. مثلّثة, Lat. *triplicitas*). A set of three signs which form a triangle, such as Aries-Leo-Sagittarius. (Arabic texts sometimes use the plural "triplicities" when they mean the singular.)
- **Triplicity lords**. A set of three planets which jointly rule a **triplicity** as a whole. One planet is primary by day, another by night, and the third lord always acts as their partner. For example, the Sun, Jupiter, and Saturn are the triplicity lords of Aries-Leo-Sagittarius: the Sun is primary by day, Jupiter by night, and Saturn is always the last, partnering lord.
- **True motion/position**. The motion or position of a planet as measured from the earth, once its **mean motion/position** has been adjusted or corrected by various types of **equations**.
- **True Sun**. The zodiacal position of the Sun, as seen from the earth, after its **mean** position has been **equated** or corrected.
- **Turn** (Ar. دور). A predictive technique in which responsibilities for being a **time lord** rotates among different planets. It may also refer to other methods in which cycles through the planets, assigning them roles as **time lords**. See **Lord of the orb**.
- **Turned away from** (Gr. *apostrophē*). See **Aversion**.
- **Turning** (Ar. دور \ إدوار, Gr. *kuklōmenon*). See **Profection**.
- **Turning signs** (Lat. *tropicus*). Normally, equivalent to **movable** or **convertible** signs. See **Quadruplicity**. But sometimes refers to the tropical signs Cancer and Capricorn, in which the Sun turns back from his most extreme **declinations**.

- **Twelfth-part** (Lat. *duodecatemorion, duodecima*; Ar. اثنى عشريّة). Signs of the zodiac defined by 2.5° divisions of other signs. For example, the twelfth-part corresponding to 4° Gemini is Cancer.
- **Two-parted signs.** Equivalent to the double-bodied or common signs: see **Quadruplicity**.
- **Under the rays.** See **Sun's rays**.
- **Underground.** Equivalent to *Imum caeli*/**IC**.
- **Unfortunate** (Lat. *infortunatus*, Ar. منحوس). When a planet's condition is made more difficult, usually by **assembly**, **square**, or **opposition** with the **infortunes**.
- **Unhealthiness** (Ar. وبال). Equivalent to **Detriment**.
- **Union** (Ar. اقتران). Usually, any **conjunction** of planets by body; but sometimes, a **mean** conjunction or even the New Moon (see **Conjunction/prevention**).
- **Unlucky.** See **Fortune/Infortune**.
- **Upright** (Ar. قائم). Describes the axis of the MC-IC, when it falls into the tenth and fourth signs, rather than the eleventh-fifth, or ninth-third.
- *Via combusta.* See **Burnt path**.
- **Victor** (Ar. مبتزّ). A planet or point identified as the most authoritative over a particular topic, **place** or **house**, or for a chart as a whole. Dykes distinguishes procedures that find victor "over" several places at once, and a victor "among" several candidate victors, usually on a ranked list.
- **Void in course.** See **Emptiness in course**.
- **Well, welled degrees** (Lat. *puteum*, Ar. بئر). A degree in which a planet is said to be more obscure in its operation. In later, English-speaking astrology, sometimes called the "pitted" degrees.
- **Western.** See **Eastern and western**.
- **Westernize, westernization** (غرّب \ تغريب). See **Easternize, easternization**.
- **Whole signs.** The oldest system of assigning house topics and **aspects**. The entire sign on the horizon (the **Ascendant**) is the first house, the entire second sign is the second house, and so on. Likewise, aspects are considered first of all according to signs: planets in Aries **look at** planets in Gemini, even if aspects which **connect** by degree are more intense.
- **Wildness** (Ar. وحشيّة, Lat. *feralitas*). When a planet is not **looked at** by any other planet.

- **Withdrawal, withdrawing** (زوال \ زائل; in some Latin translations, *recedens*). Refers to being (1) dynamically **cadent**, i.e. moving by **primary motion** away from an **axial** degree. (But occasionally might refer to being cadent by **whole signs**.) A near synonym to **retreat**. Its antonym is **Advancement**. It may also refer to (2) the **western** quadrants.
- **Zīj** (Ar. زيج). The Arabic for a Persian word meaning a set of astronomical tables for calculating planetary positions and other things. Ptolemy's *Almagest* can be considered a *zīj*.
- **Zodiac**. Three ways of dividing the **ecliptic** into signs. The "constellational" zodiac uses the actual constellations, which are of different sizes. The "sidereal" zodiac divides the ecliptic into twelve equal divisions, starting from some fixed star which acts as the **ayanamsha**. The "tropical" zodiac also uses equal divisions, but starts from the **equinoctial point**.

INDEX

'Abbāsid Caliphate...1, 4, 41, 61, 496

Abū Ma'shar...1-13, 15-30, 32-42, 44, 52, 56-57, 60-61, 64, 67-70, 74, 79, 82-83, 89, 91, 94, 103, 115, 129, 135, 137, 139, 144-45, 150, 153-54, 157, 160, 168, 171, 184, 192-95, 200, 206, 218-22, 226-27, 230, 232, 235, 237, 239, 241, 243, 245, 255-56, 261, 263-64, 266-67, 271, 283-84, 287-88, 290-91, 293-94, 304, 307, 314, 316, 318, 322-23, 328, 330, 333, 336, 339, 347-48, 353-57, 361, 363-66, 369, 371-72, 374, 377, 379-82, 385-86, 388-90, 394-96, 400, 411, 416, 422, 429-30, 432, 439-42, 444, 454, 457, 464, 471, 475, 477-79, 491-93, 503, 507, 511-16, 519, 522-23, 528, 532, 537, 539, 541-42, 548, 550-51, 553-56, 558-59, 574-75, 577, 582

Advancing...202, 278, 280, 470, 480, 520, 549, 559

Agathodaimōn...2-3, 27-28, 141-42, 144, 261, 263-68, 285, 294

Ages of Man.................... 396

al-Andarzaghar, Zādānfarrūkh 36-37, 366, 382, 523, 532, 551-52

al-Bīrūnī..................... 3, 5-6

Alexander of Aphrodisias...3, 9, 26, 440

Alexander the Great...5-6, 205, 315, 332

Alien (peregrine) planets...... 238, 481, 574

al-Kindī.......................2, 25

al-Qabīsī (Alchabitius)........ 5, 478

al-Tabarī, 'Umar . 3, 261, 454, 607

Antiochus (astrologer) 2, 29, 313

Antiscia................ 359-60, 456

Apogee/perigee...23, 25, 93, 151, 157, 162, 178, 182-83, 223-24, 243-48, 255, 352, 407-09, 430-31, 438, 480-81

Aratus.................. 2, 29, 130, 314

Aristarchus....................... 3

Aristotle...2-6, 9-10, 13-16, 18, 26, 46, 62-63, 69-70, 81, 87, 133, 145, 166, 220

Ascensions, ascensional times... 173-74, 176-77, 186-87, 276, 278, 281, 315, 329, 342-46, 355-59, 362-65, 455-56, 477, 486-87, 502, 543

Aspects
 exact aspects......30-33, 347-53, 478, 520, 536, 542-43, 547, 550
 harmonics 31, 354-55
 minor aspects 31
 no out-of-sign aspects . 30, 446, 451
 sign-to-sign 425, 444, 445

Assembly/conjunction 425, 426, 427, 430, 431, 445, 447
 no out-of-sign conjunctions 30, 425, 426, 446, 447

Astrātū 3, 284, 292

Astrology
  compared to other sciences... 50-61
  defense of.. ....78-79, 81, 89, 91, 94, 96-97, 99-103, 106, 109, 111-16
  definition........... 47-48, 153-58
  theory of ... 6-19, 62-77, 217-21
Aversion...30-31, 148, 361-64, 394, 445, 451-52, 457, 459, 462-63, 478, 481, 526, 538, 548, 574-75
Babylonians...4, 29, 163, 284, 290, 295, 314, 405, 500, 502
Besieging/enclosure 478, 483
Bizidaj...3-4, 36, 38, 40, 303, 365-66, 380, 382, 455, 523
Blocking of light...450, 464-65, 471, 474
Bonatti, Guido 35
Bounds...28, 45, 235, 237, 245-46, 255, 284-93, 397, 426, 447, 450-51, 454, 459, 466-67, 476-79, 482, 484, 554, 572
Burned path (*via combusta*) .. 341, 481, 484
Burnett, Charles........................1, 9
Burning (combustion)...25, 227, 393, 414, 417-19, 422-23, 435-38, 470-71, 480
Buzurjmihr............................ 3, 455
Calculation
  increasing and decreasing. 407, 410
Chaldeans................... 284-85, 290
Climes...101, 106, 145, 199, 237, 255, 290, 342-346, 365, 509
Collection of light 461-62
Connection (by degree) ..445-47, 449-51
  in latitude 452-54
Counteraction........................... 468
Critodemus............................... 397
Cutting of light.................... 473-74
Darījān 297-98
Darius the Great 290
Deferent circle / eccentric..........19
Degrees
  bright, dark, dusky, empty.305-06, 478, 480
  elevation and power............ 309
  increasing in good fortune. 309
  masculine/feminine..... 303-04, 478-79, 481
Detriment...25, 237-38, 240, 255, 264-66, 434, 481, 552
Distributions 579
Domain (*hayyiz*)...294, 407, 411-12, 468, 506
Dorotheus of Sidon....3, 29, 36-38, 268, 295, 313, 430, 454-55, 484, 519, 523, 525, 538, 555, 562
Eastern/western planets 230, 480
Easternization, westernization 51, 150-51, 231, 235-38, 249, 251-53, 261-62, 266-67, 273, 414-19, 430, 437, 481, 542
Eclipse 47, 453, 484
Egyptians...4, 29, 36, 178, 183-84, 284-87, 290, 293, 455, 506, 557, 570
Elements
  explanation and order... 134-36
Emptiness of course 458
Epicycle ...7, 19, 93, 218, 409, 428

Index

Equations...94, 178, 181-82, 257-58, 408-10, 579
Erasistratos 3
Escape 450, 472
Exaltation...28, 95, 230, 235, 237-38, 255, 262, 268-69, 272-84, 422, 437, 450, 454, 466-68, 475-77, 479, 543-44, 549, 551, 567, 572
Faces/decans/images 28-30, 127, 255, 295-98, 313-42, 382, 450, 454, 466-67, 476-78, 572
Fall (contrary of exaltation) 25, 230, 237-38, 240, 243, 255, 268, 272, 437, 475, 481, 551, 573
Falling (cadent)............95, 470-71
Fardārs... 487
Favor and recompense............ 475
Firmicus Maternus. 304, 430, 499
Fixed stars...2, 4-6, 28-29, 55, 117-29, 150-51, 161, 163-64, 317, 324, 372, 380-82, 425, 427, 431
  harming eyes 380
Fortunes and infortunes ...218-22, 225-27
  how they change............ .227-43
Galen..............................3, 98, 164
Halb...................................... 478, 555
Handing over
  management... 450-51, 469-72, 475-76
  nature 466, 468, 474, 476
  power 467-68
  two natures 468

Head of the Dragon.22, 152, 243, 249-50, 252, 268, 282, 482, 484, 487, 575
Hephaistion of Thebes .. 454, 484
Hermann of Carinthia.................. 1
Hermes...2-3, 27-29, 36-40, 127, 141-42, 144, 147, 258, 261, 263, 265-69, 273-82, 285, 294, 301-03, 313, 422, 479, 500, 504-05, 516-17, 523-25, 527-39, 550-51, 553, 558, 563-565, 569
Hipparchus 139
Hippocrates 4, 98, 164, 167
House-master............................ 555
Houses/places
  basic significations 387-90
  explained by opposites. 394-95
  explained by planets 390-94
Humors.. ....10, 104-05, 209-16
  black bile / melancholic.... 197, 209, 211-13, 215-16, 318, 374, 400, 488
  blood / sanguine .... .200, 209, 211-12, 321, 329, 338, 400
  phlegm.. ....21, 162, 200, 209, 211-14, 323, 332, 400, 494, 497
  tastes................................. 210-11
  yellow bile / choler ... 197, 209, 211-13, 216, 315, 325, 400, 491
In the heart (*cazimi*)...414, 417-19, 422-23, 438, 478
Indians...4, 27, 270, 284, 293, 297-98, 310, 314-28, 330-42, 404, 411
John of Spain................ 1, 219, 489

Joys/rejoicing............. 255, 478-79
  by house...... 385, 396, 481, 484
  by sign 267, 479
Kankriz.. 405
Kardajas...................................... 411
Latitude...5, 25, 128, 142, 160-62, 176-78, 182-83, 198-99, 239, 243, 255, 281-82, 294, 343-46, 365, 380-81, 407, 411, 418, 422, 431, 438, 452-55, 480-81, 484
Lemay, Richard...1, 9, 156, 163, 219, 243, 322, 325, 331-32, 334, 369, 379, 382-83, 393, 405, 418, 429, 490, 493, 496-97, 521-22, 546, 551, 554-56
Lots...2-4, 27, 35-39, 263-64, 425, 431, 444, 582
  calculation............... 501-02, 575
  explanation36, 500-01, 506-08, 516-18, 570-72
  interpretation 500, 570, 573-75
Lots (list)
  [1] Fortune......... 309, 379, 507, 509-16, 520, 530, 532, 545, 547-50, 552-53, 555, 558, 560-61, 567-69, 573, 577
  [2] Invisible (Spirit) . 379, 511, 516, 560, 573
  [3] Burdensome (Saturn) 513, 545, 561
  [4] prosperity and aid (Jupiter).................... 513, 561
  [5] courage (Mars) 514, 561
  [6] love and familiarity (Venus) ... 515, 520, 548-50, 558, 561, 570
  [7] poverty and few stratagems (Mercury) 515, 547, 551, 553, 561
  [8] life 503, 518, 528, 561, 571
  [9] support of Ascendant . 503, 519, 548-50, 561, 570
  [10] logic and reason.......... 503, 521, 559, 561
  [11] assets.........….503, 509, 519, 521, 562, 572, 574
  [12] loaning......... 503, 522, 562
  [13] found wealth 503, 522, 547, 562
  [14] siblings.39, 503, 522, 528, 562
  [15] number of siblings 503, 524, 562
  [16] death of siblings 503, 524, 562
  [17] fathers 36-39, 503, 524, 543, 545, 547, 562
  [18] death of fathers . 503, 526, 562
  [19] grandfathers 503, 526, 562
  [20] lineage 503, 526, 540, 563
  [21] immovable properties (Hermes) .. 38-39, 504, 527, 563
  [22] immovable properties (Persians)........ 504, 527, 563
  [23] agriculture. 504, 527, 535, 563
  [24] outcomes of affairs.... 504, 527, 539, 563
  [25] children 37, 39, 504, 528-29, 563, 571

INDEX

[26] time of children 504, 529, 563
[27] male children 39, 504, 529, 564
[28] female children 39, 504, 530, 536, 564
[29] sex of child. 504, 531, 564
[30] chronic illness (Hermes) 39, 504, 531, 564
[31] chronic illness (ancients) 504, 531, 564
[32] slaves 39, 504, 532, 543, 564, 571, 574
[33] prisoners 504, 532, 564
[34] men's marriage (Hermes) 39, 504, 533-34, 537, 550, 564
[35] men's marriage (Valens) 504, 534, 564
[36] men's cunning and deception 504, 534, 564
[37] men's intercourse 504, 534, 564
[38] men's debauchery and fornication 504, 534, 564
[39] women's marriage (Hermes) ... 39, 504, 535-36, 565
[40] women's marriage (Valens) ... 504, 535-36, 565, 574
[41] women's cunning and deception .504, 535-36, 565
[42] women's intercourse .504, 535-36, 565
[43] women's debauchery and indecency. 504, 535-36, 565
[44] women's abstinence. 504, 536, 565
[45] men's and women's marriage (Hermes) .39, 504, 536, 565
[46] time of marriage (Hermes) .39, 504, 537, 565
[47] marriage's stratagem 504, 537, 565
[48] in-laws 504, 537, 565
[49] contentions and contenders 504, 525, 538, 565
[50] death 39, 504, 508, 517, 538, 566
[51] killing planet 504, 517, 539, 556, 566
[52] year of death and fear. 504, 517, 539, 566
[53] burdensome place 504, 540, 566
[54] entanglement and hardship 504, 540, 566
[55] travel .. 505, 541, 566, 572
[56] traveling by water 505, 541, 566
[57] piety 505, 541, 566
[58] reason and depth of thought . 505, 542, 555, 566, 571
[59] knowledge and meditation 505, 542, 566
[60] tales, reports, superstitions .. 505, 542, 567
[61] reports, true or false 36, 505, 543, 567, 571
[62] exaltation ... 505, 543, 567

[63] rulership and authority 505, 544, 567
[64] managers, viziers, authorities 505, 544, 567
[65] authority, aid conquering 505, 526, 545, 567
[66] sudden elevation 505, 545, 567
[67] honored and known among people 505, 545, 567
[68] soldiers and conscription 505, 546, 567
[69] authority and the native's work..505, 527, 546, 556-67
[70] manual work and businesses....... 505, 547, 567
[71] businesses, buying, selling 505, 547, 567
[72] work and no escape .. 505, 547, 568
[73] mother........ 505, 548, 568
[74] nobility 505, 548-49, 550, 568
[75] ingratiation .. 505, 548-49, 550, 568
[76] being known and respected 505, 549, 568
[77] success........ 505, 549, 568
[78] passions and worldly eagerness 505, 550, 568
[79] hope 505, 550, 568
[80] friends 505, 550, 552, 568
[81] compulsion......... 505, 551, 557-58, 568
[82] plenty and good in home 505, 552, 568
[83] soul's freedom... 505, 552, 568
[84] praised and commended 505, 552, 568
[85] enemies (ancients) ... 505, 553, 569
[86] enemies (Hermes)....... 39, 505, 553, 569
[87] suffering...... 505, 553, 569
[88] the releaser. 506, 554, 569
[89] exhaustion of bodies. 506, 555, 569
[90] horsemanship and courage... 506, 555, 569, 571
[91] risk-taking . 506, 539, 556, 569
[92] cunning and deception 506, 556, 569
[93] occasion of need and desire 506, 557, 570
[94] necessity (Egyptians). 506, 557, 570
[95] necessity (Persians).. 506, 557, 570
[96] punishment 506, 558, 570
[97] work of truth 506, 559, 570
Basis 503, 519
dwelling or inhabiting (Olympiodorus)................38
Erōs (Hermes) 551
Erōs (Valens) 514, 550, 558
expedition (Dorotheus) 555
nature of the houses............ 267
Necessity (Hermes) .. 532, 558
Necessity (Valens).............. 515
Lunations (meeting and fullness) 142-43, 167, 179-81, 187, 200-03, 225, 259, 393, 527, 539, 554, 563, 566, 569

Māshā'allāh b. Atharī.. 30, 38, 476
Monomoria 301
Moon
   and animals, plants, minerals
   200-203
Motion/travel
   increasing and decreasing..407, 410
Mutual reception................ 477-78
Nawbahr .... *See* Ninth-part
Nebuchadnezzar III 290
Nebulae 431
Nechepsō 554
Neoplatonism........ 9, 14-17, 70, 81
Ninth-parts 298-300
Noah (patriarch) 290
Non-reception 475
Number
   adding and subtracting.......407, 409
Olympiodorus......................... 37-39
Overcoming............................. 482
Paul of Alexandria...37-39, 525, 532, 551, 558
Persians...4, 27, 29, 36, 198, 270, 290, 295, 307, 314-15, 329-30, 344-46, 359, 365, 368, 370, 404, 411, 414, 416-17, 419, 422, 455, 500, 502, 504, 506, 517, 527, 529, 535, 539, 547, 557, 563, 570
Pingree, David 9
Planetary hours................... 402-05
Planetary years...286, 288, 365-67, 414, 417-18, 487-88, 524, 529
Planets
   colors.............. 212, 213, 215-16

diurnal/nocturnal 22-23, 36, 160, 222-23, 227, 235, 240, 251-53, 255, 257, 260, 267, 402, 407, 411, 468, 478-79, 500, 507, 509, 511, 514, 519, 525, 530, 543
elemental principles........20-23, 151-52, 205-08, 213-14, 236-42, 244, 246-47, 249-52, 488, 490-92, 494-95, 497
masculine/feminine.. 222, 227, 250-51, 275, 294, 392, 411, 478-81, 537
mixture of qualities .. 20, 24-26, 428-42
orbs or bodies..........34-35, 283, 406, 424-27, 447-48, 450, 452
significations................... 488-98
weather 223-25
Platonism 14
Porphyry of Tyre 16
Primary directions...485-87, 500, 524, 540, 555
Profections...524, 526, 540, 554-55
Ptolemy, Claudius...3-7, 10, 20-21, 23, 27, 29, 32, 36, 44-47, 92-94, 118, 139, 205-06, 255, 258, 261, 263, 265, 269, 271-72, 284-86, 288, 290-91, 313-35, 337-43, 345-47, 350-51, 353, 380-81, 396-97, 418, 485, 502, 510-11
Pythagoreanism..................... 32-33
Qabalism 14

Quadrants...23-24, 26, 174, 186-87, 195, 201, 244-47, 251, 385-87, 397-400, 416, 424, 431-33, 480-81, 485
   as divisions and houses...... 273, 280, 385, 387, 391, 508-09, 521, 538, 541, 562, 566
Reception...450-51, 466, 469-70, 474-78, 481-82, 542, 575
Reflection of light...... 462-63, 477
Releasers...................... 543, 554-55
Resistance 472
Retrogradation...25, 35, 151, 226-27, 249, 252, 256-57, 261, 266-67, 270, 352, 393, 412, 416, 419, 437, 448, 470-73, 476, 480-81, 571, 573, 575
Returning management.... 469-71
Revoking................................ 471
Rhetorius of Egypt...4, 29, 38, 264-65, 326, 376, 379-80, 382, 397, 519, 539, 556
Right and left of Sun 412-13
Sect...18, 22, 117, 222, 234-35, 267, 291, 294, 361, 411, 468, 478-79, 506-07, 533
Sect of chart...36-38, 148, 185-87, 201-03, 231, 237-38, 240, 251-52, 291, 294-95, 309, 329, 361, 411-12, 478-81, 501, 507, 509, 511-16, 519-71, 582
Separation 446
Signs
   accumulating and becoming full 375
   agreeing in manner....... 361-64, 457

   agreeing in power 357, 359-60, 362-64, 456
   agreeing in the belt........ 357-58
   agreeing in the path............ 357
   and countries 367-70
   anxiety.................................... 382
   aquatic animals.................... 383
   as units of time 365
   commanding/obeying 355-57, 359-60
   convertible... 140-41, 143, 146, 260, 294, 299, 536, 551, 559
   culture, beguiling speech ... 382
   cut limbs 378
   dark.. 382
   directions in space 384
   diurnal/nocturnal. .28, 147-48, 237-38, 240, 255, 260, 294, 479
   double-bodied...... 140-41, 143, 146, 327, 334, 377, 523, 528, 536
   equal ascensions. .362-63, 455-56, 477
   fertile, middling, sterile 377
   fixed 140-41, 143, 145-46, 377, 536, 543
   four-footed 383
   generosity and liberality..... 374
   grace and beauty 374
   granting ease 375
   harmonizing by natural opposition and sextile.... 362
   harmonizing by square....... 364
   hooves, teeth, talons 383
   lewdness and illnesses 376
   loving, hating, hostile to each other 355-356

masculine/feminine.. 146, 148, 237-38, 240, 252, 259, 260, 266, 285, 293-95, 303, 353-54, 411-12, 478-81, 529, 531
motion and rest.................. 371
natural aspects from aversion 457
parts of human body.. 372, 374
pouring forth and emptying out....................................... 375
predatory animals................ 383
rational................................. 371
same ascensions.......... 362, 364
seizing and taking................ 375
sharpness and anger............ 378
skin and hair diseases 379
social classes 371
straight/crooked .355-56, 527-28
trees and vegetation............ 383
type of birds......................... 382
types of water 383
venomous things 383
voiced, middling, mute 378
winds..................................... 384
women's chastity and modesty 377
working by fire 384
Sindhind..............................94, 411
Solar revolutions
mundane 92, 106, 499, 512
natal........ .13, 24, 107, 435, 499, 503, 512, 520, 554, 559
Solar-lunar halves of zodiac ... 261
Spear-bearing 414, 416, 418
Stakes...95, 168-69, 172-74, 178, 186, 235, 251, 277-80, 283, 385, 387, 394-95, 398-400, 424, 470-71, 480-81, 485-86, 520, 522, 526, 536, 538, 543, 558, 565, 574-75
Stations, stationing...151, 226, 249, 412, 416, 418-19, 433, 480, 555
Stoics............ 7, 9, 13, 26, 147, 440
Sun
weather, natures, life.... ..159-66
Synodic cycle
inferiors 417-19
Moon 421-23
superiors......................... 414-17
Tail of the Dragon...22, 152, 243, 249-50, 252, 268, 282, 482, 484, 487, 575
Teucer of Babylon...4, 29, 313, 316, 318, 323, 326-27, 329-33, 336-42
Thema Mundi 260, 269, 271
Theon of Alexandria... 4, 342, 343
Theophilus of Edessa...4, 36-37, 528, 530, 532, 555
Tides...166-71, 173-81, 184-85, 188-95, 200
Transfer of light...460, 463-64, 474
Transits...13, 26-27, 57, 88, 128, 145, 163, 239, 240, 533
Triplicity (as group of signs) ...32, 34, 133, 141, 143-46, 272, 275, 291, 293-94, 299-300, 371, 375, 378, 383, 432-33
Triplicity lords...19, 95, 235, 255, 291, 294-95, 298, 450, 454, 466-67, 475-78, 549, 572

Twelfth-parts...28, 301, 303, 425, 484

Under the rays...19, 38-39, 167, 249, 379, 414, 417-19, 422-23, 436-37, 470-71, 480, 484, 525-26, 537, 543, 545, 547, 562-63, 567

Valens, Vettius...3-4, 37-40, 303, 365, 367, 430, 455, 504, 514-15, 523, 534-36, 550, 554, 564-65, 569, 574

Victors 374

Wells (degrees)............307-09, 475

Whole signs...35, 391, 444, 476, 481

Wildness 459

Withdrawing...202, 277, 387, 395, 424, 481, 520, 559, 571, 575

Yamamoto, Keiji 1

Zīj al-Shāh 411

Zodiac
   structure and justification.. 127-40

Zoroastrians, Zoroastrianism 369